MW01153212

EVENING'S EMPIRE

What does it mean to write a history of the night? *Evening's Empire* is a fascinating study of the myriad ways in which early modern people understood, experienced, and transformed the night. Using diaries, letters, and legal records together with representations of the night in early modern religion, literature, and art, Craig Koslofsky opens up an entirely new perspective on early modern Europe. He shows how princes, courtiers, burghers, and common people "nocturnalized" political expression, the public sphere, and the use of daily time. Fear of the night was now mingled with improved opportunities for labor and leisure: the modern night was beginning to assume its characteristic shape. *Evening's Empire* takes the evocative history of the night into early modern politics, culture, and society, revealing its importance to key themes from witchcraft, piety, and gender, to colonization, race, and the Enlightenment.

CRAIG KOSLOFSKY is Associate Professor in the Department of History at the University of Illinois, Urbana-Champaign. His previous publications include *The Reformation of the Dead: Death and Ritual in Early Modern Germany* (2001).

NEW STUDIES IN EUROPEAN HISTORY

Edited by

PETER BALDWIN, University of California, Los Angeles
CHRISTOPHER CLARK, University of Cambridge
JAMES B. COLLINS, Georgetown University
MIA RODRÍGUEZ-SALGADO, London School of Economics
and Political Science
LYNDAL ROPER, University of Oxford
TIMOTHY SNYDER, Yale University

The aim of this series in early modern and modern European history is to publish outstanding works of research, addressed to important themes across a wide geographical range, from southern and central Europe, to Scandinavia and Russia, from the time of the Renaissance to the Second World War. As it develops, the series will comprise focused works of wide contextual range and intellectual ambition.

A full list of titles published in the series can be found at:
www.cambridge.org/newstudiesineuropeanhistory

EVENING'S EMPIRE

A History of the Night in Early Modern Europe

CRAIG KOSLOFSKY

University of Illinois, Urbana-Champaign

CAMBRIDGE UNIVERSITY PRESS

CAMBRIDGE UNIVERSITY PRESS
Cambridge, New York, Melbourne, Madrid, Cape Town,
Singapore, São Paulo, Delhi, Tokyo, Mexico City

Cambridge University Press
The Edinburgh Building, Cambridge CB2 8RU, UK

Published in the United States of America by Cambridge University Press, New York

www.cambridge.org
Information on this title: www.cambridge.org/9780521721066

© Craig Koslofsky 2011

This publication is in copyright. Subject to statutory exception
and to the provisions of relevant collective licensing agreements,
no reproduction of any part may take place without the written
permission of Cambridge University Press.

First published 2011

Printed in the United Kingdom at the University Press, Cambridge

A catalogue record for this publication is available from the British Library

Library of Congress Cataloguing in Publication data
Koslofsky, Craig.
Evening's empire : a history of the night in early modern Europe / Craig Koslofsky.
p.   cm. – (New studies in European history)
Includes bibliographical references and index.
ISBN 978-0-521-89643-6 (hardback)
1. Night.   2. Night–Social aspects–Europe.   3. Nightlife–Europe.
4. Europe–Social life and customs.   5. Europe–History–16th century.
6. Europe–History–17th century.   I. Title.   II. Series.
GT3408.K67 2011
304.2'37094–dc22
2011008028

ISBN 978-0-521-89643-6 Hardback
ISBN 978-0-521-72106-6 Paperback

Cambridge University Press has no responsibility for the persistence or
accuracy of URLs for external or third-party Internet websites referred to in
this publication, and does not guarantee that any content on such websites is,
or will remain, accurate or appropriate.

For Dana

Contents

Figures

Maps

xiii

Acknowledgments

While writing this book I have received all sorts of assistance and support, intellectual and material, and many people deserve my thanks. My colleagues at the University of Illinois work every day to keep our history department an exciting, rewarding place to research, write, and teach. My thanks especially to the participants in our History Workshop, and to the stalwart members of the early modern reading group at Illinois, who discussed every chapter of this book in one form or another. Discussions in the Illinois German Colloquium also helped this book along; special thanks to Harry Liebersohn, Peter Fritzsche, and their graduate students. Illinois colleagues Nancy Abelmann, John Randolph, Adam Sutcliffe, Antoinette Burton, Mara Wade, Clare Crowston, David Price, and Mark Micale all read chapters and gave advice at key moments.

Some of the earliest encouragement to tackle the history of the night came from Diane Owen Hughes and Susan Karant-Nunn. Tom Tentler has been there since the beginning, of course. In Göttingen Hans Medick, Alf Lüdtke, and Jürgen Schlumbohm gave advice and inspiration. Scholars came together in Kansas City, Ithaca, Chicago, New Haven, Los Angeles, Evanston, Salt Lake City, Providence, Münster, and Seoul to share enthusiasm, healthy skepticism, and a wealth of precise details and keen observations essential to the history of everyday life. My thanks to them all.

To the undergraduate students who have taken my course on "The History of Night, Medieval to Modern" at Illinois I offer heartfelt thanks. Their rambunctious search for the night in early modern diaries, journals, and travel accounts was often more effective than my own. Likewise, over the years several graduate students have assisted my research. Some, like Sace Elder, are by now established scholars in their own right. Others, like Melissa Salrin, Amanda Eisemann, and Jacob Baum, have great careers ahead of them. They have all enriched this book with their efforts and insights. Before, during, and since her stint as my research assistant my friend and colleague Pascale Rihouet brought an amazing range of skills and insights to bear on the research and writing process. From French teacher in Tübingen to colleague in Providence, she has always been a vital force. Merci!

Along the way I have benefitted from the generosity and insights of many other scholars: Ed Muir, Mary Lindemann, and Erik Midelfort; Otto Ulbricht, Jon Mathieu, Dieter Wunder, Bjørn Westerbeek Dahl, A. Roger Ekirch, Steven Pincus, Kenneth Marcus, Isaac Land, Jacob Melish, Charles Zika, Gary Waite, Ellen McClure, Jen Hill, and Alan Stager. The comments of the anonymous reviewers of my article for the *Journal of Modern History* were exceptionally helpful, as were those of Lyndal Roper on the finished manuscript. Most recently, Alain Cabantous and Catherine Denys have proven themselves generous and gracious colleagues. Librarians and archivists from Los Angeles to Berlin have gone beyond the call of duty, especially Michael Matthaeus (Frankfurt), Klaus Dettmer (Berlin), Christoph Eggenberger (Zurich), Michel Sarter (Lille), Joe Springer (Goshen, IN), and the staff at the William Andrews Clark Library (Los Angeles) and at the Huntington Library (San Marino, CA).

The scholars and staff at the Newberry Library deserve a special thanks. They made it possible to finish this book in a superb working environment, providing everything from rare books to fresh perspectives. The participants in the 2009–10 fellows' seminar at the Newberry formed an outstanding scholarly community for the final writing process; I especially want to thank Carla Zecher, Diane Dillon, and Jim Grossman. At Cambridge University Press Michael Watson and Chloe Howell have been patient, and a pleasure to work with.

During the slow construction of this book Dana Rabin intervened at all the right moments: asking where the rural night fit in, wondering about darkness and Christianity, raising questions for every chapter – reading them all and listening to most of them as well. Imaginative and pragmatic, fearless and thoughtful, she has been the ideal intellectual travel partner for this journey into the night.

Work on this book was supported by a fellowship for University Teachers from the National Endowment for the Humanities, a grant from the William Andrews Clark Memorial Library at UCLA, and a National Endowment for the Humanities fellowship at the Newberry Library. Research support at the University of Illinois has been generous, including a released-time grant from the Department of History, funds for research assistants and leave from the Campus Research Board, and a Mellon fellowship from the College of Liberal Arts and Sciences. The new Scholarly Commons project provided essential technical support just when I needed it most.

Beyond the intellectual exchange and research support every scholar needs, there is the faith, encouragement, and humor of family and friends. In this regard I have been truly fortunate. Our children, Jonah and Eve, have put up with this project for most of their lives and have always helped keep it in perspective. They radiate excitement into their environment, and that is a wonderful thing indeed. Any expression of thanks would fall short of the warmth, love, and understanding of my brothers and sisters-in-law, my nieces and nephews, and my Rabin in-laws. Our friends in Urbana-Champaign, Lexington, Lancaster, and Bethesda/Five Islands have shared our joys and lifted our spirits.

But the gratitude I can hardly begin to express goes to Dana Rabin, who has made with me a life so rich and fulfilling that no project seems too big, no task too daunting. She is truly the one who made this book possible, and so I dedicate it to her.

CHAPTER ONE

An early modern revolution

Alone with Lady Macbeth after his disturbing encounter with Banquo's ghost (3.4.126), Macbeth asks, "What is the night?" The question is both a common way of asking the time in early modern England, and the inquiry which shapes this book. In the lives of early modern men and women, what was the night? In 1785 the Parisian writer Louis-Sébastien Mercier (1740–1814) confidently stated in an essay on "The Pillow" that "the night is the common benefactress of every thing that breathes."[1] A century earlier the barber-surgeon Johann Dietz (1665–1738), riding out of Hamburg late at night, unexpectedly came upon three hanged men on a gallows. "Filled with horror," he reminded himself in his memoir that "the night is no man's friend."[2] The ubiquity and ambiguity of the night evoked by the comments of Dietz and Mercier make the night impossible for the historian to pin down, but they also make these hours an extraordinarily revealing vantage point.

For the people of early modern Europe, the night imposed fundamental limits on daily life, at the same time serving as a many-faceted and evocative natural symbol. By connecting the quotidian with the symbolic, I examine the night at the intersection of the history of daily life and cultural history. Bringing empirical evidence from early modern daily life, drawn from diaries, letters, and legal sources, together with the immense trove of representations of the night in early modern religion, literature, and art, this study opens up a new and surprisingly consistent image of Northern Europe in the seventeenth and eighteenth centuries. With overlapping and sometimes conflicting goals poets, princes, courtiers, burghers, and common people "nocturnalized" spiritual and political expression, public space, and their use of daily time.³ My study is focused on this *noctur-nalization*, defined as the ongoing expansion of the legitimate social and symbolic uses of the night.

Nocturnalization touched all aspects of early modern culture. In the early modern centuries spiritual authors from John of the Cross to John Milton used the night to express contrariety, self-denial, and the ineffable nature of the Divine. At royal courts and in cities, noctur-nalization unfolded (and is most visible to scholars) in the years after 1650, when mealtimes, the closing schedules of city gates, the begin-ning of theatrical performances and balls, and closing times of tav-erns all moved several hours later.⁴ In the same years the nonalcoholic beverages chocolate, coffee, and tea surged in popularity – and cof-feehouses, notorious for their late hours, appeared in all European cit-ies by 1700.⁵ Of all these developments, the swift rise of public street lighting is the most salient: in 1660, no European city had perman-ently illuminated its streets, but by 1700 consistent and reliable street lighting had been established in Amsterdam, Paris, Turin, London, and Copenhagen, and across the Holy Roman Empire from Hamburg to Vienna. Fear of the night was now mingled with improved condi-tions for labor and leisure as the emerging modern night began to show its characteristic ambivalence. Devotional writers such as the Anglican minister Anthony Horneck (1641–97) praised the hours after sunset: "Now is the soul nimbler, subtler, quicker, fitter to behold things sublime and great ... Midnight prayers strangely incline God's favour."⁶ Early eighteenth-century moralists like the urbane *Tatler* editor Richard Steele (1672–1729) and the German Pietist Phillip Balthasar Sinold (1657–1742) described *as new* the regular "night life" of citizens and courtiers. Across Northern Europe in the seventeenth century we see the increased scope and legitimacy of the use of the night in spiritual and political imagery, and in everyday life.⁷ This study seeks to understand the origins, development, and effects of nocturnalization in early modern Northern Europe.⁸

1.1 AN EARLY MODERN REVOLUTION

Rooted in early modern daily life, nocturnalization was a revolution. The turn to the night changed how the people of early modern Europe ate, drank, slept, and worked, restructuring their daily lives and their mental worlds. Through nocturnalization early modern men and women found new paths to the Divine, created baroque opera and theater, formed a new kind of public sphere, and challenged the existence of an "Invisible World" of nocturnal ghosts and witches. And the imprint of nocturnalization on the early Enlightenment helped reconfigure European views of human difference and the place of humankind in the universe.

The early modern centuries began with an entirely new conception of the night. In 1540, the earliest published description of the heliocentric model of the solar system explained its implications for understanding the physical cause of the night:

> The earth, like a ball on a lathe, rotates from west to east, as God's will ordains; and … by this motion, the terrestrial globe produces day and night and the changing appearances of the heavens, accordingly as it is turned toward the sun.[9]

This text, the *Narratio prima* (1540–41) of Georg Rhäticus, was the first publication to explain the night as an effect of the earth's rotation. Rhäticus was a student of Copernicus, whose *De Revolutionibus orbium coelestium libri sex* ("Six books on the revolutions of the heavenly spheres") of 1543 described "the best-known movement of all, the revolution of day and night … as belonging wholly and immediately to the terrestrial globe."[10] The new astronomy explained that the rotation of the earth on its axis produces day and night, but it also implied another kind of night: the endless darkness of space, through which the earth moved around the sun "Like one that hath been led astray / Through the Heav'ns wide pathless way."[11]

Our deep-seated awareness of the darkness of space was unknown to the medieval world. As C.S. Lewis has observed, in the geocentric medieval view the space between the earth and the distant circle of fixed stars was illuminated: night was "merely the conical shadow cast by our Earth."[12] Solar and divine light filled the space above the earth, and the darkness of night was local, limited to the hemisphere of the earth not illuminated as the sun rotated around it. In this geocentric view, "when we look up at the night sky we are looking *through* darkness but not *at* darkness."[13] So Dante imagined the universe. But for the German shoemaker and theosopher Jacob Böhme (1575–1624), whose influential understanding of darkness and the night we will examine in chapter 3, the transition from the medieval universe to the new astronomy was deeply unsettling: "Before this [his acceptance of the heliocentric view] … I myself held that the true Heaven formed a round circle, *quite sky-blue*, high above the stars."[14] Led to "pagan thoughts" by his acceptance of the heliocentric view, Böhme was not the only pensive soul thrown into crisis by the thought of a polycentric and infinite universe of darkness: Pascal cried out that "the eternal silence of these infinite spaces fills me with dread."[15] Early modern Europeans slowly realized that the new astronomy revealed an infinite universe of endless night. As we will see in chapter 8, leading figures of the early Enlightenment, such as Bernard Le Bovier de Fontenelle (1657–1757), embraced this understanding of darkness and the night as a new basis for European cultural superiority.

This identification of the night with the earth's immanent motion signals the history of the night in early modern Europe: dynamic and revolutionary, yet tied to age-old rhythms and continuities. And like the new heliocentric understanding of the physical cause of night on earth, the nocturnalization examined in this book spread gradually from its distinct origins to widespread cultural impact. The claims made by Copernicus and elaborated by Rhäticus were understood by few and accepted by fewer still in their lifetimes. But like the new attitudes toward the night seen in nocturnalization, these revolutionary reorientations in space and time were far-reaching.

To understand nocturnalization in the early modern period we must examine the long-standing continuities of the night stretching from the ancient world to the Industrial Revolution. Compared with the effects of industrialization on the human relationship with the night, any developments within the pre-industrial period might seem trivial: the hearth, the oil-lamp, and the candle remained the only sources of artificial light before the nineteenth century. All early modern Europeans experienced the night as a natural force, with little or no way to escape its constraints. A synchronic history of the night shows how consistently the night was experienced across the pre-industrial world, from village to palace, from shepherd to sovereign.[16] But within this enduring pre-industrial night, the early modern period reveals a dynamic relationship between daily life and cultural expression that drove nocturnalization forward. This relationship gave us the modern night illuminated for labor and leisure by gas and electricity. How have scholars examined the continuity and change in this relationship between early modern Europeans and the night that surrounded them?

1.2 TAKING STOCK

Individual and social responses to the division of the day into daylight and darkness are fundamental to every culture, but scholars have just begun to examine systematically the social experience of the night in early modern Europe. References to nocturnal activity and the symbolic associations of the night in early modern Europe are scattered in research on topics ranging from Caravaggio and the history of street lighting to witch persecutions, astronomy, and coffeehouses. This research offers a fascinating but contradictory picture: we see a diabolical night, nocturnal devotion, honest labor at night, and a night of drunken excess and indiscipline. This study explores these extraordinary tensions in the early modern night, a night balanced between pre-industrial societies and the modern world, a night both devilish and divine, restful and restive, disciplined and ungovernable.

The work of scholars such as Norbert Schindler, Wolfgang Schivelbusch, A. Roger Ekirch, Daniel Ménager, and Alain Cabantous has begun to orient us to this jumbled terrain, placing the early modern night in three important contexts: in the history of sleep, as a site for every sort of quotidian activity, and as a symbol of great force in popular and learned culture. These scholars have approached nocturnal activities in early modern Europe in terms of necessity and leisure, and order and disorder. To understand the night as a symbol, these scholars have assessed its positive and negative connotations in the classical and Christian traditions. This scholarship, which has focused primarily on the night in the *longue durée*, provides an essential overview of what we already know about the quotidian and symbolic aspects of the early modern night.

Sleep is the first necessity of the night. Its history in pre-industrial times has been examined in the innovative work of A. Roger Ekirch.[17] Contrary to assumptions that pre-modern people "fled to their beds soon after sunset" and generally stayed there until sunrise, Ekirch has uncovered an age-old pattern of segmented sleep, arguing that "until the close of the early modern era, Western Europeans on most evenings experienced *two major intervals of sleep* bridged by up to an hour or more of quiet wakefulness."[18] Ekirch describes a first sleep starting after sunset and lasting several hours, followed by a short waking interval and then a second sleep until dawn. The division of the night into a "first" and "second" sleep is supported by a vast range of sources, from diaries and depositions to poetry and prose literature, and the experience of segmented sleep seems to have been familiar to all medieval and early modern Europeans.[19] The implications of segmented sleep are many. The interval of wakefulness provided time for prayer, reflection, conversation, intimacy, or activities ranging from housework to petty theft: a demarcated period of nocturnal activity in the middle of long nights. And if the feeling of well-being some described during their wakeful interval was widespread, then the baleful accounts of night's terrors must be qualified.

The second necessity of the night was work, and early modern people worked at night in countless ways. In large cities, work rhythms were uncoupled from sunrise by the end of the Middle Ages. Evidence from sixteenth-century England and France and from a detailed study of Hamburg shows that activity began around 6 a.m. regardless of the hour of sunrise. This pattern applied to merchants, clerks, masters, apprentices, and domestic servants – all rose around 5.30 a.m., often in the dark, to breakfast and begin work, perhaps attending an early church service first.[20] By the end of the seventeenth century, merchants and officials had left this common schedule by moving the start of their workday at least two hours later.[21] The urban workday included several long breaks and ended between 7 and 10 p.m.: extending the day's work after sunset by candlelight was always a possibility. Many references to late-night labor come from craftsmen and artisans working to fill an order or finish a specific job that had to done by a certain time.[22] In contrast to the intensive night work of urban artisans, those in the countryside often filled the "extra" time on long winter evenings with less skilled tasks or those that required less light, such as carding wool or spinning. Village spinning bees were an extraordinarily important part of sociability in the rural night, discussed below in chapter 7.

There were in fact many reasons to work at night in the early modern period. Harvests could not wait, especially if bad weather or pilferage threatened the crop. Once heated, furnaces and forges were used around the clock; brewing and distilling were complex tasks that could not be halted at nightfall. The tides set the work rhythms on the London docks and for rural fishermen.[23] Bakers rose very early; in eighteenth-century Paris their work "day" began between 11. 30 p.m. and 2.30 a.m., and we read of one master and his baker-boys who worked straight through from 8 p.m. to 7 a.m.[24] The domestic labor of wives and servants extended nearly around the clock.[25] Consumption also promoted work at night. The extraordinary growth of London and Paris in the eighteenth century had to be fed, and an army of local farmers and vendors traveled overnight to bring their wares into the cities' markets for the morning. In cities and villages "labor at night developed significantly at the end of the seventeenth century, and the regulations intended as safeguards quickly became obsolete,"[26] reflecting the nocturnalization of early modern daily life.

When the workday ended, some were too exhausted to do anything but sleep. But even the urban day laborers, artisans, and farmhands with the most physically demanding work looked to the evening and night for their free time. Church and state authorities recognized, at least in principle, the need for leisure time, and the service contracts of apprentices and servants gave them some expectation of free time during the day and in the evening. These servants and apprentices could hardly afford to drink in alehouses, taverns, or *cabarets*, but these public houses provided the "night life" for the more established men and women of the village or neighborhood. Among the many diversions in local public houses at night (especially conversation, singing, or dancing), card-playing stands out as near-universal by the end of the sixteenth century.[27] The increasing regulation of leisure from the Reformation onward focused on the use of the night by young people, with countless proclamations of curfews for servants and apprentices, and on holding public houses to strict closing times (usually 9 p.m. in winter and 10 p.m. in summer). The limited success of these regulations, together with the enormous growth of nocturnal leisure for the wealthy, has led Alain Cabantous to conclude that "one way or another, the vast majority of the population of Western Europe slowly began to see the night as a period of free time."[28]

The night was becoming the focus of one's free time, but it was not a time free from suspicion. In the eyes of early modern criminal courts, any night life outside the home made an individual, whether defendant, victim, or witness, suspect. But this suspicion was not distributed equally. When brought together, the existing scholarship reveals a matrix of reputation, location, class, and gender used to evaluate nocturnal activities. Wealthy or well-born men stood in one corner of this evaluative grid, with poor women "nightwalkers" in the opposite position. There was room on this grid for well-born, respectable women to attend the opera or a ball at night, and for day laborers to drink late into the night at a public house without drawing the charge of disorder. Likewise, ordinary married women frequented the drinking establishments of their neighborhood or village in the evening or at night; these visits were more respectable when the married women went as a group, perhaps to celebrate a baptism or churching. The night fascinated (and continues to fascinate) because one could move in the blink of an eye from the most legitimate and respectable locations in this nocturnal matrix to a far more disorderly, vulnerable, or exciting position.

The line between licit leisure, drunken disorder, and violent crime was easily crossed at night. Disturbances of the peace by young men or by those leaving public houses arose from masculine leisure cultures, rural and urban. Following these men further into the night, they might be the victims of theft, or perpetrators of assault. The most recent work on crime at night from Alain Cabantous seeks to distinguish between early modern perceptions of the night as criminal and the actual incidence of crime at night. According to the studies surveyed by Cabantous, in England and France homicides were not more numerous at night; nor was theft. But both crimes were classified differently and punished more severely if committed at night.[29]

Indeed, the night remained a separate jurisdiction with its own crimes, policing, and sanctions through the end of the Old Regime. The venerable watch policed the night as best it could. There was no corresponding "day watch": the cities and towns of early modern Europe did not employ any general daytime policing until the nine-teenth century. Some crimes and misdemeanors were also specific to the night – walking without a light, keeping a public house open too late, disturbing the peace, lantern-smashing, dueling (at dusk or dawn), and grave-robbing.

In cities like London, Paris, or Leipzig, the curfew was over-whelmed by a growing night life in the seventeenth century, well before the establishment of street lighting. Authorities focused on the requirement that anyone out on the streets after dark carry a light so that they could be seen, and on the closing times of public houses. In 1700 the lieutenant-general of police of Paris, d'Argenson, sought to "establish some order in the cabarets of the villages neighboring Paris." He proposed that "upon order of the King … the proprietors of those cabarets found open after midnight will be led to prison." As the legal closing time in summer was 10 p.m., he thought this a rea-sonable step.[30] D'Argenson noted that "cabarets of this sort depend for all their profits on the countryside parties," reminding us of nocturnal movement throughout Paris and out to its suburbs. This night life was facilitated by street lighting (already a generation old in Paris by this time), but as Cabantous has observed, growing nocturnal sociability and mobility also sustained and promoted assaults, brawls, and theft by night. Almost all perpetrators and victims were male; female vic-tims included shop assistants, peddlers, and prostitutes.[31] Cabantous's findings on gender and crime raise significant questions about women and the urban public sphere examined below in chapter 6.

The existing scholarship on the symbolic valences and associations of the night in the pre-modern West reveals an ambivalent legacy. All the religious traditions of early modern Europe – Roman Catholic, Protestant, Orthodox, Jewish, and Muslim – used the night to think about God and humankind, good and evil. Certainly some of the most complex and sustained discussion of darkness and the night in the West took place within the Christian tradition. The volume, complexity, and variety of writing about the night in the Christian tradition and the range of topics it understood through the night far surpass modern attempts to address the night in philosophical or literary terms. And the upheavals within early modern Christendom from the Reformations to the Enlightenment make the symbolic associations of the night in this period especially dynamic and significant.

For early modern Christians, darkness and the night had long served as powerful metaphors. From the tradition's earliest writings, darkness and the night have borne strongly -- though not exclusively – negative associations. The letters of Paul repeatedly contrast light as righteous with darkness as evil, as in 2 Corinthians 6:14: "For what fellowship hath righteousness with unrighteousness? and what communion hath light with darkness?" and 1 Thessalonians 5:5: "You are all the children of light, and the children of the day: we are not of the night, nor of darkness."[32] The night represents evil or separation from God. The light–night opposition is especially intense in the Johannine books: "Jesus answered and said unto him ... this is the condemnation, that light is come into the world, and men loved darkness rather than light, because their deeds were evil," and "Then spake Jesus again unto them, saying, I am the light of the world: he that followeth me shall not walk in darkness, but shall have the light of life" (John 3:10–19; 9:5). The betrayal and arrest of Jesus at night and the mid-day darkness that marked the crucifixion reflect the same associations.

Do these early Christian writings present any counter-associations in their use of the night? In the frame of its powerful light–darkness / good–evil oppositions, the Gospel of John introduces "a man of the Pharisees, named Nicodemus, a ruler of the Jews: The same came to Jesus by night, and said unto him, Rabbi, we know that thou art a teacher come from God." Later when he is praised for preparing the body of Jesus for burial, he is described as "Nicodemus, which at the first came to Jesus by night" (John 3:1–2; 7:50–51; 19:39). There has been little consensus among commentators on this obscure figure, on the one hand criticized for coming to Jesus only in secret, on the other

The place of communal prayer at night in the *Rule of St. Benedict* is well known.[47] The Nocturnal Office offered the opportunity to encounter the Lord at night, but it was also understood as a form of communal defense against its dangers.[48] Medieval writers in the Benedictine tradition found no opportunities to use the night as a metaphor for approaching the Divine. For example, the writings of Anselm of Canterbury (1033–1109) abound with images of divine light, but he never uses any language of apophatic darkness or envisions the dark night as a path to God, in contrast with ancient and early modern theologies of darkness.

In recent years several scholars have sought to assess the night in the high and late Middle Ages. Writing in the context of studies of other aspects of medieval culture, including collections on the monstrous and on space and place in the Middle Ages, Deborah Youngs and Simon Harris have focused on "the metaphorical and literal uses of the night in medieval society," while the Bulgarian medievalist Tzotcho Boiadjiev has examined the night in the practical texts of medieval sermons and exempla of the tenth through fifteenth centuries. Both of these studies describe a night of external threats, natural and supernatural. Using a long series of sermons and exempla Boiadjiev shows how the night transformed ambivalent places such as the road, the bridge, or the churchyard, which in other contexts might serve as symbols of progress or strength, into sites of diabolical danger and violence. For Youngs and Harris, the clerical writers of the twelfth through fifteenth centuries constructed a "dark 'other'" in their efforts to "fix what it meant to be in the light of God and part of the Christian community."[49] While they explore the wide range of negative associations with the night in the high and late Middle Ages, both of these studies go beyond the clichés of unrelenting nocturnal fear to examine the burgeoning illicit night life seen in cities beginning around the twelfth century.[50]

In the period from the sixth through fourteenth centuries, Christian writers in the West seldom drew on the few positive associations the night had acquired during the first five centuries of their tradition. The wide influence of Denys in the West issued from his writings on celestial and ecclesiastical hierarchy; his use of darkness in paradoxes to describe the Divine, whose "transcendent darkness remains hidden from all light and concealed from all knowledge" found little resonance. By the fourteenth century, however, the growth of mystical theology had renewed the use of the night in the apophatic sense first expressed by Gregory of Nyssa and Denys. Apophatic images of darkness and the night can be seen in the works of Meister Eckhart (d. 1328), in the fourteenth-century *Cloud of Unknowing* (unknown English author), in the writings of Denis the Carthusian (1402–71), and most systematically in the *De docta ignorantia* (1440) of Nicolas of Cusa (1401–64).[51] With the Dionysian corpus established and reworked by Nicolas of Cusa and other fifteenth-century mystics, early modern Christians could cite venerable authorities when using the imagery of the night to inspire or exalt, creating a counterpoint to the more widespread and traditional association of darkness and the night with evil. *How* early modern Christians drew on the theologies of darkness in their tradition has been little studied, and is the focus of chapters 2 and 3 of this book.

1.2.1 About this book

The night is emerging as a focus of scholarship in early modern Europe, creating enormous opportunities to explore the period in relation to this ubiquitous aspect of culture and daily life. How best can scholars connect the night with the salient themes and issues of the early modern centuries? To bring the history of the night into dialogue with the history of the early modern day, so to speak, we can see the night as part of a broader form of analysis, rather than as a self-contained topic. In this study I use daily life as a category of historical analysis to understand the reciprocal relationship between night and society. I show how early modern men and women mapped the contrast between darkness and light – a fundamental distinction of daily life – onto early modern culture, and how this culture in turn helped structure the distinction between night and day.[52] This approach also broadens and reorients the history of daily life itself by focusing on the imprint of everyday distinctions on complex bodies of thought and expression.[53] By moving beyond considering daily life simply as an object of study, and using it instead as a category of analysis, we can illuminate aspects of culture and society far beyond the quotidian, such as Lutheran mysticism or changing beliefs about ghosts and spirits. This approach creates new and valuable perspectives by examining the reciprocal relationships between the night and witchcraft persecutions, confessional formation, absolutism and court culture, the civilizing process, social discipline, gender and the public sphere, and colonization, race, and the early Enlightenment.

In medieval Europe, spiritual and political authorities forced the individuals and groups they excluded into the night, "physically in their movements, and metaphorically by being linked to the evil abroad in the darkness."[54] This process intensified in the sixteenth and seventeenth centuries as demonologists tied the crime of witchcraft to the nocturnal witches' sabbath (a connection never made, for example, in the fifteenth-century *Malleus maleficarum*). But as I show in chapter 2, discourses of witchcraft in this period focused on the night in another, more interior way, as the time of diabolical temptation. In the narratives of witchcraft performed on stage or extracted though the courts, the act of succumbing to this shadowy temptation and joining the Devil's nocturnal anti-society became the true crime of witchcraft. The power of this somber fiction is seen in the tens of thousands of executions for witchcraft in this age.

Early modern Europeans used the night to think profoundly about God *and* the Devil, underscoring the significance of the night to early modern culture. In chapter 3 I show how the formation of rival confessional churches led Christians to seek the Lord in the night, literally and figuratively: the widely persecuted Anabaptists provide the most concentrated example of a much broader experience. I also examine men like John of the Cross and Jacob Böhme, persecuted *within* their own churches, who brought forth an intense nocturnalization of mysticism and theology, epitomizing the wider nocturnalization of Christian piety and imagery across confessions. Like the diabolical associations of the early modern night, these mystics saw the divine night as a time of isolation in powerfully interior terms.

The visual and emotional power of imagining the night and its darkness as attributes of God quickly generated parallel political expressions. Sovereigns and courtiers mapped the contrast between

darkness and light onto the political culture of the seventeenth century, representing power and authority through fireworks, illuminations, and lavish nocturnal festivities. In chapter 4 I show how
darkness and the night were essential to baroque attempts to articulate and transcend confessional sources of authority. Nocturnal darkness intensified the light that represented God or king in spectacles
of what Jürgen Habermas called "representative publicness." At the
same time, the active use of darkness by princes to bedazzle, conceal,
and deceive expressed the fundamental political insights of the age.
The use of the night to create and represent authority reveals fundamental connections between court culture, the baroque stage, and
seventeenth-century political thought.

In chapters 4 and 5 I show how spectacular new uses of the night
slowly began to reorder everyday routines at court and in cities as
princes, courtiers, and respectable townspeople regularly extended
the legitimate social part of the day long past sunset, and often past
midnight. In the second half of the seventeenth century, parallel to
the new uses of the night at court, the rulers of the leading cities
of Northern Europe began to establish public street lighting. Most
research on street lighting has focused on the gas and electric lighting of the nineteenth and twentieth centuries, but the first European
street lighting – candles or oil-lamps in glass-paned lanterns – was an
innovation of the seventeenth century, both reflecting and promoting
new attitudes toward the night and urban space. Chapter 5 shows how
the night and its illumination thus link the representational needs of
baroque rulers with the practical expansion of urban public time and
space.

Contemporaries recognized street lighting as a "modern" security innovation. A 1692 description of Paris remarked that "the most
distant peoples should come and see … the invention of lighting
Paris during the night with an infinity of lights," explaining that
the street lighting was something "the Greeks and the Romans had
never considered for the policing of their republics."[55] In chapter 6 I
argue that this policing was part of a distinctive colonization of the
urban night. It met with immediate resistance from the urban night's
traditional inhabitants: young people – nobles, servants, apprentices,

and students – as well as tavern visitors, prostitutes, and those of all estates who sought occasional anonymity. In the ensuing struggle to colonize the urban night authorities deployed estate, age, and gender to mark the shifting lines between prohibited and respectable night life. The colonization of the urban night created a "bourgeois public sphere" whose location in daily *time*, in the evening and at night, was at least as important as its physical sites in coffeehouses or clubs. I place the arguments of Jürgen Habermas and Joan Landes on gender and the public sphere in the new context of daily time and examine how meeting at night limited respectable women's access to the emerging urban public.

The same legal-disciplinary policing underlay authorities' engagement with the night in the countryside as in the city. As with the colonization of the urban night, youth, gender, and sexuality were the key issues. But as I show in chapter 7, the encounter of church and state with the rural night was shaped by different cultural and social forces and led to outcomes distinctly different from the colonization of the night in the cities of Northern Europe. Attempts to colonize the rural night focused on social discipline and were less tied to commerce and consumption than at court or in major cities. Like their cousins in towns and cities, young people in the countryside resisted incursions into a time that had traditionally been theirs. Because neither church nor state could intervene in rural daily life as effectively as they could in cities, villagers young (and old) successfully defended their traditional night life. By 1700 the difference between the successful colonization of the urban night and the failed colonization of the rural night appeared as a real shift in patterns of daily time seen, for example, in the transformation of the age-old pattern of segmented sleep described above. References to segmented sleep are absent from the diaries of elite men like Samuel Pepys (1633–1703) and the duc de Saint-Simon (1675–1755) because their daily life was shaped by the rise of street lighting, better domestic lighting, and the spread of coffee and tea as alternatives to beer and wine. The nights of townspeople, compressed into a single sleep of seven or eight hours, began to diverge from the traditional pattern of segmented sleep reflected, for example, in rural diaries.

How did Europeans understand darkness and the night, real and symbolic, as their everyday rhythms shifted? In chapter 8 I examine the imprint of nocturnalization on the early Enlightenment through controversies over ghosts, witches, and Hell – three intertwined aspects of medieval and early modern culture deeply associated with darkness and the night.[56] For some Europeans, these manifestations of nocturnal fear were coming unmoored from their basis in everyday experience: the night and its spirits were becoming less frightening. But this seemingly straightforward connection between lighting and the Enlightenment becomes more complex and revealing as I examine the parallel unevenness of nocturnalization *and* of the universalisms of the early Enlightenment. Claims to dispel darkness, literal or figurative, lead us to darkness relocated or recreated elsewhere. Popular authors of the early Enlightenment such as Fontenelle and Balthasar Bekker (1634–98) depicted themselves as dispellers of benighted superstition, but in their works we see the displacement of darkness characteristic of nocturnalization. They created hierarchies of perception, understanding, and enlightenment that shifted the darkness of ignorance onto new differences of region and race. To recast discussions of the early Enlightenment and its radicals, I consider the tension between the universalism of light and the selective use of darkness and the night in late seventeenth-century writings on ghosts, witches, and Hell.

To trace a history of the night through these issues and developments, this book examines it as a symbol (chapters 2, 3, and 8) and in the distinct social spaces of the court, the city, and the countryside (chapters 4–7). In the early modern period the experiences, norms, and rhythms of the night at royal courts, in cities, and in the countryside – previously held in sync by sunrise and sunset – first began to diverge. By 1700 the uses of the night and its symbolic associations varied sharply across these social spaces, marking a revolution in early modern daily life. The discovery that the origins, progress, and effects of nocturnalization unfolded quite differently at courts, in cities, and in villages structures this book.

CHAPTER TWO

Darkness and the Devil, 1450–1650

Early modern Europeans thought about the night directly and indirectly under a vast range of topics. More importantly for our discussion, early modern Europeans thought *with* the night, using its lived
experience and traditional associations to articulate an extraordinary
range of values and concepts. Paradoxically, their deepest engagement
with the night and its darkness came in their discourses on witchcraft
and the Devil, and in their understanding of "the dark night of the
soul" as a path to God. Some of the most intense, transcendent, and
threatening expressions of the diabolical and the Divine were understood *in* and *through* the night in this turbulent age.[1]

The early modern authors discussed here inherited an ambiguous
image of the night – sharply negative except within the rarified world
of mystic expression. In this chapter I examine the associations of the
night with evil across European Christian culture from the fifteenth
through the seventeenth centuries, focusing on the night as a site of
diabolical temptation. In the following chapter, I turn to those who
took up and developed the "divine darkness" of Denys the Areopagite
by seeing the night, literal and figurative, as a pathway to the Divine.
In darkness, whether divine or diabolical, the night create, evoke,
and represent human isolation in solitary, individual encounters with
God and with the Devil.

2.1 THE "WITTENBERG NIGHTINGALE"

The image of the "Wittenberg Nightingale" crafted by the Nuremberg
cobbler-poet Hans Sachs (1494–1576) in 1523 was a resounding success: the pamphlet went through six printings in that year alone. The

first section of the poem describes the desolate state of Christendom through an extended allegory. As a lost flock of sheep, God's people are in the wrong place (misled from the pasture into a dark wilderness) at the wrong time (in the dark of night). The song of the nightingale can set things right by heralding the light of day:

> All through the long night
> we are all finally awakened
> as the nightingale so clearly sings
> and the light of day breaks in.[2]

Sachs immediately identifies the subject of his poem:

> Who is this dear nightingale
> who calls us to the light of day?
> It is Doctor Martin Luther
> Augustinian of Wittenberg
> Who wakes us from the night.[3]

At the end of the allegory Sachs clarifies in the margin "What the night is" ("Was die nacht sey"). For Sachs the church of Rome

> Never made clear to us the faith
> Which in Christ makes us holy
> This failure is signified by the night
> In which we all have been lost.[4]

The dawn heralded by Martin Luther dispels the night of error and confusion.

Three years earlier, the papal bull *Exsurge Domine* ("Arise, O Lord") had condemned Luther by using the same contrast between darkness and daylight, proclaiming him "blinded in mind by the father of lies." The bull explained that had Luther come to Rome personally to make his case, "we would have shown him clearer than the light of day" that the moral lapses and doctrinal errors he alleged did not exist.[5] In the reform conflicts of the 1520s all sides used this straightforward imagery of daylight and darkness as good and evil in their writing and preaching. Zwingli refers often to "clarity and light" in his *On the Clarity and Certainty of the Word of God* (*Von Klarheit und Gewißheit des Wortes Gottes*, 1522), and Luther's response to Erasmus in *The Bondage of the Will* (*De servo arbitrio*, 1525) abounds in references to the light and clarity of Scripture. He asked: "for who would say that the public fountain is not in the light, because those who are in some dark narrow lane do not see it, when all those who are in the open market place can see it plainly?"[6] For Luther darkness is the result of human failure to believe what is clearly revealed.

The first decades of the Reformation echo with this language. In his first controversial work, the 1529 *Dyaloge … touching the pestylent sect of Luther and Tyndale* (in modern editions *The Dialogue concerning Tyndale*) Thomas More attested to the derisive association of the night with spiritual blindness by the "heretics" of the 1520s:

> I … marvel at the madness of these heretics that bark against the old ancient customs of Christ's church, mocking the setting up of candles and with foolish facetiousness and blasphemous mockery demand whether God and his saints lack light or whether it be night with them that they cannot see without candle.[7]

"Whether it be night with them?" One can easily imagine the "heretical" response. As Hans Sachs explained, through the false practices arising from the cult of the saints, all Christendom stands benighted, "the holy word of God … obscured by human teaching."[8]

Later in this same dialogue More identified the night with the heretics themselves, who gather under cover of darkness. More described a carpenter of Essex whom he had personally interrogated sometime around 1521. The man "had long held diverse heresies" and confessed to frequenting "a place which he named us in London, where, he said, that such heretics were wont to resort to their readings in a chamber at midnight." The carpenter named "diverse" others who "were wont to haunt those midnight lectures," among them Richard Hunne (d. 1514) a well-known London merchant suspected of Lollardy who had died in prison while awaiting trial. In his account More underscored the heretical associations of the night: "thus there learned we … that Hunne had haunted heretics' lectures by night long before."[9] Leaving aside the veracity of More's tale of regular nocturnal gatherings, which resemble accounts of the witches' sabbath (see below, section 2.3) and descriptions of persecuted congregations gathering at night (see chapter 3), his use of the night as a sign of evil in Reformation polemic is clear.

In 1523, Erasmus wrote a short commentary on a hymn to the birth of Jesus by the fourth-century poet Aurelius Prudentius Clemens, evoking a similar sense of spiritual darkness. The hymn itself refers briefly to the winter solstice; Erasmus introduces his commentary with an extended discussion of a "world [that] lay beneath the darkness of ignorance and the shadow of sins." He refers to the era of the Nativity, describing the error, idolatry, and depravity of the pagan world. But Erasmus himself was living in dark times: accused of responsibility for the unrest in the church, challenged for his work on the New Testament, and under suspicion of heresy.[10] When he described "our darkness" in the era preceding Jesus' birth and exclaimed that "This was surely the depths of the night!" was his own age far from his thoughts? "Ignorance of the truth is night," he adds, letting this exposition of night and spiritual darkness "suffice as a kind of preface, even if it is not entirely relevant."[11]

The radicals of the early Reformation also drew on the identification of the night with evil. Given the insistence on separation from the world in Anabaptism, it is no surprise that some of the most intense uses of the darkness–light metaphor issued from the first writings of that tradition. The earliest creed of the Anabaptist movement, the Swiss-German Schleitheim Confession of 1527, proclaimed that "all those who have fellowship with the dead works of darkness have no part in the light." In the discussion of separation, the Confession explained that "there is nothing else in the world and in all creation than good and evil, believing and unbelieving, darkness and light, the world and those who are [come] out of the world, God's temple and idols, Christ and Belial, and none will have part with the other."[12] The Anabaptist congregation of Kempen (lower Rhine) described the "worldly preachers," traditional and Protestant, as "servants of the belly [Romans 16:18] ... overcome with eternal darkness" [2 Peter 2:17] in a 1545 confession submitted to the authorities of Electoral Cologne.[13] The topical biblical concordance printed in Worms c. 1540, a significant early Anabaptist text, presents a dozen Scripture passages under the topic of "light," including Romans 13 [12–14]: "The night is past, and the day is drawing near. Let us therefore cast off the works of darkness." Identifying with the light in the struggle against worldly darkness is the focus of the entry.[14]

In all of these conflicts, reformers and defenders of tradition understood their age as an immense struggle between light and darkness. Their easy reliance on the contrast between daylight and night introduces to us both the continuity and the transformation of Europeans' understanding of the night in the early modern period. The continuity is clear: as I discuss below, Christians had long associated darkness and the night with Satan, death, sin, and heresy, and continued to do so throughout the early modern period. But, as I will show in the following chapter, by the beginning of the seventeenth century mystics, poets, and theologians of all confessions expressed a renewed sense of the value of darkness and the night in ascetic, apophatic, mystical, and epistemological terms.

2.2 INSTRUMENTS OF DARKNESS

Early modern Europeans associated the night with its "black agents" of human and diabolical evil.[15] The dark hours of the day framed the most intense fears: "At night, the flying phantoms / Champing ferocious jaws, / Do by their whistling terrify my soul," as Pierre de Ronsard (1524–85) pronounced.[16] Edmund Spenser (c. 1552–99) addressed "Night, thou foule mother of annoyaunce sad / Sister of heavie Death, and nourse of Woe" in similar terms:

> Under thy mantle black there hidden lye
> Light-shonning thefte, and traiterous intent,
> Abhorred bloodshed, and vile felony,
> Shamefull deceipt, and daunger imminent.[17]

The age-old identification of night with fear and danger resonated with German poets like Simon Dach (1605–69) and Andreas Gryphius (1616–64). Writing during the Thirty Years War, they described a night of "terror, silence and dark horror": Gryphius spoke of "the hours of sad loneliness," when "black cold covers the land / and now sleep all, from labor and pain exhausted."[18] Dach expanded on the theme in the poem "Heart-Felt Lament" ("Hertzliche klage") of 1641:

> Fear I bear before the night
> I keep myself awake with fright
> My sleep is pain and sorrow,
>   I long so much
>   as no other
> night watchman, for tomorrow.[19]

This pre-modern topos has been documented by Jean Delumeau, Piero Camporesi, A. Roger Ekirch, and many others.[20] Shakespeare's contemporary, the writer Thomas Nashe, regarded this view of the night as a cliché: "When any poet would describe a horrible tragical accident," Nashe intoned, "to add the more probability and credence unto it he dismally begins to tell how it was dark night when it was done, and cheerful daylight had quite abandoned the firmament."[21] Shakespeare parodies this dismal view of the night in *A Midsummer Night's Dream* (5.1) when Bottom, playing Pyramus, awkwardly declaims:

> O grim-look'd night! O night with hue so black!
> O night, which ever art when day is not!
> O night, O night! alack, alack, alack.

Clearly, one would not want to mistake this topos for unmediated, direct evidence of the experience of the night in this period, but cliché and parody alike show its ubiquity. Can we explore this venerable identification of the night with evil, death, and despair for its distinctly early modern emphases and inflections?

Several key works reveal the developments within the continuity. Thomas Nashe described the night as a hellish time of fear and danger in his 1594 tract on *The Terrors of the Night*: "Well have poets termed night the nurse of cares, the mother of despair, the daughter of hell."[22] But Nashe expanded on these traditional associations of the night by evoking in personal, spiritual terms a night that terrified in part because it reflected the darkness within: "As touching the terrors of the night, they are as many as our sins." Nashe's night linked infernal evil, diabolical temptation, and human sin:

The devil is the special predominant planet of the night, and … Like a cunning fowler … he spreads his nets of temptation in the dark, that men might not see to avoid them.

For Nashe the "danger imminent" of the night was less physical than spiritual; less assault and more temptation. It was a time when one's sins were reckoned, and when diabolical trials (both of temptation and of despair) were the strongest:

In the quiet silence of the night he will be sure to surprise us, when he infallibly knows we shall be unarmed to resist, and that there will be full auditory granted him to undermine or persuade what he lists.[23]

Nashe concluded his tract by asserting that "the terrors of the night [are] more than of the day, because the sins of the night surmount the sins of the day." Nashe here represents a trend that makes nocturnal danger more personal, internal, and subjective: "we that live in his [the devil's] nightly kingdom of darkness must needs taste some disquiet." This interior view of the night contrasts with the traditional emphasis on the external threats, natural and supernatural, that arose at night.

Nashe's *Terrors of the Night* seems to have served as a source for Shakespeare's *Macbeth* (first performed *c.* 1603–06).[24] In this tragedy several characters comment on the night and mark its passing, while the playwright thematizes it repeatedly.[25] I argue that the play illustrates a distinctive early modern emphasis on the night as a site of temptation and surrender to the forces of darkness. Darkness is indeed the setting for much of *Macbeth*, which rehearses the older identification of the night with physical danger while building upon Nashe's association of night with temptation and sin. Each main character in *Macbeth* reminds the audience of the power of the night to tempt and corrupt, to – in Banquo's words – "win us to our harm." Shakespeare takes care to show how the dark crimes of the play are in each case preceded by dark desires, as signaled by Macbeth musing "Stars, hide your fires, / Let not light see my black and deep desires" (1.4.50). Lady Macbeth fairly personifies the power of the night to tempt in act 1, scene 7: Macbeth wavers but then succumbs to the temptation to murder Donald. This onstage scene of nocturnal persuasion, signaled by the torches in the stage directions (1.7), appears distinct from the crime itself, committed offstage. Prior to these wicked deeds come "wicked dreams" as Macbeth observes that "o'er one half-world / Nature seems dead, and wicked dreams abuse / That curtained sleep" (2.1.48–50). In contrast to the nocturnal assaults by demons or the Devil described above, the night poses no physical danger to Macbeth or Lady Macbeth. They succumb instead to nocturnal temptation.

Scholars have also noted in *Macbeth* the influence of a well-known Protestant denunciation of ghosts and purgatorial spirits, Ludwig Lavater's 1570 treatise *De spectris*. The Zurich theologian wrote to deny Catholic claims that ghosts and purgatorial spirits proved the reality of Purgatory. Widely influential, Lavater's work appeared in several Latin editions and was translated into French, German, Dutch, and English (published in 1572 under the title *Of ghostes and spirites walking by nyght*).[26] Lavater argued that any seeming ghost or magical spirit was in reality a deception of the Devil, intended to tempt Christians into false belief. "Spirits and other strange sights," he explained, "be not the souls of Men, but be either good or evil Angels, or else some secret and hidden operations."[27] These apparitions, Lavater explained repeatedly, "do appear still in these days both day and night, but especially in the night." Their affinity to the night suggested their diabolical source: "Neither may we marvel, that they are heard more in the night, than in the day time. For he who is the author of these things, is called in the holy Scriptures the Prince of darkness, and therefore he shuns the light of Gods word."[28] Lavater described a vast nocturnal conspiracy, both diabolical and human, to lure individuals into a false, "Popish" belief in ghosts and spirits. Lavater's remarks seem to frame the first meeting with the Weird Sisters in *Macbeth*, and in fact the closest parallel between *Macbeth* and Lavater's *Ghostes and spirites walking by nyght* concerns nocturnal temptation. After the encounter with the Weird Sisters Banquo warns Macbeth that

> ... oftentimes, to win us to our harm,
> The instruments of darkness tell us truths;
> win us with honest trifles, to betray us
> In deepest consequence.[29]

Here the playwright echoes Lavater's warning that "The devil sometimes utters the truth, that his words may have the more credit, and
that he may the more easily beguile them."[30] Alongside fears of danger from night's black agents grew the fear that one might be tempted
to become the Devil's own.

This association of the night with temptation and the darkness
of one's own sin appears in a range of contemporary works. In *The
Revenger's Tragedy* (1607), the protagonist Vindice comments on
lust and the temptation to incest, explaining that "if any thing /
Be damn'd, it will be twelve o'clock at night." "That twelve," he adds,
"is the *Judas* of the hours, wherein, / Honest salvation is betray'd to
sin." The dark temptation represented by the Weird Sisters in *Macbeth*
also appeared on the English stage through the nocturnal temptations
of Mephistopheles in Marlowe's *Doctor Faustus* and in the form of the
Black Dog in *The Witch of Edmonton* (c. 1621).[31]

The growing emphasis on temptation and the night is especially
clear in the development of *Doctor Faustus*. In contrast with Marlowe's
later version, neither the German *Historia von Johann Fausten* of 1587
nor the *English Faust Book* of 1588/89 connects Faust's initial temptation and fall with the night. In the German text Faustus "summoned
the devil at night between nine and ten o'clock," and at midnight
ordered the spirit to appear to him the next morning at his home.
After this morning "disputation" Faustus bade the spirit return in the
evening. Only the following morning, described in the text as "The
Third Conference of Doctor Faustus with the Spirit and the Promise
He Made" does Faust sign in blood the fatal contract.[32] The *English
Faust Book* repeats this sequence of events.[33] In the A-text of *Doctor
Faustus*, written and first performed in late 1588 or 1589, Marlowe
compresses the action into two night scenes: Faust's conjuring of
Mephistopheles ("Now that the gloomy shadow of the earth, / ...
dims the welkin with her pitchy breath, / Faustus, begin thine incan-
tations"), and the subsequent conversation ("Go and return to mighty
Lucifer, / And meet me in my study at midnight") in which Faustus
signs away his soul.[34] In Marlowe's account Mephistopheles works to
seduce Faustus by night with the full array of temptations and illusions at his disposal. The questions asked by Faustus underscore this

association: "Is it not midnight? Come, Mephistopheles" (2.1.28); "Is that the reason he tempts us thus?" (2.1.40).[35] The B-text of the play, first published in 1616, emends the setting of Faustus's first conjuration to "Now that the gloomy shadow of the *night*, / ... dims the welkin with her pitchy breath," consonant with this emphasis on nocturnal diabolical temptation.[36]

2.3 WITCHCRAFT

The emphasis by Lavater, Nashe, Marlowe, and Shakespeare on the power of the "cunning fowler ... [who] spreads his nets of temptation in the dark" was fundamental to the narratives of witchcraft which flourished in this period, especially in the understanding of the witch's pact with the Devil and the nocturnal sabbath. When our perspective on witchcraft moves from the stage to the stake we are confronted with the grim reality of witch persecution in early modern Europe. In recent decades, scholars of early modern witchcraft have given some order to the bleak record of suspicion, accusation, torture, and confession that remains from the early modern witch persecutions.[37] These scholars have identified several key aspects of early modern witchcraft, starting with witchcraft beliefs and practices in popular magic, and in rumors and accusations at the local level, where almost all trials for witchcraft began. They have also contextualized the legal sources created by the witch trials: witness testimony and the statements and confessions of defendants, coerced by torture or its threat. Demonological works and discussions of Satan and witchcraft in a broad range of other texts and images provide the intellectual and cultural background of the witch persecutions. In the crucible of the witch trials these aspects intersected to produce vivid scenes of nocturnal seduction by the Devil and shadowy gatherings in his service. Early modern theologians and jurists described the initial temptation by the Devil as leading to a pact or contract, often physically consummated, followed by participation in the witches' sabbath. Suspended between the demonology of the learned and the confessions of the accused, accounts of nocturnal temptation by the Devil and descriptions of witches gathering at night were fundamental to early modern popular culture, to the legal mechanisms of witch persecutions, and to learned demonology.

When we consider the night in each aspect of the early modern construction and persecution of witchcraft, we see some of its most distinctive contours. Here I will draw much of my evidence from the heartland of persecution for witchcraft, the area of eastern France and the Holy Roman Empire from the duchies of Luxemburg and Lorraine to the prince-bishoprics of Würzburg and Bamberg.[38] Over half of all known trials for witchcraft in all of early modern Europe took place in this politically and confessional fragmented area.[39] Influential demonological works of the period were written in the region or made reference to it, foremost Jean Bodin's *De la démonomanie des sorciers* (1580), Peter Binsfeld's *Tractat von Bekantnuss der Zauberer und Hexen* (1590), and the *Démonolâtrie* (1595) of Nicolas Remy. French, German, and English historians have published thorough local and regional studies of witchcraft in the area.[40]

The universal belief in magic and spirits was the foundation of all witch persecution. "Popular beliefs" about magic and *maleficia* were held by people of all ranks, even if they sometimes clashed with learned views on witchcraft. Witchcraft was real and threatening. From this point a key observation emerges: time and again we see peasants and other common people demonstrating both the knowledge and the desire to initiate a prosecution for witchcraft. Scholars have uncovered both a wide knowledge of demonology and demon lore and a pattern of initiative "from below" in the witch persecutions of the sixteenth and seventeenth centuries, and villagers often sought magical aid against witchcraft before turning to local authorities for help.[41]

In the witch persecutions common and learned views of witchcraft met, but they did not necessarily agree. Authorities inscribed "the witch of the church" over "the witch of the people"; the latter was dangerous but hardly diabolical.[42] In popular beliefs about magic and witchcraft, the night played an ambiguous role, corresponding to the place of the night in folk beliefs in general. One cannot generalize about the extraordinary range of associations of the night found in the multi-volume German folklore guide, the *Handwörterbuch des deutschen Aberglaubens*, except to say that the night was not uniformly associated with evil, nor did the clear light of day guarantee any protection against the Devil or his agents. Certain spells and rituals were best performed by night, but these practices were usually intended to help, not harm.[43] The extensive accounts of popular magic in Saxon witch trials show no particular correlation between *maleficia*, beneficial magic, night, and day.[44]

Specific studies in the history of folklore reveal several deep and positive associations with the night in early modern Europe. Strange references to "night journeys" in Alpine folklore and witchcraft trials give us glimpses of local popular belief in the "phantoms of the night" (*Nachtschar*), a nocturnal group of mysterious people who "danced joyously on remote meadows and mountain pastures, [and] met in certain houses for sumptuous dinners."[45] Those who saw the night phantoms and opened their homes to them received magical gifts: good luck, the ability to play music, or perhaps second sight. The idea of the phantoms of the night is not easily distinguished from other folk beliefs documented in northern Italy, the Alps, Germany, and France from the fifteenth to twentieth centuries, such as references to the *Benandanti*, "the good society" or "the blessed people." In all of these cases the groups are described as nocturnal and beneficent. Indeed, as Carlo Ginzburg's work on the *Benandanti* of Friuli and Wolfgang Behringer's study of Chonrad Stoeckhlin, a village "shaman" in the Bavarian Alps, reveal, in their first encounters with church and state authorities, these "good people" of the night did not even think to hide their nocturnal associations, so sure were they of the legitimacy of their magical night companions and journeys.[46]

But what stood behind the magical beliefs of the common people? By the middle of the sixteenth century, intellectual, ecclesiastical, and political authorities worked hard to demonstrate that the Devil underwrote all magical practices, and that all "phantoms of the night" were witches. In his *Guide to Grand-Jury Men* (1627) Richard Bernard presented the diabolical covenant as the basis of all magic: "an expressed league is made with the Devil ... that is, the Witch with spirits ... Now what other can that be, with whom the Enchanter is in league, but the Devil? ... The story of Faustus confirms it, and all the relations of Witches with us."[47] This view meant diabolizing nocturnal phantoms, practices, and symbols traditionally seen as benign or even beneficial. For scholars today, the best-known examples of this demonization appear in the work of Carlo Ginzburg and Wolfgang Behringer. Both have shown how rural folk described their roles as *Benandanti* or travelers with the *Nachtschar*, and how officials of the church and state forced these men and women into the framework of learned demonology, then condemned them.[48]

Whether *Benandanti*, flamboyant visionaries, or wise women of the village, all were aligned with the Devil in countless sermons, tracts, and ordinances.[49] The Elizabethan pastor George Gifford, writing in 1593, decried all popular magic as witchcraft:

I might reckon up her that deals with the sieve and the shears, and a number of such trumperies, in all which the most holy name of God is polluted, and if any thing be done, it is done wholly by the effectual working of Satan. God hath given natural helps, and those we may use, as from his hand against natural diseases, but things besides nature he hath not appointed.

Across the confessions of early modern Europe, this diabolization of everyday magic and superstition recast popular and elite views of the night; Ginzburg and Behringer both provide revealing studies of common people caught in the authorities' diabolization of the night. Gifford represented the diabolization as a foregone conclusion, asking: "Those which have their charms, and their night spells, what can they be but witches?"[50] As we will see below in chapter 7, villagers maintained a rich nocturnal culture despite the authorities' diabolization of the night.

Because most prosecutions for witchcraft began with local accusations, witness testimony appears frequently in trial records. In contrast with the testimony of the accused, extracted by torture or its threat, witnesses testified under less coercion and showed themselves more strategic. Their testimony often provides clear evidence of popular beliefs despite the leading questions they were asked.[51] Bernard's guide to the investigation of witchcraft advised the prosecutor to ask "the suspected witch's whole family" whether "they have heard the suspected … speak of their power to hurt this or that, or of their transportation, to this or that place, or of their meetings in the night there?"[52] This line of questioning sought to pair daytime *maleficia* with night-time gatherings. But witnesses often presented a more benign view of the night, seen for example in the 1603 witness testimony of the young Caspar Johann of Hüttersdorf.[53] At the trial of 60-year-old Schneider Augustin, he testified that after his evening meal

> he laid himself down to sleep on the hay in his master Meyer's barn. He awakened after his first sleep and saw that it was quite light in the barn; soon a great dance broke out on the threshing floor of the barn: the people danced back-to-back. In this company he, the witness, actually saw and recognized among others Schneider Augustin of Honzrath; this Schneider Augustin was by a wagon, which had been loaded with hay and stood on the threshing floor, and sat on a windowsill and blew on a huge, hideous instrument, making a terrible sound. The company discussed whether to move the wagon out, but after discussion decided to let it stay there. The whole thing lasted almost an hour and then disappeared with a great whoosh, and then it was dark in the barn again. He the witness could neither move nor spoke during all this time.[54]

As Eva Labouvie has observed, the scene described here is hardly diabolical. The dancing back-to-back to hideous music resembles an inverted peasant dance rather than a black mass or witches' sabbath. There is no reference to the Devil or to *maleficia* practiced or planned, and no emphasis on the late hour of this gathering (after the "first sleep") as particularly wicked. The relatively tame nocturnal gathering in this testimony is reflected by an English woodcut of the mid-seventeenth century showing a witches' dance by the light of the moon (Figure 2.1). This image, illustrating the chapbook tale of Robin the cobbler, "punish'd bad as Faustus with his devils" for making a diabolical pact, nonetheless resembles a peasant dance more than any diabolical witches' sabbath.[55]

However described or represented, the sabbath was key to witch trials. In Caspar Johann's testimony we see incrimination through "participation" at the gathering, which was the focus of all discussions of the dance or sabbath in trial testimony. Witchcraft persecutions needed accounts of the Sabbath to extend the chain of accusation, and this witness obliged. The protocol records that he "actually saw and recognized" Schneider Augustin of Honzrath.

Figure 2.1 Woodcut showing a witches' dance, from *The Witch of the Woodlands; or the Cobler's New Translation* (London, n.d. [early eighteenth century]), p. 2.

Confessions extracted through torture confirmed and consolidated the authorities' view of witchcraft.[56] These coerced accounts went beyond witnesses' testimony to construct a description of witchcraft from within. The true crime of witchcraft was service to the prince of darkness, and so the questions posed to accused witches and the confessions elicited focused on two typically (though not necessarily) nocturnal events: the initial agreement with the Devil (often consummated sexually), and the witches' sabbath. These confessions appear like palimpsests on which popular and legal views of witchcraft and the night overwrite one another. Their references to the night fuse the traditional sense that the Devil might appear at any time with the authorities' belief in the ubiquitous power of the Devil. Attitudes toward the night appear more uniformly negative in the testimony of accused witches, reflecting the more structured demonological writings and interrogation manuals. The Westphalian jurist Heinrich von Schultheis provided in his 1634 treatise on *How to Proceed with Interrogations into the Gruesome Blasphemy of Witchcraft,* a list of questions designed to elicit the whole nocturnal fantasy:

> Questions for interrogating the witches regarding
> their teacher
> the body of the Devil
> how they test their arts
> *maleficia*
> the place of dancing
> the worship service
> what they do after the dance
> eating and drinking
> honoring the Devil
> praying to the Devil
> blasphemy.

Schultheis also related several accounts of travelers and others who stumbled across nocturnal sabbaths.[57] A manuscript interrogatory used in the prince-bishopric of Eichstätt in 1617 included questions on "strange gatherings," asking of the accused witch "where she travelled to, and how they could get away in the dark night?" Interrogators were instructed to ask "whether and how they saw in the dark night; [and] what kind of light was present?" at the sabbath.[58]

The official narrative of witchcraft began at night. As Thomas Nashe asked in 1594: "When hath the devil commonly first appeared unto any man but in the night?" The expectation of a nocturnal encounter was ubiquitous but not rigid. Across Europe, confessed witches reported first meeting the Devil whenever they were alone, often at night but also by day.[59] The account of the widow Feylen Suin, convicted of witchcraft in the jurisdiction of the imperial abbey of St. Maximin (near Trier) in 1587, can stand for many others. "Once upon a time," her testimony began, "she was at home, sitting by the fire and her children were sleeping." She thought back on her inability to buy grain to feed her family earlier that day when "suddenly the Devil, in the form of a young apprentice with a long black robe, came to her." He consoled her and offered her money. She gave in to his temptations, denied God and "all his dear saints and the Mother of God" and had sexual relations with him ("Coitum exercuit membro frigidissimo etc.") to consummate their agreement.[60] Among the ninety-seven women and men from two villages (Longuisch and Kirsch) in the same region tried for witchcraft in the period 1587–1640, all but three confessed to first encountering the Devil alone, typically at night. Over half first met the Devil at home, including ten who encountered him in their beds at night. The interrogators of these accused witches focused relentlessly on the sexual consummation of their agreement with the Devil: all ninety-seven confessed witches in the Longuisch and Kirsch sample admitted to sexual relations with the Devil immediately upon their first encounter with him.[61]

The place of the night in these narratives varied. As the accused witch Niclas Fiedler, former mayor of Trier, confessed after repeated torture in 1591: "twelve years ago a black man came to him behind his house, between day and night, when his wife was suffering a long-lasting illness and he was very sad."[62] The accused witch was almost always described as being alone when first tempted by the Devil, and when the physical (usually sexual) consummation of the agreement between the Devil and the witch took place. This isolation, usually at night, supported narratives that confirmed the learned view of witchcraft and provided the evidence necessary for conviction, i.e., a confession of succumbing to the Devil's temptation and entering physically into an agreement with him. Two confessions from Guernsey from 1617 reveal the relative unimportance of the night in the first encounter with the Devil: Collette Du Mont confessed that "she was quite young when the Devil, in the form of a cat, appeared to her in the Parish of Torteval as she was returning from her cattle, it being still daylight, and that he took occasion to lead her astray by inciting her to avenge herself on one of her neighbors." Her co-defendant Isabel Becquet first met the Devil "in the form of a hare. [He] took occasion to tempt her, appearing to her in broad daylight in a road near her house." Isabel Becquet then confessed that the Devil later sent Collette Du Mont to her house to fetch her for the sabbath "during the ensuing night."[63]

Accounts of the witch's first encounter with the Devil stressed the physical and spiritual isolation of the accused more than a specific time of day. In contrast, the other key element in the witch's confession, the witches' dance or sabbath, was almost universally described as a gathering by night. Again, the confession of the widow Feylen Suin is representative. "Not long after [her first encounter with the Devil], on a Thursday night" the Devil returned to her "as she sat by the fire to spin and the children were asleep." Again he "had his way with her," then Suin climbed on a black dog and rode to a field beside the Mosel where "many came together ... including many important people. She danced there, leaping to the left into the air in the Devil's name."[64] In her 1617 confession Isabel Becquet of Guernsey described repeated visits to "the usual place where the Devil kept his Sabbath," but explained that "she never went to the Sabbath except when her husband remained all night fishing at sea."[65]

One cannot easily distinguish between "popular" and "learned" elements in accounts of the sabbath elicited by torture. Confessions shift between descriptions of a full-fledged "black mass," accounts of gatherings to harm crops through weather magic, and simpler accounts based on a rural dance seen in the witness testimony above. Within this range, accounts of a witches' dance far outnumber the more demonocentric confessions.[66] This suggests that despite the use of torture and leading questions designed to elicit accounts of a diabolical night, the more benign view of the night as a time for dance and sociability had deep roots. This is confirmed by the examination of rural night life below in chapter 7.

In the demonology and witch-lore of the sixteenth and seventeenth centuries, the diabolization of the night and its association with sin and temptation reached its peak. This was not a foregone conclusion, however. The influential *Malleus maleficarum* (i.e. "Hammer of sorceresses") first published in 1486 by Heinrich Institoris with Jakob Sprenger put relatively little emphasis on the night. Although Institoris felt he was writing "as the evening of the world is now declining toward sunset and the evil of men increases," the association of witchcraft with the night is quite limited in the *Malleus*.[67] The authors argue for the reality of noctivagation and include examples of nocturnal encounters with demons, but they do not attempt to theorize the night within their exposition of witchcraft. They were concerned with long-standing folk belief in nocturnal female spirits identified in canon law with "Diana, goddess of the pagans, and an innumerable multitude of women, [who] ride on certain beasts and traverse great distances … in the silence of the dead of night," as an eleventh-century confessors' guide put it. Medieval authorities stressed that Diana and the nocturnal flight were an illusion of the Devil; Institoris argued that although

women who believe that they ride on horseback with Diana or Herodias during the night-time hours are censured … adherents of the error think that because it is stated that such things happen only fantastically in the imagination, this is the case with all other effects [of witchcraft].[68]

In this first phase of the development of early modern demonology, the authors of the *Malleus* and many of their fifteenth-century contemporaries argued for the reality of nocturnal travel by witches.[69] But Institoris did not consider the night as such in the extended discussion of "incubi or succubi … [who] punish humans during the nighttime or contaminate them with the sin of debauchery" (part 1, questions 3–9), or in their review of the prosecution of witchcraft that forms part 3 of the work.[70]

It is important to note that the *Malleus* contains no discussion of the witches' sabbath, but by the second half of the sixteenth century this vision of nocturnal conspiracy had become central to the discourse on witchcraft. Shakespeare's Bolingbroke explained this in *2 Henry VI* as he and his fellow conspirators gathered to summon a spirit:

> Deep night, dark night, the silent of the night,
> The time of night when Troy was set on fire,
> The time when screech-owls cry and ban-dogs howl,
> And spirits walk, and ghosts break up their graves;
> That time best fits the work we have in hand.[71]

The fiction of the witches' sabbath (for there is no evidence of any such actual gatherings) created real and devastating possibilities for incrimination, demonization, and denunciation, based on a night of evil and fear. By Shakespeare's time the gravest crime of witchcraft was no longer conjuring or *maleficia*, but allegiance to the Devil, represented carnally by the pact, and ritualized by participation in the perverted order of the sabbath. In the twisted knot of early modern witchcraft persecution, it was surrender to nocturnal temptation and participation in the Devil's nocturnal anti-society which warranted the sentence of death, carried out on tens of thousands of victims.[72]

Thus the question of the physical reality of the witches' sabbath occupied all major demonological writers in the sixteenth and seventeenth centuries. Those who argued for the reality of the sabbath explained its secrecy by emphasizing the night in their accounts. In his *Demon-Mania of Witches* (1580) Jean Bodin addresses "Whether they [witches] are bodily transported by demons" and refers to five different cases involving witches who "had been transported many times at night to the witches' assemblies."[73] This leads Bodin to his larger point that witchcraft is exceptionally difficult to detect: "Since Satan and witches enact their mysteries at night, and witches' works are hidden and concealed and they cannot easily be sighted, the investigation and proof are difficult." Henri Boguet, judge in the county of Burgundy, agreed: "The crime of witchcraft is a crime apart, both on account of its enormity, and because it is usually committed at night and always in secret."[74] Writing in 1618 in a very different legal context, the English justice of the peace Michael Dalton also warned that "against these witches the Justices of peace may not always expect direct evidence, seeing all their works are the works of darkness, and no witnesses present with them to accuse them."[75] This emphasis on the obscurity of the crime marked it as exceptional, and Bodin and others argued that standard rules of evidence protecting the accused did not apply in witch trials.

The emphasis on the secrecy and the night also served to demonize folk beliefs. While the herdsman Chonrad Stoeckhlin and his fellow villagers distinguished carefully among good and evil forces in the

night, learned authors insisted on the identity of the Devil and darkness.[76] "It is no new or strange matter," explained Henri Boguet, "that
Satan should have his assemblies by night ... Satan is the master of
darkness and dwells in the darkness: moreover we find that he works
chiefly by night, as when he slew the first-born of Egypt and the cattle at the stroke of midnight." His experience as a judge bore this
out: "François Secretain added that she used always to go the sabbath
at about midnight ... all the other witches whom I have had in my
hands have said the same."[77] The German theologian Peter Binsfeld
summed up the theological and practical reasons for the identification
of witchcraft and the night:

Why is sorcery done much more often at night and in places abandoned by all
human traffic? There are two reasons ... After the expulsion from Paradise,
the Devil became dark and obscured, and so he does all his works in hidden
places and at dark times. The second reason is that if the wizards worked their
evil during the day, they might be seen by someone, and their wickedness
more easily discovered.[78]

These connections appear in all major demonological works of
the period. The influential work of the Jesuit Martin Del Rio, the
Disquisitiones magicae (1599–1600), which appeared in at least twenty-
four early modern editions, described witches in cities who "under
licence of night and darkness ... take pleasure in their wicked sports."[79]
Del Rio cites extensively the *Démonolâtrie* of Nicolas Remy (1595), who
provides from specific witchcraft trials in the duchy of Lorraine evidence for the reality of the witches' sabbath, including descriptions of
the food, music, dancing, masking, and homage to the Devil at "these
nocturnal assemblies and synagogues." "Just after midnight," Remy
concludes, "is the most opportune time for the activities of the Prince
of Darkness."[80] Pierre de Lancre's graphic *Tableau de l'inconstance des
mauvais anges et démons* (1612) explained that the Devil preferred the
time when "the blackest curtains of the night are drawn."[81]

Indeed, in the demonology of the age the nocturnal setting of the
sabbaths described by confessed witches seems overdetermined, as
the logic of contrariety and inversion examined so insightfully by
Stuart Clark suggests: if the servants of the Lord assembled in the

day, then the Devil's own would gather by night.[82] As Bernard presented in his *Guide to Grand-Jury Men* in parallel columns:

Behold, What the Lord doth:	What Satan doth:
1. The Lord hath his set Assemblies for his servants to meet together.	1. So the Devil hath his set meetings for his Magicians and Witches to come together.
2. The Lord hath his Sabbaths.	2. So Satan with his Witches have their times, which they call their sabbaths.[83]

Clark's study shows how early modern Europeans used the "Rule of Contraries" to understand the relationship between God and the Devil, and between the sovereign and the witch – incorporating, as Stuart notes, the inherently unstable logic of the supplement into their discourses on witchcraft and political authority.[84] Monarch and witch held parallel positions as the earthly representatives of God and Devil respectively. As contraries, sovereign and witch affirmed one another's existence. Clark has shown that this logic underpinned the endless re-creation of the sabbath (I would emphasize, the *nocturnal* sabbath) in the demonological treatises and witchcraft confessions of the sixteenth and seventeenth centuries. In chapter 8 I show how nocturnalization undermined the association of the night with witchcraft and spirits, transforming the theological and political authorities affirmed by these nocturnal forces.

For learned authors, the initial seduction of the witch by the Devil and the physical (typically sexual) consummation of their pact also followed this nocturnal logic. The French Catholic lawyer Pierre Le Loyer asked in the second (1605) edition of his monumental treatise on ghosts and specters, the *Discours et histoires des spectres, visions et apparitions des esprits, anges, demons et ames … divisez en huict livres*, "at what times and in which hours do devils appear?" Loyer responded: "The night and the darkness exist for their desires and pursuits, and Satan their prince as a title of honor is called the prince of darkness." The night, he continues

is the time when men, their bodies well-fed, sleep and rest and are subject to the ambushes of devils, inclined to their temptations, and easily moved to sensualities and the desires of the flesh.[85]

The Elizabethan bestseller *A Pensive Man's Practice* (first edn., 1584) warned that:

Mortal foes ... endeavor by all means, to entrap us by some evil or other, which we hear or see, in this vale of vanity ... whereunto we often yield, and that in the day time: much more in the dark and loathsome night, wherein all things are covered and hidden ... in which time of darkness, such as intend to work wickedness, are most ready.[86]

Given the theological and quotidian associations of sexuality with the night, the sexual confirmation of the witch's pact with the Devil would be expected at night. In the first edition of his *IIII. livres des spectres, ou apparitions et visions d'esprits, anges et démons* (1586), Loyer explained that "First of all, as the prince of darkness, he will have more force and power to make himself visible at night than by day."[87] Loyer reflected in his demonology the sense of nocturnal temptation seen above in Lavater, Nashe, Marlowe, and Shakespeare.

We see a similar association of witchcraft with the night in early modern images of witches and witchcraft. Jan Ziarnko's complex engraving of wicked acts packed into one image illustrated Pierre De Lancre's *Tableau de l'inconstance des mauvais anges et démons* (Figure 2.2, "Witches' Sabbath," 1612).[88] The image follows De Lancre's text closely and is accompanied by a guide to its grotesque details. Diurnal and nocturnal scenes overlap in the tableau, which includes two groups of men and women dancing, flying demons and witches, and the Devil enthroned as a goat (upper right). These demonological works took the nocturnal setting of the witches' sabbath quite seriously: the key to the Ziarnko illustration explains that the Devil is crowned with five horns, "the fifth one lit on fire to light all the candles and fires of the sabbath."[89] This detail helped jurists understand how witches at the sabbath could identify and incriminate other participants despite the dark of night. The sophistication and force of images such as Ziarnko's "Witches' Sabbath" notwithstanding, popular views of the Devil, the sabbath, and the night are probably better represented by Figure 2.1, resembling a simple peasants' dance.[90]

Ultimately, neither the witch of the church nor the witch of the people was confined to the night-time. As belief in the "phantoms of the night" (*Nachtschar*) indicates, early modern folklore and magical

Figure 2.2 "Description et figure du sabbat des sorciers," engraving by
Jan Ziarnko in Pierre de Lancre, *Tableau de l'inconstance des mauuais anges
et demons, ou il est amplement traicté des sorciers & de la sorcellerie* (Paris, 1612). By
permission of the Folger Shakespeare Library.

practices could associate the night with beneficial forces as much as
with human and supernatural evil. Conversely, one might encounter
the Devil by day as easily as by night. In contrast to learned views,
the night that emerges in peasant testimony about witchcraft is much
less freighted with evil and danger. When forced to testify about a
witches' sabbath, peasants generally described a witches' dance based
on a view of the night as a time for socializing and leisure. The diabolical elements added as accused witches were tortured invert various
aspects of a peasant dance by describing hideous music, preposterous
dancing, and disgusting food and drink, but these accounts do not
single out the time of the gathering *per se* as a sign of its diabolical
nature.

Learned authors described a Devil whose power was nearly unlimited on earth. They argued that the Devil most often tempted and overcame women and that this most often happened at night, but just as the Devil could and did ensnare men to serve him on earth, so too might one encounter the prince of darkness during the daylight hours. In contrast to the folk view, however, intellectual, ecclesiastical, and political authorities tended to see all popular nocturnal events as diabolical. Thus a distinct contrast emerges: while the educated demonized nocturnal folk beliefs, evidence from the common people shows no automatic association of the night with evil or temptation. As we will see below in chapter 7, gatherings at night such as spinning bees were central to licit rural sociability. The reformation of popular culture beginning in the sixteenth century challenged the nuanced folk view of the night with an intensified linkage of the night with infernal evil, diabolical temptation, and human sin. On stage, in learned demonology, and in countless confessions of witchcraft, the night became the time when women and men made themselves culpable and became the Devil's own.

Ultimately this all led to Hell. The darkness associated with Satan's servants on earth was absolute in his realm below. As Teresa of Avila (1515–82) related: "I was at prayer one day when suddenly ... I found myself, as I thought, plunged right into hell." She is granted a preview of "the place which the devils had prepared for me there" and provides a vivid description of Hell:

There was no light and everything was in the blackest darkness. I do not understand how this can be, but, although there was no light, it was possible to see everything the sight of which can cause affliction.[91]

The Elizabethan Nashe speculated that nocturnal darkness was in fact created to be a symbol of Hell: "Some divines have had this concept, that God would have made all day and no night, if it had not been to put us in mind [that] there is a Hell as well as a Heaven."[92] Descriptions of Hell often began with the punishment of the senses, sight first. Jean-Pierre Camus (1584–1652), French pastoral writer and bishop of Bellay, wrote at length on the darkness of Hell in a treatise translated into English as *A Draught of Eternity* (1632):

Now Faith doth teach us, that the damned shall be in thicker obscurities than those of Egypt, and that the deepest of darkness shall possess them forever. And in the Holy Scripture Hell is marked out in these words, *exterior darkness*. For an eternity ... light shall not be discovered therein.

This fundamental darkness required further explanation:

for although God be there [in Hell], as it were in every place; and though darkness cannot obscure his natural light, yet his will is that ... darkness cover the face of the Abyss; and that the eyes of the damned, though otherwise capable of sight, see nothing but that which may trouble and torment them.[93]

Camus went on to repeat a gloss dating back to Basil of Caesarea that the flames of Hell give heat but no light (inspired by Job 10:22, "the land of gloom and chaos, where light is as darkness"). Of course, the best-known anglophone description of the darkness of Hell appears in the first book of *Paradise Lost*:

> The dismal situation waste and wild,
> A dungeon horrible, on all sides round
> As one great furnace flamed, yet from those flames
> No light, but rather darkness visible
> Served to discover sights of woe,

Later Milton's Raphael describes the fate of the fallen angels to Adam and Eve: "Nameless in dark oblivion let them dwell."[94]

In the fallen world around them, did the men and women of this era see darkness and the night everywhere? When Marlowe's Faustus asks Mephistopheles "How comes it then, that thou art out of hell?" the spirit answers "Why, this is hell, nor am I out of it," asking in return:

> Think'st thou that I, who saw the face of God,
> And tasted the eternal joys of heaven,
> Am not tormented with ten thousand hells,
> In being depriv'd of everlasting bliss?[95]

For early modern Europeans, the night could indeed represent hell on earth. The night and its darkness expressed fundamental truths about witchcraft, spirits, Hell, and the Devil. In chapter 8 I examine the illumination of these dark features of the European mental landscape by new quotidian and metaphorical uses of the night, darkness, and light in the second half of the seventeenth century. The new truths of the resulting Enlightenment would redefine "night's black agents" for the modern world.

CHAPTER THREE

Seeking the Lord in the night, 1530–1650

3.1 DISCOVERING THE NIGHT

In the fiery exchanges of the first decades of the Reformation all sides cast their struggle as one of light against darkness, Christ against Antichrist. This was the world of the witch persecutions as well. Loud accusations of spiritual darkness or benighted ignorance drowned out the quieter tones that occasionally described darkness and the night as a path to the Divine. Yet by the end of the sixteenth century, a very different sense of darkness and the night emerged in Christian visual culture, spirituality, and literature. The art historian Maria Rzepinska was one of the first to call attention to the "'discovery of darkness' or the 'discovery of night'" in European Christian culture at the very end of the sixteenth century. She examined the use of "active darkness" to create shafts of artificial, condensed light in baroque painting, especially in the works of the late Tintoretto, Caravaggio, Ribera, Honthorst, and Georges de La Tour.[1] The use of this intense chiaroscuro suggested to Rzepinska "a powerful European trend which introduced darkness, inseparable from light, as an iconic and psychological factor of essential significance."[2] In similar terms, Chris Fitter has documented the rise of the poetic nocturne in the English Renaissance, whose "poetry, masques and painting, in revaluing the night as a time of beauty and profundity, overturn ... the construction predominant in classical and medieval traditions."[3] Fitter also dates the earliest evidence of this "nocturnal revolution" to the end of the sixteenth century. The work of Rzepinska and Fitter on this "discovery of night" sought to contextualize the development in relation to European painting and English literature respectively,

46

but their studies lead us to a broader question: how did early modern Europeans use the night to think about God in the turbulent period between the Reformation and the Enlightenment?

In this chapter I explore evidence of changing attitudes toward the night in the piety and practices of the Anabaptist movement, in the mystic theology of John of the Cross (1542–91) and Carmelite reform, and in the theosophy of Jacob Böhme (1575–1624). I then show how a wide range of writers across confessions, including John Donne (1572–1631), Johann Arndt (1555–1621), and Claude Hopil (c. 1580–after 1630) used the night in ascetic, apophatic, mystic, and epistemological terms as a powerful metaphor in the first half of the seventeenth century. This approach allows us to understand the uses of the night in early modern culture in terms more precise and revealing than those of previous scholarship and go beyond the general contrast between a positive night and a negative night.

3.2 SEEKING THE LORD IN THE NIGHT

Across Christian confessions, the confrontation with lasting division, uncertainty, and persecution in the wake of the Reformation was a painful reality. Yet in this period the few and circumscribed positive associations of the night described in chapter 1 gave way to much broader and more complex associations of darkness and the night with the Divine as Christians used the night to think about God in unprecedented and powerful ways. In this section I argue that the night became more sacred and more meaningful as an unintended consequence of the persecution and clandestine worship attendant to confessional formation. The connection between confessional division, persecution, and a new appreciation of the night is especially apparent in the new relationship with darkness and the night seen among sixteenth-century Anabaptists and Mennonites, in the mystic theology of John of the Cross, and in the complex and all-encompassing theosophy of Jacob Böhme. Their experiences and writings reveal a central set of metaphorical uses of the night that will allow us to survey the hidden terrain of darkness and devotion in the late sixteenth and seventeenth centuries.

As territorial churches established themselves in the sixteenth century, each prohibited and persecuted the others. Turbulent dynastic politics hurled kingdoms from one confession to another, and Christians of all confessions found themselves estranged from the established church of their ruler. Some chose to gather and worship in secret. For those driven "underground" by confessional conflict, the night was indispensable. Catholic, Lutheran, Anglican, and Reformed Christians all worshiped secretly at night at some point in the century after the Reformation. More importantly, members of each confessional retold and published stories of meeting at night as part of their narratives of persecution and steadfastness, faith and martyrdom. By the early seventeenth century, scattered accounts of "underground" worship at night had entered the literature of every church, subtly shifting the associations of secret services at night. As the Anglican preacher (later bishop of Norwich) Edward Reynolds (1599–1676) explained in 1632, even "in the worst times … wherein the Church was most oppressed … God found out in the wilderness a place of refuge, defence, and feeding for his Church." The faithful "did defend his truth, and … preserve his Church, though they were driven into solitary places, and forced to avoid the assemblies of Heretical and Antichristian Teachers." For Reynolds the lesson of persecution was clear: "We learn likewise not to censure persons, places or times … *Nicodemus* came to Christ *by night*, and yet even then Christ did not reject him."[4] The experience of persecution and reports of it taught this age that the persons, places, and times established by the authorities for worship might be false, and that the faithful might have to accept "persons, places or times" far from the traditional in order to worship as God intended.

Reynolds supported his point by reference to Nicodemus in the Gospel of John (3:1–3), "a man of the Pharisees, named Nicodemus, a ruler of the Jews: The same came to Jesus by night, and said unto him, Rabbi, we know that thou art a teacher come from God." Twice more identified with the night (John 7:50–51; 19:39), tradition explained that Nicodemus, like Joseph of Arimathea, came by night "secretly, for fear of the Jews" (John 19:38). In the sixteenth century this obscure figure became the exemplar for Christians forced to seek the Lord at night.

Writing in the mid 1520s, the poet Euricius Cordus was one of the first of this era to describe himself as a seeker in the night. A supporter of Luther, he felt himself "among people who persecute with ... hate every Nicodemus who seeks Christ in this night." Supporters of church reform in Hildesheim were described in 1528 as "finding their way secretly to Christ according to the example of Nicodemus." And in the town of Veere in the Netherlands in 1530 we hear of a Protestant "school" or conventicle held nightly in a home. One evening an itinerant Dutchman preached there on "how Nicodemus came at night to our Lord to be taught," combining the nocturnal meeting time with a discussion of its apostolic precedent.[5] From Catholic Albertine Saxony the redoubtable Georg Witzel, writing in 1538, compared his fellow Catholics in the surrounding Lutheran territories to Nicodemus: "they attend church at night, they sing at night, they come into their own at night; in the light of day they hide, speak under their breath, and dissimulate." In the same years Luther preached on John 3, praising Nicodemus for coming to the Lord at night.[6]

In the 1540s Calvin coined the term "Nicodemite" to rebuke Protestants in France who still attended Mass and failed to profess their faith openly.[7] He used the term figuratively, with no reference to any actual nocturnal gatherings.[8] The writings of Calvin, Farel, and Viret succeeded in giving Nicodemus a bad name, and in the second half of the sixteenth century fewer individuals identified themselves with him directly (though Calvin himself moderated his tone, later referring to Nicodemus as a true disciple).

Despite the pejorative use of "Nicodemite," the biblical scene in which Nicodemus comes to Christ by night appears in the devotional imagery of all confessions, growing in popularity well into the seventeenth century.[9] Figures 3.1 and 3.2 suggest the wide resonance of this night scene, from its use on a ceiling panel in the Carmelite convent of Himmelspforten, Würzburg (1613, Figure 3.1) to numerous prints, including one in Matthaeus Merian's engravings of biblical scenes in 1627 (Figure 3.2).

Figure 3.1 "Von Nicodemo dem Obersten. JO[hannes] 3," ceiling panel in
the Carmelite convent of Himmelspforten, Würzburg, 1613, showing
Nicodemus by candlelight.

Accounts of Christians of all confessions meeting at night to avoid
persecution abound in the second half of the sixteenth century. In
England during the reign of Mary, Protestant congregations met
in secret. Looking back from the third year of Elizabeth's reign,
William Ramsey of Devon wrote to the Protestant congregation he
served during the time of Marian persecution, reminding them that
he ministered "Early and late, privately and openly, as cause required
and occasion served."[10] A London congregation led by Thomas Rose
held a Protestant service on New Year's night, 1555, and in the remote

Figure 3.2 Matthaeus Merian, "Meeting of Christ and Nicodemus by Night," engraving in *Noui Testamenti D.N. Iesu Christi ... Des Newen Testaments vnsers Herren Jesu Christi fürnembste Historien vnd Offenbarungen in fleissigen und geschichtmesigen Figuren abgebildet, aufs Kupffer gebracht ... Durch Mattheum Merian von Basel* (Frankfurt, 1627). Photograph courtesy of the Newberry Library.

Lancashire village of Shakerly a layman named Jeffrey Hurst organized regular gatherings at his home "by night ... bringing with him some preacher or other, who used to preach unto them so long as the time would serve, and so departed by night again ... every time they came thither they were about 20 or 24 sometimes, but 16 at least, who had there also sometimes a Communion [service]."[11] In his *Ecclesiastical History* Theodore Beza described a Reformed congregation meeting at night in Tours in 1560:

[O]n the last day of September of the said year, the Holy Supper was celebrated by night with such a multitude of people that not being able to find a room large enough, they had to make do with an old temple of St. Lawrence that was not used for anything any longer ... Since then, the exhortations continued in this temple, by night, until about the twelfth of October, [when] the Church was entirely dispersed.[12]

After the accession of Elizabeth, English Catholics tended to continue to attend services in their parish church; Catholic noblemen conformed as an act of political obedience. The papal bull of 1570 deposing Elizabeth sharpened the line between English Catholics and Anglicans, and Catholic recusants began to avoid the established church and hear Mass in private or in secret, as in the county of Denbigh in Wales in 1578, where a Lady Throgmorton and others heard Mass in the house of John Edwards. Later, "upon St. Winifrid's day, Mrs. Edwards went to Halliwell by night, and there heard Mass in the night season." The recusants "carried thither with them by night, in mails and cloak-bags, all things pertaining to the saying of Mass. And ... these Mass-sayers used their audience to receive holy water, and come to confession."[13] In the same years the so-called Godly or Puritans were accused of setting up "night conventicles."[14] For Christians of all confessions, persecution or word of it showed that the true church might be driven into the night. Was it reassuring to note that "this Son of God did instruct his timorous Disciple Nicodemus, who came to him by night, more fully, than he did such as were his daily followers"?[15]

3.2.1 Anabaptists

Members of these other religious communities were sometimes forced to meet in darkness, but the Anabaptists faced a much broader exile into the night. For the persecuted Anabaptist communities of the sixteenth century, the confrontation with darkness and the night was literal. From the 1530s on, Anabaptist and Mennonite communities began to meet regularly at night, seeking in the darkness the freedom to assemble and preach denied to them during the day. They found toleration only in Moravia in the mid sixteenth century, and in the Dutch Republic from the late sixteenth century.

In the sixteenth century and for scholars today "Anabaptist" refers to Protestant radicals marked by their insistence on believer's baptism, their denial of infant baptism, their pacifism, and their understanding of their sect as the separate, "true" church.[16] From their origins in the Zurich Reformation, four Anabaptist groups emerged by the middle of the sixteenth century: the Swiss Brethren (direct successors of the first Anabaptists of Zurich), South German groups, the Hutterian or Moravian communities, and the Mennonites of northern Germany and the Low Countries. These groups sought to live a biblicist theology as a tiny minority suffering sporadic but violent persecution. The Hutterian or Moravian communities found refuge at the far eastern edge of the Holy Roman Empire in territories still controlled by the local nobility. They enjoyed a golden age in the second half of the sixteenth century before the Habsburg imposition of the Catholic Reformation forced them eastward into Hungary and Russia.[17]

The earliest reports of Anabaptist worship mention early morning services and meetings, but by the 1530s these had become too dangerous in most regions.[18] Sources from Flanders, the Rhineland, Alsace, Switzerland, Württemberg, Hesse, and Tirol document dozens of nocturnal gatherings of Anabaptists and Mennonites, including those planned around visits by Moravian/Hutterian missionaries.[19] The Strasbourg city archives, for example, describe specific gatherings at night outside the city in 1545, 1557, and 1576 and refer to at least thirty-four other nocturnal meetings in the Strasbourg area in the period before 1601.[20] The accounts came from town officials, pastors, and the simply curious who found their way into nocturnal gatherings of Anabaptists.[21] Reports of hundreds of participants are not uncommon. For example, the Lutheran pastor Elias Schad reported to the Strasbourg city council about a gathering he had infiltrated in 1576. Judging from the accents he heard, Schad thought those assembled came from across the Empire – from "Switzerland, Breisgau, Westerich [?], Württemberg, Upper and Lower Alsace, perhaps even from Moravia."[22] The intrepid Lutheran pastor described a system of passwords and sentries used to protect the gathering, evidence of practical experience built up over decades of meeting at night.[23] After Schad revealed himself to the group and initiated a lengthy theological debate over baptism and the nature of the church, he was escorted out by the Anabaptists, without whose help, he notes, he would never have found his way out of the forest at night.

Living in a state of confessional siege, the Anabaptists and Mennonites gained a new appreciation of the night in both practical and spiritual terms. A 1538 apology for Anabaptism in Hesse written by Georg Schnabel explains that their "secret gatherings in the woods, in the wilderness, or in houses" followed biblical precedents, citing among other passages "Acts 20 [verse 9], where Paul preached in the night."[24] Evidence of the re-evaluation of the night appears in one of the earliest accounts of a nocturnal gathering. As Anabaptists met outside Strasbourg on the night of July 24–25, 1545, two youths, the Lutheran pastor's son Jeremias Steinle and his friend Murwolf, snuck into the gathering "for fun" ("aus fürwitz") and described it to the city council shortly afterward. The young men reported hearing a sermon on the liberation of the children of Israel from their bondage in Egypt, and another sermon on Revelation 11.[25] The Anabaptist preaching, which lasted from about 10 p.m. until 1 a.m., contrasted the false "church of stone" established by the authorities with the true church of the spirit.[26] The assembled were told to shun their parish church and meet with their fellow believers whenever they could. The leaders of the service then explained that "one cannot find God *except in the wilderness and in the darkness*."[27] For those who gathered regularly in the night, the point was clear.[28]

By the middle of the sixteenth century, Anabaptists and their persecutors alike associated the movement with secret meetings at night.[29] The imperial warrant issued for the arrest of Menno Simons in December 1542 accused him of "deceiving the simple people with his false teaching during secret, nocturnal meetings."[30] Simons himself took up this accusation in his "A Humble and Christian Apology and Reply concerning the Bitter, Vicious Lies and False Accusations" of 1552. "In the seventh place," he explained, "they slander us and say that we are vagabonds, sneak-thieves, seducers … an ungodly sect and conspiracy." Simons used the charge to address the association of Anabaptist and Mennonite communities with the night:

As to the ugly and vicious slander of being *sneak-thieves*: sneak-thieves are thieves and murderers who secretly enter houses for the purpose of taking the property or lives of others, also adulterers and seducers who are intent upon defiling the houses of their neighbors. Such wait for the darkness, says Job, and say "No eye shall see me." In the dark they break into houses.[31]

"But we are not of that kind," Simons explained. Because in these troubled times "one cannot publicly let out a peep about the word of the Lord," the faithful must gather in secret at night. Simons justifies this with biblical authorities:

Moreover we learn from the Scriptures that Moses and all Israel ate the Passover at night [Ex. 12]; that Jesus admonished Nicodemus at night [John 3:2]; that the church assembled at night to pray [Acts 12:12]; that Paul taught the Word of the Lord all night [Acts 20]; and that the first church assembled at night to break the bread of the Lord, as the historians report.

His experience with the night led him to argue that "therefore, we confess that we must practice and promote the Word of the Lord at night as well as in the daytime, to the praise of the Lord." Acknowledging Anabaptist/Mennonite practice, he continued "And so we assemble … in the fear of God, without hindrance or harm to any man, the Lord knows, at night as well as in the daytime, in a Christian manner, to teach the Word of the Lord and to admonish and reprove in all godliness; also to pray and administer the sacraments as the word of the Lord teaches us."[32] Simons's collection of authoritative biblical accounts of gathering, teaching, and worship at night is especially significant when contrasted with the uncompromising "darkness-vs.-light" imagery of earlier Anabaptist writings.[33] In the second half of the sixteenth century, we see further evidence of a much more nuanced Anabaptist view of the night and its darkness.

A Hessian account of 1578 provides an especially clear example of Anabaptist identification with Nicodemus and the night. The Lutheran pastor Tilemann Nolte (a former priest from Fulda) accepted an invitation from a peasant named Hen Klint to go and hear the Anabaptists preach.[34] Nolte attended a gathering of about 300 people on the night of May 19, 1578 (Pentecost Monday) in a forest near the village of Schwarz. Two leaders of the group approached him and asked for his help in avoiding the authorities. They explained to Nolte that

they were poor people and they, like Nicodemus, had sought the Lord at night. Although they would well like to teach and preach openly, the authorities would not permit it.[35]

This reference to Nicodemus is especially significant. Through their deep biblicism, these Anabaptists found a scriptural reference point for lives spent "underground" avoiding persecution. Menno Simons cited John 3:1–3 in his defense of clandestine worship at night, and these Anabaptists chose to identify with Nicodemus because they "had sought the Lord at night."

The authorities did not intervene at the Hessian meeting described above, but a similar gathering in a forest outside Zurich on September 5, 1574 was encircled and broken up by the Zurich city guard: the two missionaries from Moravia who led the service were arrested. A Zurich report of the incident included a hand-colored drawing of the Moravians preaching by candlelight at a table in the forest (Figure 3.3).[36] The image of reading or preaching by candlelight in the forest recurs in other accounts.

The Hutterites of Moravia lived in relative safety and worshipped only during the day. But the Moravian Anabaptist communities sent out hundreds of missionaries in the sixteenth century, and these men moved by night, met and preached by night, and risked imprisonment, torture, and death. The authors of the *Hutterite Chronicle* described them as "hunted and driven from place to place and from land to land. They had to be like owls and night ravens, not daring to appear by day, hiding ... in the wild woods."[37] Setting out from their havens, the Hutterite settlements in Moravia, these missionaries anticipated a nocturnal life. When the missionaries Hans Arbeiter and Heinrich Schister were captured at Hainbach in the bishopric of Speyer in 1568, Arbeiter sent an account of their captivity and interrogation to his brethren in Moravia. He noted that "when we got to Kirrweiler Castle ... I, with many threats and insults, was shut into a dark dungeon deprived of all daylight, an experience familiar to many believers."[38] Describing the captivity and martyrdom of Hans Mändel in Tirol in 1560–61, the Hutterian chronicle related that while he was imprisoned in the Vellenburg, "the spirits whom God sends to terrify the ungodly at night were now sent to serve and help him," explaining that "the Lord forewarned him through such a spirit when the noblemen were coming to question him. It called him by name and told him to prepare himself and to be ready to suffer."[39] We have seen in the previous chapter the ubiquitous fear of "the spirits

Figure 3.3 Contemporary chronicle illustration of Moravian missionaries preaching by candlelight in the forest outside Zurich, 1574. Zentralbibliothek Zurich, ms F 23, s 393v/394r.

whom God sends to terrify the ungodly at night"; here the Moravian *Chronicle* records triumph over these nocturnal spirits and a sense that, with God's grace, the night and its spirits instead serve the persecuted Brethren.

The earliest writings of the Anabaptist communities, such as the Schleitheim Confession of 1527, resound with the light–darkness opposition typical of Reformation polemics: "For truly all creatures are in but two classes, good and bad … darkness and light." These early texts encouraged Anabaptists to stand firm, "so we shall not walk in darkness."[40] The transformation of the associations of darkness and the night among Anabaptists in the second half of the sixteenth century anticipates and reflects a broader appreciation of darkness across Western Europe by the start of the seventeenth century.[41] Persecution forced small groups within each confession to worship at night; for Anabaptists outside of the Dutch Republic and Moravia, this experience transformed their appreciation of darkness and the night.

3.2.2 *John of the Cross*

As Anabaptist communities from Flanders to the Austrian Alps gathered together at night, Juan de Yepes y Alvarez lay in a dark prison cell in Toledo. His daring escape, illuminated by a full moon during the night of August 15–16, 1578 symbolized a new kind of night, a night that liberated the soul to seek the Divine.[42] Following his escape John of the Cross (1542–91), as he has been known since he became a reformed Carmelite friar 1568, produced the deepest and most complex engagement with the "dark night of contemplation" in the early modern centuries.[43] His writings on darkness and the night "transformed the night into the central principle of mystic theology," crystallizing the nocturnalization of faith and piety under discussion here.[44] The works of John of the Cross epitomize the use of the night to approach and understand the Divine in the seventeenth century.

Scholars agree that the actual experience of the physical night shaped profoundly the development and expression of John's mystic theology.[45] In fact two very different aspects of John's relationship to the night emerge in his biography. Reports of his appreciation of serene nocturnal devotion (both in church before the tabernacle and outside, under the stars) contrast with the darkness of his abduction, captivity, and escape from a prison cell in the monastery of his brother Carmelites in Toledo. John's references to "the tranquil night, / at the time of the rising of the dawn, / the silent music and sounding solitude" reflect the many accounts of his excursions outside in the middle of the night with his companions to pray and observe the beauty of the heavens, as well as many nights spent in solitary prayer.[46] In violent contrast, his abduction on the night of December 2, 1577 began nine months of imprisonment in a nearly lightless cell in the fortress-like Carmelite monastery in Toledo. The period of hope and despair ended with John's daring escape on an August night in 1578. John processed the Toledo experience in several ways, writing of the sense of being kidnapped and led away in the dark, of the dark nights of imprisonment with their attendant spiritual sorrows and joys, and of the liberation of the night of August 15–16. We can examine each in turn.

By the late 1570s the movement to reform the Carmelite order led by Teresa of Avila and John of the Cross met with increasing hostility from the unreformed ("Calced") friars. The seizure of John by Calced fathers and armed men in Avila on the night of December 2, 1577 was not the first such abduction: in early 1576 John and another reformed Carmelite friar were taken from Avila to Medina del Campo by force at the instigation of the prior of the Calced friars in Avila. The two men were released after a short time – perhaps a few days. This first abduction may be reflected in one of his earliest poems, "I entered in – I knew not where," dated prior to his imprisonment in Toledo. This work speaks of a "cloud of unknowing" with the power to illuminate: "however darksome was its shroud / It illuminated all the gloomy night."[47] John might have encountered this sense of "the darkness that illuminates" in a range of authors from Denys the Areopagite to Francisco de Osuna, as discussed above in chapter 1.[48]

The abduction in December 1577 led to a much longer imprisonment. All accounts of John's cell in the Calced Carmelite monastery in Toledo stress its darkness, lit by one narrow window high above. Physical darkness, combined with the psychological pressures exerted by the unreformed Carmelites who were his jailors, informed the works John composed there and shortly after his escape. His prison works include the poems "For I Know Well the Spring" (with its refrain "Although it is the night"), the first thirty-one stanzas of *The Spiritual Canticle*, and the *Romances*. The poem "Dark Night" was written just after his nocturnal escape.[49] In eight stanzas "Dark Night" presents an account of John's escape through the words of a secular love poem. These verses also served to describe, as John explained, "the method followed by the soul in its journey upon the spiritual road to the attainment of the perfect union with God, to the extent that it is possible in this life."[50] The first five stanzas narrate a nocturnal flight that unites beloved and lover:

1 On a dark night, Kindled in love with yearnings …
   I went forth without being discovered, My house being now at rest.
2 In darkness and secure, By the secret ladder, disguised …
   In darkness and in concealment, My house being now at rest.
3 In the happy night, In secret, when none saw me,
   Nor I beheld anything, Without light or guide, save that which burned in
   my heart.
4 This light guided me – More surely than the light of noonday …
5 Oh, night that guided me, Oh, night more lovely than the dawn,
   Oh, night that joined Beloved with lover, Lover transformed in the
   Beloved!

These and other poems from the Toledo period were revised and expanded in the following years, then glossed by John in extensive prose commentaries for the benefit of reformed Carmelite nuns and monks. In these commentaries John became the theologian of his own experience of the night. His encounter with darkness, real and spiritual, led to a deep engagement with the night, expressed in this series of devotional writings and practices. John built his theology upon a set of terms, especially the "dark night of the soul" and the "dark night of the spirit," which resonate with the ascetic, apophatic, and mystic metaphors of the night articulated across early modern Europe in this period.

This engagement emerges in the two separate commentaries on the poem "Dark Night" written by John: *The Ascent of Mount Carmel* (1579–85) and *Dark Night of the Soul* (1582–85). In these complementary treatises John consolidated and refined his new use of the night as *Ursymbol* for the mystic path to union with God. The Spanish Carmelite introduced *Ascent of Mount Carmel* by outlining its use of the metaphor of night: "We may say that there are three reasons for which this journey made by the soul to union with God is called night." First, John notes that "denial and deprivation are, as it were, night to all the desires and senses of man." Second, faith, "the road along which the soul must travel to this union" is called "as dark as night to the understanding." Third, the destination of the soul's journey is "God, who, equally, is dark night to the soul in this life."[51] John's works consistently outline a threefold night: an ascetic night of purgation, an inexpressible or apophatic night, and a mystic union with God likened to the night. John elaborated this tripartite metaphor by aligning it with the lived experience of the actual night:

These three parts of the night are all one night; but, after the manner of night, it has three parts. For the first part, which is that of sense, is comparable to the beginning of the night, the point at which things begin to fade from sight. And the second part, which is faith, is comparable to midnight, which is total darkness. And the third part is like the close of night, which is God, the part which is now near to the light of day.[52]

In this metaphor the first part of the night, the "dark night of the soul" or "dark night of the senses," purges the soul of its connection to the worldly aspects of devotion. In John's experience, this could be devastating.[53] The second part of the night metaphor, the dark night of the spirit, is described by John as even more profound and disturbing than the night of the senses. That dark night of the spirit, "total darkness," serves to separate the soul from its own memory, reason, and desire so that it can be united with God.[54] The third part of this night is the mystic union of the soul and the Divine. To apply the night metaphor to the mystic path, John brought together the devotional, metaphorical, and mystical uses of the night in the Christian tradition. He retained the traditional mystic sequence (*purgatio, illuminatio, unio*) in the commentaries *Ascent of Mount Carmel* and *Dark Night of the Soul* by describing a twofold purging of the human soul (i.e., sensual nature) and spirit, moving through an ascetic night and an apophatic night to reach a mystic night of union. John's innovation is simple and powerful: the night becomes the element common to each step of the mystic's path.[55] In this way the night becomes, as Jean Baruzi has noted, the fundamental element of John's theology.[56]

Supplementing each of these metaphors of night – ascetic, apophatic, and mystic – is a deeper principle articulated by John not in direct reference to the structure and language of his work, but frequently and allusively, as for example in chapter 13 of book 1 of *Dark Night of the Soul*. Discussing the relationship between self-knowledge and knowledge of God in the night, John noted that, "As the philosophers say, one extreme can be well known by the other." With these words John cited a principle central to the philosophical, pedagogical, and rhetorical culture of the sixteenth and seventeenth centuries: contrariety, which has been so richly described by Stuart Clark in his work on the intellectual history of witchcraft.[57] The general concept of opposition in Western thought, reflected in "polarity, duality, antithesis, and contrariety" served innumerable purposes in thought and expression. Clark examines the deeply rooted "language of contraries" in early modern discourses on physics, natural magic, and medicine. Because, as Clark observes, "contrariety was thought to characterize the logic of the Creator's own thinking," it was used to understand and discuss "all natural, intellectual, and social phenomena" from cosmology and ethics to literature, rhetoric, and religion. John of the Cross's use of the *todo–nada* theme in the *Ascent of Mount Carmel* is one of countless examples.[58] In the "discovery of night" John of the Cross and his seventeenth-century successors relied on an epistemological night which illuminated through contrariety. As we will see below, Jacob Böhme elevated this device – primarily through its implications for the relationship between light and darkness – to the guiding principle of his cosmology.

Studies of John's predecessors underscore the new role the night plays in his mystic theology.[59] Although John refers to the thought of John Baconthorpe, John Tauler, and Jan van Ruysbroeck throughout his works, John's use of darkness and the night differs from these late medieval mystics.[60] Georges Tavard argues that terms similar to John's vocabulary of the night appear in the *Cloud of Unknowing* and in Walter Hilton (vernacular English writers whom John could not have known) and among the Rhenish mystics (translated into Latin by Lorenzo Surius in the mid sixteenth century), but that their conception of night "seems to diverge notably from his."[61] The key comparison is with Nicolas of Cusa, who placed the complementarity and inseparability of darkness and light near the center of his thought. The logical or conceptual value of darkness in Cusa contrasts with the place of the night, experiential and concrete, at the center of John's theology, in which it is more than merely a symbol or concept. In similar terms, Cusa's fundamental understanding of God as the "coincidentia oppositorum" in which all contradictions, including darkness and light, become one, contrasts with the irreducibility of *todo* and *nada* for John. This irreducible night seems as existential and fundamental as John's experiences of it.[62] And this night – profound and irreducible, taken without any reference to the dawn – informs a dynamic range of early modern thought and expression in the generations after John's death.

This reading of several of the major works of John of the Cross alerts us to four kinds of night – the ascetic, apophatic, mystic, and epistemological – evoked in early modern culture. The Carmelite's theology of the night allows us to understand the uses of the night in early modern culture in terms more precise and revealing than a simple contrast between positive and negative views of the night. As we will see, each of these four ways of thinking with the night resonated widely across European culture in the seventeenth century as never before. This resonance goes far beyond any question of influence by the relatively unknown Spanish Carmelite author, whose works were not published until 1618.

3.2.3 *Jacob Böhme: contrariety as cosmos*

"Nothing can be revealed to itself except through contrariety [*Wiederwärtigkeit*]." So proclaimed Jacob Böhme in his "On the

Vision of the Divine" ("Von Göttlicher Beschaulichkeit") in book 6 of the *Christosophia* (1624), one of his last writings.[63] Contrariety was fundamental to early modern thought and expression, but the German philosopher-mystic elevated this principle to the essence of divine and created nature. In his expansive theosophy, developed in a flood of prose between 1619 and 1624, Böhme envisioned contrariety as a dynamic force that shaped God, the process of creation, and all aspects of human existence. No contrariety was more important to Böhme's thought than the pair light–darkness, and a systematic, detailed cosmology of light and darkness permeates his work. In his last major work, the *Mysterium magnum* of 1623, a commentary on Genesis that elucidated "the kingdom of nature and the kingdom of grace," Böhme emphasized the power of contrariety to create and reveal:

> The darkness is the greatest enemy of the light, yet it is the means by which the light is revealed. If there were no black, then the white would not be revealed; and if there were no suffering, so also joy would not be revealed.[64]

A few pages later Böhme returns to this principle: "in the darkness the light is recognized, otherwise it would not be revealed," noting that "the basest must be the origin of the best."[65] The discussion of darkness and light in the works of the shoemaker (and later cloth merchant) of Görlitz is one of the most complex and influential of the early modern period. Böhme sought no followers and remained in outward conformity with the Lutheran church all his life. Only one of his works was published during his lifetime, but his writings circulated in manuscript copies and were quickly published in German and in translation after his death. They found admirers far and wide. In 1646 Charles I of England, after reading Böhme's *Answers to Forty Questions* (*Vierzig Fragen von der Seelen*) allegedly exclaimed, "God be praised that there are still men in existence who are able to give from their own experience a living testimony of God and His Word!"; in 1649 Oliver Cromwell's chaplain, Peter Sterry (1613–72), influenced by Böhme, preached in Behemist terms that "Darkness, and light, are both in God; not only Representatively, but really; not in their ideas only, but their Identities."[66] Böhme's life and work were shaped decisively by the confessional age into which he was born. His native region, Silesia, stood on the frontlines of religious and political conflict. As a cloth merchant he traveled across the region; he witnessed the royal entry of Frederick of the Palatinate into Prague as king of Bohemia in 1619 and saw the outbreak of what would become the Thirty Years War. In his writings he consistently sought to transcend the confessional struggles raging around him.

Böhme took the principle of contrariety, widespread in early modern culture, and elevated it to a cosmology understood through day and night, light and darkness. These pairs become inseparable and complementary. He explained his fundamental principle especially clearly in his *Quaestiones Theosophicae* (1624). In response to a question about the coexistence of God's love and wrath, Böhme began:

> The reader should understand that all things consist in Yes and No, be they divine, diabolic, terrestrial, or however they may be named. The One, as the Yes, is pure power and life, and is the truth of God or God himself. He would in himself be unknowable, and in him would be neither joy nor elevation, nor feeling, without the No.[67]

The Divine manifests itself through its creation of contraries: "The No is a counterstroke of the Yes or the truth, in order that the truth may be manifest and be a something, in which there may be a *contrarium*." This is not, however, any simple dualism:

> And yet it cannot be said that the Yes is separated from the No, and that they are two different things side by side. They are only one thing, but they separate themselves into two beginnings [*principia*], and make two centers, each of which works and wills in itself.

Böhme chose night and day to explain this reciprocity: "Just as day in relation to night, and night in relation to day, form two centers, and yet are not separated, or separated only in will and desire," so too is the relationship between the Yes and the No, which forms the basis of all existence. Continuing in reference to day and night as expressed by heat and cold, Böhme explains that:

> Neither would be manifest or operative without the other ... Without these two, which are in continual conflict, all things would be a nothing, and would

stand still without movement. The same is to be understood regarding the eternal unity of the Divine power.[68]

For light to exist, there must be darkness; and to know light, one must know darkness, because they are coexistent, not in a relationship of presence and absence, but as complements to one another. Böhme's polarized cosmos comes into being and is known through contrariety.[69]

Böhme sought to describe the dynamic relationships between God, man, and nature in images as well. In his *Answers to Forty Questions*, composed around 1620, he advises the reader to visualize his thought by contrasting darkness and light in a geometric figure: "Put the *Grimm* [a manifestation of darkness] on the left, and the light on the right …; there is no other way of drawing it, but it is a sphere."[70] The first illustration of this "Philosophische Kugel oder … Wunder = Auge der Ewigkeit" appeared in a 1632 Latin edition of the *Answers to Forty Questions* printed in Amsterdam, and the image appeared in later editions of his works in Latin, English, Dutch, and German, again showing the breadth of the reception of Böhme in the century after his death. The English adaptation of the image (1647) appears as Figure 3.4. The contrariety of light and darkness is the dominant theme of the image: one sees the "two centers," one dark and one light, as referenced above in the *Quaestiones Theosophicae*. The sixty-five specific Behemist terms brought together in the 1632 image suggest the complexity of Böhme's theosophy; at the same time, the fundamental connection between the spheres of darkness and light is apparent. In words and in images, Böhme thus presented a theology in which light and darkness are balanced and interdependent; this contrasts sharply with the imagery of light and darkness in the Lutheran and radical traditions from which he issued.[71] Given the distance of his thought from even his closest predecessors, such as Valentin Weigel and Johann Arndt, how should we assess the sources of his ideas?

Like the Anabaptists and the Carmelite reformers, Böhme knew intra- and inter-confessional strife and persecution first hand. But his experiences allow us to glimpse deeper crises and more profound solutions formed in the crucible of the confessional age. His

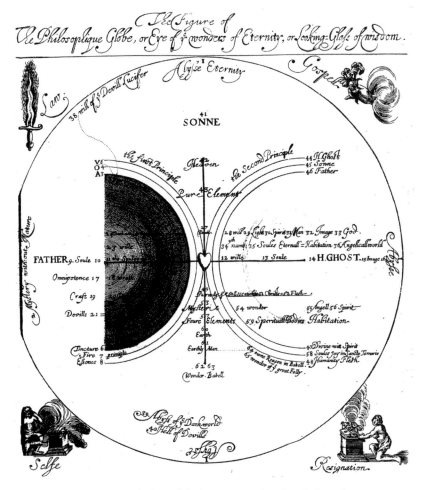

Figure 3.4 Representing light and darkness in Jacob Böhme's thought. Engraving from Jacob Böhme, *XL. questions concerning the soule* (London, 1647), pp. 22–23. University of Chicago Library, Special Collections Research Center.

theosophy, which he saw as a divine revelation, can also be understood through its personal, existential origins, and in the rich, relatively open cultural-intellectual milieu of Silesia at the end of the sixteenth century. From his first writing, the unfinished *Rising Dawn* (*Morgenröthe im Aufgang*, later referred to as *Aurora*) of 1612 to his last works in 1624, Böhme sought to explain the relationship between

God and humankind in terms of the physical world, which he understood as fundamental material reality *and* as allegory.

The decentering of the earth by the new astronomy seems to
have started Böhme's search. By his own account, Böhme's revelations followed a period of "hard melancholy and sadness" caused,
as he related in chapter 19 of the *Aurora*, when he "contemplated in
[his] spirit the vast Creation of this World." By the time he wrote
Aurora in 1612, Böhme held firmly to the new astronomy, stating
"the earth turns and courses with the other planets around the sun
as in a wheel."[72] Böhme seems to have first learned of this heliocentric view sometime before 1600: he related in the *Aurora* that he was
suddenly and deeply disturbed by his first encounter with heliocentric or polycentric astronomy, and wondered what "the little spark
of humanity" could mean to God, lost among his "great works of
heaven and earth." He described in poignant terms the loss of his
medieval Christian world view:

Before this ... I myself held that the true Heaven formed a round circle, quite
sky-blue, high above the stars, in the opinion that God had therein his specific
being, and ruled in this world solely through the power of his holy spirit.

This view was given "quite a few hard blows ("gar manchen harten
Stoß") by word of a heliocentric (or perhaps polycentric and infinite)
universe.[73]

Secure in an Aristotelian-geocentric world view, John of the Cross
contemplated the night sky with a sense of divine order that located
humankind and nature within concentric spheres of planets and fixed
stars encompassed by the celestial realm of angels, saints, and God.
Böhme looked at the same night sky with fear, "very melancholy and
intensely saddened" by the implications of the new astronomy. He
explained that as a result of his heliocentric understanding of the cosmos, the Devil would "often send pagan thoughts" (a circumlocution
for atheist conclusions about the absence of God?) to him.[74] Where
was God in this "new" universe? Infinitely distant from the earth and
humankind?[75]

Böhme feared that the absence of God was confirmed by the world
around him: "I found that good and evil were in all things, in the

elements and in the creatures, and that in this world the godless fare
as well as the pious, and that the barbarian peoples have the best
lands, and that they enjoy more happiness than the godly."[76] His crisis combined the disorientation of the new, infinite, universe with the
age-old question of theodicy. Böhme attested that "no writings, even
among those I knew so well, could console me." The cobbler-turned-
theologian described the confusion of a new, vast universe alongside
the apparent predominance of evil in the world. Böhme's contemporary John Donne evoked the same confusion at the same time in his
Anniversaries (1611):

> And new Philosophy calls all in doubt,
> The Element of fire is quite put out;
> The Sunne is lost, and th'earth, and no mans wit
> Can well direct him where to looke for it.
> And freely men confesse that this world's spent,
> When in the Planets, and the Firmament
> They seeke so many new; they see that this
> Is crumbled out againe to his Atomis.
> 'Tis all in pieces, all coherence gone;
> All just supply, and all Relation:
> Prince, Subject, Father, Sonne, are things forgot,
> For every man alone thinkes he hath got
> To be a Phoenix, and that then can be
> None of that kinde, of which he is, but he.[77]

In this passage Donne, like Böhme, fuses the "new Philosophy" with
a sense of moral or social disorder, as the proper relations between
princes and subjects, and fathers and sons have lost "All just supply,
and all Relation." With "all coherence gone," restoring order would
not be easy.[78] The solution Böhme fashioned transformed him from
troubled cobbler to influential theosopher.

The breakthrough came around 1600, as described in chapter 19 of
the *Aurora*, titled "On the created Heaven and the form of the earth
and the water, also on the light and the darkness."[79]

In a word, the solution to Böhme's crisis was immanence. God
dwelt in this world, in everything, not in a distant Heaven. This
immanence meant a new embrace of all of the natural world, both
as material and as symbol, especially – as the title of the chapter

suggests – its light *and* its darkness. This "awareness [*Erkenntnis*] and revelation from God" came after "wrestling with the love and mercy of God," a reference to Böhme's namesake Jacob wrestling at night with an angel.[80]

Immanence also shaped his new understanding of evil. Through his entire *oeuvre*, the question of evil and redemption remained central to Böhme's theosophy, as did the imagery of darkness and light. Böhme developed an understanding of evil unique within the Christian tradition, describing its generation through the unfolding of the potential within the *Ungrund* – the undifferentiated Divinity as it existed before creation. This view made evil, Satan, Hell (understood untopologically), and darkness fundamental and necessary aspects of creation. Böhme broke decisively with the traditional Christian view of evil and darkness as deficiency or privation. *Contra* Augustine, evil was in Böhme's cosmos more than the mere absence of good, and darkness more than the privation of light. Both became real in their own right as necessary aspects of creation. This cosmos and the place of evil in it stands in startling contrast to all orthodox Christian views of his age.[81]

The revelations first received around 1600 and first outlined in the unfinished *Aurora* (1612) ended the depression and confusion prompted by the new astronomy and by the seeming triumph of evil in the world. But the circulation of Böhme's ideas in manuscript marked a second turning point in the artisan's life as he faced conflict with the local Lutheran clergy over his startling, heterodox ideas. In the late sixteenth century, Böhme's Görlitz was a crossroads of heterodox ideas and beliefs where pastors, city councilors, artisans, travelers, and local nobles discussed the diverse intellectual and cultural offerings of the time: Calvinism, Lutheran mysticism, Paracelsan alchemy, the new astronomy, Catholic reform, Schwenkfeldian ideas, and more. Kepler visited the city in 1607; the city councilor Bartholomäus Scultetus and Böhme's pastor Martin Moeller (1547–1606) were among the city's leading intellectuals.

This lively, relatively open cultural-intellectual milieu was fundamental to the development of Böhme's ideas. But Görlitz was becoming less tolerant and more tied to Lutheran orthodoxy just as his writings began to circulate in 1612–13. A local nobleman, Carl Ender von Sercha, made copies of the unfinished *Aurora* manuscript. In July 1613 a copy reached the new senior Lutheran pastor of Görlitz, Gregor Richter. He immediately informed city councilor Scultetus of the cobbler's heretical work. Böhme was brought before Scultetus and questioned about his "enthusiastic beliefs." While Böhme was held briefly at the Rathaus, the *Aurora* manuscript was confiscated from his home. Böhme was warned not to dabble in theology any further and released; the manuscript was locked away. Scultetus handled Böhme fairly gently, but pastor Richter was more forceful. The following Sunday, July 28, 1613, he denounced false prophets such as Böhme from the pulpit; the cobbler-cloth merchant was then questioned by Richter and the clerical council of Görlitz on July 30. The meeting concluded with Böhme's agreement to cease writing about theological and spiritual matters. This public censure left a lasting mark on Böhme's life.[82]

In the years between his silencing in 1613 and the resumption of his writing in 1619 Böhme reflected deeply on confessional strife and war. He returned to writing with a manuscript titled *The Three Principles* (*Beschreibung der Drey Principien Göttliches Wesens*); like all his writings after 1612, it is entirely critical of the established churches and their clergy. In the theosopher's view, the world was "under the sway of a fratricidal Church of Cain."[83] Böhme now saw the revelations he received as specific to the confessional age in which he lived. All around he saw that "contention and strife in faith is arisen, that men talk much of faith, one pulling this way, another that way, making a multitude of opinions, which are altogether worse than the heathen views."[84] Confessional conflict, doctrinal rigidity, and religious persecution had emptied Christendom of true understanding of God and nature: "today titulary Christendom is full of such magi who have no natural understanding of God or nature, but only empty babbling." By reneging on his agreement to cease writing on matters of theology and faith, Böhme drew censure from the Lutheran clergy of his city. His ongoing conflict with the Lutheran churchmen of Görlitz echoes in his conclusion that through such clergy "the world is thus made stone-blind."[85]

The revelations vouchsafed to Böhme and the theosophical program he expounded were intended to illuminate a world blinded by ecclesiastical authorities and confessional strife. He placed his age in contrast with early Christianity in relation to "natural magia," i.e. the direct and allegorical understanding of the natural world: "as it was highly necessary and good that the natural magia was discontinued amongst the Christians, where the faith of Christ was manifest: so now at present it is much more necessary that the natural magia be again revealed." For Böhme "natural magia" meant a turn to the observed phenomena of the natural world, including (as described above) a new appreciation of the complementarity of darkness and light. He echoed other programs of spiritual and natural renewal circulating at this time, such as the Rosicrucian and utopian writings of Johann Valentin Andreä. The return to "natural magia" would have immense consequences:

the self-fashioned idols of titulary Christendom will be revealed and made known through nature, so that man might recognize in nature the articulated and formed Word of God, as well as the new rebirth, and the fall and perdition.[86]

Alchemy, physical and spiritual, might serve as midwife to this rebirth, which would embrace darkness as complementary to light, and night alongside day. As Böhme exhorted in his *Signatura Rerum* of 1622, here in the English translation of 1651: "Now wilt thou be a *Magus?* then thou must understand how to change the Night again into the Day," emphasizing that "the Day and Night lie in each other as one Essence."[87] Böhme saw his own age as ready to accept a new relationship between light and darkness, day and night. He would be a prophet of this nocturnalization.

The stories of the Anabaptists, John of the Cross, and Jacob Böhme alert us to a broader set of experiences across Europe in the confessional era. In each of these cases confessional conflict and ongoing persecution – from within one's own confession or across confessional lines – led to a new relationship with the night in daily life and in spiritual expression. The encounters with darkness and the night examined here show an increasing integration of the night into spiritual life and thought. The Anabaptists sought scriptural validation of their nocturnal position outside the established churches of the princes. In the midst of the brutal struggle to reform the Carmelite order, John of the Cross developed a profound theology of the night by nocturnalizing the three stages of the classic mystic sequence of purgation, illumination, and union. For Jacob Böhme, the balance between light and darkness became the basis of the cosmos: his abstract understanding of the meaning and reality of darkness and the night seeks its equal in the early modern era. Referring directly to the confessional strife around him, Böhme also presented a theory of history in which his era would see a return to "natural magia" in order to truly understand God's creation, light and dark. Böhme's writings (1612; 1619–24) take us into a period of intense occupation with the night as a path to God in Western Christendom. To chart this phenomenon in the next section, we will draw on the examples of John of the Cross and Jacob Böhme to focus on the search for God in the night in ascetic, apophatic, mystic, and epistemological terms.

3.3 THINKING WITH THE NIGHT ABOUT GOD

"Dark texts need notes," John Donne observed in a verse epistle to his patroness Lucy, countess of Bedford, in 1608. As creator of the English noun "nocturnal" to refer to a poem about the night, Donne joined unlettered Anabaptists, doctors of mystical theology, poets, and alchemical philosophers in using the night to think about God in new ways and with new intensity.[88] Each of the conceptual/metaphorical uses of the night – ascetic, apophatic, mystic, and epistemological – epitomized in the works of John of the Cross and Jacob Böhme found new or renewed expression across European culture in first half of the seventeenth century. This "discovery of the night" went far beyond the reception of the vocabulary of its most focused exponent, John of the Cross, forming a broad but distinct cultural and "spiritual undercurrent" in the period 1550–1650.[89]

Many chose poetry as the genre in which to express this new relationship with the night; John of the Cross was the forerunner in form as well as content. As Michel de Certeau observed regarding the discourse of mysticism in the period from Teresa of Avila to Angelus Silesius: "For a while, this science was sustained only by the poem (or its equivalents: the dream, the rapture, etc.). The poem was the substitute for its scientific object."[90] Much of the "discovery of the night" explicitly evoked "mystic darkness," and these "dark texts" reveal Europeans using the night to think about God in an unprecedented variety of ways. By 1640, when the Jesuit theologian Maximilian Sandaeus published an alphabetical guide to the key terms of mystic theology, the night was firmly established in the vocabulary of mysticism.[91] Under the entry for "Nox" Sandaeus presents each of the senses of the night elucidated by John of the Cross, beginning with a reference to the significance of the term: "Night. Numerous metaphors of the night can be found among the mystics; they are used most frequently by John of the Cross, distinguished mystic of our time, from whom are the books on the ascent of Mount Carmel." Sandaeus's guide also has entries for "dusk," "midnight," and "lantern," but no entry for "day."[92]

The new role of the night in devotion and theology was celebrated in verse by Richard Crashaw in the "Hymn in the Glorious Epiphanie" of his *Steps to the Temple* (1648). This English Catholic, writing in exile in Paris, brought English metaphysical poetry together with early modern Catholic mysticism.[93] He proclaimed "a most wise and well-abused Night" which he identified as the via negativa of John of the Cross, "the frugal negative Light." This "more close way" to the Divine is taught by the newborn "Child of light," whom Crashaw thanks for a night that allows us "To read more legible thine original Ray, / And make our darkness serve thy day." The poem is spoken by the three magi:

> (1.) Thus shall that reverend Child of light,
> (2.) By being Scholar first of that new night,
>   Come forth Great Master of the mistick day;
> (3.) And teach obscure Mankind a more close way
>   By the frugal negative Light
>   Of a most wise and well-abused Night,
>   To read more legible thine original Ray,
> (Chorus) And make our darkness serve thy day;
>   Maintaining 'twixt thy World and ours

A commerce of contrary pow'rs,
A mutual Trade
'Twixt Sun and Shade,
By confederate Black and White
Borrowing Day and lending Night.

In this section we will follow the undercurrent of "that new night" identified by Sandaeus and Crashaw across Europe, with a focus on its breadth in the first half of the seventeenth century, the critical period in this discovery of the night as path to the Divine.

3.3.1 The ascetic night

The "night to all the desires and senses" had a venerable place in the Christian tradition. An ascetic life of nocturnal prayer remains a fundamental aspect of Benedictine and other monastic observance. Waking in darkness for the office of nocturns held practical and eschatological significance but was foremost a physical act of self-denial.[94] This ascetic darkness is deployed by Ignatius of Loyola in the *Spiritual Exercises* (1548): in the first week of the *Exercises*, the author proposes "to deprive myself of all light ... shutting the doors and windows while I stay, except when I am to read or eat."[95] In contrast with earlier observance, however, Loyola imagines the *solitary* use of ascetic darkness, marking the key common feature of early modern nocturnal paths to the Divine. From Loyola it is a short step to the ascetic night, in which darkness serves as a metaphor for self-denial. Teresa of Avila's *Interior Castle* (1577–80) presents its first three sections or "mansions" as a descent into darkness ("the light which comes from the palace occupied by the King hardly reaches these first mansions at all"), signifying the sin the soul must overcome. At the end of the description of the second mansion Teresa reviews the ascetic value of the confrontation with darkness in a famous passage: "It is absurd to think that we can enter Heaven without first entering our own souls – without getting to know ourselves, and reflecting upon the wretchedness of our nature."[96] In darkness, self-denial leads to self-knowledge. This insight can carry a penitential tone, as in the poetry of Jesuit martyr Robert Southwell (*c.* 1561–95), whose "The Prodigal Chylde's Soule Wracke" (*c.* 1595) proclaimed:

> I, plungèd in this heavye plyght,
>   Founde in my faltes just Cause of feare;
> By darkness taught to knowe my light,
>   The loss thereof enforcèd teares.

The ascetic night echoes across the sacred writings of John Donne. In his "Hymn to Christ, at the Author's last going into Germany" (1619) Donne takes his approaching travel as the moment to rededicate himself to God, shunning the distractions of daylight in favor of the darkness and night, which allow a clearer vision of the Divine.[97]

> Seal then this bill of my divorce to all,
> On whom those fainter beams of love did fall;
> Marry those loves, which in youth scatter'd be
> On fame, wit, hopes – false mistresses – to Thee.
> Churches are best for prayer, that have least light;
> To see God only, I go out of sight:
> And to 'scape stormy days, I choose
> An everlasting night.

This night is intensely introspective, but Donne also considered the power of the ascetic night from his perspective as a preacher. In a 1629 sermon given "In the Evening" Donne addressed "atheists" and asked his listeners to look ahead to midnight:

I respite thee but a few hours, but six hours, but till midnight. Wake then; and then dark and alone, Hear God ask thee then, remember that I asked thee now, Is there a God? and if thou darest, say No.[98]

Stripped of the distractions of the daylight, alone at midnight, the "atheist" or libertine would recognize the God he scorned during the day. Donne's reference to the tolling of a "passing bell" in another sermon also evokes the shock of midnight: "A man wakes at midnight full of unclean thoughts, and hears a passing bell; this is an occasional mercy."[99] The popular English emblem book of the poet Francis Quarles (1635; many editions through the nineteenth century) took a gentler approach to the same kind of night:

> My soule, cheare up: What if night be long?
> Heav'n finds an eare, when sinners find a tongue:
> Thy teares are Morning show'rs: Heaven bids me say,
> When Peter's Cock begins to crow, 'tis Day.[100]

The Lutheran pastor, poet, and hymnist Paul Gerhardt (1607–76) looked toward an ascetic night in his "Evensong" ("Abendlied," 1667):

> Rest now all forests,
> Beasts, men, cities and fields,
> The whole world sleeps
> But you, my thoughts,
> Up, up you must begin
>   What pleases your creator most.[101]

In each stanza Gerhard presents a different theme of nocturnal meditation including Jesus as "another sun" and the stars, the body, and the bed as *memento mori*.[102]

There is no better way to visualize this ascetic night than in the devotional candlelight scenes of Georges de La Tour, especially the *Repentance of Mary Magdalene* – a popular theme, judging from the many versions and copies painted from the 1630s on.[103] La Tour's penitent Magdalene (Figure 3.5) captures the solitary nature of the ascetic night: there is no space or place in the scene into which another figure could intrude, and no light enters from outside the scene.[104] The devotional context of the night scenes produced by artists active in the duchy of Lorraine such as Jacques Bellange, Jean Le Clerc, Jacques Callot, and Georges de La Tour has been examined closely by Paulette Choné.[105] Arguing for a more careful approach to connections between painting and literature, she has identified the works of John of the Cross (which circulated in manuscript among the Discalced Carmelites of the region before their publication in 1618) and the Franciscans André de L'Auge (who preached at the ducal court of Lorraine) and Juan de Los Angeles as specific channels that brought the verbal imagery of the sacred night, ascetic and apophatic, into the visual arts of the Lorraine region.

Figure 3.5 Georges de La Tour (1593–1652), *The Magdalene with the Smoking Flame*, c. 1638–40. Los Angeles County Museum of Art.

Of course, the specific Lorraine context does not preclude a broader set of connections. Among the manuscripts of the English Benedictine Sisters in Cambrai (Flanders), we find an anonymous devotional poem of the seventeenth century that seems to gloss the solitary, ascetic night of La Tour's Magdalene:

> Alone retired within my native cell,
> At home within myself, all noyse shut out

In silent mourning I resolve to dwell,
With thoughts of death Ile hang my walls about;
All windows close, Faith shall my taper be,
At whose dim flame Ile Hell and Judgment see.
…
All windows close, Faith shall my Taper be,
On Hope Ile rest, and sleep in Charity.[106]

The abbey of Our Lady of Consolation at Cambrai was founded in 1623 by Cresacre More, great-grandson of Thomas More, and had longstanding ties to English recusant families. His daughter Dame Agnes (Grace) More (1591–1655 or 1656) and several other sisters at Cambrai were cousins of John Donne.[107] The literary works of the sisters of Cambrai use themes familiar from English metaphysical poetry, such as the contrast and reciprocity of light and darkness, "the four seasons of mankind," and the microcosm/macrocosm parallel. The sisters also drew on Spanish and French mysticism; as "Sister M.S." noted in a collection of writings "for her spiritual comfort in her several necessities": "John of the Cross. There is no better or more powerful way to increase the virtue of the mind, than … to shut fast the door of the senses, by solitude and forgetfulness of all creatures and human events."[108] She reveals a clear understanding of the "dark night of the senses" as described by John. At Cambrai, the English Benedictine sisters received and contributed to the latest currents in Western spirituality across national and confessional boundaries. The night became *a* key time and symbol in these currents: it could reveal sin and, by removing the temptations of the day, offer a path away from it. As Pascal observed in his *Pensées* (*c*. 1660): "If there were no obscurity, man would not feel his own corruption."[109]

3.3.2 *The apophatic night*

As the midpoint of the soul's dark night, faith "is compared to midnight," the darkest part of the night. "The more the soul is darkened," John explained, "the greater is the light that comes into it."[110] In his discussion of the Divine, John explained that "in order to reach Him, a soul must rather proceed by not understanding … and by blinding itself and setting itself in darkness, rather than by opening its eyes."[111]

Empowered by the sense that the path to God is as dark as night to the understanding, mystic authors made darkness and the night key apophatic terms across genres and confessions in the seventeenth century. Darkness figured in many of the oxymora and paradoxes used to express the inexpressibility of the Divine, seen for example in George Herbert's "Evensong" (*c.* 1620; the earlier of two poems with this title). Herbert begins with the more traditional negative view of "Night, earth's gloomy shade, / fouling her nest, my earth invade," but then corrects himself, noting that it is wrong to write "as if shades knew not Thee." The night is also a divine time, as he immediately asserts in apophatic terms:

> But Thou art Light and Darkness both together:
>   If that be dark we cannot see:
>   The sun is darker than a tree,
>   And thou more dark than either.
>
> Yet Thou art not so dark, since I know this,
>   But that my darkness may touch thine:
>   And hope, that may teach it to shine,
>   Since Light thy Darkness is.[112]

No one explored this theme more deeply than the French devotional poet Claude Hopil. The Parisian wrote extensively on this theme in his *The Piercings of Divine Love Expressed in One Hundred Canticles Made in Honor of the Most Holy Trinity* (*Les divins eslancemens d'amour exprimez en cent cantiques faits en l'honneur de la très saincte Trinité*) of 1629.[113] Apophatic themes and expressions from Denys the Areopagite and John of the Cross are woven into one hundred canticles in praise of the Trinity:

> In the night of faith, the ray of darkness
>   of the beautiful Trinity
> Suffices for salvation.[114]

Paradoxes of night and darkness are Hopil's primary theme:

> My spirit rises to the dungeon magnificent
> In the divine ray of mystic darkness
> All confused and ravished

> I saw what one cannot think, let alone write
> Thus I tell you all without being able to say anything
> Of all that I saw.[115]

Hopil described clearly the apophatic voice: "If I speak here only of shadow and fog, / of silence and of horror, / of dungeons and dark clouds," he explained, it is only so that "one sees the failure / that the Father causes in us through his wisdom." This failure is a "learned ignorance ... ravishing and beautiful," a "sacred darkness which reveals to us a Sun / to the heart, not to the eye."[116] Revealed to the saints by "his eternal word," the Divine is "hidden for us in the mystic night."[117] Many times Hopil refers to his own meditation "in the night not dark but mystic," suggesting that he considered the night a time of actual prayer as well as an apophatic metaphor.[118]

Despite their necessary obscurity, Hopil composed his devotional verses as canticles, meant to be sung to the tunes of popular secular chansons in the home. Scholars have noted that "individual readers were considered capable of choosing music themselves for pious chanson texts" such as those of Hopil, suggestion some circulation of his sense of the apophatic and mystic night among laypeople.[119]

Oxymora and paradoxes abounded in the popular poetry of the spiritual night. The Lutheran baroque poet Andreas Gryphius (1616–64) often wrote of the bleak shadows of the Thirty Years War, but he also chose an apophatic night in his "On the Birth of Jesus" ("Uber die Geburt Jesu"):

> Night / more than bright night! Night / brighter than the day /
> Night (brighter than the sun) / in which the light was born.
> ...
> O night, which can thwart all nights and days![120]

Other poets celebrated the night in broader terms not limited to the single, unique night of the birth of the Christian savior. As Henry Vaughan concluded his poem "The Night":

> There is in God – some say –
> A deep, but dazzling darkness; as men here
> Say it is late and dusky, because they

See not all clear.
O for that Night! where I in Him
Might live invisible and dim.

Another of the Benedictine sisters at Cambrai, Dame Clementina
Carey (d. 1671), wrote of flight from God in the night, reversing the
terms of the paradox:

If I say Darkness, and the Night,
Which shut out all, shall bar Thy sight
That Darkness, which is so to me, to Thee is Light.[121]

These baroque expressions of the inexpressible were drawn to the
night as they sought to fuse the quotidian with the sublime.

Similar insights appeared in natural philosophy, as in the alchemical treatise of Blaise de Vigenère (1523–96), *A Discovery of Fire and
Salt* (English translation, 1649).[122] Vigenère asserts that "Divinity is
so wrapped in darkness, that you cannot see day through it," citing
Psalm 17, Orpheus, and Deuteronomy 4. His comments reveal the
reception of the negative theology of Denys the Areopagite: "for in
regard of God towards us, light and darkness, are but one thing: as is
his darkness, such is his light." He adds in apophatic terms:

by … that which is equivalent to darkness, we may better apprehend something of the Divine Essence, but not by … that which relates to light … For
the Divine light is insupportable above all to all his Creatures, even down to
the most perfect, following that which the Apostle sets down in 1. of Tim. 6.
God dwells in the light inaccessible, that no man can see. So that it is to us instead
of darkness, as the brightness of the Sun is to Moles, Owls, and other night
birds.[123]

The need for darkness in the ineffable human encounter with the
Divine was a significant theme in the seventeenth century.[124] The
engravings forming the frontispiece of Daniel Cudmore's *A prayer-
song; being sacred poems on the history of the birth and passion of our
blessed Saviour* (Figure 3.6, 1655) juxtapose the sun hidden in darkness with the soldiers at Christ's tomb, blinded by the light of the
Resurrection.[125] The texts chosen place the images in an apophatic
frame. On the left "Behold the man" refers to a cloud of darkness
before the sun; on the right "He is not here but is risen" captions
the blinding physical presence of the risen Christ. The darkness that

Figure 3.6 Detail, frontispiece of Daniel Cudmore, *A prayer-song; being sacred poems on the history of the birth and passion of our blessed Saviour* (London, 1655). University of Illinois, Urbana-Champaign, Rare Books and Manuscripts Library.

covers the sun and the dazzling force that pushes back the soldiers both have their counterparts in Milton's *Paradise Lost*. Surveying their new lot in Hell, the fallen angel Mammon reminds his fellows that darkness is not confined to the infernal depths:

> This deep world
> Of darkness do we dread? How oft amidst
> Thick clouds and dark doth Heaven's all-ruling sire
> Choose to reside, his glory unobscured,
> And with the majesty of darkness round
> Covers his throne, from whence deep thunders roar
> Mustering their rage, and Heaven resembles hell?[126]

Mammon fundamentally misunderstands the origins and meaning of divine darkness, of course, describing it as a material obstacle rather than as a reflection of unconditional divine majesty.[127] Milton evokes the apophatic through Mammon's failure to understand it. Raphael's description of God is more perceptive, with its apophatic flourish:

> Fountain of light, thyself invisible
> Amidst the glorious brightness where thou sit'st
> Thron'd inaccessible, but when thou shad'st
> The full blaze of thy beams, and through a cloud
> Drawn round thee like a radiant shrine
> Dark with excessive bright thy skirts appear.[128]

As we will see below in chapter 4, the image of light blazing through a cloud was deployed by Milton's royalist contemporaries to praise earthly sovereigns as well.

3.3.3 *The mystic night*

"Although this happy night brings darkness to the spirit, it does so only to give it light in everything."[129] With these words John of the Cross opened the most advanced section of his extended nocturnal metaphor to describe the mystic union of the soul with God as night in the second book of *Dark Night of the Soul*. "On this night God … [has] put to sleep … all the faculties, passions, affections and desires which live in the soul, both sensually and spiritually." John presents the liberation of the soul through night:

> It is not to be supposed that, because in this night and darkness it has passed through so many tempests of afflictions, doubts, fears, and horrors, as has been said, it has for that reason run any risk of being lost. On the contrary … *in the darkness of this night it has gained itself.*[130]

For John and his successors, this mystic night built upon the ascetic nights of despair and purgation, and could be expressed only in the apophatic terms outlined above. As Jeanne de Cambry, an Augustinian canoness, wrote in her mystic *Ruin of Self-Love and Building of Divine Love* (1623): "But indeed they cannot be explicated by any human tongue! Nevertheless, serving myself of a similitude, I will describe this as best I can." Later in the treatise she describes a soul in mystic union: "For she will be, as it were, wrapped up in a wonderful kind of interior darkness."[131] By the early seventeenth century, more spiritual authors used similitudes of darkness and the night to describe the encounter with God.[132] Writing in 1610, the Lutheran theologian and devotional author Johann Arndt (1555–1621) described a dark night of mystical union in terms remarkably similar to those of John of the Cross:

> When the heart is still, when all senses are turned inward, in peace, and recollected in God; when no earthly light appears in the understanding, and the wisdom of the flesh is swallowed up in a night or divine darkness, then the divine light rises and gives a flash, a ray of itself, and shines in the darkness. That is the darkness in which the Lord dwells, and the night in which the will

sleeps and is in union with God. In this [state] one's memory has forgotten the world and time.[133]

The theme of darkening the self to admit the divine light is not common in Arndt's writings, but it is unmistakable. Again, it is significant that Arndt developed this metaphor of darkness without access to the works of John of the Cross, which were first printed in Spanish in 1618 and in French in 1622–23.

The writings of John of the Cross *did* clearly influence Claude Hopil's *Divins eslancemens d'amour* of 1629. Hopil described the divine union in shadowy terms: "One night in the midst of the cloud / in a superabundance of spirit / my soul was alienated of its senses." He continued: "No, I have neither heart, nor mind, nor memory / since the happy night in which I glimpsed the glory / of the King of love / a night in front of which my days are but a vain shadow / night clearer than a day."[134] In Hopil's case there is little discussion of purgation before the mystic union. As he wrote: "I like only nights and mystic clouds / To sing in silence to my God my canticles." Hopil imagines finding God "In the ray of shadow where the Essence hides, / In the *clair-obscur* where silence resides."[135] Hopil's use of phrases such as "claire obscurité" underscores the links with "clair-obscur" as key concept emerging in painting in the first half of the seventeenth century.[136]

Images of divine union in the dark night traveled across confessions. The Lutheran convert to Roman Catholicism Johannes Scheffler (1624–77), who after conversion wrote devotional poetry under the name Angelus Silesius, united the powerful sense of immanence from the heterodox spiritualist and Behemist traditions with the Catholic baroque. In his "The Blessed Silence of the Night" (1657), Scheffler provided a concise and eloquent description of the mystic night:

> Note, in the silent night, God as a man is born
> To compensate thereby for what Adam had done
> If your soul can be still as night to the created
> God becomes man in you, retrieves what's violated.[137]

Nativity, Original Sin, and mystic redemption all coincide in Scheffler's blessed night.

In all of these evocations of an ascetic "dark night of the senses" and a mystic "happy night in which I glimpsed the glory / of the King of love," the night is a solitary time in which an individual can be utterly subjected to God – but also to the Devil. The isolated figure at night, such as La Tour's Magdalene, is fundamental to contemporary narratives of diabolical temptation on stage or in witch trials. Thousands of accused witches, almost all women, inculpated themselves by describing, under torture or its threat, how they encountered the Devil alone at night and surrendered themselves to him, body and soul, in a diabolical parody of mystic union. The early modern night opened up greater heights *and* lower depths for the Christian soul, epitomizing the formation of the early modern Christian subject.[138]

3.3.4   The epistemological night

The fundamental reliance on contrariety in rhetoric and literature, in religious discourse, in sacred history, and in philosophy created an epistemological night in which "the contrary makes known the contrary, as ... the daylight by the darkness." This general understanding of contraries could shift into a sense of the value of darkness and the night, as when an author notes that "the obscurity of darkness commends the clearness of light."[139] Joshua Sylvester added this insight when he translated the *Semaines* of Huguenot poet Guillaume de Saluste Du Bartas:

> Swans seem whiter if swart crowes be by
> (For Contraries each other best discry)
> Th'All's-Architect, alternately decreed
> That Night the Day, the Day should Night succeed.[140]

Two German Catholic opponents of witchcraft persecutions, Michael Stapirius (Stappert) and Hermann Löher, produced an extraordinary print to illustrate the need to see by night and by day, i.e., to consider both guilt and innocence, in witchcraft trials (Figure 3.7). The "Brillen-Marter-Traktat" of Stappert, written around 1630 and first published with the eyeglass image by Löher in 1676, explained that judges must see with both lenses "to be able to distinguish and separate

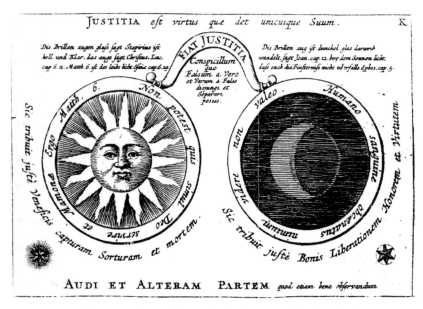

Figure 3.7 Illustrating the need to see both sides in witchcraft trials: Hermann Löher, *Hochnötige Unterthanige Wemütige Klage der Frommen Unschültigen* (Amsterdam, 1676). Jesuitenbibliothek of the St. Michael-Gymnasium, Bad Münstereifel, Germany.

the false from the true and the true from the false" ("quo Falsum a Vero et Verum a Falso disjungi et Separari posses"). Note that the night lens allows the "Bonis Liberationem Honorem et Virtutem" while the day lens is associated with the "imprisonment, torture, and death" of the witch ("Veneficis").[141]

The French Protestant theologian Lambert Daneau, author of a widely cited witchcraft treatise, placed day and night among the "contrary virtues and natures" in his *Physica Christiana* of 1576, translated as *The Wonderfull Workmanship of the World* (1578). This Calvinist treatise recognized the value of all the contraries in creation:

For God made not all things at the first of one quality, colour, and greatness, neither of one kind and nature. But he made some high some low, some moist some dry, some warm some cold, the day to be one thing and the night another. Yet God made nothing that was evil.

This mode of creation served several purposes:

The power and wisdom of God is thereby more apparent: and also the things themselves by this repugnancy of contrary virtues and natures ... For what manner [?] state of things would there have bin, if all things had bin hot? what numbness, if all things had bin cold? what misery, if all ways there had bin darkness; what wearisomness, if it had always bin day? And therefore when God had created the natures of this world, and of the things contained therein, he thought it convenient to refresh and ease them with change and course.[142]

This pattern of contrariety also structured the relations between God and humankind. In his hymn on the Epiphany, Crashaw proclaimed "a most wise and well-abused Night" that will teach "obscure Mankind ... To read more legible thine original Ray / And make our darkness serve thy day." The Lutheran poet Daniel Czepko (1605–60) captured this sense in an epigram:

> Each through the other:
> Eternity through time; life through death.
> Through the night to light, and through men I see God.[143]

By using the night to express contrariety, self-denial, and their ineffable encounters with the Divine, these seventeenth-century authors and artists profoundly enriched the scope of representation of their age, while presenting and fostering new attitudes toward the night.

3.4 A REFUGE IN THE NIGHT

Living in "these times of persecution and trial" during the Puritan Commonwealth, the royalist and Anglican poet Henry Vaughan (1622–95) turned to identify with Nicodemus in his 1655 poem "The Night":

> Wise Nicodemus saw such light
> As made him know his God by night.
> Most blest believer he!
> Who in that land of darkness and blind eyes
> Thy long-expected healing wings could see
> When Thou didst rise!

And, what can never more be done,
Did at midnight speak with the Sun![144]

Why did spiritual writers such as John of the Cross, Jacob Böhme, or John Donne see the night as a path to the Divine or insist on the complementarity of darkness and light? What happened to the clear "light overcoming darkness" imagery of the Reformation, epitomized by the "Wittenberg Nightingale" of Hans Sachs? Answering this question satisfactorily is not easy. The first step is to document the development, as I have done here, and show that it is distinct. The late medieval mystic appreciation of night in no way approaches the elevation of darkness we see in the period from the late sixteenth to the late seventeenth century.

My sense is that the valorization of darkness in Christian imagery arose from an *ongoing* sense of conflict and confusion in the confessional era. Times of apocalyptic struggle, such as the years of the early Reformation, offer a clear view of good and evil. Even if the forces of darkness threatened to triumph, at least the sides were clear. The struggle against the Antichrist was unambiguous, and it would all be settled soon. By the end of the sixteenth century, the dividing line between God's flock and the wickedness of the world was much less clear in practice. John of the Cross and Jacob Böhme faced suspicion and persecution from *within* their own churches; they, and all Christians after the Reformation, had to accept the existence of numerous confessions heretical to one another across a divided Christendom.

When we survey all those who sought the Lord by night in the pages above, does any pattern emerge? The humble Anabaptists discussed above shared little with the erudite Henry Vaughan save the bitter experience of religious persecution – and an appreciation for the night, literal and metaphorical. By the second half of the sixteenth century the clear calls to overcome the darkness surrounding God's word gave way to an appreciation of the darkness without which, as Böhme stated, the light could not be revealed, reflecting a new sense that darkness was "inseparable from light as an iconic and psychological factor of essential importance."[145] In the confessional age Christians of all churches identified themselves with Nicodemus, hoping to come to the Lord even in dark times of secrecy and persecution. Worship at night helped expand the legitimate social and symbolic uses of the night, fostering the nocturnalization of spirituality in the confessional age.

Did living in the darkness of unresolved confessional strife mean seeing darkness as a part of God's plan? In the period from the mid sixteenth through the late seventeenth century, Europeans could draw on a wide range of images and discourses to think about the Divine – the night was only one of these, and many of the contemporaries of John of the Cross, Jacob Böhme, or Henry Vaughan chose other paths to similar destinations. Darkness remains, however, an especially dynamic image and the night an especially dynamic time in this period. The new emphases on the night surveyed here (primarily, though not exclusively, in devotional texts) anticipated new forms of political expression and new uses of the night – in very material terms – in the seventeenth and eighteenth centuries.

Europeans of the seventeenth century apprehended the night and its darkness as a positive presence, a tangible reality that could be manipulated to a variety of ends. Building upon the chiaroscuro of the Renaissance, artists as diverse as Caravaggio, La Tour, and Rembrandt all used darkness (which in simple extent came to dominate many of their canvasses) to create physical and emotional depth, emphasize natural and divine light, and define space. As I have shown this was true in theological, mystical, and devotional literature as well.[146] It is clear that the appreciation of darkness and the night unfolded across the Christian West, and one of the few experiences that John of the Cross, the Anabaptists, Jacob Böhme, John Donne, Georges de La Tour, and Henry Vaughan, for example, shared was the awareness of inter- and intraconfessional division and persecution. Darkness and light had become intermixed and inseparable, and so the night became more sacred. By 1600 the straightforward "light versus darkness" imagery of the Reformation had created a confessionally fractured world in which the night took on new sacred values and, as we will see in the next chapters, secular values. The night was becoming more useful, more meaningful, and more manipulable than in the days of the "Wittenberg Nightingale." It is to these new uses of the night at court and in the city that we now turn.

CHAPTER FOUR

Princes of darkness: the night at court, 1600–1750

In 1687, John Norris of Bemerton (1657–1711), a lesser "metaphysical" poet, Anglican clergyman, and Tory pamphleteer, published an extraordinary "Hymn to Darkness."[1] Written as England's last Catholic monarch revived hopes and fears of Stuart absolutism, Norris's poem stands out from other English "poetry of night" through its praise of darkness as an awe-inspiring ruler:

> Thy *native* lot thou didst to *light resign*,
>   But still *half* of the Globe is *thine*.
> Here with a *quiet* but yet *aweful* hand
> Like the *best* Emperours thou dost command.[2]

Norris wrote within an established genre, the poetic nocturne, describing darkness, to whom "the Stars above their brightness owe," as a "most sacred Venerable thing" complementary to and inseparable from light.[3] But as a supporter of James II, Norris brought a new political message to the nocturne: he envisioned darkness as an essential aspect of divine and earthly majesty and authority:

> Tho *Light* and *Glory* be th'Almighty's *Throne*,
>   *Darkness* is his *Pavilion*.
> From that his radiant *Beauty*, but from thee
> He has his *Terrour* and his *Majesty*.[4]

Lauded as "unquestion'd Monarch" of the time before Creation, darkness was praised for fostering order, beauty, and piety: "Hail then thou Muse's and Devotion's Spring, / Tis just we should adore, 'tis just we should thee sing."[5] Norris's political appropriation of the poetic nocturne in praise of darkness and monarchy raises some valuable questions. Which early modern social, cultural, and political

developments allowed Norris to bring together divine light, nocturnal darkness, and absolute monarchy?

The virtues of the night and its darkness as attributes of God
quickly generated parallel political expressions. Through these new
symbolic associations of the night sovereigns and courtiers mapped
the contrast between darkness and light – a fundamental distinction
of daily life – onto the political culture of the seventeenth century.
Sovereigns and their servants appropriated the ascetic, mystic, and
epistemological night discussed in the previous chapter to represent
royal power and authority. This nocturnalization of political symbolism and everyday life at court in the seventeenth century arose
to strengthen and supplement established symbols of spiritual and
political sovereignty undermined by the confessional fragmen-
tation of Western Christendom. The royal courts of Europe had
long functioned as nodes in a single network, linked by kinship,
diplomacy, and a shared aristocratic culture. By the seventeenth
century no one could deny that this network was strained by permanent confessional division. Any prince who sought to act politically outside his territories, or within a multiconfessional territory,
needed to communicate persuasively about power and authority
with adherents – and indeed leading members – of other churches.
Violence was the *lingua franca* of the confessional age, spoken and
understood by almost everyone. But alongside and after the confessional and civil wars of the period 1540–1660, a new idiom of political communication was deployed by sovereigns in principalities
and city states.

This new idiom was of course the baroque, characterized by its
"enthusiasm for spectacular means of irresistible persuasion."[6] Rulers
deployed it in spiritual and secular contests across the fault lines of
Western Christendom. The baroque expression of ideas, values, and
goals sought to transcend the crisis of authority of the confessional
age by bringing new emotional and intellectual forces into play,
"shadowed" though they were "by suspicions about the pervasive-
ness of illusion or secrecy."[7] Darkness and the night were essential to
baroque attempts to articulate and transcend confessional sources of
authority: nocturnal darkness intensified the light that represented

the Divine or the prince.[8] The new uses of the night show rulers' attempts to strengthen and supplement confessional sources of authority ("most Christian king", "most Catholic king", "defender of the faith") with the "natural" authority of a "sun king." Rulers had long presented themselves as light-givers and identified themselves with the sun, but in the baroque age princes deliberately used the chiaroscuro of light in the night to intensify these images, which began to supplement (though not supplant) traditional Christian symbols of power and authority.

4.1 NOCTURNAL SPECTACLES AND PLEASURES

Performing in his first court ballet on February 23, 1653, at age fourteen, Louis XIV of France (1643–1715) presented himself for the first time as "le roi soleil." Louis danced several roles in the ballet, and in his final appearance, which concluded the play, he appeared in a radiant costume as the sun. (See Figure 4.1.) The first appearance of Louis as a sun king is striking, but its context is equally significant. The performance was the *Ballet de la Nuit* by Isaac de Benserade – and here, as in countless other spectacles of the era, a darkened background enhanced the appearance of a radiant monarch, evoking his power to dispel darkness and bedazzle his subjects.[9] The court ballet, performed in the Petit-Bourbon just outside the Louvre, was open to all, from the royal family to the commoners of Paris. And this *Ballet de la Nuit* was performed at night, using the latest staging techniques and lighting effects, designed and operated by Giacomo Torelli.[10] The Jesuit scholar of royal ceremony Claude-François Ménestrier singled it out as the finest example of the genre for the splendor of its costumes, stage décor, and lighting effects.[11] Like Norris's "Hymn to Darkness," this episode in the "fabrication of Louis XIV" calls our attention to the use of the night (both symbolic and real) in the representation of a celestial ruler. Because it was performed at night, this ballet also reveals the nocturnalization of court theater, public spectacle, and elite sociability. The *Ballet de la Nuit* thus invites an examination of darkness and the night in court spectacles and in everyday activities at court.

Figure 4.1 Louis XIV costumed as the sun in the *Ballet de la Nuit*, 1653. Pen, wash, and gouache touched with gold. Workshop of Henry de Gissey, contemporary illustration. Bibliothèque nationale de France. Photograph: Réunion des Musées Nationaux / Art Resource, NY.

How did contemporaries view the court performances and royal spectacles of the baroque era?[12] These events were meant to be "allegories of the state of the times" (as Ménestrier explained) and drew their importance, as Karl Möseneder has argued, from two fundamental political principles of the seventeenth century regarding the display and perception of power and authority. Like God, temporal rulers had to display their greatness in material creation. And common subjects had to be shown their sovereign's majesty as directly as possible because they could not otherwise comprehend the abstract authority of the prince.[13]

The comments of Louis XIV on the political role of spectacles at court addressed both the display and the perception of majesty. In the *Mémoires*, advice to the Dauphin written from 1661 on, the king described in practical terms the value of festivals and entertainment to the ruler. According to Louis, the court should be a "society of pleasures, which gives the courtiers an honest [*honnête*] familiarity with us, and touches and charms them more than one could say." He contrasted this familiarity with the distance of his lesser subjects: "the people, on the other hand, enjoy spectacles, at which we, in any event, endeavor always to please." Together, spectacles and pleasures were essential tools of government. "All our subjects in general are delighted to see that we like what they like," commented Louis: "By this we hold their minds and their hearts, sometimes more strongly than we do by rewards or kindnesses."[14] Festivities, Louis XIV continued, directed the attention of the people away from deeper political issues, which they were in any case incapable of truly understanding, accustomed as they were to perceiving only the superficial.[15] Here Louis XIV echoed Justus Lipsius (1547–1606), the influential Flemish Neostoic philosopher whose *Six Books of Politics or Civil Doctrine* (*Politicorum sive civilis doctrinae libri sex*) first appeared in 1589 and went into thirty-one Latin editions (and as many vernacular translations) in the seventeenth century. Lipsius discussed "the nature of the common people, and by what means the same may be discreetly governed" in the fourth book of the *Politicorum sive civilis doctrinae*, arguing that princes need celebrations and ceremonies to communicate with the common people, who are "void of reason ... not led to judge of any thing by discretion or wisdom." His analysis is founded on the assertion that "the common people are unstable, and nothing is more inconstant than the multitude." There follows a selective concordance of classical authors intended to show "the chiefest passions of the people," who are envious and suspicious, easily flattered and "slow of spirit."[16] Critics of increasing royal power such as Jean de La Bruyère (1645–96) also acknowledged the political role of spectacles and pleasures:

> It is a sure and ancient maxim in politics that to allow the people to be lulled by festivals, spectacles, luxury, pomp, pleasures, vanity and effeminacy, to occupy their minds with worthless things, and to let them relish trifling frivolities, is efficiently preparing the way for a despotism.[17]

As the time of both extraordinary spectacles and everyday pleasures at court, the night was, as we will see, fundamental to this political culture.

After 1650, political theorists described the distinct but complementary roles of "pleasures" and "spectacles" and began to examine these events more systematically. Michel de Pure's *Principles of Spectacles Ancient and Modern* (*Ideé des spectacles anciens et nouveaux*, 1668) lists ten forms of modern spectacle: theater, balls, fireworks, jousts, "Courses de Bague," carrousels, masquerades, military exercises, royal entries, and ballet. His contemporary Ménestrier offered a similar list.[18] The German school of *Zeremonialwissenschaft* (ceremonial studies), centered in Saxony and Brandenburg in the first half of the eighteenth century, discussed at length the relationships among spectacle, ceremony, and authority.[19] The crowning work of the *Zeremonialwissenschaftler* was Julius Bernhard von Rohr's *Introduction to the Knowledge of Ceremony of Great Rulers* (*Einleitung zur Ceremoniel-Wissenschaft der Grossen Herren*, 1729; second edn., 1733), which offers a similar analysis of courtly entertainment.[20] According to Rohr, "pleasures [and] diversions" have "certain political goals behind them. They are meant to gain the love of the better sort and the rabble, because people's spirits are more easily guided through such festivities which caress the exterior senses."[21] Rohr lists twelve types of diversions, including chivalric sports, opera, ballet and theater, and processions.[22] Old and new sit side by side in all these lists, but the nocturnalization of court entertainment and festivity is especially striking. Of the dozen listed by Rohr, six (carnival/masquerade, dances/balls/ballet, opera, costume feasts, illuminations, and fireworks) were necessarily or typically nocturnal. The remaining equestrian diversions could also be held at night inside purpose-built riding halls. Torchlit evening sleigh rides are described at the imperial court in Vienna from the early seventeenth century on.[23]

The nocturnalization of spectacle in the seventeenth century reshaped court architecture. The great spaces built for balls and celebrations at European courts (such as the Whitehall Banqueting House in London, the Herkules-Saal or the Kaiser-Saal at the Munich residence, the Hall of Mirrors at Versailles, or the Riesensaal of Dresden's Royal Palace), lit by innumerable candles, made possible more exclusive evening gatherings, allowing court society to develop and emphasize the night as never before in European civilization.[24] Richard Alewyn was the first to link innovative uses of daily time with the new secular spaces of the baroque (some of the largest constructed since antiquity) in his work on baroque festival culture.[25] He noted that between the fifteenth and the eighteenth centuries, princely celebrations show a slow shift from the street to the court and from day to night. This was "the sharpest break in the history of celebrations in the West," marking a new era in the history of the night.[26]

The slow movement of European festivals and celebrations into the night, which had begun in the fifteenth century, quickened in the seventeenth.[27] Lighting up the night had always been an elite privilege, but baroque celebrations used the night on an unprecedented scale as nocturnal entertainment began to take precedence over daytime festivities. In France a new era in the history of celebrations began on August 17, 1661, as the financier Nicolas Foucquet welcomed the young Louis XIV to Vaux-Le-Vicomte, Foucquet's magnificent estate southeast of Paris.[28] Vaux-Le-Vicomte, the first baroque chateau in France, is often described as the inspiration for Versailles. The king and his courtiers arrived at Vaux-Le-Vicomte in the late afternoon. After viewing the chateau, the royal party waited for sunset, when

Figure 4.2 Print by Israel Silvestre of firework display during "Les plaisirs de l'île enchantée. Troisième journée," 1664. © Trustees of the British Museum, 1889, 1218.139.

Foucquet's celebration was to begin.[29] The former protégé of Mazarin presented to the king an imposing nocturnal barrage of culture and luxury intended to display the wealth, power, and taste of the second-most powerful man in the kingdom. Molière wrote and performed in the evening's comedy-ballet, *The Impertinents* (*Les Fâcheux*), with music composed by Pierre Beauchamp. The set designs, lighting, and fireworks displays were the work of Charles Le Brun and Torelli. The comedy-ballet, which began after the *souper*, was followed by several fireworks displays. Accounts of the celebration carefully noted that all this took place after dark, with the king and courtiers retiring sometime after 2 a.m. The nocturnal *Gesamtkunstwerk* Foucquet had presented served as a model for the well-known baroque celebrations of Louis XIV, such as the *Plaisirs de l'île enchantée* of 1664 and the *Fête de Versailles* of 1668.[30] Rich accounts of the celebrations communicated in word and image (see Figure 4.2) the nocturnal splendor to a wider audience.

If we look back a century, we can see what was new about nocturnalization at court. On June 27, 1559, Henry II of France (1519–59) opened a five-day tournament to celebrate the weddings of his daughter Elisabeth to Philip II of Spain and his sister Marguerite to Emmanuel-Philibert, duke of Savoy. The daytime jousts were the focus of the celebration, especially on the fateful third day. According to the eyewitness account of Antoine Caraccioli, bishop of Troyes, by five o'clock in the afternoon "the hour [was] late, the weather extremely hot, and the tournament concluded." Queen Catherine and the noble spectators begged to Henry to retire, but he insisted that "he would break his lance once more," with fatal results.[31] To be sure, the festivals and celebrations of Henry II included lavish banquets at night, but the most elaborate events unfolded during the day.

English court celebrations under Henry VII and Henry VIII, like the Burgundian court practices that inspired them, could involve complex allegorical figures dancing at banquets in the evening, as at the Feast of the Pheasant at Lille in 1454 or at the court pageant celebrating the marriage of Prince Arthur and Catharine of Aragon in 1501.[32] In these cases, however, the central message of the celebration was still articulated during the day. The evening entertainments "were appendages to the basic ingredients of any festive evening, feasting and dancing," and they made no technical use of light and darkness.[33] In this way they contrast sharply with the most important English court spectacles of the seventeenth century, the masques of James I and Charles I. The Burgundian and Tudor festivals would have been incomprehensible without their daytime elements; the Stuart court masques dropped the daytime events and communicated only at night with theatrical lighting and effects.[34]

The courts of Protestant Germany show a similar expansion of the nocturnal aspects of festivals in the second half of the seventeenth century. In 1596, in celebration of the baptism of his eldest daughter, Landgrave Maurice of Hesse-Kassel held a chivalric tournament based on the myths of Jason and Perseus. Among the several days of jousting, racing, and knightly sport, only the climax of the entire celebration, marked by a spectacular fireworks display, was held at night.[35] After 1650, German princes began to shift these celebrations into the evening and night as a sign of luxury and prestige. The month-long "Festival of the Planets" celebrated at the gathering of the dukes of Saxony in Dresden in February 1678 exemplifies this development.

The "Festival of the Planets" organized by Elector John George II (1656–80) for his three brothers (dukes of the cadet lines of Saxony-Weißenfels, Saxony-Merseburg, and Saxony-Zeitz) also offered numerous jousts and other equestrian sport. But the emphasis had shifted to the evening activities. On at least thirteen evenings the festival included entertainment (opera, ballet, and theater) in Dresden's court theater, the Komödienhaus, built in 1664. These performances, in particular the court "Ballet of the Planets," were the centerpieces of the festival.[36] The Dresden "Festival of the Planets," which concluded with a massive fireworks display, was meant to demonstrate to the three younger brothers of John George II the culture and power concentrated at the Dresden court. For much of the festival, John George II and his court artists chose the night as the most effective background for this display; without these nocturnal performances the festival's theme would have made no sense.

The nocturnal celebrations of the Dresden court reached their high point under Frederick Augustus I, from 1697 also King Augustus II of Poland (1694/97–1733).[37] Through his election to the Polish throne in 1697 and his spectacular cultural politics, centered on his opulent courts at Dresden and Warsaw, Augustus sought to join the preeminent monarchs of his era.[38] Also depicting himself as a sun king, his celebrations, such as the nocturnal festivities at the Holländisches Palais during the wedding of the electoral prince in 1719, turned night into day. Even equestrian events were held at night: the Dresden Reithaus, illuminated by thousands of candles, was the scene of riding displays during Carnival in 1695 (see Figure 4.3) and during the visit of the Danish king Frederick IV (1699–1730) to the Saxon court in 1709.

Alongside these nocturnal festivities, a much older use of the night was the display of fireworks, taken to new heights at the courts of the baroque era.[39] With unintended irony, fireworks lit up the heavens for an instant before falling to earth, marrying the spectacular display of nocturnal power to a sense of the instability and illusion behind this display.[40] This period also expanded the visual

Figure 4.3 Illuminated tourney in the Dresden Reithaus, 1695. Staatliche
Kunstsammlungen Dresden, Kupferstich-Kabinett. Photo courtesy
SLUB / Dept. Deutsche Fotothek, Herbert Ludwig.

and political counterpoint to the fireworks display, the urban "illumination." Instead of the single skyward focus of the fireworks
display, the illumination placed multiple lights in the windows of a
single building or across an entire city, a massive yet precise display
of loyalty and obedience to the ruler who ordered the illumination
or was celebrated by it. (See Figure 4.4, illumination of the Hôtel de
Ville, Ghent for the entry of the Habsburg Charles VI in 1717.) A
Viennese pamphlet of 1706 lauded "true-hearted vassals / who have
illuminated your houses and palaces / with new fires of joy" – an
offering of light and loyalty to the emperor.[41] A Saxon author writing in 1736 emphasized the novelty of the practice: "It is difficult to
say when the art of illumination arose in Germany. In my opinion it
is unlikely one would have seen them before the end of the previous
seventeenth century."[42]

Two aspects of the political role of spectacles must be mentioned
here. First, it is important to note that early modern polities not

Figure 4.4 Illumination of the Hôtel de Ville, Ghent, 1717. Engraving, 1719.
Österreichische Nationalbibliothek, Bildarchiv, Vienna, 462.224-A/B.

dominated by courts, such as the Venetian Republic, the United
Provinces, and the German Free Imperial Cities, also used fireworks,
illuminations, and theater to display power and authority to domestic
and foreign audiences. Figure 4.5 shows a magnificent fireworks display in Bremen celebrating the "Respublica Bremensis" from 1668.[43]
Second, the politics of spectacle and pleasure described here did not
guarantee political success. The masques of Charles I of England
presented to the king an ideal world of authority and virtue, but they
had little meaning to important parts of the political nation. The last
masque staged for Charles I, Sir William Davenant's *Salmacida Spolia*
of 1640, was viewed with trepidation by its audience; one courtier
considered himself "being so wise as not to see it."[44] In similar terms,
the spectacular court life of King-Elector Augustus II of Poland and
Saxony did not attract the Saxon nobles who opposed his conversion
to Catholicism and his absolutist policies. Throughout his long reign,
these nobles had to be forced to attend some of his major celebrations.
Of the 112 Saxon nobles personally invited to the Dresden wedding
of the electoral prince and the Habsburg princess Maria Josephine

Figure 4.5 Firework display in Bremen, 1668, with the letters "VRPB" (Vivat
Respublica Bremensis) at right. Colored engraving. Caspar Schultz, 1668.
Staatsarchiv Marburg, Best. 4 f Bremen, Nr. 58.

in 1719, only 52 were initially willing to attend. The other 60 offered
a wide range of excuses from poverty to ill health; some later suc-
cumbed to pressure from Augustus and did appear.[45] Court festivities
demanded participation (often costly) on the terms set by the prince
as host and affirmed the sovereign's image as displayed – but subjects
could and did refuse the pleasures and spectacles offered at court. The
fact that nocturnal pleasures and spectacles were deployed by every
prince of this age – successfully or not – is further evidence of the
belief in their power.[46]

4.2 DARKNESS AND THE PERSPECTIVE STAGE

Among the nocturnal spectacles and pleasures of the court, those of
the theater deserve special attention. Nocturnal performances and
entertainment consolidated new uses of darkness in both the politics of spectacle and in everyday court life. In the seventeenth century, ministers of state, artists, and architects brought the lighting

and scenery techniques of the Italian court stage into performances north of the Alps, and darkness was essential to this new stage technology. The establishment of the baroque perspective stage can thus serve as a rough index of nocturnalization. The use of darkness in court performances unfolded in three phases: first, the use of lighting effects without a fixed perspective stage, as in the early French *ballet de cour* and the English court masque; second, the use of temporary perspective stages with movable scenery and illusionist lighting; and third, the establishment of permanent baroque perspective theaters.

These theatrical techniques arrived in England in the rarified atmosphere of the Stuart court masque, the counterpart to the French court ballet. Ben Jonson's first court masque, *The Masque of Blackness*, presented on Twelfth Night, 1605, was described by Sir Dudley Carleton: "At Night we had the Queen's Maske in the Banqueting-House, or rather her Pageant." Music and dancing were primary to the masque, and the addition of speeches from characters on stage probably led Carleton to use also the term "pageant." These court masques, with theatrical designs by Inigo Jones, "brought the full resources of Italian theatrical machinery into use for the first time on an English stage."[47] The Stuart masques were performed in the multipurpose interior of the Whitehall Banqueting House from 1622 until 1637, when a semi-permanent "Masquing Room" was built. The fall of the monarchy prevented Charles I from building a permanent court theater.[48]

In France, the *ballet de cour* developed under Catherine de'Medici and the last Valois kings. The first great example, the *Ballet comique de la reine* of October 1581, was performed from 10 p.m. to 3.30 a.m. in the Petit-Bourbon with an extraordinary range of lighting effects. Its scenery was scattered throughout the hall, however, with spectators on three sides.[49] The Grand Théâtre of Cardinal Richelieu (1585–1642) in the Palais Cardinal (inaugurated in January 1641) was the first French baroque perspective stage using "a formal proscenium and an elevated stage where scenery flats could be changed to suggest different lighting effects."[50] A remarkable grisaille shows the performance of the ballet *La Prospérité des Armes de la France* in the Grand Théâtre on February 7, 1641 (Figure 4.6). We see Louis XIII

Figure 4.6 Oil on panel (grisaille) by Juste D'Egmont, "The ballet 'La Prospérité des Armes de la France' at the Grand Théâtre du Palais Cardinal as viewed by Louis XIII and the royal family," *c.* 1641. Musée des Arts Decoratifs, Paris, France. Photograph: Erich Lessing / Art Resource, NY.

watching a darkened baroque perspective stage from the ideal central point of view, illuminated by the light from the stage, with Cardinal Richelieu to his right, and Queen Anne of Austria and the young future Louis XIV on his left.[51]

Richelieu and Mazarin both sought out the most advanced theater designers and technicians from Italy. The correspondence of Cardinal Mazarin with his agent Elpidio Benedetti in Rome during the ministry of Richelieu shows especially clearly the political interest in the darkened baroque perspective stage. Through his patronage of Roman baroque artists, his relationship with Pietro da Cortona, and his contact with Gian Lorenzo Bernini, Mazarin put into motion the artistic policies he would later pursue as minister. Bernini was important to Mazarin not only for his talents in sculpture and architecture, but also for his skill in theater technology. The cavaliere's Roman comedies of the 1630s were legendary for the "special effects" he brought to the stage. Despite their modest budgets, these performances all featured extraordinary illusions, such as the setting of the sun, the flooding of the Tiber, or a house that burst into flames (safely!) onstage. After negotiation with Mazarin and Benedetti in 1640, Bernini agreed to show Niccolò Menghi, a sculptor of his studio who was making the trip to France, how to stage some of his renowned theatrical illusions. The one that most interested Mazarin and Benedetti was "the way in which one illuminates and in which one makes the sun and the night."[52] The techniques were developed and disseminated by men like Bernini and Torelli, who installed new stage machinery in the theaters of the Petit-Bourbon (1645) and the Palais-Royal (1647) and made possible Richelieu's court ballet described above, and the *Ballet de la Nuit* which began the age of the Sun King a dozen years later.

In the Holy Roman Empire some of the earliest nocturnal court theatricals (analogous to the court ballet or masque) were performed in Darmstadt (1600), Stuttgart (1609, 1616–18), and Salzburg (1618). The darkened perspective stage is first documented at the Dresden court in 1650, and at the Munich court of the elector of Bavaria in 1651; the first performance of an Italian opera in the Empire came in Dresden in 1662, when Giovanni Bontempi's *Il paride* was presented at the wedding celebrations for the daughter of the Saxon elector.[53] The performance began on the evening of November 3 at 9 p.m. and lasted until 2 a.m.[54] In Munich and Dresden permanent baroque perspective theaters were opened in 1657 and 1664 respectively. At the imperial court in Vienna, Leopold I (1658–1705) staged an extraordinary number of operas or "dramme per musica" during his long reign, using the main ballroom of the Hofburg and the Hoftheater auf der Cortina, built in 1666–67. These nocturnal spectacles were the favored mode of self-representation of the emperor and his court.[55]

The Imperial Free City of Nuremberg inaugurated its Nachtkomödienhaus (lit. "night theater") in 1668 with the performance of a piece now lost, the *Macaria* of Johann Geuder, by the sons of its ruling patrician families.[56] The Nachtkomödienhaus contained a classic baroque perspective stage with the requisite lighting, a proscenium, an elevated stage, and movable wings to create the illusion of depth; as its name indicates, it was built to be used at night. The evening performance of *Macaria* on February 11, 1668 proclaimed the noble pretensions of the Nuremberg patricians. The city fathers sat in special boxes at the central, royal point of view while their sons declaimed the political doctrines of Justus Lipsius, affirming the hierarchy of virtuous rulers above the turbulent rabble. The play concluded with the apotheosis of the patricians:

> Not one sun stands here: many suns stand still
> In this crowded room: You Sun-Prince! Fulfill
> What our wishes desire! Let your rays of mercy
> Pour out unmerited grace upon our city.[57]

Compared with Apollo and identified as "demigods" in the play's epilogue, we see that the ruling fathers of Nuremberg found the nocturnal display of solar majesty and authority as compelling as did Louis XIV or Augustus II. Like these sun kings, the city magistrates of Nuremberg used the darkened backdrop of the baroque perspective stage to project their magnificence.

In the second half of the seventeenth century, the purpose-built baroque perspective stage displayed the highest technological and political achievements of European court theater. This stage relied on artificial illumination for its staging and special effects, and these effects were enhanced when performances were held in darkness. A contemporary described the stage equipment of the Dresden Komödienhaus in 1671:

The excellent effects of artificial perspective, the movement and transformation [of the scenery], and the machines built into the theater can be seen better at night, when performances are held with artificial light, than during the day.[58]

When the young Scotsman John Lauder, later Lord Fountainhall (1646–1722) visited "the king's comœdy house" (the theater of the Palais-Royal) in Paris in April 1665, he judged "the thing that most commended it was its rare, curious, and most conceity machines." He was amazed by "the skies, boats, dragons, wildernesses, the sun itself so artificially represented that under night with candle light nothing could appear liker them."[59] The leading guide to theater in France,

Ménestrier's *Des Ballets anciens et moderns* (1682), also emphasized the importance of darkness:

Ordinarily these performances are held at night, with artificial lighting: this is better for the machines than daylight, which reveals the theater's artifice. Artificial lighting can also be arranged where needed for maximum effect. Some lights illuminate from a hidden location, making an object appear lit by daylight. Some are arranged so that they leave in shadow the places where stage equipment is located.[60]

In Restoration London the simple staging and open-air, daytime performances familiar to us from Elizabethan theater had been supplanted by the darkened perspective stage.[61] For a production of Shakespeare's *Tempest* at the new Dorset Gardens Theatre in 1673, the stage directions of the poet laureate and dramatist Thomas Shadwell show the full use of these special effects:

Act I, Scene I. The front of the stage is opened … Behind this is the scene, which represents a thick cloudy sky, a very rocky coast, and a tempestuous sea in perpetual agitation. This Tempest … has many dreadful objects in it, as several spirits in horrid shapes flying down amidst the sailors, then rising and crossing in the air. And when the ship is sinking, the whole house is darkened, and a shadow of fire falls upon 'em. This is accompanied by lightning, and several claps of thunder to end the storm.[62]

This panoply of illusions was impossible without the ability to darken the theater.

The origins of these chiaroscuric effects take us back to the theater of the late Italian Renaissance. The Medici dukes pioneered the form, supporting their new dynasty with extraordinary displays of light and power at night.[63] At the performance of Antonio Landino's *Il Commodo* in the Medici Palace in 1539, the sun, simulated by a water-filled crystal globe, two feet in diameter, lit from behind, rose to open the play, moved across the sky, and set at the conclusion: this was one of the very first uses of a lighting effect on stage. A permanent court perspective theater, the Teatro Mediceo, was erected in the Uffizi Palace in 1589. With its proscenium arch, movable wings, single royal viewing point, and complex lighting reliant on nocturnal performances, the Teatro Mediceo was the forerunner of all the baroque perspective theaters described above. Roy Strong described its specific political role: "this highly artificial means of creating visual experience and controlling its reception by the audience [based primarily on the use of darkness and light], evolved at a court presided over by a new dynasty ever-anxious to promote itself to new levels of grandeur to conceal its bourgeois origins."[64]

The Italians also published the first description of modern theater techniques, Sebastiano Serlio's "Second Book of Architecture" (1545). Serlio discussed stage lighting in some detail and described simulating sunset and night on stage, as in the 1539 performance of *Il Commodo*. The first direct reference to the benefits of darkness for the theater is in the "Dialogues on Stage Affairs" (*c.* 1565) of Leone Di Somi (*c.* 1525–*c.* 1590), the extraordinary Jewish court physician and playwright in Mantua: "It is a natural fact ... that a man who stands in the shade sees much more distinctly an object illuminated from afar ... Wherefore I place only a few lamps in the auditorium, while at the same time I render the stage as bright as I possibly can."[65] Di Somi's advice would be expanded in theory and practice as these Italian techniques of stage illumination were brought north in the course of the seventeenth century by men like Inigo Jones and the architect Joseph Furttenbach of Ulm (1591–1667), who studied theater techniques in Italy before applying them in their native lands. In his writings on theater design, Furttenbach emphasized the utility of darkness discovered by the Italians:

No windows are placed at the sides of the front pit. The walls there are left unbroken so that the spectator will not be blinded but will sit in darkness and have greater wonder at the [simulated] daylight falling in at the streets between the houses, as well as at the light of morning coming from between the clouds ... It were better if no windows were put at the sides of the audience, so that the spectators, *left in darkness like the night*, would turn their attention to the daylight on the stage.[66]

So began a new epoch of European theater, which relied on staging at night or in darkness. Strong's reading of the visual politics of the Teatro Mediceo applies to all the chiaroscuric theaters set up at courts from Versailles to Vienna, Stockholm to Madrid: "Enclosed within the *teatro* of the Uffizi Palace, an audience of some three thousand was to be subject time and again to some amazing spectacle glorifying the Medici in whose eyes all lines of vision met."[67]

The association of the theater with darkness and illusion in the seventeenth and early eighteenth centuries becomes especially significant when we note that this age saw the theater as the supreme metaphor for human existence. Like the apocryphal last words of Cardinal Mazarin ("Tirez le rideau, mon rôle est joué"), countless funeral sermons and funeral orations of the age begin with the baroque commonplace: "Our life is well compared with a play."[68] As one scholar of German literature has observed: "At no time has the word 'Theater' or its Latin form 'theatrum' had anywhere near as wide a range of meaning as in the baroque."[69] The darkness and illusion fundamental to the theater of the age shadowed this wide range of associations.

4.3 THE NOCTURNALIZATION OF DAILY LIFE AT COURT

After these spectacular baroque celebrations came to their conclusion with a magnificent fireworks display or radiant theatrical performance, did life at court return to the dawn-to-dusk rhythm typical of early modern life? At courts before the mid seventeenth century, this was usually the case. But slowly the new emphasis on the night in court celebrations began to reorder everyday routines at court. New uses of the night at court converged with urban developments as princes and courtiers regularly extended the legitimate social part of the day long past sunset, and often past midnight.[70]

This growing emphasis on the night is reflected by a new theme in the moral criticism of court life. Long characterized as an immoral *space* (as the German proverb "bei Hof, bei Höll'" indicates),[71] the court was now condemned for its immoral use of *time*: "the night is turned into day and the day into night" at court, reversing the divine order. This misuse of daily time could be seen "in the lives of the courtiers of both sexes, who make night into day and day into night."[72] As the French Benedictine Casimir Freschot remarked in his guide to life at the imperial court in Vienna in 1705: "The brevity of the day for persons of quality, who never rise before noon, and who consequently do not have even four or five hours of daylight, makes social intercourse at night necessary."[73] Another commentator, the Pietist Phillip Balthasar Sinold, complained that "the courtiers alter the order of nature by making the day into night and the night into day." These night people "stay awake in order to indulge in their entertainments, though other people sleep: afterwards to restore the vigor lost by their sensual pleasures they sleep while other people are awake and attend to their business."[74]

The nocturnalization of court life is documented by a wide variety of sources.[75] Much of our evidence comes from the polycentric Holy Roman Empire, with its profusion of courts great and small. In their (less than constant) search for discipline, concord, and good order, most princes left detailed court ordinances and court diaries, a fairly consistent set of sources on everyday life at court. The court ordinances of the sixteenth and early seventeenth centuries prescribe a daily schedule no different from that of the other orders of society: early to bed and early to rise. At the Brandenburg court in Berlin in the late fifteenth century the Privy Council met at 6 a.m. in the summer and 7 a.m. in the winter.[76] The times set for worship, for meals, and for the closing of the palace gate are the most common indications of the course of the day at court.[77] Under the last Valois kings, the French court also kept a traditional daily schedule, reinforced by the dangers of nocturnal violence in the periods of civil war. A 1585 court ordinance of Henry III (1574–89) set the king's *souper*, the last meal of the day, at six in the evening; at 8 p.m. the king would retire to his chamber. The gates of the Louvre were to close not long after eight in the evening and open at five in the morning.[78] Members of the court, including the king, might well be out much later at night, but such activity remained clandestine.

At the Saxon court, the sixteenth- and seventeenth-century ordinances show a traditional division of the day. At the court of Elector Augustus I (1553–86), meals were to be served "in the morning around ten o'clock and in the evening at five." The 1637 court ordinance of John George I (1611–56) set the day's meals at nine in the morning and four in the afternoon; the gates were to be closed at nine

in the summer and eight in the winter.[79] Surveys of everyday life at
sixteenth-century courts confirm these impressions. By about nine at
night the court was to be quiet, with the gates locked. Any later nocturnal gatherings would have been dimly lit at best: court inventories
recorded and limited the number of tallow lights and (much more
expensive) wax candles used each week.[80]

For Saxony after 1656, court diaries are an especially rich source
on everyday life. The diaries, which recorded daily events at court,
became particularly important when the Saxon electorate was divided
among the four sons of Elector John George I upon his death in 1656.[81]
The four brothers agreed to pursue a common foreign policy and to
maintain good relations: to this end they registered the daily events
at their respective courts and regularly sent copies of these court diaries to one another. Offering a day-to-day view of Saxon court life,
the diaries describe, often in minute detail, the visitors, ceremonies,
and celebrations at each court, including the time and place of each
event. In Dresden, the birthday celebrations for Elector John George
II in 1664 and 1665 began with prayers at six or seven o'clock in the
morning. After a service lasting several hours, the court sat down to a
midday meal, followed by an afternoon worship service. No celebration in the evening is mentioned for either year.[82] At the smaller Halle
court of Duke Augustus in 1676, the court diary shows a traditional
daily schedule: no activities after the evening meal are described.[83]
Most often, the duke took his evening meal in his own chambers or
those of the duchess: the official or social part of the day had come to
an end. When a troupe of traveling actors came to the Halle court and
performed *Love's Great Garden of Confusion* and *The Two Husbands
Duped* on August 14, 1676, they did so in the afternoon. That evening, meals were again taken separately in the chambers.[84] Both norms
and practices reflected a dawn-to-dusk rhythm.

The afternoon performance of the strolling players who came
to Halle in August 1676 was far removed from the latest lighting
techniques of baroque theater seen, for example, in the Dresden
Komödienhaus or the Nuremberg Nachtkomödienhaus. The small
provincial court of Saxony-Weißenfels at Halle lagged behind the latest trends in nocturnal sociability.[85] In Saxony, these trends emerged

from the court in Dresden, where the Saxon princes and their court nobles began to exploit the expressive possibilities of the night. When John George III became elector of Saxony in 1680, he reduced court life and expenditure on festivals in favor of the military, and perform-ances in the Komödienhaus dropped off for several years.[86] But in the 1680s Dresden saw a new form of elite sociability: nobles and court officials who had attended evening performances at the Komödienhaus began to hold their own evening balls and masquerades.[87] These elites also held the city's first honorable nocturnal funerals.[88] Slowly, the social uses of the night were expanding beyond court celebra-tions and entertainment. The Saxon court diaries of John George IV (1691–94) and Augustus II (1694–1733) confirm this shift to evening entertainments in the everyday life of the Dresden court.[89] In add-ition to the court diaries, the essays of Johann Michael von Loen (dis-cussed below) describe the wide range of nocturnal entertainment the author enjoyed there during visits to Dresden from 1718 to 1723.

Nocturnalization shaped almost every aspect of life at court, from architecture to cosmetics.[90] Matthaeus Daniel Pöppelmann (1662–1736), the architect of Dresden's Zwinger, described the innovative uses of daily time and courtly space in the elegant galleries and gar-dens he had designed in Dresden, noting in 1729 that "in the com-fortable season of the year the most esteemed ladies and cavaliers of the court and many residents of the city go strolling in this garden ... until late in the evening."[91] At the imperial residence in Vienna the streets were full of traffic after dark, as Freschot observed:

in this great city ... one is underway just as often by night as by day; some to pursue the pleasures on offer, some to wait upon secret dealings, of which there can be no shortage in a place where ministers from all the powers of the world are found.[92]

Freschot also refers to audiences with the emperor scheduled for about seven to nine in the evening in winter.

At Versailles, the center of European court life, a range of sources document everyday "night life" during the reign of Louis XIV. The typical day began with the royal *lever* at nine and ended at midnight. In 1692, the duc de Saint-Simon (1675–1755) described evenings of music, cards, and billiards, called *appartements*, held thrice weekly in winter. These gatherings lasted from seven until ten in the evening in rooms that were "beautifully illuminated."[93] Saint-Simon noted that even after Louis stopped attending the *appartements* and "spent the evening with Madame de Maintenon, working with different ministers one after the other," the king "still ... wished his courtiers to attend assiduously."[94] Although she was an outsider at Versailles, Charlotte Elisabeth d'Orléans (Liselotte von der Pfalz, 1652–1722) reveals in her letters that she also lived in the fashionable new rhythm of court life, rising around 9 a.m. and retiring at midnight.[95] Research on the courts of Henry IV and Louis XIII shows that this kind of regular night life was just beginning to emerge in the last years of the reign of Louis XIII.[96] In 1641 the journalist Théophraste Renaudot observed that "all the great lords and ladies of the court, the most refined spirits and those most able to judge all things, and even most men of affairs go to bed late and rise late" – one of the very first references to the nocturnalization of daily life at court.[97]

At the Bavarian court in Munich, which vied with Dresden and Vienna to rank as the most magnificent in the Empire, Elector Max Emmanuel (1679–1726) began holding *appartements* in the mid 1680s: "five or six rooms, one after the other, all beautifully adorned and illuminated, with various tables for gaming" were set up, along with another room for dancing. As the introduction of the *appartements* suggests, daily life at the Bavarian court slowly but steadily shifted to later hours and more nocturnal activities: a 1589 court ordinance set the *coucher* of the Bavarian duke at nine in the summer and eight in winter, but by the eighteenth century, eight to ten in the evening was the normal supper hour; the *coucher* usually took place around midnight.[98]

Extending the day into the night had become a part of aristocratic style, and one's appearance by candlelight became correspondingly more important. During her stay at the electoral court in Hanover in December 1716, Lady Mary Wortley Montagu noted that "French Comedians play here every night" and remarked that

All the Woman here have literally rosy cheeks, snowy foreheads and bosoms, jet eyebrows, and scarlet lips, to which they generally add coal black hair. These perfections never leave them till the hour of their death and have a very fine effect by candlelight, but I could wish they were handsome with a little more variety.[99]

Telling time at night, which for centuries had apparently been of little concern at court, also became more important. In his 1665 diary describing the visit of Bernini to France, Paul Fréart de Chantelou mentions a novelty presented to the cavaliere: "His Eminence [the abbé Buti] showed the Cavaliere a clock for use at night, which had a dial illuminated by a lamp, so that one could tell the time at any hour."[100] These night clocks, like urban street lighting, were an invention of the seventeenth century. They were first and foremost luxury objects, but they also indicate a new interest in marking time more accurately at night.[101]

By the early eighteenth century, evening diversions and nocturnal entertainments such as gaming and dancing were considered typical of everyday life at court. In his *Introduction to the Knowledge of Ceremony of Great Rulers* (1729) Julius Bernhard von Rohr distinguishes between orderly and disorderly courts, based on the regular division of the day: "At some courts ... a certain hour is set at which the princely rulers and their servants take their rest, and in the morning arise from their beds." Fixed schedules made for orderly court life, but the pursuit of pleasure meant indulgent disorder. "The night is turned into day and the day into night" at these disorderly courts, where "a large part of the time meant for nightly rest" is spent "in eating, drinking, gambling, dancing and other divertissements" by courtiers who "then sleep almost until noon."[102]

In his *Introduction to the Knowledge of Ceremony of Great Rulers*, Rohr's criticism of night life at court is circumspect, typical of his tone when discussing "great rulers." Rohr's comments on dancing in the companion volume to the *Great Rulers*, his *Introduction to the Knowledge of Ceremony of Private Persons* (*Einleitung zur Ceremoniel-Wissenschaft der Privat-Personen*, 1728) show how disturbing the new uses of the night could be:

The balls of the well-born or the common dancing-parties are held at just that time of terror and darkness when the spirit of darkness rules: [he] arranges these [dances], and he is obeyed there ... The darkness, the snares, the masks behind which one hides often permit shameful liberties.[103]

According to Rohr, the grave moral dangers of dancing arose because "one goes too far with regard to the hour, one does not stop at the proper time, [and so] the night, which was made by God for rest, is transformed by this sensuality into day."[104] In his guide to comportment for "private persons" Rohr presents a general critique of the disorder of nocturnal sociability. Late hours at coffeehouses and nocturnal funerals also come under his criticism as widespread but improper uses of the night.

Rohr's association of night life with the well-born is reflected in the London diary (1717–21) of William Byrd of Virginia (1674–1744). After noting his attention to his evening prayers consistently for several weeks, Byrd attended a masquerade on February 6, 1718:

I dressed myself in the habit of the Marquis and went to Mrs. B-r-t, and from thence to Lady Guise's, and from thence to Lady Foley's, and at about ten went to the masquerade, where I was well diverted ... I stayed till 6 o'clock [a.m.], having kept up my spirits with chocolate. I neglected my prayers, for which God forgive me.[105]

Phillip Balthasar Sinold warned his readers of this new temptation to late hours. The division between day and night, he reminded his readers, was created by God as "a special sign of his unfathomable wisdom." Sinold then related how this divine order is ignored by two exemplary members of the "so-called beautiful world," Clorinde and Cleomenes. The two are censured equally by Sinold for staying out "nearly until morning" dancing, gossiping, and gambling, completely forgetting their evening and morning prayers, to the detriment of their bodies and souls. Their evening socializing (commencing "after seven o'clock") is an "assembly of vanity."[106] "One must realize," Sinold added,

that such nocturnal gatherings are allowed and approved in Christendom, while in contrast gatherings meant for the practice of piety [i.e., Pietist conventicles], even when they take place in broad daylight are in most places entirely forbidden.[107]

Moralists like Rohr and Sinold decried the "everyday" nature of aristocratic night life, which went far beyond the occasional use of the night at festivals or celebrations. In a tension typical of the baroque, the exclusivity and prestige of nocturnal sociability immediately evoked warnings about the illusions and deceit the night fostered.

The melancholy warnings of Rohr and Sinold about the moral dangers of "night life" contrast with the more sanguine comments of Johann Michael von Loen in his essay on *The Court at Dresden in the Year 1718* (*Der Hof zu Dresden, Im Jahr 1718*, 1749). Loen, drawing on his experiences at the opulent court of Augustus II in 1718 and 1723, describes a series of nocturnal festivities and celebrations, culminating in the Carnival season of 1723. During Carnival "every evening the so-called *Redutten* or public dances were [held]" in a "hall illuminated with countless lights." Despite the unrestrained nightly festivities, Loen points out that in Dresden "business went on uninterrupted":

Though a part of the night was spent with all manner of festivities, on the next morning one saw that every man was back at his post: the merchant in his stall, the soldier on guard, the clerks in the chancellery, the councilors in their meetings and the jurists in their chambers.[108]

The duties of daily life had come to accommodate nocturnal revelry: "only certain beauties and wandering cavaliers who had no service" stayed in bed until noon.[109] Writing in the 1730s, the courtier-author Karl Ludwig Freiherr von Pöllnitz (1692–1775) considered the late hours described here to be the norm. Pöllnitz was a vagabond courtier who visited every major court in Europe, supporting himself by gambling and publishing gossipy accounts of court romances and intrigues. At the modest court of Modena in the early 1720s he was received with all due respect by the ruling duke (Rinaldo D'Este, 1695–1737) but the "quiet" court life there drew his ridicule. He described it as nearly monastic and "inspiring melancholy": "one rises there early in the morning, goes to mass, and dines promptly at a good hour; afternoons, one takes a stroll. In the evening one plays a few games; dinner is at eight o'clock, and around ten o'clock one goes to sleep." Pöllnitz decried "this miserable way to live in monotony … which is simply not appropriate for a ruler's court."[110] These early hours were the antithesis of the nocturnal display of aristocratic style and royal majesty essential to the life of the court.

This evidence of the nocturnalization of spectacular celebrations, theatrical performances, and everyday pleasures at court could be easily multiplied, but the question would remain: why did darkness and the night become so important to the spectacles, pleasures, and daily life of Northern European court society in the seventeenth century? No single answer could address the broad international phenomenon examined here, but I suggest that new demands on the representation of power, majesty, and hierarchy explain much of the development.

The nocturnalization of political imagery and court life in the seventeenth century reflects both challenges faced by rulers and their responses to these challenges. The counterintuitive association of kings and queens not with the sun, but with darkness and the night, arose in part from what John Dryden called "adversities to Scepters," which abounded in the seventeenth century. Sovereigns found themselves eclipsed, as Samuel Pordage explained in "A Panegyrick" on the Stuart Restoration (1660): "Our regall *Sun*, since *Charles* the first was slain, / Ecclips'd has been, but now shines bright again."[111] In an ode "To The Most High and Mighty Monarch," Thomas Pecke summed up the execution of Charles I and the Commonwealth in the same terms:

> The man-headed Rabble was the *Moon*,
> Eclips'd our *Sun*; and made a glorious Noon,
> Cover its white skin with a *Midnight* vail:
> For the old *Serpent*, was the *Dragons Tail*;
> And a pretended *Parliament*, the Head:
> *Hic sita est*: *Great Britain here lies dead.*[112]

George Herbert, a poet of the divine night, provides an early example of the extension of the use of darkness as contrariety to political rhetoric. In a poem of 1621–22 in praise of Elizabeth Stuart, exiled queen of Bohemia (and daughter of James I), Herbert claims that "Through that black tiffany [the color of mourning or defeat], thy vertues shine / Fairer and richer" and that despite her exile from her kingdoms, Elizabeth's "undivided majesty" is only enhanced by this hardship "as lights do gather splendours from darkness."[113] Writing in the early seventeenth century, Herbert's use of darkness to praise an earthly ruler looks ahead to the political uses of darkness and the night in the century to come.

The political misfortunes of the Stuarts did not cease with the exile of Elizabeth from Bohemia. The vicissitudes of Charles I led royalists to claim that "we best read lustre in the shade" because "Ecclipse and suff'rings burnish Majesty."[114] The Cavalier poet John Cleveland juxtaposed the incognito Charles with the Divine Word: "Methinks in this your dark mysterious dress / I see the Gospel couched in parables."[115] Henry Vaughan's "The King Disguis'd" (1646) presaged Vaughan's loftier words on darkness and the Divine. He praised the fugitive king, who on April 27, 1646 had fled Oxford disguised as a gentleman's servant: "But full as well may we blame Night, and chide / His Wisdom, who doth light with darkness hide."[116] The mysteries of the king's flight were as impenetrable and inexpressible as those of the Lord, leading Vaughan to a dusky, apophatic political rhetoric:

> Poor, obscure shelter! if that shelter be
> Obscure, which harbours so much Majesty.
> Hence prophane Eyes! the mysterie's so deep
> Like Esdras' books, the vulgar must not see't.
> …
> Secrets of State are points we must not know;
> This vizard is thy privy Councel now.

Vaughan's references to *arcana imperii*, masking, obscurity, and the night summarize and justify the importance of illusion and deception in the political thought of the age.

Several poems celebrating the Stuart Restoration of 1660 drew on nocturnal themes, adapting images of the ascetic night and the epistemological night to the new monarch's story. John Dryden's "Astraea Redux" of 1660 sought to rehabilitate the "dark afflictions" of civil war, defeat, and exile suffered by Charles II:

> Well might the Ancient Poets then confer
> On Night the honour'd name of *Counseller*,
> Since struck with rayes of prosp'rous fortune blind
> We light alone in dark afflictions find.
> In such adversities to Scepters train'd
> The name of *Great* his famous Grandsire gain'd.

One of the very few women to publish in celebration of the arrival of Charles II, Rachel Jevon began her "Exultationis Carmen" (1660) succinctly with an epistemological night:

> Dread Soveraign *CHARLES*! O King of Most Renown!
> Your Countries Father; and Your Kingdoms Crown;
> More Splendid made by dark Afflictions Night;
> Live ever Monarch in Coelestial Light:

In his "Ode, Upon the Blessed Restoration" Abraham Cowley saw the "greatness" and "majesty" of Charles II in the wake of his defeat by Cromwell at the Battle of Worcester in 1651. Cowley draws on the vocabulary of "black Fate," clouds, and shrouds to praise the king:

> No show on Earth can sure so pleasant prove,
>   As when they *great misfortunes* see
>   With *Courage* born and *Decency.*
> So were they *born* when *Worc'ster*'s dismal *Day*
> Did all the terrors of *black Fate* display.
> So were they born when no *Disguises clowd*
>   His *inward Royalty* could *shrowd,*
> And one of th' *Angels* whom just *God* did send
>   To guard him in his noble flight,
> (A *Troop* of *Angels* did him then attend)
> Assur'd me in a *Vision* th' other night,
> That *He* (and who could better judge than *He?*)
>   Did then more *Greatness* in him see,
>   More *Lustre* and more *Majesty,*
> Than all his *Coronation Pomp* can shew to *Human Eye.*

Dryden and Jevon emphasize an ascetic "dark Afflictions Night" which makes the true majesty of the monarch "more splendid"; Cowley focuses in this passage on the power of darkness to reveal the "greatness" of Charles II in defeat – an insight granted to the poet, one notes, through the conceit of "a Vision th' other night."

Similar aspects of the ascetic and epistemological night were deployed in French royal imagery as well, especially in the aftermath of the Fronde. The Fronde's challenge to royal authority was answered on many levels, not least in the court ballets of Isaac de Benserade. In contrast with his predecessors, Benserade commented fairly directly on national politics and the court in the libretti he wrote for the ballets. In Benserade's verses for the *Ballet de la Nuit* of 1653, the king, representing a torch, refers to the Fronde as "the recent shadows / that were so celebrated" (part 3, sixth entry). "Alas!" he exclaims, "how many of the unwary ... have taken false *ardents*!" Lost in the darkness of the Fronde, his subjects exclaim: "the true one frees us from them / lighting our path."[117] In several scenes, the king's verses show how his victory over "all my rebels / fought and subdued" manifests his greatness – but each of these scenes is set at night. In the final scene of the *Ballet de la Nuit* the king, dancing as the rising sun, actually evokes future "shadows upon France" that he "will dispel," thus tying the future of the sun king to the shadows he will overcome.[118]

The adversities faced by rulers in this period were driven by the confessional divisions of Western Christendom. But the hardening of Christian confessions immediately created the need to transcend them. Paradoxically, to speak to Christians of all confessions baroque rulers had to display power and authority to one another in Christian *and* natural terms. The anonymous *Ceremoniale Brandenburgicum* (1699), an influential treatise on political ceremony, explained this in terms of light and radiance: "The authority and power of the potentates and princes of the world shines forth especially in their own lands ... But it shines even more brightly when others who are themselves powerful regard it."[119] Seventeenth-century princes, courtiers, and artists supplemented the display of traditional Christian authority with supraconfessional representations of political power, just as the secular *étatiste* thought of Hobbes served as the dark side of the divine right doctrines of Bossuet. By mapping the contrast of darkness and light onto their political displays, princes and courtiers made the night essential to what Habermas termed the "representative publicness" of the court.[120]

The hardening of confessional divisions meant that even the rulers of confessionally monolithic kingdoms like Spain needed to display their grace, power, authority, and culture in supraconfessional terms. We can see this through the experienced eyes of the duc de Saint-Simon during his embassy to the Spanish court in 1721. Invited by his Madrid host, Don Gaspard Giron, "to go and see the illuminations of the Place Mayor," Saint-Simon and his retinue "were conducted by detours to avoid the light of the illuminations in approaching them." The French courtiers' first view of the illuminated plaza was carefully arranged for maximum theatrical effect:

we arrived at a fine house which looks upon the middle of the Place, ... where the King and Queen go to see the fêtes that take place. We perceived no light in descending or in ascending the staircase. Everything had been closed, but on entering into the chamber which looks upon the Place, we were dazzled, and immediately [as] we entered the balcony speech failed me, from surprise, for more than seven or eight minutes.

The contrast between darkness and light made a powerful impression on Saint-Simon, who praised the "splendor" and "majesty" of this display. The square was lit from each of its balconies, from which "two torches of white wax were placed, one at each end of the balcony, supported upon the balustrade, slightly leaning outwards, and attached to nothing." Saint-Simon registered the desired effect: "The light that this gives is incredible; it has a splendor and a majesty about it that astonish you and impress you. The smallest type can be read in the middle of the Place, and all about, though the ground-floor is not illuminated."[121]

As the representative of Louis XV to Philip V, the duke's response was carefully registered in turn by the Spanish courtiers: "Don Gaspard Giron and the Spaniards who were with me in the house from which I saw the illumination, charmed with the astonishment I had displayed at this spectacle, published it abroad with all the more pleasure because they were not accustomed to the admiration of the French, and many noblemen spoke of it to me with great pleasure." At a royal audience the following day, Saint-Simon made certain to express to King Philip his "astonishment at an illumination so surprising and so admirable."[122]

Saint-Simon's report from Madrid suggests that the nocturnalization I have documented in Northern Europe reflects a change in style across the European court system. As confessional divisions proved unbridgeable, nocturnal displays of power and authority grew at courts across Europe. This diffusion is not surprising, as these courts were entirely international. At the time of Saint-Simon's embassy in

1721, the king of Spain was a French Bourbon, the king of England a former Lutheran from Hanover, and the king of Poland a Saxon convert to Catholicism; a few years later the Livonian Catherine I would inherit the Russian throne. For these rulers, nocturnalization was a new technique to display power and share pleasure at court and beyond. Confessional divisions led rulers, ministers, and courtiers to seek new ways to present glory – it did not matter whether the princes were Catholic Spanish Habsburgs or Calvinist Hohenzollerns: they often chose darkness and the night to display their splendor and majesty.

Nowhere is this better expressed than in the verse of John Norris of Bemerton. His "Hymn to Darkness" opened with the traditional association of darkness with maternity:

> Hail thou most *sacred Venerable* thing,
>   What Muse is worthy thee to sing?
> Thee, from whose pregnant *universal* womb
> All things, even *Light* thy *Rival* first did Come.

But for Norris, darkness and light are complementary:

> The *Vision* of the Deity is made
> More sweet and *Beatific* by thy *Shade*.

The aesthetic and political recoding of the night come together as Norris likens darkness to the ideal baroque sovereign, awesome and unchallenged by his subjects. As in the *Ballet de la Nuit*, God himself uses darkness as the backdrop for his majesty and authority. Summing up the uses of the night in baroque political symbolism, Norris makes the connection with political ceremony explicit:

> Thus when he first proclaim'd his sacred Law
>   And would his *Rebel* subjects *awe*,
> Like Princes on some great *solemnity*
> H'appear'd in's *Robes* of *State*, and Clad himself with *thee*.[123]

Norris understood well the importance of night for the supraconfessional display of power and authority in the seventeenth century. As we have seen, the use of darkness and the night as the "Robes of State" by sovereigns was a distinctive feature of baroque statecraft.

Norris's praise of divine, majestic darkness must be brought down to earth, however. Princes used the night to conceal, dissemble, or deceive – the dark side of the night's role in political culture. The utility of darkness for baroque political expression corresponds well with discussions of the political value of illusion and deception in the seventeenth century.[124] Like the darkened illusions of the perspective stage and the great European fireworks displays, this discourse of illusion and perception in political power developed first in Renaissance Italy. It was Machiavelli who advised that "in general, men judge more by sight than by touch. Everyone sees what is happening, but not everyone feels the consequences. Everyone sees what you seem to be; few have direct experience of who you really are." The Florentine then commented on the display of majesty at court: "Those few" with direct experience of a prince's true intentions "will not dare to speak out in the face of public opinion when that opinion is reinforced by the authority of the state."[125] To control what subjects see and what image the prince presented, the illusions powered by the contrast between darkness and light were vital. When Georg Rodolf Weckherlin (1584–1653), secretary to the duke of Württemberg, reported on a week-long celebration at the Württemberg court at Stuttgart in 1616, he expressed the desired effects of the baroque court festival:

My soul was amazed with marvel: mine eyes did dazzle: and all my senses were overwhelmed by the majesty, beauty, riches and magnificence of those brave Princesses, Princes, Ladies, Lords and Knights.[126]

His French contemporary Nicholas Faret's *L'honneste-homme; Ou, L'art de plaire a la court* (1630) described the court as "this theatre" in which the courtiers surround a sun king who "distributes unto them certain beams of his magnificence." At court "princes and great men are about a king like goodly stars, which receive all their light from him." But the brilliance of the monarch overwhelms the courtiers: "it is all confounded in this great light … The greatest part of the meaner sort consume themselves near this fire, before they can be warm."[127] Faret's astute description of a sun king whose light leaves "all confounded" reappears in an account of the overpowering fireworks display presented to Louis XIV by Nicolas Foucquet at Vaux-le-Vicomte in August 1661. Jean de La Fontaine (1621–95) described the scene: "Suddenly we saw the sky darkened by a dreadful cloud of rockets and serpents." He immediately asked: "Should one say 'darkened' or 'illuminated'?"[128] Light and darkness themselves were confounded as this dazzling nocturnal display left its audience blinded by the light.

The nocturnal pleasures, performances, and pyrotechnics of the court show a recurring sense that the spectacular contrast between darkness and light (real or symbolic) was an indispensable way to amaze, dazzle, and overwhelm – or dissemble. As Rohr noted, festivities can "better conceal the calamitous times that might press upon a land or city."[129] Concerns about the relationship between state power and official deception have lost none of their relevance in our own time.[130]

Seventeenth-century political writers from Justus Lipsius to Louis XIV agreed that princes need celebrations and ceremonies to communicate with the common people, who perceive only the superficial and sensual.[131] Lipsius argued that common subjects are fundamentally unable to perceive or support the common good, "not making any difference between that which is true and false."[132] The Flemish philosopher wrote in the spirit of his age. Advice on the perspective stage from Nicola Sabbatini's *Manual for Constructing Theatrical Scenes and Machines* (*Practica di Fabricar Scene e Machine ne'Teatri*, 1638) reflected Lipsius's hierarchy of perception and understanding in practical terms: "the common or less cultivated persons are set on the tiers and at the sides"; the workings of the stage machines might be visible from there, but "such people do not observe them minutely." In contrast, "the persons of culture and taste should be seated on the floor of the hall, as near the middle as possible, in the second or third rows. They will have the greatest pleasure there, since ... all parts of the scenery are displayed in their perfection."[133] The better sort could take pleasure in the illusions of the stage – or the state – while "common or less cultivated persons" would be impressed even by an imperfect display.

Scholars credit Lipsius with the spread of this educated contempt for the common people in the seventeenth century.[134] His views were

Figure 4.7 "Le Roi de France, l'Homme immortel Chef de la Ste. Ligue," print by Jacob Gole (after Dusart?) depicting Louis XIV as a hooded arsonist, 1691. © Trustees of the British Museum, S.6693.

repeated by political philosophers such as Christian Wolff (1679–1754), who legitimated the social hierarchy of their age by mapping it on to a hierarchy of perception and understanding. The lower estate recognized only superficial and immediate impressions:

The common man, who relies merely on the external senses and makes little use of reason, cannot by himself properly grasp the majesty of a king. But through *the things that come before his eyes* and that touch his other senses, he receives a clear impression of his [sovereign's] majesty, power and authority.[135]

It was in these terms that Julius Bernhard von Rohr argued that the inability of subjects to truly comprehend majesty was the primary reason for court spectacles and ceremonies.[136] This contempt for the common people fits well with prevailing argument among scholars of court society that the diverse elements of the prince's spectacles and pleasures were intended to speak simultaneously on several levels to several audiences.[137] The political philosophy behind it all stated that the display of majesty did not merely reflect political power – it created it.[138]

When we use daily life as a category of analysis, the sun kings of the age of Louis XIV and Augustus II start to look more like "princes of darkness." This was the image of Louis XIV, hooded and crowned by the moon, presented in a Netherlands caricature of 1691 (Figure 4.7). The constant use of darkness and the night by such sun kings to enhance their own (limited) brilliance invited this subversive identification. In daily life at court, the night connected autocratic rulers, aristocratic courtiers, and common subjects in a series of hierarchical fields of vision. Subjects gazed up at spectacles of light and power projected onto the night sky while princes and courtiers, seemingly face-to-face, shared an intimate "time of pleasures." Darkness was vital to each of these displays: it enabled rulers to offer pleasure, demonstrate magnificence, and deceive their subjects, combining the fundamental political strategies of this age.[139] The seventeenth-century insight that "shadows and lights are relative and reciprocal" and that "the order of nature ... has made these two conditions inseparable,"[140] extended from God to earthly rulers. This insight helps explain why in an age of "sun kings" the night became more important than ever before.

CHAPTER FIVE

"An entirely new contrivance": the rise of street lighting, 1660–1700

On April 26, 1784 the *Journal de Paris* published a letter on daylight and darkness from an anonymous subscriber. The author of the letter described an evening spent at a salon "in grand company" discussing, among other things, the new Argand oil-lamp. After considering whether this lamp would burn more efficiently and reduce lighting costs, the author returned home and went to bed "three or four hours after midnight," reflecting a daily schedule typical of persons of quality in the eighteenth century. With generous satire the author, who was accustomed to sleeping until noon every day, related his surprise upon discovering by accident the next day that the sun actually rises between six and eight in the morning (!) and that it "gives light as soon as it rises." Titling his letter "An Economical Project," the correspondent urgently sought to enlighten the journal's readers, "who with me have never seen any signs of sunshine before noon" that they could save vast sums on lighting simply by rising at dawn and having "much pure light of the sun for nothing."[1]

The author of this "Economical Project" quickly revealed himself to be Benjamin Franklin, representative of the new American republic in France.[2] His comments, which developed into the idea of daylight savings time, call our attention to the importance of nocturnal sociability in the last years of the Old Regime. They were echoed in much more critical tones by his conservative contemporaries in Italy, who complained that even the common people "profane the night either at long theater shows or at continual debaucheries" and noted that "people stay up so much later and longer that they then have to restore themselves by resting until very late the next day."[3]

When had these late hours become fashionable? Two years after Franklin's "Economical Project", the German *Journal des Luxus und der Moden* (*Journal of Luxury and Fashion*; Weimar and Gotha) published an essay on "the uses and divisions of the day and the night in various ages, and among various peoples."[4] Broadening Franklin's observations, the author and editor of the *Journal*, Friedrich Justin Bertuch (1747–1822), described "an entirely new order of things" which had replaced the traditional rhythm of daytime for work and night for rest and sleep.[5] Bertuch regarded the change as self-evident and presented several examples drawn from the courts and cities of Northern Europe. "In the fourteenth century" the merchants' stalls of Paris opened at four in the morning, "but now hardly at seven o'clock"; then, the French king retired at eight in the evening, but "now plays, visits and all social pleasures hardly even begin at that hour." From the time of Henry VIII to Bertuch's own day the English had shifted their mealtimes and sleeping times later by about seven (!) hours.[6] According to Bertuch "all these observations, which could easily be multiplied, prove clearly that the occupations of the day begin ever later, the more society is refined and luxury increases."[7] "Overall," Bertuch concluded, "the pleasures of the evening and night ... are the ruling fashion in every large city, where luxury and the need for entertainment constantly increase."[8]

The references of Bertuch and his contemporaries to monarchs, merchants, and the theater among the "grand company" and "in every large city" call attention to a fundamental shift in the rhythms of daily life in early modern courts and cities over the previous century as the hours after sunset slowly entered the regular, respectable part of daily life. With overlapping and sometimes conflicting goals princes, courtiers, burghers, and bureaucrats embraced the night, sanctioning and promoting new levels of nocturnal business and pleasure. They developed new lighting technologies for the stage and the street, and they surrounded the traditional night of natural and supernatural danger with a new aura of pleasure and respectable sociability. The aristocratic associations of street lighting, as well as its sheer cost, led some city councils to resist its imposition, sharpening the contrast between the traditional night and the origins of modern urban night life. This chapter and the next examine the opportunities and conflicts created by the nocturnalization of urban daily life.

Prescriptive and descriptive sources from European courts show mealtimes, the beginnings of theatrical performances and balls, and sleeping and rising hours moving ever later. Parallel to these developments at court, in large cities curfews and city gate closing times moved later or were given up altogether in the seventeenth century. As John Beattie observed for London, after 1660 "the idea behind the curfew – the 9pm closing down of the City – was not so much abolished as overwhelmed." His reference to the transformation of London's night life through the proliferation of "shops, taverns, and coffeehouses, theatres, the opera, pleasure gardens and other places of entertainment" could be applied, with variations of scale, to all major European cities, whether they were closely tied to court life like Paris and Vienna or independent city states such as Hamburg.[9]

Of all these developments, the rise of public street lighting was fundamental to this revolution in the rhythms of urban daily life. Its appearance was swift: in 1660, no European city had permanently illuminated its streets, but by 1700 street lighting had been established in Amsterdam, Paris, Turin, London, and Copenhagen, in French provincial cities, and across the Holy Roman Empire from Hamburg to Vienna. (See Map 5.1.) This early European street lighting – oil lamps (or, in the French case, candles) in glass-paned lanterns – was an innovation of the seventeenth century, both reflecting and promoting new attitudes toward the night and urban space.[10]

Europe's first street lighting has been studied exclusively in local and practical terms.[11] Based on evidence from the French conquest of Flanders (1667–77) under Louis XIV, and from the Electorate of Saxony during the reign of Elector Frederick Augustus I (1694–1733, as Augustus II King of Poland, 1697–1733), this chapter examines street lighting in a broader history of the night. In Lille, capital of the new French province of Flanders, the city council set up street lighting immediately after the French occupied the city in 1667. In Saxony the absolutist ruler Augustus II established public street lighting in Leipzig, the leading city of his principality, in 1701. Placing street lighting in Lille and Leipzig in a broader European context illustrates

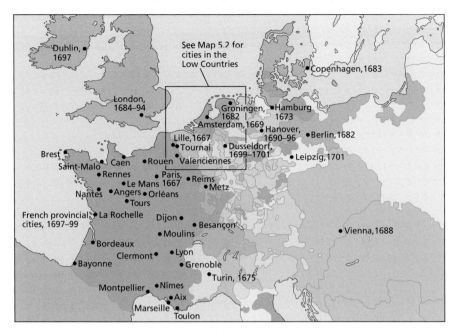

Map 5.1   Street lighting in Europe to 1700

a surprising set of relationships between security, the city, and court culture at night in seventeenth-century Europe.

5.1   LIGHTING THE STREETS OF EARLY MODERN EUROPE

In the second half of the seventeenth century, parallel to the new uses of the night at court, the rulers of the leading cities of Northern Europe also began to sanction broader uses of the night. Nocturnal illumination in general was expanding from the spectacular to the quotidian, and street lighting is the most visible example of this development.[12] The first cities to enjoy public street lighting were Paris (1667), Lille (1667), and Amsterdam (1669), followed by Hamburg (1673), Turin (1675), Berlin (1682), Copenhagen (1683), and London (1684–94).[13] In the 1670s and 1680s several other cities in the Netherlands followed Amsterdam in establishing street lighting (see Map 5.2), and by the end of the century Vienna (1688), Hanover (1690–96), Dublin

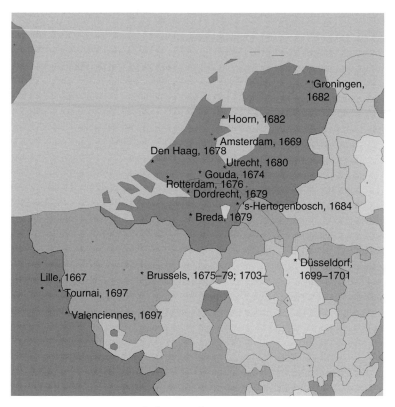

Map 5.2 Street lighting in the Low Countries to 1700

(1697), and Leipzig (1701) had illuminated their streets.[14] Several common factors appear in the emergence of street lighting in the seventeenth century. Everywhere the oil-lantern (or in the French case, the large candle-lantern) maintained at public expense, replaced the earlier candle-lanterns which city-dwellers were often required to hang outside their houses.[15] In each city, the lighting demarcated a large and consistent space which was accessible to a general public well after sunset.

Before the institution of public street lighting, the sources of light one would have seen at night on the streets of even the largest cities were few and irregular. The contrast between the few bobbing lanterns carried by individuals, the torches held by link-boys or the lights hung out in front of taverns and the more regular, uniform public lighting made a clear impression on contemporaries. The earliest published report (1690) on the "New Lights" of London noted that "There is one of these lights before the front of every tenth House on each side of the way, if the street be broad; by the regular position whereof, there is such a mutual reflection, that they all seem to be but one great Solar-Light."[16] Describing Vienna's streets in 1721, Johannes Neiner saw the affinity of street lighting with theatrical illumination: "these beautiful night lights are laid out so prettily that if one looks down a straight lane … it is like seeing a splendid theater or a most gracefully illuminated stage."[17]

The function of lighting at night had also evolved. Prior to the seventeenth century, the regulation of lighting at night was *solely* an aspect of the night watch and policing. Anyone about after dark was required to carry a torch or lantern: not to see, but to be seen.[18] This requirement appears in countless early modern ordinances. Failure to illuminate oneself was considered evidence of shadowy intentions.[19] The very limited city lighting established since medieval times (candle-lanterns or "fire-pans") was intended to deter crime and aid in fire-fighting; after the curfew ordinary citizens were to be off the streets.[20] Of course, the curfew was unenforceable in great cities like London and Paris, whose streets teemed with activity late into the night. City authorities tolerated and policed this night life, but they did not sanction it. They knew that some nocturnal activities were necessary, such as the work of midwives, doctors, or latrine-cleaners, and others unavoidable, but all nocturnal sociability could fall under the ubiquitous early modern prohibitions of "nightwalking."[21]

The new street lighting of the seventeenth century certainly was intended to promote law and order, but it also beautified a city and provided convenience and social amenity by encouraging respectable traffic on city streets after dark. Public street lighting reflected a new willingness to use the night and to reorder daily time by relaxing curfews.[22] This lighting represents both an unprecedented concession to the growing use of city streets after dark, and a renewed attempt to regulate and secure this nocturnal sociability. The meticulous street lighting schedules (see Figure 5.3) and lamplighter instructions sought to create legitimate, regular, and uniformly lighted places and times.

Surprisingly, some of the early modern roots of uniform public street lighting lie in the culture of nocturnal piety, devotion, and mysticism examined in chapter 3. The 1619 utopia of the Lutheran churchman Johann Valentin Andreä (1586–1654) reveals the cultural link between the nocturnalization of piety and devotion and the illumination of Europe's streets in the seventeenth century. The *Reipublicae christianopolitanae descriptio*, Andreä's 1619 account of an ideal Christian city, stands squarely in the tradition of utopian writing.[23] The author refers directly to More's *Utopia* and the *Civitas Solis* of Tommaso Campanella (1568–1639), and Andreä's work – usually referred to as *Christianopolis* from its German translation – has been seen as derivative of More and Campanella. But chapter 25 of *Christianopolis* presents a novel aspect of his utopia. The citizens of Christianopolis

do not allow the night to be completely dark, but light it up with lamps burning at intervals, the purpose of which is both to take care of the safety of the community and to prevent useless wandering about; they also make the night watches less worrisome.

As we will see below, the first European street lighting, established in the 1660s, marked an extraordinary turning point in the history of the night. There was no actual street lighting that could serve as a model for Andreä in 1619, and none of his predecessors imagined street lighting in their utopias. The traditional association of the night with sin and the Devil are clear, but Andreä innovates by acknowledging legitimate night work:

In this way they also set themselves against the dark kingdom and murky games of Satan, and wish to be reminded of the Eternal Light ... Let us not draw back from that arrangement [i.e., street lighting] which calms the fears of *people working in the darkness* [my emphasis], and which makes it easier to see through the veil which our own flesh is glad to draw over licentiousness and dissolute behavior.

Quite presciently, Andreä notes that street lighting will be an expensive proposition, but he imagines a night freed from moral and physical darkness:

Also there is no reason to discuss the expense here in Christianopolis, since they are extremely frugal in other respects – whereas in other places there is the greatest extravagance in almost everything. If only more were spent on light there would not be so much opportunity at night for all kinds of evil, nor such a great number of shady dealings![24]

This account of street lighting stands out because the rich utopian tradition from which Andreä drew, in particular More's *Utopia* and Campanella's "city of the sun," made no provision for such legitimate nocturnal activities.

Like his contemporary Böhme, Andreä understood the everyday world as a Christian allegory without abandoning its intrinsic significance. Each detail of Christianopolis represents an aspect of the life of the individual Christian, but Andreä also sought to realize an actual community like Christianopolis among his peers. On both levels – as allegory and as daily life – the imagined street lighting of *Christianopolis* documents a new relationship with darkness and the night emerging in the first half of the seventeenth century.

The street lighting imagined by Andreä in 1619 anticipated the actual establishment of public street lighting in European cities by a half-century. To create and maintain this sort of street lighting both technical and political problems had to be solved. The spread of street lighting across Northern Europe was based in part on the refinement of lamp and lantern design. The decisive steps were taken in Amsterdam, where the painter and inventor Jan van der Heyden (1637–1712) experimented during the 1660s with oil-lamps in glass-paned lanterns. Lamp-lanterns of his sophisticated design, which used the current of air drawn into the lantern by combustion to keep soot from collecting on the glass, made Amsterdam the first European city to install truly effective street lighting. Admiring the city, the German student Friedrich Lucae commented that "in the evening the entire city is illuminated with lanterns, so that one can pass through the crowds of people just as in broad daylight."[25] The superiority of van der Heyden's design is suggested by its rapid adoption across the United Provinces and Hamburg (under the supervision of van der Heyden), and by its unauthorized use in Berlin, Dublin, Leipzig, and elsewhere.[26] Figure 5.1 shows an overview of the van der Heyden lantern design: note the air intake hole in the lantern post.

When we see early modern street lighting as an international development, the political initiative to establish the lighting becomes especially significant. Despite its presumed benefits, city councils were not eager to incur the new expense of public lighting. Patricians in self-governing cities such as Amsterdam and Hamburg chose to set up and pay for street lighting themselves, but they were the exception. In most cases territorial rulers established the lighting in their capital cities and forced their subjects to pay for it.[27] In cities including Paris, Turin, Berlin, and Vienna, the initiative came from the monarch. In London and Westminster, private street-lighting companies contracted with the city to light specific streets and collect the corresponding fees; in Dublin (1697) and Lübeck (1704) individual entrepreneurs tried (with less success) to provide the service.[28]

The introduction of street lighting in Paris in 1667 by the "council for the reform of the policing of the city" of Louis XIV was the first of many cases of royal initiative to provide public lighting. Jean Baptiste Colbert proposed the street lighting to the council in a discussion of the night watch in December 1666, and he and his uncle Henri Pussort carried out the lighting project in 1667. The lighting and improved street cleaning were financed by a new "tax of mud and lanterns" (*taxe des boues et lanternes*), which became the only significant direct tax on householders in Paris under the Old Regime.[29] By 1702 there were 5,400 public candle-lanterns in place across the city, lit from October to March.[30] Unlike the Amsterdam lanterns mounted on posts, in Paris the lanterns held candles and were suspended about fifteen feet above the middle of the street by ropes, raised and lowered with a

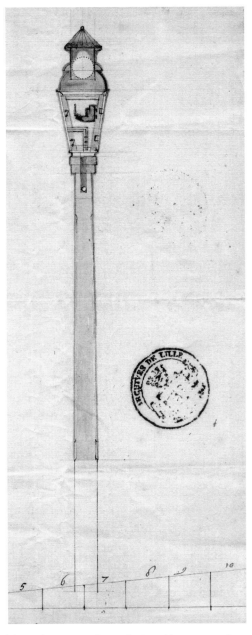

Figure 5.1 Oil-lamp, lantern, and post designed by Jan van der Heyden, 1660s. Archives municipales de Lille, Affaires Générales 1256, dossier 9, fo. 122 (*c.* 1700).

Figure 5.2 Print showing the rue Quinquempoix, Paris, 1720, with candle-
lanterns suspended above the street. From the broadsheet "Abbildung des auf
der Strasse Qvincampoix in Paris enstandenen so berühmten Actien-Handels"
(Nuremberg: Christoph Weigel, 1720). © Trustees of the British Museum,
1882,0812.461.

pulley. Figure 5.2 shows two lanterns above the rue Quinquempoix
in 1720.

Compared with Paris, Berlin was a modest provincial town in the
second half of the seventeenth century, but it was the residence of
Frederick William I, the "Great Elector" of Brandenburg-Prussia
(1640–88), who ordered in 1679 that the residents of Berlin should
hang a lantern light outside every third house at dusk each evening from September to May. The Berliners failed to comply and
on September 23, 1680 the citizenry petitioned the elector to eliminate the lighting requirement, arguing that they could not afford
it.[31] The elector responded by establishing public street lighting on
the Amsterdam model, using van der Heyden's lantern design and
maintenance plan. About 1,600 lanterns went up in the three dis-
tricts of the city (Berlin, Cölln, and Werder) – all at the citizens'
expense.[32]

As Vienna recovered from the siege of 1683, imperial authorities began to police the city more effectively. In 1685 an imperial
patent reinforced the city law requiring anyone out after the curfew

DECEMBER. Christmonat.

	Tage.	Wochen-Tage.	Monds-Unterg. Uhr viert.	Anzünden Uhr.	Monds-Aufg. Uhr viert.	Auslöschen Uhr.	Brennen Stund.
	1	Freytag	4. 2	morg. III½	am Tag. Auffgang Nachm.	morg. VII	III½
	2	Sonnab.	5. 2	morg. IV½		morg. VII	II½
	3	Sonntag	6. 2	——		——	——
Voll-mond	4	Montag	7. 2	——		——	——
	5	Dienstag	Des Monds Untergang fällt bey Tage ein.	——		——	——
	6	Mittwoch		abends V	6. 0	abends VII½	II½
	7	Donnerst.		abends V	6. 3	abends VIII½	III½
	8	Freytag		abends V	7. 2	nachts IX½	IV½
	9	Sonnab.		abends V	8. 2	nachts XI	VI
	10	Sonntag		abends IV¾	9. 3	nachts XII	VII
	11	Montag		abends IV¾	11. 0	nachts I	VIII
Letzte viertel	12	Dienstag		abends IV¾	Vormitt.	nachts II	IX
	13	Mittwoch		abends IV¾	0. 1	morg. III½	XI
	14	Donnerst.		abends IV¾	1. 2	morg. VII¼	XIV½
	15	Freytag		abends IV¾	3. 0	morg. VII¼	XIV½
	16	Sonnab.		abends IV¾	4. 1	morg. VII¼	XIV½
	17	Sonntag		abends IV¾	5. 2	morg. VII¼	XIV½
	18	Montag		abends IV¾	6. 3	morg. VII¼	XIV½
Neu-mond	19	Dienstag	Nachm.	abends IV¾	Der Mond kömmt bey Tage über den Horizont.	morg. VII¼	XIV½
	20	Mittwoch	5. 3	abends IV¾		morg. VII¼	XIV½
	21	Donnerst.	7. 0	abends IV¾		morg. VII¼	XIV½
	22	Freytag	8. 0	abends IV¾		morg. VII¼	XIV½
	23	Sonnab.	9. 1	abends IV¾		morg. VII¼	XIV½
	24	Sonntag	10. 2	abends IV¾		morg. VII¼	XIV½
	25	Montag	11. 3	nachts IX		morg. VII¼	X
Erste viertel	26	Dienstag	Vormitt.	nachts X		morg. VII¼	IX
	27	Mittwoch	1. 0	nachts XI		morg. VII¼	VIII
	28	Donnerst.	2. 0	nachts XII		morg. VII¼	VII
	29	Freytag	3. 0	nachts I½		morg. VII¼	VI
	30	Sonnab.	4. 0	morg. III		morg. VII¼	IV
	31	Sonntag	5. 0	morg. IV		morg. VII¼	III

Figure 5.3 Leipzig street-lighting schedule, December 1702. Stadtarchiv Leipzig.

bell to carry a lantern. In 1687 the imperial administrator of Lower Austria, Count Johann Quintin Jörger, began the establishment of public street lighting in Vienna. Several obstacles to the plan quickly emerged: there were not enough tinsmiths in Vienna to manufacture the lanterns, the start-up and maintenance costs were higher than expected, and the city council resisted the lighting measure because of its expense. With the support of Emperor Leopold I, Jörger was able to set up the lighting by the following spring: the streets were lit for the first time on Pentecost eve (June 5), 1688. The lighting was financed by a tax on imported wine, arranged through an intricate compromise with the city council. In 1698 the city council, which was already supplying twenty-six night-lanterns for the inner courtyard of the imperial palace (the Hofburg) itself, was asked "by the spoken request of the imperial court" to also illuminate the imperial palace of Ebersdorf, just outside the city walls, with fourteen lanterns.[33] The court made ready use of the municipal lighting system to illuminate its own representative buildings.

5.2 POLICING THE NIGHT: STREET LIGHTING IN LILLE

In 1697 the leading provincial cities of France were required by a royal edict to "immediately proceed to establish lanterns, conforming to those of our fine city of Paris."[34] This seemingly "enlightened" command from Louis XIV to set up street lighting was immediately recognized by all commentators as another revenue scheme: the thirty cities involved (see Map 5.1) would pay royal suppliers dearly for the installation and maintenance of the lanterns, with the profits going to the king.[35] As we will see below in section 5.4, local authorities in Dijon, Amiens, and other provincial cities resisted the edict; some sought to buy an exemption from it. Among the cities' protests against the edict requiring street lighting, the response of the ruling council or *Magistrat* of the city of Lille stood out: they explained that they had already established street lighting thirty years earlier and did not need the royal suppliers' assistance.[36] This was true: in 1667 Lille, capital of the French province of Flanders, became only the third city in Europe in which the complex and costly project of street lighting was realized, alongside Paris and Amsterdam. Why did Lille precede all other French provincial cities in the establishment of street lighting?

The streets of Lille were illuminated in the fall of 1667, two months after the French captured the city in the War of Devolution (1667–68). Louis XIV left Lille's ruling council in place, but the city of 50,000 was now uneasy host to a garrison of 5,000 to 10,000 French troops. Protected by a citadel built by Vauban in 1668–70,

Lille became a key French stronghold on the border with the Spanish Netherlands and near the Dutch Republic. The French occupation of Lille necessitated complex negotiations among French civil and military authorities, the governing patricians of Lille, a restive populace, and a large military presence. The policing of the night and the establishment of street lighting were an important part of this balance of overlapping authorities.[37] The Lille case reveals a close relationship between attempts to police the urban night and attempts to rule the newly conquered territories of Walloon Flanders and integrate them into the French kingdom.

In the immediate aftermath of the French capture of Lille, security at night was paramount. Three days after the surrender of the city on August 28, the *Magistrat* issued an ordinance prohibiting all movement on the streets at night. This ordinance went beyond the standard requirement to carry at light when out at night, and instead established a strict dusk-to-dawn curfew. "All residents of the countryside and foreigners who came and will come into this city" were required "to retire to their homes each day in the evening before the bell called *Le Vigneron* ('the wine-maker') sounds without thereafter finding themselves back on the streets until daylight." All residents were advised to "take care to have the things that they will need in a timely fashion, all the more [because] once the night watch has begun, they will not be free to go through the city unless it is a case of inexcusable [sic] necessity." In such a case, "they will have to go with a light and address themselves to the first watchman [they meet] in order to be escorted to wherever they need to go and then return to their home."[38] This ban on all nocturnal movement was lifted on July 23, 1668 and replaced with the standard ordinance requiring anyone out at night to carry a lantern or face a heavy fine.[39]

In September 1667 the *Magistrat* established street lighting following the Paris model of lanterns suspended by cords over the middle of street.[40] The traditional neighborhood authorities, the *maîtres des places*, were charged by the ruling council with the placement of the lanterns and their maintenance, while the responsibility for hanging out and lighting the lanterns was given to individual householders. As an update of the ordinance explained in January 1668: "wishing to obviate the insolence and disorders which occur in the evening in the said town," the *Magistrat* ordered "all those who occupy corners and the entries of streets, and other locations designated by the *maîtres des places*" to put out candle-lanterns lit "from one hour after the evening bell until after midnight."[41] The ordinance is similar to that of Paris, though it is not clear who provided the 600–700 lanterns. The 1667 lighting was limited, but it went beyond the traditional requirement that residents hang out a lantern in two ways: the local *maîtres des places* were authorized to enforce compliance, and the placement of the lanterns on special ropes "hanging above the middle of the street"[42] followed the new Paris model, lighting a street centrally from above rather than from lanterns in front of individual houses.

This street lighting arose alongside other measures intended to secure the night in Lille. In the fall of 1667 innkeepers were ordered to submit a list of their lodgers every evening, and the *Magistrat* again regulated the closing times for "Tavernes & Cabarets."[43] In the period from 1667 to 1715, the Lille *Magistrat* addressed nocturnal security in about sixty separate ordinances and resolutions; the requirement that one carry a light if out on the streets at night was repeated eleven times in this period.[44]

But whom were the authorities policing? Lillois journals and chronicles all describe violence between French officers and citizens of Lille, duels at dusk between French officers, nocturnal robberies by common soldiers, and attacks on French troops in the first months and years after the French capture of the city.[45] For French military and civil authorities, the actions of their own soldiers were of great concern, and they had to tread carefully. Following the annexation of Walloon Flanders by the French, all eyes were on the fate of Lille, "accounted the third Place of Traffic in the Low-Countries next *Amsterdam* and *Antwerp*," under French rule.[46] Louis XIV had personally accepted the city's surrender in August 1667 and confirmed the authority and privileges of the ruling *Magistrat*. Lille, described as the "capital of the conquests of his majesty,"[47] stood as a "test case" for the possible annexation of other cities of the Low Countries by France, hence the sharp concern to maintain order in the city, and especially to prevent crimes by the occupying French soldiers.

In September 1668, a few months after the Treaty of Aix-la-Chapelle confirmed the annexation of Lille and Walloon Flanders by France, Michel Le Peletier de Souzy, intendant of the new French province of Flanders, wrote to the Marquis de Louvois, secretary of state, to report on nocturnal crime in Lille: "Yesterday I handed down a judgment very stern but also very necessary – people were beginning to thieve at night in the streets of Lille as in Paris; and a citizen had been despoiled down to the shirt by four Liège horsemen from the company of Berlost."[48] Three of the four were apprehended and Le Peletier reported that he condemned two of them to be hanged, despite their rank.[49] In reply, Louvois affirmed these concerns: "Public safety during the night is so important that one would have thought they might have to be condemned to [be broken on] the wheel."[50] He considered this public spectacle of slow death, then continued, "I do not understand how in a place where the watch must do its duty as carefully as in Lille, one still dares to attempt to rob at night."[51] In this case, disciplining the night was vital to reducing the impact of the French troops on the occupied city.[52]

Turning the conquered Lillois into loyal subjects of the French king would take some time, however. In December 1669 the intendant Le Peletier complained that the *Magistrat* was disloyal and difficult to govern.[53] In 1670 the visiting Spanish ambassador (the representative of their former Habsburg rulers) was cheered in the streets, and some of the city's clergy preached against the alleged decline of public morals brought by the French.[54] We can also see the resentment of the French occupation from the street, so to speak, in the journal of the Lillois master silk weaver Pierre Ignace Chavatte (1633–93). Chavatte, like Le Peletier and Louvois, saw the night as a significant site in the negotiations between the Lillois and their new masters. Chavatte recorded numerous crimes and misdeeds by the French and observed that French attempts to police the night could themselves trigger new conflicts: in 1672 his journal notes that "on 23 July between 10 and 11 o'clock at night a French sentinel who was at the corner of the market fired his musket at a man who passed with a lit wick [of his candle or lamp] in his hand … and three to four days after he died; he was a tailor by trade and of the Flemish nation."[55] Chavatte emphasized that the unfortunate tailor was killed even though he was carrying a light as required.

Despite the French affirmation of the governance of the Lille *Magistrat*, Chavatte observed that authority over the city streets at night belonged to the French. He recorded the declaration of war between France and the United Provinces on October 16, 1673, adding resentfully "that same day in the evening servants of the *Magistrat* of the city of Lille were arrested and taken to the watch because it was forbidden to walk without a lantern."[56] Chavatte reflected a broad distrust of the French occupiers of the city, and of their policing of the night. Conflicts between French soldiers and residents of Lille often flared up at night, as on February 7, 1675, when "in the evening in the tavern *La Bourse d'Or* there was a great dispute by the citizens with the French officers in which three to four bourgeois were wounded, and a French surgeon wounded in the head; and the citizens were apprehended and taken to prison."[57] In the same year the intendant Le Peletier acknowledged the circulation of libels "prejudicial to the service of the king."[58]

In the 1680s street lighting factored into the slow détente between Lille's ruling patricians, the administrators of Louis XIV, and the common people. In 1682, the *Magistrat* established paid lamp-lighters for the city's street lighting, and the provision of street lighting gradually became more centralized and professional.[59] In 1689 the *échevins* (high judges) of the ruling council, "having noted that the establishment of lanterns to illuminate the city during the darkness of the night served not a little to prevent quarrels, thefts and other disorders that are commonly committed under cover of the night," praised the service.[60] The *Magistrat* also seems to have become more attentive to damage to the lanterns, referring in 1692 to the need to prevent people from "cutting the cords of the public lanterns."[61] In March 1697 the *Magistrat* ordered four young men "from good bourgeois homes" to pay heavy fines for destroying thirty-three lanterns in the streets of Lille during the night of November 26–27, 1696.[62]

Early modern street lighting was thought to provide both prestige and security, but in Lille, the emphasis was entirely on the latter. None of the publicity that accompanied the establishment of street lighting in Paris or Leipzig (see below) appeared in Lille; conversely, none of the Lille ordinances regarding street lighting refer to the splendor, prestige, or beauty brought by the new amenity. In the occupied city, street lighting was seen as a response to the tensions and disorder brought by the French, rather than as an urban improvement. Only after two decades did Lille's ruling council begin to refer to "the public lanterns" as a service of "the public trust."[63]

The French conquest and integration of Lille and Walloon Flanders shows how much authorities' attempts to police the night had in common with larger projects of territorial conquest and control. This comparison will be explored further in the discussion of policing, resistance, and the colonization of the night in chapters 6 and 7. In Lille, the establishment of street lighting slowly brought the French intendant and military authorities together with the city's ruling council in a common project to light and secure the city's streets.

5.3 ABSOLUTISM AND STREET LIGHTING IN LEIPZIG

In the Leipzig case, the official initiative to light the streets came from Warsaw. While in residence there on September 19, 1701 King-Elector Augustus II decreed that in Leipzig "as is common in other prominent cities, to prevent all sorts of nightly inconveniences and for beautification, lanterns shall be set up and lighted by night."[64] Interest in lighting Leipzig's streets goes back to 1695, when the Leipzig merchants' guild (the *Kaufmannschaft*), citing incessant nocturnal crime, proposed to the city council that "constantly-burning night lanterns should be maintained and the streets illuminated with them, as is established in Vienna, Hamburg, Berlin, and other places."[65]

The guild's concerns were well founded, as the 1699 attack on the traveling Strasbourg merchant Johan Eberhard Zetzner shows. The twenty-two-year-old Zetzner was bringing a letter to the post late on the evening of March 28, 1699 when he encountered a group of drunken students who challenged him "with rude and insulting words." Years later, he described what followed in his memoir:

Because I saw myself outnumbered, and had neither a knife nor a walking-stick with me, I responded with polite words and tried as much as possible to avoid them. But one drew his dagger; then I shouted for the night watch.[66]

As he called out, Zetzner felt (but did not see) a blow to his left arm. He blocked a second thrust but was badly injured; the students escaped easily. His reflections on the attack express no real surprise that the streets could be so unsafe, just anger at Leipzig's wastrel students ("these privileged hangman's knaves," as he called them).[67] Despite these dangerous conditions and the example of other leading cities, however, the fiscally conservative Leipzig city council did not take the initiative to set up street lighting.

Less than three years after the unlucky Zetzner's visit, Leipzig's streets were illuminated for the first time. A series of oil lanterns established and maintained at public expense were lit on Christmas Eve, 1701: "so it was also resolved here in Leipzig to transform the dismal night and darkness into light and bright radiance," as a Leipzig newsletter reported.[68] The decision of the absolutist King-Elector Augustus II to create "The Leipzig that Shines Forth by Night" illustrates the initiative of the court in the nocturnalization of Leipzig's daily life.[69]

Elected king of Poland in 1697, the Saxon elector Augustus II made full use of the politics of spectacle at his opulent courts at Dresden and Warsaw, and his reign illustrates both the promises and the limitations of the politics of spectacle in this era. Like his contemporary Louis XIV, Augustus styled himself a "sun king," and his celebrations sought to turn night into day. Even equestrian events could be held at night: the Dresden Reithaus, illuminated by thousands of candles, was the scene of riding displays during Carnival in 1695 (see Figure 4.3) and during the visit of the Danish king Frederick IV in 1709. The nocturnal celebrations and spectacles of the Saxon court reached their high point under Augustus.[70] But the Polish election and Augustus' lavish court swallowed immense sums of Saxon money, straining relations with the tax-weary citizens of Leipzig, the wealthiest city of the electorate.[71]

By initiating street lighting in Leipzig, Augustus followed the general pattern of royal provision of street lighting seen in Paris, Berlin, and Vienna.[72] But the actual establishment of street lighting in Leipzig was directly connected with the swift rise to power of Augustus' courtier, the appointed mayor Franz Conrad Romanus (1671–1746).

Romanus came from an established Leipzig family and studied law before entering into the service of the king-elector. Romanus is perhaps best known for the urban palace built for him at the corner of the Brühl and the Katherinenstraße: this great mansion, completed in 1704, is the most important work of Leipzig's baroque architecture.[73]

Franz Conrad Romanus was unique among the mayors of Leipzig during the Old Regime. He was not freely elected, nor had he served on the Leipzig city council (as was required) before his term as mayor began in 1701. Instead Romanus, a court official ("Appellation-Rath") of the king-elector, took office on the express command of Augustus, who overrode the resistance of the city council.[74] This was an unprecedented exercise of territorial authority over the city, intended to give the king-elector more control over the taxation of Leipzig, the single largest source of revenue in the electorate. Augustus and his privy cabinet suspected that the Leipzig city council could be more forthcoming with loans and contributions, and placed Romanus at the head of the city government to increase the flow of revenue for the unceasing expenditures of Augustus and the court. The written protests and financial counter-offers of the Leipzig city council were futile and on August 22, 1701 the council concluded that it had no choice and elected Romanus to its ranks. On August 29 Romanus took office as mayor, promising his fellow councilmen that their failed opposition to him would be "cast into the sea of oblivion."[75]

The Leipzig councilmen, on the other hand, could hardly forget the unique circumstances that brought Romanus to the office of mayor. The average age of the councilmen was well over fifty; Romanus, all of thirty years old, with no prior experience in the city council, now led its meetings. Hated and feared by his peers, he served the interests of the king-elector alone, and his task was extraordinarily difficult: to bring money into the coffers of Augustus without further alienating the citizenry or the council. With the support of Augustus, Romanus quickly sought to gain the goodwill of the citizens. A few weeks after he took office, the council received the electoral decree from Warsaw calling for the establishment of public street lighting. The decree, no doubt planned by the king-elector and Romanus, also ordered the establishment of a city drain system, the regulation of coffeehouses, and several other measures for this city of about 20,000. As mayor Romanus would oversee a range of improvements to the city which had been in discussion for some time. Of all the projects, the street lighting moved most quickly.

The city council, led by Romanus, contracted with the entire Leipzig tinsmiths' guild (7 masters), who delivered 478 lanterns: 2 van der Heyden lanterns from Amsterdam served as the models.[76] Another 222 lanterns came from Dresden, sold to the city by the banking firm of Brinck and Bodisch, Romanus' own bankers.[77] By December 24 the 700 lanterns were in place across the city: 4 lantern masters and 18 lantern keepers maintained them.[78] When the lanterns were all lit for the first time on that evening, one verse pamphlet enthusiastically reported: "away with the darkness in a brighter light ... LEIPZIG'S prosperity resounds in all lands: it shines day and night."[79]

The decree of the elector had proposed that the street lighting be funded by a new common tax or property tax. This had been the case in Vienna, for example, which led citizens to complain that those who paid the least for the lighted streets benefited the most. "The high ministers and cavaliers, who with their people frequent the imperial court at the illuminated times, are free from all contributions," as the Vienna city council protested in 1689.[80] Similar objections from Berlin underscore the initial association of street lighting and "night life" with court society. Mindful of his popularity, Romanus instead funded the Leipzig lanterns at no direct cost to the townspeople by reclaiming for the city the fees collected to enter the city after dark at the Grimma gate, the location of the main watch. These fees were under the direct authority of the king-elector, and their importance also illustrates the level of Leipzig's night life (specifically traffic between the city and its suburbs) at the turn of the century.[81] The entry fees covered the annual maintenance costs of about 3500 florins; all but 400 florins of the start-up costs of 4500 florins were paid by the king-elector directly, making the street lighting his Christmas gift to the city.[82]

Leipzig's newly illuminated streets were promptly illustrated in the clandestine news journal *Captured Letters, Exchanged between Curious Persons Regarding the Current ... Political and Learned World*

(*Aufgefangene Brieffe, welche Zwischen etzlichen curieusen Personen über den ietzigen Zustand der Staats und gelehrten Welt gewechselt worden*) published in Leipzig in 1702.[83] The journal introduces the innovation in terms of baroque spectacle:

Among other amusements ... at royal and princely solemnities and public festivals ... many thousand lights are lit – and with them often an entire city is illuminated.[84]

Calling this use of the night "the waste and great abuse of illumination" the Leipzig author presents a typical critique of the extravagance of court life.[85] But he then reveals a new bourgeois appreciation for the night by arguing that "A far better use of night-lanterns ... in cities on public lanes and streets is to replace the waning sun- and moonlight in the evening and darkness and so well and truly ward off the dangers of the night."[86] The journal included a print (Figure 5.4) which offers a visual résumé of the presumed benefits of street lighting.

The engraving is not a realistic representation of Leipzig's street lighting: instead, it brings together security, elite sociability, and the night in a single compact scene. In the foreground, left, a man reads by lantern light; couples stroll and admire the city's new baroque mansions, while two men, able to recognize each other despite the darkness, doff their hats. In the background a nightwatchman stands guard. The accompanying text emphasizes the convenience and security provided by the lanterns:

not only are we spared the private lanterns and torches, which everyone must otherwise use when going out at night, but also many sins against the Fifth, Sixth and Seventh Commandments [i.e., prohibitions of murder, adultery, and theft] are better prevented and avoided.[87]

A medal minted in 1702 to commemorate the introduction of street lighting repeats two of these scenes, showing a city watchman and a figure reading. The emphasis on reading in the print and in the medal should not be taken too literally: as Wolfgang Schivelbusch has pointed out, the *symbolic* value of lighting always supplements its visible effects.[88] Reading by the light of the lanterns was hardly practical, but this exaggeration of their power suggests that the sphere

Abbildung der Leipziger neuen Stadt Laternen.

Figure 5.4 Leipzig street-lighting scene, 1702, print from *Aufgefangene Brieffe, welche Zwischen etzlichen curieusen Personen über den ietzigen Zustand der Staats und gelehrten Welt gewechselt worden* (Wahrenberg [actually Leipzig], 1701).

of the literate was expanded by street lighting. The better sort were to benefit from it: the well-dressed men in the illustration, perhaps students, carry swords to indicate that they are not apprentices or servants. Leipzig's prosperity and prestige depended on attracting merchants and students, and this illustration promised a safer and more genteel city.

Under Romanus the Leipzig city council issued several ordinances regulating night life. During his first year in office the council forbade the fashion of "walking about the streets at night in night-shirts, masks, night-caps and other unusual clothing."[89] Repeating a 1697 ordinance, the council warned citizens and residents to "keep their own [family] at home in the evening," and the ordinance reported that "late in the evening many apprentices, boys, maids and such unmarried folk are found idly in the streets, where they practice many improper things with shouts, running about and all such mischief."[90] Another ordinance denounced the coffeehouses of the city as sites of "sexual vice ... luxurious ostentation and mischief from the early hours until late into the night."[91] The street lanterns and city ordinances were meant to civilize the city's streets and reduce this sort of "night life."[92] The verse pamphlet *The Leipzig that Shines Forth by Night*, printed to celebrate the new lanterns, also emphasizes security and order. Prostitutes "would have to shun the light"; thieves lurking would instead "go off to bed."[93] The pamphlet's author went on to praise the benefits that the visitors to Leipzig's great trade fairs would enjoy. "In security," he commented, "they can recognize friend and foe / and can go up and down the street doing business," making clear the value of street lighting for commercial uses of the night.[94]

5.4 RESISTANCE BY LOCAL AUTHORITIES

Despite the general praise of street lighting echoed here, in some cities local authorities resisted the establishment of street lighting. The innovation was associated with luxury and the aristocracy, and citizens faced with new taxes to maintain the street lighting complained that those who paid the least for the lighted streets benefited the most.[95] As a Vienna petition explained, "the citizens and artisans mostly stay at home and seldom go out after 7 o'clock in the evening, and do not benefit from the illumination as much" as the courtiers and officials.[96] These complaints underscore the association of street lighting and "night life" with court society, although the image of restrained, early-to-bed burghers is certainly qualified by many other sources.[97]

In Paris, debate arose over the schedule of the new lighting. As was common with the earliest public street lighting, all agreed that the lighting would not be used during the short nights of the summer months. The question, then, focused on when to start and end the "lighting season" in the fall and spring. The citizens of Paris, while favoring the new street lighting, sought to limit its use to about five months of the year, from October to mid March, to reduce costs. When Parisians proposed this monthly schedule for street lighting in 1671, their argument was countered by the police commissioner La Reynie, who noted that it was important for the streets to be lit through the month of March, because "during March, the season and business fill the city and the court is in Paris."[98] A Venetian traveler passing through Berlin in 1708 described the extension of the city's street lighting out to the Charlottenburg palace:

On the sides of the street stand wooden posts with glass lanterns on top; they stand along the entire four-mile-long street and burn through the entire night when the king is in Charlottenburg. That is for all who are constantly at court very commodious.[99]

The Leeds antiquarian Ralph Thoresby described a very similar sight when he visited London in 1712. He "could not but observe that all the way, quite through Hyde Park to the Queen's palace at Kensington, has lanterns for illuminating the road in the dark nights, for the coaches."[100]

When threatened with the expense of the street lighting, townspeople could resist its imposition and the increased nocturnalization it entailed. As we saw above, the oligarchs of self-governed or semi-autonomous cities such as Amsterdam, Hamburg, Dublin, or London took the initiative to establish and pay for street lighting. But one could see these cities as exceptions in light of the many (generally smaller) cities in which street lighting failed to draw sufficient public support. In Brussels, for example, public lighting was set up in 1675 but abandoned by 1680 as result of the expense.[101] Private citizens in Bremen set up street lighting on one section of a single street, the Langenstraße, in 1698; even this drew protest from one resident who did not want a lantern attached to his house. The entire city was not regularly illuminated until 1757.[102] Across France, street lighting was established in thirty cities by royal edict in 1697, but city councils resisted the imposition of the lighting and the attendant costs. Dijon, for example, was illuminated with 600 candle-lanterns in 1698, but only after the city council unsuccessfully sought to buy an exemption from the royal edict requiring the street lighting.[103] In Amiens, the city council delayed buying the lanterns from the royal supplier until 1701. Once purchased, the lanterns were placed carefully in the attic of the city hall. No further steps were taken to install them; several years later the council auctioned them off. Only in 1718 did the Amiens city council actually illuminate the city's streets – on its own initiative.[104]

These local authorities apparently preferred a traditional urban night illuminated sporadically by hand-held torches or lanterns to the cost of the street lighting. In several other cases local authorities actually removed the street lighting imposed upon them by their princes. The residence cities of Düsseldorf and Stuttgart illustrate this response to the costs and benefits of public street lighting.

Düsseldorf became the residence of John William of Pfalz-Neuberg, duke of Jülich and Berg (called "Jan Willem"; from 1690 also elector of the Palatinate) in 1679. Jan Willem transformed the modest city into a center of court culture, building a baroque theater and a new riding school while renovating the ducal palace. In 1699 he ordered the establishment of street lighting in the city. By 1701 a modest 383 lanterns were in place; 50 of these, used to light the area around the ducal palace and the court buildings, were gold-plated. The elector initially paid for the street lighting from the state budget, but in 1704 "the burden and maintenance of the aforementioned lanterns was forced upon the city."[105] In numerous petitions and at the territorial parliament representatives of the city sought to shift the cost back to the duke, or abandon the lighting altogether. After the death of the elector in 1716 the court left Düsseldorf and the city's economy collapsed. In 1718 the representatives of the city argued that the "very costly" lighting served no purpose and that the citizens did not want it at all. In the winter of 1720 the city officials finally got their wish: the street lanterns were taken down and stored in a warehouse. A few were put back in use in the 1730s but city-wide lighting did not return until decades later.[106]

In Stuttgart, traditional residence of the rulers of Württemberg, Duke Eberhard Ludwig (1693–1733) began to pressure the city magistrates to set up public lighting in 1714. The city officials demurred, arguing that the costs of the lighting far outweighed its benefits. The street lighting was finally set up in time for Carnival in 1716 at the behest of the duke. But city officials continued to argue against the lighting, claiming in July 1716 that it was even more expensive than first estimated, and that some of the lanterns had been vandalized or destroyed. Further, the city magistrates claimed that Stuttgarters were happy to carry their lanterns and torches with them, or rely on moonlight, to get around that city at night. Duke Eberhard continued to insist on public street lighting, paid for by the city. In response, in September 1717 city officials again argued that "the larger part of the residents of high and low estate recognize that the installed lanterns have little or no value to public, but they have incurred great expenses."[107] Even after the court moved to Ludwigsburg, the street lighting and its expense remained, provoking anger and anonymous placards. The city magistrates finally won out in 1732, arguing that the funds for the street lighting could instead be used to purchase a new school building. Here the state administrators sided with the Stuttgart officials, and the Duke relented: the lighting was taken down on October 29, 1732.[108]

The last word on local resistance to street lighting comes from Strasbourg, where citizens were forced after decades of struggle to support street lighting in 1779. In response, these verses were posted anonymously on the city hall:

> As our city stood in prosperity,
> It was dark out on the street,
> But as our misery has begun,
> Lanterns on the street are hung,

So that the citizen – poor man!
Can see at night to beg.
We do not need the lanterns bright,
We can see our poverty without their light.[109]

Public street lighting threatened the traditional night life and political order of these middling European cities.[110] The expansion of elite social life into the urban night described here, resisted in some cases by local authorities, was also challenged by the traditional inhabitants of the night: servants, apprentices, and students, as well as tavern visitors, prostitutes, and those who occasionally sought to escape the social legibility of early modern daily life. On city streets at night the work, leisure, and social representation patterns of courtiers, burghers, and youth could collide violently, as we see in the next chapter.

5.5 SPECTACLE, SECURITY, AND SOCIABILITY

In 1710 Richard Steele described the nocturnalization of London's daily life in a *Tatler* essay: "we have thus thrown Business and Pleasure into the Hours of Rest, and by that Means made the natural Night but half as long as it should be." The result was a shift to later rising in the morning, and Steele asserted that "near Two thirds of the Nation lie fast asleep for several hours in broad Day-light."[111] Despite some exaggeration of the numbers of leisurely late sleepers, it is clear that the pleasures of the night were emerging as a significant part of urban daily life. Princes and burghers sanctioned and promoted new levels of nocturnal "Business and Pleasure" in European courts and cities, seeking prestige or profit by lengthening the day. The hours from dusk until dawn were no longer seen only as a threatening time of semi-licit activity or supernatural danger. The old views remained, of course, but courtiers and citizens began to use the night for respectable leisure and sociability. The inclusion of street lighting in Andreä's 1619 *Christianopolis* reveals the trajectory of new relationships with the night from the sacred to the political and the practical.

The shift of respectable daily activities into the evening and night went beyond the elites who initiated it: bourgeois gentlemen imitated noble fashions, and household servants had to adjust to new cycles of daily time. Court and city authorities used street lighting to sharpen a distinction between their own growing nocturnal sociability and the night life of the "apprentices, boys, maids and such unmarried folk found idly in the streets." Their attempts to police the urban night through street lighting evoked the resistance of this indigenous nocturnal youth culture. New uses of the night by "persons of quality" thus reshaped daily life for servants, apprentices, and common people in European courts and cities.

In Lille, street lighting was intended to protect the townspeople against the nocturnal crimes associated with the thousands of troops suddenly stationed there. French administrators and Lille patricians found a common goal in the policing of the city's streets at night. The Leipzig case shows how street lighting could bring the courtly night of nocturnal spectacles together with burghers' interest in increased security and sociability. In Leipzig in 1701 (as in Paris in 1667 and Vienna in 1688) the initiative to illuminate the city came from the court, not from the city council, and the courtier-mayor Franz Conrad Romanus – the direct representative of absolutist government in Leipzig – implemented the street lighting. The Leipzig lanterns were made in imitation of the lanterns of Amsterdam, the most technically advanced of the time. But the political symbolism of the baroque court is evident in their use: the power of illumination, which bedazzled at the Dresden court, now served to secure and beautify Leipzig, at the same time muting resistance to absolutist control over the city council. The night and its illumination thus link the representational needs of baroque monarchs with the practical goals of policing urban public space and time.

CHAPTER SIX

Colonizing the urban night: resistance, gender, and the public sphere

By 1700 life at court meant late hours, and permanent public street lighting was reshaping everyday life in dozens of cities across Northern Europe. Dutch city councilors, London merchants, and the police administrators of the Sun King all sought to expand respectable daily activity into the night in the second half of the seventeenth century. This unique alignment of interests across political and economic formations attests to the powerful forces behind nocturnalization. Sovereigns and self-governing cities celebrated at night and established street lighting with the same stated goals: to reflect their own glory and to protect their subjects.

Regular public street lighting, together with an improved and expanded night-watch, was the infrastructure of urban nocturnalization.[1] It was also the most visible and expensive aspect of the project. According to its heralds, the lighting responded to "the great number of vagabonds and thieves at night … and the amount of robberies and murders that are committed in the evening and at night" (Paris), and marked a concerted effort to "detect burglaries and prevent foul play" (Amsterdam), "for the reduction and prevention of all the recently increasing nocturnal and frightening murder and theft, and for the introduction of general security" (Vienna).[2] One London enthusiast singled out the social groups that would be driven away by the lighting:

> The scatt'ring Light gilt all the Gaudy way,
> Some people rose and thought it day.
> The plying Punks crept into Holes,
> Who walk'd the streets before by sholes;
> The Night could now no longer skreen
> The Tavern-sots from being seen.[3]

The proclamations all refer to disorder and danger on city streets at night. "Plying Punks" and "Tavern-sots" were nothing new in this period, but the steps taken to control their nocturnal activities were.

In several ways, these efforts to impose a new order on city streets after dark resemble a "colonization of the night."[4] What benefits do we obtain by using this analogy to describe the nocturnalization of daily life in the cities of early modern Europe? An awareness of nocturnalization in the cities as uneven, contested, and multi-sided would be the first benefit. Any critical definition of colonization recognizes the violence necessary to colonize. Both logically and historically, the colonization of inhabited spaces means the exercise of power or authority, or both, over the people already there. Of course, many myths of colonization posit a physically "empty space" devoid of indigenous people, or natives so culturally "empty" that they embrace the cultural authority of the colonizer. Myths aside, however, the colonial exercise of power and authority is never far from violence or the threat of violence. The analogy with colonization can enhance our understanding of the urban night by taking us beyond the dire warnings and celebratory verses provided by the proponents of street lighting.

By focusing on nocturnal crime – and by defining the traditional night life of young people as criminal – early modern princes, courtiers, city councils, and merchants expanded their activities, privileges, and authority into the hours after sunset. In the deliberations and proclamations establishing the street lighting, they described the urban night as overrun with violent crime. Considering the dangerous, seemingly untamable city evoked by proponents of street lighting, it is especially significant that when commentators looked back on the process of nocturnalization, they described it as natural or inexorable. After surveying the course of nocturnalization over the previous century, Friedrich Justin Bertuch concluded that "all these observations [of nocturnalization], which could easily be multiplied, prove clearly the occupations of the day begin ever later, the more society is refined and luxury increases."[5] Bertuch does not consider the inhabitants of the space that is being colonized by a society ever more refined and "policed". This discourse of colonization depicted the night as a dangerous frontier, or, conversely, as a "natural" site of expansion for polite "society." Neither depiction of the night – as filled with violence or as an empty space – takes into account the traditional cultures of the urban night and their resistance to nocturnalization.[6] The metaphor of colonization widens our view to include those who resisted nocturnalization, shaped its boundaries, or found their daily lives caught up in it.

This is especially important in the urban context. Nocturnalization at court encountered little resistance. Rulers modified the structures of daily time in the delimited space of the court (in the narrowest sense, the royal household) without much opposition. There were few institutions within the court which could (or would seek to) resist new habits and schedules. In cities, the forces promoting and resisting nocturnalization were much more complex, aligned across class, gender, and age. As we saw in the previous chapter, some local authorities saw street lighting as an expensive luxury and resisted its establishment. In middling cities like Bremen, Amiens, Düsseldorf, and Strasbourg the most visible aspect of nocturnalization was delayed for decades, and the colonization of the night seemed far less inevitable. The traditional order of the night did not go quietly.

6.1 HAND GRENADES, HORSEWHIPS, AND THE CIVILIZING PROCESS

Focusing on the traditional order of the night leads us to a more active level of resistance to the colonization of the night. Court and city authorities used street lighting to sharpen the distinction between their own expanding "respectable" nocturnal sociability and the night life of young people. These authorities admonished heads of households to prevent "their children, namely sons and daughters, as well as male and female servants, from roaming around during night time. Also, their beds ought to be in locked and sheltered chambers, and [household heads must] check frequently in this case too."[7] These young people and servants were the natural masters of the urban night, and by all accounts had been for centuries.[8] But we must consider nocturnalization as more than a "top-down" process.

When early modern elites, from princes and courtiers to town councils and wealthy merchants, expanded their activities, privileges, and authority into the hours after sunset, they sought to secure and regulate this part of the day. But this meant regulating the young people of their own classes along with the youth of the common people. The colonization of the night took place within as well as across classes. In 1700 the *lieutenant-général de police* of Paris, Marc-René d'Argenson, reported that he was forced to intervene in the family affairs of "several bourgeois and even a few of the most distinguished merchants," who "neglect so much the education of their children that they leave them among the rascals and night-walkers." As we will see below, restraining "the debauchery and licentiousness ... of these young people" at night was a major project, led by d'Argenson, in the Paris of Louis XIV.[9]

This regulation of behavior "in the leading groups of both the nobility and the bourgeoisie – in the direction of greater foresight and a stricter regulation of libidinal impulses,"[10] which forbade "the nocturnal, beastly roaming about, shouting, yelling, and screaming in lanes and houses,"[11] has of course been described as a civilizing process. But from a nocturnal perspective the process looks quite different. A 1682 report from Justus Eberhard Passer, ambassador of Hesse-Darmstadt at the imperial court, gives us a glimpse of the violent side of the civilizing process on the streets of Vienna in the middle of the night. On February 12, 1682, Margrave Ludwig Wilhelm I of Baden celebrated Carnival and his recent promotion to imperial "Feldmarschall-Leutnant" at a "special ball and luxurious meal [*Merenda*]" at his residence in Vienna.[12] Reflecting the nocturnalization of court life, the festivities continued late into the night. Passer reported that at 3 a.m. the "lackeys" outside ("many hundreds who waited on their masters") grew restless (and cold, no doubt) and started to brawl with one another and some soldiers.[13] When the brawl on the street got the attention of the margrave and his guests inside, many "Cavalliers" came down to stop the fray by riding into it, but this only made matters worse. The fighting did not stop, Passer explained, until "Prince Louis made peace with several hand grenades, which he threw among the rioting people." As a result, Passer continued, "horses and people were damaged, and some have since died."[14]

The ambassador's laconic words – horses and people "damaged," noting that "some [humans or horses?] have since died" – show no particular shock or censure. The margrave's hand grenades sent a double message about the night: the brawling lackeys, soldiers, and other servants should accustom themselves to the late hours of their superiors. They would have to wait on their masters during a time which they had previously considered their own. To the rash cavaliers the margrave demonstrated a cooler, more civilized approach to the brutal exercise of violence. Hand grenades were more effective than directly engaging the brawlers in the dark.

The hand grenades used by the margrave themselves reflect the nocturnalization of warfare in this period. They were a relatively new weapon, developed during the Thirty Years War for siege combat. On the walls and in the trenches around besieged cities, attackers and defenders alike used the grenades when the enemy was nearby but could not be seen – as was often the case in the violent night skirmishes that accompanied a siege. The development of the hand grenade reflects the central importance of siege warfare, and of the night in siege warfare, in this period.[15] In a sense, Margrave Ludwig Wilhelm was using the grenades in a siege on the night of the February 12, 1682. He and his fellow aristocrats were occupying a new site in urban space and time by celebrating very late into the night. The lackeys who waited on them responded to this encroachment on a time of their own relative freedom with an outburst of violence. Perhaps for a moment, looking down at the fighting in the street, the margrave felt besieged in his urban palace. He responded with a siege weapon, the hand grenade.

Lackeys, pages, and other servants resisted nocturnalization in many ways, but when they disturbed the new night life of the well-born, they could face brutal violence or its threat. In London's theaters in the early eighteenth century, footmen were customarily allowed free entrance to the upper gallery, with the assumption that they were waiting on their masters. Their behavior during the plays, however, led to complaints in the periodical press, including a mock advertisement in the *Female Tatler* of December 9, 1709. In jarringly violent terms, the notice described a "lost item,"

Dropt near the Play house, in the Haymarket, a bundle of Horsewhips, designed to belabour the Footmen in the Upper Gallery, who almost every Night this Winter, have made such an intolerable Disturbance, that the Players could not be heard, and their Masters were obliged to hiss them into silence. Whoever has taken up the said Whips, is desired to leave 'em with my Lord Rake's Porter, several Noblemen resolving to exercise 'em on their Backs, the next Frosty Morning.[16]

The violence which here protects the nocturnal sociability of the masters and mistresses is only a threat – in contrast with the hand grenades of Margrave Ludwig Wilhelm – but it springs from a fantasy of brutal nocturnal discipline that erases the line between human and beast.

The Vienna incident and the London advertisement underscore the fact that, like all colonized sites, the night was contested territory. This chapter explores the violence involved in these contests and argues that urban nocturnalization is better understood as an analogue to colonization rather than as a civilizing process. Courtiers and citizens sought to control a realm already inhabited by youths (including students and other elite young men), lackeys, vagrants, prostitutes, tavern visitors, and – cutting across social distinctions – all those who sought anonymity. This colonization created spaces and times of modernity in the city, shaping access to public life in decisive new ways.

6.2 RESISTANCE

The colonization of the night met with sustained resistance from the urban night's traditional inhabitants: patrons of public houses, young people (servants, apprentices, and students), and lackeys, prostitutes, and criminals. In the struggle for the urban night estate, age, and gender were deployed to mark the shifting lines between respectable and prohibited night life.

With the introduction of public lighting and the improvement of the night watch, the streets of Paris, London, and other European cities seemed safer and more convenient to use, while the evening became a more important part of the respectable social day. The ability to free the night from its darkness testified to the power and authority of the sovereign: "so much do great spirits please themselves in striving with nature and seeming to give a law to it," as an English officer noted in his description of the projects of Louis XIV in Paris and Versailles.[17] The lighting evoked both security and sovereignty.

But did lighting the night truly provide security or glory? Whatever the benefits of street lighting in the early evening, they faded as one ventured deeper into the night. After enthusing about the superiority of Parisian street lighting over that of London, the English author of *A View of Paris* (1701) contrasted the policing of the night in the two cities:

The Streets [of Paris] are secured by Night, not by a Watch with a Lantern, as in *London*; but by a Guard of Soldiers, called *le Guet*, both Horse and Foot; the first sit … ready to start upon the least Squabble that happens; the Foot Soldiers are Distributed about … and Walk their Rounds every Hour of the Night.

Paris comes off favorably in this account, but the author immediately adds:

Yet for all this, 'tis not safe being in the Streets at *Paris*, after Eleven of the Clock, for ne're a Day passes, but we have an account of some Body or other being either stripped or Murdered the Night before.[18]

The popular Paris guide of Joachim Christoph Nemeitz (first edition, 1718) warned the traveler:

[I]f he wants to go out in the evening, it should not be too late and he should avoid finding himself alone on the streets. If, despite his intentions, he has lingered somewhere, let him send for a hackney coach or a sedan chair; if he can't get one, let him be preceded on the street by a valet holding a torch. In the evening he should avoid crossing the Pont-Neuf, the Pont-Royal, the narrow perpendicular streets, cemeteries, and the church and convent squares: these places are at night extremely dangerous.[19]

The limitations of the lighting were clear to all.

Nor did the lighting protect the image of the sovereign who established it: in the hungry winter of 1709, Saint-Simon noted that "at
night" the two statues of Louis XIV in Paris (at the place des Victoires
and the place de Vendôme) were "defiled in various ways which were
discovered in the morning" despite the unique measure of lighting
the statues themselves at night.[20] The night remained a preferred time
to undermine established authority. Anthony Wood chronicled its use
by supporters of William of Orange in May 1686, noting that "divers
scandalous papers were on Sunday night last dropt about Whitehall
and St. James," and by supporters of James II, who used the night in
the same way after the Revolution of 1688:

> [1693] May 23, Tuesd., at night, some of the Fl. [i.e., Fr.(ench)] king's dec-
> larations dispersed in Oxford streets ... On Saturday night (20 May) a great
> number of King James II's declarations were scattered about the street in all
> parts of London, as also in Whitehall; many were also laid on shopkeepers'
> stalls wrapped in brown paper; some at gentlemen's doors.[21]

Wood found the anonymity and impunity of these addresses to the
political nation especially disturbing, but the urban night resisted all
attempts to make it a silent, passive backdrop for political display.
Despite the new lighting, the night still offered boundless opportunities to challenge authority and commit crimes. Resistance to nocturnalization was everywhere.

We can categorize this resistance as traditional, criminal, or political. The traditional "nocturnal disturbances" issuing primarily from
young people, including serenading and charivaris, and their de facto
access to the night reflect long-standing uses of the night that all had
some popular sanction. Nocturnalization sought to reduce violent
crime as well – the endless succession of assaults and robberies with
no public sanction. Finally, in some cases, city authorities themselves
slowed nocturnalization by resisting the establishment of street lighting itself, underscoring the political stakes of illuminating the urban
night.[22] While keeping in mind the inherently unbounded, ambiguous nature of night life, we can use these three categories to understand the struggle over nocturnalization in the period from the mid
seventeenth century to the end of the Old Regime.

All three forms of resistance intersect in the ubiquitous problem of lantern-smashing, the most salient aspect of the conflict over the urban night. As Wolfgang Schivelbusch has noted, the Foucauldian irony is clear: a measure intended to reduce nocturnal crime immediately created a new offense.[23] A 1669 ordinance in Paris sought to protect the lanterns against "pages, lackeys and all other persons of bad life and disturbers of public peace and security who would maliciously break any lanterns."[24] In Berlin a 1702 edict, repeated five times in the next thirty years, referred to numerous attacks on lanterns and forbade all such vandalism; similar edicts were issued in Lille (1692, 1698, 1710), Frankfurt am Main (1711), and Dublin (1716).[25] In Vienna in 1688, authorities threatened to cut off the right hand of anyone caught damaging a street lantern.[26] Martin Lister, an English visitor to Paris in 1698, was impressed by the severe punishment of lantern-smashers there:

> As to these Lights, if any Man break them, he is forthwith sent to the Galleys; and there were three young Gentlemen of good families, who were in Prison for having done it in a Frolic, and could not be released thence in some Months; and that not without the diligent Application of good Friends at Court.[27]

In Leipzig in 1701, the city council feared that the street lanterns "might very easily be damaged through the depravity of wicked persons."[28] The council suspected that students would be among these "wicked persons," and arranged – even before the lanterns had been put up – for the university to issue a special warning to its "academic citizens, students and their families." The mandate promised severe – some said excessive – punishment for those who damaged lanterns, and set off a minor dispute between the Saxon privy council (on the city's behalf) and the Leipzig consistory (in support of the university's privileges). Ultimately the mandate was issued as requested by the city council.[29] Beyond their practical benefits, the lanterns were, no less than spectacular fireworks or radiant opera halls, a display of power and authority in themselves.[30] "The first and foremost law regarding the night lanterns," according to Paul Jacob Marperger's 1722 treatise on street lighting, "is their inviolability."[31] Marperger even reported that Louis XIV had had a page beheaded for smashing a lantern.[32]

Of course, the threats of draconian punishment for those who damaged street lights were not easily enforced, especially when crowds acted. On January 17, 1706 students in Vienna rioted in the streets against the Jews of the city and the court which protected them. Beginning at about 5 in the evening, they destroyed more than 300 lanterns near the Imperial Residence (the Hofburg) as other Viennese joined in, targeting the street lighting established by and for the court to show their displeasure. As evening turned to night, the mob gathered in front of the house of the court Jew Samuel Oppenheimer (the site of a similar riot in 1700). The riot ended only when soldiers and the city watch opened fire on the crowd, killing seven people and wounding many more.[33]

6.2.1 Resistance from traditional youth cultures

The association of students with the destruction of street lighting in Leipzig and Vienna calls to our attention the resistance of young people to nocturnalization. Unruly and often violent, university students stood at the intersection of noble privilege and male youth culture, which gave them an especially uninhibited relationship to the night. The custom of serenading was less objectionable (see Figure 6.1), but student drinking, gambling, brawling, and sexual license created nocturnal disorder in every city that housed them. While traveling in 1611, the English Catholic Charles Somerset commented on the nocturnal violence in Liège: "there is never a night lightly, but some one or other is killed; the town is a very ill town to live in, especially in respect of the unruliness of the students."[34]

The students of Padua enjoyed the worst reputation in Europe, at least with travelers. John Evelyn complained in 1645 that "the students themselves take a barbarous liberty in the Evenings, when they go to their strumpets, to stop all that go by the house, where any of their Companions in folly, are with them ... so as the streets are very dangerous, when the Evenings grow dark."[35] The situation was apparently no better when Andrew Balfour visited in the late 1670s – again, the "Privileges" of Padua's students allowed a relationship to the night increasingly criminalized by nocturnalization:

Figure 6.1 German students serenading, 1727, from Christian Friedrich Henrici, *Picanders Ernst-schertzhaffte und satyrische Gedichte* (Leipzig, 1727), vol. 1, p. 498. University of Illinois, Urbana-Champaign, Rare Books and Manuscripts Library.

the Scholars here have large Privileges, and many times abuse them, and become very insolent, insomuch that they have been sometimes known to threaten the Podesta himself or Governour of the Town; they have likewise a beastly custom of carrying Arms in the Night, insomuch that it is never safe to be abroad after it begins to be Dark, for many are this way unhappily Murdered without any Offence given or taken, but only by wantonness, or rather Wickedness of the Scholars.[36]

When Peter Tolstoi visited the city in 1697, he warned that "the traveling foreigner who happens to be in Padua must live cautiously, and must not walk alone late at night from house to house, because the traveler will be injured and at times even killed by a student; however, those who must walk late should do so with weapons."[37] Ultramontane visitors criticized the "barbarous liberty" students held to consider themselves masters of the night, focusing on a specific relationship to the night challenged by nocturnalization.

Padua was an eminent international university, the second oldest in Italy, but even at German Reformed universities of modest size, such as those in Herborn and Bremen, students appear as would-be masters of the urban night in a series of court records and city ordinances. All of the twenty-four students expelled from the tiny University of Herborn between 1585 and 1712 were involved in some sort of mischief at night; university records refer to specific acts of traditional student nocturnal disorder, such as fighting with the night watch and disturbing the peace at night, in seven cases.[38] In 1681 the Bremen city council singled out "the youth studying here," who numbered about 400, as the source of "wild, dissolute life and ways ... in the evening, as soon as it grows dark" in an ordinance.[39] In statute of 1607 the parlement of Toulouse forbade students to walk the streets of the city after nine at night, and to carry arms at any time; both prohibitions were oft-repeated but with little effect. The same was true in Strasbourg, where the "student-youths" and lackeys were forbidden to carry weapons in 1650.[40] Peter Heylyn complained in 1625 that the students of Paris had "regulated their villainous practices into a Common-wealth; and have their captains and other officers who command them in their night-walks."[41] Students could read about their traditional privileges in the night in Latin and dog-Latin plays and verses, such as Albert Wichgrev's comedy *Cornelius Expelled* (1600), in which a nightwatchman complains:

> My lord rector, they were three
> Who in the market place did scream,
> As the watchmen three o'clock did keep,
> And the good people would rather sleep.[42]

In late medieval and early modern Vienna students' nightly excesses were a part of daily life despite all prohibitions.[43] The immediate association of students with lantern-smashing in Leipzig anticipates their resistance to the policing of a time and place in which they had been traditionally enjoyed "large Privileges." As the evidence on student life shows, there was plenty of nocturnal activity and night life before nocturnalization (going back at least to the time of François Villon), but this youthful night of transgression was colonized to transform it into a more orderly, safe, and respectable place and time.

"And when night / Darkens the streets, then wander forth the sons Of Belial, flown with insolence and wine."[44] Milton captured concisely the relationship to the night displayed by the young sons of wealthy or noble families, and by youthful apprentices, pages, footmen, and lackeys. The night watch of Paris clashed regularly with "cliques of sons of the upper class who passed through the city at night, usually armed – in the sources they are simply referred to as *jeunes gens.*"[45] In October 1697 a patrol encountered a group of well-born young men as they emerged from a tavern with weapons drawn, drunk, with prostitutes in tow. The sergeant of the watch, one Le Guay, asked them politely to put away their weapons. The young men – members of the elite royal guards and a few from the most esteemed families of Paris – refused, and the watch patrol withdrew cautiously. Despite this show of deference, the *jeunes gens* attacked the watch. In the ensuing struggle the son of a high-ranking official was killed by the watch, and another arrested (only to be released the next morning). In the end, the patrol was rebuked for overstepping its authority by challenging the elite young men – policing the night had its social limits.[46]

The Paris police director d'Argenson included in his disciplinary ambit young men just below the status of the *jeunes gens* described above. In 1700 d'Argenson commented on the youth of "some of the bourgeois, and even a few merchants among the most distinguished." He explained:

Recently I encountered a well-born son, aged eighteen, who for more than fifteen months lodged in a house with women of public prostitution and among villains without a single effort by his father to remove him from such disorder. This discovery obliged me to issue a general ordinance urging fathers to report to the magistrate their libertine and vagabond children, under the penalty of being responsible in civil court for all the misdeeds that they may commit, and with a fine proportional to their negligence.[47]

In the colonization of the urban night, the threat to punish fathers for the crimes of their dissolute sons created a new point of leverage.[48]

6.2.2 Crime as resistance / resistance as crime

Beyond the license of apprentices, students, and servants, violent crime in general set clear limits on urban nocturnalization. In the earliest accounts of public street lighting, fantasies of controlling nocturnal crime were shadowed by persistent violence. Street lighting gave some sense of security, but violent crime at night continued to undermine the project of nocturnalization until at least the mid eighteenth century.[49]

Early modern street crime at night can serve as an index of traditional urban night life, as scholars have observed that cities faced more nocturnal crime than rural communities. In his study of crime in Cologne, one of the largest cities in the Empire, in the late sixteenth and early seventeenth centuries, Gerd Schwerhoff established a clear connection between the time of day and violent crime. Only about a quarter of all violent crimes took place before 5 p.m.; over half occurred between 5 p.m. and 10 p.m., with the remaining 20 percent in the night hours after 10 p.m.[50] The Cologne evidence is corroborated by studies of Douai (Flanders), Paris, Siegen, and Frankfurt: in these cities active traditional night life led to significant proportions of interpersonal violent crime at night.[51] Studies of crime in early modern rural regions, on the other hand, record more violent crime during the day and less in the evening or at night.[52] As Schwerhoff concludes, the social life of the early modern city continued well past sundown.

Nocturnalization meant making this part of the urban day safer for respectable people. The nocturnalization of the seventeenth century sought to pacify the urban night, but the watchmen who formed the first line of defense against nocturnal crime were often its victims. A study of homicide in Vienna reveals dozens of violent deaths by night, including about a dozen nightwatchmen killed while on duty in the period 1649–1720.[53] The street lighting established in 1687 does not seem to have had any immediate effect on the risks for watchmen in Vienna. A case from London's Old Bailey gives us a sense of the social dynamics of violence against nightwatchmen in the colonization of the night. On January 14, 1687 "after a long hearing on both sides," two accused men identified only as "J. W——." and "J. P——." were found guilty of manslaughter "for Killing one Peter Penrose Bell-man in the Parish of St. Giles's in the Fields, on the 30th. day of November last." The removal of the names of the defendants from the published record of the trial indicated their elevated status. The incident began as the nightwatchman Penrose was "ringing his Bell, and saying his Verses, on St. Andrews day, above one or two a Clock in the Morning," when he met the two accused "in the street." The two accused men "bid him not keep such a Noise, and gave him ill Language" – one imagines them "flown with insolence and wine." At this point "two other Bellmen, that came accidentally into the deceased's company, being upon the Watch not far off," tried to assist Penrose but the two accused "making up towards them with their Swords Drawn" killed him.

In their defense the accused argued that "they were abused by the Bell men and the Watch, and that they were very highly provoked to do what was done; and that the Bell man set his Dog upon them, and Knocked one of them down." They insisted that "they were set upon by the Bell men and others in the Night, and taken for Thieves, and very much abused." The accused men called well-born character

witnesses who claimed that "J. W——." and "J. P——." were respectable
and peaceable: "The Prisoners ... called several persons of very great
Quality to Evidence on their sides, that they had never been wont to
quarrel, nor to keep any unseasonable hours." As the recorder of the
Sessions Papers emphasized, they paid lip service to the norms of the
respectable urban night, keeping no "unseasonable hours" (except on
the night in question, it seems). The jury ruled the death accidental.
Despite their conviction for manslaughter, no punishment is recorded.[54] The low status of the watchmen contrasts here with the "persons of very great Quality" who testified for the accused. In the very
different system of law and policing in Paris, the low status of the
archers of the night watch meant that the *jeunes gens* they apprehended
were usually set free unpunished. In both cities, privileges of birth
and estate protected the night life of these young men.[55]

   In Paris, Vienna, London, and other large cities across Northern
Europe, the traditional night watch was augmented or reformed in
the period from the end of the seventeenth through the early eighteenth century, but its principal dimensions would remain unchanged
until the end of the Old Regime: a decentralized force of low-status
semi-professional watchmen, often unarmed, began their rounds at
sundown or at the curfew hour.[56] The most decisive expansion of
policing at night occurred in Paris, where in 1701 d'Argenson created
a new brigade of the watch that began their rounds at midnight and
patrolled until dawn. At the end of the year he reported, "I myself
cannot praise enough this new order; everyday the people testify to
their satisfaction with it." The patrols lifted the cover of darkness
from all manner of actions: "few nights go by without it [the midnight patrol] capturing or surprising some tenant who is moving out
to cheat his landlord."[57] By December 1701 several watchmen of this
patrol had been wounded on duty (considered a sign of their effectiveness); d'Argenson concluded that "the brigade that rises only at
midnight and goes off duty at daybreak does more by itself than any
of the others."[58] By early modern standards the midnight patrols were
a major step in the colonization of the night.

   As scholarship on the history of crime has shown, early modern
commentators assessed the dangers of the urban night in lurid terms.[59]
They saw urban illumination as holding back dangers ready to spring

forth the moment lighting failed. This was the case in London, where street lighting first appeared in 1684. The "Great Frost" of 1683–84 froze the Thames solid, so that booths and stalls were set up and regular traffic in coaches and sleds passed between the banks. One newsletter described "a perfect street quite Cross the Thames at Temple stairs." The frozen Thames became a public way, but one without any street lighting. As a result "Several persons going over the Ice in the night from Westminster market were set upon and robbed near Lambeth," as another newsletter reported, eager to show that the equation of "street and night" with crime still held true.[60] The entirely decentralized lighting of early modern cities was not susceptible to the power failures or blackouts first seen in the twentieth century, but early modern street lighting too could be suddenly and disturbingly absent. John Evelyn described a heavy fog that settled on London on November 8, 1699:

There happened this Week so thick a Mist & fog; that people lost their way in the streets, it being so exceedingly intense, as no light of Candle, Torches or Lanterns, yielded any or very little direction … At the Thames they beat drums, to direct the Watermen to shore, no lights being bright enough to penetrate the fog.[61]

The fog appeared around sunset and lasted until 8 p.m. By obscuring the street lighting the fog revealed, in Evelyn's account, the lurking dangers of the urban night:

I was myself in it, and in extraordinary danger, robberies were committed between the very lights which were fixed between Lond[on] & K[e]nsington on both sides, and whilst Coaches & passengers were traveling.

This sense of "extraordinary danger" evokes a night whose threats are only barely contained by the street lighting and reappear the moment it is unexpectedly extinguished. These accounts acknowledged setbacks in the struggle to colonize the urban night while reminding readers of the dangers of an uncolonized night.

To expand the legitimate social and symbolic uses of the night in early modern cities, urban elites had to actively claim the dark hours of the day and make it their own. But *for whom* was the urban night colonized? And how would the new terrain be used? These questions lead us to examine age, estate, gender, and sexuality in the formation of a new nocturnal "public."

6.3 GENDER AND THE PUBLIC SPHERE

Nocturnalization redefined what was "public" in the cities of early modern Europe. The streets seemed safer and more convenient to use, while the evening became a more important and more respectable part of the social day. The night watch and "night lanterns" helped bring together a public of individuals acting privately: street lighting was never described as facilitating either religious observance or daily manual labor.

How does the colonization of the urban night described here relate to the development of a bourgeois public sphere in the eighteenth century? Defined by Habermas as a public of private individuals who join in debate on questions of politics and letters,[62] the concept of the public sphere has proven especially stimulating because Habermas discussed it in historically specific terms, linking its development to the relations between the household, capitalism, and the state in the seventeenth and eighteenth centuries.[63] His argument contrasts the bourgeois public sphere with "representative publicness" (*repräsentative Öffentlichkeit*), the display of power or majesty to a public constituted as an audience, which he considers characteristic of the princely courts of medieval and early modern Europe.[64] Habermas's analysis of the formation of the public sphere is certainly more suggestive than historical, and he has revised his conclusions over the years,[65] but the concept of "publicness" (*Öffentlichkeit*) continues to stimulate useful research on early modern Europe.[66] In chapter 4 we saw how important the night was to early modern "representative publicness"; here I will explore the connections between the night, bourgeois publicness, and daily life in Northern Europe.

6.3.1 The rise of the coffeehouse

A sphere exists in space. From the first introduction of the concept by Habermas, the abstract space of the bourgeois public sphere has been associated with specific places like the salon, coffeehouse, or tavern. But *when* in everyday life did the discussions, debates, and exchanges of the bourgeois public sphere occur? In general, nocturnalization facilitated the evening gatherings in private homes, public houses, or clubs that Habermas thought fundamental to the formation of a public sphere composed of "private people engaged in productive work."[67] Among these meeting spaces, recent scholarship has made the coffeehouse emblematic of the public sphere.[68] This intense emphasis on the coffeehouse has been balanced by studies of the public role of taverns and other traditional public houses,[69] but the focus on public *space* seems to have pre-empted any thorough examination of the changing uses of daily *time*. Coffeehouses emerged in the second half of the seventeenth century as distinctly nocturnal spaces in urban daily life.

Commentators frequently emphasized the night in their accounts of the coffeehouse or café. As a Viennese jurist noted with concern in 1718: "The authorities should not allow the court-licensed coffee-, lemonade-, and such shops to stay open past 10 p.m. But as ... such shops do stay open, many suspicious conventicles are held in them, with highly disturbing discourses and every sort of dangerous conversation, late into the night, frequented by all sorts of suspect Nations."[70] One of the first coffeehouses associated with private citizens "grown states-men" was the Turk's Head at New Palace Yard in Westminster.[71] It was here that James Harrington's Rota Club met nightly in 1659–60 to discuss the future of the Commonwealth in England. Participants included William Petty and John Aubrey, Samuel Pepys and Sir William Poulteney. These discussions took place only in the evening: as Markman Ellis has noted, "meeting in the evening, it was reckoned, allowed those in employment or charged with affairs of state to attend."[72] This was exactly the case with Pepys, for example, who came to the Rota Club after work on the evenings of January 10 and 17, 1660.[73] Coffeehouses were open all day, of course, but their late hours attracted special attention. One of the first English publications on the new institution, the 1661 pamphlet on the *Character of Coffee and Coffee-Houses*, claimed that "the day sufficeth not some Persons to drink 3 or 4 dishes of Coffee in. They borrow of the night, though they are sure, that this drink taken so late, will not let them close their Eyes all night." Coffeehouse patrons were marked by a sort of late-night hyper-sociability ("these men are either afraid to be alone with themselves, or they to excess love Company, so that they never set apart any time to converse with themselves") which threatened Christian introspection at night.[74]

In Paris public order at night was the main concern. By the 1690s many of the city's cafés stayed open all night, marked by a lighted lantern at the door.[75] These establishments, licensed through the guild of *limonadiers*, were singled out in an ordinance of February 16, 1695 as "places of assembly and refuge for thieves, rogues, and malicious and dissolute people; this happens all the more easily because they are designated and distinguished from other houses by their private lanterns, out on the street, that are lit every evening and serve as signals."[76] Lieutenant-general of police La Reynie ordered that henceforth all *limonadiers* shops must close at 5 p.m. from November 1 to March 31 and at 9 p.m. from April 1 to October 31. After these hours it was "forbidden to admit any person of one or the other sex, whatever age or profession they might be." In the case of the cafés of Paris, the colonization of the night meant the *elimination* of private lighting at night: the 1695 ordinance required all café proprietors "who have placed private lanterns on the street in front of their homes and shops to remove them within twenty-four hours."[77] The sharp restriction of the cafés' evening hours was quickly relaxed: less than a month later the closing hours were extended to 6 p.m. (December and January), 7 p.m. (November and February–March), and 10 p.m. from April to November. In October 1695 they were extended again to 7 p.m. in the winter and 10 p.m. in the summer.[78]

By the end of the seventeenth century, coffeehouses were an established part of urban life for the well-born. The finer establishments resembled the private parlors of aristocrats' homes, transplanting an aristocratic space into bourgeois life.[79] It was in coffeehouses that many burghers first encountered billiards, for example, as well as chocolate, tea, and fine porcelain. But coffeehouses taught the aristocratic consumption of time as well, leading respectable men into late hours. A letter of Mary Jepp Clarke (1656?–1705), wife of the Whig MP Edward Clarke and lifelong friend and correspondent of John Locke, describes evening leisure for "young gentlemen" in London. Writing to her sister-in-law Ursula Clarke Venner in March 1691,

Mary agreed that her young male cousin Venner "should lodge as near us as he can" because the young man is "a perfect stranger here and to the tricks of the town which many times young gentlemen fall into at first." The risk, Clarke notes, lies in the typical use of the night by young men in London:

for want of a friend to go to when the evening draws on, [they] … so get to a coffee ["coughfy"!] house or tavern or worse to spend their time, but to prevent that necessity in my cousin while I am here at least, I will get a lodging for him in the same house where we are.[80]

Clarke considered socializing in the evening a "necessity" for young gentlemen but sought a more domestic, feminine setting for her cousin's evenings in London. Writing for young gentlemen visiting Paris in 1718, Joachim Christoph Nemeitz noted that "I approve that a young traveler goes from time to time to coffeehouses, in the late afternoon or around evening time, to listen to the conversation of the news-bearers."[81] In his *Introduction to the Knowledge of Ceremony of Private Persons* (*Einleitung zur Ceremoniel-Wissenschaft der Privat-Personen*, 1728), Julius Bernhard von Rohr advised his readers that "among the ways of passing the time that one finds in large cities, especially in the winter and in the long evenings, it might happen that a young person visits the coffeehouses."[82] The key, Rohr cautioned, was in the choice of coffeehouse, as not all were respectable.

In texts and images coffeehouses are always represented at night, suggesting that evening gatherings were the most salient part of this new institution. One of the best-known images from London, probably from the 1690s, shows numerous candles on the tables and a man illuminating a picture or notice on the wall (Figure 6.2). The cafés of Paris, with their distinctive décor and clientele, are recorded by the frontispiece of the Chevalier de Mailly's *Les entretiens des cafés de Paris et les diferens qui y surviennent* of 1702, which shows well-dressed men and women enjoying conversation and games by candlelight while served by a boy in Armenian garb (Figure 6.3).[83] An engraving by Casper Luyken (1699) published widely in the early eighteenth century shows a candlelit scene with a maid bringing a dish of coffee (Figure 6.4).[84] These two images and the Dutch

Figure 6.2 A London coffeehouse with a woman behind the counter, left; mid or late 1690s (the inscription "A.S. 1668" is false). © Trustees of the British Museum, 1931,0613.2.

illustration of *'t Koffyhuis* (Figure 6.5) are each centered on the candles that illuminate the dark space of the coffeehouse. The earliest representations of the coffeehouse on stage were also nocturnal. In London a play called *Knavery in all trades, or, The coffeehouse a comedy*, performed and printed in 1664, presented a scene of "The Coffeehouse discovered; three or four Tables set forth, on which are placed small Wax-Lights, Pipes, and Diurnals."[85] In his play *Le Caffé* (1694), Jean-Baptiste Rousseau sets much of the action at night in the Paris café of Madame Jérosme, who at midnight asks her male customers to leave because "it is the hour when women replace men in the cafés." As we will see below, this claim that women arrive at midnight includes some dramatic license, but the association of café life with the night is clear. When Madame Jérosme is asked "Do you agree with this nocturnal recreation?" She replies "Oh, certainly – if one had no other income than the expenditures made here by day, without the fortuitous income of the night, it would be foolish to aim very high."[86] The frontispiece of the play *'t Koffyhuis*, published in Amsterdam in 1712, presents a similar scene illuminated by candlesticks and a chandelier.[87]

Figure 6.3 Paris café scene with well-dressed women patrons; frontispiece of
Chevalier de Mailly, *Les entretiens des cafés de Paris* (Trevoux, 1702). Bibliothèque
nationale de France.

Figure 6.4 Dutch / German coffeehouse scene with a maid serving a dish of coffee.
Engraving by Casper Luyken, 1699. Amsterdams Historisch Museum.

Across Europe, authorities were concerned about late hours and
political conversations at coffeehouses. The attempt by Charles II
to close "the Multitude of Coffee-houses" in England in 1675 is well
known. His proclamation described them as "the great resort of
Idle and disaffected persons" which "have produced very evil and
dangerous effects; as well for that many Tradesmen and others, do
therein misspend much of their time," although there is no mention
of the night or late hours in the proclamation or any of the official
discussions leading up to their suppression.[88] As mentioned above,

Figure 6.5 Dutch coffeehouse scene from the frontispiece of Willem
Van Der Hoeven, *'t Koffyhuis: kluchtspel* (Amsterdam, 1712). Bibliothèque
nationale de France.

La Reynie imposed closing hours on the cafés of Paris in 1695; a decade earlier, a minister of Louis XIV wrote to La Reynie, explaining "The king has been informed that, in several places where coffee is served, there are assemblies of all sorts of people, and especially foreigners. Upon which His Majesty ordered me to ask whether you do not think it would be appropriate to prevent them from assembling in the future."[89] No action was taken – apparently it was not considered opportune to close these cafés in Paris.

Vienna authorities imposed a 10 p.m. closing time on coffeehouses in summer and winter in 1703; in 1706 several coffeehouses were cited for violations, and in 1707 the closing time in winter was moved to 9 p.m.[90] In his guide to the imperial court and Vienna the French Benedictine Casimir Freschot also remarked on the city's night life and on the discussion of "the conduct of generals, ministers, and even the Emperor himself" in the cafés of Vienna.[91] In Leipzig the city council was concerned to regulate coffeehouses from their first establishment in 1694. A flurry of regulation began in 1697, when the council noted that "especially in the new and unauthorized tea- and coffee-rooms … guests are kept after the hour set in the Electoral Saxon ordinance." Gambling, luxury, and "the company of suspicious women" are mentioned. Later that year and in 1701 the council issued further ordinances regulating young people on the streets at night.[92] The council's regulation of coffeehouses escalated in 1704, when it threatened to reduce number of coffeehouses in the city or forbid them entirely.[93]

The fate of the coffeehouses of Frankfurt am Main in 1703–05 reveals just how much anxiety their late hours and political associations could cause. In 1702 the Frankfurt *Rechenmeister* "ordered the owners of the coffee houses … that they … should not keep their guests longer than 9 o'clock in the evening in the winter, and in the summer only until 10 o'clock" – as we have seen, a typical regulation of the hours of coffeehouses and other public houses. There were in fact only three coffeehouses in Frankfurt at this time, but they greatly concerned the city council. The following year the council's regulation of the coffeehouses went much further. On November 20, 1703 the Frankfurt city council, citing "disturbing and dangerous times," ordered that "we shall three months from today entirely abolish the coffeehouses." In the meantime, the coffeehouse proprietors were threatened with "immediate prohibition" of their trade if they failed to close their establishments promptly at the curfew bell and further ordered "not to re-open for anyone, whomever it might be" after closing time. In the three months they would be allowed to remain open, the proprietors of the coffeehouses were warned to "set aside no special rooms for any guests other than the ordinary main room, eliminate all gaming, and serve nothing other than coffee, tea, and chocolate."[94]

Three months later, on February 21, 1704, the council reported that:

the deadline for closing the coffeehouses has passed … so today the coffeehouse keepers shall be sent to the office of the *Rechneiamt* and informed that they must immediately take in their coffee signs and serve no guests coffee or other drinks, on pain of severe punishment. And the honorable *Rechneiamt* shall be reminded to take care that none of the taverns serve any coffee or other warm drinks.[95]

The office that enforced the abolition, the *Rechneiamt*, reported on the same day that "the coffee-men have been informed by a servant of this office that the coffeehouses shall now be abolished and cease; nor shall they serve tea or chocolate any more." The coffeehouse owners were ordered "today to take down the coffee signs from their premises and be coffee-men no longer."[96] The coffeehouses remained closed for over a year. On March 24, 1705 two former coffeehouse owners were allowed to reopen under several conditions, including new closing hours of 9 p.m., summer and winter.

The city council's decision to close Frankfurt's coffeehouses in 1703 was political. Among dozens of taverns, inns, and other public houses, the city's three coffeehouses stood out as gathering places for wealthy merchants, military officers, and diplomats involved with the War of the Spanish Succession. The city's troops had just shared in the defeat of imperial forces at the Battle of Speyerbach on November 15 when the plan to close the coffeehouses was announced. Long-standing tensions between the patrician oligarchy ruling Frankfurt and the merchants and craftsmen who formed its economic base threatened to boil over, and the council saw the coffeehouses as a threat to their rule.[97] Despite scholars' concerns about an overemphasis on coffeehouses in the history of early modern public life, in the Frankfurt case the coffeehouses were singled out for closure because of the political connections of their customers.[98] In 1705 thirty-six established merchants petitioned the Frankfurt council for approval of a private club they had established. It met only in the evenings and served as a replacement for the prohibited coffeehouses, underscoring the importance of nocturnal sociability in bourgeois and coffeehouse culture.[99] In larger cities across Northern Europe these private clubs, described by Joseph Addison matter-of-factly as "nocturnal assemblies," flourished in the eighteenth century.[100]

The evidence here shows that the hours after sunset were fundamental to the sites and practices of the public sphere at the end of the seventeenth century. In a valuable intervention in the discussion of the formation of a public sphere in early modern Europe, Brian Cowan contrasted a public focused on "the magisterial realm of state power and high politics" with "the world of commercialized leisure that developed independently of the state."[101] Together, ministers of state and consumers of leisure colonized the night and created the time and space in which the bourgeois public sphere formed.[102] The process was anything but linear, of course: young people resisted the discipline that was the cutting edge of the colonization of the night, and political authorities struggled to control the "highly disturbing discourses and every sort of dangerous conversation, late into the night" that seemed an unavoidable corollary of nocturnalization.

This back-and-forth process of nocturnalization is the analogue in daily life to the rise of the bourgeois public sphere itself. The ambiguous relationship between the urban night and the state seen here mirrors a key aspect of the formation of the bourgeois public sphere:

Bourgeois publicness may be grasped first as the sphere of private people come together as a public; these [people] quickly claimed the public sphere regulated by the authorities against the public authorities themselves.[103]

Private persons used the night which the authorities had helped secure as a time to test the limits of these same authorities, and city authorities found themselves policing and restricting the very nocturnal sociability they facilitated through their colonization of the night.

Seeing the bourgeois public sphere as an aspect of nocturnalization (both in its sites and practices, as discussed here, and in its intellectual predilections, as will be discussed in chapter 8) further historicizes Habermas's arguments. At present, the most trenchant historical analysis of the rise of a public sphere has come from scholars of gender in early modern culture.[104] How does using the night as a category of analysis shape our understanding of gender and the public sphere in the seventeenth and early eighteenth centuries?

6.3.2 Gender, the night, and the public sphere

Looking back, Friedrich Justin Bertuch sought to explain the nocturnalization of early modern daily life in his 1786 essay on "the uses and divisions of the day and the night in various ages, and among various peoples." After noting that "the pleasures of the evening and night ... are the ruling fashion in France and England, and in every large city, where luxury and the need for entertainment are always on the rise,"[105] he began his analysis with the observation that "the day invites movement and the night rest." The entertainments of the daylight hours, such as tourneys, the hunt, horse-racing, and the like, he then contrasts with the pleasures of the night, such as the theater, cards, and conversation. The predominance of the nocturnal pursuits reflects, in Bertuch's understanding, the feminization of European culture: "In the past, when most nations of Europe were somewhat rawer, but also stronger and more manly, they more loved strenuous bodily exercises; now as they become more polite and refined, the calmer and more thoughtful pastimes replace the physical ones."[106]

Bertuch's connection of night life and feminization was first voiced in England and France in the second half of the seventeenth century. An early English broadside on the coffeehouse, the *News from the Coffe-House* of 1674, claimed that the culture of the coffeehouses confused gender roles:

> Here Men do talk of every Thing,
> With large and Liberal lungs,
> Like women at a Gossiping,
> With a double tyre of Tongues.[107]

Fears of feminization shaped elite culture in France and England at the end of the seventeenth century: concerns about the emasculating effects of absolute monarchy in France ran parallel to worries about politeness, commerce, and luxury in England.[108] But these concerns about feminization should not obscure a broader question: how did nocturnalization affect women's place in public and daily life? To go beyond generalizations and assess how early modern women used and experienced the urban night requires precise attention to a range of sites, from the court and the theater to the coffeehouse, salon, and street.

At court, we saw women and men together extending the day into the evening and night. Neither the favorable nor the critical descriptions of night life at court examined in chapter 4 of this book make any distinction between women and men – both are the new denizens of the night, for better or for worse (recall Faramond's "Clorinde and Cleomenes"). The aristocratic use of daily time could be seen "in the lives of the courtiers of both sexes, who make night into day and day into night."[109] No sources on the night at court suggest that there is any time for men to be active when women should not be, or vice versa.

How did the gender order of daily time at court look in the light of the street lamps? In urban spaces that served as extensions of the court, for example in Vienna or Paris, aristocratic women used the night freely to socialize and maintain social networks. Not long after street lighting was introduced in Paris, Madame de Sévigné described an evening spent chatting with her friends until midnight "chez Mme De Coulanges" – the date was December 4, 1673. Madame de Sévigné decided to escort one of their number home, although it meant a trip across Paris: "We found it pleasant to be able to go, after midnight, to the far end of the faubourg Saint-Germain." The new street lighting made this possible: "We returned merrily, thanks to the lanterns and safe from thieves."[110] One detects no sense of danger to her safety or reputation in this account. This relationship to the night was summarized by the writer Gregorio Leti in a letter to the marquise de Courcelles of 1679. Leti observed that the domestic occupations of women "constitute a state of servitude, as we have observed in all lands of the earth, in times ancient and modern." But recently the aristocratic relationship to the night had changed all this: "However, one can say that French ladies have put this state of things into good order, since three parts of the night out of four, and two out of the four parts of the day are spent in strolls, visits, late evenings, balls, and games."[111] Leti's slightly critical tone underscores the novelty of this night life.

A contemporary of Madame de Sévigné, the Austrian countess Johanna Theresia Harrach (1639–1716), made and received countless evening social visits in Vienna and spent time at the imperial court and its theater on long winter nights from about 1665 on. As the wife of the imperial ambassador to Spain, she maintained a wide social network and presence at court, especially during her husband's absences in Spain. Her detailed daily letters show that she usually returned home between nine and ten at night: when the court was in Vienna from November through April, this schedule meant regularly traveling through the city by carriage long after dark.[112] In similar terms, in a letter written from London on February 13, 1710 Lady Mary Wortley Montagu considered herself to be "the only young woman in town ... in my own house at ten o'clock to-night." It was "the night of Count Turrucca's ball," a "Splendid ... entertainment" hosted by the Portuguese ambassador. Lady Mary's narrow conception of "the town" gives us a clear indication of which women were out after 10 p.m. with their reputations intact.[113] John Vanbrugh's unfinished play *A Journey to London* (written in the early 1720s) satirized the night life of aristocratic women in a lively exchange between "Lord Loverule" and his wife, Lady Arabella:

LORD LOVERULE: But, madam, can you think it a reasonable thing to be abroad till two o'clock in the morning, when you know I go to bed at eleven?

LADY ARABELLA: And can you think it a wise thing (to talk your own way now) to go to bed at eleven, when you know I am likely to disturb you by coming there at three?

LORD LOVERULE: Well, the manner of women's living of late is insupportable, and some way or other –

LADY ARABELLA: It's to be mended, I suppose. – Pray, my lord, one word of fair argument. You complain of my late hours; I of your early ones;

so far we are even, you'll allow. But which gives us the best figure in the eye of the polite world? My two o'clock speaks life, activity, spirit, and vigour; your eleven has a dull, drowsy, stupid, good-for-nothing sound with it. It savours much of a mechanic, who must get to bed betimes that he may rise early to open his shop, faugh!

LORD LOVERULE: I thought to go to bed early and rise so, was ever esteemed a right practice for all people.

LADY ARABELLA: Beasts do it.

After comparing her husband to a low "mechanic," Lady Arabella responds to her husband's concerns about her late-night companions: "I'll have you to know I keep company with the politest people in the town, and the assemblies I frequent are full of such."[114]

The daily rhythms of a well-born couple in London emerge from the diary of James Brydges (1674–1744; made first duke of Chandos, 1719). Brydges and his wife Mary maintained a busy social life in London, recorded in Brydges's diary for the years 1697 to 1702. Coffeehouses were fundamental to James Brydges's daily life; he records visiting them during the day and at night, traveling across London with his wife by coach. As Brian Cowan has noted, Mary Brydges never accompanied her husband into any of the coffee-houses. Her evenings were spent in domestic visits, which were no less important for the socially aspiring couple. They make similar use of the evening and night for socializing and leisure, but the public houses visited by the husband contrast with the domestic socializing of the wife.[115]

The purported freedom of "French ladies" over "three parts of the night out of four" carried over into the first cafés of Paris as well. As historians of coffee have established, the cafés of Paris presented a distinctly aristocratic décor which contrasted with the more utilitarian furnishings of English coffeehouses. The first truly successful café in Paris, the Procope, opened in a former Turkish bath in the rue des Fossés-Saint-Germain in 1686. The proprietor kept the mirrors, chandeliers, and marble table-tops of the bathhouse, and these "well-furnished rooms" quickly attracted a well-to-do clientele.[116] As noted above, Jean-Baptiste Rousseau's play *Le Caffé* (1694) revolves around the presence of women as customers at night in the café of Madame Jérosme.[117] An ephemeral style journal, *Le porte-feuille galant*, explained in 1700 that "cafes are places frequented by honest people of both sexes." The social variety mentioned so often in accounts of coffeehouses and cafés appears here as well. "You can see all sorts of characters," including

gallant men, coquettish women, polite abbots and others who are not, soldiers, news-mongers, officers, provincials, foreigners, lawyers, drinkers and professional gamblers, parasites, adventurers, knights of industry, wealthy young men, amorous old women, Gascons, and sham heroes, demi-beaux esprits, and many other figures whose varied portraits could be multiplied infinitely.[118]

The variety reflects a distinct Parisian gender order, as women are clearly part of the clientele. The frontispiece of the Chevalier de Mailly's *Les entretiens des cafés de Paris et les diferens qui y surviennent* of 1702 (see Figure 6.3.) emphasizes (like Rousseau's play of a few years earlier) women in cafés at night. The interlocutors in the *Entretiens* visit the cafes between the evening and the late night and mention the dangers of the streets at night, suggesting the cafés were oases of relative safety. The last conversation in Mailly's collection is narrated by a woman, suggesting their active place in elite café culture. The author explains that "It may be said that it is improper to introduce a woman in a café; however, I have seen there … women who were quite pretty and spiritual."[119] In France, where the social life of the nobility was most integrated by gender, nocturnalization brought well-born women access to urban sites such as balls, theater and opera, and cafés (which were themselves more closely aligned with aristocratic culture than in Britain).[120] In Figure 6.6 we see the new association of a "woman of quality" with the evening and night.

But Paris and London, as well as Vienna and Leipzig, were also shaped by citizens and their values. The bourgeois gender order of the night contrasted sharply with the freedoms of elite women to use the night as they wished. Non-noble women active at night in the city, for work or leisure, were suspect – and increasingly so – in the seventeenth century. For England, the development has been examined by Paul Griffiths in his work on the prosecution of nightwalking in the sixteenth and seventeenth centuries.[121] In seventeenth-century

A Paris chez J. Mariette, rue S.t Jacques aux Colonnes d'Hercules

Le Soir
Dame de Qualité joüant aux Cartes

Figure 6.6 Pierre-Jean Mariette, "Le Soir: Dame de Qualité jouant aux Cartes"
(Paris: chez J. Mariette, rue St Jacques aux Colonnes d'Hercules, *c.* 1690).
Bibliothèque nationale de France.

London arrests and prosecutions for nightwalking began to focus almost exclusively on women: a crime overwhelmingly associated with men in the late Middle Ages had become feminized and sexualized. Griffiths's work underscores the intricate relationships between estate and gender that shaped access to the urban night. As the trials recorded in the Sessions Papers of the Old Bailey show, the reputation of being "a common nightwalker" had lost none of its force in the second half of the seventeenth century: in 1687, for example, Dorothy Hall was charged with theft: her claims of innocence notwithstanding, "being known to be a common Night-walker, she was found Guilty."[122] The career of one Jane King is instructive. She was described as "a notorious Night-walker" when charged with the robbery of Hilkiah Osmonton in May 1688. Acquitted on that charge, she was tried again at the same session along with Mary Batters for the robbery of Richard Beale, who testified that "as he was going over Holborn Bridge about Eleven a Clock at Night, as he was making Water against the Wall, the Prisoners with some other Women Assaulted him, and took away the above said Moneys." Beale cried out for help and the watch appeared and arrested some of the women, including King and Batters. The sessions recorder explained that "The Prisoners made a very slight Defence for themselves; and being known in Court to be old and Notorious Night-walkers and Debauched Livers, they were found Guilty." King was tried again in December 1688 for picking the pocket of "one Mr. Church." According to the sessions account:

the Proof against the Prisoner was, That being one that practiced the Trade of Night walking, she invited him to a Tavern in St. Martins le Grand, in order to partake of a Bottle of Wine, But they had scarcely begun to grow familiar, before she had dived into his Pocket, and getting his Purse of Gold, she gave him the slip.

She was caught soon afterwards. At trial she claimed never to have seen Mr. Church and alleged that "some Common Women that had been abroad that Night described him to her, saying, That a whole Cluster of them had been with him in an Alley" and had robbed him. Church was "positive she was the very Woman, the Jury found her guilty of the Felony."[123]

The trends uncovered by Griffiths were fully developed by the first half of the eighteenth century, as seen for example in the comments of Bernard Mandeville on crime and its prevention. Mandeville and his contemporaries assumed that the victims of nocturnal crime were men; Mandeville was happy to blame them for their carelessness, describing them as "unthinking" because they "never mind what companies they thrust themselves into." Such men included "such as will be drunk, [or] go home late in the dark unattended." In Mandeville's accounts, women were either perpetrators of, or accomplices to, nocturnal crime. Foolish victims "scruple not to talk and converse with lewd women, as they meet them; or that are careless of themselves as well as of the securing and fastening of their houses."[124] Safest from urban crime, Mandeville explained, was a man "temperate in his liquor; [who] avoids, as much as is possible, unseasonable hours; never gives ear to night-walkers; a man that abroad is always watchful over himself, and every thing about him."[125] Mandeville makes no reference to women as victims of nocturnal crime in this pamphlet.

Operating with a subtle set of indicators of age, marital status, dress, and familiarity, the bourgeois order of the night cast renewed suspicion on women outside the home at night. This suspicion had an important function: given the emphasis on respectable nocturnal sociability in coffeehouses, one might assume that women could participate in coffeehouse culture, thereby benefiting from better access to respectable night life that nocturnalization provided. Indeed, several scholars have argued that women did share in English coffeehouse life.[126] But the work of scholars such as Brian Cowan and Markman Ellis indicates otherwise – women were excluded from coffeehouse sociability in London and, as we will see below, in German-speaking Europe as well.[127] Suspicion helped create new times and spaces for men to gather from which women of their own class were excluded. The aristocratic women of Paris were a significant exception that warrants further research.

The bourgeois and moralizing approach to nocturnalization should not, however, obscure the women who were part of coffeehouse culture: not as customers and interlocutors, but as coffeehouse-keepers,

servants, prostitutes, and pamphlet-hawkers. In London, women coffeehouse keepers were relatively common but subject to satire and
accusations of prostitution.[128] Gallant pamphlet-writers were happy
to maintain the association of prostitution with coffeehouses, claiming for example that "There being scarce a Coffee-Hut but affords a
Tawdry Woman, a wanton Daughter, or a Buxom Maid, to accommodate Customers."[129] Visitors to London tended to confirm this
association.[130]

Female pamphlet-hawkers supported the circulation of news and
rumor vital to coffeehouse culture, and they sold their wares day
and night on the streets and in coffeehouses: in 1684 Judith Jones
was described as "a hawker that serves the Amsterdam coffeehouse."[131] When John Roberts walked along Bow Lane at about
10 p.m. on October 2, 1722, he encountered two women crying
pamphlets. The first announced "a full and true Account of a horrid barbarous and bloody Plot, against the King and Government";
the second, Sarah Turbat, was selling a different pamphlet and
responded "Damn ye there's no Plot, who should be the Author of
it, George? Damn him, who made him King? The Devil: For he's
his Uncle." Another witness confirmed this outburst and added
that Turbat "used several other vile and scandalous Expressions
against His Majesty not fit to be repeated."[132] These "mercury-
women" or pamphlet- hawkers, among the poorest of London's
poor, supported the public sphere – and were, as Paula McDowell
has shown, "anything but the passive purveyors of others' ideas,"
as Sarah Turbat's words above show. Still, as Cowan has noted, one
cannot characterize these women as participants in the respectable
public sphere of their city.

Attitudes toward women and coffeehouses in the Empire follow
the associations and exclusions seen in Britain and can serve as an
index of the place of women in urban nocturnalization. The unknown
author of the *Caffée- und Thée-Logia* (Hamburg, 1691) praised the
coffeehouses of Germany and claimed that "in England, Holland,
and Italy I have seen ... women dressed in men's clothing in the coffeehouses; in some the owner keeps a gallant lady for the amorous
pleasures of his guests."[133] A critic wrote in 1701 that the coffeehouses

led young men astray and that "in the winter during the long nights, many poor whores wait in these houses in such quantity, as if they displayed themselves in a formal procession."[134] In his *Useful, Fashionable, and Novel Ladies' Lexicon* of 1715, Gottlieb Siegmund Corvinus discussed coffee in the domestic sphere in a dozen entries but provided no entry for "coffeehouse." The reason becomes clear under the entry for "Caffe-Menscher," defined as "those suspicious and disorderly painted women who wait upon the men present in coffeehouses and render them all services willingly."[135] Corvinus informed his female audience in no uncertain terms that all women in coffeehouses were morally suspect. The Leipzig city council in 1704 ordered that "all visits to and work in coffeehouses by female persons, whether preparing beverages, waiting tables, or under any other pretext ... are forbidden." Women were simply banned from coffeehouses, as customers and as servants.[136] Enforcement of this was another matter, but the Leipzig ordinance reflects an extreme expression of Cowan's conclusion that it is "difficult to conceive of a role for women in the ideal coffeehouse society that did not fit into the existing stereotypes of either the virtuous servant or the vicious prostitute."[137]

How does attention to daily time deepen our understanding of the gendering of the public sphere in the seventeenth and early eighteenth centuries? The evidence examined here reveals a changing gender order at night in Europe's cities, but nocturnalization did not affect all women in the same way. On the one hand, unattached women out on the streets at night were seen at the looser end of the scale of sexual morality by authorities and by men seeking sex. Women in coffeehouses and taverns might face the same assumptions, depending on their age, dress, and company: evidence of respectable women entering coffeehouses alone and at night is very rare.[138] On the other hand, elite women passed freely through the urban night on their way to or from domestic sociability, including the rarified world of the salons. Estate or social rank were fundamental to access to nocturnal spaces: when Madame de Sévigné and her friends rode across Paris from the home of Madame Coulanges to the home of Madame LaFayette after midnight in December 1673, their transport, lighting, servants, and destination made it clear that they were honorable women of the highest rank. Elite women participated in the nocturnalization radiating out from the court and the *haute bourgeoisie*, but for middling women, respectable access to the "public night" did not expand with nocturnalization.

Writing in 1988, Joan Landes was the first to consider the history of the modern public sphere in terms of gender. She concluded that "the bourgeois public is essentially, not just contingently, masculinist." In his Introduction to the 1990 edition of *Strukturwandel der Öffentlichkeit* [*The Structural Transformation of the Public Sphere*], Habermas agreed. He asked if women were excluded from bourgeois publicness "*in the same way* as workers, peasants, and the 'crowd,' i.e., the 'dependent' men."[139] Citing Carol Pateman and Landes, Habermas concluded that the exclusion of women from the political public sphere "has also been constitutive" because their relegation to the "private core of the nuclear family's interior space" ("privaten Kernbereich des kleinfamilialen Binnenraumes") is fundamental to the private subjectivity that constitutes the public sphere.[140] Their exclusion differs from that of men excluded by class because their exclusion creates a specific form of family and private sphere which is the essential, suppressed counterpart of the public sphere.

How, historically speaking, did this exclusion occur? This is the question Landes sets out to answer in *Women and the Public Sphere*. The line of inquiry is all the more intriguing because in the French case, which is Landes's focus, aristocratic women played crucial (though sometimes exaggerated) roles in the culture and politics of the Old Regime, for example in the conversational gatherings known then as "*le monde*," i.e., the salon. Landes sees the salon as the most traditional of the new practices and institutions that arose between civil society and the state, such as the coffeehouse, the literary club, and the periodical press; it was certainly the most domestic of these. Significantly, contemporaries emphasized the "pronounced feminine character" of salon culture in contrast with the other public sites, suggesting to Landes "an implicit gender dynamic within the institutional and cultural geography of the oppositional bourgeois public sphere."[141] Landes then pursues this gender dynamic on the level of the symbolic politics of the emerging bourgeois public sphere – a rich line of inquiry, to be sure, but not the only way to trace the exclusion of women from the public sphere in the last century of the Old Regime. Given the importance of the family and private life in the formation of the bourgeois public, daily life would be a logical approach. By using daily life as a category of analysis, we can see how nocturnalization served to exclude women from the times and places fundamental to the formation of the bourgeois public – especially those outside the home.

The rise of the coffeehouse can serve as an index of bourgeois publicness and nocturnalization. The varying place of women in coffeehouse or café culture, ranging from aristocratic inclusion in Paris to legal and de facto exclusion in Leipzig, reveals the importance of the night in the formation of a bourgeois public sphere that was regularly nocturnal.

The night was the setting for many of the institutions and practices that formed bourgeois publicness. Indeed, the night appears as a visible analogue to bourgeois or polite publicness on the level of daily life. The new urban nights of respectable sociability after dark were, to quote historians of the public sphere, "the contingent products of a process of exclusion and containment in which members of alternate 'impolite' publics were shut out from the reconstructed 'public sphere as a polite zone'."[142] The colonization of the night described here redefined the long-standing youth cultures of the night as "impolite" and often criminal, revealing, to paraphrase Paula McDowell, "a whole host of overlapping relationships to the night, some of which had to be shut down to create the established order" of the polite urban night.[143] All means, from the most violent to the most subtle, were used to carve out a night that would serve "as a polite zone" for some men while eliminating the traditional relationship with the night exemplified by apprentices, servants, and students. This colonization of the urban night reshaped youth, gender, and the public sphere in the last century of the Old Regime.[144] The successes and limitations of this colonization of the urban night leads us consider similar attempts to colonize the rural night (chapter 7), and the cultural and intellectual implications of a new urban night for the early Enlightenment (chapter 8).

CHAPTER SEVEN

Coloni*ing the rural night?*

On the night of Thursday, January 13, 1603, "early in the morning, roughly between two and three o'clock," the innkeeper Barthel
Dorfheilige of the Hessian town of Wanfried awoke to the sound of
splintering wood.[1] He quickly discovered two young noblemen, Hans
Werner von Eschwege (*c.* 1581–*c.* 1624) and his cousin Eberhard von
Alten (*c.* 1583–?), smashing in the window of the main room of his
inn. Dorfheilige reported that he "hastily lit a lamp and ran into the
room in his nightshirt, and shined his light out the broken window to
see the malefactors." He recognized "Hans Werner, son of Reinhard
von Eschwege zu Aue" and then Eberhard von Alten. Hans Werner
greeted him and apologized for the broken window while Eberhard
demanded that Dorfheilige open the door. Hans Werner said he
would vouch for his cousin's good conduct, so Dorfheilige let them
in and called for one of his servants to see to their horses.[2]

Once inside, the two young "Junkers" (as Dorfheilige called them)
continued their harassment of the innkeeper, breaking another window from the inside and assaulting Dorfheilige's wife, children, and
servants. The two young men then forced the innkeeper to accompany
them on a similar visit to awaken the local miller, then returned to the
inn for more wine and a meal. When the servants of the noblemen began
to beat one of Dorfheilige's children, the innkeeper defended his son
with a bread knife: the two noblemen and two more of their servants
joined the fray and Dorfheilige fled into the streets of the town. Hans
Werner and Eberhard mounted their horses and followed him. Several
neighbors came out of their houses to aid the innkeeper, but paid the
price as the young noblemen fired at them, broke out more windows,
and screamed threats. "Finally the *Schultheiss* [village administrator]

and soldiers came to town and sounded the bell," and the noblemen and their servants rode off, shouting abuse behind them.[3]

This violent incident, in which the "Junkers" shoved Dorfheilige's pregnant wife into a pile of manure, beat one of his children bloody, and unleashed terror on his "house and home," reveals several fundamental aspects of the early modern rural night. We see the association of violence with the night, and importance of the public house to the life of a village, both day and night. Towns like Wanfried had no regular night watch and Hans Werner and Eberhard had plenty of time to lash out at the villagers before any local authorities appeared. From the perspective of the local authorities, the rural night was simply much harder to police.

But the assault on the inn led by the young Hans Werner von Eschwege was no random act of nocturnal violence. His father Reinhard von Eschwege zu Aue (d. 1607) was entangled in several bitter legal disputes with the peasants of Wanfried over grazing, hunting, and fishing rights.[4] Early modern German law insisted on the daytime character of all legal proceedings. One could not convene a court, prepare a will, or pronounce a verdict at night.[5] Parallel with the legal disputes of the day, this rural conflict was carried into the night by the actions of young men. Hans Werner said as much while drinking in Barthel Dorfheilige's inn in the middle of the night. The complaint recorded his words in direct discourse:

In particular he [Hans Werner von Eschwege] said: "You peasants of Wanfried or *Bürger* – whatever you want to be – last summer you gave my father some trouble. If I had known, I had some good fellows with me back then ... You'll get very little out of it [i.e., the lawsuit], and I'll pay back each one of you, one after the other. It's your *Vogt* [county administrator] who's leading you into this. If I run into him, I'll put a bullet through his hat."[6]

By day the lawsuits worked their way through the courts; at night – the domain of young men – other pressures were brought to bear. This incident at Wanfried suggests that despite broad attempts to regulate nocturnal disorder, in the villages of early modern Europe young "guardians of disorder" ruled the night.[7] More often than in cities, their "order" prevailed over that of the church or the state when the sun went down.

The ungovernable aspects of the rural night became more prominent after 1650 as a new contrast between urban and rural night emerged. The preceding chapters on the night at royal courts and in cities have shown a series of seventeenth- and eighteenth-century developments I describe as nocturnalization: an ongoing expansion of the symbolic and respectable social uses of the night. As we saw in the previous chapter, nocturnalization in cities evoked significant resistance from the young people who had made the night streets their domain. This dialectic of nocturnalization and resistance is best described as a colonization of the urban night. By 1700, contemporaries observed that this colonization was reshaping everyday life in the cities of Northern Europe.

Nocturnalization affected daily life in the villages of early modern Europe as well, but with a different set of priorities and outcomes. The agents of nocturnalization were church and state, but the development was less tied to commerce and consumption than at court or in major cities. As in cities, young people resisted incursions into a time that had traditionally been theirs. Because neither church nor state could intervene in rural daily life as effectively as they could in cities, villagers young and old more successfully defended their traditional night life. City and countryside were both sites of nocturnalization, but this process unfolded very differently in rural areas.

7.1 PATTERNS

How was the night understood and experienced in the villages of early modern Europe? Some scholars have emphasized that "The night is no man's friend," as a French proverb put it, and the unfortunate innkeeper of Wanfried might agree.[8] But historians of popular culture and daily life such as Norbert Schindler and A. Roger Ekirch have argued that far too many common people were active at night – by choice or necessity – to allow us to characterize the early modern night as universally threatening.[9] Early modern women and men did much more at night than sleep or fear for their lives and goods. As Alain Cabantous has shown, the first hours after sunset do not reveal the expected retreat into the home. In the city and in the countryside work continued, entertainment and socializing began, and groups of young people regularly disturbed the settling calm.[10] The literary formula of nocturnal fear and insecurity must be balanced by an understanding of actual nocturnal activity – although this kind of rural "night life" is more difficult to assess.

When we survey the material from Ekirch, Cabantous, and others, several patterns emerge. Night life in the early modern countryside was shaped by the tensions between necessity and leisure, and between order and disorder. Here we will consider the necessities of sleep and labor, then survey a range of activities extending from leisure and sociability to disorder and crime: it is between these poles that the distinct features of the rural night emerge. Village spinning bees and public houses, as well as the courtship customs of the youth, characterized the rural night as its contrast with the night in the city began to emerge in the late seventeenth and eighteenth centuries.

7.1.1 Necessity

Labor and rest shaped the rural night. The age-old pattern of segmented sleep documented by A. Roger Ekirch (described in chapter 1) appears in rural and urban sources alike until the end of the seventeenth century. At that point, as we will see below, rural and urban sleep patterns began to diverge. Labor at night was ubiquitous. Despite the comment in the Gospel of John (9:4) – "I must work the works of him that sent me, while it is day: the night cometh, when no man can work" (King James Bible) – some forms of work at night were unavoidable. Blacksmiths worked at night, in part because they could.[11] And as Alain Cabantous has shown, rural labor at night was on the rise at the end of the seventeenth century, encompassing a range of tasks, including fishing, sowing, or harvesting by moonlight, and spinning, weaving, sewing, or knitting by firelight.[12] In winter, the hearth might provide enough light for the indoor tasks; otherwise common people would use rush lights or oil-lamps, the rich candles.[13] Casual labor on long winter evenings was, as we will see below, a key feature of rural night.

The regulation of labor and rest was recognized as an important aspect of household management. The Protestant Austrian noble-man Wolfgang Helmhard von Hohberg (1612–88) explained in his well-known *Georgica curiosa* (1682, editions through the eighteenth century) that "The father of the house is like the clock of the house, which everyone must follow when rising, going to sleep, working, eating and all other business."[14] The immensely popular *Five Hundred Points of Good Husbandry* (1557, editions through the eighteenth century) of Thomas Tusser (1524?–80) advised mas-ters to "Declare after supper, take heed thereunto / what work in the morning each servant shall do." This guide gives us some idea what hours of sleep were expected in the sixteenth and seventeenth centuries:

> In winter at nine, and in summer at ten
> to bed after supper, both maidens and men.
> In winter at five a clock servants arise,
> in summer at four it is very good guise.[15]

The Tyrolean physician Hippolyt Guarinoni (1571–1654) recom-mended that adults retire between 8 and 9 p.m. and wake at 5 a.m.[16] Across Northern Europe, the traditional curfew hour was 9 p.m., but it is difficult to say anything conclusive about the bedtimes of early modern people in the countryside. Prescriptions are common, but their relation to practice is not clear. The limited evidence we have from diaries and legal records suggests that, in practice, most country folk went to bed between 9 and 10 p.m.[17] But, as we will see below, when the household of John Wright of Brixworth, Northamptonshire was thrown into confusion by an errant dog at "eleven or twelve o'clock" on the night of December 13, 1672, the servant maids were still awake washing dishes, though the master of the house was already in his nightshirt and most rooms were no longer lit.

Those with leisure and light might extend the day. Mary Jepp Clarke described long winter evenings at Chipley, the Clarkes's Somerset estate, in a letter of April 1700: "we have had all this winter our proper times for everything in our chamber, which is good, and in the evening while Nanny and I did work she [Elizabeth] read plays and what else diverted us which made the long nights pass a way the more pleasantly to us all."[18]

Making long winter nights pass more pleasantly was a common desire in the early modern countryside. Beyond small gatherings in private homes, two sites emerge as especially important for "night life" in the countryside: the spinning bee and the public house. Spinning bees were a peripatetic but vital place for the nocturnal courtship customs of early modern rural youth, while public houses were more fixed locations for the adult sociability of the village. Rural night life was shaped by the contrast between the mobile sociability of the young and the relative stability of mature socializing in the public house.

Spinning bees were fundamental to rural night life in many parts of early modern Northern Europe, especially in Germany, France, and the Swiss cantons.[19] When a fire broke out in the Norman village of Basly late on the evening of February 4, 1684, we learn that most of the women of the village were at a spinning bee, including the unmarried Le Petit sisters and Anne Jouvin, whose homes were destroyed by the blaze.[20] Such spinning bees (*Spinnstube*, *veillée*) combined labor with socializing on long winter evenings.[21] Evidence from the Basle countryside and southern Germany suggests a fixed season for spinning bees, roughly from Advent to Carnival, with special celebrations on the first and last gatherings of the season; in other areas the winter gatherings appear more spontaneous.[22] The form of the spinning bee varied: as many as a dozen women young and old would meet to spin wool or flax, knit, or sew by candlelight.[23] "When there is a shortage of light," as a Swabian ordinance of 1651 explained, "neighbors and their families" might gather "by a common tallow candle" to work – but in a very modest circle "not to exceed six or at most eight persons, who keep a reasonable hour and completely avoid all idle chatter and other extravagances."[24] While sharing light, heat, and conversation, the women and girls might be visited by the young men of the village. (See Figures 7.1 and 7.2.)

Figure 7.1 "Kurtzweilige Beschreibung der löblichen Spinn- vnd Rockenstuben," broadside engraved after Sebald Beham, Nuremberg, seventeenth century.

This – in the authorities' view – is where the trouble began. In 1661 the bishop of Châlons issued an ordinance forbidding "men and boys" from joining or visiting "the vigils [*veillées*] when women and girls spin or do other work in the winter." Likewise, "women and girls are not to let them in, play, or dance with them during the night."[25] In Calvinist Guernsey in 1637, the Royal Court forbade the "vueilles" "because of the regular and scandalous debauchery which is committed at the assemblies of young people ... during the night." Marriageable young people met and courted at these "vigils"; a less judgmental English visitor to Guernsey noted that "from these meetings many marriages are contracted."[26] A contemporary French engraving (Figure 7.2) shows the scene just after the young men have arrived. A hanging oil-lamp illuminates the young women, distaffs in hand, one at a spinning wheel, just interrupted by the swains, who have begun to dance and show their affections. The text below claims that such visits, if handled wisely, transform "the most toilsome labor" into "more even than an amusement." Images and accounts from Germany (such as Figure 7.1) focus on sexual morality, adding concerns about disrespectful gossip, bawdy songs, rude pranks, and gluttony. At the spinning bees young

Figure 7.2 The arrival of the young men at the spinning bee: "Decembre: La Veillée," engraving by Jean Mariette, seventeenth century. Bibliothèque nationale de France.

servants "cook, eat, and drink what they have stolen at home," as one reported.[27] French and German sources record such courting customs as the "brushing off," in which each unmarried woman gave one of the young men the honor of brushing the stray bits of flax or wool off her lap while she worked.[28]

From the perspective of the participants, spinning bees combined labor, leisure, and important courtship customs; village elders tolerated them, arguing that "the young must have their diversions and merriment."[29] In Figure 7.1, first printed *c.* 1524 by Sebald Beham, then copied and reprinted in the mid seventeenth century with new verses, the older "shepherd's mother Elizabeth" (figure Y) looks at the disarray around her but then "thinks back to the good old days / when she had such fun herself."[30] The spinning bees were denounced by pastors and administrators (outsiders to the village) not simply on moral grounds, but also because the gatherings sustained local nocturnal countercultures. In Figures 7.1 and 7.2 and in many written accounts of spinning bees the authority figures of family, church, and

state are absent or obscured by the "rural plebian culture of laughter."[31]
In Beham's print the village administrator (the *Schultheiss*, figure G)
sits asleep beside the stove and "the priest is off taking care of his
cook." Sexual license is everywhere in Beham's scene: the maid of the
Schultheiss (E) is there with her lover Fritz (F); Curdt (L) "wants to
sneak behind the stove and sleep with Elßgen," and Ulrich (W) "so
pleases ... Appel [Apollonia, figure X] that she is about to put out her
light." The Beham print singles out each these figures for criticism,
but offers no hope of any moral improvement.

Figure 7.3 shows a more orderly peasant home at night: the
women are working flax while a group of men seated around the
table drink. The young woman and man standing at the back converse discretely under more watchful eyes. In Figure 7.4 we see an
ideal spinning bee: an all-female scene (an author, far left, looks
on) with well-lighted and industrious figures. In the accompanying
text the women give their legitimate reasons for gathering to spin.
Several say their husbands are out drinking; a maid explains that
she has been frightened by a ghost and does not want to stay in her
room alone. Other women have come to socialize, leaving snoring
husbands home in bed.

Condoned or criticized, and despite its many local variations (it
might be more or less focused on productive work, and more or less
planned or scheduled) all the evidence agrees that the spinning gatherings were always held on long winter nights.[32]

These gatherings are richly documented on the Continent.[33] In the
British Isles, peasants gathered at night for spinning or knitting in
Ireland, Scotland, and Wales.[34] In England – with the exception of
Yorkshire and Lancashire – spinning bees do not seem to have been
an established practice,[35] but their key features – women establishing an evening space for work or socializing, then inviting unmarried
men to join them – do appear. In Norfolk in the spring of 1665 we
learn that

Margaret Barkle, the servant of James Money of Gresham, butcher, was
charged to have taken an handkerchief with flour & late in the night with Ellen
Berston & Katherine Wilson to have gone to the widow Thoulder's house in
Sustead, intending a merry meeting there with some fellows.[36]

Figure 7.3 Spinning bee scene; engraving by Claudine Bouzonnet Stella, seventeenth century. Bibliothèque nationale de France.

Figure 7.4 An orderly spinning bee: Jacob von der Heyden, "KunckelBrieff oder SpinnStuben," *c.* 1620. Kunstsammlungen der Veste Coburg, Inventar Nr. XIII,441,8; Neg. Nr. 8685.

The gatherings of young people in the evening for work or conversation could easily turn into an impromptu dance or a "merry meeting."[37]

Indeed, when young men and women met at a spinning bee, they took part in one of several related and widely documented early modern customs of nocturnal courtship. The spinning bee overlapped with the south German *Heimgarten* (in other parts of Germany, *Nachtfreien* or *Kiltgang*), an evening gathering of unmarried young men and women at the house of a married couple. The term *Heimgarten* could also refer to time spent together by a courting couple at night after the larger gathering broke up, or to night-time visits by young single men to the homes – or beds – of young women.[38] Thus the *Heimgarten* could shade into the practice of bundling, the most intimate of early modern nocturnal courtship customs.[39] In France examples of the custom of allowing courting couples to share a bed for the night appear in the Protestant county of Montbéliard, and in Champagne, Burgundy, and Savoy.[40] Bundling was a rural custom, arising in part from the long distances suitors traveled to visit young women, which then necessitated an overnight stay. This seems to have been the excuse Leonard Wheatcroft used when staying overnight at the home of his future wife, Elizabeth Hawley, during their courtship in 1656–57.[41]

Wheatcroft's detailed courtship narrative describes many evening gatherings and nights spent together with his "beloved paramour, sweet Betty." They met at the "wakes" (i.e., church ales, notorious for lasting well into the night) in Wheatcroft's hometown of Ashover. One evening Wheatcroft waited at Elizabeth's house for her to return from a walk, "it being a fine warm evening for maids to delight themselves in." To Wheatcroft's great joy she returned "when the evening drew towards an end, and the glorious sun withdrew himself from my sight."[42] They went to her uncle's house, where they stayed the night and "did lovingly embrace each other." On another occasion, after Wheatcroft pretended to be engaged to another woman, he reported that "these and suchlike expressions [of Elizabeth's exasperation] did keep us waking all night. She, being then so vexed at me, would not so much as afford me one kiss."[43] Much of Wheatcroft's courtship of Elizabeth Hawley took place at night.

Indeed, the night was the accepted time for courtship. A notary describing a street fight and ensuing homicide in the village of Septfontaines (in the Franche-Comté) on the night of December 7, 1623 acknowledged that the night was the time "for visiting homes where there were girls or widows available for marriage." In this case an unwanted suitor named Pierre Révillon was asked repeatedly to leave a private home where he was courting a young widow, "for which … Pierre Révillon was truly dissatisfied because *it was only around seven or eight o'clock in the evening*" and "other young people were [still] drinking in the kitchen … Nothing about leaving had been said to them so that he, the said Pierre Révillon, thought that it was insulting to ask him to leave."[44] It was already several hours after sunset, and the gathering continued well after Révillon was expelled. The late hour was not the issue, but the frustrated Révillon started a fight outside which ended with a death, producing our record of the events of that night.[45]

In the many ways described here, young adults got to know potential sexual or marriage partners, both personally and physically. As historians of early modern marriage and sexuality have established, "the majority of the … population did not make arranged marriages."[46] Parental consent became more important in the confessional era, but this was consent to a match based on some kind of personal choice. With the exception of the wealthy or the nobility, young people sought out their own marriage partners within a group circumscribed by status, trade, and locale. Once mutual interest was established, courting couples enjoyed considerable physical intimacy with one another; sexual relations often began with the engagement.[47] The night significantly facilitated all aspects of the passage from single youth to husband or wife. From meeting a group of potential spouses at a spinning bee or village dance, to getting to know a specific individual in the dim intimacy of a chamber during a *Heimgarten* visit or while bundling, to the physical consummation of the relationship (ending, it was hoped, in marriage), the night was constant companion to the couple. Church and state gave their sanction to the marriage during the day, but husbands and wives were made at night.

Seen in these terms, the night was much more than an accidental or contingent part of rural servants' lives. In comparison with young servants in the city, rural youth had less contact with their peers during the working day, and fewer opportunities to socialize.[48] They relied more on the evening and night hours for the serious business of meeting potential marriage partners, and for less serious pursuits as well.[49] In Norfolk in 1665 a justice of the peace noted that he had

> sent Robert Coe, Sir John Palgrave's man, to Bridewell for having on two nights run out to dancings, & the first time he was out all night & the last time till midnight, for he would not come home until the dancing was over, though Sir John sent for him. The last time he carried away the key of the hall door to get in again.[50]

Here we catch a glimpse of the struggle between servants and masters over access to the night. Coe's insistence on having his night life reflected a frequent demand by servants. In Bavaria, for example, the Bishop of Augsburg complained in 1603 that when servants negotiated their contracts, they demanded (and received) explicit permission to go out at night and meet with unmarried persons of the opposite sex, or at least to talk with one another at night through a window.[51] These are all well-known aspects of rural courtship, of course, but the servants' contracts and authorities' complaints make the importance of the night explicit. A shortage of servants made these negotiations possible, as a Bavarian mandate of 1635 explained: "so too the farmers, if they want to keep their servants, are expected to allow [morally] suspect gatherings and *Heimgarten*, both day and night."[52] In his collection of sermons for country folk, the *Tuba rustica* (1701), Bavarian parish priest Christoph Selhamer gave several examples of courtship by night, all of which ended badly for the young women involved. In a sermon titled "The Bedroom Window" he came to the root of the problem: "I know quite well: in some places wicked servants set the terms when they enter into service, saying: 'Yes, farmer, I will serve you well for a year … but I'll tell you right now: you won't forbid me from running around the streets at night.'"[53] An Augsburg print of the seventeenth century shows this nocturnal courtship at a maid's window (Figure 7.5).

Figure 7.5 "Nacht": lovers meet at a window ("Fensterln"). Augsburg print, seventeenth century.

In 1760 the Lutheran pastor in Swabian Oberrot (near Hall) complained bitterly to the territorial authorities about the spinning bees and unrestrained night life of the local youth and begged them to impose some discipline: "You can start with my own servant, who is a nightwalker. I am at my wit's end trying to contain loose servants: as soon as an honest man says something [to them], they simply quit, and no one else wants the job."[54] At the end of the century, Graf Preysing reported the same problem on his Hohenaschau estate in

1796.[55] He also blamed the shortage of servants for this demand, suggesting that when their bargaining power rose, rural servants tried to secure their access to the spinning bees and "merry meetings" of the social night.

Like the spinning bee, the night life of the public house was condemned from the pulpit. But the importance of the public house was also well recognized: these institutions served the village throughout the day and evening.[56] Even in a single region they showed great variety, including alehouses, taverns (originally associated primarily with the sale of wine), and inns authorized to provide meals and lodging.[57] Subject to licensing and regulation in all European polities, public houses were of tremendous economic importance locally and served as hubs for communication and travel.[58] The men (and often the women) of a village spent much of their leisure time there, and public houses were at their busiest on Sundays, feast days, and in the evenings.[59] Closing times were an issue at all public houses, underscoring their association with night life. Mandated closing times were remarkably consistent across early modern Europe, generally 8 p.m. in the winter and 9 p.m. in the summer.[60] These mandates were honored only in the breach, however.[61] Patrons leaving public houses at closing time (or after) were the most common disturbers of the peace in early modern Europe, urban or rural.[62] As we will see below, the evening hours of the public house correspond with the higher incidence of violent crime in the evening rather than late at night.

Dancing linked all sites and forms of nocturnal sociability, from the spinning bee to the public house and beyond. Young and old took part in dances scheduled and spontaneous. We learn from court records of a late-night "dancing match" in 1639 at a mill in Wiltshire. When examined, Jane Lawes explained "that on St. John's Day last at night she was invited to the mill at Broad Chalke to a dancing match where there were diverse of the young men and maidens of the p[ar]ish, where she saw no abuse offered or incivility committed by any." Another examinant gives us an idea how these impromptu dances ended: "Joane Deane confirms the above and says further that 'about two hours before day, the candles being burnt out, she heard some of the maids cry out, but who they were or what caused them to cry out she knows not, being in the dark'."[63] Again we see youth-centered night life as more itinerant than that of married folk.[64]

7.1.3 Disorder

From distracted spinners to violent suitors and riotous dancers out all night, the rural night was a time of disorder. Of course, "disorder" is in the eye of the beholder; here it refers to the category used by church and secular authorities. Some of the night-time practices classified by authorities as disorder, such as the charivari, were seen by the participants as in fact affirming a village order which had been upset by a problematic marriage. Other sources of disorder, such as spinning bees, were important to villagers for economic and social reasons. Beyond these group practices, disorderly individuals appear across the rural night. By examining what constitutes "disorder" in the rural night we can better understand the conflicting claims made on it.

As Norbert Schindler has observed, in towns or villages the disturbers of the nightly peace fell into two distinct groups: young men and tavern visitors.[65] The two groups were separated by the cost of drinking in the tavern, which exceeded the means of most young men. As Beat Kümin has shown, drinking beer or wine at a public house regularly was a luxury for most peasants: a few glasses could easily exceed a day's wages.[66] Those who could afford to drink at a public house often left singing, shouting, blaspheming, or quarreling, often well after the mandated closing time.[67] For the young men of the village, on the other hand, the sheer disruptive exuberance of making noise under the cover of darkness sometimes bursts out of the records, as in a 1732 church council report from Gruorn, a Württemberg village in the Swabian Alps: "The servants from the Aglishardt farm raced through the village at eleven-thirty at night with bellowing cries, which greatly angered the residents."[68] Singing also could disturb the relative peace of the village at night. The 1732 church council report from Gruorn mentions "Johannes Grießinger, mason" who "almost every night, and especially on Sundays, sings improper street songs."[69] These songs might be as lewd as the "The Chimney-Sweep" (a "knave's ditty" sung by servants at spinning bees across southern Germany in the first half of the seventeenth century) or pious but unorthodox, such as the "Jörg Wagner," an Anabaptist hymn sung by Hans Ankelin at the top of his lungs one night in 1598.[70]

When night fell the contrast between the order of the state and the order of the village became especially clear.[71] The various shaming rituals of early modern rural society, such as the charivari (also "skimmington" or "riding") or the "groaning" were meant to restore order upset by some individual or relationship. In France the charivari was typically nocturnal, but the best-documented "ridings" and "groanings" in early modern England were all daytime events.[72] The cover of darkness allowed individual villagers to reproach their neighbors anonymously, and these practices could be quite refined. In 1639 a tavern servant named Bastian Scheckenbach was fined heavily by the parish of Frickenhausen (near Würzburg) for "strewing straw at night as mischief."[73] This sounds insignificant to modern ears, but in fact the practice was well known: villagers would awake one morning to find their muddy lanes marked with paths of straw connecting various houses, suggesting or revealing illicit relationships among their inhabitants – the rural equivalent, one might say, of posting political placards at night in London or Paris.

In this case, the young Scheckenbach seems to have gone too far: someone turned him in for creating a disturbance at night.[74] These nocturnal disturbances threatened the order of the day, as the local clergy felt most keenly. For priests, pastors, and preachers all this disorderly night life resulted in drowsy churchgoers who fell asleep during services. Among the published sermons of the seventeenth and eighteenth centuries, sleeping in church was a familiar topic. In 1709 the Swiss Reformed pastor Conradin Riola published a "spiritual trumpet" against the habit of sleeping during services. Riola, writing from the village of Sent, explained that God had ordained the night for rest and the day for labor: those who roamed about at night like wild animals and slept during the day disturbed the divine order.[75] Catholic preachers in Bavaria repeated such condemnations, as did the Reformed Scottish kirk sessions studied by Margo Todd.[76] All referred to the misuse of the night as the cause of daytime slumber.

7.1.4 Violence and crime

Sociability at night flowed easily into nocturnal violence. On December 9, 1666 in the Hessian village of Ebsdorf, two men emerged from a house "in the evening in the twilight."[77] Andreas Keiser, a Lutheran, and Hans Caspar Hägelich, "calvinisch," had been drinking beer in the house of Hans Kiß. They had begun to argue about religion and had already come to blows. They each left the alehouse to go home but met up outside, where the dispute continued. Hägelich, the Calvinist, pulled a hatchet out from his tunic and swung; Keiser, unarmed, tried to flee but received a deep wound in the back, from which he died two days later.

The victim Keiser was the husband of the niece of Caspar Preis of Stausebach, a pious Catholic peasant whose diary recorded this typical outburst of "one-on-one" nocturnal violence.[78] Robert Muchembled was one of the first to note that dusk, rather than the late night, was the critical time for violent crime in the countryside. Based on a study of judicial records in Artois from 1401 to 1660, he observed that among cases of homicide in which the time of the violence is indicated (37 percent of the total cases), about 17 percent of these deadly encounters took place in the afternoon, 22 percent at night, and 55 percent in the evening.[79] Alain Cabantous has made a more detailed comparison of eight studies of rural crime at night in seventeenth- and eighteenth-century France and England and concluded that about half of all crimes recorded took place at night, about equally divided between the evening hours and later at night.[80] In other words, the rural night was no more criminal than the rural day.

But nocturnal crime was more frightening, if not more frequent, than crime during the day. Records of criminal proceedings confirm the real potential for violence in any encounter involving young men in the evening or after dark. In the Artois village of Lorgies in 1602, on March 17 at around eight in the evening, the young Pierre Soix mistakenly attacked Philippe Carpentier, the village farrier, mortally wounding him. Their exchange captures some of the tension of these nocturnal encounters. Soix was walking along, singing, when he heard someone approaching and called out "Who goes there?" Carpentier, well known to Soix but unrecognized in the dark, responded with "What have you?" ["Que veux-tu avoir?"] Soix responded hopefully "friends," but Carpentier replied "I know of no friends" ["Je ne cognois nulz amis"] and knocked Soix to the ground. In defense, Soix fatally stabbed him.[81] In 1616 in the upper Bavarian village of Siegsdorf, a certain "Wolf, servant of Pämer" stabbed another young servant "for no other reason" than that they came together in the lane and did not recognize each other. Earlier that year in the same village Adam Aufhaimer attacked the weaver Stephan Peutner "at night in the street," breaking one of his ribs with a stone.[82] In the dark villagers tended to attack first, assuming that anyone whom they did not recognize had shadowy intentions.[83]

Early modern authorities condoned this kind of defensive or preemptive nocturnal violence, even at its most extreme. On April 30, 1666 William Knaggs and Thomas Bell, a blacksmith, "together with several young men and boys of the town of Birdsall [Yorkshire] … being about the number of fourteen" went into a forest belonging to the Eddlethorpe farm at "about eleven o'clock in the night." Knaggs and Bell separated from the group, "their intention then being to choose and get a young ash tree for a Maypole to carry to the town of Birdsall." The search proved fatal for Knaggs: he and Bell "heard someone speak but did not well understand what they said and immediately after a gun was discharged and the said William Knaggs being then close by … gave a shriek and turned around and fell down dead." Bell could not see who shot Knaggs, but "immediately after the gun was discharged, one Mr. Edward Ruddock and another person" came up to Birdsall, saying "'Ho rogues! Ho rogues! Have we met with you? I'll make rogues on you. It's more fit you were in your beds than here at this time of night.'"[84] Ruddock asked Bell where the rest of the group was, then set off after them, "in his hand one gun," and fired again a few minutes later.[85] Ruddock was tried for the homicide. Despite the evidence given here by Thomas Bell, he was acquitted, underscoring the expectation of danger at night reflected in all these deadly encounters.

In addition to this interpersonal violence, the rural night also saw communal violence that enforced group identities or village boundaries. The young Thomas Isham of Lamport kept a diary of country life in Northhamptonshire in 1671–73, recording on April 30, 1673 a particularly brutal encounter between the young men of two villages:

> Last night the servants of four farmers, with Mr. Baxter's man and Henry Lichfield, went to Draughton [about a mile northwest] to bring home the first drawing of beer, which they bought from Palmer. On the way back sixteen or seventeen Draughton men met them with stakes and began to lay about them; but being few and unarmed against a greater number of armed men, they were easily beaten, and Mr. Baxter's man has had his skull laid bare in several places and almost fractured.[86]

The diarist does not explain what score the Draughton men had to settle with the six young men of Lamport; a slight to village pride, or perhaps the visitors were courting the young women of Draughton. The chronicle of the Dötschel brothers of Mitwitz, a village in rural Franconia, recorded violent brawls after their village's church fair (kermesse, *Kirchweihfest*) on August 31, 1628 and in 1670: "Anno 1670 year [sic], at our church fair in the night, Erhart Bauer … became unruly with Attam and Michael, the two Jüng brothers from Rotschreuth … and it became a great brawl." Each of these "battles" (as the Dötschels described them) between neighboring villages ended with several men seriously injured.[87]

Nocturnal crimes against property were associated with nightwalkers, suspicious persons who might eavesdrop, "cast men's gates, carts or the like into ponds, or commit other outrages or misdemeanors in the night, or shall be suspected to be pilferers, or otherwise likely to disturb the peace."[88] When the term first appeared in the late Middle Ages, nightwalkers were assumed to be men, but, as discussed in chapter 6, in seventeenth-century London the term came to refer to "lewd and idle women." In the provinces the term retained its masculine associations through the eighteenth century: as the Justice of the Peace Robert Doughty explained to Norfolk jurors at a quarter session in 1664, nightwalkers were "rogues … such as slept on the day & watched on the night, & such as frequented alehouses &

2

fared well & had no visible means of livelihood."[89] In the countryside nightwalking shaded into poaching, a widespread nocturnal crime issuing from deep social tensions.[90]

Whatever the actual level of interpersonal nocturnal crime in the countryside, early modern villagers were quick to defend themselves against perceived nocturnal threats to themselves or their goods.[91] Thomas Isham recorded an "uproar" on the night of December 13, 1672:

About eleven or twelve o'clock tonight a noise was heard in Mr. Wright's yard. The maids, who were washing dishes, heard someone beating on the window, breaking it as if trying to get in. They were terrified.

The entire household, and the village, sprang into action:

[O]ne beat on the bell, another blew a horn, a third put candles in every room. Meanwhile Wright, clad only in a nightshirt, ran through the house like a madman, and his son waited in the hall with a sword and holding a gun, ready to receive them with a volley ... the neighbors, aroused by the horn and thinking that the house was being attacked by thieves, assembled with forks, sticks, and spits.

Armed and ready, when the villagers investigated the yard they found "a dog that had been shut out and had broken a window." Isham notes that "this sent them away with roars of laughter,"[92] but the retrospectively ridiculous preparation for violence clearly shows that such a situation could be dangerous. In the Bavarian town of Traunstein in 1698 the apprentice carpenter Ruepp Jähner lost the fingers on his right hand when he took an ill-considered shortcut over a fence late one night: he was attacked without warning by his neighbor, Sylvester Schneiderpaur. After dark, any "intruder" to a domestic space could reckon with a violent response.

7.2 COLONIZING THE RURAL NIGHT?

The rural night belonged to the common people. When church and state authorities sought to discipline the night in the countryside, they spoke and acted as if they faced a "dark continent" of rural superstition, excess, and intransigence. All the activities just described drew the authorities' attention as they sought to regulate and police labor, leisure, disorder, and crime in villages and farms, and in the rural night's uninhabited spaces, such as forests and roads.[93] This focus on the rural night increased in the seventeenth and eighteenth centuries.[94] In Catholic areas church leaders tried to reinforce their moral discipline by co-opting or introducing nocturnal forms of popular piety.[95] How does this engagement with the rural night compare with the colonization of the urban night examined in previous chapters? The same legal-disciplinary framework underlay authorities' engagement with the night in the countryside as in the city. But the encounter of church and state with the rural night was shaped by different cultural and social forces and led to outcomes distinctly different from the colonization of the night in the cities of Northern Europe.

In these cities, the colonization of the night was based on settlement, achieved when courtiers and respectable burghers shifted their daily activities later into the evening and night. Respectable activity after dark reoriented the use of the evening and night hours away from young people and toward a new kind of homosocial, respectable man. The result was a new period of urban time based on public street lighting and private consumption. This engagement with the night sought to create an urban site of *activity* for respectable men, who eagerly occupied its taverns, coffeehouses, clubs, and theaters, now more safely connected by lighted streets.[96] Unlike the colonization of the urban night, which was based on the expansion of the nocturnal activity of one group at the expense of another, the colonization of the rural night was a struggle to *clear* the rural night of its traditional activities (such as spinning bees, courtship customs, and popular nocturnal celebrations) and create an ordered time largely empty of activity.[97]

Efforts to colonize the rural night required a sharp focus on young people. Youth were the "indigenous" people of the early modern night, and limiting their night life was a constant concern. The Bavarian priest Christof Selhammer epitomized this view when he preached that rural servants should be locked in at night: "Among the peasants, the master of the house should keep careful watch over his servants. At night every house-door should be locked and bolted so that no one goes out and no one can sneak in."[98] The administrators and pastors who sought to discipline the rural night had little interest in supplanting traditional village night life with their own sociability. The colonization of the rural night was not based on settlement. Indeed, as we will see below, the rural gentry began to slip out of step with the daily rhythms of their urban cousins at the start of the eighteenth century.

The means by which spiritual and secular authorities sought to colonize the rural night have been described as "social discipline." The early modern colonization of the night – urban and rural – began on paper with a stream of legal writing on the dangers of the night and its fundamental association with sin and crime in the early seventeenth century.[99] These works proposed, both implicitly and explicitly, that policing could and should combat the disorder of the night. In theory and practice, the colonization of the rural night sought to reclassify nocturnal leisure, sociability, and disorder as crime.

7.2.1 Disciplining the rural night

The sexuality of young adults was at the center of these attempts to discipline the rural night. As we have seen, young people in the countryside depended on the night for courtship, social exchange, and leisure, and they defended their access to the night in negotiations with their masters. In response, church and state authorities repeatedly tried to restrict all forms of rural "night life."

The prescriptions of church and state maintained an intense focus on spinning bees and similar gatherings. Across France a succession of bishops condemned these gatherings from the sixteenth century through the end of the Old Regime.[100] The statutes published by the bishop of Saint-Malo in 1619 were especially florid, describing the spinning bees as "assemblies of the night invented by the prince of darkness whose sole aim is to cause the fall of man."[101] Worse even than the public house was the "intolerable corruption and detestable, hideous debauchery committed under the guise of what is known in this country as spinning [and] scutching [hemp] ... done at night, where men, women, and girls flock." "We have heard from reliable people," the statutes continued, "that going to such a ... spinning bee is [the same as] going to a brothel."[102] The parlement of Brittany prohibited them entirely in 1670.[103] The synodal statutes issued for the diocese of Troyes in 1680 forbade

men and boys, under pain of excommunication ... to be with women and girls in the places where they assemble at night to spin or work, to linger there in any way, or to wait to walk them back home. As we also forbid under the same penalties women and girls to receive [the men and boys]. We urge them to behave during the time of their work with all the modesty befitting the faithful, and even to sanctify their meetings by a few prayers.[104]

This statute reflects a modest hope that casual labor at night could be "sanctified" once the sexes were rigorously separated. Most other authorities, less optimistic, simply forbade the gatherings entirely.[105] German authorities also focused on the sexual associations of the spinning bee, "in which all kinds of immorality and fornication are carried on."[106] In a personal plea, a Lutheran pastor bedeviled by the spinning bees begged the state authorities for a decree that "every servant who would be found on the streets or in public houses, or other such places after 9 p.m. should be condemned to pay a fixed fine." Recognizing that masters were not especially interested in separating young people from the rural night, the pastor continued: "and those heads of households whose servants were not home at the aforementioned time, and who keep silent about it and do not report [their servants] should just as well be punished with a fine."[107]

Church authorities challenged all forms of nocturnal courtship across Europe in the seventeenth century, with some success: in France bishops threatened bundling and prenuptial sex with excommunication, and they had all but disappeared by the mid eighteenth century.[108] In electoral Cologne the nocturnal courtship customs of the spring, such as the *Mailehen* (a mock marriage for courting couples) were successfully separated from the church's celebration of Pentecost, though not eliminated entirely.[109]

We might suspect that the focus on the sexuality of village youth made the night itself incidental to this program of social discipline.

But the official abhorrence of youthful rural night life was so prevalent in the sixteenth and seventeenth centuries that we can see the night disciplined *as night*. As the council of Schwäbisch Hall ordered in 1684:

> If any unmarried servants go out to drink wine, and otherwise do only what is right, and in the evening each one goes home alone, nonetheless the male servants shall pay 1 fl. and the maids 15 ß as punishment.[110]

In this small city, most servants came from the surrounding countryside and continued to socialize there – hence the rural context of this decree. The authorities focused directly on the night rather than on excesses in nocturnal sociability in their attempts to contain their young servants: even if nothing improper was done and all returned home by a reasonable hour, nocturnal gatherings would still be an offense.

These attempts to discipline the rural night faced sharp limits. The proliferation of laws, ordinances, and statutes focused on the night life of rural youth began in the first third of the seventeenth century. As many scholars have noted, this legislation remained in place, relatively unchanged, for 150 years or more.[111] Spinning bees and similar nocturnal gatherings were forbidden everywhere, but with little effect. Scholars have documented their persistence through the eighteenth century in German-speaking Switzerland, in the Vorarlberg, in rural France, and across Germany.[112] Disciplining night life in rural public houses was equally unsuccessful. These inns and taverns were too deeply rooted and performed too many acknowledged functions to be challenged directly. Specific complaints about late hours did not lead to any general restriction of opening times on paper or in practice.[113]

This failure to discipline the rural night is part of a key feature of the early modern state first discussed by Jürgen Schlumbohm in 1997: countless laws and regulations promulgated but not enforced.[114] Yet the limited effectiveness of early modern administration only partially explains the enormous gap between prescription and enforcement seen in these attempts to discipline the rural night. As

Schlumbohm has argued, early modern administrators valued laws, ordinances, and proclamations as symbols of the state's authority. As symbols, these laws were not limited by modern-rational expectations of what could be enforced or effected in practice. The act of making or proclaiming law *in itself* showed the state to be Christian and benevolent.

For these laws to be more than symbols of state authority, local cooperation between rulers and subjects was essential. Church and state authorities proclaimed their baleful view of the moral and physical dangers of the night in countless laws and ordinances. But local support for limiting the night life of village youth was quite limited. Priests, pastors, and administrators noted that when pressed, heads of households sometimes defended spinning bees. One Lutheran pastor complained that "the fornication and license of the youth are made into a praiseworthy custom by parents [who claim that] from it many Christian marriages are made, as the nightly gatherings and noise bear witness."[115] Every spinning bee or *Heimgarten* had at least the tacit approval of the head of the household in which it was held, and the concluding verses of the Beham spinning bee print (Figure 7.1) explain: "how could it be finer for these servants / after all, the whole community of the village is with them / high and low alike. And so they like their fun at all hours / in the evening as in the morning." With the whole village involved, who would prevent this night life? Village courts almost never prosecuted young men for nocturnal visits to court young women at their windows, or in their bedchambers. Indeed, these visits were not met with the sort of condoned violence seen above in cases of nocturnal intruders, suggesting some level of acceptance. In the specific case of Leonard Wheatcroft and Elizabeth Hawley, we know that her parents allowed them to spend the night together on many occasions once their courtship had begun. As long as spinning bees, late nights in taverns, nocturnal courtship customs, and similar night life received the tacit approval of village elders, neither church nor state could do much to discipline the rural night.

7.2.2 Sanctifying the rural night

Alongside these widespread attempts to discipline the rural night and limit nocturnal activity, a more ambitious aspect of the colonization of the rural night unfolded in Catholic territories, driven by the baroque piety of Catholic reform. As we saw in chapter 3, pious laymen, Capuchin missionaries, and reforming bishops all sought new uses for the night in a program of spiritual renewal and ecclesiastical intensification. The spiritual uses of darkness discussed in chapter 3, ascetic and aesthetic, inspired new forms of nocturnal lay piety in Italy, France, and Catholic Germany.[116] This interest in sanctifying the rural night went beyond the purely disciplinary aims shared by church and state. New practices, such as the devotion of the Forty Hours and nocturnal lay processions during Holy Week, played a major role in the public piety of the seventeenth century, urban and rural. The continuous veneration of the Host day and night, formalized in the Forty Hours' Devotion, has been described as "an incomparable means to gather the faithful," while the nocturnal processions of the lay penitent brotherhoods on Holy Thursday or Good Friday represented "Catholic ritual's most massive venture into the night" in the early modern centuries.[117] Here we will examine the rise and fall of rural nocturnal devotion in the sixteenth and seventeenth centuries.

The devotion of the Forty Hours is a period of continual prayer before the Eucharist augmented with preaching, processions, and other displays of piety.[118] From its origins in Milan in the 1520s and 1530s, the devotion spread with the reforms of Trent. As Pope Clement VIII explained in the Papal Constitution "Graves et diuturnae" of 1592: "We have determined to establish publicly in this Mother City of Rome an uninterrupted course of prayer in such wise that ... there be observed the pious and salutary devotion of the Forty Hours ... at every hour of the day and night."[119] The devotion was an ideal expression of the visual, emotional, and Eucharistic piety of the Catholic Reformation: performed in commemoration of the forty hours between the death and resurrection of the Christian savior, the penitential devotion served the missionary efforts of Capuchins, Jesuits, and Barnabites in the century after Trent.

The Forty Hours' Devotion was practiced in French-speaking lands from the late sixteenth century on.[120] In the duchy of Chablais, for example, the devotion played a vital role in missions to the Protestant region around Geneva in 1597–98, performed twice in the town of Thonon and once in the village of Annemasse. Held across France in episcopal cities and towns, the devotions were intended to draw the faithful from rural parishes and involved confraternities from nearby towns and villages.[121] The literal span of forty hours meant prayer through at least one full night. Public prayers and processions in darkness served to "render the site [of the devotion] more venerated through this clear dark obscurity," as one Catholic account explained in apophatic terms.[122] The night served the emotional, penitential, and missionary goals of the Forty Hours' Devotion.

In France this devotion, though "established and developed by the church, gained a popular character."[123] But the very popularity of the practice with clergy and lay people led to a nocturnal collision between the devotional and the disciplinary imperatives of Catholic reform. Clergy often scheduled the Forty Hours' Devotion to counter the start of Carnival or on Mardi Gras, seeking to draw revelers away from the traditional masquerades and nocturnal revelry and into the churches for continual prayer before the consecrated host. But by the mid seventeenth century some churches chose to interrupt the devotion at night, arguing that it was better "to avoid unpleasant encounters ... in the evening on the streets and to close the church and avoid the disorder that might be committed there later."[124] These concerns grew, and in 1686 the Capuchin order of France received official permission from Rome to interrupt the Forty Hours' Devotion at night. Instead, the forty hours of prayer and preaching would occur only during daylight hours. But interrupting the "around-the-clock" veneration of the Eucharist robbed the practice of its unique theme and intensity, and surrendered the night back to the spinning bees, Carnival revelry, and tavern visits described above.[125] By the end of the seventeenth century the Forty Hours' Devotion was in decline.

Despite the popularity of the Forty Hours' Devotion and the willingness of lay people to gather in churches for prayer and veneration of the Eucharist at night, the French clergy of the age of Louis XIV were convinced that no good could come from a gathering of common people at night, no matter how pious the context. By the end of the seventeenth century, numerous episcopal ordinances and statutes prohibited all lay prayer in churches at night, as the synodal statutes of the diocese of Amiens of 1697 indicate: "we urge all parish priests in the countryside to make public in their churches an evening prayer (at least on holidays and Sundays) at the sound of the bell, at the time they deem most convenient, *and always before dark*."[126] The interruption of the Forty Hours' Devotion at night and the statutes prohibiting public prayer in churches after dark reflect the deep suspicion of French clergy of the late seventeenth century toward popular nocturnal gatherings of any kind.

In the Catholic territories of the Holy Roman Empire the same pattern emerges. Forays into the night by the clergy and pious laypeople, reflecting the baroque piety of Catholic reform, were followed by a retreat from popular nocturnal piety at the end of the seventeenth century. In the Empire nocturnal penitential processions were the most salient aspect of this attempt to sanctify the rural night. The Jesuits introduced these processions in cities such as Augsburg and Würzburg, but confraternities and lay brotherhoods soon followed suit in small towns and villages in Swabia, Bavaria, Franconia, Austria, and Tirol.[127]

The drama of these nocturnal processions, with costumed participants and illuminated images of the Passion, put baroque devotion in motion. The Good Friday procession of the confraternity of the Holy Rosary in the town of St. Johann in Tirol is especially well documented. Between 1645 and 1756 the confraternity held seventy-nine processions. All seventeen processions held between 1667 and 1686 took place "in the evening," but the practice was then moved permanently to the daytime.[128] In the Bavarian city of Traunstein, the processions of the Corpus Christi confraternity were viewed with wonder by local peasants, but they showed "poor reverence and respect" for the evening spectacle (1667). In 1676, in hopes of a "more attractive" procession, the confraternity considered moving its start from 7 p.m. to "the daytime, soon after matins … because people could see everything better, and it would be easier to maintain order than at night, and would also save on lights, and avoid the danger of fire."[129] The brotherhood decided to keep the spectacle at night, but in 1680 tried processing in the afternoon before returning again to nocturnal processions. In Mindelheim the Good Friday procession of the Corpus Christi brotherhood, documented as nocturnal in 1686, was moved to the early afternoon sometime in the early eighteenth century.[130] The nocturnal processions of confraternities in France, usually held on the night of Holy Thursday, suffered the same relocation.[131]

The confident, Tridentine attempt to sanctify popular nocturnal customs and initiate new nocturnal rituals was overshadowed in the course of the seventeenth century by the defensive action described as an "obsessive denial of the night."[132] As a result, the Catholic church, like its Protestant relations, had little relationship with the rural night by the early eighteenth century. A 1671 ordinance of Antoine Godeau, bishop of Vence, sums up the Catholic withdrawal from the rural night:

Being advised that in our diocese every year many irreverences are committed on the night of Holy Thursday in the churches where the people linger under the pretext that the Blessed Sacrament is exposed, we have ordered as a remedy, first, that … the Blessed Sacrament will no longer be exposed after the Mass of Holy Thursday but … will be deposited in the chalice which will be covered by a white veil and placed upon the altar.

[Second,] We prohibit any sort of person from sleeping in the church under pain of excommunication, [and] order that it will close at ten o'clock precisely. The penitent brothers who are accustomed to come in procession to the church will have to come before nine o'clock to sing the litany of the Passion as they are accustomed and will then return to their chapels with modesty and without noise.[133]

By the end of the seventeenth century the church's colonization of the night was in full retreat. The very practices curtailed by this bishop – prayer vigils before the Eucharist at night and nocturnal processions by confraternities – had been promoted by pious laymen and missionary clergy during the previous century.

The colonization of the rural night was less ambitious than that in the city. It was also less successful, even in its limited terms. By and large, attempts to rid the rural night of its courting couples and drunken tavern-goers failed. Attempts to sanctify certain rural nights during Holy Week or at Christmas also had little effect on rural youth and village culture.[134] Most of the ordinances, statutes, and decrees aimed at clearing the rural night of its disorder were in place by the early seventeenth century; most of the goals described in these regulations, such as the elimination of women's spinning bees or "alley-catting" by young men, were unmet at the end of the eighteenth century, with the ordinances and prohibitions repeated and reprinted through the end of the Old Regime.

The sources of this failure to colonize the rural night are easy to see. The colonization of the urban night was driven by the settlement of urban elites in the night, reflecting powerful forces of conspicuous consumption of goods and time, supported by the disciplinary efforts of the state. In the countryside, settlement was not a priority and village elites often winked at the nocturnal customs of their youth. The disciplinary reach of the state was notoriously limited.[135] As a result, country life moved in traditional rhythms, creating a new contrast with the nocturnalized pulse of the better-policed and illuminated streets of the great cities of the eighteenth century.

7.3 COUNTRY FOLK, CITY NIGHTS: DAILY TIME DIVERGES IN THE EIGHTEENTH CENTURY

By 1700 a new literary formula was emerging. Authors embellished the age-old comparison between urban and rural life with a new contrast between the nights of the city and those of the countryside. In 1714 Alexander Pope (1688–1744) penned an "Epistle to Miss Blount, on her leaving the Town, after the Coronation." Addressing "some fond Virgin, whom her mother's care / Draggs from the town to wholesome country air," Pope describes the fate of Miss Blount in the country:

She went, to plain-work, and to purling brooks,
Old-fashion'd halls, dull aunts, and croaking rooks:
She went from Op'ra, park, assembly, play,
To morning walks, and pray'r three hours a day:
To part her time 'twixt reading and bohea,
To muse, and spill her solitary tea,
Or o'er cold coffee trifle with the spoon,
Count the slow clock, and dine exact at noon:
Divert her eyes with pictures in the fire,
Hum half a tune, tell stories to the squire;
Up to her godly garret after sev'n,
There starve and pray, for that's the way to heav'n.[136]

The daily rhythms of country life seem especially deadening here, with dinner at noon and bedtime not long after seven.

Were the urban and rural nights truly drifting apart? Pope's comments clearly reflect the divergence of city and country time as a literary theme, but also reveal a real shift in patterns of daily time. In the *Tatler* of December 12, 1710, Richard Steele mentioned "an old friend … being lately come to town" from the countryside. "I went to see him on Tuesday last about eight o'clock in the evening," continued the author, "with a design to sit with him an hour or two and talk over old stories":

but upon inquiring after him, his servant told me he was just gone up to bed. The next morning, as soon as I was up and dressed, and had dispatched a little business, I came again to my friend's house about eleven o'clock, with a design to renew my visit; but upon asking for him, his servant told me he was just sat down to dinner.

Clearly, London and the country are out of step in this case. Steele continued:

In short, I found that my old-fashioned friend religiously adhered to the example of his forefathers, and observed the same hours that had been kept in his family ever since the Conquest.[137]

When the Newcastle curate Henry Bourne published his thoughts on *Antiquitates vulgares; or, the antiquities of the common people* (Newcastle, 1725) he sought to give "an account of several of their opinions and ceremonies." The common people are in his understanding country folk (and there is nothing new in this assumption), but Bourne's comments suggest that he sees a different daily rhythm in the countryside. Discussing the belief that the evil spirits of the night are banished by cockcrow, he notes

that in Country-Places, where the Way of Life requires more early Labour, they always go cheerfully to Work at that time [i.e. cockcrow]; whereas if they are called abroad sooner, they are apt to imagine every Thing they see or hear, to be a wandering Ghost.[138]

Rural folk also spend their long winter evenings differently, as Bourne notes in his tenth chapter, "Of the Country Conversation in a Winter's Evening: Their Opinions of Spirits and Apparitions." Bourne claims that "Nothing is commoner in Country Places, than for a whole family in a Winter's Evening, to sit round the Fire, and tell stories of Apparitions and Ghosts."[139] Physician and poet Mark Aikenside's *The Pleasures of the Imagination* (1744) presents a similar scene:

> Hence finally, by night
> The village-matron, round the blazing hearth,
> Suspends the infant-audience with her tales,
> Breathing astonishment! of witching rhymes,
> And evil spirits ...
>   of shapes that walk
> At dead of night, and clank their chains, and wave
> The torch of hell around the murderer's bed.[140]

The connection these authors make between the absence of nocturnalization and the belief in ghosts and witches plays a key role in the disenchantment of the night discussed in the next chapter. By creating the stereotype of rustic superstition at night, these commentators reflected a new divergence of daily schedules between city and village. In the cities, nocturnalization was promoted by the state on one hand, and by a deepening public consumer culture on the other – a powerful combination of discipline and distinction.[141] Both forces were attenuated in the countryside.

Curioſes Geſpräch
Zwiſchen Hänſel und Lippel
Zweyen
Oberländiſchen Bauren /
Bey der
Den 14. Märtzen 1745. in der Königl. Haupt⸗ und
Reſidentz⸗Stadt Wienn
Solenniſer gehaltenen Illumination,
Uber die ſo glücklich⸗als höchſt⸗erfreuliche Geburt eines
Zweyten Königl. Printzen und Ertz⸗Hertzogen
CAROLI JOSEPHI &c.

Wienn / gedruckt bey Johann Jacob Jahn / Univerſitäts⸗Buchdruckern / im
Pfeifferiſchen Hauß untern Tuchläden.

Figure 7.6 Two peasants marvel at an illumination in Vienna. *Curioses Gespräch: ʒwischen Hänsel und Lippel ʒweyen oberländischen Bauern bey der den 14.Märʒen in … Wien … gehalten Illumination* (Vienna, 1745), fo. 2.

The spread of street lighting and festive illuminations in cities also created a new contrast with the night in the countryside. In a 1745 pamphlet celebrating the birth of a Habsburg prince, two "peasants from the highlands" view the illumination of Vienna (see Figure 7.6). The first is astounded: "wherever I look, wherever I go, lights shine without end / and the houses all around are like the heavens." The other adds "in our village there's never been a church fair ('kermes') like this!"[142]

Ekirch has shown that the age-old pattern of segmented sleep was disrupted by artificial light beginning in the late seventeenth century (coincident with the rise of street lighting, better domestic lighting, and coffeehouses). "Divided sleep," he argued, "would grow less common with the passage of time, first among the propertied classes in the better-lit urban neighborhoods, then slowly among other social strata."[143] References to segmented sleep are absent from the diaries of elite men because their daily life was extended well past sunset by artificial lighting, indoors and out. The nights of townspeople, compressed by artificial light into a single sleep of seven or eight hours, began to diverge from the age-old pattern of segmented sleep found everywhere else.

By the middle of the century, the well-born might encounter early rising and rural daily time as something "new." In 1740 Anne Donnellan (*c.* 1700–62), daughter of a chief baron of the Exchequer, discovered rising with the sun during a visit to Spa. Writing to Elizabeth Robinson Montagu, Donnellan explained:

I like Spa exceedingly; 'tis a mere country village, with a very romantic country about it. I like the way of living, which is new to me; we are all out by six in the morning in our chaises, and go three miles to the Geronstere waters; we come home at nine, and take a cup of chocolate, dine between twelve and one, go to the assembly at four, where there are all countries, and all languages, half a dozen card tables, and no crowd; from the assembly we take a walk in the Capuchin's garden; all are in before eight to supper, and to bed at ten.[144]

In her reply Elizabeth Robinson imagines herself at Spa and seems quite touched by the "new" country schedule of rising by 6 a.m.:

I like the manner of living, it is quite new, and the place so romantic! I cannot say I am fond of such early rising, or that I delight in cards, but custom would, in a week's time, make the first easy, and I suppose for the other it is not worse than Bath.[145]

In the summer 6 a.m. would be just after sunrise, which would have scarcely seemed early to the sixteenth-century ancestors of these women.

Summing up these developments in 1786 the fashion writer Friedrich Justin Bertuch explained that "an entirely new order of things" had supplanted the traditional rhythm of daytime for work and night for rest and sleep.[146] As discussed in chapter 5, Bertuch regarded the change as self-evident and presented numerous examples drawn from the courts and cities of Northern Europe, noting that people of quality in England had shifted their mealtimes and sleeping times later by about seven (!) hours over the past two centuries.[147] This nocturnalization was inevitable: "the occupations of the day begin ever later, the more society is refined and luxury increases."[148] This refinement was perceived and presented as urban and European: "the king of Yemen, ruler of Arabia Felix, dines early at nine for a midday meal, at five for the evening [meal], and goes to sleep around eleven," whereas "the pleasures of the evening and night are the ruling fashion in France and England, and indeed in every great city."[149] The shift to later hours does not include the rural population.[150]

By the eighteenth century the temporal markers of daily life – the traditional times for labor, meals, and sleep – in the two sites were slipping out of step as townspeople used artificial lighting, indoors and out, to shift their daily schedule into the night. The nightward shift of daily times for dinner (i.e., the main, "midday" meal), supper, and sleep by social class is underscored by the view from Napoleon's Paris:

Two hundred years ago the Parisians had their dinner at noon: today the craftsman dines at two o'clock, the great merchant at three, the clerks at four, the parvenu, the businessman, and the exchange agent at five o'clock; the minister, the legislator, the rich bachelor, at six, and the last usually leave the dinner table at the time when our fathers sat down for their last meal of the day.

Emphasizing the late hours of the city's well-to-do, the author continued, "those who do have supper sit down at the table at eleven o'clock, and in the summer they go to bed when the worker rises."[151] In the *Tatler* essay quoted above, Steele elaborated on the development by creating a contrast with rural life:

For this reason I desired a friend of mine in the country to let me know, whether the lark rises as early as he did formerly? and whether the cock begins to crow at his usual hour? My friend has answered me, that his poultry are as regular as ever, and that all the birds and beasts of his neighborhood keep the same hours that they have observed in the memory of man."[152]

Steele recognized that waking, dining, and sleeping hours were now dictated by location and class as they had not been a generation earlier. Moral commentators like Steele may have criticized the nocturnalization of urban daily life, but they were too invested in social discipline and social distinction to actually challenge the process. The resulting tensions between urban and rural time persist to this day, as rural resistance to daylight savings time suggests.

In 1658 the peasant Michl Bruckhay sued the Jewish livestock dealer Hudel Hitzig before the Imperial Aulic Court (*Hofgericht*) in Rottweil. Both men lived in the village of Kriegshaber, near Augsburg, and as the dispute moved through the imperial legal system, Bruckhay's son and his son's friends lashed out against their Jewish neighbor. On the night before Easter 1659 they threw a pig in Hitzig's well and broke his windows. The local authorities did not condone this nocturnal assault, levying a 45-gulden fine on Michl Bruckhay for his son's actions.[153] Little had changed between the invasion of Barthel Dorfheilige's inn at Wanfried in 1603 and this incident in 1659, and young men would continue to serve as the "guardians of disorder" in villages through the end of the Old Regime.

When darkness fell over the early modern countryside, the characteristic ambivalence of the night emerged. Fear waxed alongside pleasure, leisure merged with labor, and limitations created opportunities. An intense combination of discipline and distinction drove nocturnalization at courts and in cities. From a rural perspective, however, the illuminated courts and cities resembled another vitreous innovation of the seventeenth century, the greenhouse. The concentrated administrative energy and dynamic conspicuous consumption at courts and in large cities produced an exotic bloom of night life. This growth could not be sustained in the early modern countryside, where rural folk instead tended hardy, native nocturnal traditions. Attempts to colonize the rural night were fewer and less successful. At the end of the eighteenth century the spinning bees had endured, rural publicans and customers continued to ignore closing hours, and the night remained a time and place for youth, especially young men. The expansion of respectable night life at the expense of the nocturnal elements of traditional youth culture in cities created a new contrast between city and country nights.

CHAPTER EIGHT

Darkness and Enlightenment

How did Europeans understand darkness and the night, real and symbolic, as the rhythms of daily time shifted? This chapter examines several key controversies of the early Enlightenment in the context of daily experiences and popular beliefs associated with the night and its shadows. The imprint of nocturnalization on these controversies reveals the unevenness of nocturnalization *and* of the universal claims made by the New Philosophy. Claims to dispel darkness, literal or figurative, lead us to darkness relocated or recreated elsewhere. The tension between the universalism of light and the selective use of the night refigures our understanding of the origins of the Enlightenment and the special place of its early or radical phase.

The study of nocturnalization in the preceding chapters has revealed two contrasting but ultimately complementary responses to darkness and the night in the seventeenth century. Two sets of discourses and practices arose: one which sought to dispel darkness and transform the night, and another focused on creating and manipulating darkness, whether in devotion or spectacle. These two faces of nocturnalization left their imprint on the form and content of the early Enlightenment. In the first set of discourses and practices, the new street lighting was often described as vanquishing the darkness by transforming night into day: "The night will be lit up as bright as day, in every street," as a 1667 report on the new street lighting of Paris exclaimed.[1] This sense of triumph over darkness is reflected on an intellectual level by Spinoza, for example, who defined darkness as a nonentity in a 1663 treatise, arguing that "We imagine nonentities positively, as beings ... we imagine as if they were beings all those modes which the mind uses for negating, such as blindness, extremity, or ... darkness, etc."[2] In his *Essay Concerning Human Understanding* Locke made clear that the association of the night with frightening supernatural beings was entirely contingent: "The ideas of goblins and sprites have really no more to do with darkness than light," he explained. The problem was a false association created by young women:

yet let but a foolish maid inculcate these often on the mind of a child, and raise them there together, possibly he shall never be able to separate them again so long as he lives, but darkness shall ever afterwards bring with it those frightful ideas, and they shall be so joined, that he can no more bear the one than the other.[3]

Darkness itself has no innate qualities for Locke. In similar terms the readers of London's popular *Athenian Mercury* were told in an article on darkness published in the 1690s that darkness was "a mere Privation of light."[4]

In contrast to the proclaimed elimination of darkness, baroque piety and the perspective stage used darkness as a real presence to create visual and emotional effects, as did the fireworks and illuminations that crowned court celebrations and political displays. Nocturnalization thus describes a dual relationship to darkness, encompassing the discourses and practices that dispelled or denied darkness as well as those that created, maintained, and manipulated it. This chapter examines the influence of both sides of nocturnalization on European culture at the start of what Herder called "our enlightened century."[5] The seemingly straightforward connection between lighting and the Enlightenment becomes more complex and revealing when we examine both aspects of nocturnalization in the milieu, intellectual content, and controversies of the early Enlightenment.[6] I do this by tracing the cultural and intellectual fates of ghosts, witches, and Hell – three intertwined aspects of medieval and early modern culture deeply associated with darkness and the night – in the seventeenth and early eighteenth centuries.[7] These manifestations of nocturnal fear, now separated from their basis in the darkness of everyday life, became weak links in the chain of traditional belief. But the discourses which challenged traditional ideas about ghosts, witches, and Hell all used or evoked darkness and the night to supplement their claims. In the same terms, I examine the imprint of nocturnalization on two key texts of the early Enlightenment: Bernard Le Bovier de Fontenelle's *Entretiens sur la pluralité des mondes* (*Conversations on the Plurality of Worlds*) of 1686 and Balthasar Bekker's *De betoverde weereld* (*The World Bewitched*, 1691–94). Both of these self-consciously "global" works redrew intellectual and cultural boundaries, creating new zones of insight and darkness.

8.1 GHOSTS

In early modern Europe, ghosts made eschatology apparent to the senses. They revealed the meaning of death and the reality of the afterlife in physical reality: ghosts could be seen, heard, or felt. Their place in early modern European culture (learned and popular) was especially sharply debated across the period from the Reformation through the Enlightenment.

The association of ghosts with the night was axiomatic. Across the Western cultural tradition, the night has long served as a fundamental symbol of death and the afterlife,[8] and the experience of the night shaped descriptions of death, purgatory, Hell, and ghosts in popular and learned accounts alike. In 1643 a baker in the Bavarian town of Altomünster reported to his confessor that he had been visited by a ghost from Purgatory. The spirit asked the baker to fulfill a vow so that it could rest in peace. As David Lederer observed in his valuable 2002 article on ghosts in early modern Bavaria, the baker seems to have understood the apparition as a true purgatorial spirit in orthodox Catholic terms, but the Ecclesiastical Council in Freising did not agree. When the confessor reported the baker's experience to the Ecclesiastical Council, the learned clerics of the Council responded with a list of ten problems with the account. Among them, "the baker claimed that the spirit appeared brightly lit and joyous during the day as well as at night. Ghosts from Purgatory, the Council reminded the father confessor, were spirits of the dark, tending to sadness and usually showing themselves around midnight."[9] The leading Protestant denunciation of ghosts from Purgatory, Ludwig Lavater's 1570 treatise *De Spectris*, argued that any seeming ghost was in reality the Devil or a demon assuming the form of deceased person to deceive the living.[10] As described above in chapter 2, Lavater agreed that such apparitions "do appear still in these days both day & night, but especially in the night ... For he who is the author of these things, is called in the holy Scriptures the Prince of darkness, and therefore he shunneth the light of Gods word."[11] Lavater warned that "Spirits and other strange sights, be not the Souls of Men, but be either good or evil Angels," or else some human trickery.[12] In other words, Lavater and most sixteenth-century Protestants agreed that the Devil could visit the living in any guise, including that of a familiar deceased person; some persons might also fake an apparition of some kind, but the souls of the dead could not leave the afterlife and appear to the living: "neither the souls of the faithful, nor of infidels, do walk upon the earth after they are once parted from their bodies." The meaning of ghosts and other nocturnal apparitions became the focus of fierce Protestant–Catholic debate in the second half of the sixteenth century with the publication of Pierre Le Loyer's Catholic response to Lavater, the 1586 *IIII. livres des spectres, ou apparitions et visions d'espirits, anges et démons* (*Four Books on Specters or Apparitions and Visions of Spirits, Angels, and Demons*). Despite the controversy surrounding the issue, Protestants and Catholics agreed that apparitions (whether ghosts from Purgatory or devils from Hell) were most likely to walk the earth at night.[13]

The deep association of ghosts with the night across the confessional divisions of early modern culture linked the new ghost controversies that arose in the late seventeenth century with nocturnalization. The ideas and values of the early Enlightenment, whether inspired by Descartes, Hobbes, or by general skepticism, found ready expression in debates over ghosts and spirits. In comparison with discussions about the reality of witchcraft and the existence of Hell, the stakes were a bit lower when expressing skepticism about spirits or their abilities, and queries about the reality of ghosts and the abilities of spirits could be aired in a broader forum. At the same time, as we will see, skepticism about the "nature, power, administration, and operation" of spirits could serve as the thin end of the wedge of unbelief.[14]

The rise of skeptical, Cartesian, and empiricist views challenged ghost beliefs in new ways, and the beliefs found new defenders in Protestant Europe. Two new positions on the reality of specters and ghosts, running parallel to the nocturnalization examined above, emerged in the second half of the seventeenth century. Skepticism about the existence or physical abilities of spirits might arise from even a superficial brush with Hobbes or Descartes; defenders of the spirit world associated this skepticism with libertines like the English "town-gallant," who "Till Noon ... lies a Bed to digest his over-nights Debaucht" – a night spent in brothels, playhouses, coffeehouses, and taverns. Denounced as a blasphemous skeptic in the 1675 pamphlet *The Character of a town-gallant*, the gallant's "religion (for now and then he will be prattling of that too) is pretendedly Hobbian." He actually understands nothing of the New Philosophy, our critic explains, but "the rattle of it at Coffee-houses has taught him to Laugh at Spirits, and maintain there are no Angels, but those in Petticoats. And therefore he defies Heaven ... imagines Hell, only a Hot-house to Flux in for a Clap, and calls the Devil, the Parsons Bug-Bear."[15] Often associated with the worst of debauchery and unbelief, the denial of spirits by free-thinkers and "esprits forts" in taverns and coffeehouses led to broader and more sophisticated forms of unbelief. To counter this position, conservatives began to emphasize the reality of spirits as evidence of the reality of Heaven, Hell, and the entire "invisible world." As we will see, the café at night was a key site for these debates over the implications of the New Philosophy for belief in ghosts and spirits across Northern Europe.

In 1701 the clandestine Leipzig newsletter *Geheime Briefe, So zwischen curieusen Personen über notable Sachen ... gewechselt worden* (*Secret Letters, Exchanged among Curious Persons on Notable Issues*) defended the existence of ghosts to a broader public, providing us with an extraordinary visual overview of the issues in the form of an illustration of a ghost appearing to three men at night (Figure 8.1).

The unnamed author of the *Secret Letters* insisted that ghosts and spirits were real, and that the denial of their existence was pernicious: "The denial of ghosts is the subtle profession of atheism" ("Spectrorum negatio est subtilis Atheismi professio") is the title of

Figure 8.1 Facing-page illustration, *Geheime Briefe, So zwischen curieusen Personen über notable Sachen … gewechselt worden* (Freystadt [i.e. Leipzig], 1701), after p. 829.

Figure 8.2 Detail: illustration title, *Geheime Briefe, So zwischen curieusen Personen über notable Sachen ... gewechselt worden* (Freystadt [i.e. Leipzig], 1701), after p. 829.

the illustration (Figure 8.2). The illustration offers a unique visualization of the ghost controversy. As the three men drink and smoke their pipes by candlelight, a libertine raises a toast, unaware of the headless apparition just seen by the companion on his left. The dark time of drink, sin, and atheism becomes a moment when the reality of spirits (and of God) is revealed: the libertine night becomes a mystic time. The corresponding text in the 1701 *Secret Letters* asks "What we should think of those Christians who do not believe in ghosts and the appearance of spirits and deny their physical actions?"[16] The response denounces such Christians as a "disturbing and dangerous swarm," and attacks the "ghost-busters" ("Gespenst-Stürmer") who deny the appearance and effects of spirits. Such persons

are not really subtle but in fact truly crude atheists, who must either deny the witness of the Holy Scripture, Old and New Testaments, or twist [Scripture] in an unreasonable and scurrilous way.[17]

The author emphasizes the evidence in the Christian Scriptures:

accounts of ghosts appear in the Old Testament (such as the appearance of the prophet Samuel and similar, etc.), not to speak of the New Testament ... which must be mere fables to such a "ghost-buster" if he wants to deny the appearance of spirits.[18]

The association of late-night conversation with the debate over ghosts and spirits extends beyond this image, appearing in several diaries of the period. Far from the intellectual centers of Leipzig or London, for example, the West Country physician Claver Morris of Wells in Somerset noted a similar exchange in his diary on September 6,

1709: "At the [weekly Tuesday night] Music-Meeting there happened to be Captain James Coward; And his asking how a Spirit could throw a Bed-Staff gave me an occasion to prove beyond his denying, & I hope to his satisfaction, that the World was not eternal and that there were future rewards & Punishments after Death."[19] The conversation recorded in Morris's terse entry starts with Coward posing a question raised by Descartes and Spinoza: how could an immaterial spirit interact with the physical world? We do not know exactly what followed this question, but one way or another, the conversation led to Morris shoring up several pillars of Christian doctrine by asserting the last judgment and the reality of *post mortem* punishments, including Hell. As the *Secret Letters* article warned, there seemed to be a slippery slope from skepticism about ghosts to the outright denial of Christian verities.

Only one "ghost-buster" was mentioned by name in the *Secret Letters* article: the Amsterdam Reformed minister Balthasar Bekker (1634–98), who had unleashed an enormous controversy with the publication of his *De betoverde weereld* (*The World Bewitched*, 1691–94).[20] Across the four volumes of this work Bekker argued that "the apparitions of Evil Spirits are contrary to true Reason, and that the Holy Scripture affords no proofs of it."[21] Bekker's work was immediately translated into German, French, and English and was read and discussed widely in the 1690s.[22] Bekker was an orthodox Reformed minister, but the intellectual basis of *The World Bewitched* was an explosive combination of Cartesian pneumatology and Spinoza's accomodationalist biblical exegesis. On Cartesian grounds he questioned whether "a Spirit, as a Spirit, and so much the more as it is a Spirit, can without Body act upon all sorts of Bodies, and upon other Spirits," concluding that "the operations of such Spirits, as are not joined to a Body; either Angels or Devils" cannot "act upon other Bodies, either of Men, or other matter."[23] Denounced as a "Spinozist" and atheist for the claims in *The World Bewitched*, which we will examine below, Bekker was permanently suspended from his post in Amsterdam in 1692.[24] The contrast between Bekker and his predecessor Lavater is especially revealing: these two Reformed pastors and theologians, separated by a century of concentrated intellectual ferment, held completely opposed views of the existence and effects of demons and spirits in this world.

The denunciations of Bekker's work in the Netherlands, England, and Germany were intense. His claim that neither reason nor Scripture could prove "that Men have any commerce with Spirits"[25] deeply disturbed Protestant authors who saw in such spirits proof of all things spiritual, and in their denial the prelude to atheism. Some argued for guilt by association: in 1692 the Amsterdam Reformed minister Jacobus Koelman claimed that ideas in *The World Bewitched* "have a lot in common with atheists, Sadducees, Epicureans, Libertines, and other Scripture despisers, and especially with Thomas Hobbes, Benedict Spinoza, Adrian Koerbach, David Joris, and the like."[26]

Indeed, in the 1690s conservative English Protestants were responding to the same intellectual threats generated by "atheists, Sadducees, Epicureans, [and] Libertines" homegrown and imported. The number of ghost publications in Britain surged and the *Athenian Mercury* (an English periodical similar to the *Secret Letters*) began trading in ghost stories. But the English ghost controversy had its origins a generation earlier. As ghost-story collector John Aubrey (1626–97) explained:

When I was a child … before the Civil Wars … the fashion was for old women and maids to tell fabulous stories nighttimes, of Sprites and walking of Ghosts, etc. … When the wars came, and with them Liberty of Conscience and Liberty of inquisition [inquiry], the phantoms vanished. Now children fear no such things, having heard not of them.[27]

The Interregnum unleashed a torrent of heterodox ideas from Thomas Hobbes, the Ranters, other antinomians, and Christian mortalists like Richard Overton and John Milton – all in one way or another denied the existence of ghosts, spirits, demons, the afterlife, or the immortality of the soul. Responding to the "Liberty of Conscience and Liberty of inquisition" that had begun in the 1640s, the Cambridge theologian Henry More (1614–87) began promoting ghost belief in his 1653 *An antidote against atheisme, or, An appeal to the natural faculties of the minde of man*. This was the first Protestant defense of the belief in ghosts and spirits:

I thought fit to fortify and strengthen the Faith of others as much as I could; being well assured that a contemptuous misbelief of such like Narrations concerning *Spirits*, and an endeavour of making them all ridiculous and incredible, is a dangerous Prelude to *Atheisme* it self, or else a more close and crafty Profession or Insinuation of it.[28]

For writers like More, the night took on a new value as the time of the appearance of ghosts and spirits. Among the defenders of established Christianity in the latter half of the seventeenth century, the spirits of the night held a new meaning. No longer seen as diabolical illusions or as bearers of messages of repentance, justice, or vengeance, now the specters were seen as proof of the immortality of the soul, and of the existence of God and the afterlife as well. As penitential spirits or diabolic apparitions, they drew their meaning from a larger system of belief; now, in an ominous reversal of signification, these apparitions had to serve as evidence of that larger invisible reality.

For many Protestant authors in Britain, the Netherlands, and the Empire, the threat of popery that once surrounded such apparitions was utterly overshadowed by the Christian mortalism of Milton or the "atheism" of Hobbes, Spinoza, or even Bekker. The utility of the ghost to preserve faith in God – and in divine mystery and majesty – became paramount. This utility was initially supported by hopes that the circulation of enough "well-attested" ghost stories would prove their reality *within* the empiricism on the rise at the end of the century.

In this debate, both positions reflected fundamental changes in everyday life for the learned and urbane. As noted earlier, nocturnalization encompassed two seemingly contradictory trends: on the one hand the conquest of the darkness and the night through vastly improved street and domestic lighting, and on the other the creation and manipulation of darkness at royal spectacles, on baroque perspective stages, and in absolutist political display in general. The ghost literature of the seventeenth century presents a similar contrast between dispellers and promoters of the shadowy spirit world. The "ghost-busters" (such as Spinoza and Bekker) claimed to shine the light of Cartesian analysis or rational Scriptural exegesis onto the shadowy existence of ghosts and reveal them to be, in the words of

Spinoza "but dreams, which differ from God as totally, as that which *is not* differs from that which *is*."[29] Whether materialist, rationalist, or empiricist, the radical Enlightenment promised the elimination of the shadowy world of ghosts, demons, and spirits. The discourses which denied the existence of ghosts circulated in the most nocturnalized spaces of this period. Many issued from the cities of the Netherlands, which enjoyed the oldest and most effective street lighting in Europe. (See Map 5.2.) From this dense concentration of nocturnalized daily life, the ideas of the radical Enlightenment radiated through the night, from the genteel evening gatherings of Claver Morris in Somerset to the coffeehouses and taverns of London, Paris, and Leipzig.

In contrast, sovereigns who used darkness and the night to enhance their displays of light and power – such as Charles I, Louis XIV, Augustus the Strong of Saxony, or even Frederick William I of Prussia – mirror those anxious Protestants who assessed the dangers of "atheism" as much greater than those of popery and so emphasized the reports of ghosts and spirits in their own times as "sensible proof of spirits" and therefore of God. In a 1678 treatise on angels Benjamin Camfield referred to "the Supreme Spirit, and Father of Spirits":

'tis to be observed, among our modern Atheists and Sadducees especially, that their antipathy and aversation, as to the notion and being of Spirits universally, hath carried them on (and naturally doth so) to the dethroning of God, the Supreme Spirit, and Father of Spirits.[30]

Terrified by the dethroning of kings and heavenly king alike, apologists for monarchy and revealed Christianity praised darkness as fundamental to divine and earthly majesty. Dryden's "Astraea Redux" of 1660 presented the night as a time when the truth of monarchy was revealed ("Well might the Ancient Poets then confer / On Night the honour'd name of *Counseller*"), rehabilitating the Stuarts, "In such adversities to Scepters train'd," by claiming that "We light alone in dark afflictions find." Rachel Jevon's poem in celebration of the restoration of Charles II pairs darkness and splendor by proclaiming Charles "More Splendid made by dark Afflictions Night; / Live ever Monarch in Coelestial Light." The royal spectacles of Louis XIV, beginning with the *Ballet de la Nuit* of 1653, used darkness to enhance the brilliance of the Sun King.[31] The parallel between the importance of darkness to baroque royal spectacle and the importance of ghosts and spirits to Christian faith was first made explicit by Henry More in his 1653 *Antidote against atheisme*. More chose to end his 160-page treatise with a ringing simile:

For assuredly that Saying was nothing [i.e., never] so true in Politicks, *No Bishop, no King*; as this is in Metaphysics, *No Spirit, no God*.[32]

Countless Protestant divines had denounced all apparitions as human or diabolical trickery, but More, Camfield, Koelman and other Protestants writing in response to the New Philosophy saw these specters as heaven-sent evidence of the Divine. By the end of the seventeenth century, Protestant supporters of monarchy and the divine monarch had embraced the night and its ghosts in terms that would have been unthinkable a half-century earlier.

8.2 WITCHES

The debate over ghosts and spirits shaded into the more weighty issue of witchcraft. This is no surprise: for early modern people the ghost and the witch were "not merely allied beliefs, but intrinsic parts of the same system."[33] The Devil might appear in the form of a ghost, or directly to a witch; witches might summon the spirits of the dead (as the witch of Endor did) – all were manifestations of the same metaphysical order, sharing deep associations with the night.

Though closely associated in popular and learned belief, the stakes were higher when witchcraft was at issue. Ghost belief could have serious theological and political implications, but there were no major legal issues tied to it. Witchcraft, in contrast, was a crime described and denounced in every body of Western law. Its ties to the political order were explicit. By the middle of the seventeenth century, Protestants and Catholics alike had created a stable context for witchcraft that demanded its persecution, despite the publications of skeptics from several confessions. This context framed witches as the Devil's servants on earth, with their *maleficia*, gatherings, and rituals recognized as inverted reflections of the legitimate servants and proper worship of God. Imagined nocturnal gatherings were a key part of this inversion. In these terms Stuart Clark has elucidated the political logic behind the persecution of witches, which helps account for the violence of both the persecutions and the flare-ups of debate over it. In response to criticism of the execution of several witches in Scotland in 1697, minister Robert Wylie argued that "unless a man hath so far renounced humanity as well as religion as to deny invisible Spirits, and the being of witches," the actions of the Scots authorities were irreproachable.[34] The legal and practical context of witchcraft persecution, as well as its theoretical underpinnings in learned demonology, all emphasized the night as the time of diabolical temptation and the witches' sabbath. The tie between witchcraft and the night intensified at the end the sixteenth century as the learned demonization of the night made its way into popular culture through witch trials and publications.

After 1650, the stable framework of learned demonology and legal persecution was shaken by new challenges that went beyond the humane skepticism of Montaigne, Scot, Wier, or Spee. On an intellectual level, these challenges arose from Cartesian or materialist thought; on a quotidian level, increasing use of the night for respectable sociability undercut its demonization. Spinoza provides some of the most striking expressions, arguing in his *Korte Verhandeling* (*c.* 1660) that "devils cannot possibly exist" and refuting arguments about the existence of spirits in series of letters in 1674.[35] Such authors challenged the possibility of witchcraft on an abstract level, and they presented their arguments as light overcoming the darkness of superstition.

In response to these new challenges, witchcraft took on new meanings in the law and learned discourse.[36] More and more, stories about witches became assertions of the reality of witchcraft. As with ghosts and spirits, supporters of traditional, revealed Christianity saw witchcraft itself as evidence of the reality of their faith and their God. The nocturnal crimes and gatherings of witches were inverted testimony to the divine order preached by the established churches. To preface accounts of witchcraft and witch trials in New England and Sweden *The Compleat Library, or, News for the Ingenious* (December, 1692) explained the stakes:

As we are troubled in this Age by a great many Atheists, or pretenders to Atheism, so we are no less pestered with a multitude of Pretenders to Reason and Christianity both, which yet against both Reason and Scripture ... do strangely *Sadducise*, and dogmatically, and confidently maintain, there are no witches.[37]

By publishing these accounts of sorcery, "being attested in the most Authentic manner that is possible," the author hoped to "satisfy them [i.e., the skeptics] of the Reality of the Being of such wicked Creatures, and of the lamentable Effects of their horrid Confederacy with wicked Spirits." Despite this author's reference to "the lamentable Effects" of human alliance with evil spirits, these alliances served an important new purpose by generating accounts of witchcraft which could now be used in the name of established Christianity to support a system of beliefs that seemed (to traditional defenders at least) to be challenged on all sides. As a Scots author explained in a 1698 account of witchcraft, after "Seeing Devils take so much pains to contract for the Souls of Witches; the Saducee's tho' judicially blinded in their Reason, are hereby rendred inexcusable by very sense."[38]

Conversations with free-thinkers confirmed the fear that denial of the reality of ghosts and witches was a slippery slope to graver errors. This was the conclusion of Ralph Thoresby, the nonconformist antiquary of Leeds, who noted in his diary on June 13, 1712 that he was "troubled." Visiting London, he had spent that evening and the one before at a coffeehouse in the company of learned men like himself, including one Obadiah Oddy (a classicist), a "Mr. Gale," and Edmond Halley, Savilian Professor at Oxford. Halley had a reputation as a free-thinker, but the trouble came from Oddy. Thoresby wrote that Oddy, who had been "very zealous in opposing even the best attested narratives of apparitions, witchcraft, etc." on the previous evening, "now confessed he believed there was no Devil." Thoresby responded in his diary: "the Lord enlighten him!"[39] Could accounts of devils and witches counter this unbelief? In conversation with the free-thinker Oddy, Thoresby (and perhaps other interlocutors) presented "the best attested narratives of apparitions, witchcraft, etc." as proof of the invisible world of God and spirits, but to no avail.

Apparently concerned by his nocturnal encounter with skepticism, Thoresby began *the next day* to read "Mr. Beaumont of Genii," a reference to John Beaumont's *An historical, physiological and theological treatise of spirits, apparitions, witchcrafts, and other magical practices ... With a refutation of Dr. Bekker's World bewitch'd; and other authors that have opposed the belief of them* of 1705.[40] Ten days later he noted that he had "Finished the perusal of Mr. Beaumont's History of Genii, or spirits, presented to me, and recommended by the pious Bishop of Gloucester, from whom I had also an account of that very remarkable apparition mentioned in the postscript. His Lordship says this curious treatise has done much good in this skeptical age."[41]

Beaumont's treatise began with an engraving of divination by night (Figure 8.3, "Jews Going Out in the Moonshine to Know their Fortune" by Michael van der Gucht) which reinforced the traditional association of the night with the reality of magic and divination. Here Beaumont cited a Jewish tradition of nocturnal divination during Sukkoth after repeating accounts of contemporary "second-sighted persons" about whom he had been "credibly informed."[42] Thoresby would have found in Beaumont many accounts of spirits and witches, including detailed reports of the Essex witch trials of 1645. The treatise spoke in the empirical tone of the time with many well-attested narratives, including an account of the author's own experience with spirits and a report from the bishop of Gloucester, with whom Thoresby had spoken personally about "that very remarkable apparition mentioned in the postscript."

Accounts like these were nothing new, but now they bore the additional function of affirming an entire system of belief in spirits, witches, the Devil, and God. Thoresby's conversation with Oddy suggests that these nocturnal accounts would never persuade Cartesians or materialists, however. As Jean Le Clerc explained in the first French review of Bekker's *World Bewitched*, several scholars were preparing to answer Bekker, but "one would wish that in order to refute him, they would not adopt all the stories that have been made and are made every day regarding Sorcerers & Magicians ... They will not persuade our *Esprits forts* by this path."[43] Instead, Le Clerc argued that

Figure 8.3 Illustration of "Jews going out in the Moonshine to know their
Fortune" in John Beaumont, *An historical, physiological and theological treatise
of spirits, apparitions, witchcrafts, and other magical practices … With a
refutation of Dr. Bekker's World bewitch'd; and other authors that have opposed
the belief of them* (London, 1705), frontispiece. University of Illinois,
Urbana-Champaign, Rare Books and Manuscripts Library.

"to answer Mr. Becker solidly, they must … prove that the nature of
a spirit is such, that it necessarily has a certain power over bodies,
though limited; or that, at least, God has established, with regard to
pure spirits and their relation to the body, a law much like that of the
human spirit's relationship to the body with which it is united."[44] This
was a tall order.

As in the debate over ghosts and spirits, supporters *and* deniers of
witchcraft reflected fundamental changes in everyday life. The intellectual conquest of the night defined darkness and witchcraft alike as
nonentities, and no amount of empirical evidence could change this
definition. Supporters of traditional Christianity turned to the terrors of the night for "proofs" of their understanding of God and the
invisible world, but the landscape of darkness was beginning to shift
beneath them.

8.3 HELL

In early modern Christian doctrine, Hell was suspended in a thick network of concepts and connotations. The immortality of the soul, divine judgment, *post mortem* punishment, the resurrection of the body, revealed doctrine, and a morally static afterlife – all these concepts were woven together in the traditional teaching on Hell. And all these concepts and connotations were questioned as never before in the seventeenth century – first by radical Christians, then by the radical Enlightenment. A challenge to any one of the concepts could have seismic effects on the entire concept of Hell, and the stakes were high. Unlike the belief in ghosts or witches, the doctrine of Hell was preached quite deliberately to deter sin, stir consciences, and maintain the social order. In a 1686 letter the devotional author Matthew Henry presented the accepted view that "Heaven and Hell are great things indeed, and should be much upon our hearts, and improved by us as a spur of constraint to put us upon duty, and a bridle of restraint to keep us from sin."[45] The famously dissolute free-thinker Matthew Tindal said the same in his 1697 tract on religious toleration, though with less straightforward conviction.[46] He placed atheists and deists outside the bounds of toleration because they denied "the Existence of a God, or that he concerns himself with Humane Affairs; it being the belief of these things that preserveth them in Peace and Quiet, and more effectually obliges them to be true to their Promises and Oaths, and to perform all their Covenants and Contracts."[47] Denying the efficacy of ghosts, spirits, and witches was already dangerous – witness the career of Balthasar Bekker – but denying openly the existence of divine *post mortem* punishment in Hell went beyond the limits of even radical Enlightenment discourse. Confounding Hell's dark existence meant unleashing on an already troubled world all the crime, excess, lust, and deceit kept in check by fear of eternal punishment. Was Hell a nocturnal illusion that even the most enlightened had to maintain?

We are accustomed to think of the challenges to Hell in the seventeenth century as theological and intellectual, originating in extra-confessional Christianity and in the radical Enlightenment. But

traditional Christian Hell as understood and preached by the established churches of early modern Europe was built from the raw mate-
rials of daily life, not merely from Christian doctrine and Scripture.
When Christians described Hell, they spoke to all five senses, creating a *bricolage* of experiences. Early modern authors, following a
long tradition, distinguished between the *poena damni* (internal suffering) and the *poena sensi* (external sensual suffering) that would be
experienced in Hell.[48] Some of the most significant challenges to Hell
in this period arose from the same realms of experience used to make
traditional Hell real.

The constitution of Hell through the senses and through lived
experience has already been discussed by scholars of early modern culture and belief. Carlos Eire has argued that early modern
Christians might "relate experiences in this world to what they had
seen and heard about the infernal regions, thereby receiving a fore-
taste of what might await the five senses after death."[49] As Eire has
suggested, the moans and wails of criminals punished in the town
square, the smell of the burnt flesh of a heretic, the pain of passing a
kidney stone (or of giving birth), the bitterness of an herbal remedy –
all could be part of the experience of Hell.[50] Eire and other scholars
have suggested that early modern people imagined Hell in terms of
extreme experiences of torture, pain, and suffering. Using daily life as
a category of analysis broadens this approach by considering Hell in
terms of mundane early modern experience rather than focusing on
the extreme experiences.

Early modern descriptions of Hell drew their force from the often
terrifying experience of darkness and the night in everyday life. How
did shifts in attitudes toward darkness and the night relate to changing beliefs in Hell? I argue that the "dark foundations"[51] of Hell in
daily life and experience were shifting in the second half of the seventeenth century – with profound implications for Hell itself.

Darkness and the night evoked many emotions in early modern
Europe, but fear was assumed to be foremost. It was an easy leap
from fear to Hell. The Scottish Presbyterian Elizabeth Nimmo (née
Brodie, d. 1717) fused everyday darkness with Hell in an incident
recounted in her journal or "spiritual narrative":

I was afraid I had sinned the sin unto death. One Sabbath night when my trouble was very great ... I was immediately challenged, though the challenge seemed to come from the Devil: "O," says the enemy, "you have now sinned the sin unto death." I knew not how to go alone ... and after I had lighted my candle, and had read half a side of a book in octavo, then the temptation came in sorely upon me that the room was full of devils to carry me to Hell. I thought I had no comfort but the burning candle, and out it went without any visible cause, whereupon I thought I should have dropt down to the pit.[52]

Nimmo's account of a solitary nocturnal encounter with diabolical temptation resembles both the confessions of accused witches and La Tour's penitent Magdalene (Figure 3.5). Nocturnal Hell was still very real to Nimmo in rural Scotland in the late seventeenth century, but for some of her learned and urbane contemporaries, the night was now associated with the freedom to question the very existence of the Hell she so feared.[53]

From Milton to Spinoza, seventeenth-century Europe produced both vivid evocations of Hell and the first truly resonant denials of its existence. Europeans challenged the orthodox doctrine of Hell in the seventeenth century as never before. Denunciations of eternal torment issued from both radical Christian and secular pens. Positions ranged from the annihilationist argument (represented, for example, by Thomas Hobbes) that the wicked would be destroyed (usually after some time in Hell) and only the saved would enjoy eternal life, to the universalist claim (first advanced by Origen) that eventually all souls would be saved.[54]

But these denials of Hell present a strange paradox. After assessing the range of denials in his masterful study of *The Decline of Hell*, D.P. Walker examines the early modern understanding of the social function of the orthodox doctrine. Aside from a few millenarian Christians, all agreed that without the fear of Hell, society would collapse. As a deterrent to sin and crime, eternal damnation was too important to be questioned publicly. As Henry Dodwell put it in 1698: "in this age of licentiousness, there is hardly any doctrine ... of more pernicious consequence than that ... concerning *the finiteness of hell torments*."[55] Learned doubts about the duration or existence of Hell were too dangerous to be shared with the common people. The conflict between learned disbelief and the social function of eternal punishment led to a "double doctrine" of Hell in which those who denied its existence privately affirmed it publicly.

Authors were quite clear about the double doctrine of Hell. The English Platonist and clergyman Thomas Burnet (1635?–1715) printed his universalist treatise *De Statu Mortuorum et Resurgentium* (*Of the State of the Dead and of Those who are to Rise*) privately and in Latin.[56] Translated and published in English, Dutch, and French after his death, in its pages readers found this warning:

> whatever you decide, in your own mind, about these punishments being eternal or not, the received doctrine and words must be used for the people and when preaching to the populace, which is inclined to vice and can be deterred from evil only by the fear of punishment.

Burnet's attempt to limit access to his writings about Hell failed, despite his warning that "if anyone translates these things, which are addressed to the learned, into the vulgar tongue, I shall consider it done with ill will and evil intent."[57] Even Anthony Ashley Cooper, third earl of Shaftesbury, who denied *post mortem* rewards and punishments alike as contrary to disinterested virtue practiced for its own sake, admitted that "the principle of fear of future punishment, and the hope of future reward … is yet in many circumstances a great advantage, and support to virtue" for those too impulsive or weak to strive for virtue for its own sake.[58] The issue also figured in debates between French Protestants and Catholics in the second half of the seventeenth century. When confronted with Pierre Jurieu's publication of Origen's denial of eternal torment, the French Protestant pastor Elie Saurin agreed with Bossuet, bishop of Meaux:

> The crime, or rather the imprudence, consists in M. Jurieu's having informed the people of a thing which could only scandalize and could not in any way edify.[59]

A range of seventeenth-century writers agreed that the denial of the orthodox doctrine of Hell should be presented in terms either intellectual or esoteric, so that "none of the Wicked shall understand, but the Wise shall understand."[60]

Rare were men like F.M. Van Helmont, who in 1684 denounced this secrecy, asking:

Is it sufficient ground for preaching this Doctrine [of eternal damnation], to concede that it will terrify and affright people from sin? Does God need any Lie of man's making, to deter people from sin? Or shall we lie for God?[61]

In similar terms Pierre Bayle denounced the self-interest which led Arminian theologians like Jean Le Clerc and Issac Jaquelot to conceal their belief in universal salvation. If they revealed that they agreed with Origen and would "exclude no one from the bliss of paradise," they would be driven from the Netherlands by the "Ministers of the Flemish and Walloon Churches ... [because] the dogma of eternal torment seems too precious and too important to allow it to be attacked."[62] Bayle then rehearses the social defense of the orthodox Hell, which "restrains vice by the fear of eternal damnation"; denial of eternal punishment "opens the door to all crimes [and] encourages all criminals."[63] Of course, Bayle did not believe that the denial of divine punishment necessarily led to immorality and vice, but his challenges to the theological foundations of Hell were always concealed or indirect.

Working with anonymous, posthumous, and unpublished works, Walker carefully exposes a variety of intellectuals who concealed or obscured their disbelief in orthodox Hell. In England personal ties connected Samuel Clarke (1675–1729), John Locke, and Isaac Newton in shared disbelief in orthodox Hell.[64] On the Continent debates and denunciations shed light on the disbelief of Spinoza, Bayle, and many Arminian theologians. Walker argues that "probably many disbelieved in eternal punishment, but none of them published against it in his lifetime and under his own name."[65] In 1730 William Whiston quoted Samuel Clarke as having said that "few or no thinking men" affirmed the doctrine of eternal torment.[66] Many followed Burnet's advice and publicly affirmed the traditional doctrine while privately denying it.[67] For the learned, this "double doctrine" of Hell – one for the enlightened, another for the common people – presented to the vulgar a simulated inferno designed to deter them from sin.[68]

The "double doctrine" reveals the imprint of nocturnalization on the intellectuals' loss of faith in Hell during the seventeenth and early eighteenth centuries. For men such as Spinoza, Burnet, or Newton, Hell, like darkness, had become a nonentity, with no existence of its own. But the double doctrine unearthed by Walker reveals that Hell, if not real, was still important for its social functions. Like darkness on the baroque perspective stage, Hell was created and dispelled to produce specific effects. When men who did not believe in Hell encouraged preaching and teaching about Hell as if it were real, they staged eternal damnation.

Threats of eternal damnation functioned like stage effects, reliant on the manipulation of darkness in the night. The utility of darkness in baroque theater merged with the utility of the fear of Hell in the comments of the master theater designer Joseph Furttenbach. In a guide to theater techniques published in 1663, he described how "Lucifer would be brought on quickly from Hell and let down again amidst flames and smoke. Especially when the lights are dimmed for night, this gives quite a terrifying effect."[69] The double doctrine of useful lies about Hell simulated the realm of the prince of darkness for an audience of the ignorant and undisciplined, like a flash of fire from a staged Hell, to produce "a terrifying effect."

Hell had become a theatrical display, a simulation based on darkness and illusion. This was clear to someone like Burnet. Writing against the orthodox teaching on Hell (but in Latin), Burnet was especially angered by the orthodox claim that the elect will take pleasure in viewing the eternal torment of the damned. Burnet cast this whole scene – the saved looking down on the torments of the damned in Hell – as a "spectacle on the stage." Driven to irony, he asks:

Consider a little ... what a theatre of providence this is: by far the greatest part of the human race burning in flames for ever and ever. Oh what a spectacle on the stage, worthy of an audience of God and angels! And then to delight the ear, while this unhappy crowd fills heaven and earth with wailing and howling, you have a truly divine harmony.

Of course, the double doctrine itself was ironic, affirming Hell on one level while denying it on another. Hell had become a useful artifice or a necessary evil – much like the darkness of which it was made.

8.4 DARKNESS AND ENLIGHTENMENT

Nocturnalization promoted the expression of key concepts of the early Enlightenment. Many of these ideas could be traced back to the New Philosophy of Descartes, Hobbes, or Spinoza. But the abstract, complex, and contradictory arguments of these authors could challenge just about everything in the traditional learned culture of their time. Why did issues such as ghosts, witches, and Hell emerge, among others, as key controversies?[70] A specific aspect of Hell's "dark foundations," resting on an ancient bedrock of fear, looked a little less frightening to all who experienced nocturnalization – a significant minority of Europeans in 1700. A primordial feature of daily life was now pushed back, however slightly, by the new street lighting and by improved domestic lighting. In this new era of the history of the night, women accused of witchcraft evoked pity rather than Satan's dark powers, and one could now "laugh at spirits."[71] The "esprits forts," libertines, and skeptics who challenged the reality of ghosts, witches, Hell, and the Devil were at home in the night when these conversations flourished.

Contemporaries understood the effects of nocturnalization on the religious and philosophical debates of the time. As Lewis Theobald, editor of the London journal the *Censor* complained in 1717:

> It is too frequent a provocation to a Man of my Gravity … to be obliged to sit up with a Mixture of Company, who, when the *Watchman* has gone his Round, and the Sparks are entering on their *Third* Bottle, will trouble the Board with Debates of Religion, and the Power of Faith.

At this late hour serious topics arose: "How unfit a Time is it, when either Reason nods, or is bewildered, to launch out into Subjects of such a Nature; and play the Skeptics, when Notions must be so confused." Theobald saw the clear effects of these conversations:

> I doubt not but this Custom of trifling with Immortality and Themes above the Sphere of common Reason, when the Powers of Wine have made the Tongue licentious, has been the Cause of many a Free-thinker among the alert and sanguine.[72]

He did not, however, suggest reversing the nocturnalization of London's cultured life: he goes on to explain that late hours per se are not the issue. Instead the late-night conversations on "themes above the sphere of common reason" have helped change the intellectual tone of the times, creating free-thinkers and "bigots" alike: the former are too emboldened, and the latter too frightened, by late-night "trifling with Immortality."[73] His French contemporary, the abbé Jean Terrasson (1670–1750), claimed that street lighting had led to the decline of letters: "Before this age … everyone returned home early for fear of being murdered on the street, which redounded in favor of one's work. Now, one stays out at night and works no more."[74] Social banter was replacing solitary reflection in the learned night.

The association of the night with free-thinking was widespread. The guide to Paris published in 1718 by the German Nemeitz advised young men to visit the city's "infinite number of cafés" in the afternoon or evening.[75] In particular, he noted that "the widow Lawrence in the rue Dauphine keeps a café, called the 'café des beaux esprits' where assemble certain persons who discuss all sorts of curious and spiritual matters."[76] A police report of August 1729 described such café conversations in a more alarmed tone:

There are in Paris self-proclaimed wits who talk in cafés and elsewhere of religion as a chimera … and if order is not restored, the number of atheists or deists will increase, and many people will make a religion according to their own fashion, as in England.[77]

Like the night print from the *Secret Letters* and the accounts of Morris and Thoresby examined above, these authors testify to effects of nocturnalization on the form and content of the debates of the early Enlightenment.

The magnitude of this change is revealed by comparison with a 1629 sermon of John Donne (cited in chapter 3). Preaching "in the evening" at St. Paul's in London, Donne called on the power of midnight, solitary and profound, to strip away the vanity of the day. Addressing an "atheist," Donne asked him to look ahead "but a few hours, but six hours, but until midnight." Donne assumed that at midnight his listener would be asleep, "dark and alone" in an ascetic or penitential night. Donne taunted: "Wake then; and then dark and alone, Hear God ask thee then, remember that I asked thee now, Is there a God?

and if thou darest, say No."[78] By the end of the seventeenth century, nocturnalization had transformed the scene imagined by Donne. In London midnight was precisely the time when the society of gallants, free-thinkers, and "atheists" thrived. They confronted not God, but one another in drink and conversation. Worldly banter replaced sacred introspection as a key nocturnal activity, and the late hour was more likely to strengthen their free-thinking than to challenge it. For Donne and his listeners, it was "an occasional mercy" when "A man wakes at midnight full of unclean thoughts, and hears a passing bell."[79] But by the end of the century, the social din of the coffeehouse had drowned out the lonely sound of the passing bell.[80]

The imprint of nocturnalization upon the discussions of ghosts, witchcraft, and Hell also appears in the framing concepts and rhetorical strategies of important works of the early Enlightenment. Here I examine early Enlightenment thought in terms of nocturnalization through two popular texts, Bernard Le Bovier de Fontenelle's *Entretiens sur la pluralité des mondes* (*Conversations on the Plurality of Worlds*) of 1686 and Balthasar Bekker's *De betoverde weereld* (*The World Bewitched*, 1691–94). These works, which reached especially wide audiences, present the same tension between the two aspects of nocturnalization – the discourses and practices that dispelled or denied darkness and those that created, maintained, and manipulated it – seen in the discussions of witchcraft, ghosts, and Hell above. Fontenelle presents an intellectual seduction by night, lifting the veils of nature but counseling secrecy from "les esprits ordinaires." To refute accounts of spirits, ghosts, and witches, Bekker emphasizes repeatedly that these encounters often take place "at night and in nightmares" when reason is obscured.[81] Both authors created hierarchies of perception, understanding, and enlightenment that shifted the darkness of ignorance onto differences of region and race.

8.4.1 Nature: Fontenelle's Conversations on the Plurality of Worlds

Bernard Le Bovier de Fontenelle (1657–1757) combined talents and connections in literature (he was the nephew of the brothers Corneille) with interests in astronomy, geometry, and physics. The *Conversations on the Plurality of Worlds* was his first major success when published in 1686. In 1691 he was elected to the Académie française and in 1697 appointed permanent secretary of the Académie des Sciences – a testament to his skill as an elucidator of science. He published widely as a moralist, advocate of *les modernes*, Cartesian, and biographer of science. Voltaire and Diderot hailed him as a true pioneer of the Enlightenment.

Fontenelle's extraordinarily popular *Conversations* went through thirty-two editions during the author's long lifetime; translations appeared in every major European language throughout the eighteenth century. In the year following its publication, the book was placed on the Index of Prohibited Books, and in this year Fontenelle added a sixth chapter that reinforced the book's enlightened-aristocratic tone.[82] This work and his other writings of the 1680s – some clandestine, some popular – marked "the gateway to the French Enlightenment."[83] Like the larger intellectual movement of which it is emblematic, *Conversations* engages with darkness, the night, and nocturnalization on several levels.

Consisting of six conversations at night between an unnamed marquise and a scientifically informed narrator, Fontenelle's work teaches the fundamentals of a Copernican–Cartesian universe, infinite and dynamic. Fontenelle explained astronomy through his narrator's intellectual seduction of the marquise, who is untutored in natural philosophy but possesses a keen intellect and ready curiosity. (Fontenelle's narrator describes her as "a blond ... the most beautiful woman I know.") In his Preface Fontenelle explains that "the ideas of this book are less familiar to most women than those of *The Princess of Cleves*, but they're no more obscure." His narrator then leads the marquise from ignorance and disbelief to a clear understanding of the heliocentric solar system, the movement of the earth, geographic features on the moon, eclipses, the six known planets, and the possibility of life in other solar systems. Fontenelle's conversations between the amiable narrator and his bright pupil reveal a clear parallel between the darkness deployed in the theater and the use of darkness in the presentation and transmission of natural philosophy in the

Enlightenment. As in the theater and in court culture in general, the relationship between the creation of darkness and the illumination of darkness is central to the project, yet carefully hidden.

The text opens with a letter from the narrator to a "Monsieur L***" describing the narrator's conversations with the marquise. "I'll divide them for you by evenings," the narrator explains, "because in fact we had these conversations only at night."[84] The nocturnal setting evokes the expansion of legitimate nocturnal activity in the period, as well as nightly pursuits ranging from astronomy and the theater to court life. The use of darkness – intellectual, metaphoric, and represented – to create the *Conversations* shows the text to be an intellectual expression of *both* aspects of nocturnalization. Like the nocturnal spectacles of the opera or the court, Fontenelle's nocturnal *Conversations* depict the triumph of light over darkness on one level, while on other levels fostering, maintaining, and manipulating darkness. Indeed, in the first of these nightly conversations, the narrator uses an analogy with theater to persuade the marquise to accept a new epistemology based on darkness and obscurity. Before he can explain anything about the movement of the earth or the position of the sun, he must convince the marquise to leave her "common-sense" views behind. He does this by comparing the natural world to the theater:

I have always thought that nature is very much like an opera house. From where you are at the opera you don't see the stages exactly as they are; they're arranged to give the most pleasing effect from a distance, and the wheels and counter-weights that make everything move are hidden out of sight. You don't worry, either, about how they work. Only some engineer in the pit, perhaps, may be struck by some extraordinary effect and be determined to figure out for himself how it was done. That engineer is like the philosophers. But what makes it harder for the philosophers is that, in the machinery that Nature shows us, the wires are better hidden.[85]

Fontenelle summarizes the central insight that underwrites his text: "'Whoever sees nature as it truly is simply sees the backstage area of the theater.'"[86] His frame of reference is the baroque perspective stage, with its reliance on darkness and illusion.

With the help of Fontenelle's narrator the young marquise comes to understand that there is more to nature than meets the eye. But the analogy "nature–theater" also incorporated a hierarchy of perception. As a guide to the opera published in Hamburg in 1702 explained:

Nowadays all persons of distinction seek entertainment from the opera, but among the thousands found in the boxes and seats one would scarcely meet ten who understand what happens there and how to evaluate it. Indeed, a great many in the audience do not understand one bit of it. The most important things to note at an opera are … the sets, which no one can rightly assess unless he understands painting and perspective … Above all the machines [must be] considered, as they are the best thing about the opera, filling the spirits of all members of the audience with wonder.[87]

One had to learn how to see the opera, just as Fontenelle's narrator teaches the marquise (and his many readers) how to see the natural world.

But this learning is not meant to be shared widely. When the marquise reports on the sixth evening that two "men of wit" ridiculed her knowledge of astronomy, the narrator advises her to do as he does and keep their insights secret from the ignorant: "Let us content ourselves with being a little select party who believe and not divulge our mysteries to the common people."[88] The artificial illusions of the theater, dependent on darkness, become in the *Conversations* a model for nature in a discussion that dispels intellectual darkness for the marquise while maintaining it for "the vulgar."

The hierarchy of perception presented by Fontenelle was perhaps most fully expressed in the darkness of the baroque theater. The influential guide to the baroque stage, Nicola Sabbatini's *Practica di Fabricar Scene e Machine ne'Teatri* (*Manual for Constructing Theatrical Scenes and Machines*) of 1638 makes this hierarchy explicit in practical terms:

the common or less cultivated persons are set on the tiers and at the sides, since the machines give a less perfect appearance in these places, and because such people do not observe them minutely. The persons of culture and taste should be seated on the floor of the hall, as near the middle as possible, in the second or third rows. They will have the greatest pleasure there, since … all parts of the scenery and the machines are displayed in their perfection.[89]

Sabbatini's advice maps a political and cultural hierarchy onto the perception of the stage or the world. The "cultured" see beyond the surface when they view the sets and special effects of the opera or theater. They appreciate what is concealed as well as what is visible. In the same terms, many scholars have noted Fontenelle's oblique style, discretion, and use of irony. The author expected his proper audience of *raisonneurs* to be able to read between the lines. Those at the top of the hierarchy of perception would see the more radical scope of Fontenelle's views.[90] His clandestine philosophical writings of the 1680s reveal his anticlericalism and deep skepticism regarding all systems of metaphysical thought, including revealed Christianity.[91]

8.4.2 Scripture: Bekker's The World Bewitched

The Amsterdam Reformed minister Balthasar Bekker (1634–98) unleashed an extraordinary controversy with the 1691–94 publication of his *De betoverde weereld* (*The World Bewitched*). Bekker, son of a Friesian village pastor, studied at the universities of Groningen and Franeker. He became a Cartesian but was also strongly influenced by the biblical philology of Cocceius. He earned a doctorate and served as pastor in Franeker before taking a position in Amsterdam in 1678.

When Bekker published the first two books of *The World Bewitched* in 1691, he was an experienced author with several catechisms and a work on comets to his credit. Nothing prepared him, however, for the extraordinary popularity or violent responses generated by *The World Bewitched*.[92] Across the four books of *The World Bewitched* Bekker argued "upon the same foundation of Scripture and Reason" that "the Empire of the Devil is but a Chimera, and that he has neither such a Power, nor such an Administration as is ordinarily ascribed to him."[93] As Bekker's work was translated into German, French, and English, dozens of refutations were published, as well as a few defenses of Bekker from authors more radical than he. Another edition published in England in 1700 as *The world turn'd upside down, or, A plain detection of errors, in the common or vulgar belief, relating to spirits, spectres or ghosts, daemons, witches, &c.* kept the controversy going, with an important response published by John Beaumont in 1705 (the book to which Ralph Thoresby turned for reassurance in 1712).

In *The World Bewitched* Bekker sought to make "an exact enquiry after whatever is falsely believed in the World, and the Erroneous

Opinions that are entertained without any other ground than that they are every day told and heard of."[94] Specifically, Bekker intended to deny the supposed effects of Satan and evil spirits in the world. He saw this work as a continuation of the Protestant Reformation, "a new and perhaps final phase in the perfection of Christianity."[95] As with the *Conversations*, Bekker's *World Bewitched* engages with darkness, the night, and nocturnalization on several levels. Bekker proposes to illuminate "the frightful Darkness of Paganism" while creating darkness in new hierarchies of interpretation, perception, and revelation. His attitude toward the common people, his approach to Scripture, and his understanding of the night all reveal the imprint of nocturnalization, as does the place of "pagans" in this work.

Bekker's challenge to belief in witchcraft, evil spirits, and the power of the Devil has been depicted as reflecting growing popular skepticism and disbelief in the Netherlands. But Bekker himself complained of the credulity of his congregants and the cases of supposed possession and bewitchment they brought to him. He made clear in *World Bewitched* that he was "rejecting the Opinion commonly received amongst the Vulgar, concerning the Craft and Power of the Devil." In his survey of belief in witches and demons, past and present, he noted that "for as to the common People, either Papists, Jews, or Pagans, they know nothing for the most part, but a little by hear-say; so that there is no relying upon them." Even among Protestants, "it is sure without mistake, that for the most part, what the most illiterate believe and practice, is contrary to the sense of Divines, and of all those that understand any thing in the Holy Scripture." He sounds a resigned tone: "I will have nothing to do with them [the common people] upon this subject, having often tried my self how many follies our own People say and believe, upon this account."[96] Despite the popular response to *World Bewitched*, he sought an audience among the learned – as the four detailed volumes of his study suggest. He addressed "our Doctors and our Men of letters [among whom] ... there are none so credulous as the Vulgar; however there is a very considerable difference to be seen in their Opinions, some believing almost every thing, and others almost nothing at all" about ghosts and witches.[97] Even among the most free-thinking Christians in the

Netherlands, the Collegiants, belief in spirits and diabolic possession was widespread and vigorously defended.[98]

Bekker's frustration with the credulity of the common people echoes in his sense that his own tradition has utterly misunderstood the biblical testimony regarding spirits and the Devil: "But to our great shame, most ... of us, as well as of other Sects, that pretend a Veneration for the Holy Writ, search not in it after its Sense, being satisfied with the vulgar Interpretations, and such as they have received from others." To correct this misinterpretation, Bekker proposed, like Fontenelle, to look beyond the deceptive surface of his object of study to a deeper understanding of Scripture heretofore obscured from view. This is the work of books II and III of *World Bewitched*.

From the first, Bekker's critics noted that he used an extreme accomodationist hermeneutic associated with Spinoza or Cocceius to radically reinterpret all scriptural references to angels, the Devil, and evil spirits.[99] It was this approach to Scripture, rather than his Cartesian pneumatology, that most provoked Bekker's fellow divines. As Le Clerc noted in the first French review of Bekker, "to answer Mr. Bekker solidly, they must ... prove ... that according to the rules of criticism, and the spirit of the Hebrew and Greek Languages, it is impossible to give the Scripture the sense which our author gives it."[100] A battalion of theologians proceeded to do just that. The intensity and extent of their responses made Bekker a target of attack decades after his death in 1698. A satire of 1730–31 imagined a conversation with his ghost, illustrated with a visual lampoon showing what was wrong with Bekker's approach to demons and Scripture. In Figure 8.4 Bekker is shown sieving or sifting demons out of the Christian Scriptures. Below the sieve are a series of terms used by Bekker to interpret away apparent references to evil spirits, possession, demons, etc. in the Bible: "frenzy," "melancholy," "lunacy," "enthusiasm," and "epilepsy" are among them. In this lampoon of Bekker, he is unaware that the real Devil and demons are hovering just above him. The caption reads "So Becker sorts out the devils by his art; / But the spirit of lies alone makes more doubt." This remarkable representation of Bekker's

So sichtet Becker zwar nach seiner Kunst die Teufel;
Allein, der Lügen-Geist vermehret nur den Zweifel.

Figure 8.4 Balthasar Bekker sieving devils, from *Curieuse Gespräche im Reiche derer Todten. Zweyte Unterredung oder Gespräche im Reiche derer Todten* (Leipzig and Braunschweig: s.n., 1731), frontispiece to part 2. Wellcome Library, London.

approach to Scripture directly challenges the accomodationist hermeneutic of Spinoza and Cocceius, denying the esoteric knowledge hidden from the vulgar and the hierarchy of perception on which it was based.

More broadly, Bekker's insistence on natural or physical explanations for all supposed encounters with spirits, angels, and devils led him to emphasize the power of the night and sleep to cloud the mind. Dark times and places became the antipode to the Cartesian rationality he took as his method. The accounts of Jacob wrestling with an angel (Genesis 32; Hosea 12) "occurred, as in every case before and after, in a divine night-vision," Bekker explained.[101] Likewise "the Devil … does not have the freedom to haunt the world or appear to people, except in sleep or in a dream." In books II–IV of *The World Bewitched* he explains dozens of biblical, historical, and contemporary encounters with angels, devils, or spirits as nocturnal dreams, visions, or misperceptions. Examining an account from the early church, Bekker asks "At what time" did the Devil appear to Theodoretus? "At night. He was perhaps sleeping or dreaming." One must consider the time of day when examining any account of a ghost or demon, Bekker insists.

In his refutation of dozens of ghost stories in book IV, Bekker articulates the role of the night in his analysis:

For example, when the will-o'-the-wisp sometimes pops and crackles and gives off a strange and unpleasant noise, like the whimpering or sighing of a person, it seems to some, because man's fearfulness is greater at night than by day and hinders him from using his judgment and reason properly (so that the true cause is not recognized) that all these … are the antics of Satan.

Bekker follows this observation with a series of accounts concerning ghosts and specters, emphasizing that each occurred "in the evening, while lying in bed," "in the evening hours," "in the evening twilight," or "at night in front of the bed."[102] Signaling a key theme in the later Enlightenment understanding of the night, Bekker demonstrates in example after example that the dreams and fears of the night check the use of reason. Night became the shadowy supplement to the light of reason, always dispelled but ever-present.

8.5 DARKNESS AND RACE IN THE EARLY ENLIGHTENMENT

Fontenelle and Bekker shared a mission to reorient their world by placing the familiar in a startling new contexts. The secularizing, disenchanting force of their works redrew lines of intellectual and cultural division between men and women, between Europeans and the wider world, and between the enlightened and the superstitious. Questions of human difference by gender, region, and culture play a key role in *The Conversations* and in *The World Bewitched*. Fontenelle and Bekker figure very differently in the early Enlightenment, but in their projects of education and enlightenment they both propose new zones of ignorance and new boundaries between light and darkness. Both rely on a hierarchy of perception to break down old barriers and create new divisions.

References to region and race set the stage for the last lesson in Fontenelle's explication of astronomy. At the end of the final evening, the marquise asks "'haven't I always heard that the Chinese were very great astronomers?'" The narrator agrees as to their reputation, but corrects the marquise. He explains:

In truth, I am more and more persuaded there is a certain Genius which has hitherto been confined within our Europe, or which at least has extended very little beyond it.[103]

Here the fundamental distinction between the *raisonneurs* and the vulgar is generalized across the earth. Among the Europeans some few would be enlightened; among other peoples, likely none. The Europeans stand in the same relationship to other peoples as the *raisonneurs* to the vulgar, at the summit of a hierarchy of perception and understanding. This European claim on enlightenment is underscored throughout the *Conversations* by reference to the astrological and cosmological "fallacies" of other peoples, for example in the discussion of the fear caused by eclipses or comets. Indeed, Fontenelle describes the earth itself demarcated by "complexions." Looking down from the height of understanding, Fontenelle explained:

I sometimes imagine that I'm suspended in the air, motionless while the Earth turns under me for twenty-four hours, and that I see passing under my gaze all the different faces: white, black, tawny, and olive complexions. At first there are hats, then turbans; wooly heads, then shaved heads.

The text brings the "certain Genius" of the Europeans together with the visible contrast between "societies." Trying to imagine what inhabitants of other worlds would look like, Fontenelle's narrator generalizes about human variety, observing that "'All faces in general are made on the same model, but those of two large societies – European, if you like, and African – seem to have been made on two specific models'."[104] Visible difference and intellectual superiority coincide in the construction of race.

In Fontenelle's most popular work the intellectual darkness of "the vulgar" serves as a backdrop to the glittering intellects of the marquise and the narrator, who agree not to even address the irrational masses. On a larger scale, the absurd beliefs, barbaric practices, and scientific ignorance of the "Africans and Tartars," "Iroquois," and Chinese which decorate the *Conversations* reveal the new hierarchies of race and region built into this fundamental Enlightenment text.

The relationship between gender and race in the *Conversations* is mirrored in the contemporary *Code noir* regulating slavery in France's American colonies, also published in 1687.[105] The gender inclusion of the *Conversations*, in which the beautiful blond marquise becomes the intellectual superior of the waggish noblemen who fail to understand the solar system, is consolidated as the marquise takes her place in the European superiority asserted by Fontenelle. The inclusion of enlightened women takes place in a new hierarchy which is based on European knowledge of the natural world and marked by race. The authors of the *Code noir* sought to consolidate difference through gender in similar terms by decreeing that slave status followed the maternal line. Articles 8–13 of the code asserted that all persons born in the French Caribbean colonies "will follow the condition of their mother." The maternal transmission of status in the *Code noir* contrasted sharply with French practice and noble ideology, which relentlessly emphasized the male line of descent.[106] In the colonies, however, concubinage with female slaves was an overriding factor. The *Code noir* punished such "free men who will have one or several children from their concubinage with their slaves," fining them heavily. "Beyond the fine, they [would] be deprived of the slave and the children, and … she and they be confiscated for the profit of the [royal] hospital, without ever being manumitted." Creating race as a category of division shifted the transmission of civil status from men to women in the *Code noir*. In practice, racial separation in the French Caribbean hardened in the following years, making the *Code noir* appear relatively liberal in its tolerance for mixed-race marriages, for example. The *Conversations* and the *Code noir* use gender in similar ways to draw new boundaries between learning and ignorance, or between freedom and slavery, in order to consolidate the category "European" or "French," defined in opposition to extra-European ignorance, superstition, dark skin, and servility.

In *The World Bewitched* Bekker also redefined the relationship between enlightened Europeans and "all the Pagans in the World ... in Asia ... in Africa ... and at last in America" in far-reaching terms. Bekker considered the place of these "Modern Pagans" in the first book of *The World Bewitched*, described by an English reviewer as "being but a collection of the various Opinions of Men about this Matter."[107] The reviewer thought that this first book of *The World Bewitched* "has not been attended with great Difficulties." Compared to the furor created by the Cartesian and exegetical arguments in books II and III, that was true, and few scholars today have examined the argument Bekker makes in the first book.

Contemporaries *did* respond to his discussion of belief in the Devil by "Pagans as well Ancient as Modern," however. These contemporaries, such as Benjamin Binet and John Beaumont, saw that, far from being a noncommittal survey of beliefs in demons, the Devil, ghosts, and witches in all times and places, this first section makes a bold and startling argument that redraws the dividing lines between knowledge and ignorance, shifting the "the frightful Darkness of Paganism" onto the beliefs of the other peoples of world, ancient and modern.[108]

In the first book of *The World Bewitched* Bekker assembles evidence about pagan beliefs in the Devil, demons, ghosts, witches, and spirits. He argues that "the difference to be found amongst them is not material, and must be accounted as inconsiderable, comparatively to the conformity that is betwixt them all." Bekker interprets the consistent pagan belief in evil spirits in light of his assertion, "certain and undoubted, that every Opinion that proceeds from Paganism as from its Original, cannot at the same time be founded upon the Holy Scripture." Bekker implies here and argues later that pagan belief in spirits is "contrary to true Reason, and ... Holy Scripture affords no proofs of it."[109] These pagan beliefs are thus entirely false, not merely distorted misperceptions of a Christian reality that includes ghosts, demons, and witches. The overall claim of *The World Bewitched* that spirits and demons can affect nothing material, and that the Devil's reach does not extend to the physical world, is supported in book I by this evidence, leading Bekker to conclude, for example, that "It is … sufficiently proved, by all the quotations of this Book, that there are no Miracles, Oracles, purging Fires, Apparitions of Hobgoblins or Souls, Witchcraft by Letters and Characters, or choice of Days, either in Judaism or Popery; but they draw their Original from Paganism."[110] Rooted in paganism, these beliefs had no place in the further reformation of Christianity Bekker proposed.

The place of the practices and beliefs of modern-day pagans in Bekker's argument presented the strange reversal of the well-known proof of the existence of God "by universal consent." The argument from "universal consent" functioned as a "moral proof" of the existence of God, quite familiar to Protestant and Catholic theologians alike.[111] According to this proof all nations, ancient and modern, demonstrated some belief in a god or gods. However mistaken these pagan conceptions of the Divine might be, taken as a whole they showed an inescapable underlying truth. No reasonable person would conclude that all these peoples were mistaken; therefore, there must be a real God. Among the many proofs of the existence of God taught by early modern theologians, that from universal consent was a widely cited and seen as a meta-proof, a "consequence of the force of all proofs of God."[112] Theologians distinguished, of course, between the proper Christian understanding of God based on revelation, and the misconceived, anthropomorphic pagan gods. Nonetheless, "the abuse which one does to a truth does not destroy it," as the Huguenot theologian Benjamin Binet explained, and pagan beliefs testified indirectly to the reality of the Christian God.[113] This argument for the existence of God underscored, however tentatively, the fundamental unity of humankind. Belief in the Divine was universal and evident – the only partial exceptions were the European "atheists," real or imagined, against whom seventeenth-century theologians sharpened their arguments.[114] A flicker of the true God was visible even in the darkest pagan idolatry.

Recognition of a common truth united all peoples, however distorted or idolatrous pagan understandings of God might be.

Bekker divided this unity. In his view ancient and modern pagans joined most Christians in the common and false belief in the power of the Devil, spirits, and witches. Bekker opposed himself and an enlightened minority of his readers to the superstitious pagans and Christians of his age. He proposed "to the Reader and myself, the lesson of the Apostle in his first Epistle to Timothy. 4:7: 'Reject prophane, and Old Wives Fables, and exercise thy self to Godliness.'" In the first book or section of *The World Bewitched* Bekker argued from universal error: the age-old and world-wide belief in spirits and the Devil was, according to his Cartesian understanding of spirits, impossible; according to his reading of the Bible it was unscriptural as well. Reason and Scripture showed pagans to be in utter darkness on this issue, and their ignorant belief in ghosts and spirits could only be cleared up from Cartesian and scriptural starting points. Bekker's reliance on these two sources of authority, the New Philosophy and Scripture, led him to forthrightly deny any truth or value in the beliefs of the "Pagans as well Ancient as Modern" he surveyed. This denial distinguished him from the detached but respectful tone of eighteenth-century works which developed the concept of "comparative religion," such as Picart and Bernard's *Religious Ceremonies of the World* (1723–37).[115]

Alongside the outraged responses to Bekker's application of Descartes, Spinoza, and Cocceius to questions of the Devil, ghosts, and spirits, contemporaries noted his transformation of the well-known argument from universal consent into something quite ominous: after all, Bekker's claim that belief in physically active ghosts and spirits was a universal error could be expanded by a skeptic or atheist to argue that the universal belief in a deity was just as erroneous. The most widely circulated clandestine manuscript of the early Enlightenment, the *Traité des Trois Imposteurs*, succinctly made just such a case:

Those who ignore physical causes have a natural fear born of doubt. Where there exists a power which to them is dark or unseen, from thence comes a desire to pretend the existence of invisible Beings, that is to say their own phantoms which they invoke in adversity, whom they praise in prosperity, and of whom in the end they make Gods. And as the visions of men go to extremes, must we be astonished if there are created an innumerable quantity of Divinities?[116]

The rationalist theologian Benjamin Binet responded to Bekker with a variation on the proof of the existence of God by universal consent, arguing that:

all the peoples of the world are steeped in the opinion of demons. One can infer from this confession that what they know [of demons], however erroneous it might be, must be known to them through the [demons'] operations. And to put this truth in full light, please note the following: It is impossible that one and the same belief universally spread and constantly received may be entirely false in its content.

Following the argument from universal consent, Binet explains "if demons have been universally and constantly accepted by all the peoples of the world, this knowledge must proceed from some solid cause."[117]

Evidence from other peoples was important to Bekker and to those who sought to refute the claims he made in book 1 of *The World Bewitched*. Binet accused Bekker of trying to "evade the entire supernatural order that our travelers tell us regarding the wizardry of the peoples and the operations of the devils who, they report, molest them." Binet notes that Bekker "makes fun everywhere of the credulity of humankind." Indeed, Bekker introduces his work by claiming that only with a proper (Cartesian) perspective can one understand "the inconsistency of the Properties of Bodies with those of Spirits … as I do here … as was necessary … to lay a firm foundation to this work, that is wholly grounded upon that Principle, at least as to those things that are the object of the Light of Reason." This leads Binet to argue for the universality of human experience with the Devil, unconstrained by the claims of European enlightenment. He rebukes Bekker:

Thus Sir, you mean to make us laugh by denying the operations of demons on the Brazilian peoples, for example, because they are not good enough theologians to rise to the knowledge of God and the mysteries that His word has revealed us, or because they ignore the true [i.e., Cartesian] doctrine of demons.

Binet refuses to accept the division of the world proposed by Bekker (and in the same terms by Fontenelle) into the few (European) enlightened and the many ignorant on such fundamental issues.[118] But in the course of the following century the divisions Europeans perceived between themselves and the other peoples of the world would be intensified by adding the opposition enlightened–superstitious to the existing dualities based on religion, race, and civilization.

For a few learned Europeans and a wider circle of readers and fellow-travelers, a new relationship with the night put the prince of darkness and his attendant ghosts, spirits, demons, and witches into a new light. All these shadowy figures were linked in a wave of controversy that helped define the first generation of the Enlightenment. Representations of darkness and the night – literal and metaphorical – shaped key works of the early Enlightenment, such as Fontenelle's *Conversations on the Plurality of Worlds* and Bekker's *The World Bewitched*, revealing the imprint of nocturnalization on the new ways of understanding the book of Nature and the book of Scripture at the end of the seventeenth century. Living and working in the most nocturnalized sites on earth, authors like Fontenelle and Bekker depicted themselves as conquerors of darkness, but in their works we see the displacement of darkness characteristic of nocturnalization. They each created hierarchies of perception, understanding, and enlightenment that shifted the darkness of ignorance onto new differences of region and race. And by taking the victory of light over darkness as the very emblem of their heterogeneous movement, the authors of the European Enlightenment invoked both sides of nocturnalization, dispelling and creating darkness in discourses that contrasted the light of reason with the allegedly benighted peoples of the wider world, whose beliefs about ghosts, witches, and spirits were "proof of the obscurity, that is spread over their understanding."[119]

CHAPTER NINE

Conclusion

Nocturnalization was a revolution in early modern Europe. In the seventeenth century princes and urban oligarchs alike projected their glory onto the night with illuminations and fireworks displays, while purpose-built baroque theaters could be fully darkened, day or night, to enable the complex "special effects" and illusions of baroque opera or theater. These practices reveal a new willingness to deploy and manipulate darkness and the night. And as the eighteenth century began, Europeans in cities and at royal courts – and even a few in the countryside – encountered the night equipped with more domestic lighting, new street lighting, and new, sober beverages like coffee and tea. In cities, the abandonment of curfews and the rise of the club and the coffeehouse transformed late hours into a time of polite sociability and conversation. For those exposed to increased domestic lighting, sleep itself reflected this new relationship with the night. The traditional biphasic sleep pattern of a "first" and "second" sleep began to give way to a single compressed period of nightly slumber.[1] These are all signs of the uneven but distinct march of nocturnalization.

The sources of this nocturnalization were many. In the fractured Christendom of the confessional age, religious persecution and a disorientingly heterodox world led some to seek refuge, literal or allegorical, in the night. Nicodemus, the disciple "which at the first came to Jesus by night" became the byword for those who sought the Lord at night. The persecution which sporadically drove early modern Christians into the night marks the growth of both the scope and the ambitions of the early modern state, as state churches replaced or buttressed the authority of Rome. The expanding reach of these states, focused on moral and social discipline, included the policing of the urban night. Sweeping disciplinary ambitions were seldom realized, but the policing of the urban night rested on a long tradition and was one area of relatively successful oversight. Supported by this oversight, the elites of the court and city colonized the urban night, displaying their conspicuous consumption of time (and, materially, lighting) alongside their enjoyment of coffee, tea, fine porcelain, and other luxuries. The evening and night became the time of the emerging public sphere as the respectable public used the night which the authorities had helped colonize to gather and critique those same authorities, from the most mundane to the most exalted. The breadth of nocturnalization arose from its sources in state, public, and private initiative as a key site where projects of discipline and consumption overlapped.

A 1702 article on street lighting in an anonymous Leipzig newsletter summarizes these sources of nocturnalization. Written from a burgher standpoint that criticizes both the extravagance of the court and the folly of the poor, this feigned letter from the *Captured Letters, Exchanged between Curious Persons Regarding the Current … Political and Learned World* addresses the use of the night to display status, as well as the nocturnalization of daily life at court and in cities.[2] Its title is its program: "On the vanity and waste of illuminations / and in contrast regarding the useful and necessary employment of harbor lights and also the night lanterns set up here in Leipzig."[3] It concludes with a moralizing "madrigal" on the recent history of the night:

> The Epicurean makes
> The day into his night
> Vanity likes to turn things upside-down
> These folk let themselves be fooled
> > into thinking that they can turn night into day
> > through their illuminations.
> Whoever cannot afford so much
> > that he can buy wax candles
> But despite that wants to ape the rich
> > (also gladly feasting)
> He burns boldly little oil-lights or lamps.

> The folly has spread so far
> > that even the poor must follow it
> > Although some are already stuck in direst need.
> These are the fruits of such solemnities!
> This rubbish was invented by the papists
> > and so the land was disgraced.
> It would be fine, if the money for it had to be paid
> > by the priests and not the lay folk.[4]

A far better use of artificial illumination, intoned this author, would be street lighting, which indeed was beginning in Leipzig as he wrote.

These comments identify the use of the night for spectacle with the "papists." Nocturnal spectacles and urban illuminations were used by rulers of all confessions, but the references to "papists" and "priests" by this Lutheran author remind us that religious conflict and baroque culture alike forced or led early modern Europeans into the night, and into new attitudes toward the night. The references to "illuminations" and "solemnities" also link lighting with court culture. Finally, we are told that conspicuous consumption and its imitation by social inferiors account for the spread of nocturnalization – a familiar comment in an age which satirized bourgeois gentlemen for striving to appear noble. Taken together, "commercial and urban vigor, a trend towards political absolutism, and an emphasis on orthodox, textual religions" formed a distinctly early modern compound.[5]

The nocturnalization which reshaped daily life for a significant minority of seventeenth-century Europeans separated darkness from the night as never before in Western culture. Darkness was slowly transformed from a primordial presence to a more manageable aspect of life, acquiring in the process new associations within mysticism and popular devotion, political display, respectable sociability, and learned exchange. In each of these areas nocturnalization encompassed both the triumph over darkness and the deliberate evocation or manipulation of it. Symbolically and historically, this pairing reveals a supplemented process in which stated goals were always shadowed by their contradiction or inversion.

Alone and isolated in a literal or figurative night, early modern women and men could encounter the Devil or God on an intensely personal level – be it through seduction or revelation. The early modern night opened up greater heights *and* lower depths for the Christian soul, as mystics and witches alike were made in the dark night of illumination or temptation. Georges de La Tour's popular "penitent Magdalene" (Figure 3.5), isolated by candlelight, reappears in contemporary narratives of nocturnal diabolical temptation on stage or in witch trials. The promise of the night as a path to the Divine presented by John of the Cross, Johann Arndt, John Donne, or Claude Hopil was shadowed by the demonology of their churches, which shaped the interrogations of the thousands of accused witches who confessed to attending nocturnal sabbaths and to nocturnal pacts with the Devil sealed by sexual relations. By the early modern logic of contrariety, the night that could unite the soul with God could also unite the body with Satan.

As the sovereigns of the seventeenth century embraced the night for their displays of power and provision of pleasure at court, they also articulated the supplemented process of nocturnalization – in two different ways. First, princes moved their spectacles and celebrations into the night during a century of unprecedented challenges to the very principle of royal authority. Forced by these challenges to claim that "Ecclipse and suff'rings burnish Majesty," and that "we best read the lustre in the shade,"[6] these princes and their panegyrists evoked the darkness to claim victory over it. Writing in praise of Louis XIV in 1665, André Félibien repeated a now-familiar theme: "his majesty has destroyed the grim clouds [of rebellion] which have darkened this entire kingdom for so many years, and illuminated it with rays of joyful light."[7] Figuratively and literally, the darkened backdrop enhanced the luster of would-be sun kings. Second, from Machiavelli on, the principles of statecraft emphasized the ruler's need to conceal and dissemble, and nocturnal spectacles and pleasures also served to divert both the common people and the political nation, leaving them blinded by the light of their radiant monarch.

The dark side of the colonization of the urban night can be seen in its exclusions, as the new urban nights of respectable sociability were carved out of the youthful, undisciplined, violent night life known in European cities since the high Middle Ages. The blithe comments in the *Tatler* about the movement of urban sociability into the night are shadowed by the fates of the individuals and alternate publics excluded from the nocturnal "public sphere as a 'polite zone'."[8] This new respectable night life required the discipline of even elite young men, and fostered sites with very little access for women, such as the club or coffeehouse, as well as the salon, theater, or evening ball, open only to well-born ladies. The contrast with the traditional order of the night in the countryside underscored the fashionable distinction of this urbane night.

In the taverns, coffeehouses, and clandestine printing workshops of the urban night, a respectable public discussed claims to dispel the darkness of ignorance and superstition. Despite its insistent rhetoric of light and clarity, darkness and the night were key to the early Enlightenment. Arguments that threatened established political or spiritual authority had to be expressed carefully, and many relied on the darkness of anonymity or the shadows of discretion. Enlightenment authors like Fontenelle proposed a hierarchy of perception, with troubling truths hidden from the benighted masses. And these early Enlightenment works supplemented their claims that physical darkness was a nonentity by stressing differences of region and race, sometimes marked by contrasting "white, black, tawny, and olive complexions."[9] Nocturnalization marked Enlightenment claims to dispel darkness while actually deploying it elsewhere as a deficiency that could not be corrected through the light of reason.

The early modern expansion of the legitimate social and symbolic uses of the night described in this book created new centers of power and new margins of exclusion. This supplemented process always combined the elimination of darkness with its deliberate evocation or manipulation. As Europeans consolidated the expansion of respectable daily activity into the night in the eighteenth century, they identified their intellectual and political achievements with the light of reason and the torch of civilization. As Pope's "Epitaph. Intended for Sir Isaac Newton" (1730) exclaimed: "Nature, and Nature's Laws lay hid in Night / God said, *Let Newton be!* and All was Light."

The Enlightenment's rhetoric of illumination adapted the received Christian theology of light without much appreciation for its corresponding theology of darkness. In 1796 the first Christian missionaries to the islands of the South Pacific set sail from England. Reports of the "mental ignorance and moral depravity" of the Polynesians had impressed upon the missionaries "the obligation we lay under to endeavour to call them from darkness into marvelous light."[10] To go into the night and dispel its darkness was foundational to nocturnalization. But for the peoples of this vast region between Hawai'i, Tahiti, and New Zealand, the night itself was sacred, a reflection of the creation of the world and its gods. Darkness represented a sacral connection between creation, death, and the ancestors of the living. In contrast, the light of day was profane and ordinary.[11] Ill-equipped to grasp the exalted place of darkness in Polynesian cosmology, these first missionaries could only report on the "dreadful ... darkness that envelopes the minds of those poor heathens."[12] Success was limited, and seventy-five years later another English missionary to the Polynesians encountered the same cosmology while visiting an island near Samoa:

As evening deepened into night, the heathen became quite friendly and chatty ... When pressed to embrace Christianity, they affectingly said, "We know that your God is stronger than ours; but we love darkness. To us darkness is good, light is bad."

This Polynesian exaltation of the night evoked the other side of European nocturnalization – the discourses and practices that embrace or manipulate darkness. But in response, the missionaries turned to the dominant associations of light and darkness in their tradition:

We thought of the inspired declaration, "And this is the condemnation, that light is come into the world, and men loved darkness rather than light, because their deeds were evil. For every one that doeth evil hateth the light, neither cometh to the light, lest his deeds should be reproved" (John 3:19–20).[13]

Always two-sided, the nocturnalization examined here fostered a culture ever more identified with diurnal reason, power, and authority, generating its dark others in encounters at home and around the globe.

Given the significance of the night in Western culture and its ubiquity in daily life, perhaps it is not surprising that the night intersects so many themes and developments in early modern Europe. In contrast with the attempts of some scholars to find a coherent theme in the night's history, I have approached it as part of a fundamental distinction within early modern daily life. The contrariety between daylight and darkness has served, like gender, as a category of analysis. With no claim to completeness, I have shown how this contrast between night and day was used to order and express key aspects of early modern culture, and, reciprocally, how this culture structured the multiple meanings of night and day. The night is heuristic: it provides unexpected perspectives on diurnal discourses, authorities, and institutions, whether as a view from the margins, or as those authorities and institutions seek to enter the night itself, literally or figuratively. To follow on the conclusion of Bryan Palmer in his *Cultures of Darkness: Night Travels in the Histories of Transgression* (2000): "The night can be grasped historically as both a figment of power's imaginative fears … and as an actual place and space in which the ubiquitous contestations of everyday life were fought out."[14] Understanding the content of those fears, and the outcomes of those struggles provides an incisive and encompassing perspective on early modern Europe and on the origins of modernity.

Notes

1 AN EARLY MODERN REVOLUTION

1. Louis-Sébastien Mercier, *Mon bonnet de nuit* (Neuchatel: De l'Imprimerie de la Société Typographique, 1785), ii: 7. Mercier's observation was noted by A. Roger Ekirch, *At Day's Close: Night in Times Past* (New York: W.W. Norton, 2005), p. 185.

2. Johann Dietz, *Mein Lebenslauf*, ed. Friedhelm Kemp (Munich: Kosel, 1966), pp. 156–57.

3. In 1989 Corinne Walker noted that "L'histoire de la vie nocturne sous l'Ancien Régime reste à écrire," in her "Du plaisir à la nécessité. L'apparition de la lumière dans les rues de Genève à la fin du XVIIIe siècle," in *Vivre et imaginer la ville XVIIIe–XIXe siècles*, ed. François Walter (Geneva: Éditions Zoé, 1988), pp. 97–124, p. 99, but in the last twenty years scholars have begun to conceptualize and explore the topic, foremost Alain Cabantous, *Histoire de la nuit: XVIIe–XVIIIe siècle* (Paris: Fayard, 2009); Ekirch, *Day's Close*; Daniel Ménager, *La Renaissance et la nuit*, Seuils de la modernité 10 (Geneva: Droz, 2005); Norbert Schindler, "Nächtliche Ruhestörung. Zur Sozialgeschichte der Nacht in der frühen Neuzeit," in *Widerspenstige Leute: Studien zur Volkskultur in der frühen Neuzeit* (Frankfurt: Fischer Taschenbuch Verlag, 1992), pp. 215–57, Paulette Choné, *L'Atelier des nuits. Histoire et signification du nocturne dans l'art d'Occident* (Presses universitaires de Nancy, 1992), and Mario Sbriccoli, ed., *La Notte: Ordine, sicurezza e disciplinamento in eta moderna* (Florence: Ponte alle grazie, 1991).

4. See Roman Sandgruber, "Zeit der Mahlzeit. Veränderung in Tagesablauf und Mahlzeiteinteilung in Österreich im 18. und 19. Jahrhundert," in *Wandel der Volkskultur in Europa. Festschrift für Günter Wiegelmann*, ed. Nils-Arvid Bringéus and Günter Wiegelmann (Münster: Coppenrath, 1988), pp. 459–72, and Peter Reinhart Gleichmann, "Nacht und Zivilisation," in *Soziologie: Entdeckungen im Alltäglichen. Festschrift für Hans Paul Bahrdt*, ed. Martin Baethge and Wolfgang Essbach (Frankfurt and New York: Campus, 1983), pp. 174–94.

5. See the article on coffee, tea, and chocolate by Simon Varey, "Three Necessary Drugs," *1650–1850: Ideas, Aesthetics, and Inquiries in the Early Modern Era* 4 (1998): 3–51, and the literature cited there. See also Peter Albrecht, "Coffee-Drinking as a Symbol of Social Change in Continental Europe in the Seventeenth and Eighteenth Centuries," *Studies in Eighteenth-Century Culture* 18 (1989): 91–103.

6. Anthony Horneck, *The Happy Ascetick: or, The Best Exercise, To Which Is Added, A Letter to a Person of Quality, Concerning the Holy Lives of the Primitive Christians. By Anthony Horneck, Preacher at the Savoy* ([London]: Printed by T[homas]. N[ewcomb]. for Henry Mortlock at the Phaenix in St. Paul's Church-yard, and Mark Pardoe at the Black Raven over against Bedford-House in the Strand, 1681), p. 397; the work appeared in five editions through 1724.

7. In his discussion of European night life Wolfgang Schivelbusch refers to the simultaneous rise of the "lighting of order" (i.e., street lighting) and the "lighting of festivity" and suggests that "the baroque culture of the night spawned modern night life." See his pioneering *Disenchanted Night: The Industrialization of Light in the Nineteenth Century*, trans. Angela Davies (Berkeley: University of California Press, 1988), pp. 137–39.

8. The crisis of authority which began with the Reformations of the sixteenth century created the key cultural and political conditions for nocturnalization. This study focuses on the polities which struggled, through civil war, to define and represent political power and authority in relation to Christian legitimacy in the period from 1540 to 1660: the Holy Roman Empire, the Swiss Confederation, France and the Low Countries, and the British Isles.

9. Georg Joachim Rhäticus, *Narratio Prima*, trans. Edward Rosen, in *Three Copernican Treatises*, ed. Edward Rosen (Mineola, NY: Dover Publications, 2004), p. 148. The *Narratio Prima* was first published in Danzig (1540) and Basle (1541).

10. Nicolaus Copernicus, *On the Revolutions of Heavenly Spheres*, trans. Charles Glen Wallis, ed. Stephen Hawking (Philadelphia: Running Press, 2004), p. 60 (introduction to book 2).

11. John Milton, *Il Penseroso*, 69–70, in *Complete Shorter Poems*, ed. Stella P. Revard (Malden, MA: Wiley-Blackwell, 2009), p. 55.

12. C.S. Lewis, *The Discarded Image: An Introduction to Medieval and Renaissance Literature* (Cambridge University Press, 2000), p. 111: "nowhere in medieval literature have I found any suggestion that, if we could enter the translunary world, we should find ourselves in an abyss of darkness."

13. *Ibid.*, p. 112, my emphasis.

14. Jacob Böhme, *Aurora oder Morgenröthe im Aufgang*, 1: 265; ch. 19, §4, italics mine. Böhme's works are cited from the 1730 edition as published in

facsimile: Jacob Böhme, *Sämtliche Schriften*, ed. August Faust and Will-
Erich Peuckert (Stuttgart: Fromman, 1955–61). References are by volume
and page of the facsimile edition and by book, chapter, and section of the
1730 edition.

15. Blaise Pascal, *Pensées*, ed. and trans. Roger Ariew (Indianapolis, IN:
    Hackett, 2005), p. 64 (*Pensées* S233/L201).
16. See Ekirch, *Day's Close*, pp. xxviii–xxix.
17. A. Roger Ekirch, "Sleep We Have Lost: Pre-Industrial Slumber in the
    British Isles," *American Historical Review* 106, 2 (2001): 343–86.
18. *Ibid.*, p. 364.
19. Ekirch provides more evidence in *Day's Close*, pp. 261–323. Ekirch's
    discovery of segmented or biphasic sleep raises further questions. The
    varying length of the night at northern European latitudes would seem to
    leave little time for two intervals of sleep in a summer night lasting only
    eight or nine hours.
20. In Hamburg, for example, the daily "early sermon" was given at 6 a.m.
    Wolfgang Nahrstedt, *Die Entstehung der Freizeit. Dargestellt am Beispiel
    Hamburgs* (Göttingen: Vandenhoeck & Ruprecht, 1972), pp. 103–04,
    116–18. Those who worked entirely outdoors were still tied to the start
    of the natural day. In all cities and some villages, public clocks struck the
    hours around the clock, thus making it possible to rise before dawn at a
    relatively consistent time.
21. *Ibid.*, pp. 114–41.
22. On labor at night see Hans-Joachim Voth, *Time and Work in England
    1750–1830* (Oxford: Clarendon Press, 2000). This sort of night work
    reflects the growth of domestic consumption and production proposed
    by Jan de Vries, *The Industrious Revolution: Consumer Behavior and the
    Household Economy, 1650 to the Present* (Cambridge University Press,
    2008), esp. pp. 125–30.
23. Ekirch, *Day's Close*, pp. 155–85; Cabantous, *Histoire de la nuit*, pp.
    53–68.
24. Steven Laurence Kaplan, *The Bakers of Paris and the Bread Question,
    1700–1775* (Durham, NC: Duke University Press, 1996), pp. 227–28.
25. Ekirch, *Day's Close*, pp. 163–64.
26. Cabantous, *Histoire de la nuit*, p. 54.
27. On cards see Alessandro Arcangeli, *Recreation in the Renaissance:
    Attitudes towards Leisure and Pastimes in European Culture, c. 1425–1675*
    (Basingstoke: Palgrave Macmillan, 2003), pp. 55–61, and Gary S. Cross,
    A Social History of Leisure since 1600 (State College, PA: Venture Publish-
    ing, 1990).
28. Cabantous, *Histoire de la nuit*, p. 305.
29. *Ibid.*, pp. 140–84.

30. Marc-René de Voyer d'Argenson, *Notes de René d'Argenson, lieutenant général de police, intéressantes pour l'histoire des moeurs et de la police de Paris à la fin du règne de Louis XIV* (Paris: Imprimerie Emile Voitelain et cie, 1866), p. 51.

31. Cabantous, *Histoire de la nuit*, p. 179; on London see Jennine Hurl-Eamon, *Gender and Petty Violence in London: 1680–1720* (Columbus: Ohio State University Press, 2005), pp. 165–66.

32. Quotations from the Christian Bible are taken from the 1611 King James Bible unless otherwise noted.

33. Jean-Marie Auwers, "La nuit de Nicodème (Jean 3, 2; 19, 39) ou l'ombre du langage," *Revue biblique* 97, 4 (1990): 481–503, and J.M. Bassler, "Mixed Signals: Nicodemus in the Fourth Gospel," *Journal of Biblical Literature* 108 (1989): 635–46.

34. Wolfgang Speyer, "Mittag und Mitternacht als heilige Zeiten in Antike und Christentum," in *Vivarium: Festschrift Theodor Klauser, Jahrbuch fur Antike und Christentum, Erganzungsband* 11 (Münster: Aschendorff, 1984), pp. 314–26. Speyer goes on to examine the history of noon as a liminal and dangerous time in early Christian culture and the medieval denial of noontime demons.

35. Augustine, *Confessions*, trans. F.J. Sheed, ed. Michael P. Foley (Indianapolis, IN: Hackett, 2006), p. 299.

36. Augustine, *Concerning the Nature of the Good*, in *A Select Library of the Nicene and Post-Nicene Fathers of the Christian Church*, ed. Philip Schaff (New York: The Christian Literature Co., 1886–90), IV: 354 (ch. 16) on God as the "perfect framer of all things, [who] fittingly make[s] privations of things." See Augustine, *De natura boni*, in *Corpus scriptorum ecclesiasticorum latinorum* (Vienna: Hoelder-Pichler-Tempsky, 1892), XXV, ii: 861.

37. Augustine, *Concerning the Nature of the Good*, ch. 15.

38. Alongside the Neoplatonic influences, renewed insistence on the Nicene doctrine of divine creation *ex nihilo* encouraged the growth of negative or apophatic theology, first expressed in terms of darkness in the writings of Gregory of Nyssa (d. 394). These two streams — Neoplatonic and Nicene — merged most influentially in the writings of Denys the Areopagite. See the discussions in Denys Turner, *The Darkness of God: Negativity in Christian Mysticism* (Cambridge University Press, 1995), and Andrew Louth, *The Origins of the Christian Mystical Tradition from Plato to Denys* (Oxford: Clarendon Press, 1981).

39. Denys the Areopagite, "The Mystical Theology," in *Pseudo-Dionysius: The Complete Works*, trans. Colm Luibheid; foreword and notes by Paul Rorem, Classics of Western Spirituality 54 (New York: Paulist Press, 1987), p. 138.

40. Denys the Areopagite, "Mystical Theology," in *Pseudo-Dionysius*, p. 139.
41. *Ibid.*, p. 135.
42. See Jean Verdon, *Night in the Middle Ages*, trans. George Holoch (University of Notre Dame Press, 2002), p. 212. Denys continued to influence political thought on spectacle and the display of majesty through the seventeenth century.
43. Paul Edward Dutton, *The Politics of Dreaming in the Carolingian Empire* (Lincoln: University of Nebraska Press, 1994), p. 20.
44. Thietmar of Merseburg, *Chronicon*, ed. Friedrich Kurze and J.M. Lappenberg (Hanover: Hahn, 1889), p. 9 (book 1, §12), cited in Ekirch, *Day's Close*, p. 18. See Theodore Andersson, "The Discovery of Darkness in Northern Literature," in *Old English Studies in Honour of John C. Pope*, ed. Robert B. Burlin and Edward B. Irving, Jr. (University of Toronto Press, 1974), pp. 1–14, and Alois Niederstätter, "Notizen zu einer Rechts- und Kulturgeschichte der Nacht," in *Das Recht im kulturgeschichtlichen Wandel: Festschrift für Karl Heinz Burmeister zur Emeritierung*, ed. Bernd Marquardt and Alois Niederstätter (Konstanz: UVK, 2002), pp. 173–90.
45. As quoted in Arno Borst, *Lebensformen im Mittelalter* (Frankfurt: Propyläen, 1973), pp. 146–47.
46. Chris Fitter, "The Poetic Nocturne: From Ancient Motif to Renaissance Genre," *Early Modern Literary Studies* 3, 2 (1997): 2.1–61. Online at http://purl.oclc.org/emls/03-2/fittnoct.html.
47. Mary W. Helms, "Before the Dawn: Monks and the Night in Late Antiquity and Early Medieval Europe," *Anthropos* 99 (2004): 177–91, and Verdon, *Night in the Middle Ages*, pp. 208–15.
48. Helms, "Before the Dawn," pp. 179, 181, 185. See below, ch. 3, n. 59.
49. Deborah Youngs and Simon Harris, "Demonizing the Night in Medieval Europe: A Temporal Monstrosity?" in *The Monstrous Middle Ages*, ed. Bettina Bildhauer and Robert Mills (University of Toronto Press, 2003), pp. 134–54; Tzotcho Boiadjiev, "Loca nocturna – Orte der Nacht," in *Raum und Raumvorstellungen im Mittelalter*, ed. Jan A. Aertsen and Andreas Speer, Miscellanea Mediaevalia 25 (Berlin: de Gruyter, 1997): 439–51.
50. Their conclusions agree with the overview provided by the French medievalist Jean Verdon in his *Night in the Middle Ages*, p. 3.
51. Josef Koch, "Über die Lichtsymbolik im Berich der Philosophie und der Mystik des Mittelaters," *Studium Generale* 13, 11 (1960): 653–70. Nicolas of Cusa moved decisively from the dominant light–dark opposition to a sense of the complementarity and inseparability of light and darkness. This renewed sense of the value of darkness appears in the two central principles of his theology: his emphasis on the infinite distance

between human knowledge and the Divine (which can therefore only be approached through a "docta ignorantia"), and his fundamental understanding of God as the "coincidentia oppositorum" in which all contradictions become one.

52. I see the expansion of "daily life" from the subject of research to a category of historical analysis as analogous to the development from women as the subject of "women's history" to gender as a "useful category of historical analysis" – drawing on the landmark article of Joan W. Scott, "Gender: A Useful Category of Historical Analysis," *American Historical Review* 91, 5 (1986): 1053–75.

53. Recent surveys suggest that *Alltagsgeschichte* focuses more on everyday agency *in response to* complex ideologies, and less on the role of the everyday in the intellectual and cultural constitution of those ideologies. See Paul Steege, Andrew Stuart Bergerson, Maureen Healy, and Pamela E. Swett, "The History of Everyday Life: A Second Chapter," *Journal of Modern History* 80, 2 (2008): 358–78, esp. "Agency," pp. 368–73; and Alf Lüdtke, "Alltagsgeschichte – ein Bericht von unterwegs," *Historische Anthropologie* 11, 2 (2003): 278–95.

54. Youngs and Harris, "Demonizing the Night," p. 150.

55. Giovanni Paolo Marana, *Lettre d'un Sicilien à un de ses amis*, ed. Valentin Dufour, Anciennes descriptions de Paris 9 (Paris: A. Quantin, 1883), pp. 50–51. See Yvonne Bellenger, "La description de Paris dans la 'Lettre d'un Sicilien' datée de 1692," in *La découverte de la France au XVIIe siècle*, ed. Centre méridional de rencontres sur le XVIIe siècle (Paris: CNRS, 1980), pp. 119–32.

56. See Gillian Bennett, "Ghost and Witch in the Sixteenth and Seventeenth Centuries," in *New Perspectives on Witchcraft, Magic and Demonology*, ed. Brian P. Levack, vol. III, *Witchcraft in the British Isles and New England* (New York: Routledge, 2001), pp. 259–70.

2 DARKNESS AND THE DEVIL, 1450–1650

1. Thinking with the night about the secular world, ranging from romantic love to astronomy, is an immense aspect of this topic which must be left for discussion in a later project. Important work on the secular night in early modern Europe has been done by Daniel Ménager, *La Renaissance et la nuit*, Seuils de la modernité 10 (Geneva: Droz, 2005).

2. Hans Sachs, *Die Wittenbergisch Nachtigall*, ed. Gerald H. Seufert (Stuttgart: Reclam, 1974), p. 17: "Durch auß und auß die lange nacht / Und synd auch aller erst erwacht / So die Nachtigall so hell synget / Und des tages gelentz her dringet."

3. *Ibid.*, p. 19: "Wer die lieplich nachtigall sey / Die uns den liechten tag auß schrey / Ist Doctor Martinus Luther / Zu Wittenberg Augustiner / Der uns auffwecket von der nacht."

4. *Ibid.*, p. 27, vv. 326–29: "Hond uns den glauben nye erklert / In Christo der uns sälig macht / Diser mangel bedeüt die nacht / Darinn wir alle irr seind gangen."

5. *Exsurge Domine*, from www.papalencyclicals.net/Leo10/l10exdom.htm.

6. *D. Martin Luthers Werke. Kritische Gesamtausgabe* (Weimar: H. Böhlaus Nachfolger, 1883–), XVIII: 551–787 (see section 3 of *De servo arbitrio*).

7. Thomas More, *The Dialogue Concerning Tyndale by Sir Thomas More, Reproduced in Black Letter Facsimile from the Collected Edition (1557) of More's English Works*, ed. W.E. Campbell and A.W. Reed (London: Eyre and Spottiswoode, 1927), p. 23.

8. Sachs, *Wittenbergisch Nachtigall*, p. 18.

9. More, *Dialogue Concerning Tyndale*, p. 240.

10. Desiderius Erasmus, *Collected Works of Erasmus. Literary and Educational Writings*, ed. Craig Ringwalt Thompson, Jesse Kelley Sowards, Anthony Levi, Elaine Fantham, Erika Rummel, and Jozef Ijsewijn (University of Toronto Press, 1978), pp. xix–xx.

11. *Ibid.*, pp. 175–76.

12. "Schleitheim Articles / Brotherly Union (1527)," trans. Cornelius J. Dyck *et al.*, in *Confessions of Faith in the Anabaptist Tradition, 1527–1660*, ed. with an Introduction by Karl Koop, Classics of the Radical Reformation 11 (Kitchener, Ontario: Pandora Press, 2006), p. 28.

13. "Wismar Articles (1554)," *ibid.*, p. 103.

14. C. Arnold Snyder, ed., *Biblical Concordance of the Swiss Brethren, 1540*, trans. Gilbert Fast and Galen Peters; Introduction by Joe Springer, Anabaptist Texts in Translation 2 (Kitchener, Ontario: Pandora Press, 2001), pp. 48–49 on "light".

15. "Good things of the day begin to droop and drowse, / Whiles night's black agents to their preys do rouse." *Macbeth* 3.2.52–53.

16. "La nuit des fantômes volans / Claquetans leurs becs violans / En sifflant mon âme espovantent," cited in Robert Mandrou, *Introduction to Modern France 1500–1640. An Essay in Historical Psychology*, trans. R.E. Hallmark (New York: Holmes & Meier, 1976), p. 56.

17. Edmund Spenser, *The Faerie Queen. Books Three and Four*, ed. Dorothy Stephens (Indianapolis, IN: Hackett Publishing, 2006), p. 87 (book 3, canto 4).

18. "Schrecken und Stille und dunkeles Grausen, finstere Kälte bedecket das Land, / Izt schläft, was Arbeit und Schmerzen ermüdet, diß sind der traurgien Einsamkeit Stunden." Andreas Gryphius, "Mitternacht,"

in *Lyrische Gedichte von Andreas Gryphius*, ed. Julius Tittmann (Leipzig: F.A. Brockhaus, 1880), p. 25.

19. Simon Dach, *Werke*, ed. Hermann Oesterley (Hildesheim and New York: Georg Olms Verlag, 1977), pp. 151–52:

> Ich trage grauen für der nacht
> Und habe gantz mich außgewacht,
> Mein schlaff ist pein und sorgen,
> Ich sehne mich
> So sehr, als sich
> Kein wächter, nach dem morgen.

20. See A. Roger Ekirch, *At Day's Close: Night in Times Past* (New York: W.W. Norton, 2005), pp. 7–30; Piero Camporesi, *The Fear of Hell: Images of Damnation and Salvation in Early Modern Europe* (University Park, PA: Pennsylvania State University Press, 1991); and Jean Delumeau, *La Peur en Occident (XIVe–XVIIIe siècles): Une cité assiégée* (Paris: Fayard, 1978), esp. pp. 87–97, "La peur de la nuit."

21. Thomas Nashe, *The Terrors of the Night, or A Discourse of Apparitions*, in *Selected Writings*, ed. Stanley Wells (Cambridge, MA: Harvard University Press, 1965), pp. 141–75, p. 175.

22. *Ibid.*, p. 146.

23. *Ibid.*, pp. 146–48.

24. Ann Pasternak Slater, "Macbeth and the Terrors of the Night," *Essays in Criticism* 28 (1978): 112–28.

25. See Jean-Marie Maguin, *La nuit dans le théâtre de Shakespeare et de ses prédécesseurs* (Lille: Service de reproduction des thèses, Université de Lille III, 1980), pp. 742–96, 931–42, and the essays by Abiteboul, Costa de Beauregard, and Mailhol in Simone Kadi, ed., *La nuit dans les oeuvres de Shakespeare et de ses contemporains, l'invisible présence*. Recherches valenciennoises 5 (Presses universitaires de Valenciennes, 2000).

26. Pasternak Slater, "Macbeth," pp. 114, 125–27. See Ludwig Lavater (1527–86), *Of ghostes and spirites walking by nyght, 1572*, ed. with an Introduction and Appendix by J. Dover Wilson and May Yardley (Oxford University Press, 1929). The 1572 edition is titled *Of ghostes and spirites walking by nyght, and of strange noyses, crackes and sundry forewarnynges, whiche commonly happen before the death of menne, great slaughters, & alterations of kyngdomes. One booke, written by Lewes Lauaterus of Tigurine. And translated into Englyshe by R.H.* [i.e., Robert Harrison]. Thomas Nashe seems to have read the book; Shakespeare may have been familiar with the second English edition of 1596.

27. Lavater, *Of ghostes and spirites*, p. 98. Thomas Browne denounces ghosts in similar terms in his *Religio medici*: "those apparitions and ghosts of

departed persons are not the wandering souls of men, but the unquiet walks of devils." [*A true and full copy of that which was most imperfectly and surreptitiously printed before vnder the name of*] Religio medici ([London]: Printed for Andrew Crook, 1643), pp. 85–86.

28. Lavater, *Of ghostes and spirites*, p. 90. The author sometimes presents the night as an active deceiver: "for the night beguileth mens eyes. And therefore none ought to maruell, if trauellers towardes night or at midnight, mistake stones, trees, stubbes, or such like to be sprites or elues" (p. 20).

29. Pasternak Slater, "Macbeth," pp. 127–28, makes this comparison.

30. Lavater, *Of ghostes and spirites*, p. 173.

31. Jean-Claude Mailhol, "Les créatures des ténèbres dans la tragédie domestique élisabéthaine et jacobéenne," in *La nuit dans les oeuvres de Shakespeare*, ed. Kadi, pp. 231–76, and Anthony Harris, *Night's Black Agents: Witchcraft and Magic in Seventeenth-Century English Drama* (Manchester University Press, 1980), p. 50.

32. Faustus "beschwuer also den Teuffel inn der Nacht zwischen Neun unnd zehen Uhr," H.G. Haile, ed., *Das Faustbuch nach der Wolfenbüttler Handschrift* (Berlin: E. Schmidt Verlag, 1963), p. 33; "Das Dritte *Colloquium Doctor Faustii* mit dem Gaist und seiner gethonen *Promission*," p. 38.

33. David Wootton, ed., *Doctor Faustus with The English Faust Book* (Indianapolis, IN: Hackett Publishing, 2005), pp. 67–154 (the text of the *English Faust Book*); here pp. 69–75.

34. David Scott Kastan, ed., *Doctor Faustus: A Two-Text Edition (A-text, 1604; B-text, 1616)* (New York: W.W. Norton, 2005), p. 63.

35. See Richard Halpern, "Marlowe's Theater of Night: Doctor Faustus and Capital," *English Literary History* 71, 2 (2004): 455–95; here 473–82.

36. Kastan, ed., *Doctor Faustus*, 1.3 (emphasis mine), p. 63. In Marlowe's text the pact that begins at midnight also ends at midnight, twenty-four years later, as Roy T. Eriksen has noted in his "'What resting place is this?' Aspects of Time and Place in *Doctor Faustus* (1616)," *Renaissance Drama* n.s. 16 (1985): 49–74.

37. Recent surveys are provided by Robin Briggs, *The Witches of Lorraine* (Oxford University Press, 2007), pp. 1–8, and Jonathan B. Durrant, *Witchcraft, Gender, and Society in Early Modern Germany*, Studies in Medieval and Reformation Traditions 124 (Leiden: Brill, 2007), Introduction and pp. 243–54. See the recent debate between Monika Neugebauer-Wölk, "Wege aus dem Dschungel: Betrachtungen zur Hexenforschung," *Geschichte und Gesellschaft* 29, 2 (2003): 316–47 and Gerd Schwerhoff, "Esoterik statt Ethnologie? Mit Monika Neugebauer-Wölk unterwegs im Dschungel der Hexenforschung," online at www.historicum.net/themen/hexenforschung/thementexte/forschungsdebatten/ (text dated August 1, 2007).

38. See Robin Briggs, *Witches and Neighbors: The Social and Cultural Context of European Witchcraft* (New York: Viking Press, 1996), p. 328.

39. See also William Monter, "Witch Trials in Continental Europe 1560–1660," in *Witchcraft and Magic in Europe: The Period of the Witch Trials*, ed. Bengt Ankarloo and Stuart Clark (Philadelphia: University of Pennsylvania Press, 2002), pp. 1–52. Scholars regard England as a variation within the patterns of European witch beliefs, but not as an exception to the discourses and practices that drove witchcraft persecutions. See Stuart Clark, *Thinking with Demons: The Idea of Witchcraft in Early Modern Europe* (Oxford: Clarendon Press, 1997) on the integration of English, Scottish, and Continental evidence.

40. Including Briggs, *Witches of Lorraine*; Elisabeth Biesel, *Hexenjustiz, Volksmagie und soziale Konflikte im lothringischen Raum*, Trierer Hexenprozesse 3 (Trier: Spee, 1997); Jean-Claude Diedler, *Démons et sorcières en Lorraine. Le bien et le mal dans les communautés rurales de 1550 à 1660* (Paris: Messene, 1996); Eva Labouvie, *Zauberei und Hexenwerk. Ländlicher Hexenglaube in der frühen Neuzeit* (Frankfurt: Fischer Taschenbuch Verlag, 1991); and Walter Rummel, *Bauern, Herren und Hexen: Studien zur Sozialgeschichte sponheimischer und kurtrierischer Hexenprozesse 1574–1664* (Göttingen: Vandenhoeck & Ruprecht, 1991).

41. Franz Irsigler, "Einführung," in *Methoden und Konzepte der historischen Hexenforschung*, ed. Herbert Eiden, Rita Voltmer, Gunther Franz, and Franz Irsigler, Trierer Hexenprozesse 4 (Trier: Spee, 1998), p. 10, and Walter Rummel, "Vom Umgang mit Hexen und Hexerei. Das Wirken des Alltags in Hexenprozessen und die alltägliche Bedeutung des Hexenthemas," *ibid.*, p. 102.

42. Labouvie, *Zauberei und Hexenwerk*, pp. 14–154.

43. Hanns Bächtold-Stäubli, V. Knoblauch-Matthias, and Eduard Hoffmann-Krayer, *Handwörterbuch des deutschen Aberglaubens* (Berlin: de Gruyter, 1932), similar material in Paul Sébillot, *Le folk-Lore de France*, vol. 1, *Le Ciel et la Terre* (Paris: Librairie orientale & américaine, 1904), pp. 134–64, "La Nuit".

44. Manfred Wilde, *Die Zauberei- und Hexenprozesse in Kursachsen* (Cologne, Weimar, and Vienna: Böhlau, 2003), pp. 253–65.

45. Wolfgang Behringer, *Shaman of Oberstdorf: Chonrad Stoeckhlin and the Phantoms of the Night*, trans. H.C. Erik Midelfort (Charlottesville, VA: University Press of Virginia, 1998), p. 36.

46. Carlo Ginzburg, *The Night Battles: Witchcraft and Agrarian Cults in the Sixteenth and Seventeenth Centuries*, trans. John and Anne Tedeschi (London: Routledge & Kegan Paul, 1983), pp. 1–16, and Behringer, *Shaman*, pp. 91–104.

47. Richard Bernard, *A guide to grand-iury men diuided into two bookes: in the first, is the authors best aduice to them what to doe, before they bring in a billa vera in cases of witchcraft … In the second, is a treatise touching witches good and bad, how they may be knowne, euicted, condemned, with many particulars* (London: Printed by Felix Kingston, 1627), p. 115.

48. Ginzburg, *Night Battles*, chs. 3–4, and Behringer, *Shaman*, pp. 89–118.

49. See Clark, *Thinking with Demons*, pp. 457–88, and the literature cited there.

50. George Gifford, *A dialogue concerning [H]witches and witchcrafts* (London: Printed by Iohn Windet for Tobie Cooke and Mihil Hart, 1593), fo. G(1). See Alan Macfarlane, "A Tudor Anthropologist: George Gifford's *Discourse* and *Dialogue*," in *The Damned Art: Essays in the Literature of Witchcraft*, ed. Sydney Anglo (London: Routledge & Kegan Paul, 1977), pp. 140–55, and Scott McGinnis, "'Subtiltie' Exposed: Pastoral Perspectives on Witch Belief in the Thought of George Gifford," *Sixteenth Century Journal* 33, 3 (2002): 665–86.

51. Malcolm Gaskill, "Witches and Witnesses in Old and New England," in *Languages of Witchcraft: Narrative, Ideology and Meaning in Early Modern Culture*, ed. Stuart Clark (Basingstoke: Macmillan, 2001), pp. 55–80, and Rummel, *Bauern, Herren und Hexen*, pp. 284ff.

52. Bernard, *Guide to grand-iury men*, pp. 235–36.

53. Eva Labouvie, "Hexenspuk und Hexenabwehr: Volksmagie und volkstümlicher Hexenglaube," in *Hexenwelten: Magie und Imagination vom 16.–20. Jahrhundert*, ed. Richard van Dülmen (Frankfurt: Fischer Taschenbuch-Verlag, 1987), pp. 49–93.

54. See the complete original text, *ibid.*, p. 84. Labouvie describes the trial in *Zauberei und Hexenwerk*, pp. 161–65.

55. Like the demonological works they sometimes illustrated, images of the witches and the sabbath reflected both popular and learned views of the relationship between witchcraft, the Devil, and the night. Representations of individual witches encountering the Devil or practicing *maleficia* were less often set at night; images of the witches' dance or sabbath either indicate no time of day or are clearly nocturnal. Space does not permit a full review of the rich scholarship on the visual side of early modern witchcraft; see Charles Zika, *The Appearance of Witchcraft: Print and Visual Culture in Sixteenth-Century Europe* (London: Routledge, 2007), and the literature cited there.

56. See Virginia Krause, "Confessional Fictions and Demonology in Renaissance France," *Journal of Medieval and Early Modern Studies* 35, 2 (2005): 327–48.

57. Heinrich von Schultheis, *Eine Außführliche Instruction Wie in Inquisition Sachen des grewlichen Lasters der Zauberey gegen Die Zaubere der Göttlichen*

*Majestät und der Christenheit Feinde ohn gefahr der Unschuldigen ʒu proce-
diren ... In Form eines freundlichen Gesprächs gestelt* (Cologne: bey Hinrich
Berchem, 1634).

58. Durrant, *Witchcraft, Gender, and Society*, p. 258. Several of the eighty-four
    items in this Eichstätt interrogatory focus on the connection between sex
    and the night, for example "On what occasion did she come to know her
    spouse ...? Whether they did not meet together at night and confer with
    each other alone [before marriage]?" (pp. 256–57, 259).

59. Richard van Dülmen, "Imaginationen des Teuflischen," in *Hexenwelten*,
    ed. van Dülmen, pp. 94–130; here p. 102.

60. The confession is published with Jürgen Macha, *Deutsche Kanʒleisprache
    in Hexenverhörprotokollen der Frühen Neuʒeit* (Berlin and New York: de
    Gruyter, 2005) on the enclosed CD-ROM, under "St. Maximin 1587."
    For a nearly identical confession from Barbara Erbin of the Alpine vil-
    lage of Oberstdorf (home of Chonrad Stoeckhlin) in 1587, see Behringer,
    Shaman, pp. 107–08.

61. Elisabeth Biesel, "'Die Pfeifer seint alle uff den baumen gesessen':
    Hexensabbat in der Vorstellungswelt einer ländlichen Bevölkerung," in
    Methoden und Konʒepte der historischen Hexenforschung, ed. Eiden *et al.*, pp.
    298–302.

62. "Hat also gebondenn gestanden, vnndt bekendt, eß sei ein Schwartzer
    man hinder seinem hauß vur Zwolff Jahrn, Zwischent tag vnnd nachtt Zu
    Ime Kommenn, alß er Seiner hausfrauwen Langwirriger Krankheit hal-
    ben beschwerdtt, vnnd bekummertt geweßen, derselb hab gesagt, solt nit
    so Zaghafftt sein, Die Sachenn wurden Zum besten Kommen, derselb hab
    Ime Zugemuutet, er soll gott Verlaugnenn, vnnd seiner Motter, vnnd Ime
    Zustendig sein, er habs aber nit gethann." Macha, *Hexenverhörprotokollen*,
    enclosed CD-ROM, under "Trier 1591".

63. John Linwood Pitts, *Witchcraft and Devil Lore in the Channel Islands*
    (Guernsey: Guille-Allès Library, 1886), pp. 33–51.

64. Macha, *Hexenverhörprotokollen*, enclosed CD-ROM, under "St. Maximin
    1587."

65. Pitts, *Witchcraft*, p. 22.

66. As Dülmen has in his "Imaginationen des Teuflischen." See also Nicole
    Jacques-Lefèvre and Maxime Préaud, eds., *Le sabbat des sorciers en Europe
    (XVe–XVIIIe siècles)* (Grenoble: Éditions Jérôme Millon, 1993).

67. Heinrich Institoris and Jacob Sprenger, *Malleus maleficarum*, ed. and
    trans. Christopher S. Mackay (Cambridge University Press, 2006), II:
    63. Daniel Ménager has observed that the *Malleus* "does not establish a
    relationship between the Sabbath and the night," *La renaissance et la nuit*,
    p. 153, n. 5., challenging Jean Delumeau's association of the witches' sab-
    bath with the night before the second half of the sixteenth century.

68. Institoris and Sprenger, *Malleus maleficarum*, ed. and trans. Mackay, II: 45.

69. See Hans Peter Broedel, *The Malleus Maleficarum and the Construction of Witchcraft: Theology and Popular Belief* (Manchester University Press, 2003), pp. 101–21.

70. Institoris and Sprenger, *Malleus maleficarum*, ed. and trans. Mackay, II: 248, 73–111. Even in this discussion of incubi and succubi, the traditional theme of nocturnal assault predominates over the sense of seduction in the night.

71. *2 Henry VI*, 1.4.19–23. Fitter, "Poetic Nocturne," refers to this same passage to illustrate a more general point about darkness and evil in early modern literature.

72. Current scholarship estimates that between 40,000 and 60,000 persons were executed during the sixteenth and seventeenth centuries. See Merry E. Wiesner, *Witchcraft in Early Modern Europe* (Boston: Houghton Mifflin, 2007), p. 1.

73. Jean Bodin, *On the Demon-Mania of Witches*, trans. Randy A. Scott with an Introduction by Jonathan L. Pearl, Renaissance and Reformation Texts in Translation 7 (Toronto: Centre for Reformation and Renaissance Studies, 1995), pp. 114–17.

74. Henry Boguet, *Discours exécrable des sorciers: ensemble leur procez, faits depuis deux ans en ça, en divers endroicts de la France ... Seconde édition* (Paris: D. Binet, 1603), p. 168.

75. Michael Dalton, *The Countrey Justice* (London: Printed for the Societie of Stationers, 1618), p. 243.

76. Behringer, *Shaman*, pp. 23–34.

77. Boguet, *Discours exécrable des sorciers*, p. 47.

78. Peter Binsfeld, *Tractat von Bekanntnuss der Zauberer unnd Hexen*, ed. Hiram Kümper (Vienna: Mille Tre Verlag, Schächter, 2004), p. 218.

79. Martin Del Rio, *Investigations into Magic*, ed. and trans. P.G. Maxwell-Stuart (Manchester University Press, 2000), p. 269.

80. Nicolas Remy, *Demonolatry*, ed. Montague Summers, trans. E.A. Ashwin (London: J. Rodker, 1930), pp. 54–55.

81. Pierre de Lancre, *Tableau de l'inconstance des mauvais anges et démons: où il est amplement traité des sorciers et de la sorcellerie*, ed. Nicole Jacques-Lefèvre (Paris: Aubier, 1982), p. 96.

82. Clark, *Thinking with Demons*, pp. 11–105. This logic was especially coherent for Protestants, who had largely eliminated regular night-time worship from their traditions. Christians forced by persecution to meet at night used their lived experience to refigure the association of nocturnal gatherings with evil; see below, chapter 3.

83. Bernard, *Guide to grand-iury men*, p. 263.

84. Clark, *Thinking with Demons*, pp. 134–35.
85. Pierre Le Loyer, *Discours et histoires des spectres, visions et apparitions des esprits, anges, démons et ames, se monstrans visibles aux hommes: divisez en huict livres … par Pierre Le Loyer* (Paris: Chez Nicolas Buon, 1605), p. 356: "La nuict & les tenebres sont par eux desirees & cherchees, & Satan leur Prince pour tiltres d'honneur s'appelle Prince des tenebres. C'est le temps où les hommes & leurs corps bien nourris dorment & reposent subjects aux embusches des Diables, enclins à leurs tentations, & faciles à esmouvoir aux sensualitez & defits de la chair."
86. John Norden, *A pensiue mans practise Very profitable for all personnes* (London: Printed by Hugh Singleton, 1584), fo. 13.
87. Pierre Le Loyer, *IIII. livres des spectres, ou apparitions et visions d'esprits, anges et démons se monstrans sensiblement aux hommes* (Angers: G. Nepueu, 1586), p. 515.
88. The article by Lyndal Roper, "Witchcraft and the Western Imagination," *Transactions of the Royal Historical Society* 16 (2006): 117–41, opens with Ziarnko's sabbath image and De Lancre's treatise (pp. 117–19).
89. Pierre de Lancre, *Tableau de l'inconstance des mauuais anges et démons, ou il est amplement traicté des sorciers & de la sorcellerie* (Paris: Chez Iean Berjon, 1612), engraving by Jan Ziarnko facing title page, legend "A". The accused sometimes tried to avoid naming other suspects by claiming it was too dark at the sabbath to recognize anyone else: see van Dülmen, "Imaginationen des Teuflischen," pp. 114–15.
90. See Labouvie, "Hexenspuk und Hexenabwehr," p. 87, on printed and popular representations of the sabbath.
91. Teresa of Avila, *The Complete Works of St Teresa of Jesus*, 3 vols., trans. and ed. E. Allison Peers (London: Sheed and Ward, 1972–75), I: 215–16.
92. Nashe, *Terrors of the Night*, p. 146.
93. Jean-Pierre Camus, *A Draught of Eternity*, trans. Miles Carr (Douai: By the widowe of Marke Wyon, at the signe of the Phœnix, 1632), pp. 100–01.
94. John Milton, *Paradise Lost*, ed. David Scott Kastan and Merritt Yerkes Hughes (Indianapolis, IN: Hackett Publishing, 2005), pp. 10, 192; I.61–63, VI.380.
95. Kastan, ed., *Doctor Faustus*, p. 17; 1.3.76–80 (A-text).

3 SEEKING THE LORD IN THE NIGHT, 1530–1650

1. Maria Rzepinska, "Tenebrism in Baroque Painting and Its Ideological Background," *Artibus et Historiae* 13, 7 (1986): 91–112. See also Paulette Choné, *L'Atelier des nuits. Histoire et signification du nocturne dans l'art*

d'Occident (Presses universitaires de Nancy, 1992), and Brigitte Borchhardt-Birbaumer, "Braunlicht und Seelenfunke – Das Nachtstück zur Zeit der Gegenreformation," in *Die Nacht,* ed. Peter-Klaus Schuster, Christoph Vitali, and Ilse von Zur Mühlen (Munich: Haus der Kunst, 1998), pp. 83–94.

2. Rzepinska, "Tenebrism," p. 92.
3. Chris Fitter, "The Poetic Nocturne: From Ancient Motif to Renaissance Genre," *Early Modern Literary Studies* 3, 2 (1997): paragraphs 1, 62. Online at http://purl.oclc.org/emls/03-2/fittnoct.html.
4. Edward Reynolds, *An explication of the hundreth and tenth Psalme ... Being the substance of severall sermons preached at Lincolns Inne* (London: Imprinted by Felix Kyngston for Robert Bostocke, 1632), p. 371 (original emphasis).
5. Carl Krause, *Euricius Cordus: Eine biographische Skizze aus der Reformationszeit* (Hanau: König, 1863), p. 92; Ulman Weiss, "Nicodemus Martyr – ein unbekanntes Pseudonym Sebastian Francks?" *Archiv für Reformationsgeschichte* 85 (1994): 163–79, 167; Frederik Casparus Wieder, *De Schriftuurlijke liedekens, de liederen der Nederlandsche hervormden tot op het jaar 1566* ('s-Gravenhage: M. Nijhoff, 1900), pp. 53–54.
6. Erika Rummel, *The Confessionalization of Humanism in Reformation Germany* (Oxford University Press, 2000), pp. 75, 102–20; *D. Martin Luthers Werke. Kritische Gesamtausgabe* (Weimar: H. Böhlaus Nachfolger, 1883–), XLVII: 1–28.
7. See Stefania Tutino, "Between Nicodemism and 'Honest' Dissimulation: The Society of Jesus in England," *Historical Research* 79, 206 (2006): 534–53; Nikki Shepardson, "The Rhetoric of Martyrdom and the Anti-Nicodemite Discourses in France, 1550–1570," *Renaissance and Reformation/ Renaissance et Reforme* 27, 3 (2003): 37–61; John S. Oyer, "Nicodemites among Württemberg Anabaptists," *Mennonite Quarterly Review* 71, 4 (1997): 487–514, and the literature cited there.
8. The name "Huguenot" itself, in use by about 1552, was associated with worship at night. Beza reported that "At Tours there was a superstitious belief that the ghost of Hugh Capet roamed through the city at night. As the Protestants held their meetings in the night, they were derisively called Huguenots, as if they were the troop of King Hugh." George Park Fisher, *The Reformation* (New York: C. Scribner's Sons, 1906), p. 227. See also Philip Benedict, *Christ's Churches Purely Reformed: A Social History of Calvinism* (New Haven: Yale University Press, 2002), p. 143.
9. See Charles L. Kuhn, "The Mairhauser Epitaph: An Example of Late Sixteenth-Century Lutheran Iconography," *Art Bulletin* 58, 4 (1976): 542–46.

10. Patrick Collinson, *The Elizabethan Puritan Movement* (London: Routledge, 1982), p. 21.

11. John Foxe, *Actes and monuments of matters most speciall and memorable, happenyng in the Church … from the primitiue age to these latter tymes of ours, with the bloudy times, horrible troubles, and great persecutions agaynst the true martyrs of Christ, sought and wrought as well by heathen emperours, as nowe lately practised by Romish prelates, especially in this realme of England and Scotland. Newly reuised and recognised, partly also augmented, and now the fourth time agayne published*, 2 vols. (London: Imprinted by Iohn Daye, dwellyng ouer Aldersgate beneath S. Martins, 1583), pp. 2075–76. See J.W. Martin, "The Protestant Underground Congregations of Mary's Reign," *Journal of Ecclesiastical History* 35, 4 (1984): 522–23.

12. Théodore de Bèze, *Histoire ecclésiastique des églises réformées au royaume de France*, ed. G. Baum and Eduard Cunitz (Paris: Librairie Fischbacher, 1883), 1: 345. For evidence of Reformed services at night in Paris in 1557, see Barbara Diefendorf, *The Saint Bartholomew's Day Massacre: A Brief History with Documents* (Boston, MA: Bedford/St Martin's, 2009), pp. 48–56. On the massacre as nocturnal state violence, see Alain Cabantous, *Histoire de la nuit: XVIIe–XVIIIe siècle* (Paris: Fayard, 2009), p. 148.

13. John Strype (1643–1737), *The Life and Acts of John Whitgift … Digested, Compiled, and Attested from Records, Registers, Original Letters and Other Authentic Mss* (Oxford: Clarendon Press, 1822), 1: 165–66.

14. Collinson, *Elizabethan Puritan Movement*, pp. 372–80; for more examples, see Patrick Collinson, John Craig, and Brett Usher, eds., *Conferences and Combination Lectures in the Elizabethan Church: Dedham and Bury St. Edmunds, 1582–1590*, Church of England Record Society 10 (Woodbridge: Boydell Press, 2003), p. 218.

15. Thomas Jackson (1579–1640), *The humiliation of the Sonne of God by his becomming the Son of man, by taking the forme of a servant, and by his sufferings under Pontius Pilat … by Thomas Jackson Dr. in Divinitie, chaplaine to his Majestie in ordinarie, and president of Corpus Christi Colledge in Oxford* (London: Printed by M. Flesher for John Clark, 1635), p. 355.

16. On the most recent scholarship, see R. Emmet McLaughlin, "Radicals," in *Reformation and Early Modern Europe: A Guide to Research*, ed. David M. Whitford (Kirksville, MO: Truman State University Press, 2008), pp. 103–10.

17. Anabaptists first settled in Moravia in the 1530s. By 1545 there were thirty-one Hutterite communities on noble estates there. After decades of pressure from Habsburg supporters of the Catholic Reformation, the last Anabaptists were driven out of Moravia in 1622; most resettled in Hungary. See Claus Peter Clasen, *Anabaptism: A Social History, 1525–1618: Switzerland, Austria, Moravia, South and Central Germany* (Ithaca, NY: Cornell University Press, 1972), pp. 211–13.

18. For an example of Anabaptists arrested at an afternoon gathering ("nachmittage umb iii slege") in 1535, see Paul Wappler, *Die Täuferbewegung in Thüringen von 1526–1584* (Jena: Fischer, 1913), p. 128.

19. A survey of published primary sources reveals thirty-four specific documented gatherings by night in the period before 1618, as well as references to other specific meetings and to regular meetings at night. These must represent only a fraction of the total number of Anabaptists' nocturnal gatherings.

20. Stephen F. Nelson and Jean Rott, "Strasbourg: The Anabaptist City in the Sixteenth Century," *Mennonite Quarterly Review* 58 (1984): 230–40.

21. See the list in Jean Rott and Marc Lienhard, "La communauté de 'frères suisses' de Strasbourg de 1557 à 1660," *Saisons d'Alsace* 76 (1981): 30.

22. *Ibid.*, p. 32.

23. Elsa Bernhofer-Pippert, *Täuferische Denkweisen und Lebensformen im Spiegel oberdeutscher Täuferverhöre*, Reformationsgeschichtliche Studien und Texte 96 (Münster: Aschendorff, 1967), pp. 90–92.

24. Günther Franz, ed., *Wiedertäuferakten, 1527–1626*, Urkundliche Quellen zur hessischen Reformationsgeschichte 4 (Marburg: Elwert, 1951), p. 178.

25. The sermon on Revelation 11 might have stressed the measuring of the temple of God and its altar (Rev. 11:1) or the prophets identified as "two candlesticks [or torches] standing before the God of the earth" (Rev. 11:4).

26. On this theme see Bernhofer-Pippert, *Täuferische Denkweisen*, pp. 38, 56, 98.

27. Abraham Hulshof, *Gescheidenis van de Doopsgezinden te Straatsburg van 1525 tot 1557* (Amsterdam: Clausen, 1905); for the Steinle account see pp. 208–11 (my emphasis).

28. In 1600 the church council of the Palatinate noted the mocking tone of Anabaptist Niclaus Weitzel in a report on the growth of the movement in the principality: "When they [the Anabaptists] are told to go to church, they say they have a vast church; it has a great roof, and that is where they go." Acknowledging this reference to the outdoor, typically nocturnal gatherings of the Anabaptists, the council remarked with resignation that "they too have their nocturnal assemblies in the area around Erpolzheim." Manfred Krebs, ed., *Baden und Pfalz*, Quellen zur Geschichte der Täufer 4 (Gütersloh: Bertelsmann, 1951), p. 233.

29. In his "Dialog on Drunkenness" (1551) the Colmar poet Jörg Wickram explained that "the custom of Anabaptists is to meet in dark forests in old abandoned shacks." See Jörg Wickram, *Sämtliche Werke*, vol. x, *Kleine Spiele*, ed. Hans-Gert Roloff (Berlin: de Gruyter, 1997), p. 285.

30. Gary K. Waite, *Eradicating the Devil's Minions: Anabaptists and Witches in Reformation Europe, 1525–1600* (University of Toronto Press, 2007), p. 67.

31. The title of the Dutch edition of 1576; printed as "Reply to False Accusations," in Menno Simons, *The Complete Writings of Menno Simons, c. 1496–1561*, trans. Leonard Verduin, ed. John C. Wenger, with a bibliography by Harold S. Bender (Scottdale, PA: Herald Press, 1956), pp. 541–77; here pp. 566–67.

32. *Ibid.*

33. Despite the rifts between Dutch–North German Mennonites and Swiss Anabaptism, shared persecution led to similar arguments, seen for example in a Swiss confession of 1588, the "Einfache Bekenntnis" of an unknown representative of the rural Zurich Anabaptist community. The confession explained that "we do our best [to gather] with thanks and praise in the forests, in stables or other places, wherever God gives us space and place." When "the clear and pure truth ... is neither heard nor accepted, but persecuted instead" then the "pious servants of Christ ... shall preserve themselves from the persecutors and their enemies with caution and humility." Urs B. Leu and Christian Scheidegger, *Die Zürcher Täufer 1525–1700* (Zurich: Theologischer Verlag Zürich, 2007), Appendix, p. 381: "sonder werden sich nach maß und bescheidenheit vor den vervolgeren und iren fynden hütten."

34. Hessian authorities discovered to their dismay that *both* Swiss Brethren and Moravians were meeting secretly at night in Hesse; Nolte attended a gathering of the Swiss Brethren. See Theodor Sippel, "The Confession of the Swiss Brethren in Hesse, 1578," *Mennonite Quarterly Review* 23 (1949): 22–34.

35. *Ibid.*, p. 23, and Franz, ed., *Wiedertaüferakten*, p. 400. See David Mayes, "Heretics or Nonconformists? State Policies toward Anabaptists in Sixteenth-Century Hesse," *Sixteenth Century Journal* 32, 4 (2001): 1003–26.

36. See Heinold Fast, "Die Aushebung einer nächtlichen Täuferversammlung 1574," *Mennonitische Geschichtsblätter* 31 (1974): 103–06.

37. *The Chronicle of the Hutterian Brethren (Das große Geschichtbuch der Hutterischen Brüder)* (Rifton, NY: Plough Publishing House, 1987), I: 223–24. The entries discussed here were written between 1542 and *c.* 1580 by Hans Kräl and Hauprecht Zapf (p. xv).

38. *Ibid.*, I: 398–401.

39. *Ibid.*, I: 373.

40. "Schleitheim Articles/Brotherly Union (1527)," trans. Cornelius J. Dyck *et al.*, in *Confessions of Faith in the Anabaptist Tradition, 1527–1660*, ed. with an Introduction by Karl Koop, Classics of the Radical Reformation 11 (Kitchener, Ontario: Pandora Press, 2006), p. 28.

41. John D. Derksen sees 1540 as a turning point in nonconformist and Anabaptist culture in the Strasbourg region, citing "a more 'survivalist' world view among "settled nonconformists." Their nocturnal meetings

arose as "the radicals' physical circumstances ... affected their world-view." "After 1535, with defeat, dislocation, numerical decrease and socio-economic decline, the dissidents' goal became more to survive than to change the world." This corresponds to the shift from a stark "light against darkness" view to a more nuanced appreciation of the night. John D. Derksen, *From Radicals to Survivors: Strasbourg's Religious Nonconformists over Two Generations*, Bibliotheca Humanistica & Reformatorica 61 ('t Goy-Houten: Hes & de Graaf, 2002), pp. 255–57.

42. For a detailed account of John's escape see Crisógono de Jesús, *The Life of St. John of the Cross*, trans. Kathleen Pond (London: Longmans, 1958), pp. 108–13.

43. John of the Cross, *Dark Night of the Soul*, in *The Complete Works of Saint John of the Cross, Doctor of the Church*, trans. and ed. E. Allison Peers (Westminster, MD: Newman Press, 1964), p. 413 (book 2, ch. 13).

44. See Alois M. Haas, "'Die dunkle Nacht der Sinne und des Geistes.' Mystische Leiderfahrung nach Johannes vom Kreuz," in *Die dunkle Nacht der Sinne: Leiderfahrung und christliche Mystik*, ed. Alois M Haas (Düsseldorf: Patmos-Verlag, 1989), pp. 108–25, here p. 109, and the extensive literature cited there.

45. Such as Ruud Welten, "The Night in John of the Cross and Michel Henry," *Studies in Spirituality* 13 (2003), pp. 213–16.

46. Michel Florisoone, *Esthétique et mystique d'après Sainte Thérèse d'Avila et Saint Jean de la Croix: suivi d'une note sur Saint Jean de la Croix et le Greco et d'une liste commentée des oeuvres de Saint Jean de la Croix* (Paris: Éditions du Seuil, 1956), pp. 24–30.

47. John of the Cross, *Complete Works*, trans. and ed. Peers, pp. 425–26: "I entered in – I knew not where – / And, there remaining, knew no more, / Transcending far all human lore."

48. See Haas, "'Dunkle Nacht der Sinne und des Geistes'," p. 113; George H. Tavard, *Poetry and Contemplation in St. John of the Cross* (Athens: Ohio University Press, 1988), pp. 76–79; Laura Calvert, "Images of Darkness and Light in Osuna's *Spiritual Alphabet Books*," *Studia Mystica* 8, 2 (1985) 38–44; and Giovanna Della Croce, "Johannes vom Kreuz und die deutsch-niederländische Mystik," *Jahrbuch für mystische Theologie* 6 (1960): 21–30.

49. Kieran Kavanaugh, "Introduction," in John of the Cross, *The Collected Works of St. John of the Cross*, trans. Kieran Kavanaugh (Garden City, NY: Doubleday, 1964), p. 33.

50. John of the Cross, *Dark Night of the Soul*, in *Complete Works*, trans. and ed. Peers, p. 325.

51. *Ibid.*, pp. 325–26.

52. John of the Cross, *Ascent of Mount Carmel*, in *Complete Works*, trans. and ed. Peers, pp. 20–21.

302 *Notes to pages 61–64*

53. John of the Cross, *Dark Night of the Soul*, in *Complete Works*, trans. and ed. Peers, pp. 349–61.
54. *Ibid.*, pp. 349, 376–96.
55. Haas, "'Dunkle Nacht der Sinne und des Geistes'," pp. 113–24.
56. Jean Baruzi, *Saint Jean de la Croix et le problème de l'expérience mystique*, second edn. (Paris: Alcan, 1931), p. 300.
57. Stuart Clark, *Thinking with Demons: The Idea of Witchcraft in Early Modern Europe* (Oxford University Press, 1997), pp. 43–68; on Clark's discussion of witchcraft see above, chapter 2. See Tavard, *Poetry and Contemplation*, pp. 76–78.
58. John of the Cross, *Ascent of Mount Carmel*, in *Complete Works*, trans. and ed. Peers, pp. 58–60, and Tavard, *Poetry and Contemplation*, pp. 64–68, 75–92.
59. High medieval authors did not use the imagery of darkness and the night to express spiritual truth. For example, Anselm of Canterbury grappled with the sense of Divine withdrawal described by John as "the dark night of the soul." But Anselm had no sense of a purgative or beneficial Divine absence or night. For Anselm, images of darkness help to convey the problem ("Still thou art hidden, O Lord, from my soul in thy light and thy blessedness; and therefore my soul still walks in its darkness and wretchedness") but not the solution, which Anselm describes as the soul's return to the light of God. As a contemporary Benedictine scholar explains, "the seeming separation that constitutes that state [i.e., the 'dark night'] cannot be instigated by perfect God, only by fallible humanity." See Paschal Baumstein, "Anselm on the Dark Night and Truth," *Cistercian Studies Quarterly* 35, 2 (2000): 239–49; here 244.
60. On the reception of John Baconthorpe, John Tauler, and Jan van Ruysbroeck by John of the Cross, see Alois Winkelhofer, "Johannes vom Kreuz und die Surius-Übersetzung der Werke Taulers," in *Theologie in Geschichte und Gegenwart; Michael Schmaus zum sechzigsten Geburtstag*, ed. Johann Auer and Hermann Volk (Munich: K. Zink, 1957), pp. 317–48; here pp. 317–23.
61. Elizabeth Wilhelmsen, *Knowledge and Symbolization in Saint John of the Cross* (Frankfurt: Lang, 1993), pp. 15–34; Tavard, *Poetry and Contemplation*, p. 77.
62. Tavard, *Poetry and Contemplation*, pp. 76–79.
63. Böhme's works are cited from the 1730 edition as published in facsimile: Jacob Böhme, *Sämtliche Schriften*, ed. August Faust and Will-Erich Peuckert (Stuttgart: Frommann, 1955–61). References are by volume and page of the facsimile edition and by book, chapter, and section of the 1730 edition. Böhme, *Christosophia, oder Der Weg zu Christo*, IV: 167, book 6 ("Von Göttlicher Beschaulichkeit" ["On the visibility of God"]),

ch. 1, §8: "Kein Ding ohne Wiederwärtigkeit mag ihme selber offenbar werden ..."

64. Böhme, *Mysterium Magnum*, VII: 45, ch. 8, §27. See also *Mysterium Magnum*, VII: 25, ch. 5, §7: "Die Finsterniß ist die gröste Feindschaft des Lichts, und ist doch die Ursach, daß das Licht offenbar werde. Denn so kein Schwartzes wäre, so möchte ihme das Weisse nicht offenbar seyn; und wenn kein Leid wäre, so wäre ihr die Freude auch nicht offenbar."

65. Böhme, *Mysterium Magnum*, VII: 45, ch. 8, §27 and VII: 66, ch. 10, §62: "in der Finsterniß wird das Licht erkant, sonst wäre es ihme nicht offenbar," and "das Böseste muß das Beste Ursache seyn."

66. Bernhard Pünjer, *Geschichte der christlichen Religions-philosophie seit der Reformation* (Braunschweig: C.A. Schwetschke, 1880), p. 195; Peter Sterry, *The commings* [sic] *forth of Christ in the power of his death. Opened in a sermon preached before the High Court of Parliament, on Thursday the first of Novem. 1649* (London: Printed by Charles Sumptner, for Thomas Brewster and Gregory Moule, 1650 [i.e., 1649]), fo. aa1r.

67. Böhme, *Quaestiones Theosophicae, oder Betrachtung Göttlicher Offenbarung*, IX: 6–7, "Die 3. Frage," §§2–3.

68. *Ibid.*, §3.

69. Ernst-Heinz Lemper, "Voraussetzungen zur Beurteilung des Erfahrungs- und Schaffensumfelds Jakob Böhmes," in *Gott, Natur und Mensch in der Sicht Jacob Böhmes und seiner Rezeption*, ed. Jan Garewicz and Alois M. Haas, Wolfenbütteler Arbeiten zur Barockforschung 24 (Wiesbaden: Harrassowitz, 1994), pp. 41–69; here pp. 57–61.

70. Christoph Geissmar, "The Geometrical Order of the World: Otto van Veen's *Physicae et theologicae conclusiones*," *Journal of the Warburg and Courtauld Institutes* 56 (1993): 168–82, here 180–81: "Setze den Grimm zur Lincken, und das Licht zur Rechten ...; dann anderst kann mans nicht mahlen; aber es ist eine Kugel." See Böhme, *Viertzig Fragen von der Seelen*, III: 31, Frage 1, §105.

71. For those who preceded and influenced Böhme on the themes of light, darkness, immanence, and contrariety, see Andrew Weeks, *Boehme. An Intellectual Biography of the Seventeenth-Century Philosopher and Mystic* (Albany, NY: State University of New York Press, 1991); Lemper, "Voraussetzungen," in *Gott, Natur und Mensch*, ed. Garewicz and Haas; Günther Bonheim, *"ward Jch dero wegen Gantz Melancolisch. Jacob Böhmes Heidnische gedancken* bei Betrachtung des Himmels und die Astronomie seiner Zeit," *Euphorion* 91 (1997): 99–132; Sibylle Rusterholz, "Jacob Böhmes Deutung des Bösen im Spannungsfeld von Tradition und Innovation," in *Contemplata aliis tradere. Studien zum Verhältnis von Literatur und Spiritualität*, ed. Claudia Brinker (Berne: Lang, 1995), pp. 225–40; Livia Datteri Rasmussen, "Jacob Böhme: doch ein Beispiel für

den 'heliozentrischen Chok'? Zur Interaktion von Naturwissenschaft, Theologie, Mystik und Literatur in der Frühen Neuzeit," *Morgen-Glantz: Zeitschrift der Christian Knorr von Rosenroth-Gesellschaft* 3 (1993): 189–205; Russell Hvolbek, "Being and Knowing: Spiritualist Epistemology and Anthropology from Schwenckfeld to Böhme," *Sixteenth Century Journal* 22 (1991): 97–110; Herbert Deinert, "Die Entfaltung des Bösen in Böhmes *Mysterium Magnum*," *PMLA* 79, 4 (1964): 401–10; and Kurt Goldammer, "Lichtsymbolik in philosophischer Weltanschauung, Mystik und Theosophie vom 15. bis zum 17. Jahrhundert," *Studium Generale* 13 (1960): 670–82, and Josef Koch, "Über die Lichtsymbolik im Bereich der Philosophie und der Mystik des Mittelalters," *Studium Generale* 13 (1960): 653–70.

72. Böhme, *Aurora oder Morgenröthe im Aufgang*, I: 376–77, ch. 25, §61; Weeks, *Boehme*, p. 54.
73. Böhme, *Aurora oder Morgenröthe im Aufgang*, I: 265, ch. 19, §§4–5.
74. See Sibylle Rusterholz, "Jakob Böhmes spirituelle Erfahrung als 'Grund' seiner schriftstellerischen Existenz," in *Die Morgenröte bricht an: Jakob Böhme, naturnaher Mystiker und Theosoph*, Herrenalber Forum 24 (Karlsruhe: Evangelische Akademie Baden, 1999), pp. 100–20, and Bonheim, "Böhmes *Heidnische gedancken*," pp. 99–132.
75. The legacy of Giordano Bruno's *De l'infinito universo e mondi* (1584) also figured in these concerns.
76. Böhme, *Aurora oder Morgenröthe im Aufgang*, I: 266, ch. 19, §§8–9.
77. John Donne, "The First Anniversary: An Anatomy of the World," in *John Donne's Poetry*, ed. Donald R. Dickson, Norton Critical Edition (New York: Norton, 2007), pp. 125–26.
78. See Andreas Mahler, "Jahrhundertwende, Epochenschwelle, epistemischer Bruch? England um 1600 und das Problem überkommener Epochenbegriffe," in *Europäische Barock-Rezeption*, ed. Klaus Garber, Wolfenbütteler Arbeiten zur Barockforschung 20 (Wiesbaden: Harrassowitz, 1991), II: 1008.
79. Böhme, *Aurora oder Morgenröthe im Aufgang*, I: 266–67, ch. 19 ("Von dem erschaffenen Himmel und der Gestalt der Erden und des Wassers, sowol von dem Lichte und der Finsterniß"), §§10–14.
80. Genesis 32:35: "And Jacob was left alone; and there wrestled a man with him until the breaking of the day."
81. See Rusterholz, "Jacob Böhmes Deutung des Bösen," in *Contemplata aliis tradere*, ed. Brinker, pp. 236–27, on darkness as an eternal aspect of the Divine.
82. Weeks, *Boehme*, pp. 93–98.
83. *Ibid.*, p. 97.
84. Böhme, *Mysterium Magnum*, VIII: 745, ch. 68, §6: "As at this very day titulary Christendom is full of such magi as have no natural understanding,

either of God or of nature more among them, but only an empty babbling of a supernatural magic ground … that indeed titulary Christendom's idols which it maketh to itself might, through nature, be made manifest and known, that man might know in nature the outspoken or expressed formed Word of God, as also the new regeneration, and also the fall and perdition."

85. *Ibid.* On Böhme's critique of the "Belly-Servants of the Antichrist," which he saw in all churches of his age, see Weeks, *Boehme*, pp. 97–98, and G. Haensch, "Gesellschaftskritik und Reformationsidee in der Philosophie Jakob Böhmes," *Deutsche Zeitschrift für Philosophie* 36, 1 (1988): 66–72.

86. Böhme, *Mysterium Magnum*, VIII: 746, ch. 68, §7.

87. Jacob Böhme, *Signatura rerum, or, The signature of all things shewing the sign and signification of the severall forms and shapes in the creation, and what the beginning, ruin, and cure of every thing is*, trans. John Ellistone (London: Printed by John Macock for Gyles Calvert, 1651), p. 53, and Böhme, *De Signatura Rerum*, VI: 67, ch. 7, §43.

88. Donne was the first to use "nocturnal" as a noun to refer to a poem about the night in his "A Nocturnal upon St. Lucy's Day, Being the Shortest Day." See Fitter, "Poetic Nocturne," paragraphs 24–28, and Clarence H. Miller, "Donne's 'A Nocturnall upon S. Lucies Day' and the Nocturns of Matins," *Studies in English Literature, 1500–1900* 6, 1 [The English Renaissance] (1966): 77–86.

89. Rzepinska, "Tenebrism," p. 93. Michel de Certeau's *The Mystic Fable*, trans. Michael B. Smith (University of Chicago Press, 1995) focuses on this period as marked by the formation and decline of *mystics* as a discourse. His survey of mysticism from Teresa of Avila to Angelus Silesius opens and closes with authors who used darkness and the night to describe their path to the divine. See pp. 16–26, 75–150.

90. Certeau, *Mystic Fable*, p. 77. See also Michael Kapeller, *Auch Finsternis finstert dir nicht: ein Versuch über die Nacht des Glaubens und die Reflexion dieser Erfahrung in der Dogmatik*, Theologie der Spiritualität 7 (Münster: Lit, 2004), pp. 94–95.

91. Maximilianus Sandaeus, *Pro theologia mystica clavis: elucidarium onomasticon vocabulorum et loquutionum obscurarum* (Louvain: Éditions de la Bibliotheque S.J., 1963; facsimile of Cologne: Officina Gualteriana, 1640), pp. 288–89.

92. "Nox. Multa apud Mysticos indicari possunt metaphora Noctis, qua frequentissimè utitur Iohannes à Cruce, excellens nostri temporis Mysticus, cuius sunt Libri de Asensu Montis Carmeli." *Ibid.*, "Index Vocabulorum."

93. Richard Crashaw, *The Complete Poetry of Richard Crashaw*, ed. George Walton Williams (New York: Norton, 1972), p. 45.

94. Mary W. Helms, "Before the Dawn: Monks and the Night in Late Antiquity and Early Medieval Europe," *Anthropos* 99 (2004): 177–91.

95. Ignatius of Loyola, *The Spiritual Exercises of S. Ignatius of Loyola. Founder of the Society of Jesus* (Saint-Omers: Printed by Nicolas Joseph Le Febvre, 1736), p. 22. The deliberate use of darkness was integral to Jesuit culture in this period. See below, chapter 4, section 4.2, "Darkness and the perspective stage."

96. Teresa of Avila, *Interior Castle*, in *The Complete Works of St Teresa of Jesus*, ed. and trans. E. Allison Peers (London: Sheed and Ward, 1972), II: 210, 218; Joseph Chorpenning, "The Image of Darkness and Spiritual Development in the *Castillo interior*," *Studia Mystica* 8, 2 (1985): 45–58.

97. John Donne, "A Hymn to Christ, at the Author's Last Going into Germany" (1619), in *John Donne's Poetry*, ed. Dickson, pp. 154–55. See Jeffrey Johnson, "Gold in the Washes: Donne's Last Going into Germany," *Renascence* 46, 3 (1994): 199–207. For similar comments by Luther and Calvin, see Daniel Ménager, *La Renaissance et la nuit*, Seuils de la modernité 10 (Geneva: Droz, 2005), pp. 164–65, although these sixteenth-century Protestants describe the spiritual night in more passive terms, in contrast with Catholic baroque references to actively seeking or creating darkness and the night for spiritual benefit.

98. Note that the sermon was preached "in the evening." John Donne, *Complete Poetry and Selected Prose*, ed. Charles M. Coffin (New York: Random House, 1978), p. 629.

99. *Ibid.*, p. 585.

100. Francis Quarles, *Emblemes by Fra. Quarles* (London: Printed by G[eorge] M[iller] and sold at Iohn Marriots shope, 1635), p. 131.

101. Paul Gerhardt, "Abend-Lied," in *Gedichte des Barock*, ed. Ulrich Maché and Volker Meid (Stuttgart: Reclam, 1980), pp. 174–75:

> Nun ruhen alle Wälder /
> Vieh / Menschen / Städt und Felder /
> Es schläfft die gantze Welt:
> Ihr aber meine Sinnen /
> Auf / auf ihr solt beginnen
> Was eurem Schöppfer wol gefällt.

See Martha Mayo Hinman, "The Night Motif in German Baroque Poetry," *Germanic Review* 42, 3 (1967): 83–95.

102. Gerhardt, "Abend-Lied," p. 175. Almost as an afterthought, Gerhard offers in the penultimate stanza a more traditional prayer for protection from "Satan."

103. See Stuart McClintock, *The Iconography and Iconology of Georges De La Tour's Religious Paintings, 1624–1650*, Studies in Art and Religious Interpretation 31 (Lewiston, NY: Edwin Mellen Press, 2003), and Paulette Choné, ed., *L'âge d'or du nocturne* (Paris: Gallimard, 2001).

104. Georges de La Tour (1593–1652), *The Magdalen with the Smoking Flame*, *c.* 1638–40. Painting, oil on canvas, 46 $\frac{1}{16}$ × 36 $\frac{1}{8}$ in. Los Angeles County Museum of Art.

105. See Choné, *L'Atelier des nuits*, and her articles on "La lanterne et le flambeau," in *Georges de La Tour, ou, La nuit traversée*, ed. Anne Reinbold (Metz: Éditions Serpenoise, 1994), pp. 145–58, and on "Exégèse de la ténèbre et luminisme nocturne: les 'nuits' lorraines et leur contexte spirituel," in *Les signes de Dieu aux XVIe et XVII siècles*, ed. Geneviève Demerson and Bernard Dompnier (Association des Publications de la Faculté des Lettres et Sciences Humaines de Clermont-Ferrand, 1993), pp. 89–99.

106. Dorothy L. Latz, ed., *Glow-Worm Light: Writings of 17th Century English Recusant Women from Original Manuscripts*, Salzburg Studies in English Literature 92: 21 (Institut für Anglistik und Amerikanistik, Universität Salzburg, 1989), p. 70.

107. Donne's maternal grandfather John Heywood died a recusant in Flanders in 1578.

108. Latz, ed., *Glow-Worm Light*, p. 142.

109. Blaise Pascal, *Pensées*, ed. and trans. Roger Ariew (Indianapolis, IN: Hackett, 2005), p. 225. In this passage Pascal balanced darkness with the traditional value of light: "if there were no illumination, man would not hope for a remedy."

110. John of the Cross, *Ascent of Mount Carmel*, in *Complete Works*, trans. and ed. Peers, p. 69.

111. *Ibid.*, p. 92.

112. George Herbert, *The Complete English Poems*, ed. John Tobin (London: Penguin Books, 1991), p. 191. The poem was composed before 1633.

113. Claude Hopil, *Les divins eslancemens d'amour exprimez en cent cantiques saints en l'honneur de la Tres-saincte Trinité* (Paris: S. Hure, 1629). For an introduction to Hopil, see François Bouchet, "Claude Hopil ou l'éclat des ténèbres," *Conférence* 1 (1995): 155–91.

114. Translated from the modern edition: Claude Hopil, *Les divins élancements d'amour*, ed. F. Bouchet (Grenoble: Millon, 2001), canticle 41, 4. See Werner Indermühle, *Essai sur l'oeuvre de Claude Hopil* (Zurich: Juris-Verlag, 1970), pp. 21–31.

115. Hopil, *Divins élancements*, canticle 74, 1:

> Mon Esprit s'eslevant aux cachots magnifiques
> Dans le rayon divin des tenebres mistiques,
> Tout confus & ravy,
> Je vy ce qu'on ne peut penser ny moins escrire,
> Ainsi je vous du tout en ne pouvant rien dire:
> De tout ce que je vy.

116. *Ibid.*, canticle 31, 10.

117. *Ibid.*, canticle 96, 3.
118. *Ibid.*, canticle 54, 8. Hopil describes prayer at night in canticles 49, 54, 72, 74, 75, 89, and 91.
119. Dorothy S. Packer, "Collections of Chaste Chansons for the Devout Home (1613–1633)," *Acta Musicologica* 16, 2 (1989): 175–216, here 178. In contrast with John of the Cross, Hopil scarcely mentions the ascetic night. The painful passages through the darkness of the senses and spirit central to John's encounter with the night seem to play no role in Hopil's mysticism.
120. Andreas Gryphius, "Über die Geburt Jesu," in *Gedichte des Barock*, ed. Maché and Meid, p. 113:

> Nacht / mehr denn lichte Nacht! Nacht / lichter als der Tag /
> Nacht / heller als die Sonn' / in der das Licht geboren.
> …
> O Nacht, die alle Nächt' und Tage trotzen mag!

See Vereni Fässler, *Hell-Dunkel in der barocken Dichtung. Studien zum Hell-Dunkel bei Johann Klaj, Andreas Gryphius und Catharina Regina von Greiffenberg.* Europäische Hochschulschriften 44 (Berne: Lang, 1971), pp. 47–68.
121. Latz, ed., *Glow-Worm Light*, p. 81.
122. Blaise de Vigenère, *A discovery of fire and salt discovering many secret mysteries, as well philosophicall, as theologicall*, trans. Edward Stephens (London: Printed by Richard Cotes, and are to be sold by Andrew Crooke, 1649), p. 24. First edn. (posthumous), Paris, 1618.
123. Blaise de Vigenère, *Traicté du feu et du sel* (Paris: Chez la veufue A. l'Angelier, 1618), p. 38.
124. Graeme J. Watson makes a similar point in his "The Temple in 'The Night': Henry Vaughan and the Collapse of the Established Church," *Modern Philology* 84, 2 (1986): 144–61, in reference to the Cudamore illustration.
125. Daniel Cudmore, *Euchodia. Or, A prayer-song; being sacred poems on the history of the birth and passion of our blessed Saviour, and several other choice texts of Scripture* (London: Printed by J.C. for William Ley in Paul's Chain, 1655). Note that the reference to "Iohn 20. 5" in the frontispiece corresponds to John 19:5 ("Behold the man") in modern editions of the text.
126. John Milton, *Paradise Lost*, ed. David Scott Kastan and Merritt Yerkes Hughes (Indianapolis, IN: Hackett, 2005), p. 50; II.263–68.
127. William Flesch, "The Majesty of Darkness," in *John Milton*, ed. Harold Bloom (New York: Chelsea House, 1986), pp. 293–311.
128. Milton, *Paradise Lost*, ed. Kastan and Hughes, p. 94; III.375–80.
129. John of the Cross, *Dark Night of the Soul*, in *Complete Works*, trans. and ed. Peers, p. 396.

130. *Ibid.*, pp. 419–20.
131. In the seventeenth-century English translation: Dorothy L. Latz, ed., *The Building of Divine Love, As Translated by Agnes More*, Salzburg Studies in English Literature. Elizabethan and Renaissance Studies 92: 17 (Institut für Anglistik und Amerikanistik, Universität Salzburg, 1992), pp. 48, 81.
132. For example, John's works were used extensively by the influential Francisan spritual writer Juan de Los Angeles (d. 1609). See Irene Behn, *Spanische Mystik: Darstellung und Deutung* (Düsseldorf: Patmos-Verlag, 1957), pp. 160–68.
133. Johann Arndt, *Vier Bücher von wahrem Christenthumb: die erste Gesamtausgabe (1610)*, ed. Johann Anselm Steiger, Johann Arndt-Archiv 2 (Hildesheim: G. Olms, 2007), book 3, pp. 48–49.
134. Hopil, *Divins élancements*, canticles 74, 1 and 75, 1.
135. *Ibid.*, canticles 66, 11 and 86, 1.
136. Rzepinska, "Tenebrism," pp. 97–100.
137. Angelus Silesius, *The Cherubinic Wanderer*, trans. Maria Shrady (New York: Paulist Press, 1986), pp. 71–72.
138. On subjectivity see Patricia Fumerton, *Unsettled: The Culture of Mobility and the Working Poor in Early Modern England* (University of Chicago Press, 2006), pp. 3–5, 47–59, Gen Doy, *Picturing the Self: Changing Views of the Subject in Visual Culture* (London: I. B. Tauris, 2005), pp. 35–62, Lyndal Roper, *Oedipus and the Devil: Witchcraft, Sexuality and Religion in Early Modern Europe* (London: Routledge, 2003), pp. 1–36.
139. Daniel Drovin, *Les Vengeances divines, de la transgression des sainctes ordonnances de Dieu* (Paris: J. Mettayer, 1595), fos. 108v–109r (= 189v–190r), as quoted in Clark, *Thinking with Demons*, p. 137, and Louis LeRoy, *Of the interchangeable course, or variety of things in the whole world and the concurrence of armes and learning ... Written in French by Loys le Roy called Regius: and translated into English by R.A.* (London: Printed by Charles Yetsweirt, 1594), as quoted in Clark, *Thinking with Demons*, p. 55.
140. Guillaume de Saluste Du Bartas, seigneur (1544–90), *La Semaine* (1578); complete English translation by Joshua Sylvester, *Devine Weekes and Workes* (1605), here from the 1621 edition (London: Printed by Humphray Lownes, 1621), p. 12. See Michel Braspart, ed., *Du Bartas, poète chrétien* (Neuchâtel: Delachaux et Niestlé, 1947), p. 86.
141. Rainer Decker, "Der Brillen-Traktat des Michael Stappert," Introduction to Hermann Löher, *Hochnötige Unterthanige WEMÜTIGE KLAGE der Frommen Unschültigen* (Amsterdam, 1676), ed. Thomas P. Becker, online at http://extern.historicum.net/loeher.
142. Lambert Daneau, *The wonderfull woorkmanship of the world wherin is conteined an excellent discourse of Christian naturall philosophie*, trans.

Thomas Twyne (London: for Andrew Maunsell, in Paules Church-
yard, 1578).

143. Daniel Czepko, "Jedes durchs andere," in *Geistliche Schriften*, ed. Werner
     Milch (Darmstadt: Wissenschaftliche Buchgesellschaft, 1963), p. 224.
     See Hinman, "Night Motif in German Baroque Poetry," p. 87.

144. Henry Vaughan, "The Night," in *The Works of Henry Vaughan*, ed. L.C.
     Martin, second edn. (Oxford: Clarendon Press, 1957), pp. 522–23. On
     Vaughan's sense of persecution in the Commonwealth era, see Watson,
     "Henry Vaughan and the Collapse of the Established Church," pp. 144–61,
     and Geoffrey Hill, "A Pharisee to Pharisees: Reflections on Vaughan's
     'The Night'," *English* 38 (1989): 97–113. As Hill notes, Vaughan refers to
     "these times of persecution and trial" in *The Mount of Olives* (1652), and
     in his 1654 *Flores Solitudinis* the poet explains that "there are bright stars
     under the most palpable clouds, and light is never so beautiful as in the
     presence of darkness."

145. Rzepinska, "Tenebrism," p. 93. Historians of art and philosophy have
     described this development in painting, astronomy, and optics, and in
     hermetic and alchemical thought. Goldammer's "Lichtsymbolik in phi-
     losophischer Weltanschauung" describes especially clearly the wholly
     negative view of darkness in fifteenth- and sixteenth-century thinkers
     from Ficino and Paracelsus to Valentin Weigel.

146. Catholics also developed popular forms of nocturnal piety in this period,
     most prominently the Devotion of the Forty Hours, which spread from
     its origins in Milan through Italy and France, and the evening Good
     Friday processions of southern Germany and the Rhineland. See below,
     chapter 7, for further discussion of these literal incursions into the night,
     urban and rural. On the importance of darkness and the night to these
     practices, see Mark S. Weil, "The Devotion of the Forty Hours and
     Roman Baroque Illusions," *Journal of the Warburg and Courtauld Institutes*
     37 (1974): pp. 218–48; Bernard Dompnier, "Un Aspect de la dévotion
     Eucharistique dans la France du XVIIe siècle: les Prières des Quarante-
     Heures," *Revue d'histoire de l'Eglise de France* 67 (1981): 5–31; and Fred
     G. Rausch, "Karfreitagsprozessionen in Bayern," in *Hört, sehet, weint
     und liebt: Passionsspiele im alpenländischen Raum*, ed. Michael Henker,
     Eberhard Dünninger, and Evamaria Brockhoff, Veröffentlichungen zur
     bayerischen Geschichte und Kultur 20 (Munich: Süddeutscher Verlag,
     1990), pp. 87–93, and the literature cited there.

4 PRINCES OF DARKNESS: THE NIGHT
AT COURT, 1600–1750

1. Norris's first publication was a crude anti-Whig burlesque, *A Murnival of
   Knaves*, published in June 1683. See George R. Wasserman, "A Critical

Edition of the Collected Poems of John Norris of Bemerton", PhD thesis, University of Michigan, 1957, pp. 1–27.

2. John Norris of Bemerton, "Hymn to Darkness," in *A Collection of Miscellanies* (Oxford: J. Crosley, 1687), pp. 37–38.

3. Chris Fitter, "The Poetic Nocturne: From Ancient Motif to Renaissance Genre," *Early Modern Literary Studies* 3, 2 (1997): 2.1–61. Online at http://purl.oclc.org/emls/03–2/fittnoct.html. Fitter outlines the development of the poetic nocturne through Milton, distinguishing between "Cavalier" and "sacred" approaches within the genre, but he does not go on to examine its political inflection by Norris.

4. Here Norris echoed a poem by John Walton of 1678: "So the *first Light himself* has for his Throne / Blackness, and Darkness his Pavilion." I. W. [i.e., John Walton], "To my worthy friend, Mr. Henry Vaughan the Silurist" (1678), in *The Works of Henry Vaughan*, ed. L.C. Martin, second edn. (Oxford: Clarendon Press, 1957), p. 620. The use of darkness to emphasize majesty contrasts clearly with an earlier emphasis on darkness as concealing authority and hierarchy – seen for example when Shakespeare's Henry V walks unrecognized among his troops the night before battle of Agincourt (act 4, scene 1). See Raymond Gardette, "Ténèbres lumineuses: quelques repères shakespeariens," in *Penser la nuit: XVe–XVIIe siècles*, ed. Dominique Bertrand, Colloques, Congrès et Conférences sur la Renaissance 35 (Paris: H. Champion, 2003), pp. 343–65.

5. Norris, "Hymn to Darkness," in *Collection*, p. 38.

6. Massimo Ciavolella and Patrick Coleman, "Guide to the programs on 'Culture and Authority in the Baroque'" held at the Center for Seventeenth and Eighteenth Century Studies, UCLA, 2000–01.

7. *Ibid.* See Maria Goloubeva's overview of the scholarship on the baroque as style and culture in *The Glorification of Emperor Leopold I in Image, Spectacle, and Text*, Veröffentlichungen des Instituts für Europäische Geschichte Mainz 184 (Mainz: von Zabern, 2000), pp. 15–21, and the literature cited there.

8. Jesuit culture played an important role in the use of darkness to intensify Christian imagery and devotion. The application of Ignatian spirituality to baroque theater was promoted by seventeenth-century Jesuits such as Emanuele Tesauro of Turin: see Sebastian Neumeister, "*Tante belle inuentioni di Feste, Giostre, Balletti e Mascherate*: Emmanule Tesauro und die barocke Festkultur," in *Theatrum Europaeum: Festschrift für Elida Maria Szarota*, ed. Richard Brinkmann *et al.* (Munich: W. Fink, 1982), pp. 153–68.

9. On the *Ballet de la Nuit* see Marie-Claude Canova-Green, "Le Ballet de cour en France," in *Spectaculum Europaeum: Theatre and Spectacle in Europe (1580–1750)*, ed. Pierre Béhar and Helen Watanabe-O'Kelly, Wolfenbütteler Arbeiten zur Barockforschung 31 (Wiesbaden: Harrassowitz, 1999), pp. 485–512; Dominik Keller, "Unter dem Zeichen der Sonne," in

Die schöne Kunst der Verschwendung, ed. Georg Kohler and Alice Villon-Lechner (Zurich and Munich: Artemis, 1988), pp. 57–58, and Kathryn A. Hoffmann, *Society of Pleasures: Interdisciplinary Readings in Pleasure and Power during the Reign of Louis XIV* (New York: St. Martin's Press, 1997), pp. 13–40.

10. See Marianne Closson, "Scénographiques nocturnes du baroque: l'exemple du ballet français (1580–1650)," in *Penser la nuit*, ed. Bertrand, pp. 425–47; Ian Dunlop, *Louis XIV* (London: Chatto & Windus, 1999), p. 31; and Isaac de Benserade, *Ballets pour Louis XIV*, ed. Marie-Claude Canova-Green (Toulouse: Société de Littératures Classiques, 1997), 1: 7–35, 91–160.

11. Benserade, *Ballets pour Louis XIV*, ed. Canova-Green, 1: 94.

12. See Helen Watanabe-O'Kelly, "From 'Société de plaisir' to 'Schönes Neben-Werck' – The Changing Purpose of Court Festivals," *German Life and Letters* 45, 3 (1992): 216–19.

13. This is discussed most clearly in Roy Strong, *Art and Power: Renaissance Festivals 1450–1650* (Woodbridge: Boydell Press, 1984), p. 4, and Karl Möseneder, *Zeremoniell und monumentale Poesie: die "Entrée solennelle" Ludwigs XIV. 1660 in Paris* (Berlin: Gebr. Mann, 1983), pp. 34–43.

14. "Cette société de plaisirs, qui donne aux personnes de la cour une honnête familiarité avec nous, les touche et les charme plus qu'on peut dire. Les peuples, d'un autre côté, se plaisent au spectacle," as quoted in Hoffmann, *Society of Pleasures*, pp. 13, 30, 173–74.

15. Möseneder, *Zeremoniell*, p. 36.

16. From a contemporary English translation: Justus Lipsius, *Sixe Bookes of Politickes or Civil Doctrine*, trans. William Jones (London: Richard Field, 1594), pp. 68–70.

17. Jean de La Bruyère, *Les Caractères*, ed. Robert Garapon (Paris: Garnier, 1962), pp. 275f. See also the comments of Gabriel Naudé (1639) on "seduction and deception by appearances," as cited in Möseneder, *Zeremoniell*, p. 36.

18. Michel de Puré (1634–80), *Idée des spectacles anciens et nouveaux* (Paris, 1668, repr. Geneva: Minkoff Reprint, 1972), pp. 161–318, and Claude-François Ménestrier (1631–1705), *Traité des tournois, joustes, carrousels et autres spectacles publics* (Lyon, 1669; repr. New York: Garland, 1979).

19. See the valuable study by Miloš Vec, *Zeremonialwissenschaft im Fürstenstaat. Studien zur juristischen und politischen Theorie absolutistischer Herrschaftsrepräsentation*, Studien zur Europäischen Rechtsgeschichte 106 (Frankfurt: Klostermann, 1998).

20. Julius Bernhard von Rohr (1688–1742), *Einleitung zur Ceremoniel-Wissenschaft der Grossen Herren*, ed. with a commentary by Monika Schlechte (Leipzig: Edition Leipzig, 1990; reprint of the second edn., Berlin, 1733), pp. 732–880.

21. *Ibid.*, pp. 733f., as cited in Möseneder, *Zeremoniell*, p. 39.

22. Rohr discusses (1) processions, (2) tourneys and chivalric sport, (3) Carrousels, Ringrennen, and equestrian ballet, (4) carnivals and masquerades, (5) concerts, dances, balls and ballets, (6) operas and comedies, (7) costume feasts and "peasant weddings", (8) sleigh rides, (9) illuminations, (10) fireworks, (11) target shooting, and finally (12) hunting. *Ibid.*, "Verzeichniß der Capitel" and pp. 732–875.

23. See Jean-Louis Sponsel, *Der Zwinger, die Hoffeste und die Schloßbaupläne zu Dresden* (Dresden: Stengel, 1924), pp. 73–98, and Beatrix Bastl, "Feuerwerk und Schlittenfahrt: Ordnungen zwischen Ritual und Zeremoniell," *Wiener Geschichtsblätter* 51 (1996): 197–229.

24. Richard Alewyn and Karl Sälzle, *Das große Welttheater: Die Epoche der höfischen Feste in Dokument und Deutung* (Hamburg: Rowohlt, 1959), pp. 30–31. See Samuel John Klingensmith, *The Utility of Splendor: Ceremony, Social Life and Architecture at the Court of Bavaria, 1600–1800* (University of Chicago Press, 1993); and Hellmut Lorenz, "Barocke Festkultur und Repräsentation im Schloß zu Dresden," *Dresdner Hefte* 12, 38 (1994): 48–56.

25. Innovative organizations of space and time often develop together: consider the communal monastery and the daily schedule of Benedict's Rule or the work of Jacques LeGoff on medieval cities and "merchants' time." The "spatial turn" in recent scholarship calls to our attention the range of baroque innovations in the measurement, structuring, and management of time, in all its divisions.

26. Richard Alewyn, *Das große Welttheater: Die Epoche der höfischen Feste*, second edn. (Munich: Beck, 1985), pp. 37–39.

27. Alewyn sees "the transition from Renaissance to baroque" as "the decisive phase" in the nocturnalization of court festivals: *ibid.*, p. 37.

28. Jean Cordey, *Vaux-le-Vicomte*, Preface by Pierre de Nolhac (Paris: Éditions Albert Morancé, 1924), and Peter-Eckhard Knabe, "Der Hof als Zentrum der Festkultur. Vaux-le-Vicomte, 17. August 1661," in *Geselligkeit und Gesellschaft im Barockzeitalter*, ed. Wolfgang Adam, Wolfenbütteler Arbeiten zur Barockforschung 28 (Wiesbaden: Harrassowitz, 1997) II: 859–70.

29. Knabe, "Der Hof als Zentrum," p. 861.

30. See Alewyn and Sälzle, *Welttheater*, pp. 98–102, and E. Magne, *Les Fêtes en Europe au XVIIe siècle* (Paris: Martin-Dupuis, 1930).

31. The account of Antoine Caraccioli, bishop of Troyes, is published in H. Noel Williams, *Henri II: His Court and Times* (London: Methuen, 1910), pp. 341–43. On the time of day of the accident see also Lucien Romier, *Les origines politiques des guerres de religion*, 2 vols. (Paris: Perrin, 1913–14), II: 379–80.

32. See Gordon Kipling, *The Triumph of Honour: Burgundian Origins of the Elizabethan Renaissance*, Publications of the Sir Thomas Browne Institute, Leiden: General Series 6 (The Hague: Leiden University Press, 1977), pp. 74–136; Strong, *Art and Power*, pp. 16–19; Jean Verdon, *Night in the Middle Ages*, trans. George Holoch (University of Notre Dame Press, 2002), pp. 127–34.

33. Strong, *Art and Power*, p. 18.

34. As Strong notes, daytime spectacles such as royal entries and tournaments were replaced by court entertainments under the first two Stuarts (*ibid.*, pp. 153–70, p. 154).

35. Alewyn and Sälze, *Welttheater*, pp. 91–97. In sixteenth-century Germany town and village dances, including those of the elites of German cities such as Augsburg and Nuremberg, were held on Sunday afternoon. See Wolfgang Brunner, "Städtisches Tanzen und das Tanzhaus im 16. Jahrhundert," in *Alltag im 16. Jahrhundert. Studien zu Lebensformen in mitteleuropäischen Städten*, ed. Alfred Kohler and Heinrich Lutz (Vienna: Verlag für Geschichte und Politik, 1987), pp. 45–64, 52.

36. See Sponsel, *Der Zwinger*, pp. 32–42, Helen Watanabe-O'Kelly, *Court Culture in Dresden: From Renaissance to Baroque* (New York: Palgrave, 2002), pp. 30–34, 130–65, and Horst Richter, *Johann Oswald Harms. Ein deutscher Theaterdekorateur des Barock* (Emsdetten: Lechte, 1963), pp. 28–52. See also the *Dresdner Hefte* 11, 33 (1993), special volume on "Johann Georg II und sein Hof." The Festival of the Planets is described in Gabriel Tzschimmer, *Die Durchlauchtigste Zusammenkunft, oder: Historische Erzehlung, was der durchlauchtigste furst und herr, Herr Johann George der Ander, herzog zu Sachsen* (Nuremberg: J. Hoffmann, 1680), which specifies the time of each day's events.

37. See Sponsel, *Der Zwinger*; Georg Kohler, "Die Rituale der fürstlichen Potestas. Dresden und die deutsche Feuerwerkstradition," in *Die schöne Kunst der Verschwendung*, ed. Kohler and Villon-Lechner (Zurich and Munich: Artemis, 1988), pp. 101–34; and Katrin Keller, "La Magnificence des deux Augustes: Zur Spezifik höfischer Kultur im Dresden des Augusteischen Zeitalters (1694–1763)," *Cahiers d'études germaniques* 28 (1995): 55–66.

38. See Watanabe-O'Kelly, *Court Culture in Dresden*, pp. 193–237, and Karlheinz Blaschke, "Die kursächsische Politik und Leipzig im 18. Jahrhundert," in *Leipzig: Aufklärung und Bürgerlichkeit*, ed. Wolfgang Martens (Heidelberg: Schneider, 1990), pp. 23–38.

39. On fireworks, see Kevin Salatino, *Incendiary Art: The Representation of Fireworks in Early Modern Europe* (Santa Monica, CA: Getty Research Institute for the History of Art and the Humanities, 1997), Kohler and Villon-Lechner, eds., *Die schöne Kunst der Verschwendung*, and Eberhard

Fähler, *Feuerwerke des Barock: Studien zur öffentlichen Fest und seiner litera-rischen Deutung vom 16.–18. Jahrhundert* (Stuttgart: Metzler, 1974).

40. As an "absolutist" ruler whose displays of power always exceeded his real political impact, Augustus the Strong noted this irony at an intimate fête with thirteen of his courtiers and his mistress in July 1711. At the meal each person was asked to write a phrase or motto in the guestbook. Without comment, Augustus wrote "la feuse tierre (et) ies ne Reste que la feusme," i.e. "the rocket climbs high, and nothing remains but smoke" – a realistic appraisal of the politics of spectacle from a monarch to his courtiers? See Paul Haake, *August der Starke im Urteil der Gegenwart* (Berlin: Curtius, 1929), pp. 121–23.

41. Johann Neiner, *Brachium Dexterae Excelsi, Oder die … Sieghaften Entset-zung Barcellone … und nächtlicher Illumination der gantzen Stadt Wienn* (Vienna: Christian Barthlmae Pruckner, 1706), 4v: "Ihr treu-gesinnte Vasallen aber / die Ihr heut eure Häuser und Palläste / mit neuen Freuden-Feuern beleuchtet."

42. See the contemporary survey from Christian Schoettgen, *Historische Nachricht von denen Illuminationen, wie solche zu alten und neuen Zeiten … in Gebrauch gewesen* (Dresden: Hekel, 1736), p. 29. Schoettgen notes that the illumination of Magdeburg in 1701 was the first in the city's history, for example.

43. See Herbert Schwarzwälder, "Oberstleutnant Johann Georg von Bendeleben und sein großes Feuerwerk in Bremen zur Erinnerung an den Frieden von Habenhausen am 20. Oktober 1668," *Bremisches Jahrbuch* 58 (1980): 9–22, and Thomas Lediard, *Eine Collection curieuser Vorstellungen in Illuminationen und Feier-Wercken … bey Gelegenheit eini-ger publiquen Festins und Rejouissances, in Hamburg* (Hamburg: Stromer, 1730).

44. Its designer Inigo Jones thought it "generally approved of, especially by all strangers." Strong, *Art and Power*, pp. 169–70. See Kevin Sharpe, *The Personal Rule of Charles I* (New Haven: Yale University Press, 1992), pp. 209–74.

45. Monika Schlechte, "Barocke Festkultur in Dresden. Quellenforschung zu einem kulturgeschichtlichen Phänomen," *Wissenschaftliche Zeitschrift der Technischen Universität Dresden (Separatreihe 1 "Gesellschaftswissenschaften")* 39, 6 (1990): 7–11.

46. Even the parsimonious soldier-king Frederick William I of Prussia, 1713–40, is only a partial exception. Recent studies have noted that Frederick William I, though legendary for his thrift and reduction of court life, also displayed the expected luxury and ceremony when receiv-ing foreign ambassadors or princes. For a state visit of Augustus II in 1728, the Prussian king prepared a nocturnal shooting competition at

the Charlottenburg illuminated by 8,000 lanterns. See Sponsel, *Zwinger*, p. 135, and Barbara Stollberg-Rillinger, "Höfische Öffentlichkeit. Zur zeremoniellen Selbstdarstellungen des brandenburgischen Hofes vor dem europäischen Publikum," *Forschungen zur Brandenburgischen und Preussischen Geschichte* n.s. 7, 2 (1997): 145–76. On the nocturnal "Tabakskollegium" of Frederick I and Frederick William I, see Franziska Windt, *Preußen 1701 – eine europäische Geschichte: Katalog* (Berlin: Henschel, 2001), pp. 181–82.

47. Stephen Orgel, ed., "Introduction," *Ben Jonson: The Complete Masques* (New Haven: Yale University Press, 1969), p. 3. See Russell West, "Perplexive Perspectives: The Court and Contestation in the Jacobean Masque," *Seventeenth Century* 18, 1 (2003): 25–43.

48. For permanent, purpose-built baroque stages the English would have to wait until the Restoration: the Theatre Royal opened in Drury Lane in 1663, and the more elaborate Dorset Gardens Theater in Blackfriars opened in 1671. See Edward J. Dent, *Foundations of English Opera: A Study of Musical Drama in England during the Seventeenth Century* (New York: Da Capo Press, 1965), pp. 137–40.

49. Strong, *Art and Power*, pp. 119–22, and Gösta M. Bergmann, *Lighting in the Theatre* (Stockholm: Almqvist & Wiksell International, 1977), pp. 117–19.

50. Hilliard T. Goldfarb, "Richelieu and Contemporary Art: 'Raison d'état' and Personal Taste," in Hilliard T. Goldfarb, ed., *Richelieu: Art and Power* (Montreal Museum of Fine Arts, 2002), p. 240.

51. See *ibid.*, pp. 240–42, illustration 107.

52. Madeleine Laurain-Portemer, "Mazarin, militant de l'art baroque au temps de Richelieu (1634–1642)," *Bulletin de la Société de l'Histoire de l'Art français* (1975): 65–100, here 72–74, 95, citing a letter of Benedetti to Mazarin dated March 7, 1640. See also Paul Fréart de Chantelou (1609–94), *Diary of the Cavaliere Bernini's visit to France*, ed. with an Introduction by Anthony Blunt, annotated by George C. Bauer, trans. Margery Corbett (Princeton University Press, 1985), Appendix B, "Bernini and the Theatre," pp. 339–41.

53. Helen Watanabe-O'Kelly has underscored Werner Braun's point that it is difficult to generalize about the state of opera in the Empire before 1660. See Werner Braun, "Opera in the Empire," and Sara Smart, "Ballet in the Empire," in *Spectaculum Europaeum*, ed. Béhar and Watanabe-O'Kelly, pp. 437–64, 547–70; Watanabe-O'Kelly, *Court Culture in Dresden*, pp. 166–92; and H.A. Frenzel, "The Introduction of the Perspective Stage in the German Court and Castle Theatres," *Theatre Research* 3 (1961): 88–100.

54. Jörg Jochen Berns, Frank Druffner, Ulrich Schütte, and Brigitte Walbe, eds., *Erdengötter: Fürst und Hofstaat in der Frühen Neuzeit im Spiegel*

von Marburger Bibliotheks- und Archivbeständen. Ein Katalog (Marburg Universitätsbibliothek, 1997), p. 489.

55. Goloubeva, *The Glorification of Emperor Leopold I*, pp. 23–25, 45–81.
56. Markus Paul, *Reichsstadt und Schauspiel: Theatrale Kunst im Nürnberg des 17. Jahrhunderts* (Tübingen: Niemeyer, 2002), pp. 292–325.
57. *Ibid.*, p. 323:

> Nicht eine Sonn hier steht: Viel Sonnen stehen stille /
> In diesen engen Raum: Du Sonnen-Prinz! Erfülle /
> Was unser Wünschen wünscht! Laß deine Gnadenstrahlen /
> Die unverdiente Gnad an unsrer Statt bezahlen.

58. Tobias Beutel, *Chur-Fürstlicher Sächsicher stets grünender hoher Cedern-Wald* (Dresden: Bergen, 1671), fo. R4. See also Moritz Fürstenau, *Zur Geschichte der Musik und des Theaters am Hofe zu Dresden* (Dresden, 1861–62; repr. edn., Leipzig: Edition Peters, 1979), pp. 217–33, and Irmgard Becker-Glauch, *Die Bedeutung der Musik für die Dresdener Hoffeste bis in die Zeit Augusts des Starken* (Kassel and Basle: Bärenreiter-Verlag, 1951), pp. 30–79.
59. John Lauder, Lord Fountainhall, *Journals of Sir John Lauder, Lord Fountainhall … 1665–1676*, ed. with Introduction by Donald Crawford, Publications of the Scottish History Society 36 (Edinburgh: Printed at the University Press by T. and A. Constable for the Scottish History Society, 1900), pp. 3–5.
60. Claude-François Ménestrier, *Des ballets anciens et moderns selon les règles du théâtre* (Paris: R. Guignard, 1682), cited in Jan Clarke, "Illuminating the Guénégaud Stage: Some Seventeenth-Century Lighting Effects," *French Studies* 53, 1 (1999): 3–15, here 7.
61. See the rich and detailed study by R.B. Graves, *Lighting the Shakespearean Stage, 1567–1642* (Carbondale, IL: Southern Illinois University Press, 1999).
62. Quoted in Dent, *Foundations of English Opera*, pp. 139–40.
63. See Strong, *Art and Power*, pp. 5–6, 126–52; Bergmann, *Lighting*, pp. 44–88. Of course, the other northern Italian courts shared in the development of these theater techniques.
64. Strong, *Art and Power*, p. 140.
65. Leone di Somi, "Dialogues," in Allardyce Nicoll, ed., *The Development of the Theatre* (New York: Harcourt, Brace & World, 1966), p. 275.
66. Joseph Furttenbach the Elder, *Mannhafter Kunstspiegel*, in *The Renaissance Stage: Documents of Serlio, Sabbattini and Furttenbach*, trans. Allardyce Nicoll, John H. McDowell, and George R. Kernodle, ed. Barnard Hewitt (Coral Gables, FL: University of Miami Press, 1958), p. 206 (emphasis mine).

67. Strong, *Art and Power*, p. 140. On Madrid see Margaret Rich Greer, *The Play of Power: Mythological Court Dramas of Calderón de la Barca* (Princeton University Press, 1991), and the literature cited there.

68. See the model funeral sermon (based on the funeral sermon for Agnes von Dohrstadt) in Balthasar Kindermann's *Der Deutsche Redner*, first edn. (Wittenberg: Fincelius, 1660), p. 275. On Mazarin see Johann Michael von Loen, *Gesammelte kleine Schriften*, ed. Johann Caspar Schneider (Frankfurt and Leipzig: Zu finden bey Philipp Heinrich Huttern, 1750), §3, p. 45.

69. Thomas Kirchner, "Der Theaterbegriff des Barocks," *Maske und Kothurn* 31 (1985): 131–41. Jonathan Dewald also emphasizes theater as the image of political life in his study of *Aristocratic Experience and the Origins of Modern Culture: France 1570–1715* (Berkeley: University of California Press, 1993), pp. 37–38.

70. Everyday lighting at court was especially conspicuous consumption. Scholars are just beginning to assess its place among the material expenses of court life. See William Ritchey Newton, *Derrière la façade: vivre au château de Versailles au XVIIIe siècle* (Paris: Perrin, 2008), pp. 131–73, Jeroen Duindam, *Vienna and Versailles: The Courts of Europe's Dynastic Rivals, 1550–1780* (Cambridge University Press, 2003), pp. 63–89, and Hanns Leo Mikoletzky, "Der Haushalt des kaiserlichen Hofes zu Wien (vornehmlich im 18. Jahrhundert)," *Carinthia* 146 (1956): 658–83.

71. "At court – in hell": see Helmuth Kiesel, *"Bei Hof, bei Höll"*. *Untersuchungen zur literarischen Hofkritik von Sebastian Brant bis Friedrich Schiller* (Tübingen: Niemeyer, 1979).

72. Rohr, *Grossen Herren*, pp. 18–19, and Théophraste Renaudot, ed., *Quatriesme centurie des questions traitées aux conférences du Bureau d'Adresse, depuis le 24e Ianvier 1639, jusques au 10e Iuin 1641* (Paris: Bureau d'adresse, 1641), p. 416: "en la vie des courtizans de l'un et l'autre sexe qui font de la nuit jour et du jour la nuit."

73. Casimir Freschot (1640?–1720), *Mémoires de la cour de Vienne, ou Remarques faites par un voyageur curieux sur l'état présent de cette cour* (Cologne: Chez Guillaume Etienne [actually The Hague], 1705), p. 91. German translation as *Relation von dem kayserlichen Hofe zu Wien* (Cologne: bey W. Stephan [actually Amsterdam or Leipzig], 1705), pp. 51–52. On Freschot see Erich Zöllner, "Das barocke Wien in der Sicht französischer Zeitgenossen," in *Probleme und Aufgaben der österreichischen Geschichtsforschung: ausgewählte Aufsätze*, ed. Heide Dienst and Gernot Heiss (Munich: R. Oldenbourg, 1984), pp. 383–94.

74. The author of several devotional tracts and a Pietist utopia, Sinold also published an manual of advice, *Die Wissenschaft zu leben ... und ... ein tüchtiges Mitglied der menschlichen Gesellschaft zu seyn* (Frankfurt and

Leipzig: "in den Buchläden zu finden," 1739), p. 212. On Sinold von Schütz, see Hans Wagener, "Faramonds Glukseligste (sic) Insel: Eine pietistische Sozialutopie," *Symposium* 26 (1972): 78–89, and the literature cited there.

75. See for example the 1640 oil painting of a nocturnal banquet at court by Wolfgang Heimbach (1615–78), Kunsthistorisches Museum, Vienna.

76. Julius von Pflugk-Harttung, *Im Morgenrot der Reformation*, fourth edn. (Basle: A. Rohde, 1922), pp. 182f.

77. On the shift from two to three meals per day, see Roman Sandgruber, "Zeit der Mahlzeit. Veränderung in Tagesablauf und Mahlzeiteinteilung in Österreich im 18. und 19. Jahrhundert," in *Wandel der Volkskultur in Europa. Festschrift für Günter Wiegelmann*, ed. Nils-Arvid Bringéus and Günter Wiegelmann (Münster: Coppenrath, 1988), pp. 459–72.

78. Jacqueline Boucher, "La nuit dans l'imagination et le mode de vie de la cour des derniers Valois," in *Penser la Nuit*, ed. Bertrand, pp. 413–24, p. 418; see the overview in Duindam, *Vienna and Versailles*, pp. 150–60.

79. Arthur Kern, ed., *Deutsche Hofordnungen des 16. und 17. Jahrhunderts* (Berlin: Weidmann, 1905–07), II: 49, 71, 79.

80. Kurt Treusch von Buttlar, "Das tägliche Leben an den deutschen Fürstenhöfen des 16. Jahrhunderts," *Archiv für Kulturgeschichte* 4 (1899): 15–19.

81. The eldest son, John George II, inherited the bulk of the territory, the electoral dignity, and the Dresden court; the three younger sons (Augustus, Christian, and Maurice) founded the cadet lines of Saxony-Weißenfels, Saxony-Merseburg, and Saxony-Zeitz, with their courts at Halle, Merseburg, and Zeitz, respectively. Typically the three younger brothers sent their court diaries to John George II in Dresden, who in turn sent reports of the comings and goings at his court to Halle, Merseburg, and Zeitz. See Gabriele Henkel, "Die Hoftagebücher Herzog Augusts von Sachsen-Weißenfels," *Wolfenbüttler Barock-Nachrichten* 18, 2 (1991): 75–114, and Watanabe-O'Kelly, *Court Culture in Dresden*, pp. 30–34.

82. Eberhard Schmidt, *Der Gottesdienst am Kurfürstlichen Hofe zu Dresden* (Göttingen: Vandenhoeck & Ruprecht, 1961), pp. 32–34.

83. Henkel, "Hoftagebücher," pp. 106–14.

84. *Ibid.*, pp. 111–12: "Der Liebe großer Irrgarten und darauff das Poßenspiel: Die 2 betrogene Ehemänner gennant, agiert."

85. In 1680 the court moved from Halle to Weißenfels on the accession of Duke John Adolph, and in 1685 a small Komödiensaal was opened in the Weißenfels palace. See Klaus-Peter Koch, "Das Jahr 1704 und die Weißenfelser Hofoper," in *Weißenfels als Ort literarischer und künstlerischer Kultur im Barockzeitalter*, ed. Roswitha Jacobsen (Amsterdam and Atlanta, GA: Rodopi, 1994), pp. 75–95.

86. See Fähler, *Feuerwerke des Barock*, p. 125.

87. Sponsel, *Der Zwinger*, p. 43.

88. In Dresden and in other Lutheran cities such as Berlin, court nobles and urban elites began to stage torch-lit nocturnal funeral processions in the 1680s. They were quickly imitated by citizens and townspeople, despite the vehement resistance of the clergy, and by 1700 nocturnal funerals were the norm in Lutheran cities. See Craig Koslofsky, *The Reformation of the Dead: Death and Ritual in Early Modern Germany* (New York: St. Martin's Press, 2000), pp. 133–59.

89. So for example the evening ball attended by John George IV on Tuesday, January 10, 1693: "Hat Abends Herr Ober-Jägermeister von Erdtmannsdorff in seinem Hause den Ball gegeben, wobey Ihr Churfürstl. Durchl. zu Sachsen unser gnädigster Herr auch erschienen." Sächsisches Haupstaatsarchiv Dresden, OHMA, O IV, Nr. 69, Hofdiarium, 1693.

90. Two aspects of court life relatively unaffected by nocturnalization were the hunt and the schedule of Christian worship services.

91. Matthaeus Daniel Pöppelmann, *Vorstellung und beschreibung des ... Zwinger Gartens Gebdäuden oder Der königl. Orangerie ʒu Dresden* (Dresden: Pöppelmann, 1729), cited in Peter Lahnstein, *Das Leben im Barock: Zeugnisse und Berichte 1640–1740* (Stuttgart: W. Kohlhammer, 1974), p. 110.

92. Freschot, *Relation von dem Kayserlichen Hofe ʒu Wien*, p. 51.

93. Klingensmith, *Utility of Splendor*, p. 171.

94. Louis de Rouvroy, duc de Saint-Simon (1675–1755), *Memoirs of Louis XIV and the Regency, by the Duke of Saint-Simon*, trans. Bayle St. John (Washington, D.C.: M.W. Dunne, 1901), I: 34, and *Mémoires de M. le duc de Saint-Simon*, 42 vols., ed. A. de Boislisle and Léon Lecestre (Paris: [Montpensier], 1975–; reprint of the 1879–1930 Hachette edn.): I: 70–71. For a similar description of the *appartements* from Elisabeth Charlotte, Princess Palatine and duchess of Orléans, see her letter to Wilhemine Ernestine of the Palatinate, sent from Versailles, December 6, 1682, as reproduced in *Letters from Liselotte*, ed. and trans. Maria Kroll (New York: McCall, 1971), p. 40.

95. Maria Fürstenwald, "Liselotte von der Pfalz und der französische Hof," in *Europäische Hofkultur im 16. und 17. Jahrhundert*, ed. August Buck *et al.*, Wolfenbütteler Arbeiten zur Barockforschung 8–10 (Hamburg: Hauswedell, 1981), III: 468.

96. See Boucher, "La cour des derniers Valois," and Émile Magne, *La Vie quotidienne au temps de Louis XIII* (Paris: Hachette, 1942), pp. 50–90.

97. Renaudot, ed., *Quatriesme centurie des questions*, p. 413.

98. Klingensmith, *Utility of Splendor*, pp. 155–59, 171. On *appartements* at the court of Charles XII (1697–1718) of Sweden, see Fabian Persson, *Servants*

of Fortune: The Swedish Court between 1598 and 1721 (Lund: Wallin & Dalholm, 1999), p. 53.

99. Lady Mary Wortley Montagu, *The Complete Letters of Lady Mary Wortley Montagu*, ed. Robert Halsband, 3 vols. (Oxford: Clarendon Press, 1965–67), I: 288, to Lady Rich, December 1, 1716. On cosmetics see Melissa Hyde, "The Make-Up of the Marquise: Boucher's Portrait of Pompadour at her Toilette" *Art Bulletin* 82, 3 (2000): 453–75, and the literature cited there. See also Piero Camporesi on "the revenge of the night," in *Exotic Brew: The Art of Living in the Age of Enlightenment*, trans. Christopher Woodall (Cambridge: Polity Press, 1994), pp. 12–19.

100. Chantelou, *Diary of the Cavaliere Bernini's Visit*, p. 179.

101. Night clocks were first designed in Rome, reportedly at the request of Pope Alexander VII (Chigi, 1655–67). On an early eighteenth-century Florentine night clock (case and mosaics by Giovanni Battista Foggini; woodwork by Leonard van der Vinne) in the Getty Museum collection, see Peter Fusco, "Curator's Report: Proposed Purchase, Night Clock," May 6, 1997, J. Paul Getty Museum, Permanent Collection, Object File, Acc. No. 97.DB.37, pp. 1–5. See also Alessandra Mazzonis, "Un orologio del XVII secolo al Museo Correale di Sorrento: il notturno di Pietro T. Campani," *Kermes* 14, 44 (2001): 17–26, 69, for a survey of European night clocks from the seventeenth and eighteenth centuries.

102. Rohr, *Grossen Herren*, pp. 18–19.

103. Julius Bernhard von Rohr, *Einleitung zur Ceremoniel-Wissenschaft der Privat Personen*, ed. with a commentary by Gotthart Frühsorge (Berlin, 1728; repr. Leipzig: Edition Leipzig, 1990), pp. 467–68.

104. *Ibid.*, p. 468.

105. William Byrd, *The London Diary (1717–1721) and Other Writings*, ed. Louis B. Wright and Marion Tinling (New York: Oxford University Press, 1958), p. 76.

106. Sinold, *Die Wissenschaft zu leben*, p. 337.

107. *Ibid.*, pp. 337–38.

108. Loen, *Kleine Schriften*, §3, pp. 62–66. On Loen, see Christiane Buchel, "Johann Michael von Loen im Wandel der Zeiten: Eine kleine Forschungsgeschichte," *Das Achtzehnte Jahrhundert: Mitteilungen der Deutschen Gesellschaft für die Erforschung des Achtzehnten Jahrhunderts* 16, 1 (1992): 13–37.

109. Loen, *Kleine Schriften*, §3, p. 66.

110. Karl Ludwig Freiherr von Pöllnitz, *Nouveaux Mémoires du Baron de Pollnitz, contenant l'histoire de sa vie*, new edn. (Frankfurt: "Aux Dépens de la Compagnie," 1738), II: 151–52.

111. Samuel Pordage, "A Panegyrick on his Majesties Entrance Into London," in *Poems upon several occasions by S.P.* (London: Printed by W.G. for Henry Marsh, and Peter Dring, 1660).

112. Thomas Pecke, *To the Most High and Mighty Monarch, Charles the II, by the grace of God, King of England, Scotland, France and Ireland, defender of the faith* (London: Printed by James Cottrel, 1660), p. 2.

113. Ted-Larry Pebworth, "Herbert's Poems to the Queen of Bohemia: A Rediscovered Text and a New Edition" [with text], *ELR* 9, 1 (1979): 108–20; see also George Herbert, *The Complete English Poems*, ed. John Tobin (London: Penguin Books, 1991), pp. 196–97. In his letters to Elizabeth, Henry Wotton regularly addressed her as "Most resplendent Queen, even in the darkness of Fortune," and in 1629 spoke of "beholding how her virtues overshine the darkness of her fortune." Henry Wotton, *The Life and Letters of Sir Henry Wotton*, ed. Logan Pearsall Smith (Oxford: Clarendon Press, 1907), II: 293, 325.

114. I. W. [i.e., John Walton], "To my worthy friend, Mr. Henry Vaughan the Silurist" (1678), in *Works of Henry Vaughan*, p. 620.

115. John Cleveland, "The King's Disguise," in *The Poems of John Cleveland*, ed. John M. Berdan (New Haven: Yale University Press, 1911), p. 164.

116. Vaughan, "The King Disguis'd," in *Works of Henry Vaughan*, p. 626.

117. Benserade, *Ballets pour Louis XIV*, ed. Canova-Green, I: 91–160; here p. 135 (note the reference to Psalm 119: 105, "Your word [is] a lamp to my feet / And a light to my path"). As Charles Silin has noted, there are "at least five allusions to the successful issue of the recent difficulties" in the *Ballet de la Nuit*: Charles I. Silin, *Benserade and His Ballets de Cour* (Baltimore: Johns Hopkins University Press, 1940), p. 219.

118. Could this evocation of the darkness of rebellion to underscore the importance of the monarch at some point deconstruct itself, emphasizing instead the dark origins of the Sun King? See Aurélia Gaillard, "Le Soleil à son coucher: la nuit réversible de la mythologie solaire sous Louis XIV," in *Penser la nuit*, ed. Bertrand, pp. 449–64, and Hélène Merlin, "Nuit de l'État et Roi-Soleil," in *La Nuit*, ed. François Angelier and Nicole Jacques-Chaquin (Grenoble: Millon, 1995), pp. 203–18.

119. As cited in Vec, *Zeremonialwissenschaft*, p. 139: "Die Hoheit und Macht der Potentaten und Fürsten der Welt / leuchtet zwar sonderlich in dero Landen hervor … Aber es gläntzet dieselbiger noch heller wann andere Mächtige selbst dieselbe considerieren."

120. Habermas described this specific relationship between representation, authority, and audience as "representative publicness" (*repräsentive Öffentlichkeit*), "the display of inherent spiritual power or dignity before an audience," though he did not consider daily time or the night in its development. See *The Structural Transformation of the Public Sphere: An Inquiry into a Category of Bourgeois Society*, trans. Thomas Burger with Frederick Lawrence (Cambridge, MA: MIT Press, 1989), pp. xv, 5–13. As we will see below in chapter 6, the night was equally vital to the development of a bourgeois public sphere in early modern cities.

121. Saint-Simon, *Memoirs*, trans. St. John, III: 307–8, and *Mémoires*, XXXIX: 2–4.

122. *Ibid*. For the court, the illumination was followed by nocturnal entertainment: "Scarcely had I time to return home and sup after this fine illumination than I was obliged to go to the palace for the ball that the King had prepared there, and which lasted until past two in the morning." Evidence suggests that the Spanish court also nocturnalized its spectacles, theater, and daily routines during the seventeenth century. See for example Hannah E. Bergman, "A Court Entertainment of 1638," *Hispanic Review* 42, 1 (1974): 67–81, in which a young woman at court complains that her mother expects her to go to sleep by midnight (p. 70).

123. Norris, "Hymn to Darkness," in *Collection*, pp. 37–38.

124. See Dewald, *Aristocratic Experience*, pp. 33–40. This corresponds with the understanding of the baroque presented by José Antonio Maravall, *Culture of the Baroque: Analysis of a Historical Structure*, trans. Terry Cochran, Theory and History of Literature 25 (Minneapolis: University of Minnesota Press, 1986).

125. Machiavelli, *The Prince*, ch. 18, in *Selected Political Writings*, ed. and trans. David Wootton (Indianapolis, IN: Hackett, 1994), p. 55.

126. In a contemporary English translation – see Ludwig Krapf and Christian Wagenknecht, eds., *Stuttgarter Hoffeste: Texte und Materialen zur höfischen Repräsentation im frühen 17. Jahrhundert* (Tübingen: Niemeyer, 1979).

127. From the contemporary English translation: Nicholas Faret (1596–1646), *The Honest Man or the Art to Please at Court*, trans. Edward Grimstone (London: Thomas Harper, 1632), as quoted in Margaret Lucille Kekewich, ed., *Princes and Peoples: France and British Isles, 1620–1714* (Manchester University Press, 1994), pp. 29–30.

128. Salatino, *Incendiary Art*, p. 19. La Fontaine's response is discussed by Gaillard, "Le Soleil à son coucher".

129. Rohr, *Grossen Herren*, p. 733, as cited in Möseneder, *Zeremoniell*, p. 39.

130. From Machiavelli on, realist discussions of the display of power and majesty were kept separate from actual presentations of a prince's (simulated) greatness. Baroque political theory "revealed" and discussed the very mechanisms and techniques of power that it advised rulers to conceal. Michael Stolleis has discussed this paradox in his *Arcana imperii und Ratio status: Bemerkungen zur politischen Theorie des frühen 17. Jahrhunderts* (Göttingen: Vandenhoeck & Ruprecht, 1980). Political theorists resolved the issue through their strategic contempt for the perceptions and awareness of the common people. The formation in the eighteenth century of a public sphere gradually challenged this contempt and the concomitant darkness and secrecy of absolutist political culture. See Jörg Jochen Berns, "Der nackte Monarch und die nackte Wahrheit – Auskünfte der deutschen Zeitungs- und

Zeremoniellschriften des späten 17. und frühen 18. Jahrhunderts zum Verhältnis von Hof und Öffentlichkeit," *Daphnis* 11, 1–2 (1982): 315–50, Andreas Gestrich, *Absolutismus und Öffentlichkeit: politische Kommunikation in Deutschland zu Beginn des 18. Jahrhunderts*, Kritische Studien zur Geschichtswissenschaft 103 (Göttingen: Vandenhoeck & Ruprecht, 1994), pp. 34–77, and James Van Horn Melton, *The Rise of the Public in Enlightenment Europe* (Cambridge University Press, 2001).

131. The mystic writings of Denys the Areopagite also contributed to this understanding of spectacle in French political discourse in this period: see Yves Durand, "Mystique et politique au XVIIe siècle: l'influence du Pseudo-Denys," *XVIIe Siècle* 173 (1991): 323–50, who argues for their direct influence on Louis XIV.

132. Lipsius, *Sixe Bookes of Politickes*, trans. Jones, pp. 68–70.

133. Nicola Sabbatini's *Practica di Fabricar Scene e Machine ne' Teatri* (*Manual for Constructing Theatrical Scenes and Machines*, 1638) as translated in Hewitt, ed. *Renaissance Stage*, pp. 96–97.

134. For further examples in French political thought see Möseneder, *Zeremoniell*, pp. 38–39. Johann Heinrich Zedler's *Grosses vollständiges Universal-Lexikon* (Leipzig: Zedler, 1732–50) defined the masses ("Pöbel") as "die gemeine Menge niederträchtiger und aller höhern Achtbarkeit geraubter Leute" ("the common crowd of base people deprived of all higher perception"), XXVIII: col. 948.

135. Rohr, *Grossen Herren*, p. 2.

136. See Christian Freiherr von Wolff, *Vernünfftige Gedancken von dem Gesellschafftlichen Leben der Menschen, und insonderheit dem gemeinen Wesen zu Beforderüng der Gluckseeligkeit des menschlichen Geschlechtes* (Halle: Renger, 1721). Rohr opened his *Introduction to the Knowledge of Ceremony of Great Rulers* with a long citation from Wolff's *Vernünfftige Gedancken*.

137. See the overview provided by Jörg Jochen Berns, "Die Festkultur der deutschen Höfe zwischen 1580 und 1730," *Germanisch-Romanische Monatsschrift* n.s. 34, 3 (1984): 295–311.

138. See Stollberg-Rilinger, "Höfische Öffentlichkeit," pp. 147–50, and the concise remarks of Ulrich Schütte, "Das Fürstenschloß als 'Pracht-Gebäude'," in *Die Künste und das Schloss in der frühen Neuzeit*, ed. Lutz Unbehaun with the assistance of Andreas Beyer and Ulrich Schütte, Rudolstädter Forschungen zur Residenzkultur 1 (Munich: Deutscher Kunstverlag, 1998), pp. 15–29.

139. The scarcity of any direct discussion of the role of the night in the con-temporary theorists of baroque court spectacle (such as Ménestrier or Rohr) is not surprising. Discussion of the night in the literature of

spectacles was analogous (on the level of daily life) to the discussions of deception, illusion, and "image" in baroque political theory discussed above. Thus a tract could recommend the use of illusions of majesty and power, confident that the common people would see only the illusions – never the political advice behind them. Proclamations of a monarch's greatness and advice on the importance of burnishing this image existed side by side, but never in the same text. Analogously, on the technical level references to the utility of darkness to create illusion, spectacle, and wonder are frequent; on the theoretical level we see a keen sense of the power of spectacle, but little explicit discussion of the need for darkness itself. On the gaze, landscape, and power, see Dianne S. Harris and D. Fairchild Ruggles, "Introduction," in *Sites Unseen: Landscape and Vision* (University of Pittsburgh Press, 2007), pp. 23–29.

140. From a 1668 lecture on Poussin's *Rebecca and Eliezer at the Well* (1648) given by the painter Philippe de Champaigne at the French royal academy of painting and sculpture, as quoted in John Rupert Martin, *Baroque* (New York: Harper & Row, 1977), pp. 295–96.

5 "AN ENTIRELY NEW CONTRIVANCE": THE RISE OF STREET LIGHTING, 1660–1700

1. Benjamin Franklin, *Writings*, ed. J.A. Leo Lemay (New York: Literary Classics of the United States, 1987), pp. 984–88.
2. See Camille Couderc, "Economies proposées par B. Franklin et Mercier de Saint-Léger pour l'éclairage et la chauffage à Paris," *Bulletin de la Société de l'histoire de Paris et de l'Ile-de-France* 43 (1916): 93–101. Franklin promoted the establishment of Philadelphia's street lighting, the first in North America, in 1757.
3. Cristoforo Muzani (1724–1813), cited in Piero Camporesi, *Exotic Brew: The Art of Living in the Age of Enlightenment*, trans. Christopher Woodall (Cambridge: Polity Press, 1994), pp. 12–19, 14–15.
4. Friedrich Justin Bertuch, "Moden in Gebrauche und Eintheilung des Tages und der Nacht zu Verschiedenen Zeiten, und bey verschiedenen Völkern," *Journal der Moden* [after 1786 *Journal des Luxus und der Moden*] 1 (May 1786): 199–201. See Gerhard Wagner, *Von der Galanten zur Eleganten Welt. Das Weimarer "Journal des Luxus und der Modern" (1786–1827)* (Hamburg: Bockel, 1994).
5. Cf. the comment of Johann Beckmann, *Beyträge zur Geschichte der Erfindungen* (Leipzig: P.G. Kummer, 1782), 1: 62: "Gemeiniglich hält man die Erleuchtung der Straßen für eine ganz neue Einrichtung" ("The illumination of the streets is generally considered an entirely new contrivance").

6. "eine ganz neue Ordnung der Dinge eingeführt," Bertuch, "Moden," p. 200.
7. *Ibid.*
8. *Ibid.*, p. 201.
9. J.M. Beattie, *Policing and Punishment in London 1660–1750: Urban Crime and the Limits of Terror* (Oxford University Press, 2001), p. 172. On coffeehouses, see below, chapter 6.
10. On modern street lighting see Mark J. Bouman, "Luxury and Control: The Urbanity of Street Lighting in Nineteenth-Century Cities," *Journal of Urban History* 14, 1 (1987): 7–37, and Wolfgang Schivelbusch, *Disenchanted Night: The Industrialization of Light in the Nineteenth Century*, trans. Angela Davies (Berkeley: University of California Press, 1988).
11. There is no comparative work on early modern street lighting as an international and interurban development. Schivelbusch and Bouman offer comparative analyses of modern street lighting; Schivelbusch begins with a discussion of early modern street lighting in Paris. With an analysis indebted to Foucault, he emphasizes its relationship to absolutist surveillance and policing, but he does not consider the practical developments in Amsterdam detailed by Lettie S. Multhauf, "The Light of Lamp-Lanterns: Street Lighting in Seventeenth-Century Amsterdam," *Technology and Culture* 26 (1985): 236–52. Eighteenth-century comparative discussions of street lighting include Paul Jacob Marperger, *Abermahliger Versuch zur Abhandlung einer nützlichen Policey-Materia, nehmlich von denen Gassen Laternen, Strand- und Wacht-Feuern, und andern nächtlichen Illuminationibus oder Erleuchtungen der Gassen und Strassen* (Dresden and Leipzig: "Verlegung des Authoris," 1722), and P. Patte, *De la manière la plus avantageuse d'èclairer les rues d'une ville pendant la nuit* (Amsterdam: s.n., 1766).
12. My comparison is indebted to Schivelbusch, who refers to the parallel rise of the "lighting of order" (street lighting) and the "lighting of festivity" in the seventeenth century. See *Disenchanted Night*, pp. 137–43.
13. The beginnings of public street lighting are documented for Paris by Auguste Philippe Herlaut, "L'éclairage des rues de Paris à la fin du XVIIe siècle et au XVIIIe siècle," *Mémoires de la Société de l'histoire de Paris et de l'Ile-de-France* 43 (1916): 130–240, and for Amsterdam by Multhauf, "Street Lighting in Seventeenth-Century Amsterdam." On Turin see Davide Bertolotti, *Descrizione di Torino* (Turin, 1840; repr. Bologna: A. Forni, 1976), p. 63 (my thanks to Geoffrey Symcox for this reference); on London see Malcolm Falkus, "Lighting in the Dark Ages of English Economic History: Town Streets before the Industrial Revolution," in *Trade, Government, and Economy in Pre-Industrial England. Essays presented to F. J. Fisher*, ed. D.C. Coleman

and A.H. John (London: Weidenfeld and Nicolson, 1976), pp. 187–211; for Copenhagen see Johann Georg Krünitz, *Ökonomisch-Technologische Encyklopädie*, vol. LXV (Berlin: Pauli, 1794), and Stadtarchiv Leipzig [hereafter SdAL], Urkunden, 97, 811, fos. 124–32 (manuscript copy of the 1683 Copenhagen street-lighting ordinance).

14. See W. Leybold, "Hamburgs öffentliche Gassenbeleuchtung. Von den Anfängen bis zur Franzosenzeit, 1673–1816," *Nordalbingia* 5 (1926): 455–75, and Wolfgang Nahrstedt, *Die Entstehung der Freizeit. Dargestellt am Beispiel Hamburgs* (Göttingen: Vandenhoeck & Ruprecht, 1972), pp. 88–95; on Vienna see Ludwig Böck, "Zur Geschichte der öffentlichen Beleuchtung Wiens," *Wiener Neujahrs-Almanach* 4 (1898): 1–27, and Margit Altfahrt and Karl Fischer, "'Illuminations-Anfang der Stadt Wien' (Zur Einführung der Straßenbeleuchtung in Wien im Jahre 1687)," *Wiener Geschichtsblätter* 42 (1987): 167–70; on Berlin see Herbert Liman, *Mehr Licht: Geschichte der Berliner Straßenbeleuchtung* (Berlin: Haude & Spener, 2000); on Hanover, see Siegfried Müller, *Leben in der Residenzstadt Hannover: Adel und Bürgertum im Zeitalter der Aufklärung* (Hanover: Schlüter, 1988), pp. 42, 102.

15. See Falkus, "Lighting in the Dark Ages," pp. 251–53, and Schivelbusch, *Disenchanted Night*, p. 82.

16. Thomas DeLaune, *Angliæ Metropolis: or, The Present State of London … First written by … Tho. Delaune, gent. and continued to this present year by a careful hand* (London: Printed by G.L. for J. Harris and T. Howkins, 1690), pp. 365–66. On perceptions of eighteenth-century street lighting, see Schivelbusch, *Disenchanted Night*, pp. 95–96.

17. Johannes Neiner, *Vienna Curiosa & Gratiosa, Oder Das anjetzo Lebende Wienn* (Vienna: Joann. Baptistae Schilgen, 1720), pp. 17–18.

18. See for example the Berlin/Cölln ordinance of 1636 in Christian Otto Mylius, ed., *Corpus Constitutionum Marchicarum* (Berlin and Halle: Buchladen des Waisenhauses, 1737–55), part 5, section 2, cols. 633–34; and Falkus, "Lighting in the Dark Ages," pp. 249–51.

19. See Johann Heinrich Zedler, *Grosses vollstandiges Universal-Lexikon*, vol. XVI (Halle and Leipzig: Verlegts Johann Heinrich Zedler, 1737), article on "Laterne" and the description of the "Diebeslaterne" (thieves' lantern).

20. A Leipzig city ordinance of 1544 set the curfew bell at 9 p.m. in the summer and 8 p.m. in the winter. P.G. Müller, "Die Entwicklung der künstlichen Straßenbeleuchtung in den sächsischen Städten," *Neues Archiv für Sächsische Geschichte und Altertumskunde* 30 (1909): 144–45.

21. On England, see the work of Paul Griffiths, "Meanings of Nightwalking in Early Modern England," *Seventeenth Century* 13, 2 (1998): 212–38, and Elaine A. Reynolds, *Before the Bobbies: The Night Watch and Police Reform in Metropolitan London, 1720–1830* (Basingstoke: Macmillan, 1998).

22. For example, the general Leipzig curfew described above was simply not renewed after the establishment of street lighting in 1701; instead the city council focused on the regulation of youth at night.

23. Johann Valentin Andreä, *Reipublicae christianopolitanae description* (Strasbourg: Zetzner, 1619), dedicated to the Lutheran devotional theologian Johann Arndt. See the excellent English edition: J.V. Andreae, *Christianopolis*, ed. with an Introduction by Edward H. Thompson, Archives internationales d'histoire des idées 162 (Dordrecht: Kluwer Academic Publishers, 1999), pp. 143–45.

24. Andreae, *Christianopolis*, ed. Thompson, pp. 185–86. An earlier Rosicrucian work by Andreä, the *Chymische Hochzeit* of 1616, also carefully described outdoor lighting along a pathway within the grounds of a castle. See *The hermetick romance, or, The chymical wedding written in High Dutch by Christian Rosencreutz*, trans. E. Foxcroft (London: Printed by A. Sowle, 1690), p. 28.

25. Friedrich Lucae, *Der Chronist Friedrich Lucae: ein Zeit- und Sittenbild aus der zweiten Hälfte des siebenzehnten Jahrhunderts*, ed. Friedrich Lucae II (Frankfurt: Brönner, 1854), p. 99. Lucae visited Amsterdam in 1665 or 1666 and again in 1667, observing the street lighting before it was completed in 1669.

26. Multhauf, "Street Lighting in Seventeenth-Century Amsterdam," pp. 249–50; M.G. Niessen, "Straatverlichting," *Ons Amsterdam* 18 (1966), pp. 82–85; Patrick Meehan, "Early Dublin Public Lighting," *Dublin Historical Record* 5 (1943): 130–36.

27. On royal cities see Leon Bernard, *The Emerging City: Paris in the Age of Louis XIV* (Durham, NC: Duke University Press, 1970) and John P. Spielman, *The City and the Crown: Vienna and the Imperial Court, 1600–1740* (West Lafayette, IN: Purdue University Press, 1993).

28. Marperger's 1722 treatise on street lighting presents nine different schemes to pay for the lighting. (Marperger, *Von denen Gassen Laternen*, pp. 22–7.) On the English approach see William Robert Scott, *The Constitution and Finance of English, Scottish and Irish Joint-Stock Companies to 1720* (Cambridge, 1912; repr. Gloucester, MA: Peter Smith, 1968), III: 52–60, as placed in the context of urban development by Paul Slack, *From Reformation to Improvement: Public Welfare in Early Modern England* (Oxford: Clarendon Press, 1999), pp. 102–04. On Dublin and Lübeck see Meehan, "Dublin Public Lighting," pp. 130–36, and W. Brehmer, "Beiträge zu einer Baugeschichte Lübecks. 3. Die Straßen," *Zeitschrift des Vereins für Lübeckische Geschichte und Alterthumskunde* 5, 2 (1887): 254–58.

29. Bernard, *Paris*, pp. 53–54, and Herlaut, "L'éclairage," pp. 137–48. Louis XIV sold a major exemption from the *taxe des boues et lanternes* in 1704.

30. Bernard, *Paris*, pp. 162–66, and Herlaut, "L'éclairage," p. 163.

31. Geheimes Staatsarchiv Preussischer Kulturbesitz Berlin, I. HA, Rep. 21, Nr. 24b1, Fasc. 5, September 23, 1680. Greater Berlin was originally divided by the Spree river into the separate towns of Berlin and Cölln. Confusion between Cölln on the Spree and Köln/Cologne on the Rhine has led some scholars to mistakenly claim that street lighting was also established in Cologne in 1682. In fact, Cologne had no municipal street lighting until the early nineteenth century. See F. Joly, *Die Beleuchtung und Wasserversorgung der Stadt Köln* (Cologne: J.P. Bachem, 1895).

32. See *300 Jahre Strassenbeleuchtung in Berlin* (Berlin: Senator für Bau- und Wohnungswesen, 1979), pp. 8–14.

33. Böck, "Beleuchtung Wiens," p. 14. By the early eighteenth century there were about 1,650 street lanterns in the city. Conrad Richter, "Die erste öffentliche Beleuchtung der Stadt Wien," *Alt-Wien* 6 (1897): 9–11.

34. Archives Municipales de Lille [hereafter AM Lille], Affaires Générales 1256, dossier 9, fo. 3.

35. See Régine Martin, "Les débuts de l'éclairage des rues de Dijon," *Annales de Bourgogne* 25, 4 (1953): 253–55, and Joseph Thomas, *L'éclairage des rues d'Amiens à travers les âges* (Cayeux-sur-Mer: P. Ollivier, 1908), pp. 12–14.

36. Catherine Denys, *Police et sécurité au XVIIIe siècle dans les villes de la frontière franco-belge* (Paris: Harmattan, 2002), pp. 276–77.

37. *Ibid.*, pp. 192–200.

38. Archives Départmentales du Nord [hereafter ADN], C w.305/2899, ordinance of August 31, 1667.

39. ADN, C 2899, ordinance of July 23, 1668.

40. AM Lille, Affaires Générales 1256, dossier 1, fos. 1–3.

41. ADN, C 2899, ordinance of January 17, 1668.

42. AM Lille, Affaires Générales 1256, dossier 1, fo. 3. With 600–700 lanterns for a population of about 55,000 in 1667, Lille compares favorably with Rouen (population 60,000 and 800 lanterns in 1700), but less so with Leipzig (21,000 residents and 700 lanterns in 1701).

43. ADN, C 2899, ordinance of September 23, 1667 regarding innkeepers; ordinance of October 27, 1667 on closing time for "Tavernes & Cabarets"; see also Philippe Jessu, *Louis XIV en Flandre: Exposition historique … à Lille, 28 octobre 1967–30 avril 1968* (Société des amis des musées de Lille, 1967), p. 93. All these ordinances issued from the *Magistrat*; in some cases the initiative of the French governor or intendant is apparent, as for example the announcement on September 22, 1667 of a reward for the denunciation of those guilty of assaulting a French officer. ADN, C 2899.

44. Denys, *Police et sécurité*, pp. 193–95.

45. Albert Croquez, *Histoire politique et administrative d'une province française, la Flandre*, vol. II, *Louis XIV en Flandres* (Paris: Champion, 1920), pp. 50–58.

46. Laurence Echard, *Flanders, or the Spanish Netherlands, most accurately described shewing the several provinces* (London: Printed for Tho. Salusbury, 1691), pp. 17–18.

47. Louis Trénard, *Histoire de Lille: De Charles Quint à la conquête française (1500–1715)*, Histoire de Lille 2 (Toulouse: Privat, 1981), p. 407.

48. Croquez, *Louis XIV en Flandres*, p. 56, and Alain Lottin, *Vie et mentalité d'un Lillois sous Louis XIV* (Lille: É. Raoust & cie, 1968), p. 356. The victim was probably the young man Weimel mentioned in the journal of the silk weaver Pierre Ignace Chavatte on August 24, 1668 ("Weimel fut descoutrez tout nud"). The journal of Chavatte covers the years 1657–93 and has been published in Gerhard Ernst and Barbara Wolf, eds., "Pierre Ignace Chavatte: *Chronique memorial (1657–1693)*," in *Textes français privés des XVIIe et XVIIIe siècles*, Beiheft zur Zeitschrift für romanische Philologie 310, CD 1–3 (Tübingen: Max Niemeyer Verlag, 2005).

49. Croquez, *Louis XIV en Flandres*, p. 56, and Lottin, *Vie et mentalité*, p. 356.

50. Lottin, *Vie et mentalité*, p. 356.

51. *Ibid.*

52. In the same period Le Peletier reported on three soliders hanged for plundering a house near their barracks late one night. Croquez, *Louis XIV en Flandres*, p. 55.

53. On the relationship between the French and the Lille *Magistrat*, see Victoria Sanger, "Military Town Planning under Louis XIV: Vauban's Practice and Methods, 1668–1707," PhD thesis, Columbia University, 2000, pp. 64–68; Gail Bossenga, *The Politics of Privilege: Old Regime and Revolution in Lille* (Cambridge University Press, 1991), pp. 1–25; here p. 21; and Albert Croquez, *La Flandre wallonne et les pays de l'intendance de Lille sous Louis XIV* (Paris: H. Champion, 1912), pp. 80–81.

54. Trénard, *Histoire de Lille*, pp. 287–92, and Lottin, *Vie et mentalité*, pp. 171–88.

55. "Un homme tuè dune centinel au marchè," Ernst and Wolf, ed., "Chavatte: *Chronique memorial*," in *Textes français privés*, July 23, 1672. Spelling and punctuation as original.

56. *Ibid.*, October 16, 1673, "La guerre declarè contre la france." The following year the French completed the Saint-Sauveur bastion overlooking the workers' quarter of the city – a reminder of their distrust of Lillois artisans like Chavatte. See Sanger, "Military Town Planning under Louis XIV," pp. 46–47.

57. Ernst and Wolf, ed., "Chavatte: *Chronique memorial*," in *Textes français privés*, February 7, 1675, "Un debat a la bourse d'or des bourgeois avec des officiers francois."

58. Trénard, *Histoire de Lille*, p. 290; see also Croquez, *Louis XIV en Flandres*, pp. 50–58.
59. A. Crapet, "La vie à Lille de 1667 à 1789," *Revue du Nord* 6 (1920): 126–54, 198–221; and 7 (1921): 266–322, here 135; Denys, *Police et sécurité*, pp. 199, 277; and Catherine Denys, "La sécurité en ville: les débuts de l'éclairage public à Lille au XVIIIe siècle," *Les Cahiers de la sécurité* 61, 1 (2006): 143–50.
60. Catherine Denys, "Le bris de lanternes dans les villes du Nord au XVIIIe siècle: quelques réflexions sur la signification d'un délit ordinaire," in *La petite délinquance du moyen âge à l'époque contemporaine*, ed. Benoît Garnot and Rosine Fry, Publications de l'Université de Bourgogne 90 (Dijon: EUD, 1998), pp. 309–19; here p. 311.
61. Lottin, *Vie et mentalité*, p. 356.
62. Denys, "Le bris de lanternes," p. 314.
63. Lottin, *Vie et mentalité*, p. 356, and Denys, "Le bris de lanternes," p. 316, citing the *Magistrat* in 1710.
64. SdAL, Urkundensammlung, 97, 1–7, "Laternen. 1701–1702," fo. 1. Augustus also oversaw the introduction of street lighting in Dresden in 1705. See Müller, "Die Entwicklung der künstlichen Straßenbeleuchtung," pp. 144–51; cf. P.G. Hilscher, *Chronik der Königlich Sächsischen Residenzstadt Dresden* (Dresden: In Commission der Ch. F. Grimmer'schen Buchhandlung, 1837), pp. 313–14. No other Saxon cities established any regular street lighting until the late eighteenth century.
65. SdAL, Sekt. K 252, Bl. 1–16., here fo. 6.
66. Rudolf Reuss, ed., *Aus dem Leben eines strassburger Kaufmanns des 17. und 18. Jahrhunderts: "Reiss-Journal und Glücks- und Unglücksfälle,"* Beiträge zur Landes- und Volkeskunde von Elsass-Lotharingen und den angrenzenden Gebieten 43 (Strasbourg: J.H.E. Heitz, 1913), p. 14.
67. Why was Zetzner out to mail a letter so late at night? No doubt he was following the schedule of a post-coach. The coaches came and went at fixed times according to published schedules, picking up post and passengers at all hours of the day and night. They connected the insular time of individual cities with regional schedules and movement, and their regular travel brought a new kind of legitimate nocturnal activity to cities. See Wolfgang Behringer, "Bausteine zu einer Geschichte der Kommunikation. Eine Sammelrezension zum Postjubiläum," *Zeitschrift für historische Forschung* 21, 1 (1994): 92–112, and the literature cited there. On students and the night, see below, chapter 6.
68. "Also hat man auch nunmehr allhier zu Leipzig die düstere Nacht und Finsternüß in Licht und hellen Schein zu verwandeln resolviert." *Aufgefangene Brieffe, welche Zwischen etzlichen curieusen Personen über den ietzigen Zustand der Staats und gelehrten Welt gewechselt worden*

(Wahrenberg: J.G. Freymunden [actually Leipzig: Groschuff], 1701), p. 890.

69. The title of a verse pamphlet, *Das bey der Nacht Hervorleuchtende Leipzig* (Leipzig: Immanuel Tietze, 1701), held in the SdAL, Tit. xxvi, Nr. 3, fos. 21r–22v.

70. See Jean-Louis Sponsel, *Der Zwinger, die Hoffeste und die Schloßbaupläne zu Dresden* (Dresden: Stengel, 1924); Georg Kohler, "Die Rituale der fürstlichen Potestas. Dresden und die deutsche Feuerwerkstradition," in *Die schöne Kunst der Verschwendung*, ed. Georg Kohler and Alice Villon-Lechner (Zurich and Munich: Artemis, 1988), pp. 101–34; and Katrin Keller, "La Magnificence des deux Augustes: Zur Spezifik höfischer Kultur im Dresden des Augusteischen Zeitalters (1694–1763)," *Cahiers d'études germaniques* 28 (1995): 55–66.

71. See Karlheinz Blaschke, "Die kursächsische Politik und Leipzig im 18. Jahrhundert," in *Leipzig: Aufklärung und Bürgerlichkeit*, ed. Wolfgang Martens (Heidelberg: Schneider, 1990), pp. 23–38.

72. Dresden, sixty miles to the southeast of Leipzig, had been the primary residence of the Saxon electors since the mid sixteenth century. Leipzig, with its three annual trade fairs, was the commercial center of the territory (and indeed of Central Europe as a whole) and the Saxon princes, including Augustus, usually visited Leipzig during the trade fairs. Augustus preferred to rent one of the city's luxurious baroque palaces, the Appel'schen Haus on the market square, rather than stay in his own official residence in the city, the medieval Moritz castle on the city wall, which he considered too old-fashioned. See Karl Czok, *Am Hofe Augusts des Starken* (Stuttgart: Deutsche Verlags-Anstalt, 1990), pp. 135–39. The court moved with Augustus when he came to Leipzig, renting the finest merchants' houses on the market square, and court life was superimposed on the places and spaces of the city's merchant elites: the opera house, the coffeehouses and merchants' courtyards, and the city's main churches.

73. Nikolaus Pevsner, *Leipziger Barock: Die Baukunst der Barockzeit in Leipzig* (Dresden: W. Jess, 1928). After a series of court intrigues still not clearly understood, Franz Conrad Romanus was accused of embezzlement, removed from office, and arrested in 1705. Unable to regain the favor of Augustus, Romanus was imprisoned at the Königsstein fortress and held there until his death in 1746. See Gustav Wustmann, ed., *Quellen zur Geschichte Leipzigs* (Leipzig: Duncker & Humblot, 1889–95) ii: 263–352.

74. *Ibid.*, ii: 264–67.

75. *Ibid.*, ii: 267: "ins Meer der Vergessenheit geworfen sein möchte."

76. SdAL, "Acten, die Einrichtung der orthen Straßenbeleuchtung betr. 1701," fo. 2.

77. *Ibid.*, fo. 5.

78. Wustmann, ed., *Quellen*, II: 269.
79. SdAL, *Das bey der Nacht Hervorleuchtende Leipzig*. The street lighting of Paris was celebrated in very similar terms in 1667: "Il fera comme en plein midi / Clair la nuit dedans chaque rue." ("The night will be lit up as bright as day, in every street.") *Gazette de Robinet*, October 29, 1667, cited in Schivelbusch, *Disenchanted Night*, p. 90.
80. Quoted in Böck, "Beleuchtung Wiens," pp. 10–12.
81. See Verena Kriese, "Die Vorstädte Leipzigs im 18. Jahrhundert," *Jahrbuch für Regionalgeschichte* 16, 2 (1989): 110–25. The suburbs were not illuminated until the late eighteenth century. The early modern street lighting was limited to the area within the city walls.
82. Wustmann, ed., *Quellen*, II: 269–70. In comparison, in 1701 the Leipzig city council contributed 6,000 florins toward the construction of a major new public building, the poorhouse, orphanage, asylum, and workhouse of St. George. See Tanya Kevorkian, "The Rise of the Poor, Weak, and Wicked: Poor Care, Punishment, Religion and Patriarchy in Leipzig, 1700–1730," *Journal of Social History* 34, 1 (2000): 163–81.
83. *Aufgefangene Brieffe*, pp. 890–91.
84. *Ibid*. For an example of this temporary festive street lighting in Hanover in 1665, see Siegfried Müller, *Leben im alten Hannover: Kulturbilder einer deutschen Stadt* (Hanover: Schlüter, 1986), pp. 22, 146, and the examples above in chapter 4.
85. *Aufgefangene Brieffe*, pp. 890–91. The article is titled "Von der Illuminations-Pracht und Mißbrauch / und hingegen von nützlichen und nöthigen Gebrauch der See-Lichter und Nacht-Laternen auch nunmehr zu Leipzig aufgesteckt worden."
86. *Ibid*., p. 888.
87. *Ibid*.
88. Schivelbusch, *Disenchanted Night*, pp. 93–96.
89. Wustmann, ed., *Quellen*, II: 271, quoting from the *Ratspatente* of 1701–02. Richard Steele describes a similar fashion in London coffeehouses: "the students … come in their night-gowns to Saunter away their time … One would think these young Virtuoso's take a gay Cap and Slippers, with a scarf and party-colour'd Gown, to be the Ensigns of Dignity." "Hominem pagina nostra sapit," *Spectator* 49 (April 26, 1711), ed. Donald F. Bond (Oxford: Clarendon Press, 1965), I: 209. See Ariane Fennetaux, "Men in Gowns: Nightgowns and the Construction of Masculinity in Eighteenth-Century England," *Immediations: Research Journal of the Courtauld Institute of Art* 1, 1 (2004): 77–89.
90. The Leipzig ordinances regulating "night life" were all directed at heads of households and refer to nocturnal youthful disorder. Wustmann, ed., *Quellen*, II: 271. Young people in the urban night are examined in chapter 6.

91. Wustmann, ed., *Quellen*, II: 271.

92. Of course, the success of these attempts to police a city's night life is another matter, as the following chapter will show.

93. "Es wird manch Huren-Packt die Lichter müssen scheuen / Manch Dieb zu Bette gehen / der in die Nacht gelaurt." *Das bey der Nacht Hervorleuchtende Leipzig*, SdAL, Tit. XXVI, Nr. 3, fo. 22v.

94. *Ibid.*: "Wenn sie bey Sicherheit / sich Freund und Feind zu kennen / Die Strassen auff und ab zu handeln können gehn."

95. See the Vienna petition noted above and Gerhard Tanzer, *Spectacle müssen seyn: die Freizeit der Wiener im 18. Jahrhundert*, Kulturstudien 21 (Vienna: Böhlau, 1992), p. 58.

96. *Ibid.*

97. After all, the "citizens and artisans" of early modern cities had been, not long before, the "many apprentices, boys ... and such unmarried folk ... found idly in the streets ... late in the evening," as the 1697 and 1702 Leipzig ordinances described them.

98. Herlaut, "L'éclairage," p. 166: "en mars, la saison et les affaires remplissent la ville et la Cour est à Paris." The longer court schedule was adopted.

99. Irene Schrattenecker, ed., *Eine deutsche Reise Anno 1708* (Innsbruck: Haymon, 1999), p. 131. The author is an unknown Venetian.

100. Ralph Thoresby, *The Diary of Ralph Thoresby, F.R.S., Author of the Topography of Leeds: (1677–1724)*, ed. Joseph Hunter (London: H. Colburn and R. Bentley, 1830), II: 120 (June 15, 1712).

101. Léon Clerbois, "Histoire de l'éclairage public à Bruxelles," *Annales de la société royale d'archéologie de Bruxelles* 24 (1910): 91–106. Public street lighting was re-established in Brussels in 1703.

102. Johann Georg Kohl, *Alte und Neue Zeit. Episoden aus der Cultur-Geschichte der freien Reichs-Stadt Bremen* (Bremen: Müller, 1871), pp. 22–25. See Staatsarchiv Bremen 2-D.20.b.1.e.2.a., Bd.1: "Rechnungs-buch der Beleuchtungsabgabe," indicating that funds were collected for lanterns and oil starting in 1698.

103. On French provincial street lighting see Daniel Bontemps and Hubert Beylier, *Lanternes d'éclairage public: XVIIe et XVIIIe siècles* (Paris: Ministère de la Culture et de la Communication, Direction du Patrimoine, 1986), pp. 2–10, and Martin, "Les débuts de l'éclairage des rues de Dijon," pp. 253–55. On Caen, see Gabriel Vanel, ed., *Recueil de journaux caennais, 1661–1777: publiés d'après les manuscrits inédits* (Rouen: A. Lestringant, 1904), pp. 43–44.

104. Thomas, *L'éclairage des rues d'Amiens*, pp. 11–15. On resistance to the street lighting in Tournai (annexed to France 1668–1713), see A. de la Grange, "Historire de l'éclairage public à Tournai (1275–1890),"

Bulletins de la Société historique et archéologique de Tournai 25 (1894): 392–98.

105. Friedrich Lau, *Geschichte der Stadt Düsseldorf* (Düsseldorf: Bagel, 1921), I: 131. By 1701 the other leading princes of the Empire had established street lighting in their main cities (Berlin, Vienna, and Hanover, with Leipzig in the works) and the Wittelsbach elector John William of Pfalz-Neuberg sought to keep up with his peers.

106. Lau, *Geschichte der Stadt Düsseldorf*, I: 132; Hugo Weidenhaupt and Manfred Fey, *Düsseldorf: Geschichte von den Ursprüngen bis ins 20. Jahrhundert* (Düsseldorf: Schwann im Patmos-Verlag, 1988), II: 71.

107. Paul Sauer and Hansmartin Decker-Hauff, *Geschichte der Stadt Stuttgart*, vol. III, *Vom Beginn des 18. Jahrhunderts bis zum Abschluss des Verfassungsvertrags für das Königreich Württemberg 1819* (Stuttgart: Kohlhammer, 1993), pp. 139–40: "der größere Teil der Einwohnerschaft hohen und niederen Standes erkenne, was für schlecten oder gar keinen Nutzen die ... eingeführten Laternen dem Publikum gebracht, welch große Kosten sie dagegen verursacht hätten."

108. The city agreed that the specific "lighting tax" would still be assessed, however, until 1744, suggesting that the objection to the street lighting went beyond its cost. *Ibid.*

109. The original verse:

> Als unsre Stadt im Wohlstand sass,
> Da war es finster auf der Strass,
> Doch als das Unglück angefangen
> Hat man Laternen aufgehangen,
> Damit der arme Bürgersmann
> Des Nachts zum Bettlen sehen kann.
> Wir brauchen die Laternen nicht,
> Wir sehn das Elend ohne Licht.

Hermann Ludwig, *Strassburg vor hundert Jahren. Ein Beitrag zur Kulturgeschichte* (Stuttgart: Frommann, 1888), p. 277.

110. See Christian Casanova, *Nacht-Leben: Orte, Akteure und obrigkeitliche Disziplinierung in Zürich, 1523–1833* (Zürich: Chronos, 2007), pp. 11–206. In Zurich no public street lighting was established until the French occupation in 1799.

111. *Tatler* 263 (December 14, 1710).

6 COLONIZING THE URBAN NIGHT: RESISTANCE, GENDER, AND THE PUBLIC SPHERE

1. On the expansion of the night watch, see J. M. Beattie, *Policing and Punishment in London 1660–1750: Urban Crime and the Limits of Terror*

(Oxford University Press, 2001), pp. 169–207, Gerhard Sälter, *Polizei und soziale Ordnung in Paris: zur Entstehung und Durchsetzung von Normen im städtischen Alltag des Ancien Régime (1697–1715)* (Frankfurt: Klostermann, 2004), pp. 181–200, and Christian Casanova, *Nacht-Leben: Orte, Akteure und obrigkeitliche Disziplinierung in Zürich, 1523–1833* (Zurich: Chronos, 2007), pp. 141–206.

2. Eugène Defrance, *Histoire de l'éclairage des rues de Paris* (Paris: Imprimerie nationale, 1904), p. 36: "le grand nombre de vagabonds et voleurs de nuit … et la quantité de vols et meutres qui s'y sont faits le soir et la nuit"; Lettie S. Multhauf, "The Light of Lamp-Lanterns: Street Lighting in Seventeenth-Century Amsterdam," *Technology and Culture* 26 (1985): 239; *Codex Austriacus, Supplementum Codicis Austriaci Sammlung Oesterreichischer Gesetze und Ordnungen … bis auf das Jahr 1720* (Leipzig: Eisfeld, 1748), III: 239: "zu Abwendung und Verhütung aller, nächtlicher weil eine Zeit her häufig in Schwang gegangen, und noch befürchtenden Mord und Diebereyen, wie auch Einführung einer allgemeinen Sicherheit."

3. *State-Poems; Continued from the Time of O. Cromwel, to this Present Year 1697* ([London]: s.n., 1697), pp. 243–46, 245.

4. I draw an analogy between the colonization of the night and the early modern understanding of the colonization of space and place, as seen for example in the 1694 *Dictionnaire de l'Académie française*: "Colonie. Peuple & habitans d'un païs qui se sont establis dans un autre." ("Colony. People and inhabitants of one country who are established in another.") For earlier references to "the colonization of the night" see Murray Melbin, *Night As Frontier: Colonizing the World after Dark* (New York: Free Press, 1987), who accepts the image of the frontier as an unoccupied space; Norbert Schindler, "Nocturnal Disturbances: On the Social History of the Night in the Early Modern Period," in *Rebellion, Community and Custom in Early Modern Germany* (Cambridge University Press, 2002), p. 195: "Alongside the court aristocracy, the Counter-Reformation church … also sought to colonise the night and to extend into the evening its disciplinary grip on the everyday lives of subjects"; and Peter Clark, *British Clubs and Societies, 1580–1800: The Origins of an Associational World* (Oxford University Press, 2000), p. 171: "The colonization of the night was an essential part of the refashioned world of urban sociability." On similar themes seen in the colonization of the night and in European colonization of Asia, America, and Africa, see below, n. 141, surveying the relevant scholarship on colonization and empire.

5. Friedrich Justin Bertuch, "Moden in Gebrauche und Eintheilung des Tages und der Nacht zu Verschiedenen Zeiten, und bey verschiedenen Völkern," *Journal der Moden* [after 1786 *Journal des Luxus und der Moden*] 1 (May 1786): 200: "die Geschäfte des Tages allenthalben und immer desto später anfangen, jemehr sich die Societät verfeinert und der Luxus steigt."

6. On "casual time" as resistance to structured public places and times, a "night that causes an 'accident'," see Michel de Certeau, *The Practice of Everyday Life*, trans. Steven Rendall (Berkeley: University of California Press, 1984), pp. 202–03.

7. Ulrike Strasser, *State of Virginity: Gender, Religion, and Politics in an Early Modern Catholic State* (Ann Arbor: University of Michigan Press, 2007), p. 102, citing a Munich edict of 1630.

8. On apprentices, servants, and maids in London night life, see Paul Griffiths, *Youth and Authority: Formative Experiences in England, 1560–1640* (Oxford: Clarendon Press, 1996), pp. 198–221. On nocturnal youthful disorder in smaller cities and towns see David Underdown, *Fire from Heaven: Life in an English Town in the Seventeenth Century* (New Haven: Yale University Press, 1992), pp. 79–84, 147–49; Frédérique Pitou, "Jeunesse et désordre social: les coureurs de nuit à Laval au XVIIIe siècle," *Revue d'histoire moderene et contemporaine* 47, 1 (2000): 69–92; and Norbert Schindler, "Guardians of Disorder: Rituals of Youthful Culture at the Dawn of the Modern Age," in *A History of Young People in the West*, ed. Giovanni Levi and Jean-Claude Schmitt, trans. Camille Naish (Cambridge, MA and London: Belknap Press of Harvard University Press, 1997), I: 240–82.

9. Sälter, *Polizei und soziale Ordnung*, pp. 414, 194. D'Argenson served as *lieutenant-général de police* of Paris from 1697 to 1715; he was preceded by the first *lieutenant-général de police*, Gabriel Nicolas de La Reynie (served 1667–97).

10. Norbert Elias, *The Civilizing Process: Sociogenetic and Psychogenetic Investigations*, trans. Edmund Jephcott (Oxford: Blackwell, 2000), p. 413.

11. From a Strasbourg ordinance of 1651 forbidding "das nächtliche, unmänschliche graßieren, Jauchzen, Jählen und Schreien in Gassen und Häusern" quoted in Johannes Beinert, "Moscherosch im Dienste der Stadt Straßburg," *Jahrbuch für Geschichte, Sprache und Literatur Elsass-Lothringens* 23 (1907): 138–46, here 144.

12. High-ranking imperial officials like Ludwig Wilhelm usually rented suitable accomodations in Vienna, as near the Hofburg as possible, but housing in the city was extraordinarily scarce. See John P. Spielman, *The City and the Crown: Vienna and the Imperial Court, 1600–1740* (West Lafayette, IN: Purdue University Press, 1993), esp. pp. 75–100.

13. As armed and liveried servants, lackeys were often singled out as especially violent and associated with night-time violence. As Scarron remarked:

> Pages, laquais, voleurs de nuit;
> Carosses, chevaux et grand bruit:
> C'est là Paris. Que vous en semble?

See Léon Hilaire, "Pages et laquais," *L'Investigateur: Journal de l'Institut historique* 52 (1881): 149–54, and Stuart Carroll, *Blood and Violence in Early Modern France* (Oxford University Press, 2006).

14. "Printz Louis mit Einigen Handkranaten (Unter die tumultierenden werffend) frieden gemacht, wodurch Pferde und Menschen beschädiget, Und etliche schon gestorben sind." Ludwig Baur, "Berichte des Hessen-Darmstädtischen Gesandten Justus Eberhard Passer an die Landgräfin Elisabeth Dorothea über die Vorgänge am kaiserlichen Hofe und in Wien von 1680 bis 1683," *Archiv für Österreichische Geschichte* 37 (1867): 271–409, 331–32.

15. It is no coincidence that Ludwig Wilhelm gained some of his first miliary experience at the siege of Philippsburg in 1676.

16. *Female Tatler* 67 (December 9, 1709), [p. 2]. See Fidelis Morgan, *The Female Tatler* (London: Dent, 1992).

17. John Childs, ed., "Captain Henry Herbert's Narrative of His Journey through France with his Regiment, 1671–3," *Camden Fourth Series* 30 (1990): 271–369, here 304–05.

18. *A view of Paris, and places adjoining ... Written by a gentleman lately residing at the English Ambassador's at Paris* (London: Printed for John Nutt, near Stationers-Hall, 1701), p. 11.

19. Joachim Christoph Nemeitz, *Séjour de Paris: c'est à dire, instructions fidèles, pour les voiageurs de condition, comment ils se doivent conduire, s'ils veulent faire un bon usage de leur tems & argent, durant leur Séjour à Paris* (Leiden: J. Van Abcoude, 1727), ed. Alfred Franklin as *La vie de Paris sous la Régence* (Paris: Éditions Plon, Nourrit et cie, 1897), p. 230.

20. Louis de Rouvroy, duc de Saint-Simon, *Mémoires de M. le duc de Saint-Simon*, 42 vols., ed. A. de Boislisle and Léon Lecestre (Paris: [Montpensier], 1975–; reprint of the 1879–1930 Hachette edn.), XVII: 396.

21. Anthony Wood, *The Life and Times of Anthony Wood, Antiquary, of Oxford, 1632–1695, Described by Himself*, ed. Andrew Clark. Oxford Historical Society Publications 19 (Oxford: Clarendon Press, 1894), III: 187, 423; entries for May 25, 1686 and May 23, 1693. See A. Roger Ekirch, *At Day's Close: Night in Times Past* (New York: W.W. Norton, 2005), p. 228.

22. See above, chapter 5, section 5.4.

23. Wolfgang Schivelbusch, *Disenchanted Night: The Industrialization of Light in the Nineteenth Century*, trans. Angela Davies (Berkeley: University of California Press, 1988), pp. 97–114.

24. Auguste Philippe Herlaut, "L'éclairage des rues de Paris à la fin du XVIIe siècle et au XVIIIe siècle," *Mémoires de la Société de l'histoire de Paris et de l'Ile-de-France* 43 (1916): 130–240; here 226.

25. Christian Otto Mylius, ed. *Corpus Constitutionum Marchicarum* (Berlin and Halle: Buchladen des Waisenhauses, 1737–55), part 6, section 2,

cols. 37–38, 73–74, 169, and part 1, section 1, cols. 171–72; Catherine Denys, "Le bris de lanternes dans les villes du Nord au XVIIIe siècle: quelques réflexions sur la signification d'un délit ordinaire," in *La petite délinquance du moyen âge à l'époque contemporaine*, ed. Benoît Garnot and Rosine Fry, Publications de l'Université de Bourgogne 90 (Dijon: EUD, 1998), pp. 309–19; Achilles Augustus von Lersner and Georg August von Lersner, *Achill. Augusti von Lersner nachgehohlte, vermehrte und continuirte Frankfurthische Chronica Zweyter Theil* (Frankfurt: Johann Adam Recksroth, 1734), p. 27; Patrick Meehan, "Early Dublin Public Lighting," *Dublin Historical Record* 5 (1943): 130–36.

26. Conrad Richter, "Die erste öffentliche Beleuchtung der Stadt Wien," *Alt-Wien* 6 (1897): 10. In Clermont in 1698 lantern vandals were threatened with excommunication: André-Georges Manry, *Histoire de Clermont-Ferrand* (Clermont-Ferrand: Bouhdiba, 1993), pp. 166–67.

27. Martin Lister, *A Journey to Paris in the Year 1698*, ed. Raymond Phineas Stearns (Urbana: University of Illinois Press, 1967), p. 25.

28. Sächsisches Hauptstaatsarchiv Dresden [hereafter SHAD], Loc. 1779, "Acta, das zu Conservation der Nachtlaternen …", fo. 3: "aus Muthwillen boßhafter Leuthe gar leicht gekränket werden möchten."

29. SHAD, Loc. 1779, fo. 5; Theodor Distel, "Miscellen 5," *Archiv für sächsische Geschichte* n.s. 5, 1 (1878): 90–92.

30. Schivelbusch (*Disenchanted Night*, pp. 86, 98, 121) makes this point. The political symbolism and practical value of the street lighting help explain the initial distribution of the lighting evenly across a city. As symbols of the power and authority of the monarch and city government, and as a practical deterrent to crime, it could hardly have been otherwise. To be sure, politically or commercially important streets and squares were better lit, but leaving a street or section of the city dark would imply that it was somehow outside the power and authority of the lights, and it would certainly offer a place for those "shy of the light" to gather. On the density of street lighting in Paris and Rouen, see Daniel Roche, *A History of Everyday Things: The Birth of Consumption in France, 1600–1800*, trans. Brian Pearce (Cambridge University Press, 2000), p. 120, and Jean-Pierre Bardet, *Rouen aux XVIIe et XVIIIe siècles: les mutations d'un espace social*, Regards sur l'histoire 50 (Paris: Société d'édition d'enseignement supérieur, 1983), pp. 125–27 and tables 60–61.

31. Paul Jacob Marperger, *Abermahliger Versuch zur Abhandlung einer nützlichen Policey-Materia, nehmlich von denen Gassen Laternen, Strand- und Wacht-Feuern, und andern nächtlichen Illuminationibus oder Erleuchtungen der Gassen und Strassen* (Dresden and Leipzig: "Verlegung des Authoris," 1722), pp. 27–8.

32. *Ibid.*, p. 28.

33. Carl Eduard Vehse, *Geschichte des Östereichischen Hofs und Adels und der östereichischen Diplomatie* (Hamburg: Hoffman und Campe, 1851), VII: 66–67, citing the *Lettres historiques*. See Spielman, *City and the Crown*, pp. 123–36 on anti-Jewish violence in Vienna.

34. Charles Somerset, *The Travel Diary (1611–1612) of an English Catholic, Sir Charles Somerset*. Edited from the Manuscript in the Brotherton Collection, University of Leeds, ed. Michael G. Brennan (Leeds Philosophical and Literary Society, 1993), p. 281.

35. John Evelyn, *The Diary of John Evelyn. In Six Volumes*, ed. E.S. de Beer (Oxford: Clarendon Press, 1955), II: 472.

36. Andrew Balfour, *Letters write* [sic] *to a friend by the learned and judicious Sir Andrew Balfour ... containing excellent directions and advices for travelling thro' France and Italy* (Edinburgh: s.n., 1700), p. 230.

37. Petr Andreevich Tolstoi, *The Travel Diary of Peter Tolstoi: A Muscovite in Early Modern Europe*, trans. Max J. Okenfuss (DeKalb, IL: Northern Illinois University Press, 1987), p. 102. Padua's reputation extended into the early eighteenth century, when another English visitor noted that "The City is ... well Fortified, but thinly Inhabited; which is occasion'd by the frequent Tumults and Quarrels of the Scholars, who usually walk the Streets arm'd in the Night-time, and even seek Occasions of doing Mischief." Ellis Veryard, *An account of divers choice remarks ... taken in a journey through the Low-Countries, France, Italy, and part of Spain* (London: S. Smith and B. Walford, 1701), p. 124.

38. Carl Heiler, "Der Herborner Student 1584–1817," *Nassauischen Annalen* 55 (1935): 79–85.

39. Herbert Schwarzwälder, *Sitten und Unsitten, Bräuche und Missbräuche im alten Bremen in den Proklamen eines hochedlen, hochweisen Rathes dieser Stadt* (Bremen: Schünemann, 1984), p. 69.

40. Sophie Cassagnes-Brouquet, "La violence des étudiants à Toulouse à la fin du XVe et au XVIe siècle (1460–1610)," *Annales du Midi* 94 (1982): 243–62, and Beinert, "Moscherosch," p. 144.

41. As cited in John Lough, *France Observed in the Seventeenth Century by British Travelers* (Stocksfield, UK: Oriel Press, 1985), pp. 103–04.

42. Neil Brough and R.J. Kavanagh, "Kreuzgang's Precursors: Some Notes on the *Nachtwachen* des Bonaventura," *German Life and Letters* 39, 3 (1986): 173–92, here 185.

43. Alois Niederstätter, "Notizen zu einer Rechts- und Kulturgeschichte der Nacht," in *Das Recht im Kulturgeschichtlichen Wandel: Festschrift für Karl Heinz Burmeister zur Emeritierung*, ed. Bernd Marquardt and Alois Niederstätter (Konstanz: UVK, 2002), pp. 173–90; here p. 182; Uta Tschernuth, "Studentisches Leben in den Bursen," in *Das alte Universitätsviertel in Wien 1385–1985*, ed. Günther Hamann, Kurt

Mühlberger, and Franz Skacel, Schriftenreihe des Universitätsarchivs 2 (Vienna: Universitätsverlag für Wissenschaft und Forschung, 1985), pp. 153–62.

44. John Milton, *Paradise Lost*, ed. David Scott Kastan and Merritt Yerkes Hughes (Indianapolis, IN: Hackett Publishing, 2005), p. 24; 1.500–02

45. Sälter, *Polizei und soziale Ordnung*, p. 192.

46. *Ibid.*, pp. 193–95.

47. Marc-René de Voyer d'Argenson, *Notes de René d'Argenson, intéressantes pour l'histoire des moeurs et de la police de Paris: à la fin du règne de Louis XIV* (Paris: Imprimerie Émile Voitelain et cie, 1866), p. 36.

48. In the transition from *Fremdzwang* to *Selbstzwang* proposed by Elias in *The Civilizing Process*, this pressure on fathers to control sons could be seen as a key intermediate step. See further evidence in Sälter, *Polizei und soziale Ordnung*, pp. 410ff.

49. See Robert Shoemaker, "Male Honour and the Decline of Public Violence in Eighteenth-Century London," *Social History* 26, 2 (2001): 190–208, and Gustav Gugitz, "Mord und Totschlag in Alt-Wien. Ein Beitrag zur Geschichte der öffentlichen Sicherheit und Kriminalität in Wien im 17. und 18. Jahrhundert," *Jahrbuch des Vereins für Geschichte der Stadt Wien* 14 (1958): 141–55.

50. Gerd Schwerhoff, *Köln im Kreuzverhör: Kriminalität, Herrschaft und Gesellschaft in einer frühneuzeitlichen Stadt* (Bonn and Berlin: Bouvier, 1991), pp. 300–01.

51. Claude Fouret, "Douai au XVIe siècle: une sociabilité de l'agression," *Revue d'histoire moderne et contemporaine* 34 (1987): 3–29; Joachim Eibach, *Frankfurter Verhöre: städtische Lebenswelten und Kriminalität im 18. Jahrhundert* (Paderborn: Schöningh, 2003), pp. 222–24, and the studies cited there.

52. Sébastien Cabantous, "Crimes et délits nocturnes en pays tarnais au siècle des lumières," *Revue du Tarn*, third series, 181 (2001): 107–31, and Julius R. Ruff, *Crime, Justice, and Public Order in Old Regime France: The Sénéchaussées of Libourne and Bazas, 1696–1789* (London: Croom Helm, 1984), pp. 83–85.

53. Gugitz, "Mord und Totschlag in Alt-Wien"; cf. the Totenbeschauprotokolle (coroners' reports) in the Wiener Stadt- und Landesarchiv.

54. *The Proceedings on the King's Commissions of the Peace, Oyer and Terminer, and Gaol Delivery for the City of London; and also Gaol Delivery for the County of Middlesex, held at Justice-Hall in the Old Bailey* [hereafter OBSP], January 14, 1687: "J. W—— and J. P—— were Indicted for Killing one Peter Penrose Bell-man in the Parish of St. Giles's in the Fields, on the 30th. day of November last." On attitudes toward nightwatchmen, see Brough and Kavanagh, "Kreuzgang's Precursors."

55. Sälter, *Polizei und soziale Ordnung*, pp. 193–95, citing cases from 1696 and 1697.

56. See Catherine Denys, "The Development of Police Forces in Urban Europe in the Eighteenth Century," *Journal of Urban History* 36, 3 (2010): 332–44, and Catherine Denys, Brigitte Marin, and Vincent Milliot, eds., *Réformer la police. Les mémoires policiers en Europe au XVIIIe siècle* (Presses universitaires de Rennes, 2009). On the end of the night watch see Joachim Schlör, *Nights in the Big City: Paris, Berlin, London 1840–1930*, trans. Pierre Gottfried Imhoff and Dafydd Rees Roberts (London: Reaktion Books, 1998), pp. 73–86.

57. d'Argenson, *Notes*, pp. 63–64.

58. Sälter, *Polizei und soziale Ordnung*, pp. 183–84.

59. Beattie, *Policing and Punishment*, pp. 167–97.

60. Anne Emily Garnier Newdigate-Newdegate, *Cavalier and Puritan in the Days of the Stuarts; Compiled from the Private Papers and Diary of Sir Richard Newdigate, Second Baronet, with Extracts from Ms. News-Letters Addressed to Him between 1675 and 1689* (New York: Longmans, Green, and Co., 1901), pp. 234–38.

61. Evelyn, *Diary*, ed. de Beer, vol. v, *Kalendarium, 1690–1706*, p. 363.

62. Jürgen Habermas, *Strukturwandel der Öffentlichkeit. Untersuchungen zu einer Kategorie der bürgerlichen Gesellschaft. Mit einem Vorwort zur Neuauflage 1990* (Frankfurt: Suhrkamp, 1990), p. 18.

63. See Karin Sennefelt, "Citizenship and the Political Landscape of Libelling in Stockholm, c. 1720–70," *Social History* 33, 2 (2008): 145–63, and the literature cited there. See also the essays by Hohendahl, Baker, Zaret, and Eley in Craig Calhoun, ed., *Habermas and the Public Sphere* (Cambridge, MA: MIT Press, 1992), and Kurt Imhof, "'Öffentlichkeit' als historische Kategorie und als Kategorie der Historie," *Schweizerische Zeitschrift für Geschichte* 46, 1 (1996): 3–25.

64. Habermas, *Strukturwandel*, pp. 58–69; Jürgen Habermas, *The Structural Transformation of the Public Sphere: An Inquiry into a Category of Bourgeois Society*, trans. Thomas Burger with Frederick Lawrence (Cambridge, MA: MIT Press, 1989), pp. 5–14.

65. See the "Vorwort zur Neuauflage 1990" in Habermas, *Strukturwandel der Öffentlichkeit*, pp. 11–50; see Peter Uwe Hohendahl, "The Theory of the Public Sphere Revisited," in *Sites of Discourse – Public and Private Spheres – Legal Culture*, ed. Uwe Böker and Julie A. Hibbard (Amsterdam and New York: Rodopi, 2002), pp. 13–33, and Geoff Eley, "Politics, Culture, and the Public Sphere," *Positions* 10, 1 (2002): 219–36.

66. For example, the essays in Peter Lake and Steven C. A. Pincus, eds., *The Politics of the Public Sphere in Early Modern England* (Manchester University Press, 2007).

67. *Structural Transformation*, p. 34; *Strukturwandel*, p. 95: "Privatleuten, die produktive Arbeit tun."
68. Brian William Cowan, *The Social Life of Coffee: The Emergence of the British Coffeehouse* (New Haven: Yale University Press, 2005).
69. See the valuable study by Beat Kümin, *Drinking Matters: Public Houses and Social Exchange in Early Modern Central Europe* (Basingstoke: Palgrave Macmillan, 2007), pp. 185–88, arguing that alehouses and taverns, rather than coffeehouses or salons, were the leading sites of social and cultural exchange in the last century of the Old Regime.
70. Johann Baptist Suttinger, *Consuetudines Austriacae ad stylum excelsi regiminis infra anasum olim accommodatae* (Nuremberg: Martin Endter, 1718), p. 23. The *Réflexions morales, satiriques et comiques, sur les moeurs de notre siècle* of Jean Frédéric Bernard (Amsterdam: chez Jean Frederic Bernard, 1713) describes the coffeehouses of the Dutch Republic as filled with "a spirit of sedition and discord … an anarchy of libertine discourse," as quoted in Lynn Hunt, Margaret C. Jacob, and Wijnand Mijnhardt, *The Book That Changed Europe: Picart and Bernard's Religious Ceremonies of the World* (Cambridge, MA: Belknap Press of Harvard University Press, 2010), p. 37.
71. Steve Pincus, "'Coffee Politicians Does Create': Coffeehouses and Restoration Political Culture," *Journal of Modern History* 67 (1995): 807–34.
72. Markman Ellis, *The Coffee House: A Cultural History* (London: Phoenix, 2004), p. 47.
73. *Ibid.*, pp. 49–50. Of course, the gatherings essential to a public sphere did not take place only at night.
74. M.P., *Character of Coffee and Coffee-Houses* (London: John Starkey, 1661). See below, chapter 8, on the implications of coffeehouse sociability at night for the early Enlightenment.
75. Alfred Franklin, *Le café, le thé et le chocolat*, La vie privée d'autrefois 13 (Paris: Éditions Plon, Nourrit et cie, 1893), pp. 73–74.
76. *Ibid.*, p. 73.
77. *Ibid.*, p. 74.
78. *Ibid.*, p. 76.
79. Peter Albrecht, "Coffee-Drinking As a Symbol of Social Change in Continental Europe in the Seventeenth and Eighteenth Centuries," *Studies in Eighteenth-Century Culture* 18 (1989): 91–103, and "Kaffee und Kaffeehäuser in der Universitätsstadt Helmstedt vom Ende des 17. bis zum Anfang des 19. Jahrhunderts," *Braunschweigisches Jahrbuch* 72 (1991): 95–118.
80. Mary Jepp Clarke, "Letter from Mary Jepp Clarke to Ursula Clarke Venner, March 01, 1691," in *Clarke Family Letters* (Alexandria, VA: Alexander Street Press, 2002), record numer S7378-D180.

81. Nemeitz, *Séjour de Paris*, ed. Franklin, p. 52. On news-men or "nouvellistes" in French cafés see François Fosca, *Histoire des cafés de Paris* ([Paris]: Firmin-Didot et cie, 1934), p. 20.

82. Julius Bernhard von Rohr, *Einleitung zur Ceremoniel-Wissenschaft der Privat Personen*, ed. with a commentary by Gotthart Frühsorge (Berlin, 1728; repr. Leipzig: Edition Leipzig, 1990), pp. 467–68.

83. Chevalier de Mailly, *Les entretiens des cafés de Paris et les diferens qui y surviennent* (Trévoux: Chez Etienne Ganeau, 1702).

84. Abraham a Sancta Clara, *Etwas für alle, das ist: Eine kurtze beschreibung allerley stands- ambts- und gewerbs-persohnen: mit beygeruckter sittlichen lehre und biblischen concepten* (Würzburg: druckts Martin Frantz Hertz, 1711), p. 152. See Pieter van Eeghen and Johan Philip van der Kellen, *Het werk van Jan en Casper Luyken* (Amsterdam: F. Muller & Co., 1905), II: 407–13.

85. John Tatham, *Knavery in all trades, or, The coffee-house a comedy: as it was acted in the Christmas holidays by several apprentices with great applause* (London: Printed by J.B. for W. Gilbertson and H. Marsh, 1664), fo. D3r.

86. Franklin, *Le café*, pp. 65–69.

87. Willem van der Hoeven, *'t Koffyhuis: kluchtspel* (Amsterdam: de erfg. van J. Lescailje, 1712). See Pim Reinders and Thera Wijsenbeek-Olthuis, *Koffie in Nederland: vier eeuwen cultuurgeschiedenis* (Zutphen: Walburg Pers, 1994), p. 49.

88. *A proclamation for the suppression of coffee-houses* (London: Printed by the assigns of John Bill, and Christopher Barker, 1675); see *Calendar of State Papers, Domestic Series, of the Reign of Charles II, 1660–1685* (London: HMSO, 1860–1939), XVII: 465, 503. A report of December 12, 1674 does refer to "much talk abroad" which "seems the nocturnal exercises at the coffee houses." *Calendar of State Papers, Domestic Series, of the Reign of Charles II*, XVI: 459.

89. Jean-Baptiste Antoine Colbert, marquis de Seignelay, writing on December 27, 1685, as cited in Jean Leclant, "Coffee and Cafés in Paris, 1644–1693," in *Food and Drink in History*, Selections from the Annales, Économies, Sociétes, Civilisations 5, ed. Robert Forster and Orest A. Ranum (Baltimore: Johns Hopkins University Press, 1987), p. 91.

90. Gustav Gugitz, *Das Wiener Kaffeehaus; ein Stück Kultur- und Lokalgeschichte* (Vienna: Deutscher Verlag für Jugend und Volk, 1940), p. 31.

91. Casimir Freschot (1640?–1720), *Mémoires de la cour de Vienne, ou Remarques faites par un voyageur curieux sur l'état present de cette cour* (Cologne: Chez Guillaume Etienne [actually The Hague], 1705), pp. 31–32.

92. Stadtarchiv Leipzig [hereafter SdAL], Tit. I, Nr. 37, "Thee- und Caffe-Stuben," May 18, 1697.

93. SdAL, Tit. I, Nr. 37, and Tit. LX B 3b, "in denen sogenandten Caffee-Häusern," August 19, 1704. Closing hours were set at 9 p.m. in winter and 10 p.m. in the summer.

94. Stadtarchiv Frankfurt, Bmb 1703, fos. 93v–94v.

95. Stadtarchiv Frankfurt, Bmb 1703, fo. 142r: "ihre caffèschilde sovort einziehen und sich furters gaste auff den caffè, und anders getrancke zu setzen, bey hoher straffe enthalt(en) sollen."

96. Stadtarchiv Frankfurt, Rechneiamt Bücher Nr. 7, fo. 69v (old fo. 67v): "Abschaffung der The und Caffee Häußer."

97. See Gottlieb Schnapper-Arndt, *Studien zur Geschichte der Lebenshaltung in Frankfurt a. M. während des 17. und 18. Jahrhunderts*, ed. Karl Bräuer, Veröffentlichungen der Historischen Kommission der Stadt Frankfurt a.M. 2: 1–2 (Frankfurt: Baer, 1915), I: 352.

98. The coffeehouses of Cologne were likewise closed by an edict of August 23, 1706: see the reference to "Abschaffung der Coffehäuser" in Karl Härter and Michael Stolleis, eds., *Repertorium der Policeyordnungen der Frühen Neuzeit*, vol. VI, *Reichsstädte 2 Köln*, ed. Klaus Militzer, Studien zur europäischen Rechtsgeschichte 191 (Frankfurt: Klostermann, 2005), p. 1061.

99. Alexander Dietz, *Frankfurter Handelsgeschichte* (Frankfurt: Hermann Minjon, 1910–25), IV: 206–07.

100. *Spectator* 9 (March 10, 1711), as quoted in Valérie Capdeville, "Les clubs londoniens: vie nocturne et transgression," in *La nuit dans l'Angleterre des lumières*, ed. Suzy Halimi (Paris: Presses Sorbonne nouvelle, 2008), pp. 21–34. The majority of these clubs met in private rooms in taverns or pubs, rather than in coffeehouses. See Kümin, *Drinking Matters*, pp. 187–88.

101. Cowan, *Social Life of Coffee*, p. 250.

102. In Europe's very largest cities, retail trade helped light up the night. Schivelbusch (*Disenchanted Night*, pp. 144–46) cites Defoe's *Complete Tradesman* (1728) on London shopkeepers' use of lavish lighting to attract customers. The account of Paris by Nemeitz notes that "Many shops and most of the cafés, cookshops, and public houses are open until 10 or 11 o'clock, and the windows of these establishments are adorned with an infinity of lights, which shed a great light in the streets." Nemeitz, *Séjour de Paris*, ed. Franklin, p. 57.

103. "Bürgerliche Öffentlichkeit läßt sich vorerst als die Sphäre der zum Publikum versammelten Privatleuten begreifen; diese beanspruchen die obrigkeitlich reglementierte Öffentlichkeit alsbald gegen die öffentliche Gewalt selbst," Habermas, *Strukturwandel*, p. 86.

104. As initiated by Joan Landes, *Women and the Public Sphere in the Age of the French Revolution* (Ithaca, NY: Cornell University Press, 1988).

105. Bertuch, "Moden in Gebrauche und Eintheilung des Tages und der Nacht," pp. 199–201.

106. *Ibid.* See Piero Camporesi, *Exotic Brew: The Art of Living in the Age of Enlightenment*, trans. Christopher Woodall (Cambridge: Polity Press, 1994), pp. 12–26 on feminization and "the Revenge of the night."

107. For much more see Ellis, *Coffee-House*, pp. 137–38; Lawrence Klein, "Coffeehouse Civility, 1660–1714: An Aspect of Post-Courtly Culture in England," *Huntington Library Quarterly* 59, 1 (1996): 30–52, here 38.

108. E. J. Clery, *The Feminization Debate in Eighteenth-Century England: Literature, Commerce and Luxury* (New York: Palgrave Macmillan, 2004), and Landes, *Women and the Public Sphere.*

109. Julius Bernhard von Rohr, *Einleitung zur Ceremoniel-Wissenschaft der Grossen Herren.* Reprint of the second edn., Berlin, 1733, ed. with a commentary by Monika Schlechte (Leipzig: Edition Leipzig, 1990), pp. 18–19: "die Nacht in Tag, und der Tag in Nacht verwandelt," and Théophraste Renaudot, ed., *Quatriesme centurie des questions traitées aux conférences du Bureau d'Adresse, depuis le 24e Ianvier 1639, jusques au 10e Iuin 1641* (Paris: Bureau d'adresse, 1641), p. 416: "en la vie des courtizans de l'un et l'autre sexe qui font de la nuit jour et du jour la nuit."

110. "Nous revînmes gaiement à la faveur des lanternes et dans la sûreté des voleurs." Marie de Rabutin-Chantal Sévigné, *Correspondance: texte établi, presenté et annoté par Roger Duchene* (Paris: Gallimard, 1970), 1: 623.

111. Letter dated Paris, August 26, 1679. The writer and satirist Leti was a Milanese convert to the Reformed church, writing to the marquise while she was in prison. C.H. de Saint-Dider, ed., *Mémoires de la marquise de Courcelles ... et sa correspondance, précédés d'une histoire de sa vie et de son procès. Revue et augmentée d'après des documents inédits* (Paris: Académie des Bibliophiles, 1869), pp. 287–304, 341ff.; here p. 292.

112. See Susanne Claudine Pils, *Schreiben über Stadt. Das Wien der Johanna Theresia Harrach 1639–1716*, Forschungen und Beiträge zur Wiener Stadtgeschichte 36 (Vienna: Deuticke, 2002), pp. 227–32, 253–55 on the evening and night life of the Countess Harrach.

113. Lady Mary Wortley Montagu, *The Complete Letters of Lady Mary Wortley Montagu*, ed. Robert Halsband, 3 vols. (Oxford: Clarendon Press, 1965–67), 1: 20–21.

114. John Vanbrugh, *A Journey to London*, 2.1, in John Vanbrugh, *The Relapse; The Provoked Wife; The Confederacy; A Journey to London; The Country House*, ed. Brean Hammond (Oxford University Press, 2004), pp. 274–75.

115. Cowan, *Social Life of Coffee*, p. 250.

116. Albrecht, "Coffee-Drinking," p. 94; Leclant, "Coffee and Cafés," pp. 89–90; Ellis, *Coffee House*, pp. 80–81.

117. Franklin, *Le café*, pp. 65–69.

118. *Ibid.*, p. 62, quoting *Le porte-feuille galant, ouvrage mêlé de prose et de vers. Avec plusieurs questions sérieuses et galantes* (June 15, 1700), p. 3.

119. Mailly, pp. 367–68, and Marie-Pascale Pieretti, "Is That Seat Taken? Women and Café Life in Early Eighteenth-Century Paris," unpublished paper, 2004.

120. On salons, see Benedetta Craveri, *The Age of Conversation*, trans. Teresa Waugh (New York: New York Review Books, 2006). These national and regional contrasts call for more research on gender and the early modern night.

121. Paul Griffiths, "Meanings of Nightwalking in Early Modern England," *Seventeenth Century* 13, 2 (1998): 212–38.

122. OBSP, "Dorothy Hall, of the Parish of St. Clement Danes," May 12, 1687.

123. OBSP, "Jane King, a notorious Night-walker," May 31, 1688.

124. Bernard Mandeville, *An enquiry into the causes of the frequent executions at Tyburn* (London: Printed and sold by J. Roberts in Warwick-Lane, 1725), pp. 10–11.

125. *Ibid.*, p. 10.

126. For an overview of the debate, see Brian William Cowan, "What Was Masculine about the Public Sphere? Gender and the Coffeehouse Milieu in Post-Restoration England," *History Workshop Journal* 51 (2001): 127–57. See also Helen Berry, "'Nice and Curious Questions': Coffee Houses and the Representation of Women in John Dunton's *Athenian Mercury*," *Seventeenth Century* 12, 2 (1997): 257–76.

127. Ellis, *Coffee House*, pp. 66–67.

128. On satires of women who kept coffeehouses, see *ibid.*, pp. 109–10, especially *re* London's Amsterdam Coffee House.

129. *Ibid.*, p. 124.

130. César de Saussure, *A Foreign View of England in the Reigns of George I. and George II. The Letters of Monsieur César De Saussure to His Family*, ed. and trans. Madame Van Muyden (London: J. Murray, 1902), pp. 164–65.

131. Paula McDowell, *The Women of Grub Street: Press, Politics, and Gender in the London Literary Marketplace, 1678–1730* (Oxford: Clarendon Press, 1998), p. 60.

132. The case of Sarah Turbat, OBSP, October 10, 1722, is noted in McDowell, *Women of Grub Street*, p. 73. Cf. pp. 58–62 on "Hawkers and Ballad-Singers."

133. As quoted in Peter Albrecht, "Die 'Caffe-Menscher' im. 18. Jahrhundert," in *Coffeum wirft die Jungfrau um: Kaffee und Erotik in Porzellan und Grafik aus drei Jahrhunderten*, ed. Ulla Heise (Leipzig: Kiepenheuer, 1998), pp. 36–46; here p. 39.

134. *Die Verschlemmerte und bezauberte Koffe- und Thee-Welt: welche eine Menge artiger Begebenheiten enthält, so sich seit kurzem zu Amsterdam, Rotterdam, in dem Haage, zu Uitrecht, und in denen benachbarten Orten, sowohl unter verheyratheten als ledigen Personen, zugetragen* (Frankfurt and Leipizig, 1737; first edn., Frankfurt and Leipzig, 1701), as quoted in Albrecht, "Die 'Caffe-Menscher'," p. 39.

135. Gottlieb Siegmund Corvinus, *Nutzbares, galantes und curiöses Frauenzimmer-Lexicon: Worinnen nicht nur Der Frauenzimmer geistlich- und weltliche Orden, Aemter, Würden, Ehren-Stellen, Professionen und Gewerbe … Nahmen und Thaten der Göttinnen … gelehrter Weibes-Bilder … auch anderer … Trachten und Moden … Gewohnheiten und Gebräuche … Ergötzlichkeiten … Gebrechen … und alles … was einem Frauenzimmer vorkommen kan, und ihm nöthig zu wissen … Ordentlich nach dem Alphabet … abgefaßt* (Leipzig: bey Joh. Friedrich Gleditsch und Sohn, 1715), col. 285. Albrecht, "Die 'Caffe-Menscher'," p. 44, quotes Braunschweig records from 1698 and 1711 expelling from the city "Caffeejungfer" and a "Caffeeschenkerin" for moral offenses.

136. SdAL, Tit. I, Nr. 37, and Tit. LX B 3b, "in denen sogenandten Caffee-Häusern," August 19, 1704.

137. Cowan, *Social Life of Coffee*, p. 244.

138. On respectable women in English alehouses and taverns, see Bernard Capp, "Gender and the Culture of the English Alehouse in Late Stuart England," in *The Trouble with Ribs: Women, Men and Gender in Early Modern Europe*, ed. Anu Korhonen and Kate Lowe, Collegium: Studies across Disciplines in the Humanities and Social Sciences 2 (Helsinki: Helsinki Collegium for Advanced Studies, 2007): 103–27. E-publication accessed at www.helsinki.fi/collegium/e-series/volumes/volume_2/index.htm.

139. Habermas, *Strukturwandel*, p. 18: "*in derselben Weise* wie Arbeiter, Bauern und der "Pöbel", also die "unselbstständigen" Männer."

140. *Ibid.*, pp. 18–19.

141. Landes, *Women and the Public Sphere*, p. 40.

142. Cowan, "What Was Masculine," p. 132, citing McDowell, *Women of Grub Street*, pp. 285–86.

143. McDowell, *Women of Grub Street*, p. 285.

144. The rich scholarship on colonial cultures and European empires has identified several features of early modern and modern colonization that resonate with the colonization of the night described here. The most prominent feature is the role of gender; for the British empire see Kathleen Wilson, "Empire, Gender, and Modernity in the Eighteenth Century," in *Gender and Empire*, ed. Philippa Levine (Oxford University Press, 2004), pp. 14–45, and the literature cited there on the co-production of

colonized spaces (and times!) by state and private actors, and by colonizer and colonized, and on gendered access to colonized sites. Other key issues which suggest valuable comparisons, such as respectability, the control of sexuality, mobility, and the role of the middle class, are discussed in Tony Ballantyne and Antoinette M. Burton, eds., *Moving Subjects: Gender, Mobility, and Intimacy in an Age of Global Empire* (Urbana: University of Illinois Press, 2009); Adelle Perry, *On the Edge of Empire: Gender, Race, and the Making of British Columbia, 1849–1871* (University of Toronto Press, 2001); and Frederick Cooper and Ann Laura Stoler, eds., *Tensions of Empire: Colonial Cultures in a Bourgeois World* (Berkeley: University of California Press, 1997). These comparisons warrant further investigation.

7 COLONIZING THE RURAL NIGHT?

1. Hessisches Staatsarchiv Marburg [hereafter HstAM], Bestand 17d Reg Cassel Familienrep. von Eschwege, Paket 5 ("Causa Criminalis"), fo. 1: "Morgens fruhe vortage ungefehr zwischen zwey undt drey Uhr."

2. HstAM, Bestand 17d Reg Cassel Familienrep. von Eschwege, Paket 5, fo. 1.

3. HstAM, Bestand 17d Reg Cassel Familienrep. von Eschwege, Paket 5, fos. 2–4

4. Hermann Grebe, "Ein Erbvergleich zwischen den Adelshäusern von Eschwege zu Aue und Reichensachsen," *Zeitschrift des Vereins für hessische Geschichte und Landeskunde* 95 (1990): 233–58, here 233–34.

5. Alois Niederstätter, "Notizen zu einer Rechts- und Kulturgeschichte der Nacht," in *Das Recht im kulturgeschichtlichen Wandel. Festschrift für Karl-Heinz Burmeister zur Emeritierung*, ed. Bernd Marquardt and Alois Niederstätter (Constance: UVK, 2002), pp. 173–90; here p. 177.

6. HstAM, Bestand 17d Reg Cassel Familienrep. von Eschwege, Paket 5, fo. 2.

7. The phrase is from Norbert Schindler, "Guardians of Disorder: Rituals of Youthful Culture at the Dawn of the Modern Age," in *A History of Young People in the West*, ed. Giovanni Levi and Jean-Claude Schmitt, trans. Camille Naish (Cambridge, MA and London: Belknap Press of Harvard University Press, 1997), 1: 240–82.

8. Robert Muchembled, "La violence et la nuit sous l'Ancien Régime," *Ethnologie française* 21, 3 (1991): 237–42, 238; see above, chapter 1, for a similar comment from the Halle barber-surgeon Johann Deitz.

9. Norbert Schindler, "Nächtliche Ruhestörung. Zur Sozialgeschichte der Nacht in der frühen Neuzeit," in *Widerspenstige Leute: Studien zur Volkskultur in der frühen Neuzeit* (Frankfurt: Fischer Taschenbuch-Verlag, 1992), pp. 215–57.

10. Alain Cabantous, *Histoire de la nuit: XVIIe–XVIIIe siècle* (Paris: Fayard, 2009), pp. 307–10.

11. Cornelius Novelli, "Sin, Sight, and Sanctity in the *Miller's Tale*: Why Chaucer's Blacksmith Works at Night," *Chaucer Review* 33, 2 (1998): 168–75.

12. Alain Cabantous, "La nuit rustique. Monde rural et temps nocturne aux XVIIe et XVIIIe siècles," in *Les fruits de la récolte. Études offertes à Jean-Michel Boehler*, ed. Isabelle Laboulais and Jean-François Chauvard (Presses universitaires de Strasbourg, 2007), pp. 53–56. A south German guide from 1705 advised that "what can be done under the roof by night and during a storm shall neither be done during clear, beautiful weather nor outside in the fields." See Bernd Roeck, *Civic Culture and Everyday Life in Early Modern Germany* (Leiden: Brill, 2006), pp. 239–40.

13. See Renate Müller, *Licht und Feuer im ländlichen Haushalt: Lichtquellen und Haushaltsgeräte* (Hamburg: Altonaer Museum, 1994).

14. "Ein Hausvater gleichet einer Hausuhr, darnach sich jedermann mit Aufstehen, Schlafengehen, Arbeiten, Essen und allen Geschäften richten muß," as cited in Otto Brunner, *Adeliges Landleben und europäischer Geist; Leben und Werk Wolf Helmhards von Hohberg, 1612–1688* (Salzburg: O. Müller, 1949), p. 285. See also Heimo Cerny, "Wolf Helmhard von Hohberg (1612–1688). Ein niederösterreichischer Landedelmann, Schriftsteller und Agronom," *Jahrbuch für Landeskunde von Niederösterreich* n.s 54/55 (1988/89): 59–84.

15. Thomas Tusser (1524?–1580), *Five hundred points of good husbandry as well for the champion or open countrey, as also for the woodland or several, mixed, in every moneth, with huswifery, over and besides the book of huswifery* (London: Printed by J.M. for the Company of Stationers, 1663), pp. 133–34.

16. See Jürgen Bücking, *Kultur und Gesellschaft in Tirol um 1600: des Hippolytus Guarinonius' Grewel der Verwüstung menschlichen Geschlechts (1610) als kulturgeschichtliche Quelle des frühen 17. Jahrhunderts* (Lübeck: Matthiesen, 1968), pp. 153–54, and Alwin Schulz, *Das Häusliche leben der europäischen Kulturvölker vom Mittelalter bis zur zweiten Hälfte des XVIII. Jahrhunderts* (Munich: R. Oldenbourg, 1903), p. 337.

17. See Birgit Emich, "Zwischen Disziplinierung und Distinktion: Der Schlaf in der Frühen Neuzeit," *Werkstatt Geschichte* 34 (2003): 53–75, and the literature cited there.

18. Mary Jepp Clarke, "Letter from Mary Jepp Clarke to Edward Clarke, April 13, 1700," in *Clarke Family Letters* (Alexandria, VA: Alexander Street Press, 2002), record number S7378-D368.

19. Early modern spinning bees have been examined primarily within the various national and regional traditions. The most recent studies

are Cabantous, *Histoire de la nuit*, pp. 64–68; Michel Vernus, *La Veillée: découverte d'une tradition* (Yens-sur-Morges: Cabédita, 2004); Carl-Jochen Müller, "'Rechte Pflanzschulen aller Laster'? Lichtstuben im Limpurgischen – Bekämpfung und Behauptung einer ländlichen Institution," in *Stadt und Land: Bilder, Inszenierungen und Visionen in Geschichte und Gegenwart: Wolfgang von Hippel zum 65. Geburtstag*, ed. Sylvia Schraut and Bernhard Stier (Stuttgart: Kohlhammer, 2001), pp. 373–89; Albert Schnyder, "Lichtstuben im alten Basel. Zu einer von Frauen geprägten Form frühneuzeitlicher Geselligkeit," *Schweizerisches Archiv für Volkskunde* 92, 1 (1996): 1–13; and Uwe Henkhaus, *Das Treibhaus der Unsittlichkeit: Lieder, Bilder und Geschichte(n) aus der hessischen Spinnstube* (Marburg: Hitzeroth, 1991).

20. John Cashmere, "Sisters Together: Women without Men in Seventeenth-Century French Village Culture," *Journal of Family History* 21, 1 (1996): 44–62.

21. Achim Landwehr, *Policey im Alltag: die Implementation frühneuzeitlicher Policeyordnungen in Leonberg* (Frankfurt: Klostermann, 2000), p. 254, and Henkhaus, *Treibhaus der Unsittlichkeit*, pp. 16–23, emphasize the importance of labor at spinning bees as a balance to the authorities' fixation on sociability at the gatherings.

22. Schnyder, "Lichtstuben im alten Basel." The season for the spinning bees thus matched that of the court in residence in Paris or Vienna.

23. See *ibid.* and Edward Shorter, "The 'Veillée' and the Great Transformation," in *The Wolf and the Lamb: Popular Culture in France, from the Old Régime to the Twentieth Century*, ed. Jacques Beauroy, Marc Bertrand, and Edward T. Gargan, Stanford French and Italian Studies 3 (Saratoga, CA: Anma Libri, 1977), pp. 127–40.

24. As quoted in Müller, "Lichtstuben im Limpurgischen," p. 376.

25. Felix Vialart de Herse, "Ordonnances et règlements faits dans le cours de sa visite en l'anné 1661," in *Statuts, ordonnances, mandements, règlements et lettres pastorales du diocèse de Châlons* (Châlons: s.n., 1693), pp. 19–20, as published in Dominique Julia, "La réforme posttridentine d'après les procès-verbaux de visites pastorales: ordre et résistances," in *La società religiosa nell'età moderna: atti del Convegno studi di storia sociale e religiosa, Capaccio-Paestum, 18–21 maggio 1972* (Naples: Guida, 1973), pp. 403–04.

26. Darryl Ogier, "Night Revels and Werewolfery in Calvinist Guernsey," *Folklore* 109 (1998): 53–62, here 54, quoting from the travel journal (1677) of Charles Trumbull.

27. Hans Medick, "Village Spinning Bees: Sexual Culture and Free Time among Rural Youth in Early Modern Germany," in *Interest and Emotion: Essays on the Study of Family and Kinship*, ed. Hans Medick and David

Warren Sabean (Cambridge University Press, 1984), pp. 317–39; here p. 322.

28. Wilhelm Rudeck, *Geschichte der öffentlichen Sittlichkeit in Deutschland: moralhistorische Studien* (Jena: Costenoble, 1897), p. 62.

29. C. Scott Dixon, *The Reformation and Rural Society: The Parishes of Brandenburg-Ansbach-Kulmbach, 1528–1603* (Cambridge University Press, 1996), p. 114.

30. "Dann sie weiß noch wol Zeit und Tag / Daß sie auch so zu Leben pflag. Denckt / auch noch wol der guten Zeit / Darinn sie hät gar manche Frewd." On this print see Alison G. Stewart, "Distaffs and Spindles: Sexual Misbehavior in Sebald Beham's *Spinning Bee*," in *Saints, Sinners, and Sisters: Gender and Northern Art in Medieval and Early Modern Europe*, ed. Jane L. Carroll and Alison G. Stewart (Aldershot: Ashgate, 2003), pp. 127–54.

31. Medick, "Village Spinning Bees," pp. 322–23.

32. Schnyder, "Lichtstuben im alten Basel," pp. 7–10.

33. On the Netherlands see Gerard Rooijakkers, "Spinningen in de Pre-Industriële Plattelandssamenleving," *Focaal: Tijdschrift voor Antropologie* 4 (1986): 43–61

34. A. Roger Ekirch, *At Day's Close: Night in Times Past* (New York: W.W. Norton, 2005), pp. 178–79.

35. The description of spinning bees in Guernsey by the English traveler Charles Trumbull in 1677 suggests they were unknown to him from his experiences in England, for example. See Richard Hocart, ed., "The Journal of Charles Trumbull," *Transactions of la Société Guernesiaise* 21 (1984): 566–85.

36. Barkle was convicted of theft, sent to a Bridewell, and whipped. See James Rosenheim, ed., *The Notebook of Robert Doughty 1662–1665*, Norfolk Record Society 54 ([Norwich]: Norfolk Record Society, 1991), p. 49.

37. See Müller, "Lichtstuben im Limpurgischen," p. 381.

38. See Niederstätter, "Rechts- und Kulturgeschichte der Nacht," pp. 182–85; Stefan Breit, *"Leichtfertigkeit" und ländliche Gesellschaft: voreheliche Sexualität in der frühen Neuzeit*, Ancien Régime, Aufklärung und Revolution 23 (Munich: Oldenbourg, 1991), pp. 87–89; and Thomas Paul Becker, *Konfessionalisierung in Kurköln: Untersuchungen zur Durchsetzung der katholischen Reform in den Dekanaten Ahrgau und Bonn anhand von Visitationsprotokollen 1583–1761*, Veröffentlichungen des Stadtarchivs Bonn 43 (Bonn: Edition Röhrscheid, 1989), pp. 176–79, on village dances in the Cologne region.

39. See Cabantous, *Histoire de la nuit*, pp. 88–93; Ekirch, *Day's Close*, pp. 197–202; Yochi Fischer-Yinon, "The Original Bundlers: Boaz and Ruth, and Seventeenth-Century English Courtship Practices," *Journal of*

Social History 35, 3 (2002): 683–705; Breit, *"Leichtfertigkeit" und ländliche Gesellschaft*, pp. 97–98 ("Bettfreien"); Arie Theodorus van Deursen, *Plain Lives in a Golden Age: Popular Culture, Religion, and Society in Seventeenth-Century Holland*, trans. Maarten Ultee (Cambridge University Press, 1991), p. 94 ("night-courting" in North Holland); Eduard Fuchs, *Illustrierte Sittengeschichte vom Mittelalter bis zur Gegenwart. Renaissance* (Munich: A. Langen, Verlag für Literatur und Kunst, 1909), pp. 230–38.

40. Jean-Louis Flandrin, "Repression and Change in the Sexual Life of Young People in Medieval and Early Modern Times," *Journal of Family History* 2, 3 (1977): 199–203.

41. George A.E. Parfitt and Ralph A. Houlbrooke, eds., *The Courtship Narrative of Leonard Wheatcroft, Derbyshire Yeoman* (Reading: Whiteknights Press, 1986), pp. 21, 52–54.

42. *Ibid.*, p. 61.

43. *Ibid.*, p. 64.

44. Paul Delsalle, *La Franche-Comté au temps des archiducs Albert et Isabelle, 1598–1633: documents choisis et présentés* (Besançon: Presses universitaires franc-comtoises, 2002), pp. 59–60.

45. *Ibid.*, p. 60.

46. Robin Briggs, *Communities of Belief: Cultural and Social Tension in Early Modern France* (New York: Oxford University Press, 1989), p. 264.

47. On France, see *ibid.*, pp. 235–76; on England, Parfitt and Houlbrooke, eds., *Courtship Narrative*, pp. 19–22; on southern Germany, Govind Sreenivasan, *The Peasants of Ottobeuren, 1487–1726: A Rural Society in Early Modern Europe* (Cambridge University Press, 2004), pp. 246–54.

48. Cabantous makes this point for rural life in general: *Histoire de la nuit*, p. 302.

49. See Medick, "Village Spinning Bees," p. 323.

50. See Rosenheim, ed., *Notebook of Robert Doughty*, p. 47: "28 January 1665: [I] sent Robert Coe, Sir John Palgrave's man, to Bridewell."

51. Josephus Antonius Steiner, ed., *Acta selecta ecclesiae Augustanae: accedit synopsis episcopalium decretorum per eandem ecclesiam a tempore Concilii Tridentini usque in praesentem annum promulgatum* (Augsburg: M. Rieger, 1785), p. 257; cited in Rainer Beck, "Illegitimität und voreheliche Sexualität auf dem Land: Unterfinning, 1671–1770," in *Kultur der einfachen Leute: bayerisches Volksleben vom 16. bis zum 19. Jahrhundert*, ed. Richard van Dülmen (Munich: Beck, 1983), pp. 112–50; here p. 126.

52. As cited in Breit, *"Leichtfertigkeit" und ländliche Gesellschaft*, p. 217. Beck, "Unterfinning," p. 235, n. 23 cites similar Bavarian mandates from 1643, 1654, 1671, and 1682.

53. Christoph Selhamer, *Tuba Rustica. Das ist: Neue Gei-Predigen* (Augsburg: Verlag Georg Schlüters, 1701), as excerpted in Karl Böck, *Das Bauernleben*

in den Werken bayerischer Barockprediger (Munich: Schnell & Steiner, 1953), p. 79. See Thomas Groll, "Der Salzburger Dompfarrvikar, Weilheimer Stadtpfarrer u. Vilgertshofener Wallfahrtspriester Christoph Selhamer (1638–1708) als ausdrucksstarker Barockprediger," *Jahrbuch des Vereins für Augsburger Bistumsgeschichte* 43 (2009): 545–81.

54. Müller, "Lichtstuben im Limpurgischen," p. 380.

55. Breit, *"Leichtfertigkeit" und ländliche Gesellschaft*, p. 217.

56. See Robert Muchembled, *La violence au village: sociabilité et comportements populaires en Artois du XVe au XVIIe siècle* ([Turnhout]: Brepols, 1989), p. 219.

57. See the valuable study by Beat A. Kümin, *Drinking Matters: Public Houses and Social Exchange in Early Modern Central Europe* (Basingstoke: Palgrave Macmillan, 2007).

58. See Beat Kümin and B. Ann Tlusty, "Introduction," in *The World of the Tavern: Public Houses in Early Modern Europe*, ed. Beat Kümin and B. Ann Tlusty (Burlington, VT: Ashgate, 2002), pp. 8–9, and Susanne Rau and Gerd Schwerhoff, eds., *Zwischen Gotteshaus und Taverne. Öffentliche Räume in Spätmittelalter und Früher Neuzeit*, Norm und Struktur. Studien zum sozialen Wandel in Mittelalter und früher Neuzeit 21 (Cologne: Böhlau, 2004).

59. Sébastien Cabantous, "Crimes et délits nocturnes en pays tarnais au siècle des lumières," *Revue du Tarn*, third series, 181 (2001): 107–31, here 110–12; Kümin, *Drinking Matters*, p. 65; Michael Frank, "Satan's Servant or Authorities' Agent? Publicans in Eighteenth-Century Germany," in *The World of the Tavern*, ed. Kümin and Tlusty, p. 31. The main light at public houses in the evening came from the hearth, but inventories from seventeenth-century English public houses, for example, mention great and small candlesticks as well. See Janet Pennington, "Inns and Taverns of Western Sussex, 1550–1700: A Documentary and Architectural Investigation," in *The World of the Tavern*, ed. Kümin and Tlusty, p. 125.

60. Kümin, *Drinking Matters*, p. 65, as seen in the north German county of Lippe, for example, where public houses were to close at 8 p.m. in the winter and 9 p.m. in the summer: Frank, "Satan's Servant or Authorities' Agent?" p. 36, and Hans Heiss, "The Pre-Modern Hospitality Trade in the Central Alpine Region: The Example of Tirol," in *The World of the Tavern*, ed. Kümin and Tlusty, pp. 170–71, citing a complaint about "raucous and reckless games, boozing, and dancing until late in the night hours" from Brixen, 1785.

61. S. Cabantous, "Crimes et délits nocturnes," p. 111, describing *cabarets* "never empty all night long" in 1764.

62. Kümin, *Drinking Matters*, p. 132.

63. B. Howard Cunnington, ed., *Records of the County of Wilts: Being Extracts from the Quarter Sessions Great Rolls of the Seventeenth Century* (Devizes:

G. Simpson & Co., 1932), pp. 131–32. Perhaps dancing until the candles went out added a thrill absent from dancing in a public house.

64. Becker, *Konfessionalisierung*, pp. 176ff. In 1677 a Polish royal entourage was traveling near the small city of Schwangau late at night when they heard a distant rhythmic noise. Riding toward it, they found a large wooden hall built atop a local peak, filled with Bavarian peasants dancing. Michel Komaszynski, "Das Bayern des XVII. Jahrhunderts in polnischen Reisebeschreibungen," *Zeitschrift für bayerische Landesgeschichte* 56, 3 (1993): 635–48.

65. Schindler, "Nächtliche Ruhestörung," pp. 230–33 on brawls after tavern visits. On the nocturnal excesses of young men, see also Eva Lacour, "Faces of Violence Revisited. A Typology of Violence in Early Modern Rural Germany," *Journal of Social History* 34, 3 (2001): 649–67, here 657.

66. Kümin, *Drinking Matters*, p. 65.

67. Ekirch, *Day's Close*, pp. 233–36; Schindler, "Nächtliche Ruhestörung," pp. 230–33; Karl-S. Kramer, "Rechtliches Gemeindeleben im Maindreieck zwischen Reformation und Aufklärung," *Bayerisches Jahrbuch für Volkskunde* (1953): 136–48, here 140.

68. Peter Lahnstein, ed., *Das Leben im Barock: Zeugnisse und Berichte 1640–1740* (Stuttgart: W. Kohlhammer, 1974), p. 148.

69. *Ibid.*

70. Müller, "Lichtstuben im Limpurgischen," pp. 382–84; Peter Burschel, *Sterben und Unsterblichkeit: zur Kultur des Martyriums in der frühen Neuzeit*, Ancien Régime, Aufklärung und Revolution 35 (Munich: Oldenbourg, 2004), pp. 117–18.

71. As Schindler has commented in his "Guardians of Disorder."

72. See the examples in Jacques Le Goff and Jean Claude Schmitt, eds., *Le Charivari: actes de la table ronde organisée à Paris, 25–27 avril 1977*, Civilisations et sociétés 67 (Paris: L'Ecole, 1981). The riding described by Justice of the Peace William Holcroft in Essex in 1682 took place during the day, as did a well-documented "groaning" (a mock childbirth meant to accuse a man of sodomy) held in Gloucestershire in 1716. See J.A. Sharpe, *"William Holcroft, His Booke": Local Office-Holding in Late Stuart Essex*, Essex Historical Documents 2 (Chelmsford: Essex Record Office, 1986), pp. xv, 73, and David Rollison, "Property, Ideology, and Popular Culture in a Gloucestershire Village 1660–1740," *Past & Present* 93, 1 (1981): 70–97.

73. Kramer, "Rechtliches Gemeindeleben," pp. 139–40, as cited in Hermann Heidrich, "Grenzübergänge: Das Haus und die Volkskultur in der frühen Neuzeit," in *Kultur der einfachen Leute*, ed. van Dülmen, pp. 17–19.

74. Kramer, "Rechtliches Gemeindeleben," p. 140.

75. Jon Mathieu, "In der Kirche schlafen. Eine sozialgeschichtliche Lektüre von Conradin Riolas 'Geistlicher Trompete' (Strada im Engadin, 1709),"

Schweizerisches Archiv für Volkskunde 87, 3/4 (1991): 121–43. See also Emich, "Schlaf in der Frühen Neuzeit," pp. 62–63, and Keith Thomas, *Man and the Natural World: A History of the Modern Sensibility* (New York: Pantheon Books, 1983), p. 39.

76. Elfriede Moser-Rath, *Predigtmärlein der Barockzeit: Exempel, Sage, Schwank und Fabel in geistlichen Quellen des oberdeutschen Raumes* (Berlin: de Gruyter, 1964), Urs Herzog, *Geistliche Wohlredenheit: die katholische Barockpredigt* (Munich: Beck, 1991), and Margo Todd, *The Culture of Protestantism in Early Modern Scotland* (New Haven: Yale University Press, 2002), pp. 39–40.

77. Wilhelm A. Eckardt and Helmut Klingelhöfer, ed. *Bauernleben im Zeitalter des Dreissigjährigen Krieges: die Stausebacher Chronik des Caspar Preis, 1636–1667*, Beiträge zur hessischen Geschichte 13 (Marburg: Trautvetter und Fischer, 1998), pp. 100–01. See also Kümin, *Drinking Matters*, p. 136.

78. Malcolm Greenshields describes a remarkably similar incident from the rural Haute Auvergne in 1654; see his *An Economy of Violence in Early Modern France: Crime and Justice in the Haute Auvergne, 1587–1664* (University Park, PA: Pennsylvania State University Press, 1994), pp. 80–83.

79. Muchembled, *Violence au village*, pp. 20, 29–32; Muchembled, "Violence et la nuit," p. 237. The majority of homicides in Muchembled's sample probably occurred during the day, but violence was more common in the evening than later at night.

80. Cabantous, *Histoire de la nuit*, p. 162.

81. Muchembled, *Violence au village*, pp. 122–23.

82. Schindler, "Nächtliche Ruhestörung," p. 229.

83. *Ibid.*, pp. 242–45; Muchembled, *Violence au village*, p. 122.

84. James Raine, ed., *Depositions from the Castle of York, Relating to Offenses Committed in the Northern Counties in the Seventeenth Century*, Publications of the Surtees Society 40 (Durham: Published for the Society by F. Andrews, 1861), pp. 141–42.

85. The Ruddock family had long held the Eddlethorpe farm; see Charles Jackson, ed., *The Autobiography of Mrs. Alice Thornton of East Newton, Co. York*, Publications of the Surtees Society 62 (Durham: Published for the Society by Andrews and Co., 1875), p. 355.

86. Thomas Isham, *The Diary of Thomas Isham of Lamport (1658–81), kept by him in Latin from 1671 to 1673 at his father's command*, trans. Norman Marlow, with Introduction, Appendixes and Notes by Sir Gyles Isham (Farnborough: Gregg, 1971), p. 207. Eva Lacour describes a similar encounter in the village of Onse (Rheinland-Pfalz) in "Faces of Violence Revisited," pp. 655–56.

87. See Rainer Hambrecht, "'Das Papier ist mein Acker …' Ein Notizbuch des 17. Jahrhunderts von Handwerker-Bauern aus dem nordwestlichen Oberfranken," *Jahrbuch der Coburger Landesstiftung* 29 (1984): 317–450, here 350, 388. Serge Dontenwill describes a similar clash at a church fair in Ambierle (near Roanne) on June 25, 1683, in his article "Aspects de la vie quotidienne et de l'organisation sociale des communautés paysannes du centre sud-est de la France au temps de Louis XIV (1638–1715)," *Dix-septième siècle* 234, 1 (2007): 97–134, here 132.
88. Paul Griffiths, "Meanings of Nightwalking in Early Modern England," *Seventeenth Century* 13, 2 (1998): 212–38, here 213.
89. Rosenheim, ed., *Notebook of Robert Doughty*, p. 110.
90. See J.H. Porter, "Crime in the Countryside, 1600–1800," and John E. Archer, "Poachers Abroad," in *The Unquiet Countryside*, ed. G.E. Mingay (London and New York: Routledge, 1989), pp. 9–22, 52–64. Poaching and other rural nocturnal activities that unfolded outside the village, such as the clandestine gatherings of Anabaptists, the wanderings of lone travellers, and groups travelling by post-coach also came under increasing scrutiny in the eighteenth century. See below, section 7.2, on attempts to colonize the rural night.
91. Schindler, "Nächtliche Ruhestörung," p. 244.
92. Isham, *Diary*, p. 180.
93. On rural travel at night, and on post-coaches and messengers' access to cities after their gates had closed for the night, see Cabantous, *Histoire de la nuit*, pp. 245–49; Roland Racevskis, *Time and Ways of Knowing under Louis XIV: Molière, Sévigné, Lafayette* (Lewisburg, PA: Bucknell University Press, 2003), pp. 90–106; and Klaus Gerteis, "Das 'Postkutschenzeitalter': Bedingungen der Kommunikation im 18. Jahrhundert," *Aufklärung* 4, 1 (1989): 55–78.
94. See Emich, "Schlaf in der Frühen Neuzeit," pp. 57–67.
95. Norbert Schindler has described the entire process, urban and rural, as an attempt "to colonise the night" – see above, chapter 6, note 4. See also the discussion of the "colonial context" of the attempts by Sir Richard Holford, a London businessman and Master in Chancery, to "civilize" his Gloucestershire estates, in Rollison, "Property, Ideology, and Popular Culture," pp. 87–94.
96. For England, the importance of gender in the new contrast between the rural and the urban night can be seen in the shifting meaning of the term "nightwalker," which came to refer exclusively to women in seventeenth-century London while keeping its centuries-old association with idle men in rural usage. See Griffiths, "Meanings of Nightwalking."
97. More villages established regular night watches in the seventeenth and eighteenth centuries, but we see no establishment of any village street

lighting intended to facilitate labor or leisure at night. See Cabantous, "Nuit rustique," p. 63, and David Warren Sabean, *Property, Production, and Family in Neckarhausen, 1700–1870*, Cambridge Studies in Social and Cultural Anthropology 73 (Cambridge University Press, 1990), p. 58.

98. Selhamer, *Tuba Rustica*, in Böck, *Bauernleben*, p. 79.

99. See Cabantous, *Histoire de la nuit*, pp. 140–46, and the essays in Mario Sbriccoli, ed., *La Notte: Ordine, sicurezza e disciplinamento in eta moderna* (Florence: Ponte alle grazie, 1991).

100. Briggs, *Communities of Belief*, p. 263.

101. Nancy Locklin, *Women's Work and Identity in Eighteenth-Century Brittany* (Burlington, VT: Ashgate, 2007), p. 132.

102. François Lebrun, "La religion de l'évêque de Saint-Malo et de ses diocé-sains au début du XVIIe siècle, à travers les statuts synodaux de 1619," in *La religion populaire. Actes du colloque international ... Paris, 17–19 octo-bre 1977*, Colloques internationaux du Centre National de la Recherche Scientifique 576 (Paris: Éditions du Centre National de la Recherche Scientifique, 1979), pp. 45–51; here p. 48. Also cited in Locklin, *Women's Work*, p. 132.

103. Locklin, *Women's Work*, p. 132.

104. Charles Lalore, ed., *Ancienne et nouvelle discipline du diocèse de Troyes, de 1785 à 1843. Statuts et règlements* (Troyes: Au Secrétariat de l'evêché, 1882–83), III: 257–58.

105. Medick, "Village Spinning Bees," pp. 321–29.

106. *Ibid.*, pp. 321–22.

107. Müller, "Lichtstuben im Limpurgischen," p. 380.

108. Flandrin, "Repression and Change," pp. 201–02.

109. Becker, *Konfessionalisierung*, p. 297.

110. Renate Dürr, *Mägde in der Stadt: das Beispiel Schwäbisch Hall in der frühen Neuzeit* (Frankfurt: Campus-Verlag, 1995), p. 265.

111. Beck, "Unterfinning," p. 126.

112. See Niederstätter, "Rechts- und Kulturgeschichte der Nacht," p. 186 (Alpine Switzerland and Austria); Briggs, *Communities of Belief*, p. 263 (France); and Henkhaus, *Treibhaus der Unsittlichkeit*, pp. 133–50 (Hesse).

113. Kümin, *Drinking Matters*, pp. 74–114, 193.

114. Jürgen Schlumbohm, "Gesetze, die nicht durchgesetzt werden – ein Strukturmerkmal des frühneuzeitlichen Staates?" *Geschichte und Gesellschaft* 23 (1997): 647–63.

115. Müller, "Lichtstuben im Limpurgischen," p. 381.

116. In this period no other established church attempted anything as ambi-tious as the Catholic program of public nocturnal devotion.

117. Bernard Dompnier, "Un aspect de la dévotion eucharistique dans la France du XVIIe siècle: les prières des Quarante-Heures," *Revue*

d'histoire de l'Eglise de France 67 (1981): 5–31; here 31; Schindler, "Nächtliche Ruhestörung," p. 218.

118. See Jill R. Fehleison, "appealing to the Senses: The Forty Hours Celebrations in the Duchy of Chablais, 1597–98," *Sixteenth Century Journal* 36, 2 (2005): 375–96, and Dompnier, "Dévotion eucharistique."

119. As quoted in Herbert Thurston, "Forty Hours' Devotion," in *The Catholic Encyclopedia*, ed. Charles Herbermann *et al.* (New York: Encyclopedia Press, 1913), VI: 152.

120. Dompnier, "Dévotion eucharistique," pp. 12–31.

121. Fehleison, "Appealing to the Senses," and Dompnier, "Dévotion eucharistique."

122. Dompnier, "Dévotion eucharistique," p. 11, quoting the contemporary account of Charles de Genève, *Les trophées sacrés ... en la conversion du duché de Chablais et pays circonvoisins de Genève.*

123. Dompnier, "Dévotion eucharistique," p. 31.

124. *Ibid.*, p. 24, quoting a Paris document of 1633.

125. Briggs, *Communities of Belief*, p. 269.

126. *Actes de l'église d'Amiens; recueil de tous les documents relatifs à la discipline du diocèse* (Amiens: Caron, 1848–49), II: 51 (emphasis mine). Rural services at night were also prohibited in the diocese of Troyes in 1706; see Lalore, ed., *Ancienne et nouvelle discipline du diocèse de Troyes*, III: 311.

127. For an overview see Fred G. Rausch, "Karfreitagsprozessionen in Bayern," in *Hört, sehet, weint und liebt. Passionsspiele im alpenländischen Raum*, ed. Michael Henker, Eberhard Dünninger, and Evamaria Brockhoff (Munich: Süddeutscher Verlag, 1990), pp. 87–93. Friedrich Zoepfl, "Die Feier des Karfreitags im Mindelheim des 17. und 18. Jahrhunderts," *Jahrbuch des Historischen Vereins Dillingen an der Donau* 30 (1917): 79–94, notes the importance of participants and spectators from neighboring villages at these processions.

128. Norbert Hölzl, "Das Jahrhundert der Passionsspiele und Karfreitagsprozessionen in St. Johann," *Österreichische Zeitschrift für Volkskunde* n.s. 23, 2 (1969): 116–32. For an account of a nocturnal procession in a Steiermark village in 1671, see Roswitha Stipperger, "Eine Karfreitagsprozession in Schladming aus dem Jahre 1671," *Österreichische Zeitschrift für Volkskunde* n.s. 33 (1979): 95–102.

129. Norbert Schindler, "'Und daß die Ehre Gottes mehrers befördert würde ...'. Mikrohistorische Bemerkungen zur frühneuzeitlichen Karfreitagsprozession in Traunstein," *Mitteilungen der Gesellschaft für Salzburger Landeskunde* 136 (1996): 171–200; here 185.

130. Zoepfl, "Feier des Karfreitags im Mindelheim," p. 85.

131. Julia, "La réforme posttridentine," p. 383 on forbidding nocturnal processions in the dioceses of Senez, Aix, and Fréjus. On rural piety and confraternities in villages, see Joseph Aulagne, *La réforme catholique du dix-septième siècle dans le diocèse de Limoges* (Paris: H. Champion, 1908).
132. Julia, "La réforme posttridentine," p. 396.
133. Published *ibid.*, "Pièce annexe n. 8," p. 396.
134. The struggle in France to make Christmas night a time of devotion rather than festivity needs further research. See the comments in Louis Pérouas, ed., *Pierre Robert (1589–1658). Un Magistrat du Dorat entre érudition et observation*, Foreword by Michel Cassan (Limoges: PULIM, 2001) and Michèle Bardon, ed., *Journal (1676–1688) de Jean-Baptiste Raveneau* (Étrépilly: Presses du Village, 1994).
135. Cf. Schlumbohm, "Gesetze," pp. 653–56.
136. Alexander Pope, *The Poems of Alexander Pope: A One-Volume Edition of the Twickenham Text with Selected Annotations*, second edn., ed. John Butt (London: Routledge, 1968), p. 243.
137. The essay is "… Minimâ contentos Nocte Britannos," *Tatler* 263 (December 14, 1710).
138. Henry Bourne, *Antiquitates vulgares; or, the antiquities of the common people. Giving an account of several of their opinions and ceremonies* (Newcastle: Printed by J. White for the author, 1725), p. 38.
139. *Ibid.*, p. 76
140. Mark Aikenside (1721–70), *The Pleasures of Imagination. A Poem. In Three Books* (London: Printed for R. Dodsley, 1744), p. 24.
141. Birgit Emich pairs these terms in her article on "Schlaf in der Frühen Neuzeit," pp. 57–74. The divergence of urban and rural daily rhythms has also been noted by Peter Clark, *British Clubs and Societies, 1580–1800: The Origins of an Associational World* (Oxford University Press, 2000), pp. 169–71. See also John E. Crowley, *The Invention of Comfort: Sensibilities and Design in Early Modern Britain and Early America* (Baltimore, MD: Johns Hopkins University Press, 2001), section 11 on windows, mirrors, and domestic lighting.
142. *Curioses Gespräch: zwischen Hänsel und Lippel zweyen oberländischen Bauern bey der den 14.Märzen in … Wien … gehalten Illumination* (Vienna: J.J. Jahn, 1745), fo. 2.
143. A. Roger Ekirch, "Sleep We Have Lost: Pre-Industrial Slumber in the British Isles," *American Historical Review* 106, 2 (2001): 343–86; here 383.
144. *The Letters of Mrs. E. Montagu, with Some of the Letters of Her Correspondence*, ed. Matthew Montagu (London: T. Cadell & W. Davies, 1809), 1: 109 (July 11, 1740).
145. *Ibid.*, pp. 113–14 (August 21, 1740).

146. Friedrich Justin Bertuch, "Moden in Gebrauche und Eintheilung des Tages und der Nacht zu Verschiedenen Zeiten, und bey verschiedenen Völkern," *Journal der Moden* [after 1786 *Journal des Luxus und der Moden*] 1 (May 1786): 199–201.
147. *Ibid.*, p. 200.
148. *Ibid.*
149. *Ibid.*, pp. 200–01.
150. See Emich, "Schlaf in der Frühen Neuzeit," p. 73.
151. Jean Baptiste Pujoulx, *Paris à la fin du XVIIIe siècle; ou, Esquisse historique et morale des monumens et des ruines de cette capitale; de l'etat des sciences, des arts de l'industrie à cette époque, ainsi que des moeurs et des ridicules de ses habitans* (Paris, Mathé: 1801).
152. Steele, "… Minimâ contentos Nocte Britannos."
153. Sabine Ullmann, "Kontakte und Konflikte zwischen Landjuden und Christen in Schwaben während des 17. und zu Anfang des 18. Jahrhunderts," in *Ehrkonzepte in der frühen Neuzeit: Identitäten und Abgrenzungen*, ed. Sibylle Backmann *et al.* (Berlin: Akademie Verlag, 1998), pp. 299–300.

8 DARKNESS AND ENLIGHTENMENT

1. "Il fera comme en plein midi / Clair la nuit dedans chaque rue …" *Gazette de Robinet*, October 29, 1667, as cited in Wolfgang Schivelbusch, *Disenchanted Night: The Industrialization of Light in the Nineteenth Century*, trans. Angela Davies (Berkeley: University of California Press, 1988), p. 90.
2. Baruch Spinoza, "Metaphysical Thoughts," in *Complete Works*, ed. Michael L. Morgan, trans. Samuel Shirley (Indianapolis, IN: Hackett, 2002), p. 178.
3. John Locke, *An Essay Concerning Human Understanding*, ed. Pauline Phemister (Oxford University Press, 2008), p. 251.
4. *The Athenian Oracle: being an entire collection of all the valuable questions and answers in the old Athenian mercuries … By a member of the Athenian Society. In three volumes. The third edition corrected* (London: Printed for Andrew Bell, 1706–16), III: 429–30. This *Athenian Mercury* article does consider the possibility of divine or supernatural darkness, corresponding to its cautious stance on the existence of ghosts; see below, section 8.1.
5. Johann Gottfried von Herder, "This Too a Philosophy of History for the Formation of Humanity," in *Philosophical Writings*, ed. and trans. Michael N. Forster (New York: Cambridge University Press, 2002), p. 324. On the sources of the light metaphors used in the Enlightenment, see Fritz Schalk, "Zur Semantik von Aufklärung," in *Studien zur französischen Aufklärung* (Frankfurt: Klosterman, 1977), pp. 323–39.

6. On periodization, see Jonathan Irvine Israel, *Radical Enlightenment: Philosophy and the Making of Modernity 1650–1750* (Oxford University Press, 2001), pp. 14–22, 159–66, and the literature cited there.

7. See Gillian Bennett, "Ghost and Witch in the Sixteenth and Seventeenth Centuries," in *New Perspectives on Witchcraft, Magic and Demonology*, ed. Brian P. Levack, vol. III, *Witchcraft in the British Isles and New England* (New York: Routledge, 2001), pp. 259–70.

8. See Ernst Thomas Reimbold, *Die Nacht im Mythos, Kultus, Volksglauben und in der transpersonalen Erfahrung; eine religionsphänomenologische Untersuchung* (Cologne: Wison, 1970).

9. David Lederer, "Ghosts in Early Modern Bavaria," in *Werewolves, Witches, and Wandering Spirits: Traditional Belief and Folklore in Early Modern Europe*, ed. Kathryn A. Edwards (Kirksville, MO: Truman State University Press, 2002), pp. 25–53; here pp. 46–47.

10. Lavater's treatise appeared in English editions in 1572 and 1596. See Ludwig Lavater, *Of ghostes and spirites walking by nyght, 1572*, ed. with an Introduction and Appendix by J. Dover Wilson and May Yardley (Oxford University Press, 1929).

11. *Ibid.*, p. 90.

12. *Ibid.*, p. 98.

13. Pierre Le Loyer, *IIII. livres des spectres, ou apparitions et visions d'esprits, anges et démons se monstrans sensiblement aux hommes* (Angers: G. Nepueu, 1586). See Bennett, "Ghost and Witch," p. 267.

14. Balthasar Bekker, *The World Turn'd Upside Down, or, A Plain Detection of Errors, in the Common or Vulgar Belief, Relating to Spirits, Spectres or Ghosts, Dæmons, Witches, &C.: In a Due and Serious Examination of Their Nature, Power, Administration, and Operation* (London: Printed for Eliz. Harris, 1700).

15. *The Character of a town-gallant exposing the extravagant fopperies of som[e] vain self-conceited pretenders to gentility and good breeding* (London: Printed for W.L., 1675), p. 4.

16. *Geheime Briefe, So zwischen curieusen Personen über notable Sachen … gewechselt worden* (Freystadt [i.e. Leipzig]: Hüllsen, 1701), pp. 904–10: "Was von denen jenigen Christen zuhalten sey / welche keine Gespenste und Erscheinungen der Geister glauben auch derselben thätliche Verrichtungen leugnen."

17. *Ibid.*, p. 905.

18. *Ibid.*, p. 906.

19. Edmund Hobhouse, ed., *Diary of a West Country Physician, A.D. 1684–1726* (London: Simpkin, Marshall, 1934), pp. 55–56, 18–19.

20. Balthasar Bekker, *De betoverde weereld, zynde een grondig ondersoek van 't gemeen gevoelen aangaande de geesten, derselver aart en vermogen, bewind en*

bedrijf: als ook 't gene de menschen door derselver kraght en gemeenschap doen. In vier boeken ondernomen (Amsterdam: Daniel van den Dalen, 1691–94).

21. Balthasar Bekker, *The World Bewitched; or, An Examination of the Common Opinions Concerning Spirits: Their Nature, Power, Administration, and Operations* ([London]: R. Baldwin, 1695), p. [liv].

22. The first translations were into German (1693), French (1694), and English (1695, 1700). References to this work are to the English edition of 1695, and to the French edition of 1694: Balthasar Bekker, *Le monde enchanté ou Examen des communs sentimens touchant les esprits, leur nature, leur pouvoir, leur administration, & leurs opérations* (Amsterdam: Chez Pierre Rotterdam, 1694).

23. Bekker, *World Bewitched*, p. 256.

24. See Israel, *Radical Enlightenment*, pp. 375–405.

25. Bekker, *World Bewitched*, p. [lvi].

26. As quoted in Andrew C. Fix, "Bekker and Spinoza," in *Disguised and Overt Spinozism around 1700*, ed. Wiep van Bunge and Wim Klever (Leiden: Brill, 1996), p. 23. In these controversies "Sadducism" (Sadduceeism) referred to the denial of the doctrine of the Resurrection or the immortality of the soul in general, hence the denial of spirits or ghosts.

27. As quoted in Christopher Hill, *The Century of Revolution, 1603–1714*, second edn. (London: Routledge, 2001), p. 245.

28. Henry More, *An antidote against atheisme, or, An appeal to the natural faculties of the minde of man, whether there be not a God by Henry More* (London: Printed by Roger Daniel, 1653), p. 164.

29. Letter to Hugo Boxel, September 1674, in Baruch Spinoza, "Correspondence," in *Complete Works*, ed. Morgan, p. 899, letter 54. See Gunther Coppens, "Spinoza et Boxel. Une histoire de fantômes," *Revue de Métaphysique et de Morale* 41, 1 (2004): 59–72.

30. Benjamin Camfield, *A theological discourse of angels and their ministries wherein their existence, nature, number, order and offices are modestly treated of … by Benjamin Camfield* (London: Printed by R.E. for Hen. Brome, 1678), p. 172.

31. See above, chapter 4.

32. More, *Antidote against atheisme*, p. 164.

33. Bennett, "Ghost and Witch," p. 262.

34. Michael F. Graham, *The Blasphemies of Thomas Aikenhead: Boundaries of Belief on the Eve of the Enlightenment* (Edinburgh University Press, 2008), p. 139.

35. Israel, *Radical Enlightenment*, p. 375 and Spinoza, "Correspondence," in *Complete Works*, ed. Morgan, pp. 893–906, letters 51–56.

36. Recent scholarship has argued that focusing on the changing purposes for which the idea of witchcraft was deployed is more productive than merely pursuing simple questions of belief or unbelief in witchcraft, or

to associate its decline with a single outlook, whether Cartesian, materialist, or empiricist. See Ian Bostridge, *Witchcraft and Its Transformations: c. 1650–c. 1750* (Oxford University Press, 1997), and Thomas Jefferson Wehtje, "Out of Darkness, Light: The Theological Implications of (Dis) Belief in Witchcraft in Early Modern English Literature and Thought", PhD thesis, Stony Brook University, 2004.

37. *The Compleat Library, or, News for the Ingenious* 2 (December, 1692): 50.

38. Francis Grant, *Sadducimus debellatus: or, a true narrative of the sorceries and witchcrafts exercis'd by the devil and his instruments upon Mrs. Christian Shaw, daughter of Mr. John Shaw, of Bargarran in the County of Renfrew in the West of Scotland, from Aug. 1696 to Apr. 1697* (London: Printed for H. Newman and A. Bell, 1698), p. vi.

39. Ralph Thoresby, *The Diary of Ralph Thoresby, F.R.S., Author of the Topography of Leeds*, 2 vols., ed. Joseph Hunter (London: H. Colburn and R. Bentley, 1830), II: 118–19 (June 13, 1712). See also entry for June 12, 1712: "Was after with Mr. Gale and Mr. Oddy, a learned gentleman at the Coffeehouse."

40. John Beaumont, *An historical, physiological and theological treatise of spirits, apparitions, witchcrafts, and other magical practices … With a refutation of Dr. Bekker's World bewitch'd; and other authors that have opposed the belief of them* (London: Printed for D. Browne, 1705). The compendious work was published in a German translation in 1721.

41. Thoresby, *Diary*, II: 119.

42. Beaumont reported that "it's a custom of the Jews" during Sukkoth "to go forth in the Night, because they think all things that will happen to them that year, are revealed to them that Night in the Moonshine." In this case, if a man's shadow in the moonlight appeared headless (as suggested in the illustration), this foretold his death within the year. Beaumont, *Treatise of Spirits*, pp. 88–89.

43. *Bibliothèque Universelle et Historique* 21 (1691): 122–51; here 150.

44. *Ibid.*, p. 150.

45. J.B. Williams, ed., *Memoirs of the Life, Character and Writings of the Rev. Matthew Henry* (Boston: Peirce & Williams, 1830), pp. 56–57.

46. As noted in the *Oxford Dictionary of National Biography*, the poet Abel Evans denounced Tindal in his poem *The Apparition* (Oxford: Printed and sold by the booksellers of London and Westminster, 1710). His verses associated free-thinking, debauchery, and the night, referring to Tindal as follows: "In Vice and Error from his *Cradle* Nurs'd: / He studies hard, and takes extreme Delight, / In Whores, or Heresies to spend the Night." (p. 3)

47. Matthew Tindal, *An essay concerning the power of the magistrate* (London: Printed by J.D. for Andrew Bell, 1697), p. 6.

48. Philip C. Almond, "The Contours of Hell in English Thought, 1660–1750," *Religion* 22, 4 (1992): 297–311; here 304.
49. Carlos Eire, "The Good Side of Hell: Infernal Meditations in Early Modern Spain," *Historical Reflections/Réflexions Historiques* 26 (2000): 286–310; here 290.
50. *Ibid.*, pp. 286–91.
51. John Milton, *Paradise Lost*, ed. David Scott Kastan and Merritt Yerkes Hughes (Indianapolis, IN: Hackett, 2005), p. 209; VI.870.
52. William George Scott-Moncrieff, ed., *Narrative of Mr. James Nimmo written for his own satisfaction to keep in some remembrance the Lord's way dealing and kindness towards him, 1654–1709*, Publications of the Scottish History Society 6 (Edinburgh: Printed by T. and A. Constable for the Society, 1887), pp. xiii–xiv, quoting "from a copy of Mrs. Nimmo's Narrative, in which the spelling has been adapted."
53. See the references to nocturnal conversations among free-thinkers at this time in Edinburgh in Graham, *Blasphemies of Thomas Aikenhead*, pp. 60–65.
54. D.P. Walker, *The Decline of Hell: Seventeenth-Century Discussions of Eternal Torment* (University of Chicago Press, 1964), pp. 3–51.
55. *Ibid.*, p. 226.
56. *Ibid.*, pp. 158–59.
57. Walker, *Decline of Hell*, p. 159, quoting Thomas Burnet, *De statu mortuorum et resurgentium tractatus* (London: A. Bettesworth and C. Hitch, 1733), p. 309.
58. Walker, *Decline of Hell*, pp. 171–72.
59. *Ibid.*, pp. 182–83, n. 5.
60. *Ibid.*, p. 247. On concealing radical belief, see Stephen D. Snobelen, "Isaac Newton, Heretic: The Strategies of a Nicodemite," *British Journal for the History of Science* 32 (1999): 381–419.
61. Walker, *Decline of Hell*, p. 144.
62. *Ibid.*, p. 190.
63. *Ibid.*
64. *Ibid.*, pp. 93–103; Snobelen, "Newton," pp. 401–12.
65. Walker, *Decline of Hell*, p. 262.
66. *Ibid.*, p. 96.
67. *Ibid.*, p. 262.
68. Snobelen, "Newton," pp. 408–19.
69. See his *Mannhafter Kunstspiegel* (*Noble Mirror of Art*) (Augsburg: Schultes, 1663), as translated in Allardyce Nicoll, John H. McDowell, and George R. Kernodle, trans. and Barnard Hewitt, ed., *The Renaissance Stage: Documents of Serlio, Sabbattini and Furttenbach* (Coral Gables, FL: University of Miami Press, 1958), p. 229.

70. As Jonathan Israel has shown, seemingly obscure intellectual and cultural issues, such as the diabolical basis of pagan oracles, could bring the commitments of the early Enlightenment into sharp focus. See his *Radical Enlightenment*, pp. 359–74.

71. The most widely circulated clandestine philosophical manuscripts of the period 1680–1750 "devote considerable space to … condemning belief in demons, spirits, sorcery, divination, and the Devil" – all issues tied to the night and its associations. See Israel, *Radical Enlightenment*, pp. 690–91.

72. *Censor* (London, 1715–) 3, 67 (March 26, 1717): 20–21.

73. *Ibid.*, p. 21. He adds that late-night conversations like these "no less encourag'd *Superstition* in Those, who have imbib'd odd Sentiments from the Weakness of their own Constitutions, or swallow'd them from the Imposition of their Teachers."

74. Cited in Edouard Fournier, *Les lanternes: histoire de l'ancien éclairage de Paris* (Paris: Dentu, 1854), p. 25.

75. Joachim Christoph Nemeitz, *Séjour de Paris: c'est à dire, instructions fidèles, pour les voiageurs de condition, comment ils se doivent conduire, s'ils veulent faire un bon usage de leur tems & argent, durant leur Séjour à Paris* (Leiden: J. Van Abcoude, 1727), ed. Alfred Franklin as *La vie de Paris sous la Régence* (Paris: Éditions Plon, Nourrit et cie, 1897), p. 52.

76. *Ibid.*, p. 51.

77. As quoted in Alan Charles Kors, *Atheism in France, 1650–1729*, vol. I, *The Orthodox Sources of Disbelief* (Princeton University Press, 1990), p. 12.

78. John Donne, *Complete Poetry and Selected Prose*, ed. Charles M. Coffin (New York: Random House, 1978), p. 629.

79. *Ibid.*, p. 585.

80. As suggested by a query in the *Athenian Gazette* which began, "Being in company the other Night, among other discourse, one of the company said a man might be too Godly, and quoted that text for it, Eccl. 7:16, 'Be not Righteous overmuch.'" The editors of the *Gazette* replied that this was "an old objection of the Atheists," and sought to bring sound Christian virtue into this nocturnal coffeehouse conversation. *Athenian Gazette* 6, 18 (March 16, 1692): 119–20.

81. Bernard Le Bovier de Fontenelle, *Entretiens sur la pluralité des mondes. Digression sur les anciens et les modernes*, ed. Robert Shackleton (Oxford: Clarendon Press, 1955), p. 147; Bekker, *Le monde enchanté*, book IV, p. 49.

82. English translations from Bernard Le Bovier de Fontenelle, *Conversations on the Plurality of Worlds*, trans. H.A. Hargreaves (Berkeley: University of California Press, 1990); see p. xxiv on the early editions.

83. Werner Krauss, *Fontenelle und die Aufklärung* (Munich: Fink, 1969), p. 7.

84. Fontenelle, *Entretiens*, p. 59: "A Monsieur L***"; Fontenelle, *Conversations*, p. 8.

85. Fontenelle, *Entretiens*, p. 63; Fontenelle, *Conversations*, p. 11, first evening.

86. Fontenelle, *Entretiens*, p. 64; Fontenelle, *Conversations*, p. 12, first evening.

87. *Des eröfneten Ritter-Platz. Anderer Theil, Welcher zu Fortsetzung der vorigen noch andere galante Wissenschaften anweiset* (Hamburg: Benjamin Schiller, 1702), pp. 43f., as quoted in Jörg Jochen Berns, Frank Druffner, Ulrich Schütte, and Brigitte Walbe, eds., *Erdengötter: Fürst und Hofstaat in der Frühen Neuzeit im Spiegel von Marburger Bibliotheks- und Archivbeständen. Ein Katalog* (Marburg Universitätsbibliothek, 1997), pp. 487–88, 151.

88. Fontenelle, *Entretiens*, pp. 144–45.

89. Nicola Sabbatini's *Practica di Fabricar Scene e Machine ne' Teatri* (*Manual for Constructing Theatrical Scenes and Machines*, 1638) as translated in Hewitt, ed. *Renaissance Stage*, pp. 96–97.

90. See Claire Cazanave, "Une publication invente son public: les *Entretiens sur la pluralité des mondes*," in *De la publication: entre Renaissance et Lumières*, ed. Christian Jouhaud and Alain Viala (Paris: Fayard, 2002), pp. 267–80, and Steven F. Rendall, "Fontenelle and His Public," *MLN* 86, 4 (1971): 496–508.

91. Israel, *Radical Enlightenment*, pp. 592–93, 684.

92. On the reception of *The World Bewitched* see *ibid.*, pp. 374–405 and Jonathan Israel, "Les controverses pamphlétaires dans la vie intellectuelle hollandaise et allemande à l'époque de Bekker et Van Leenhof," *XVIIe Siècle* 49, 2 (1997): 254–64.

93. Bekker, *World Bewitched*, pp. [liii–lvii].

94. *Ibid.*, p. [xvi].

95. Han van Ruler, "Minds, Forms, and Spirits: The Nature of Cartesian Disenchantment," *Journal of the History of Ideas* 61, 3 (2000): 381–95; here 382.

96. Bekker, *World Bewitched*, p. 311.

97. *Ibid.*, p. 224.

98. Andrew C. Fix, *Prophecy and Reason: The Dutch Collegiants in the Early Enlightenment* (Princeton University Press, 1991).

99. Spinoza explained that the miracles described in Scripture were "adapted to the beliefs and judgment of the historians who recorded them. The revelations, too, were adapted to the beliefs of the prophets." Neither miracles nor revelations could be accepted at face value, since the biblical accounts reflect the limitations of those who recorded them and of the audience addressed by them. Baruch Spinoza, *Theological-Political Treatise*, trans. Samuel Shirley with an Introduction by Seymour Feldman (Indianapolis, IN: Hackett, 2001), p. 87.

100. *Bibliothèque Universelle et Historique* 21 (1691): 150; see the translation in the *Athenian Gazette* 4, 18 (November 28, 1691): 17–23. See also the sympathetic critique of Philippus van Limborch in his letter to John Locke, July 27, 1691, in *The Correspondence of John Locke*, ed. E.S. de Beer (Oxford University Press, 1976–1989), IV: 294–301.

101. Bekker, *Le monde enchanté*, book II, p. 187.

102. *Ibid.*, book IV, pp. 385–474. In his debunking of witch and ghost stories in book IV Bekker mentions the night as the time of the incident in about fifty cases. Beaumont noticed this emphasis on the night as a time of confusion and error and sought to respond in his *Treatise of spirits*, pp. 307–09.

103. Fontenelle, *Entretiens*, p. 157 (sixth evening).

104. Fontenelle, *Entretiens*, p. 107; Fontenelle, *Conversations*, p. 46 (third evening).

105. *Édit du Roi, touchant la police des isles de l'Amérique Française. Du mois de Mars 1685. Registré au Conseil Souverain de S. Domingue, le 6 Mai 1687* (Paris, 1687), 28–58. See the modern edition of Louis Sala-Molins, ed., *Le Code Noir ou le calvaire de Canaan* (Paris: Presses universitaires de France, 1987).

106. See Guillaume Aubert, "The Blood of France: Race and Purity of Blood in the French Atlantic World," *William and Mary Quarterly* 61, 3 (2004), and the literature cited there.

107. *Miscellaneous Letters* 1, 7 (November 28, 1694): 120.

108. Bekker, *World Bewitched*, p. 8. The English translation of *The World Bewitched* included only this first book and a summary of the rest, suggesting that author and publishers thought its arguments were coherent on their own.

109. *Ibid.*, pp. 237, 256, and in the Preface, "An Abridgement of the Whole Work," pp. [xxiii–lxxiii].

110. *Ibid.*, p. 259.

111. Kors, *Atheism in France*.

112. *Ibid.*, p. 93.

113. Benjamin Binet, *Idée Genérale de la Théologie Payenne, Servant de Refutation au Systeme de Mr. Bekker. Touchant L'existence & l'Operation Des Demons. Ou Traitté Historique des Dieux du Paganisme* (Amsterdam: Du Fresne, 1699), p. 222.

114. Kors, *Atheism in France*.

115. See Lynn Hunt, Margaret C. Jacob, and Wijnand Mijnhardt, *The Book That Changed Europe: Picart and Bernard's* Religious Ceremonies of the World (Cambridge, MA: Belknap Press of Harvard University Press, 2010).

116. Samuel Briggs, ed., *De Tribus Impostoribus … The Three Impostors: Translated (with Notes and Comments) from a French Manuscript of the Work Written in 1716 with a Dissertation on the Original Treatise and a Bibliography of the Various Editions* ([Cleveland?]: Privately printed for the subscribers, 1904), p. 44. On its publication see Hunt *et al.*, *The Book That Changed Europe*, pp. 39–43. See also Abraham Anderson, *The Treatise of the Three Impostors and the Problem of Enlightenment: A New Translation of the Traité des trois Imposteurs (1777 Edition) with Three Essays in Commentary* (Lanham, MD: Rowman & Littlefield, 1997).

117. Binet, *Idée Generale de la Théologie Payenne*, pp. 212–17.

118. Another critic of Bekker's argument from universal error, John Beaumont, was no theologian, and his approach to refuting the arguments of Bekker focused not on Cartesianism or the interpretation of Scripture, but on the argument in the first book of *The World Bewitched*, regarding the widespread belief in witches and the relationship between paganism and Christianity, citing the works of authors who challenged Bekker on those terms, especially Benjamin Binet. Beaumont translated long sections of Binet's *Idée Generale de la Théologie Payenne* into his *Treatise of Spirits*.

119. Bekker, *World Bewitched*, p. 91. This theme is discussed by Rolf Reichardt, "Light against Darkness: The Visual Representations of a Central Enlightenment Concept," *Representations* 61 (1998): 95–148, though without reference to European views of the larger world.

9 CONCLUSION

1. A. Roger Ekirch, "Sleep We Have Lost: Pre-Industrial Slumber in the British Isles," *American Historical Review* 106, 2 (2001): 343–86. See above chapters 1 and 7.

2. *Aufgefangene Brieffe, welche Zwischen etzlichen curieusen Personen über den ietzigen Zustand der Staats und gelehrten Welt gewechselt worden* (Wahrenberg: J.G. Freymunden [actually Leipzig: Groschuff], 1701), p. 890.

3. "Von der Illuminations-Pracht und Mißbrauch / und hingegen von nützlichen und nöthigen Gebrauch der See-Lichter und Nacht-Laternen auch nunmehr zu Leipzig aufgesteckt."

4. *Aufgefangene Brieffe*, p. 890:

> Der Epicurer macht
> Den Tag zu seiner Nacht.
> Die Eitelkeit pflegt solches umzukehren.
> Denn diese lässet sich bethoren /
> Das sie die Nacht verwandelt in den Tag /
> Und zwar durch die Illuminationen.

Wer aber nicht so viel vermag /
Daß er Wachslichter kan bezahlen /
Und will doch die Reichen prahlen /
Darneben gern auch mit schlampampen /
Der brennet Kühn / Oel-Funtzeln oder Lampen.
So weit ist nun die Thorheit eingerissen /
Daß ihr so gar die Armen folgen müssen /
Steckt mancher auch schon in den grössten Nöthen.
Das sind die Früchte der Solennitäten!
Den Unrath hat das Pabsthum erst erfunden /
Darüber wird das Land so sehr geschunden.
Es bleiebe wohl / wenn nur hierzu die Pfaffen
Das Geld / und nicht die Layen müsten schaffen.

5. Victor Lieberman has argued convincingly that the combination of forced conformity in religion, the growth of the state's disciplinary ambitions, and commerce tied to urban consumption shaped polities across Eurasia in a global early modern period. See his Introduction to *Beyond Binary Histories: Re-Imagining Eurasia to c. 1830*, ed. Victor B. Lieberman (Ann Arbor: University of Michigan Press, 1999), p. 2: "between c. 1450 and 1670 societies across Southeast Asia experienced a commercial and urban vigor, a trend towards political absolutism, and an emphasis on orthodox, textual religions that in combination gave birth to an 'Age of Commerce,' also termed the "early modern period." See also Victor Lieberman, "Transcending East–West Dichotomies: State and Culture Formation in Six Ostensibly Disparate Areas," in *Beyond Binary Histories*, ed. Lieberman, pp. 19–102, esp. pp. 53–63, and Victor B. Lieberman, *Strange Parallels: Southeast Asia in Global Context, c. 800–1830*, vol. II, *Mainland Mirrors: Europe, Japan, China, South Asia, and the Islands* (Cambridge University Press, 2009).
6. I.W. [i.e., John Walton], "To my worthy friend, Mr. Henry Vaughan the Silurist" (1678), in *The Works of Henry Vaughan*, ed. L.C. Martin, second edn. (Oxford: Clarendon Press, 1957), p. 620.
7. André Félibien, *Tapisseries Du Roy, Ou Sont Representez Les Quatre Elemens Et Les Quatre Saisons. Avec Les devises Qvi Les Accompagnent Et Leur Explication = Königliche Französische Tapezereyen, Oder überaus schöne Sinn-Bilder, in welchen Die vier Element, samt den Vier Jahr-Zeiten ... vorgestellet werden ... Aus den Original-Kupffern nachgezeichnet* (Augsburg: Krauß / Koppmayer, 1690), p. 2.
8. See Paula McDowell, *The Women of Grub Street: Press, Politics, and Gender in the London Literary Marketplace, 1678–1730* (Oxford: Clarendon Press, 1998), pp. 285–87.

9. Bernard Le Bovier de Fontenelle, *Entretiens sur la pluralité des mondes. Digression sur les anciens et les modernes*, ed. Robert Shackleton (Oxford: Clarendon Press, 1955), p. 107 (third evening).

10. *A missionary voyage to the Southern Pacific Ocean, performed in the years 1796, 1797, 1798, in the ship Duff, commanded by Captain James Wilson. Compiled from journals of the officers and missionaries; and Illustrated with Maps, Charts, and Views … by a Committee Appointed for the Purpose by the Directors of the Missionary Society* (London: The Missionary Society, 1799), p. 3.

11. Christa Bausch, "Das Nachtmythologem in der polynesischen Religion und seine Auswirkungen auf protestantische Missionstätigkeit," *Zeitschrift für Religions- und Geistesgeschichte* 22 (1970): 244–66, and Christa Bausch, "*Po* and *Ao*. Analysis of an Ideological Conflict in Polynesia," *Journal de la Société des Océanistes* 34 (1978): 169–85.

12. *A missionary voyage to the Southern Pacific Ocean*, p. 240.

13. William Wyatt Gill, *Jottings from the Pacific* (London: Religious Tract Society, 1885), p. 21, describing travels in 1875.

14. Bryan D. Palmer, *Cultures of Darkness: Night Travels in the Histories of Transgression, from Medieval to Modern* (New York: Monthly Review Press, 2000), p. 454.

Bibliography

PRIMARY SOURCES

ARCHIVES CONSULTED

Archives Départmentales du Nord, Lille [ADN]
Archives Municipales de Lille [AM Lille]
Geheimes Staatsarchiv Preussischer Kulturbesitz Berlin [GStAB]
Hessisches Staatsarchiv Marburg [HstSM]
Sächsisches Hauptstaatsarchiv Dresden [SHAD]
Staatsarchiv Bremen [StAB]
Stadtarchiv Frankfurt [SdAF]
Stadtarchiv Leipzig [SdAL]
Wiener Stadt- und Landesarchiv [WSL]

PRINTED SOURCES

Abraham a Sancta Clara, *Etwas für alle, das ist: Eine kurtze beschreibung allerley stands- ambts- und gewerbs-personhen: mit beygeruckter sittlichen lehre und biblischen concepten* (Würzburg: druckts Martin Frantz Hertz, 1711).

Actes de l'église d'Amiens: recueil de tous les documents relatifs à la discipline du diocèse, 2 vols. (Amiens: Caron, 1848–49).

Aikenside, Mark. *The Pleasures of Imagination. A Poem. In Three Books* (London: Printed for R. Dodsley, 1744).

Anderson, Abraham. *The Treatise of the Three Impostors and the Problem of Enlightenment: A New Translation of the Traité des trois Imposteurs (1777 Edition) with Three Essays in Commentary* (Lanham, MD: Rowman & Littlefield, 1997).

Andreä, Johann Valentin. *Christianopolis*, ed. with an Introduction by Edward H. Thompson, Archives internationales d'histoire des idées 162 (Dordrecht: Kluwer Academic Publishers, 1999).

The hermetick romance, or, The chymical wedding written in High Dutch by Christian Rosencreutz, trans. E. Foxcroft (London: Printed by A. Sowle, 1690).

Reipublicae christianopolitanae descriptio (Strasbourg: Zetzner, 1619).

Angelus Silesius. *The Cherubinic Wanderer*, trans. Maria Shrady (New York: Paulist Press, 1986).

Arndt, Johann. *Vier Bücher von wahrem Christenthumb: die erste Gesamtausgabe (1610)*, ed. Johann Anselm Steiger, Johann Arndt-Archiv 2 (Hildesheim: G. Olms, 2007).

Athenian Oracle: being an entire collection of all the valuable questions and answers in the old Athenian mercuries ... By a member of the Athenian Society. In three volumes. The third edition corrected (London: Printed for Andrew Bell, 1706–16).

Aufgefangene Brieffe, welche Zwischen etzlichen curieusen Personen über den ietzigen Zustand der Staats und gelehrten Welt gewechselt worden (Wahrenberg: J.G. Freymunden [actually Leipzig: Groschuff], 1699–1703).

Augustine, *Concerning the Nature of the Good*, in *A Select Library of the Nicene and Post-Nicene Fathers of the Christian Church*, vol. IV, ed. Philip Schaff (New York: The Christian Literature Co., 1886–90).

Confessions, trans. F.J. Sheed, ed. Michael P. Foley (Indianapolis, IN: Hackett, 2006)

De natura boni, in *Corpus scriptorum ecclesiasticorum latinorum*, ed. Michael Petschenig *et al.* (Vienna: Hoelder-Pichler-Tempsky, 1892).

Balfour, Andrew. *Letters write* [sic] *to a friend by the learned and judicious Sir Andrew Balfour ... containing excellent directions and advices for travelling thro' France and Italy* (Edinburgh: s.n., 1700).

Bardon, Michèle, ed. *Journal (1676–1688) de Jean-Baptiste Raveneau* (Étrépilly: Presses du Village, 1994).

Baur, Ludwig. "Berichte des Hessen-Darmstädtischen Gesandten Justus Eberhard Passer an die Landgräfin Elisabeth Dorothea über die Vorgänge am kaiserlichen Hofe und in Wien von 1680 bis 1683," *Archiv für Österreichische Geschichte* 37 (1867): 271–409.

Beaumont, John. *An historical, physiological and theological treatise of spirits, apparitions, witchcrafts, and other magical practices ... With a refutation of Dr. Bekker's World bewitch'd; and other authors that have opposed the belief of them* (London: Printed for D. Browne, 1705).

Beckmann, Johann. *Beyträge zur Geschichte der Erfindungen*, 5 vols. (Leipzig: P.G. Kummer, 1782–1805).

Bekker, Balthasar. *Balthasar Bekkers bezauberte Welt*, 3 vols. (Leipzig: Weygand, 1781–1782).

De betoverde weereld, zynde een grondig ondersoek van 't gemeen gevoelen aangaande de geesten, derselver aart en vermogen, bewind en bedrijf: als ook 't gene de menschen door derselver kraght en gemeenschap doen. In vier boeken ondernomen, 4 vols. (Amsterdam: Daniel van den Dalen, 1691–94).

Le monde enchanté ou Examen des communs sentimens touchant les esprits, leur nature, leur pouvoir, leur administration, & leurs opérations, 4 vols. (Amsterdam: Chez Pierre Rotterdam, 1694).

The World Bewitched; or, An Examination of the Common Opinions Concerning Spirits: Their Nature, Power, Administration, and Operations ([London]: R. Baldwin, 1695).

The World Turn'd Upside Down, or, A Plain Detection of Errors, in the Common or Vulgar Belief, Relating to Spirits, Spectres or Ghosts, Dæmons, Witches, &C.: In a Due and Serious Examination of Their Nature, Power, Administration, and Operation (London: Printed for Eliz. Harris, 1700).

Benserade, Isaac de. *Ballets pour Louis XIV*, ed. Marie-Claude Canova-Green (Toulouse: Société de Littératures Classiques, 1997).

Bernard, Jean Frédéric. *Réflexions morales, satiriques et comiques, sur les moeurs de notre siècle* (Amsterdam: chez Jean Frédéric Bernard, 1713).

Bernard, Richard. *A guide to grand-iury men diuided into two bookes: in the first, is the authors best aduice to them what to doe, before they bring in a billa vera in cases of witchcraft ... In the second, is a treatise touching witches good and bad, how they may be knowne, euicted, condemned, with many particulars* (London: Printed by Felix Kingston, 1627).

Bertuch, Friedrich Justin. "Moden in Gebrauche und Eintheilung des Tages und der Nacht zu Verschiedenen Zeiten, und bey verschiedenen Völkern," *Journal der Moden* 1 (May 1786): 199–201.

Beutel, Tobias. *Chur-Fürstlicher Sächsicher stets grünender hoher Cedern-Wald* (Dresden: Bergen, 1671).

Das bey der Nacht Hervorleuchtende Leipzig (Leipzig: Immanuel Tietze, 1701).

Bèze, Théodore de. *Histoire ecclésiastique des églises réformées au royaume de France*, ed. G. Baum and Eduard Cunitz, 3 vols. (Paris: Librairie Fischbacher, 1883–89).

Binet, Benjamin. *Idée Générale de la Théologie Payenne, Servant de Refutation au Systeme de Mr. Bekker. Touchant L'existence & l'Operation Des Demons. Ou Traitté Historique des Dieux du Paganisme* (Amsterdam: Du Fresne, 1699).

Binsfeld, Peter. *Tractat von Bekanntnuss der Zauberer unnd Hexen*, ed. Hiram Kümper (Vienna: Mille Tre Verlag, Schächter, 2004).

Böck, Karl. *Das Bauernleben in den Werken bayerischer Barockprediger* (Munich: Schnell & Steiner, 1953).

Bodin, Jean. *On the Demon-Mania of Witches*, trans. Randy A. Scott, with an Introduction by Jonathan L. Pearl, Renaissance and Reformation Texts in Translation 7 (Toronto: Centre for Reformation and Renaissance Studies, 1995).

Boguet, Henry. *Discours exécrable des sorciers: ensemble leur procez, faits depuis deux ans en ça, en divers endroicts de la France ... Seconde édition* (Paris: D. Binet, 1603).

Böhme, Jacob. *Sämtliche Schriften*, ed. August Faust and Will-Erich Peuckert (Stuttgart: Fromman, 1955–61).

Signatura rerum, or, The signature of all things shewing the sign and significa-tion of the severall forms and shapes in the creation, and what the beginning, ruin, and cure of every thing is, trans. John Ellistone (London: Printed by John Macock for Gyles Calvert, 1651).

Bourne, Henry. *Antiquitates vulgares; or, the antiquities of the common people. Giving an account of several of their opinions and ceremonies* (Newcastle: Printed by J. White for the author, 1725).

Braspart, Michel, ed. *Du Bartas, poète chrétien* (Neuchâtel: Delachaux et Niestlé, 1947).

Briggs, Samuel, ed. *De Tribus Impostoribus ... The Three Impostors: Translated (with Notes and Comments) from a French Manuscript of the Work Written in 1716 with a Dissertation on the Original Treatise and a Bibliography of the Various Editions* ([Cleveland?]: Privately printed for the subscribers, 1904).

Browne, Thomas. *[A true and full copy of that which was most imperfectly and surreptitiously printed before vnder the name of] Religio medici* ([London]: Printed for Andrew Crook, 1643).

Burnet, Thomas. *De statu mortuorum et resurgentium tractatus* (London: A. Bettesworth and C. Hitch, 1733).

Byrd, William. *The London Diary (1717–1721) and Other Writings*, ed. Louis B. Wright and Marion Tinling (New York: Oxford University Press, 1958).

Calendar of State Papers, Domestic Series, of the Reign of Charles II, 1660–1685, 28 vols. (London: HMSO, 1860–1939).

Camfield, Benjamin. *A theological discourse of angels and their ministries wherein their existence, nature, number, order and offices are modestly treated of ... by Benjamin Camfield* (London: Printed by R.E. for Hen. Brome, 1678).

Camus, Jean-Pierre. *A Draught of Eternity*, trans. Miles Carr (Douai: By the widowe of Marke Wyon, at the signe of the Phœnix, 1632).

Case of Edmund Heming [The], who first set up the new lights in the City of London (London: s.n., 1689).

Chantelou, Paul Fréart de. *Diary of the Cavaliere Bernini's visit to France*, ed. with an Introduction by Anthony Blunt, annotated by George C. Bauer, trans. Margery Corbett (Princeton University Press, 1985).

Character of a town-gallant [The] exposing the extravagant fopperies of som[e] vain self-conceited pretenders to gentility and good breeding (London: Printed for W.L., 1675).

Character of Coffee and Coffee-Houses [by M.P.] (London: John Starkey, 1661).

Charlotte Elisabeth d'Orléans, *Letters from Liselotte*, ed. and trans. Maria Kroll (New York: McCall, 1971).

Childs, John, ed. "Captain Henry Herbert's Narrative of His Journey through France with His Regiment, 1671–3," *Camden Fourth Series* 30 (1990): 271–369.

Chronicle of the Hutterian Brethren (Rifton, NY: Plough Publishing House, 1987).

Clarke Family Letters (Alexandria, VA: Alexander Street Press, 2002).

Cleveland, John. *The Poems of John Cleveland*, ed. John M. Berdan (New Haven: Yale University Press, 1911).

Codex Austriacus, Supplementum Codicis Austriaci Sammlung Oesterreichischer Gesetze und Ordnungen ... bis auf das Jahr 1720 (Leipzig: Eisfeld, 1748).

Copernicus, Nicolaus. *On the Revolutions of Heavenly Spheres*, trans. Charles Glen Wallis, ed. Stephen Hawking (Philadelphia: Running Press, 2004).

Corvinus, Gottlieb Siegmund. *Nutzbares, galantes und curiöses Frauenzimmer-Lexicon: Worinnen nicht nur Der Frauenzimmer geistlich- und weltliche Orden, Aemter, Würden, Ehren-Stellen, Professionen und Gewerbe ... Nahmen und Thaten der Göttinnen ... gelehrter Weibes-Bilder ... auch anderer ... Trachten und Moden ... Gewohnheiten und Gebräuche ... Ergötzlichkeiten ... Gebrechen ... und alles ... was einem Frauenzimmer vorkommen kan, und ihm nöthig zu wissen ... Ordentlich nach dem Alphabet ... abgefaßt* (Leipzig: bey Joh. Friedrich Gleditsch und Sohn, 1715).

Crashaw, Richard. *The Complete Poetry of Richard Crashaw*, ed. George Walton Williams (New York: Norton, 1972).

Cudmore, Daniel. *Euchodia. Or, A prayer-song; being sacred poems on the history of the birth and passion of our blessed Saviour, and several other choice texts of Scripture* (London: Printed by J.C. for William Ley in Paul's Chain, 1655).

Cunnington, B. Howard, ed. *Records of the County of Wilts: Being Extracts from the Quarter Sessions Great Rolls of the Seventeenth Century* (Devizes: G. Simpson & Co., 1932).

Curioses Gespräch: zwischen Hänsel und Lippel zweyen oberländischen Bauern bey der den 14. Märzen in ... Wien ... gehalten Illumination (Vienna: J.J. Jahn, 1745).

Czepko, Daniel. *Geistliche Schriften*, ed. Werner Milch (Darmstadt: Wissenschaftliche Buchgesellschaft, 1963).

Dach, Simon. *Werke*, ed. Hermann Oesterley (Hildesheim and New York: Georg Olms Verlag, 1977).

Dalton, Michael. *The Countrey Justice* (London: Printed for the Societie of Stationers, 1618).

Daneau, Lambert. *The wonderfull woorkmanship of the world wherin is conteined an excellent discourse of Christian naturall philosophie*, trans. Thomas Twyne (London: for Andrew Maunsell, in Paules Church-yard, 1578).

d'Argenson, Marc-René de Voyer. *Notes de René d'Argenson, lieutenant général de police, intéressantes pour l'histoire des moeurs et de la police de Paris à la fin du règne de Louis XIV* (Paris: Imprimerie Émile Voitelain et cie, 1866).

Del Rio, Martin. *Investigations into Magic*, ed. and trans. P.G. Maxwell-Stuart (Manchester University Press, 2000).

DeLaune, Thomas. *Angliæ Metropolis: or, The Present State of London ... First written by ... Tho. Delaune, gent. and continued to this present year by a careful hand* (London: Printed by G.L. for J. Harris and T. Howkins, 1690).

Denys the Areopagite, *Pseudo-Dionysius: The Complete Works*, trans. Colm Luibheid; Foreword and Notes by Paul Rorem, Classics of Western Spirituality 54 (New York: Paulist Press, 1987).

Dietz, Johann. *Mein Lebenslauf*, ed. Friedhelm Kemp (Munich: Kosel, 1966).

Donne, John. *Complete Poetry and Selected Prose*, ed. Charles M. Coffin (New York: Random House, 1978).

    John Donne's Poetry, ed. Donald R. Dickson, Norton Critical Edition (New York: Norton, 2007).

Drovin, Daniel. *Les Vengeances divines, de la transgression des sainctes ordonnances de Dieu* (Paris: J. Mettayer, 1595).

Du Bartas, Guillaume de Saluste. *Devine Weekes and Workes*, trans. Joshua Sylvester (London: Printed by Humphray Lownes, 1621).

Echard, Laurence. *Flanders, or the Spanish Netherlands, most accurately described shewing the several provinces* (London: Printed for Tho. Salusbury, 1691).

Eckardt, Wilhelm A., and Helmut Klingelhöfer, eds. *Bauernleben im Zeitalter des Dreissigjährigen Krieges: die Stausebacher Chronik des Caspar Preis, 1636–1667*, Beiträge zur hessischen Geschichte 13 (Marburg: Trautvetter und Fischer, 1998).

Erasmus, Desiderius. *Collected Works of Erasmus. Literary and Educational Writings*, 7 vols., ed. Craig Ringwalt Thompson, Jesse Kelley Sowards, Anthony Levi, Elaine Fantham, Erika Rummel, and Jozef Ijsewijn (University of Toronto Press, 1978–).

Ernst, Gerhard, and Barbara Wolf, eds. "Pierre Ignace Chavatte: *Chronique memorial (1657–1693)*," in *Textes français privés des XVIIe et XVIIIe siècles*, Beiheft zur Zeitschrift für romanische Philologie 310, CD 1–3 (Tübingen: Max Niemeyer Verlag, 2005).

Evelyn, John. *The Diary of John Evelyn. In Six Volumes*, ed. E.S. de Beer (Oxford: Clarendon Press, 1955).

Faret, Nicholas. *The Honest Man or the Art to Please at Court*, trans. Edward Grimstone (London: Thomas Harper, 1632).

Félibien, André. *Tapisseries Du Roy, Ou Sont Representez Les Quatre Elemens Et Les Quatre Saisons. Avec Les devises Qvi Les Accompagnent Et Leur*

Explication = *Königliche Französische Tapezereyen, Oder überaus schöne Sinn-Bilder, in welchen Die vier Element, samt den Vier Jahr-Zeiten … vorgestellet werden … Aus den Original-Kupffern nachgezeichnet* (Augsburg: Krauß / Koppmayer, 1690).

Fontenelle, Bernard Le Bovier de. *Conversations on the Plurality of Worlds*, trans. H.A. Hargreaves (Berkeley: University of California Press, 1990).

   Entretiens sur la pluralité des mondes. Digression sur les anciens et les modernes, ed. Robert Shackleton (Oxford: Clarendon Press, 1955).

Foxe, John. *Actes and monuments of matters most speciall and memorable, happenyng in the Church … from the primitiue age to these latter tymes of ours, with the bloudy times, horrible troubles, and great persecutions agaynst the true martyrs of Christ, sought and wrought as well by heathen emperours, as nowe lately practised by Romish prelates, especially in this realme of England and Scotland. Newly reuised and recognised, partly also augmented, and now the fourth time agayne published*, 2 vols. in 1 (London: Imprinted by Iohn Daye, dwellyng ouer Aldersgate beneath S. Martins, 1583).

Franklin, Alfred, ed. *La vie de Paris sous la Régence* (Paris: Éditions Plon, Nourrit et cie, 1897).

Franklin, Benjamin. *Writings*, ed. J.A. Leo Lemay (New York: Literary Classics of the United States, 1987).

Franz, Günther, ed. *Wiedertäuferakten, 1527–1626*, Urkundliche Quellen zur hessischen Reformationsgeschichte 4 (Marburg: Elwert, 1951).

Freschot, Casimir. *Mémoires de la cour de Vienne, ou Remarques faites par un voyageur curieux sur l'état présent de cette cour* (Cologne: Chez Guillaume Etienne [actually The Hague], 1705).

   Relation von dem kayserlichen Hofe zu Wien (Cologne: bey W. Stephan [actually Amsterdam or Leipzig], 1705).

Geheime Brieffe, so zwischen curieusen Personen über notable Sachen der Staats- und gelehrten Welt gewechselt worden (Freystadt [i.e. Leipzig]: Hülssen, 1701–05).

Gifford, George. *A dialogue concerning [H]witches and witchcraftes* (London: Printed by Iohn Windet for Tobie Cooke and Mihil Hart, 1593).

Gill, William Wyatt. *Jottings from the Pacific* (London: Religious Tract Society, 1885).

Grant, Francis, Lord Cullen. *Sadducimus debellatus: or, a true narrative of the sorceries and witchcrafts exercis'd by the devil and his instruments upon Mrs. Christian Shaw, daughter of Mr. John Shaw, of Bargarran in the County of Renfrew in the West of Scotland, from Aug. 1696 to Apr. 1697* (London: Printed for H. Newman and A. Bell, 1698).

Gryphius, Andreas. *Lyrische Gedichte von Andreas Gryphius*, ed. Julius Tittmann (Leipzig: F.A. Brockhaus, 1880).

Haile, H.G., ed. *Das Faustbuch nach der Wolfenbüttler Handschrift* (Berlin: E. Schmidt Verlag, 1963).

Hambrecht, Rainer. "'Das Papier ist mein Acker ...' Ein Notizbuch des 17. Jahrhunderts von Handwerker-Bauern aus dem nordwestlichen Oberfranken," *Jahrbuch der Coburger Landesstiftung* 29 (1984): 317–450.

Herbert, George. *The Complete English Poems*, ed. John Tobin (London: Penguin Books, 1991).

Herder, Johann Gottfried von. "This Too a Philosophy of History for the Formation of Humanity," in *Philosophical Writings*, ed. and trans. Michael N. Forster (New York: Cambridge University Press, 2002), pp. 272–359.

Herse, Felix Vialart de. "Ordonnances et règlements faits dans le cours de sa visite en l'anné 1661," in *Statuts, ordonnances, mandements, règlements et lettres pastorales du diocèse de Châlons* (Châlons: s.n., 1693).

Hewitt, Barnard, ed. *The Renaissance Stage: Documents of Serlio, Sabbattini and Furttenbach*, trans. Allardyce Nicoll, John H. McDowell, and George R. Kernodle (Coral Gables, FL: University of Miami Press, 1958).

Hobhouse, Edmund, ed. *Diary of a West Country Physician*, A.D. *1684–1726* (London: Simpkin, Marshall, 1934).

Hocart, Richard, ed. "The Journal of Charles Trumbull," *Transactions of la Société Guernesiaise* 21 (1984): 566–85.

Hoeven, Willem van der. *'t Koffyhuis: kluchtspel* (Amsterdam: de erfg. van J. Lescailje, 1712).

Hopil, Claude. *Les divins élancements d'amour*, ed. François Bouchet (Grenoble: Millon, 2001).

   Les divins eslancemens d'amour exprimez en cent cantiques saints en l'honneur de la Tres-saincte Trinité (Paris: S. Hure, 1629).

   Méditations sur le Cantique des cantiques, et Les Douces extases de l'âme spirituelle, ed. Guillaume Peyroche d'Arnaud (Geneva: Droz, 2000).

Horneck, Anthony. *The Happy Ascetick: or, The Best Exercise, To Which Is Added, A Letter to a Person of Quality, Concerning the Holy Lives of the Primitive Christians. By Anthony Horneck, Preacher at the Savoy* ([London]: Printed by T[homas] N[ewcomb] for Henry Mortlock at the Phoenix in St. Paul's Church-yard, and Mark Pardoe at the Black Raven over against Bedford-House in the Strand, 1681).

Ignatius of Loyola. *The Spiritual Exercises of S. Ignatius of Loyola. Founder of the Society of Jesus* (Saint-Omers: Printed by Nicolas Joseph Le Febvre, 1736).

Institoris, Heinrich, and Jacob Sprenger, *Malleus maleficarum*, ed. and trans. Christopher S. Mackay, 2 vols. (Cambridge University Press, 2006).

Isham, Thomas. *The Diary of Thomas Isham of Lamport (1658–81), kept by him in Latin from 1671 to 1673 at his father's command*, trans. Norman Marlow, with Introduction, Appendixes and Notes by Sir Gyles Isham (Farnborough: Gregg, 1971).

Jackson, Charles, ed. *The Autobiography of Mrs. Alice Thornton of East Newton, Co. York*, Publications of the Surtees Society 62 (Durham: Published for the Society by Andrews and Co., 1875).

Jackson, Thomas. *The humiliation of the Sonne of God by his becomming the Son of man, by taking the forme of a servant, and by his sufferings under Pontius Pilat ... by Thomas Jackson Dr. in Divinitie, chaplaine to his Majestie in ordinarie, and president of Corpus Christi Colledge in Oxford* (London: Printed by M. Flesher for John Clark, 1635).

John of the Cross. *The Collected Works of St. John of the Cross*, trans. Kieran Kavanaugh (Garden City, NY: Doubleday, 1964).

The Complete Works of Saint John of the Cross, Doctor of the Church, trans. and ed. E. Allison Peers (Westminster, MD: Newman Press, 1964).

Kern, Arthur, ed. *Deutsche Hofordnungen des 16. und 17. Jahrhunderts*, 2 vols. (Berlin: Weidmann, 1905–07).

Kindermann, Balthasar. *Der Deutsche Redner* (Wittenberg: Fincelius, 1660).

Kircher, Athanasius. *Ars Magna Lucis Et Vmbrae In Decem Libros Digesta* (Rome: Scheus, 1646).

Koop, Karl, ed. *Confessions of Faith in the Anabaptist Tradition, 1527–1660*, ed. with an Introduction by Karl Koop, Classics of the Radical Reformation 11 (Kitchener, Ontario: Pandora Press, 2006).

Krapf, Ludwig, and Christian Wagenknecht, eds. *Stuttgarter Hoffeste: Texte und Materialen zur höfischen Repräsentation im frühen 17. Jahrhundert* (Tübingen: Niemeyer, 1979).

Krebs, Manfred, ed. *Baden und Pfalz*, Quellen zur Geschichte der Täufer 4 (Gütersloh: Bertelsmann, 1951).

Krünitz, Johann Georg. *Ökonomisch-Technologische Encyklopädie*, 242 vols. (Berlin: Pauli, *et al.*, 1773–1858).

La Bruyère, Jean de. *Les Caractères*, ed. Robert Garapon (Paris: Garnier, 1962)

Lahnstein, Peter. *Das Leben im Barock: Zeugnisse und Berichte 1640–1740* (Stuttgart: W. Kohlhammer, 1974).

Lalore, Charles, ed. *Ancienne et nouvelle discipline du diocèse de Troyes, de 1785 à 1843. Statuts et règlements* (Troyes: Au Secrétariat de l'évêché, 1882–83).

Lancre, Pierre de. *Tableau de l'inconstance des mauuais anges et démons, ou il est amplement traicté des sorciers & de la sorcellerie* (Paris: Chez Iean Berjon, 1612).

Tableau de l'inconstance des mauvais anges et démons: où il est amplement traité des sorciers et de la sorcellerie, ed. Nicole Jacques-Lefèvre (Paris: Aubier, 1982).

Latz, Dorothy L., *Glow-Worm Light: Writings of 17th Century English Recusant Women from Original Manuscripts*, Salzburg Studies in English Literature 92: 21 (Institut für Anglistik und Amerikanistik, Universität Salzburg, 1989).

Latz, Dorothy L., ed. *The Building of Divine Love, As Translated by Agnes More*, Salzburg Studies in English Literature. Elizabethan and Renaissance Studies 92: 17 (Institut für Anglistik und Amerikanistik, Universität Salzburg, 1992).

Lauder, John, Lord Fountainhall. *Journals of Sir John Lauder, Lord Fountainhall ... 1665–1676*, ed. with Introduction by Donald Crawford, Publications of the Scottish History Society 36 (Edinburgh: Printed at the University Press by T. and A. Constable for the Scottish History Society, 1900).

Lavater, Ludwig. *Of ghostes and spirites walking by nyght, 1572*, ed. with an Introduction and Appendix by J. Dover Wilson and May Yardley (Oxford University Press, 1929).

Lediard, Thomas. *Eine Collection curieuser Vorstellungen in Illuminationen und Feier-Wercken ... bey Gelegenheit einiger publiquen Festins und Rejouissances, in Hamburg* (Hamburg: Stromer, 1730).

LeRoy, Louis. *Of the interchangeable course, or variety of things in the whole world and the concurrence of armes and learning ... Written in French by Loys le Roy called Regius: and translated into English by R.A.* (London: Printed by Charles Yetsweirt, 1594).

Lersner, Achilles Augustus von, and Georg August von Lersner, *Achill. Augusti von Lersner nachgehohlte, vermehrte und continuirte Frankfurthische Chronica Zweyter Theil* (Frankfurt: Johann Adam Recksroth, 1734).

Lipsius, Justus. *Sixe Bookes of Politickes or Civil Doctrine*, trans. William Jones (London: Richard Field, 1594).

Lister, Martin. *A Journey to Paris in the Year 1698*, ed. Raymond Phineas Stearns (Urbana: University of Illinois Press, 1967).

Locke, John. *An Essay Concerning Human Understanding*, ed. Pauline Phemister (Oxford University Press, 2008).

Loen, Johann Michael von. *Gesammelte kleine Schriften*, ed. Johann Caspar Schneider (Frankfurt and Leipzig: Zu finden bey Philipp Heinrich Huttern, 1750).

Lough, John, ed. *France Observed in the Seventeenth Century by British Travelers* (Stocksfield, UK: Oriel Press, 1985).

Loyer, Pierre Le. *IIII. livres des spectres, ou apparitions et visions d'esprits, anges et démons se monstrans sensiblement aux hommes* (Angers: G. Nepueu, 1586).

    Discours et histoires des spectres, visions et apparitions des esprits, anges, démons et ames, se monstrans visibles aux hommes: divisez en huict livres ... par Pierre Le Loyer (Paris: Chez Nicolas Buon, 1605).

Lucae, Friedrich. *Der Chronist Friedrich Lucae: ein Zeit- und Sittenbild aus der zweiten Hälfte des siebenzehnten Jahrhunderts*, ed. Friedrich Lucae II (Frankfurt: Brönner, 1854).

Luther, Martin. *D. Martin Luthers Werke. Kritische Gesamtausgabe*, 4 divisions (Weimar: H. Böhlaus Nachfolger, 1883–).

Maché, Ulrich, and Volker Meid, eds. *Gedichte des Barock* (Stuttgart: Reclam, 1980).

Machiavelli, Niccolò. *The Prince*, in *Selected Political Writings*, ed. and trans. David Wootton (Indianapolis, IN: Hackett, 1994).

Mailly, Chevalier de. *Les entretiens des cafés de Paris et les diferens qui y surviennent* (Trévoux: Chez Etienne Ganeau, 1702).

Mandeville, Bernard. *An enquiry into the causes of the frequent executions at Tyburn* (London: Printed and sold by J. Roberts in Warwick-Lane, 1725).

Marana, Giovanni Paolo. *Lettre d'un Sicilien à un de ses amis*, ed. Valentin Dufour, Anciennes descriptions de Paris 9 (Paris: A. Quantin, 1883).

Marlowe, Christopher. *Doctor Faustus: A Two-Text Edition (A-text, 1604; B-text, 1616)*, ed. David Scott Kastan (New York: W.W. Norton, 2005).

Marperger, Paul Jacob. *Abermahliger Versuch zur Abhandlung einer nützlichen Policey-Materia, nehmlich von denen Gassen Laternen, Strand- und Wacht-Feuern, und andern nächtlichen Illuminationibus oder Erleuchtungen der Gassen und Strassen* (Dresden and Leipzig: "Verlegung des Authoris," 1722).

Ménestrier, Claude-François. *Des ballets anciens et modernes selon les règles du théâtre* (Paris: R. Guignard, 1682).

Traité des tournois, joustes, carrousels et autres spectacles publics (Lyon, 1669; repr. New York: Garland, 1979).

Mercier, Louis-Sébastien. *Mon bonnet de nuit* (Neuchatel: De l'Imprimerie de la Société Typographique, 1785).

Milton, John. *Il Penseroso*, in *Complete Shorter Poems*, ed. Stella P. Revard (Malden, MA: Wiley-Blackwell, 2009), pp. 53–58.

Paradise Lost, ed. David Scott Kastan and Merritt Yerkes Hughes (Indianapolis, IN: Hackett Publishing, 2005).

Missionary voyage to the Southern Pacific Ocean [A], performed in the years 1796, 1797, 1798, in the ship Duff, commanded by Captain James Wilson. Compiled from journals of the officers and missionaries; and Illustrated with Maps, Charts, and Views ... by a Committee Appointed for the Purpose by the Directors of the Missionary Society (London: The Missionary Society, 1799).

Montagu, Elizabeth. *The Letters of Mrs. E. Montagu, with Some of the Letters of Her Correspondents*, ed. Matthew Montagu, 4 vols. (London: T. Cadell & W. Davies, 1809–13).

Montagu, Mary Wortley. *The Complete Letters of Lady Mary Wortley Montagu*, ed. Robert Halsband, 3 vols. (Oxford: Clarendon Press, 1965–67).

More, Henry. *An antidote against atheisme, or, An appeal to the natural faculties of the minde of man, whether there be not a God by Henry More* (London: Printed by Roger Daniel, 1653).

More, Thomas. *The Dialogue Concerning Tyndale by Sir Thomas More, Reproduced in Black Letter Facsimile from the Collected Edition (1557) of More's English Works*, ed. W.E. Campbell and A.W. Reed (London: Eyre and Spottiswoode, 1927).

Mylius, Christian Otto, ed. *Corpus Constitutionum Marchicarum* (Berlin and Halle: Buchladen des Waisenhauses, 1737–55).

Nashe, Thomas. *The Terrors of the Night, or A Discourse of Apparitions*, in *Selected Writings*, ed. Stanley Wells (Cambridge, MA: Harvard University Press, 1965), pp. 141–75.

Neiner, Johann. *Brachium Dexterae Excelsi, Oder die … Sieghaften Entsetzung Barcellone … und nächtlicher Illumination der gantzen Stadt Wienn* (Vienna: Christian Barthlmae Pruckner, 1706).

Vienna Curiosa & Gratiosa, Oder Das anjetzo Lebende Wienn (Vienna: Joann. Baptistae Schilgen, 1720).

Nemeitz, Joachim Christoph. *Séjour de Paris: c'est à dire, instructions fidèles, pour les voiageurs de condition, comment ils se doivent conduire, s'ils veulent faire un bon usage de leur tems & argent, durant leur Séjour à Paris* (Leiden: J. Van Abcoude, 1727).

Newdigate-Newdegate, Anne Emily Garnier. *Cavalier and Puritan in the Days of the Stuarts: Compiled from the Private Papers and Diary of Sir Richard Newdigate, Second Baronet, with Extracts from Ms. News-Letters Addressed to Him between 1675 and 1689* (New York: Longmans, Green, and Co., 1901).

Nicoll, Allardyce, ed. *The Development of the Theatre* (New York: Harcourt, Brace & World, 1966).

Norden, John. *A pensiue mans practise Very profitable for all personnes* (London: Printed by Hugh Singleton, 1584).

Norris, John, of Bemerton. "Hymn to Darkness," in *A Collection of Miscellanies* (Oxford: J. Crosley, 1687), pp. 37–38.

Parfitt, George A. E., and Ralph A. Houlbrooke, eds. *The Courtship Narrative of Leonard Wheatcroft, Derbyshire Yeoman* (Reading: Whiteknights Press, 1986).

Pascal, Blaise. *Pensées*, ed. and trans. Roger Ariew (Indianapolis, IN: Hackett, 2005).

Patte, P. *De la manière la plus avantageuse d'éclairer les rues d'une ville pendant la nuit* (Amsterdam: s.n., 1766).

Pecke, Thomas. *To the Most High and Mighty Monarch, Charles the II, by the grace of God, King of England, Scotland, France and Ireland, defender of the faith* (London: Printed by James Cottrel, 1660).

Pérouas, Louis, ed. *Pierre Robert (1589–1658). Un Magistrat du Dorat entre érudition et observation*, Foreword by Michel Cassan (Limoges: PULIM, 2001).

Pöllnitz, Karl Ludwig Freiherr von. *Nouveaux Mémoires du Baron de Pollnitz, contenant l'histoire de sa vie*, new edn., 2 vols. (Frankfurt: "Aux Dépens de la Compagnie," 1738).

Pope, Alexander. *The Poems of Alexander Pope: A One-Volume Edition of the Twickenham Text with Selected Annotations*, second edn., ed. John Butt (London: Routledge, 1968).

Pöppelmann, Matthaeus Daniel. *Vorstellung und beschreibung des … Zwinger Gartens Gebdäuden oder Der königl. Orangerie zu Dresden* (Dresden: Pöppelmann, 1729).

Pordage, Samuel. "A Panegyrick on his Majesties Entrance Into London," in *Poems upon several occasions by S.P.* (London: Printed by W.G. for Henry Marsh, and Peter Dring, 1660).

Proceedings of the King's Commission of the Peace and Oyer and Terminer, and Gaol Delivery of Newgate, held for the City of London and also Gaol Delivery for the County of Middlesex, at Justice-Hall, in the Old Bailey (London: Court of Aldermen of the City of London, 1674–1834).

Pujoulx, Jean Baptiste. *Paris à la fin du XVIIIe siècle; ou, Esquisse historique et morale des monumens et des ruines de cette capitale; de l'etat des sciences, des arts de l'industrie à cette époque, ainsi que des moeurs et des ridicules de ses habitans* (Paris: Mathé, 1801).

Puré, Michel de. *Idée des spectacles anciens et nouveaux* (Paris, 1668; repr. Geneva: Minkoff Reprint, 1972).

Quarles, Francis. *Emblemes by Fra. Quarles* (London: Printed by G[eorge] M[iller] and sold at Iohn Marriots shope, 1635).

Raine, James, ed. *Depositions from the Castle of York, Relating to Offenses Committed in the Northern Counties in the Seventeenth Century*, Publications of the Surtees Society 40 (Durham: Published for the Society by F. Andrews, 1861).

Remy, Nicolas. *Demonolatry*, ed. Montague Summers, trans. E.A. Ashwin (London: J. Rodker, 1930).

Renaudot, Théophraste, ed. *Quatriesme centurie des questions traitées aux conférences du Bureau d'Adresse, depuis le 24e Ianvier 1639, jusques au 10e Iuin 1641* (Paris: Bureau d'adresse, 1641).

Reuss, Rudolf, ed. *Aus dem Leben eines strassburger Kaufmanns des 17. und 18. Jahrhunderts: "Reiss-Journal und Glücks- und Unglücksfälle,"* Beiträge zur Landes- und Volkeskunde von Elsass-Lotharingen und den angrenzenden Gebieten 43 (Strasbourg: J.H.E. Heitz, 1913).

Reynolds, Edward. *An explication of the hundreth and tenth Psalme ... Being the substance of severall sermons preached at Lincolns Inne* (London: Imprinted by Felix Kyngston for Robert Bostocke, 1632).

Rhäticus, Georg Joachim. *Narratio Prima*, trans. Edward Rosen, in *Three Copernican Treatises*, ed. Edward Rosen (Mineola, NY: Dover Publications, 2004).

Rohr, Julius Bernhard von. *Einleitung zur Ceremoniel-Wissenschaft der Grossen Herren*, ed. with a commentary by Monika Schlechte (Leipzig: Edition Leipzig, 1990; reprint of the second edn., Berlin, 1733).

Einleitung zur Ceremoniel-Wissenschaft der Privat Personen, ed. with a commentary by Gotthart Frühsorge (Berlin, 1728; repr. Leipzig: Edition Leipzig, 1990).

Rosenheim, James, ed. *The Notebook of Robert Doughty 1662–1665*, Norfolk Record Society 54 ([Norwich]: Norfolk Record Society, 1991).

Sachs, Hans. *Die Wittenbergisch Nachtigall*, ed. Gerald H. Seufert (Stuttgart: Reclam, 1974).

Saint-Dider, C.H. de, ed. *Mémoires de la marquise de Courcelles ... et sa correspondance, précédés d'une histoire de sa vie et de son procès. Revue et augmentée d'après des documents inédits* (Paris: Académie des Bibliophiles, 1869).

Saint-Simon, duc de [Louis de Rouvroy]. *Mémoires de M. le duc de Saint-Simon*, 42 vols., ed. A. de Boislisle and Léon Lecestre (Paris: [Montpensier], 1975–; reprint of the 1879–1930 Hachette edn.).

Memoirs of Louis XIV and the Regency, by the Duke of Saint-Simon, trans. Bayle St. John, 3 vols. (Washington, D.C.: M.W. Dunne, 1901).

Sala-Molins, Louis, ed. *Le Code Noir ou le calvaire de Canaan* (Paris: Presses universitaires de France, 1987).

Sandaeus, Maximilianus. *Pro theologia mystica clavis: elucidarium onomasticon vocabulorum et loquutionum obscurarum* (Louvain: Éditions de la Bibliotheque S.J., 1963; facsimile of Cologne: Officina Gualteriana, 1640).

Saussure, César de. *A Foreign View of England in the Reigns of George I. & George II. The Letters of Monsieur César De Saussure to His Family*, ed. and trans. Madame Van Muyden (London: J. Murray, 1902).

Schoettgen, Christian. *Historische Nachricht von denen Illuminationen, wie solche zu alten und neuen Zeiten ... in Gebrauch gewesen* (Dresden: Hekel, 1736).

Schrattenecker, Irene, ed. *Eine deutsche Reise Anno 1708* (Innsbruck: Haymon, 1999).

Schultheis, Heinrich von. *Eine Außführliche Instruction wie in Inquisition Sachen des grewlichen Lasters der Zauberey gegen die Zaubere der Göttlichen Majestät und der Christenheit Feinde ohn gefahr der Unschuldigen zu procediren ... In Form eines freundlichen Gesprächs gestelt* (Cologne: bey Hinrich Berchem, 1634).

Scott-Moncrieff, William George, ed. *Narrative of Mr. James Nimmo written for his own satisfaction to keep in some remembrance the Lord's way dealing and kindness towards him, 1654–1709*, Publications of the Scottish History Society 6 (Edinburgh: Printed by T. and A. Constable for the Society, 1887).

Selhamer, Christoph. *Tuba Rustica. Das ist: Neue Gei-Predigen* (Augsburg: Verlag Georg Schlüters, 1701).

Sévigné, Marie de Rabutin-Chantal. *Correspondance: texte établi, presenté et annoté par Roger Duchene*, 3 vols. (Paris: Gallimard, 1972–78).

Sharpe, J.A., ed. *"William Holcroft, His Booke": Local Office-Holding in Late Stuart Essex*, Essex Historical Documents 2 (Chelmsford: Essex Record Office, 1986).

Simons, Menno. *The Complete Writings of Menno Simons, c. 1496–1561*, trans. Leonard Verduin, ed. John C. Wenger, with a bibliography by Harold S. Bender (Scottdale, PA: Herald Press, 1956).

Sinold von Schütz, Phillip Balthasar. *Die Wissenschaft zu leben ... und ... ein tüchtiges Mitglied der menschlichen Gesellschaft zu seyn* (Frankfurt and Leipzig : "in den Buchläden zu finden," 1739).

Snyder, C. Arnold, ed. *Biblical Concordance of the Swiss Brethren, 1540*, trans. Gilbert Fast and Galen Peters; Introduction by Joe Springer, Anabaptist Texts in Translation 2 (Kitchener, Ontario: Pandora Press, 2001).

Somerset, Charles. *The Travel Diary (1611–1612) of an English Catholic, Sir Charles Somerset*. Edited from the Manuscript in the Brotherton Collection, University of Leeds, ed. Michael G. Brennan (Leeds Philosophical and Literary Society, 1993).

Spectator, The. Ed. Donald Bond, 5 vols. (Oxford: Clarendon Press, 1965).

Spenser, Edmund. *The Faerie Queen. Books Three and Four*, ed. Dorothy Stephens (Indianapolis, IN: Hackett Publishing, 2006).

Spinoza, Baruch. "Appendix Containing Metaphysical Thoughts," in *Complete Works*, ed. Michael L. Morgan, trans. Samuel Shirley (Indianapolis, IN: Hackett, 2002), pp. 177–212.

    Theological-Political Treatise, trans. Samuel Shirley, with an Introduction by Seymour Feldman (Indianapolis, IN: Hackett, 2001).

State-Poems; Continued from the Time of O. Cromwel, to this Present Year 1697 ([London]: s.n., 1697).

Steiner, Josephus Antonius, ed. *Acta selecta ecclesiae Augustanae: accedit synopsis episcopalium decretorum per eandem ecclesiam a tempore Concilii Tridentini usque in praesentem annum promulgatum* (Augsburg: M. Rieger, 1785).

Sterry, Peter. *The commings* [sic] *forth of Christ in the power of his death. Opened in a sermon preached before the High Court of Parliament, on Thursday the first of Novem. 1649* (London: Printed by Charles Sumptner, for Thomas Brewster and Gregory Moule, 1650 [i.e. 1649]).

Strien, C.D. van. *Touring the Low Countries: Accounts of British Travellers, 1660–1720* (Amsterdam University Press, 1998).

Strype, John. *The Life and Acts of John Whitgift … Digested, Compiled, and Attested from Records, Registers, Original Letters and Other Authentic Mss* (Oxford: Clarendon Press, 1822).

Suttinger, Johann Baptist. *Consuetudines Austriacae ad stylum excelsi regiminis infra anasum olim accommodatae* (Nuremberg: Martin Endter, 1718).

Tatham, John. *Knavery in all trades, or, The coffee-house a comedy: as it was acted in the Christmas holidays by several apprentices with great applause* (London: Printed by J.B. for W. Gilbertson and H. Marsh, 1664).

Teresa of Avila, *The Complete Works of St Teresa of Jesus*, 3 vols., trans. and ed. E. Allison Peers (London: Sheed and Ward, 1972–75).

Thietmar of Merseburg, *Chronicon*, ed. Friedrich Kurze and J.M. Lappenberg (Hanover: Hahn, 1889).

Thoresby, Ralph. *The Diary of Ralph Thoresby, F.R.S., Author of the Topography of Leeds (1677–1724)*, ed. Joseph Hunter (London: H. Colburn and R. Bentley, 1830).

Tindal, Matthew. *An essay concerning the power of the magistrate* (London: Printed by J.D. for Andrew Bell, 1697).

Tolstoi, Petr Andreevich. *The Travel Diary of Peter Tolstoi: A Muscovite in Early Modern Europe*, trans. Max J. Okenfuss (DeKalb, IL: Northern Illinois University Press, 1987).

Tusser, Thomas. *Five hundred points of good husbandry as well for the champion or open countrey, as also for the woodland or several, mixed, in every moneth, with huswifery, over and besides the book of huswifery* (London: Printed by J.M. for the Company of Stationers, 1663).

Tzschimmer, Gabriel. *Die Durchlauchtigste Zusammenkunft, oder: Historische Erzehlung, … der durchlauchtigste furst und herr, Herr Johann George der Ander, herzog zu Sachsen* (Nuremberg: J. Hoffmann, 1680).

Vanbrugh, John. *The Relapse; The Provoked Wife; The Confederacy; A Journey to London; The Country House*, ed. Brean Hammond (Oxford University Press, 2004).

Vanel, Gabriel, ed. *Recueil de journaux caennais, 1661–1777: publiés d'après les manuscrits inédits* (Rouen: A. Lestringant, 1904).

Vaughan, Henry. *The Works of Henry Vaughan*, ed. L.C. Martin, second edn. (Oxford: Clarendon Press, 1957).

Verschlemmerte und bezauberte Koffe- und Thee-Welt [Die]: welche eine Menge artiger Begebenheiten enthält, so sich seit kurzem zu Amsterdam, Rotterdam, in dem Haage, ʒu Uitrecht, und in denen benachbarten Orten, sowohl unter verheyratheten als ledigen Personen, ʒugetragen (Frankfurt and Leipzig, 1737; first edn., Frankfurt and Leipzig, 1701).

Veryard, Ellis. *An account of divers choice remarks ... taken in a journey through the Low-Countries, France, Italy, and part of Spain* (London: S. Smith and B. Walford, 1701).

View of Paris [A], and places adjoining ... Written by a gentleman lately residing at the English Ambassador's at Paris (London: Printed for John Nutt, near Stationers-Hall, 1701).

Vigenère, Blaise de. *A discovery of fire and salt discovering many secret mysteries, as well philosophicall, as theologicall,* trans. Edward Stephens (London: Printed by Richard Cotes, and are to be sold by Andrew Crooke, 1649).

Traicté du feu et du sel (Paris: Chez la veufue A. l'Angelier, 1618).

Vogel, Johann Jacob. *Leipʒigisches Geschicht-Buch oder Annales, Das ist: Jahr- und Tage-Bücher der Weltberühmten Königl. und Churfürstlichen sächsischen Kauff- und Handels-Stadt Leipʒig ... biß in das 1714. Jahr* (Leipzig: Lanckisch, 1714).

Walton, John. "To my worthy friend, Mr. Henry Vaughan the Silurist," in *The Works of Henry Vaughan,* ed. L.C. Martin, second edn. (Oxford: Clarendon Press, 1957), p. 620.

Wasserman, George R. "A Critical Edition of the Collected Poems of John Norris of Bemerton," PhD thesis, University of Michigan, 1957.

Wickram, Jörg. *Sämtliche Werke,* vol. x, *Kleine Spiele,* ed. Hans-Gert Roloff (Berlin: de Gruyter, 1997).

Williams, J.B., ed. *Memoirs of the Life, Character and Writings of the Rev. Matthew Henry* (Boston: Peirce & Williams, 1830).

Wolff, Christian Freiherr von. *Vernünfftige Gedancken von dem Gesellschafftlichen Leben der Menschen, und insonderheit dem gemeinen Wesen ʒu Beförderung der Gluckseeligkeit des menschlichen Geschlechtes* (Halle: Renger, 1721).

Wood, Anthony. *The Life and Times of Anthony Wood, Antiquary, of Oxford, 1632–1695, Described by Himself,* ed. Andrew Clark, Oxford Historical Society Publications 19 (Oxford: Clarendon Press, 1894).

Wootton, David, ed. *Doctor Faustus with The English Faust Book* (Indianapolis, IN: Hackett Publishing, 2005).

Wotton, Henry. *The Life and Letters of Sir Henry Wotton,* ed. Logan Pearsall Smith (Oxford: Clarendon Press, 1907).

Wustmann, Gustav, ed. *Quellen ʒur Geschichte Leipʒigs,* 2 vols. (Leipzig: Duncker & Humblot, 1889–95).

Zedler, Johann Heinrich. *Grosses vollständiges Universal-Lexikon,* 64 vols. (Leipzig: Zedler, 1732–50).

SECONDARY SOURCES

300 Jahre Strassenbeleuchtung in Berlin (Berlin: Senator für Bau- und Wohnungswesen, 1979).

Albrecht, Peter. "Coffee-Drinking As a Symbol of Social Change in Continental Europe in the Seventeenth and Eighteenth Centuries," *Studies in Eighteenth-Century Culture* 18 (1989): 91–103.

"Die 'Caffe-Menscher' im 18. Jahrhundert," in *Coffeum wirft die Jungfrau um: Kaffee und Erotik in Porzellan und Grafik aus drei Jahrhunderten*, ed. Ulla Heise (Leipzig: Kiepenheuer, 1998), pp. 36–46.

"Kaffee und Kaffeehäuser in der Universitätsstadt Helmstedt vom Ende des 17. bis zum Anfang des 19. Jahrhunderts," *Braunschweigisches Jahrbuch* 72 (1991): 95–118.

Alewyn, Richard. *Das große Welttheater: Die Epoche der höfischen Feste*, second edn. (Munich: Beck, 1985).

Alewyn, Richard, and Karl Sälzle. *Das große Welttheater: Die Epoche der höfischen Feste in Dokument und Deutung* (Hamburg: Rowohlt, 1959).

Almond, Philip C. "The Contours of Hell in English Thought, 1660–1750," *Religion* 22, 4 (1992): 297–311.

Altfahrt, Margit, and Karl Fischer. "'Illuminations-Anfang der Stadt Wien' (Zur Einführung der Straßenbeleuchtung in Wien im Jahre 1687)," *Wiener Geschichtsblätter* 42 (1987): 167–70.

Andersson, Theodore. "The Discovery of Darkness in Northern Literature," in *Old English Studies in Honour of John C. Pope*, ed. Robert B. Burlin and Edward B. Irving, Jr. (University of Toronto Press, 1974), pp. 1–14.

Arcangeli, Alessandro. *Recreation in the Renaissance: Attitudes towards Leisure and Pastimes in European Culture, c. 1425–1675* (Basingstoke: Palgrave Macmillan, 2003).

Archer, John E. "Poachers Abroad," in *The Unquiet Countryside*, ed. G.E. Mingay (London and New York: Routledge, 1989), pp. 52–64.

Aubert, Guillaume. "The Blood of France: Race and Purity of Blood in the French Atlantic World," *William and Mary Quarterly* 61, 3 (2004): 439–78.

Aulagne, Joseph. *La réforme catholique du dix-septième siècle dans le diocèse de Limoges* (Paris: H. Champion, 1908).

Auwers, Jean-Marie. "La nuit de Nicodème (Jean 3, 2; 19, 39) ou l'ombre du langage," *Revue biblique* 97, 4 (1990): 481–503.

Bächtold-Stäubli, Hanns, V. Knoblauch-Matthias, and Eduard Hoffmann-Krayer. *Handwörterbuch des deutschen Aberglaubens*, 10 vols. (Berlin: de Gruyter, 1927–42).

Baldwin, Peter C. "How Night Air Became Good Air, 1776–1930," *Environmental History* 8, 3 (2003): 412–29.

Ball, Daniela, ed. *Kaffee im Spiegel europäischer Trinksitten* (Zurich: Johann Jacobs Museum, 1991).

Ballantyne, Tony, and Antoinette M. Burton, eds. *Moving Subjects: Gender, Mobility, and Intimacy in an Age of Global Empire* (Urbana: University of Illinois Press, 2009).

Bardet, Jean-Pierre. *Rouen aux XVIIe et XVIIIe siècles: les mutations d'un espace social*, Regards sur l'histoire 50 (Paris: Société d'édition d'enseignement supérieur, 1983).

Baruzi, Jean. *Saint Jean de la Croix et le problème de l'expérience mystique*, second edn. (Paris: Alcan, 1931).

Bassler, J.M. "Mixed Signals: Nicodemus in the Fourth Gospel," *Journal of Biblical Literature* 108 (1989): 635–46.

Bastl, Beatrix. "Feuerwerk und Schlittenfahrt: Ordnungen zwischen Ritual und Zeremoniell," *Wiener Geschichtsblätter* 51 (1996): 197–229.

Bath, Jo, and John Newton, eds. *Early Modern Ghosts: Proceedings of the "Early Modern Ghosts" Conference Held at St. John's College, Durham University on 24 March 2001* (Durham: Centre for Seventeenth-Century Studies, 2003).

Baumstein, Paschal. "Anselm on the Dark Night and Truth," *Cistercian Studies Quarterly* 35, 2 (2000): 239–49.

Bausch, Christa. "Das Nachtmythologem in der polynesischen Religion und seine Auswirkungen auf protestantische Missionstätigkeit," *Zeitschrift für Religions- und Geistesgeschichte* 22 (1970): 244–66.

 "*Po* and *Ao*. Analysis of an Ideological Conflict in Polynesia," *Journal de la Société des Océanistes* 34 (1978): 169–85.

Baxandall, Michael. *Shadows and Enlightenment* (New Haven: Yale University Press, 1995).

Beattie, J.M. *Policing and Punishment in London 1660–1750: Urban Crime and the Limits of Terror* (Oxford University Press, 2001).

Beck, Rainer. "Illegitimität und voreheliche Sexualität auf dem Land: Unterfinning, 1671–1770," in *Kultur der einfachen Leute: bayerisches Volksleben vom 16. bis zum 19. Jahrhundert*, ed. Richard van Dülmen (Munich: Beck, 1983), pp. 112–50.

Becker, Thomas Paul. *Konfessionalisierung in Kurköln: Untersuchungen zur Durchsetzung der katholischen Reform in den Dekanaten Ahrgau und Bonn anhand von Visitationsprotokollen 1583–1761*, Veröffentlichungen des Stadtarchivs Bonn 43 (Bonn: Edition Röhrscheid, 1989).

Becker-Glauch, Irmgard. *Die Bedeutung der Musik für die Dresdener Hoffeste bis in die Zeit Augusts des Starken* (Kassel and Basle: Bärenreiter-Verlag, 1951).

Behn, Irene. *Spanische Mystik: Darstellung und Deutung* (Düsseldorf: Patmos-Verlag, 1957).

Behringer, Wolfgang. "Bausteine zu einer Geschichte der Kommunikation. Eine Sammelrezension zum Postjubiläum," *Zeitschrift für historische Forschung* 21, 1 (1994): 92–112.

Shaman of Oberstdorf: Chonrad Stoeckhlin and the Phantoms of the Night, trans. H.C. Erik Midelfort (Charlottesville, VA: University Press of Virginia, 1998).

Beinert, Johannes. "Moscherosch im Dienste der Stadt Straßburg," *Jahrbuch für Geschichte, Sprache und Literatur Elsass-Lothringens* 23 (1907): 138–46.

Bellenger, Yvonne. "La description de Paris dans la 'Lettre d'un Sicilien' datée de 1692," in *La découverte de la France au XVIIe siècle*, ed. Centre méridional de rencontres sur le XVIIe siècle (Paris: CNRS, 1980), pp. 119–32.

Benedict, Philip. *Christ's Churches Purely Reformed: A Social History of Calvinism* (New Haven: Yale University Press, 2002).

Bennett, Gillian. "Ghost and Witch in the Sixteenth and Seventeenth Centuries," in *New Perspectives on Witchcraft, Magic and Demonology*, ed. Brian P. Levack, vol. III, *Witchcraft in the British Isles and New England* (New York: Routledge, 2001), pp. 259–70.

Bergman, Hannah E. "A Court Entertainment of 1638," *Hispanic Review* 42, 1 (1974): 67–81.

Bergmann, Gösta M. *Lighting in the Theatre* (Stockholm: Almqvist & Wiksell International, 1977).

Bernard, Leon. *The Emerging City: Paris in the Age of Louis XIV* (Durham, NC: Duke University Press, 1970).

Bernhofer-Pippert, Elsa. *Täuferische Denkweisen und Lebensformen im Spiegel oberdeutscher Täuferverhöre*, Reformationsgeschichtliche Studien und Texte 96 (Münster: Aschendorff, 1967).

Berns, Jörg Jochen. "Der nackte Monarch und die nackte Wahrheit – Auskünfte der deutschen Zeitungs- und Zeremoniellschriften des späten 17. und frühen 18. Jahrhunderts zum Verhältnis von Hof und Öffentlichkeit," *Daphnis* 11, 1–2 (1982): 315–50.

"Die Festkultur der deutschen Höfe zwischen 1580 und 1730," *Germanisch-Romanische Monatsschrift* n.s. 34, 3 (1984): 295–311.

Berns, Jörg Jochen, Frank Druffner, Ulrich Schütte, and Brigitte Walbe, eds. *Erdengötter: Fürst und Hofstaat in der Frühen Neuzeit im Spiegel von Marburger Bibliotheks- und Archivbeständen. Ein Katalog* (Marburg Universitätsbibliothek, 1997).

Berry, Helen. *Gender, Society, and Print Culture in Late Stuart England: The Cultural World of the Athenian Mercury* (Aldershot: Ashgate, 2003).

"'Nice and Curious Questions': Coffee Houses and the Representation of Women in John Dunton's *Athenian Mercury*," *Seventeenth Century* 12, 2 (1997): 257–76.

Bertolotti, Davide. *Descrizione di Torino* (Turin, 1840; repr. Bologna: A. Forni, 1976).

Bertrand, Dominique, ed. *Penser la nuit: XVe–XVIIe siècles*, Colloques, Congrès et Conférences sur la Renaissance 35 (Paris: H. Champion, 2003).

Bibl, Viktor. *Die Wiener Polizei: eine kulturhistorische Studie* (Leipzig: Stein-Verlag, 1927).

Biesel, Elisabeth. "'Die Pfeifer seint alle uff den baumen gesessen': Hexensabbat in der Vorstellungswelt einer ländlichen Bevölkerung," in *Methoden und Konzepte der historischen Hexenforschung*, ed. Herbert Eiden, Rita Voltmer, Gunther Franz, and Franz Irsigler, Trierer Hexenprozesse 4 (Trier: Spee, 1998), pp. 289–302.

Hexenjustiz, Volksmagie und soziale Konflikte im lothringischen Raum, Trierer Hexenprozesse 3 (Trier: Spee, 1997).

Biet, Christian, and Vincent Jullien, eds. *Le siècle de la lumière, 1600–1715* (Fontenay-aux-Roses: ENS Éditions Fontenay/Saint-Cloud, 1997).

Blaschke, Karlheinz. "Die kursächsische Politik und Leipzig im 18. Jahrhundert," in *Leipzig: Aufklärung und Bürgerlichkeit*, ed. Wolfgang Martens (Heidelberg: Schneider, 1990), pp. 23–38.

Böck, Ludwig. "Zur Geschichte der öffentlichen Beleuchtung Wiens," *Wiener Neujahrs-Almanach* 4 (1898): 1–27.

Boiadjiev, Tzotcho. "Loca nocturna – Orte der Nacht," in *Raum und Raumvorstellungen im Mittelalter*, ed. Jan A. Aertsen and Andreas Speer, Miscellanea Mediaevalia 25 (Berlin: de Gruyter, 1997): 439–51.

Bonheim, Günther. "*ward Jch dero wegen Gantz Melancolisch*. Jacob Böhmes *Heidnische gedancken* bei Betrachtung des Himmels und die Astronomie seiner Zeit," *Euphorion* 91 (1997): 99–132.

Bontemps, Daniel, and Hubert Beylier. *Lanternes d'éclairage public: XVIIe et XVIIIe siècles* (Paris: Ministère de la Culture et de la Communication, Direction du Patrimoine, 1986).

Borchhardt-Birbaumer, Brigitte. "Braunlicht und Seelenfunke – Das Nachtstück zur Zeit der Gegenreformation," in *Die Nacht: Bilder der Nacht in den Bayerischen Staatsgemäldesammlungen*, ed. Peter-Klaus Schuster, Christoph Vitali, and Ilse von Zur Mühlen (Munich: Haus der Kunst, 1998), pp. 83–94.

Imago noctis. Die Nacht in der Kunst des Abendlandes: vom Alten Orient bis ins Zeitalter des Barock (Vienna: Böhlau, 2003).

Borsay, Peter. *The English Urban Renaissance: Culture and Society in the Provincial Town, 1660–1770* (Oxford: Clarendon Press, 1989).

Borst, Arno. *Lebensformen im Mittelalter* (Frankfurt: Propyläen, 1973).

Bossenga, Gail. *The Politics of Privilege: Old Regime and Revolution in Lille* (Cambridge University Press, 1991).

Bostridge, Ian. *Witchcraft and Its Transformations: c. 1650–c. 1750* (Oxford University Press, 1997).

Bouchet, François. "Claude Hopil ou l'éclat des ténèbres," *Conférence* 1 (1995): 155–91.

Bouman, Mark J. "City Lights and City Life: A Study of Technology and Society," PhD thesis, University of Minnesota, 1984.

"Luxury and Control: The Urbanity of Street Lighting in Nineteenth-Century Cities," *Journal of Urban History* 14, 1 (1987): 7–37.

Bowers, Brian. *Lengthening the Day: A History of Lighting Technology* (Oxford University Press, 1998).

Braun, Werner. "Opera in the Empire," in *Spectaculum Europaeum: Theatre and Spectacle in Europe (1580–1750) = Histoire du spectacle en Europe (1580–1750)*, ed. Pierre Béhar and Helen Watanabe-O'Kelly, Wolfenbütteler Arbeiten zur Barockforschung 31 (Wiesbaden: Harrassowitz, 1999), pp. 437–64.

Brehmer, W. "Beiträge zu einer Baugeschichte Lübecks. 3. Die Straßen," *Zeitschrift des Vereins für Lübeckische Geschichte und Alterthumskunde* 5, 2 (1887): 254–58.

Breit, Stefan. *"Leichtfertigkeit" und ländliche Gesellschaft: voreheliche Sexualität in der frühen Neuzeit*, Ancien Régime, Aufklärung und Revolution 23 (Munich: Oldenbourg, 1991).

Brewer, Daniel. "Lights in Space," *Eighteenth-Century Studies* 37, 2 (2004): 171–86.

Briggs, Robin. *Witches and Neighbors: The Social and Cultural Context of European Witchcraft* (New York: Viking Press, 1996).

The Witches of Lorraine (Oxford University Press, 2007).

Broeck, Sabine. "When Light Becomes White: Reading Enlightenment through Jamaica Kincaid's Writing," *Callaloo* 25, 3 (2002): 821–43.

Broedel, Hans Peter. *The Malleus Maleficarum and the Construction of Witchcraft: Theology and Popular Belief* (Manchester University Press, 2003).

Brough, Neil, and R.J. Kavanagh. "Kreuzgang's Precursors: Some Notes on the *Nachtwachen* des Bonaventura," *German Life and Letters* 39, 3 (1986): 173–92.

Brunner, Otto. *Adeliges Landleben und europäischer Geist; Leben und Werk Wolf Helmhards von Hohberg, 1612–1688* (Salzburg: O. Müller, 1949).

Brunner, Wolfgang. "Städtisches Tanzen und das Tanzhaus im 16. Jahrhundert," in *Alltag im 16. Jahrhundert. Studien zu Lebensformen in mitteleuropäischen Städten*, ed. Alfred Kohler and Heinrich Lutz (Vienna: Verlag für Geschichte und Politik, 1987), pp. 45–64.

Buchel, Christiane. "Johann Michael von Loen im Wandel der Zeiten: Eine kleine Forschungsgeschichte," *Das Achtzehnte Jahrhundert: Mitteilungen der Deutschen Gesellschaft für die Erforschung des achtzehnten Jahrhunderts* 16, 1 (1992): 13–37.

Bücking, Jürgen. *Kultur und Gesellschaft in Tirol um 1600: des Hippolytus Guarinonius'* Grewel der Verwüstung menschlichen Geschlechts *(1610) als kulturgeschichtliche Quelle des frühen 17. Jahrhunderts* (Lübeck: Matthiesen, 1968).

Burke, Peter. *The Fabrication of Louis XIV* (New Haven: Yale University Press, 1992).

Burke, Thomas. *English Night-Life: From Norman Curfew to Present Black-Out* (London: B.T. Batsford, 1941).

Burschel, Peter. *Sterben und Unsterblichkeit: zur Kultur des Martyriums in der frühen Neuzeit*, Ancien Régime, Aufklärung und Revolution 35 (Munich: Oldenbourg, 2004).

Buttlar, Kurt Treusch von. "Das tägliche Leben an den deutschen Fürstenhöfen des 16. Jahrhunderts," *Archiv für Kulturgeschichte* 4 (1899): 15–19.

Cabantous, Alain. *Histoire de la nuit: XVIIe–XVIIIe siècle* (Paris: Fayard, 2009).

"La nuit rustique. Monde rural et temps nocturne aux XVIIe et XVIIIe siècles," in *Les fruits de la récolte. Études offertes à Jean-Michel Boehler*, ed. Isabelle Laboulais and Jean-François Chauvard (Presses universitaires de Strasbourg, 2007), pp. 49–64.

Cabantous, Sébastien. "Crimes et délits nocturnes en pays tarnais au siècle des lumières," *Revue du Tarn*, third series, 181 (2001): 107–31.

Calhoun, Craig, ed. *Habermas and the Public Sphere* (Cambridge, MA: MIT Press, 1992).

Calvert, Laura. "Images of Darkness and Light in Osuna's *Spiritual Alphabet Books*," *Studia Mystica* 8, 2 (1985) 38–44.

Camporesi, Piero. *Exotic Brew: The Art of Living in the Age of Enlightenment*, trans. Christopher Woodall (Cambridge: Polity Press, 1994).

The Fear of Hell: Images of Damnation and Salvation in Early Modern Europe (University Park, PA: Pennsylvania State University Press, 1991).

Canova-Green, Marie-Claude. "Le Ballet de cour en France," in *Spectaculum Europaeum: Theatre and Spectacle in Europe (1580–1750)* = *Histoire du spectacle en Europe (1580–1750)*, ed. Pierre Béhar and Helen Watanabe-O'Kelly, Wolfenbütteler Arbeiten zur Barockforschung 31 (Wiesbaden: Harrassowitz, 1999), pp. 485–512.

Capdeville, Valérie. "Les clubs londoniens: vie nocturne et transgression," in *La nuit dans l'Angleterre des lumières*, ed. Suzy Halimi (Paris: Presses Sorbonne nouvelle, 2008), pp. 21–34.

Capp, Bernard. "Gender and the Culture of the English Alehouse in Late Stuart England," in *The Trouble with Ribs: Women, Men and Gender in Early Modern Europe*, ed. Anu Korhonen and Kate Lowe, Collegium: Studies across Disciplines in the Humanities and Social Sciences 2 (Helsinki: Helsinki Collegium for Advanced Studies, 2007): 103–27. E-publication accessed at http://www.helsinki.fi/collegium/e-series/volumes/volume_2/index.htm.

Carroll, Stuart. *Blood and Violence in Early Modern France* (Oxford University Press, 2006).

Casanova, Christian. *Nacht-Leben: Orte, Akteure und obrigkeitliche Disziplinierung in Zürich, 1523–1833* (Zurich: Chronos, 2007).

Cashmere, John. "Sisters Together: Women without Men in Seventeenth-Century French Village Culture," *Journal of Family History* 21, 1 (1996): 44–62.

Cassagnes-Brouquet, Sophie. "La violence des étudiants à Toulouse à la fin du XVe et au XVIe siècle (1460–1610)," *Annales du Midi* 94 (1982): 243–62.

Cazanave, Claire. "Une publication invente son public: les *Entretiens sur la pluralité des mondes*," in *De la publication: entre Renaissance et Lumières*, ed. Christian Jouhaud and Alain Viala (Paris: Fayard, 2002), pp. 267–80.

Cerny, Heimo. "Wolf Helmhard von Hohberg (1612–1688). Ein niederösterreichischer Landedelmann, Schriftsteller und Agronom," *Jahrbuch für Landeskunde von Niederösterreich* n.s. 54/55 (1988/89): 59–84.

Certeau, Michel de. *The Mystic Fable*, trans. Michael B. Smith (University of Chicago Press, 1995).

The Practice of Everyday Life, trans. Steven Rendall (Berkeley: University of California Press, 1984).

Choné, Paulette. "Exégèse de la ténèbre et luminisme nocturne: les 'nuits' lorraines et leur contexte spirituel," in *Les signes de Dieu aux XVIe et XVIIe siècles*, ed. Geneviève Demerson and Bernard Dompnier (Association des Publications de la Faculté des Lettres et Sciences Humaines de Clermont-Ferrand, 1993), pp. 89–99.

L'Atelier des nuits. Histoire et signification du nocturne dans l'art d'Occident (Presses universitaires de Nancy, 1992).

Choné, Paulette, ed. *L'âge d'or du nocturne* (Paris: Gallimard, 2001).

Chorpenning, Joseph. "The Image of Darkness and Spiritual Development in the *Castillo interior*," *Studia Mystica* 8, 2 (1985): 45–58.

Clark, Peter. *British Clubs and Societies, 1580–1800: The Origins of an Associational World* (Oxford University Press, 2000).

Clark, Stuart. *Thinking with Demons: The Idea of Witchcraft in Early Modern Europe* (Oxford: Clarendon Press, 1997).

Clarke, Jan. "Illuminating the Guénégaud Stage: Some Seventeenth-Century Lighting Effects," *French Studies* 53, 1 (1999): 3–15.

Clasen, Claus Peter. *Anabaptism: A Social History, 1525–1618: Switzerland, Austria, Moravia, South and Central Germany* (Ithaca, NY: Cornell University Press, 1972).

Clerbois, Léon. "Histoire de l'éclairage public à Bruxelles," *Annales de la société royale d'archéologie de Bruxelles* 24 (1910): 91–106.

Clery, E.J. *The Feminization Debate in Eighteenth-Century England: Literature, Commerce and Luxury* (New York: Palgrave Macmillan, 2004).

Collinson, Patrick. *The Elizabethan Puritan Movement* (London: Routledge, 1982).

Collinson, Patrick, John Craig, and Brett Usher, eds. *Conferences and Combination Lectures in the Elizabethan Church: Dedham and Bury St. Edmunds, 1582–1590*, Church of England Record Society 10 (Woodbridge: Boydell Press, 2003).

Cooper, Frederick, and Ann Laura Stoler, eds. *Tensions of Empire: Colonial Cultures in a Bourgeois World* (Berkeley: University of California Press, 1997).

Coppens, Gunther. "Spinoza et Boxel. Une histoire de fantômes," *Revue de Métaphysique et de Morale* 41, 1 (2004): 59–72.

Cordey, Jean. *Vaux-le-Vicomte*, Preface by Pierre de Nolhac (Paris: Éditions Albert Morancé, 1924).

Couderc, Camille. "Economies proposées par B. Franklin et Mercier de Saint-Léger pour l'éclairage et la chauffage à Paris," *Bulletin de la Société de l'histoire de Paris et de l'Ile-de-France* 43 (1916): 93–101.

Cowan, Brian William. "Mr. Spectator and the Coffeehouse Public Sphere," *Eighteenth-Century Studies* 37, 3 (2004): 345–66.

    The Social Life of Coffee: The Emergence of the British Coffeehouse (New Haven: Yale University Press, 2005).

    "What Was Masculine about the Public Sphere? Gender and the Coffeehouse Milieu in Post-Restoration England," *History Workshop Journal* 51 (2001): 127–57.

Crapet, A. "La vie à Lille de 1667 à 1789," *Revue du Nord* 6 (1920): 126–54, 198–221; and 7 (1921): 266–322.

Craveri, Benedetta. *The Age of Conversation*, trans. Teresa Waugh (New York: New York Review Books, 2006).

Crisógono de Jesús. *The Life of St. John of the Cross*, trans. Kathleen Pond (London: Longmans, 1958).

Croquez, Albert. *Histoire politique et administrative d'une province française, la Flandre*, vol. 11, *Louis XIV en Flandres* (Paris: Champion, 1920).

    La Flandre wallonne et les pays de l'intendance de Lille sous Louis XIV (Paris: H. Champion, 1912).

Cross, Gary S. *A Social History of Leisure since 1600* (State College, PA: Venture Publishing, 1990).

Crouzet-Pavan, Elisabeth. *"Sopra le acque salse": espaces, pouvoir et société à Venise à la fin du Moyen Âge* (Rome: Istituto storico italiano per il Medio Evo, 1992).

Crowley, John E. *The Invention of Comfort: Sensibilities and Design in Early Modern Britain and Early America* (Baltimore, MD: Johns Hopkins University Press, 2001).

Czok, Karl. *Am Hofe Augusts des Starken* (Stuttgart: Deutsche Verlags-Anstalt, 1990).

Datteri Rasmussen, Livia. "Jacob Böhme: doch ein Beispiel für den 'heliozentrischen Chok'? Zur Interaktion von Naturwissenschaft, Theologie, Mystik und Literatur in der Frühen Neuzeit," *Morgen-Glantz: Zeitschrift der Christian Knorr von Rosenroth-Gesellschaft* 3 (1993): 189–205.

De Beer, Esmond Samuel. "The Early History of London Street Lighting," *History* 25 (1941): 311–24.

Decker, Rainer. "Der Brillen-Traktat des Michael Stappert," Introduction to Hermann Löher, *Hochnötige Unterthanige WEMÜTIGE KLAGE der Frommen Unschültigen* (Amsterdam, 1676), ed. Thomas P. Becker, online at http://extern.historicum.net/loeher.

Defrance, Eugène. *Histoire de l'éclairage des rues de Paris* (Paris: Imprimerie nationale, 1904).

Deinert, Herbert. "Die Entfaltung des Bösen in Böhmes *Mysterium Magnum*," *PMLA* 79, 4 (1964): 401–10.

Delattre, Simone. *Les douze heures noires: la nuit à Paris au XIXe siècle* (Paris: Albin Michel, 2000).

Della Croce, Giovanna. "Johannes vom Kreuz und die deutsch-niederländische Mystik," *Jahrbuch für mystische Theologie* 6 (1960): 21–30.

Delsalle, Paul. *La Franche-Comté au temps des archiducs Albert et Isabelle, 1598–1633: documents choisis et présentés* (Besançon: Presses universitaires franc-comtoises, 2002).

Delumeau, Jean. *La Peur en Occident (XIVe–XVIIIe siècles): Une cité assiégée* (Paris: Fayard, 1978).

Dent, Edward J. *Foundations of English Opera: A Study of Musical Drama in England during the Seventeenth Century* (New York: Da Capo Press, 1965).

Denys, Catherine. "The Development of Police Forces in Urban Europe in the Eighteenth Century," *Journal of Urban History* 36, 3 (2010): 332–44.

"La sécurité en ville: les débuts de l'éclairage public à Lille au XVIIIe siècle," *Les Cahiers de la sécurité* 61, 1 (2006): 143–50.

"Le bris de lanternes dans les villes du Nord au XVIIIe siècle: quelques réflexions sur la signification d'un délit ordinaire," in *La petite délinquance du moyen âge à l'époque contemporaine*, ed. Benoît Garnot and Rosine Fry, Publications de l'Université de Bourgogne 90 (Dijon: EUD, 1998), pp. 309–19.

Police et sécurité au XVIIIe siècle dans les villes de la frontière franco-belge (Paris: Harmattan, 2002).

Denys, Catherine, Brigitte Marin, and Vincent Milliot, eds. *Réformer la police. Les mémoires policiers en Europe au XVIIIe siècle* (Presses universitaires de Rennes, 2009).

Deppe, Uta. *Die Festkultur am Dresdner Hofe Johann Georgs II. von Sachsen (1660–1679)* (Kiel: Ludwig, 2006).

Derksen, John D. *From Radicals to Survivors: Strasbourg's Religious Nonconformists over Two Generations*, Bibliotheca Humanistica & Reformatorica 61 ('t Goy-Houten: Hes & de Graaf, 2002).

Deursen, Arie Theodorus van. *Plain Lives in a Golden Age: Popular Culture, Religion, and Society in Seventeenth-Century Holland*, trans. Maarten Ultee (Cambridge University Press, 1991).

Dewald, Jonathan. *Aristocratic Experience and the Origins of Modern Culture: France 1570–1715* (Berkeley: University of California Press, 1993).

Diedler, Jean-Claude. *Démons et sorcières en Lorraine. Le bien et le mal dans les communautés rurales de 1550 à 1660* (Paris: Éditions Messene, 1996).

Dietz, Alexander. *Frankfurter Handelsgeschichte*, 4 vols. in 5 (Frankfurt: Hermann Minjon, 1910–25).

Distel, Theodor. "Miscellen 5," *Archiv für sächsische Geschichte* n.s. 5, 1 (1878): 90–92.

Dixon, C. Scott. *The Reformation and Rural Society: The Parishes of Brandenburg-Ansbach-Kulmbach, 1528–1603* (Cambridge University Press, 1996).

Dohrn-van Rossum, Gerhard. *Die Geschichte der Stunde: Uhren und moderne Zeitordnung* (Munich: C. Hanser, 1992).

Dompnier, Bernard. "Un aspect de la dévotion eucharistique dans la France du XVIIe siècle: les prières des Quarante-Heures," *Revue d'histoire de l'Eglise de France* 67 (1981): 5–31.

Dontenwill, Serge. "Aspects de la vie quotidienne et de l'organisation sociale des communautés paysannes du centre sud-est de la France au temps de Louis XIV (1638–1715)," *Dix-septième siècle* 234, 1 (2007): 97–134.

Doy, Gen. *Picturing the Self: Changing Views of the Subject in Visual Culture* (London: I.B. Tauris, 2005).

Druffner, Frank. "Gehen und Sehen bei Hofe: Weg- und Blickführungen im Barockschloss," in *Johann Conrad Schlaun, 1695–1773: Architektur des Spätbarock in Europa*, ed. Klaus Bußmann, Florian Matzner, and Ulrich Schulze (Stuttgart: Oktagon, 1995), pp. 542–51.

Duindam, Jeroen. *Myths of Power: Norbert Elias and the Early Modern European Court* (Amsterdam University Press, 1994).

Vienna and Versailles: The Courts of Europe's Dynastic Rivals, 1550–1780 (Cambridge University Press, 2003).

Dülmen, Richard van. "Imaginationen des Teuflischen: Nächtliche Zusammenkünfte, Hexentänze, Teufelssabbate," in *Hexenwelten: Magie und Imagination vom 16.–20. Jahrhundert*, ed. Richard van Dülmen (Frankfurt: Fischer Taschenbuch-Verlag, 1987), pp. 94–130.

Dunlop, Ian. *Louis XIV* (London: Chatto & Windus, 1999).

Durand, Yves. "Mystique et politique au XVIIe siècle: l'influence du Pseudo-Denys," *XVIIe Siècle* 173 (1991): 323–50.

Dürr, Renate. *Mägde in der Stadt: das Beispiel Schwäbisch Hall in der frühen Neuzeit* (Frankfurt: Campus-Verlag, 1995).

Durrant, Jonathan B. *Witchcraft, Gender, and Society in Early Modern Germany*, Studies in Medieval and Reformation Traditions 124 (Leiden: Brill, 2007).

Dutton, Paul Edward. *The Politics of Dreaming in the Carolingian Empire* (Lincoln: University of Nebraska Press, 1994).

Eeghen, Pieter van, and Johan Philip van der Kellen. *Het werk van Jan en Casper Luyken* (Amsterdam: F. Muller & Co., 1905).

Eibach, Joachim. *Frankfurter Verhöre: städtische Lebenswelten und Kriminalität im 18. Jahrhundert* (Paderborn: Schöningh, 2003).

Eiden, Herbert, Rita Voltmer, Gunther Franz, and Franz Irsigler, eds. *Methoden und Konzepte der historischen Hexenforschung*, Tierer Hexenprozesse 4 (Trier: Spee, 1998).

Eire, Carlos. "The Good Side of Hell: Infernal Meditations in Early Modern Spain," *Historical Reflections/Réflexions Historiques* 26 (2000): 286–310.

Ekirch, A. Roger. *At Day's Close: Night in Times Past* (New York: W.W. Norton, 2005).

"Sleep We Have Lost: Pre-Industrial Slumber in the British Isles," *American Historical Review* 106, 2 (2001): 343–86.

Eley, Geoff. "Politics, Culture, and the Public Sphere," *Positions* 10, 1 (2002): 219–36.

Elias, Norbert. *The Civilizing Process: Sociogenetic and Psychogenetic Investigations*, trans. Edmund Jephcott (Oxford: Blackwell, 2000).

Ellis, Markman. *The Coffee House: A Cultural History* (London: Phoenix, 2004).

Emich, Birgit. "Zwischen Disziplinierung und Distinktion: Der Schlaf in der Frühen Neuzeit," *Werkstatt Geschichte* 34 (2003): 53–75.

Engel, Gisela, Ursula Kern, and Heide Wunder, eds. *Frauen in der Stadt: Frankfurt im 18. Jahrhundert* (Königstein im Taunus: Helmer, 2002).

Eriksen, Roy T. "'What resting place is this?' Aspects of Time and Place in *Doctor Faustus* (1616)," *Renaissance Drama* n.s. 16 (1985): 49–74.

Fähler, Eberhard. *Feuerwerke des Barock: Studien zur öffentlichen Fest und seiner literarischen Deutung vom 16.–18. Jahrhundert* (Stuttgart: Metzler, 1974).

Falkus, Malcolm. "Lighting in the Dark Ages of English Economic History: Town Streets before the Industrial Revolution," in *Trade, Government, and Economy in Pre-Industrial England. Essays presented to F.J. Fisher*, ed. D.C. Coleman and A.H. John (London: Weidenfeld and Nicolson, 1976), pp. 187–211.

Faroqhi, Suraiya. *Subjects of the Sultan: Culture and Daily Life in the Ottoman Empire* (London: I.B. Tauris, 2000).

Fässler, Vereni. *Hell-Dunkel in der barocken Dichtung. Studien zum Hell-Dunkel bei Johann Klaj, Andreas Gryphius und Catharina Regina von Greiffenberg*, Europäische Hochschulschriften 44 (Berne: Lang, 1971).

Fast, Heinold. "Die Aushebung einer nächtlichen Täuferversammlung 1574," *Mennonitische Geschichtsblätter* 31 (1974): 103–06.

Faudemay, Alain. *Le clair et l'obscur à l'âge classique*, Travaux des universités suisses 8 (Geneva: Éditions Slatkine, 2001).

Fehleison, Jill R. "Appealing to the Senses: The Forty Hours Celebrations in the Duchy of Chablais, 1597–98," *Sixteenth Century Journal* 36, 2 (2005): 375–96.

Fennetaux, Ariane. "Men in Gowns: Nightgowns and the Construction of Masculinity in Eighteenth-Century England," *Immediations: Research Journal of the Courtauld Institute of Art* 1, 1 (2004): 77–89.

Fischer-Yinon, Yochi. "The Original Bundlers: Boaz and Ruth, and Seventeenth-Century English Courtship Practices," *Journal of Social History* 35, 3 (2002): 683–705.

Fisher, George Park. *The Reformation* (New York: C. Scribner's Sons, 1906).

Fitter, Chris. "The Poetic Nocturne: From Ancient Motif to Renaissance Genre," *Early Modern Literary Studies* 3, 2 (1997): 2.1–61. Online at http://purl.oclc.org/emls/03-2/fittnoct.html.

Fix, Andrew C. "Bekker and Spinoza," in *Disguised and Overt Spinozism around 1700*, ed. Wiep van Bunge and Wim Klever (Leiden: Brill, 1996), pp. 23–40.

  Fallen Angels: Balthasar Bekker, Spirit Belief, and Confessionalism in the Seventeenth Century Dutch Republic (Dordrecht: Kluwer, 1999).

  Prophecy and Reason: The Dutch Collegiants in the Early Enlightenment (Princeton University Press, 1991).

Flake, Otto. *Türkenlouis: Gemälde einer Zeit* (Berlin: S. Fischer, 1937).

Flandrin, Jean Louis. *Les amours paysannes: amour et sexualité dans les campagnes de l'ancienne France (XVIe–XIXe siècle)* ([Paris]: Gallimard/ Julliard, 1975).

  "Repression and Change in the Sexual Life of Young People in Medieval and Early Modern Times," *Journal of Family History* 2, 3 (1977): 196–210.

Flather, Amanda. *Gender and Space in Early Modern England* (Woodbridge: Royal Historical Society/Boydell Press, 2007).

Flesch, William. "The Majesty of Darkness," in *John Milton*, ed. Harold Bloom (New York: Chelsea House, 1986), pp. 293–311.

Florisoone, Michel. *Esthétique et mystique d'après Sainte Thérèse d'Avila et Saint Jean de la Croix: suivi d'une note sur Saint Jean de la Croix et le Greco et d'une liste commentée des oeuvres de Saint Jean de la Croix* (Paris: Éditions du Seuil, 1956).

Fosca, François. *Histoire des cafés de Paris* ([Paris]: Firmin-Didot et cie, 1934).

Fouret, Claude. "Douai au XVIe siècle: une sociabilité de l'agression," *Revue d'histoire moderne et contemporaine* 34 (1987): 3–29.

Fournier, Edouard. *Les lanternes: histoire de l'ancien éclairage de Paris* (Paris: Dentu, 1854).

Franklin, Alfred. *Le café, le thé et le chocolat*, La vie privée d'autrefois 13 (Paris: Éditions Plon, Nourrit et cie, 1893).

Frenzel, H.A. "The Introduction of the Perspective Stage in the German Court and Castle Theatres," *Theatre Research* 3 (1961): 88–100.

Fuchs, Eduard. *Illustrierte Sittengeschichte vom Mittelalter bis zur Gegenwart. Renaissance*, 3 vols. in 6 (Munich: A. Langen, Verlag für Literatur und Kunst, 1909–12).

Fumerton, Patricia. *Unsettled: The Culture of Mobility and the Working Poor in Early Modern England* (University of Chicago Press, 2006).

Fürstenau, Moritz. *Zur Geschichte der Musik und des Theaters am Hofe zu Dresden*, 2 vols. in 1 (Dresden, 1861–62; repr. Leipzig: Edition Peters, 1979).

Fürstenwald, Maria. "Liselotte von der Pfalz und der französische Hof," in *Europäische Hofkultur im 16. und 17. Jahrhundert*, ed. August Buck *et al.*, Wolfenbütteler Arbeiten zur Barockforschung 8–10 (Hamburg: Hauswedell, 1981), pp. 467–74.

Garnert, Jan. "Seize the Day: Ethnological Perspectives on Light and Darkness," *Ethnologia Scandinavica* 24 (1994): 38–59.

"Über die Kulturgeschichte der Beleuchtung und des Dunkels," *Historische Anthropologie* 5, 1 (1997): 62–82.

Gaskill, Malcolm. "Witches and Witnesses in Old and New England," in *Languages of Witchcraft: Narrative, Ideology and Meaning in Early Modern Culture*, ed. Stuart Clark (Basingstoke: Macmillan, 2001), pp. 55–80.

Geissmar, Christoph. *Das Auge Gottes: Bilder zu Jakob Böhme*, Wolfenbütteler Arbeiten zur Barockforschung 23 (Wiesbaden: Harrassowitz, 1993).

"The Geometrical Order of the World: Otto van Veen's *Physicae et theologicae conclusiones*," *Journal of the Warburg and Courtauld Institutes* 56 (1993): 168–82.

Gerteis, Klaus. "Das 'Postkutschenzeitalter': Bedingungen der Kommunikation im 18. Jahrhundert," *Aufklärung* 4, 1 (1989): 55–78.

Gestrich, Andreas. *Absolutismus und Öffentlichkeit: politische Kommunikation in Deutschland zu Beginn des 18. Jahrhunderts*, Kritische Studien zur Geschichtswissenschaft 103 (Göttingen: Vandenhoeck & Ruprecht, 1994).

Gibbons, B.J. *Gender in Mystical and Occult Thought: Behmenism and Its Development in England* (New York: Cambridge University Press, 1996).

Ginzburg, Carlo. *The Night Battles: Witchcraft and Agrarian Cults in the Sixteenth and Seventeenth Centuries*, trans. John and Anne Tedeschi (London: Routledge & Kegan Paul, 1983).

Gleichmann, Peter Reinhart. "Nacht und Zivilisation," in *Soziologie: Entdeckungen im Alltäglichen. Festschrift für Hans Paul Bahrdt*, ed. Martin Baethge and Wolfgang Essbach (Frankfurt and New York: Campus, 1983), pp. 174–94.

Goldammer, Kurt. "Lichtsymbolik in philosophischer Weltanschauung, Mystik und Theosophie vom 15. bis zum 17. Jahrhundert," *Studium Generale* 13 (1960): 670–82.

Goldfarb, Hilliard T., ed. *Richelieu: Art and Power* (Montreal Museum of Fine Arts, 2002).

Goloubeva, Maria. *The Glorification of Emperor Leopold I in Image, Spectacle, and Text*, Veröffentlichungen des Instituts für Europäische Geschichte Mainz 184 (Mainz: von Zabern, 2000).

Graham, Michael F. *The Blasphemies of Thomas Aikenhead: Boundaries of Belief on the Eve of the Enlightenment* (Edinburgh University Press, 2008).

Grange, A. de la. "Histoire de l'éclairage public à Tournai (1275–1890)," *Bulletins de la Société historique et archéologique de Tournai* 25 (1894): 392–98.

Graves, R.B. *Lighting the Shakespearean Stage, 1567–1642* (Carbondale, IL: Southern Illinois University Press, 1999).

Grebe, Hermann. "Ein Erbvergleich zwischen den Adelshäusern von Eschwege zu Aue und Reichensachsen," *Zeitschrift des Vereins für hessische Geschichte und Landeskunde* 95 (1990): 233–58.

Greenshields, Malcolm. *An Economy of Violence in Early Modern France: Crime and Justice in the Haute Auvergne, 1587–1664* (University Park, PA: Pennsylvania State University Press, 1994).

Greer, Margaret Rich. *The Play of Power: Mythological Court Dramas of Calderón de la Barca* (Princeton University Press, 1991).

Griffiths, Paul. "Meanings of Nightwalking in Early Modern England," *Seventeenth Century* 13, 2 (1998): 212–38.

  Youth and Authority: Formative Experiences in England, 1560–1640 (Oxford: Clarendon Press, 1996).

Groll, Thomas. "Der Salzburger Dompfarrvikar, Weilheimer Stadtpfarrer u. Vilgertshofener Wallfahrtspriester Christoph Selhamer (1638–1708) als ausdrucksstarker Barockprediger," *Jahrbuch des Vereins für Augsburger Bistumsgeschichte* 43 (2009): 545–81.

Gugitz, Gustav. *Das Wiener Kaffeehaus; ein Stück Kultur- und Lokalgeschichte* (Vienna: Deutscher Verlag für Jugend und Volk, 1940).

"Mord und Totschlag in Alt-Wien. Ein Beitrag zur Geschichte der öffentlichen Sicherheit und Kriminalität in Wien im 17. und 18. Jahrhundert," *Jahrbuch des Vereins für Geschichte der Stadt Wien* 14 (1958): 141–55.

Haake, Paul. *August der Starke im Urteil der Gegenwart* (Berlin: Curtius, 1929).

Haas, Alois M., ed. *Die dunkle Nacht der Sinne: Leiderfahrung und christliche Mystik* (Düsseldorf: Patmos-Verlag, 1989).

Habermas, Jürgen. *The Structural Transformation of the Public Sphere: An Inquiry into a Category of Bourgeois Society*, trans. Thomas Burger with Frederick Lawrence (Cambridge, MA: MIT Press, 1989).

Strukturwandel der Öffentlichkeit. Untersuchungen zu einer Kategorie der bürgerlichen Gesellschaft. Mit einem Vorwort zur Neuauflage 1990 (Frankfurt: Suhrkamp, 1990).

Haensch, G. "Gesellschaftskritik und Reformationsidee in der Philosophie Jakob Böhmes," *Deutsche Zeitschrift für Philosophie* 36, 1 (1988): 66–72.

Halpern, Richard. "Marlowe's Theater of Night: Doctor Faustus and Capital," *English Literary History* 71, 2 (2004): 455–95.

Harris, Anthony. *Night's Black Agents: Witchcraft and Magic in Seventeenth-Century English Drama* (Manchester University Press, 1980).

Harris, Dianne S., and D. Fairchild Ruggles, eds. *Sites Unseen: Landscape and Vision* (University of Pittsburgh Press, 2007).

Härter, Karl, and Michael Stolleis, eds. *Repertorium der Policeyordnungen der Frühen Neuzeit*, vol. VI, *Reichsstädte 2 Köln*, ed. Klaus Militzer, Studien zur europäischen Rechtsgeschichte 191 (Frankfurt: Klostermann, 2005).

Harvey, Simon, and Elizabeth Grist. "The Rainbow Coffee House and the Exchange of Ideas in Early Eighteenth-Century London," in *The Religious Culture of the Huguenots, 1660–1750*, ed. Anne Dunan-Page (Aldershot: Ashgate, 2006), pp. 163–72.

Hazewinkel, H.C. "Het begin van de straatverlichting te Rotterdam," *Rotterdamsch Jaarboekje* 5, 10 (1952): 183–200.

Heidrich, Hermann. "Grenzübergänge: Das Haus und die Volkskultur in der frühen Neuzeit," in *Kultur der einfachen Leute: bayerisches Volksleben vom 16. bis zum 19. Jahrhundert*, ed. Richard van Dülmen (Munich: Beck, 1983), pp. 17–41.

Heiler, Carl. "Der Herborner Student 1584–1817," *Nassauischen Annalen* 55 (1935): 79–85.

Helms, Mary W. "Before the Dawn: Monks and the Night in Late Antiquity and Early Medieval Europe," *Anthropos* 99 (2004): 177–91.

Henkel, Gabriele. "Die Hoftagebücher Herzog Augusts von Sachsen-Weißenfels," *Wolfenbüttler Barock-Nachrichten* 18, 2 (1991): 75–114.

Henkhaus, Uwe. *Das Treibhaus der Unsittlichkeit: Lieder, Bilder und Geschichte(n) aus der hessischen Spinnstube* (Marburg: Hitzeroth, 1991).

Herlaut, Auguste Philippe. "L'éclairage des rues de Paris à la fin du XVIIe siècle et au XVIIIe siècles," *Mémoires de la Société de l'histoire de Paris et de l'Ile-de-France* 43 (1916): 130–240.

Herzog, Urs. *Geistliche Wohlredenheit: die katholische Barockpredigt* (Munich: Beck, 1991).

Hilaire, Léon. "Pages et laquais," *L'Investigateur: Journal de l'Institut historique* 52 (1881): 149–54.

Hill, Christopher. *The Century of Revolution, 1603–1714*, second edn. (London: Routledge, 2001).

Hill, Geoffrey. "A Pharisee to Pharisees: Reflections on Vaughan's 'The Night'," *English* 38 (1989): 97–113.

Hilscher, P.G. *Chronik der Königlich Sächsischen Residenzstadt Dresden* (Dresden: In Commission der Ch. F. Grimmer'schen Buchhandlung, 1837).

Hinman, Martha Mayo. "The Night Motif in German Baroque Poetry," *Germanic Review* 42, 3 (1967): 83–95.

Hoffmann, Kathryn A. *Society of Pleasures: Interdisciplinary Readings in Pleasure and Power during the Reign of Louis XIV* (New York: St. Martin's Press, 1997).

Hohendahl, Peter Uwe. "The Theory of the Public Sphere Revisited," in *Sites of Discourse – Public and Private Spheres – Legal Culture*, ed. Uwe Böker and Julie A. Hibbard (Amsterdam and New York: Rodopi, 2002), pp. 13–33.

Hölzl, Norbert. "Das Jahrhundert der Passionsspiele und Karfreitagsprozessionen in St. Johann," *Österreichische Zeitschrift für Volkskunde* n.s. 23, 2 (1969): 116–32.

Horowitz, Elliot. "Coffee, Coffeehouses and the Nocturnal Rituals of Early Modern Jewry," *AJS Review* 14, 1 (1989): 17–46.

"The Eve of the Circumcision: A Chapter in the History of Jewish Nightlife," *Journal of Social History* 23, 1 (1989): 45–69.

Hulshof, Abraham. *Gescheidenis van de Doopsgezinden te Straatsburg van 1525 tot 1557* (Amsterdam: Clausen, 1905).

Hunt, Lynn, Margaret C. Jacob, and Wijnand Mijnhardt. *The Book That Changed Europe: Picart and Bernard's Religious Ceremonies of the World* (Cambridge, MA: Belknap Press of Harvard University Press, 2010).

Hurl-Eamon, Jennine. *Gender and Petty Violence in London: 1680–1720* (Columbus: Ohio State University Press, 2005).

Hvolbek, Russell. "Being and Knowing: Spiritualist Epistemology and Anthropology from Schwenckfeld to Böhme," *Sixteenth Century Journal* 22 (1991), pp. 97–110.

Hyde, Melissa. "The Make-Up of the Marquise: Boucher's Portrait of Pompadour at her Toilette," *Art Bulletin* 82, 3 (2000): 453–75.

Imhof, Kurt. "'Öffentlichkeit' als historische Kategorie und als Kategorie der Historie," *Schweizerische Zeitschrift für Geschichte* 46, 1 (1996): 3–25.

Indermühle, Werner. *Essai sur l'oeuvre de Claude Hopil* (Zurich: Juris-Verlag, 1970).

Israel, Jonathan. "Les controverses pamphlétaires dans la vie intellectuelle hollandaise et allemande à l'époque de Bekker et Van Leenhof," *XVIIe Siècle* 49, 2 (1997): 254–64.

Radical Enlightenment: Philosophy and the Making of Modernity 1650–1750 (Oxford University Press, 2001).

Jacques-Lefèvre, Nicole, and Maxime Préaud, eds. *Le sabbat des sorciers en Europe (XVe–XVIIIe siècles)* (Grenoble: Éditions Jérôme Millon, 1993).

Jeanclos, Yves. "La nuit pénale en France: éléments d'analyse historique," in *Le temps et le droit*, ed. Anne Guineret-Brobbel Dorsman (Besançon: Presses universitaires franc-comtoises, 2003), pp. 63–84.

Jessu, Philippe. *Louis XIV en Flandre: Exposition historique … à Lille, 28 octobre 1967–30 avril 1968* (Société des amis des musées de Lille, 1967).

Johnson, Jeffrey. "Gold in the Washes: Donne's Last Going into Germany," *Renascence* 46, 3 (1994): 199–207.

Joly, F. *Die Beleuchtung und Wasserversorgung der Stadt Köln* (Cologne: J.P. Bachem, 1895).

Jubert, Paul. *L'illumination publique à Rouen; notes sur l'éclairage public de la ville de 1697 à 1789* (Rouen: A. Lainé, 1933).

Julia, Dominique. "La réforme posttridentine d'après les procès-verbaux de visites pastorales: ordre et résistances," in *La società religiosa nell'età moderna: atti del Convegno studi di storia sociale e religiosa, Capaccio-Paestum, 18–21 maggio 1972* (Naples: Guida, 1973), pp. 311–415.

Kadi, Simone, ed. *La nuit dans les oeuvres de Shakespeare et de ses contemporains, l'invisible présence*, Recherches valenciennoises 5 (Presses universitaires de Valenciennes, 2000).

Kantorowicz, Ernst H. "Oriens Augusti – Lever du Roi," *Dumbarton Oaks Papers* 17 (1963): 117–78.

Kapeller, Michael. *Auch Finsternis finstert dir nicht: ein Versuch über die Nacht des Glaubens und die Reflexion dieser Erfahrung in der Dogmatik*, Theologie der Spiritualität 7 (Münster: Lit, 2004).

Kaplan, Steven Laurence. *The Bakers of Paris and the Bread Question, 1700–1775* (Durham, NC: Duke University Press, 1996).

Keller, Dominik. "Unter dem Zeichen der Sonne," in *Die schöne Kunst der Verschwendung*, ed. Georg Kohler and Alice Villon-Lechner (Zurich and Munich: Artemis, 1988), pp. 57–100.

Keller, Katrin. "La Magnificence des deux Augustes: Zur Spezifik höfischer Kultur im Dresden des Augusteischen Zeitalters (1694–1763)," *Cahiers d'études germaniques* 28 (1995): 55–66.

"Mein Herr befindet sich gottlob gesund und wohl": *sächsische Prinzen auf Reisen* (Leipziger Universitäts-Verlag, 1994).

Kevorkian, Tanya. "The Rise of the Poor, Weak, and Wicked: Poor Care, Punishment, Religion and Patriarchy in Leipzig, 1700–1730," *Journal of Social History* 34, 1 (2000): 163–81.

Kiesel, Helmuth. *"Bei Hof, bei Höll"*. *Untersuchungen zur literarischen Hofkritik von Sebastian Brant bis Friedrich Schiller* (Tübingen: Niemeyer, 1979).

Kipling, Gordon. *The Triumph of Honour: Burgundian Origins of the Elizabethan Renaissance*, Publications of the Sir Thomas Browne Institute, Leiden: General Series 6 (The Hague: Leiden University Press, 1977).

Kirchner, Thomas. "Der Theaterbegriff des Barocks," *Maske und Kothurn* 31 (1985): 131–41.

Klein, Lawrence. "Coffeehouse Civility, 1660–1714: An Aspect of Post-Courtly Culture in England," *Huntington Library Quarterly* 59, 1 (1996): 30–52.

Klingensmith, Samuel John. *The Utility of Splendor: Ceremony, Social Life and Architecture at the Court of Bavaria, 1600–1800* (University of Chicago Press, 1993).

Knabe, Peter-Eckhard. "Der Hof als Zentrum der Festkultur. Vaux-le-Vicomte, 17. August 1661," in *Geselligkeit und Gesellschaft im Barockzeitalter*, ed. Wolfgang Adam, Wolfenbütteler Arbeiten zur Barockforschung 28 (Wiesbaden: Harrassowitz, 1997), II: 859–70.

Koch, Josef. "Über die Lichtsymbolik im Bereich der Philosophie und der Mystik des Mittelalters," *Studium Generale* 13, 11 (1960): 653–70.

Koch, Klaus-Peter. "Das Jahr 1704 und die Weißenfelser Hofoper," in *Weißenfels als Ort literarischer und künstlerischer Kultur im Barockzeitalter*, ed. Roswitha Jacobsen (Amsterdam and Atlanta, GA: Rodopi, 1994), pp. 75–95.

Kohl, Johann Georg. *Alte und Neue Zeit. Episoden aus der Cultur-Geschichte der freien Reichs-Stadt Bremen* (Bremen: Müller, 1871).

Kohler, Georg. "Die Rituale der fürstlichen Potestas. Dresden und die deutsche Feuerwerkstradition," in *Die schöne Kunst der Verschwendung*, ed. Georg Kohler and Alice Villon-Lechner (Zurich and Munich: Artemis, 1988), pp. 101–34.

Komaszynski, Michel. "Das Bayern des XVII. Jahrhunderts in polnischen Reisebeschreibungen," *Zeitschrift für bayerische Landesgeschichte* 56, 3 (1993): 635–48.

Korff, Gottfried. "Einige Bemerkungen zum Wandel des Bettes," *Zeitschrift für Volkskunde* 77 (1981): 1–16.

Kors, Alan Charles. *Atheism in France, 1650–1729*, vol. 1, *The Orthodox Sources of Disbelief* (Princeton University Press, 1990).

Koslofsky, Craig. "Court Culture and Street Lighting in Seventeenth-Century Europe," *Journal of Urban History* 28, 6 (2002): 743–68.

"Princes of Darkness: The Night at Court, 1650–1750," *Journal of Modern History* 79, 2 (2007): 235–73.

The Reformation of the Dead: Death and Ritual in Early Modern Germany (New York: St. Martin's Press, 2000).

"Von der Schande zur Ehre: Nächtliche Begräbnisse im lutherischen Deutschland, 1650–1700," *Historische Anthropologie* 5, 3 (1997): 350–69.

Kramer, Karl-Siegfried. "Rechtliches Gemeindeleben im Maindreieck zwischen Reformation und Aufklärung," *Bayerisches Jahrbuch für Volkskunde* (1953): 136–48.

Krause, Carl. *Euricius Cordus: Eine biographische Skizze aus der Reformationszeit* (Hanau: König, 1863).

Krause, Virginia. "Confessional Fictions and Demonology in Renaissance France," *Journal of Medieval and Early Modern Studies* 35, 2 (2005): 327–48.

Krauss, Werner. *Fontenelle und die Aufklärung* (Munich: Fink, 1969).

Kriese, Verena. "Die Vorstädte Leipzigs im 18. Jahrhundert," *Jahrbuch für Regionalgeschichte* 16, 2 (1989): 110–25.

Krusenstjern, Benigna von. *Selbstzeugnisse der Zeit des dreissigjährigen Krieges: Beschreibendes Verzeichnis* (Berlin: Akademie, 1997).

Kuhn, Charles L. "The Mairhauser Epitaph: An Example of Late Sixteenth-Century Lutheran Iconography," *Art Bulletin* 58, 4 (1976): 542–46.

Kümin, Beat A. *Drinking Matters: Public Houses and Social Exchange in Early Modern Central Europe* (Basingstoke: Palgrave Macmillan, 2007).

Kümin, Beat A., and B. Ann Tlusty, eds. *The World of the Tavern: Public Houses in Early Modern Europe* (Burlington, VT: Ashgate, 2002).

Labouvie, Eva. "Hexenspuk und Hexenabwehr: Volksmagie und volkstümlicher Hexenglaube," in *Hexenwelten: Magie und Imagination vom 16.–20. Jahrhundert*, ed. Richard van Dülmen (Frankfurt: Fischer Taschenbuch-Verlag, 1987), pp. 49–93.

Zauberei und Hexenwerk. Ländlicher Hexenglaube in der frühen Neuzeit (Frankfurt: Fischer Taschenbuch-Verlag, 1991).

Lacour, Eva. "Faces of Violence Revisited. A Typology of Violence in Early Modern Rural Germany," *Journal of Social History* 34, 3 (2001): 649–67.

Laitinen, Riitta. "Night-Time Street Fighting and the Meaning of Place: A Homicide in a Seventeenth-Century Swedish Provincial Town," *Journal of Urban History* 33, 4 (2007): 602–19.

Lake, Peter, and Steven C.A. Pincus, eds. *The Politics of the Public Sphere in Early Modern England* (Manchester University Press, 2007).

Landes, David S. *Revolution in Time: Clocks and the Making of the Modern World* (Cambridge, MA: Belknap Press of Harvard University Press, 1983).

Landes, Joan. *Women and the Public Sphere in the Age of the French Revolution* (Ithaca, NY: Cornell University Press, 1988).

Landwehr, Achim. *Policey im Alltag: die Implementation frühneuzeitlicher Policeyordnungen in Leonberg* (Frankfurt: Klostermann, 2000).

Lau, Friedrich. *Geschichte der Stadt Düsseldorf*, 2 vols. (Düsseldorf: Bagel, 1921).

Laurain-Portemer, Madeleine. "Mazarin, militant de l'art baroque au temps de Richelieu (1634–1642)," *Bulletin de la Société de l'Histoire de l'Art français* (1975): 65–100.

Layer, Adolf. "Passionsspiele und Passionsumzüge in Schwaben," *Jahrbuch des Historischen Vereins Dillingen a. d. Donau* 82 (1980): 210–37.

Le Goff, Jacques, and Jean Claude Schmitt, eds. *Le Charivari: actes de la table ronde organisée à Paris, 25–27 avril 1977*, Civilisations et sociétés 67 (Paris: L'Ecole, 1981).

Lebrun, François. "La religion de l'évêque de Saint-Malo et de ses diocésains au début du XVIIe siècle, à travers les statuts synodaux de 1619," in *La religion populaire. Actes du colloque international ... Paris, 17–19 octobre 1977*, Colloques internationaux du Centre National de la Recherche Scientifique 576 (Paris: Éditions du Centre National de la Recherche Scientifique, 1979), pp. 45–51.

Leclant, Jean. "Coffee and Cafés in Paris, 1644–1693," in *Food and Drink in History*, Selections from the Annales, Économies, Sociétes, Civilisations 5, ed. Robert Forster and Orest A. Ranum (Baltimore, MD: Johns Hopkins University Press, 1987), pp. 86–97.

Lederer, David. "Ghosts in Early Modern Bavaria," in *Werewolves, Witches, and Wandering Spirits: Traditional Belief and Folklore in Early Modern Europe*, ed. Kathryn A. Edwards (Kirksville, MO: Truman State University Press, 2002), pp. 25–53.

Lemper, Ernst-Heinz. "Voraussetzungen zur Beurteilung des Erfahrungs- und Schaffensumfelds Jakob Böhmes," in *Gott, Natur und Mensch in der Sicht Jacob Böhmes und seiner Rezeption*, ed. Jan Garewicz and Alois M. Haas, Wolfenbütteler Arbeiten zur Barockforschung 24 (Wiesbaden: Harrassowitz, 1994), pp. 41–69.

Leu, Urs B. and Christian Scheidegger. *Die Zürcher Täufer 1525–1700* (Zurich: Theologischer Verlag Zürich, 2007).

Levere, Trevor Harvey. "Natural Philosophers in a Coffee House: Dissent, Radical Reform and Pneumatic Chemistry," in *Science and Dissent in*

England, 1688–1945, ed. Paul Wood (Aldershot: Ashgate, 2004), pp. 131–46.

Lewis, C.S. *The Discarded Image: An Introduction to Medieval and Renaissance Literature* (Cambridge University Press, 2000).

Lexutt, Athina. "Friedensstifterin Mystik? Die Rezeption mystischer Literatur als mögliche Brücke zwischen den Konfessionen," *Monatshefte für evangelische Kirchengeschichte des Rheinlandes* 51 (2002): 67–86.

Leybold, W. "Hamburgs öffentliche Gassenbeleuchtung. Von den Anfängen bis zur Franzosenzeit, 1673–1816," *Nordalbingia* 5 (1926): 455–75.

Lieberman, Victor B. *Strange Parallels: Southeast Asia in Global Context, c. 800–1830*, vol. ɪɪ, *Mainland Mirrors: Europe, Japan, China, South Asia, and the Islands* (Cambridge University Press, 2009).

Lieberman, Victor B., ed. *Beyond Binary Histories: Re-Imagining Eurasia to c. 1830* (Ann Arbor: University of Michigan Press, 1999).

Liman, Herbert. *Mehr Licht: Geschichte der Berliner Straßenbeleuchtung* (Berlin: Haude & Spener, 2000).

Lintsen, Harry. *Geschiedenis van de techniek in Nederland: de wording van een moderne samenleving, 1800–1890*, 6 vols. ('s-Gravenhage: Stichting Historie der Techniek, 1992–93).

Locklin, Nancy. *Women's Work and Identity in Eighteenth-Century Brittany* (Burlington, VT: Ashgate, 2007).

Lorenz, Hellmut. "Barocke Festkultur und Repräsentation im Schloß zu Dresden," *Dresdner Hefte* 12, 38 (1994): 48–56.

Lottin, Alain. *Etre et croire à Lille et en Flandre: XVIe–XVIIIe siècle: recueil d'études* (Arras: Artois Presses Université, 2000).
    Vie et mentalité d'un Lillois sous Louis XIV (Lille: É. Raoust & cie, 1968).

Louth, Andrew. *The Origins of the Christian Mystical Tradition from Plato to Denys* (Oxford: Clarendon Press, 1981).

Lüdtke, Alf. "Alltagsgeschichte – ein Bericht von unterwegs," *Historische Anthropologie* 11, 2 (2003): 278–95.

Lüdtke, Alf, ed. *The History of Everyday Life: Reconstructing Historical Experiences and Ways of Life*, trans. William Templer (Princeton University Press, 1995).

Ludwig, Hermann. *Strassburg vor hundert Jahren. Ein Beitrag zur Kulturgeschichte* (Stuttgart: Frommann, 1888).

McClintock, Stuart. *The Iconography and Iconology of Georges De La Tour's Religious Paintings, 1624–1650*, Studies in Art and Religious Interpretation 31 (Lewiston, NY: Edwin Mellen Press, 2003).

McClure, Ellen M. *Sunspots and the Sun King: Sovereignty and Mediation in Seventeenth-Century France* (Urbana: University of Illinois Press, 2006).

McDowell, Paula. *The Women of Grub Street: Press, Politics, and Gender in the London Literary Marketplace, 1678–1730* (Oxford: Clarendon Press, 1998).

Macfarlane, Alan. "A Tudor Anthropologist: George Gifford's *Discourse* and *Dialogue*," in *The Damned Art: Essays in the Literature of Witchcraft*, ed. Sydney Anglo (London: Routledge & Kegan Paul, 1977), pp. 140–55.

McGinnis, Scott. "'Subtiltie' Exposed: Pastoral Perspectives on Witch Belief in the Thought of George Gifford," *Sixteenth Century Journal* 33, 3 (2002): 665–86.

Macha, Jürgen. *Deutsche Kanzleisprache in Hexenverhörprotokollen der Frühen Neuzeit* (Berlin and New York: de Gruyter, 2005).

McLaughlin, R. Emmet. "Radicals," in *Reformation and Early Modern Europe: A Guide to Research*, ed. David M. Whitford (Kirksville, MO: Truman State University Press, 2008), pp. 103–10.

Magne, Émile. *Les Fêtes en Europe au XVIIe siècle* (Paris: Martin-Dupuis, 1930).

La Vie quotidienne au temps de Louis XIII (Paris: Hachette, 1942).

Maguin, Jean-Marie. *La nuit dans le théâtre de Shakespeare et de ses prédécesseurs* (Service de reproduction des thèses, Université de Lille III, 1980).

Mahler, Andreas. "Jahrhundertwende, Epochenschwelle, epistemischer Bruch? England um 1600 und das Problem überkommener Epochenbegriffe," in *Europäische Barock-Rezeption*, ed. Klaus Garber, Wolfenbütteler Arbeiten zur Barockforschung 20 (Wiesbaden: Harrassowitz, 1991), II: 995–1026.

Mailhol, Jean-Claude. "Les créatures des ténèbres dans la tragédie domestique élisabéthaine et jacobéenne," in *La nuit dans les oeuvres de Shakespeare, l'invisible présence*, ed. Simone Kadi, Recherches valenciennoises 5 (Presses universitaires de Valenciennes, 2000), pp. 231–76.

Mandrou, Robert. *Introduction to Modern France 1500–1640. An Essay in Historical Psychology*, trans. R.E. Hallmark (New York: Holmes & Meier, 1976).

Manry, André-Georges. *Histoire de Clermont-Ferrand* (Clermont-Ferrand: Bouhdiba, 1993).

Maravall, José Antonio. *Culture of the Baroque: Analysis of a Historical Structure*, trans. Terry Cochran, Theory and History of Literature 25 (Minneapolis: University of Minnesota Press, 1986).

Martens, Wolfgang. "Bürgerlichkeit in der frühen Aufklärung," in *Aufklärung, Absolutismus und Bürgertum in Deutschland. Zwölf Aufsätze*, ed. Franklin Kopitzsch (Munich: Nymphenburger Verlagshandlung, 1976), pp. 347–63.

Martin, J.W. "The Protestant Underground Congregations of Mary's Reign," *Journal of Ecclesiastical History* 35, 4 (1984): 519–59.

Martin, John Rupert. *Baroque* (New York: Harper & Row, 1977).

Martin, Régine. "Les débuts de l'éclairage des rues de Dijon," *Annales de Bourgogne* 25, 4 (1953): 254–58.

Mathieu, Jon. "In der Kirche schlafen. Eine sozialgeschichtliche Lektüre von Conradin Riolas 'Geistlicher Trompete' (Strada im Engadin, 1709)," *Schweizerisches Archiv für Volkskunde* 87, 3/4 (1991): 121–43.

Maurer, Michael. *Die Biographie des Bürgers: Lebensformen und Denkweisen in der formativen Phase des deutschen Bürgertums (1680–1815)* (Göttingen: Vandenhoeck & Ruprecht, 1996).

Mayes, David. "Heretics or Nonconformists? State Policies toward Anabaptists in Sixteenth-Century Hesse," *Sixteenth Century Journal* 32, 4 (2001): 1003–26.

Mazzonis, Alessandra. "Un orologio del XVII secolo al Museo Correale di Sorrento: il notturno di Pietro T. Campani," *Kermes* 14, 44 (2001): 17–26, 69.

Medick, Hans. "Village Spinning Bees: Sexual Culture and Free Time among Rural Youth in Early Modern Germany," in *Interest and Emotion: Essays on the Study of Family and Kinship*, ed. Hans Medick and David Warren Sabean (Cambridge University Press, 1984), pp. 317–39.

Meehan, Patrick. "Early Dublin Public Lighting," *Dublin Historical Record* 5 (1943): 130–36.

Melbin, Murray. *Night As Frontier: Colonizing the World after Dark* (New York: Free Press, 1987).

Melton, James Van Horn. *The Rise of the Public in Enlightenment Europe* (Cambridge University Press, 2001).

Ménager, Daniel. *La Renaissance et la nuit*, Seuils de la modernité 10 (Geneva: Droz, 2005).

Menninger, Annerose. *Genuss im kulturellen Wandel: Tabak, Kaffee, Tee und Schokolade in Europa, 16.–19. Jahrhundert*, second edn. (Stuttgart: Steiner, 2008).

Merlin, Hélène. "Nuit de l'État et Roi-Soleil," in *La Nuit*, ed. François Angelier and Nicole Jacques-Chaquin (Grenoble: Millon, 1995), pp. 203–18.

Mikoletzky, Hanns Leo. "Der Haushalt des kaiserlichen Hofes zu Wien (vornehmlich im 18. Jahrhundert)," *Carinthia* 146 (1956): 658–83.

Miller, Christopher R. *The Invention of Evening: Perception and Time in Romantic Poetry* (Cambridge University Press, 2006).

Miller, Clarence H. "Donne's 'A Nocturnall upon S. Lucies Day' and the Nocturns of Matins," *Studies in English Literature, 1500–1900* 6, 1 [The English Renaissance] (1966): 77–86.

Monter, William. "Witch Trials in Continental Europe 1560–1660," in *Witchcraft and Magic in Europe: The Period of the Witch Trials*, ed. Bengt Ankarloo and Stuart Clark (Philadelphia: University of Pennsylvania Press, 2002), pp. 1–52.

Morgan, Fidelis. *The Female Tatler* (London: Dent, 1992).

Mortier, Roland. *Clartés et ombres du siècle des Lumières. Études sur le 18e siècle littéraire* (Geneva: Droz, 1969).

Möseneder, Karl. *Zeremoniell und monumentale Poesie: die "Entrée solennelle" Ludwigs XIV. 1660 in Paris* (Berlin: Gebr. Mann, 1983).

Moser-Rath, Elfriede. *Predigtmärlein der Barockzeit: Exempel, Sage, Schwank und Fabel in geistlichen Quellen des oberdeutschen Raumes* (Berlin: de Gruyter, 1964).

Muchembled, Robert. *La violence au village: sociabilité et comportements populaires en Artois du XVe au XVIIe siècle* ([Turnhout]: Brepols, 1989).

"La violence et la nuit sous l'Ancien Régime," *Ethnologie française* 21, 3 (1991): 237–42.

Müller, Carl-Jochen. "'Rechte Pflanzschulen aller Laster'? Lichtstuben im Limpurgischen – Bekämpfung und Behauptung einer ländlichen Institution," in *Stadt und Land: Bilder, Inszenierungen und Visionen in Geschichte und Gegenwart: Wolfgang von Hippel zum 65. Geburtstag*, ed. Sylvia Schraut and Bernhard Stier (Stuttgart: Kohlhammer, 2001), pp. 373–89.

Müller, P.G. "Die Entwicklung der künstlichen Straßenbeleuchtung in den sächsischen Städten," *Neues Archiv für Sächsische Geschichte und Altertumskunde* 30 (1909): 144–51.

Müller, Renate. *Licht und Feuer im ländlichen Haushalt: Lichtquellen und Haushaltsgeräte* (Hamburg: Altonaer Museum, 1994).

Müller, Siegfried. *Leben im alten Hannover: Kulturbilder einer deutschen Stadt* (Hanover: Schlüter, 1986).

Leben in der Residenzstadt Hannover: Adel und Bürgertum im Zeitalter der Aufklärung (Hanover: Schlüter, 1988).

Multhauf, Lettie S. "The Light of Lamp-Lanterns: Street Lighting in Seventeenth-Century Amsterdam," *Technology and Culture* 26 (1985): 236–52.

Nahrstedt, Wolfgang. *Die Entstehung der Freizeit. Dargestellt am Beispiel Hamburgs* (Göttingen: Vandenhoeck & Ruprecht, 1972).

Nelson, Stephen F., and Jean Rott, "Strasbourg: The Anabaptist City in the Sixteenth Century," *Mennonite Quarterly Review* 58 (1984): 230–40.

Neugebauer-Wölk, Monika. "Wege aus dem Dschungel: Betrachtungen zur Hexenforschung," *Geschichte und Gesellschaft* 29, 2 (2003): 316–47.

Neumeister, Sebastian. "*Tante belle inuentioni di Feste, Giostre, Balletti e Mascherate*: Emmanule Tesauro und die barocke Festkultur," in *Theatrum Europaeum: Festschrift für Elida Maria Szarota*, ed. Richard Brinkmann *et al.* (Munich: W. Fink, 1982), pp. 153–68.

Newton, William Ritchey. *Derrière la façade: vivre au château de Versailles au XVIIIe siècle* (Paris: Perrin, 2008).

Niderst, Alain. *Fontenelle à la recherche de lui-même (1657–1702)* (Paris: A.-G. Nizet, 1972).

Niederstätter, Alois. "Notizen zu einer Rechts- und Kulturgeschichte der Nacht," in *Das Recht im kulturgeschichtlichen Wandel: Festschrift für Karl Heinz Burmeister zur Emeritierung*, ed. Bernd Marquardt and Alois Niederstätter (Konstanz: UVK, 2002), pp. 173–90.

Niessen, M.G. "Straatverlichting," *Ons Amsterdam* 18 (1966): 82–85.

Nieto, José C. *Mystic, Rebel, Saint: A Study of St. John of the Cross*, Travaux d'humanisme et Renaissance 168 (Geneva: Droz, 1979).

"St John of the Cross' Poem 'Dark Night': The Dark Night of the Soul, or the Senses' Delight?" in *Probing the Reformed Tradition: Historical Studies in Honor of Edward A. Dowey, Jr.*, ed. Elsie Anne McKee and Brian G. Armstrong (Louisville, KY: Westminster/John Knox Press, 1989), pp. 292–312.

Novelli, Cornelius. "Sin, Sight, and Sanctity in the *Miller's Tale*: Why Chaucer's Blacksmith Works at Night," *Chaucer Review* 33, 2 (1998): 168–75.

O'Dea, William T. *The Social History of Lighting* (London: Routledge and Paul, 1958).

Ogborn, Miles. *Spaces of Modernity: London's Geographies, 1680–1780* (New York: Guilford Press, 1998).

Ogier, Darryl. "Night Revels and Werewolfery in Calvinist Guernsey," *Folklore* 109 (1998): 53–62.

Reformation and Society in Guernsey (Rochester, NY: Boydell Press, 1996).

Orgel, Stephen. "Introduction," in *Ben Jonson: The Complete Masques*, ed. Stephen Orgel (New Haven: Yale University Press, 1969).

Oyer, John S. "Nicodemites among Württemberg Anabaptists," *Mennonite Quarterly Review* 71, 4 (1997): 487–514.

Packer, Dorothy S. "Collections of Chaste Chansons for the Devout Home (1613–1633)," *Acta Musicologica* 16, 2 (1989): 175–216.

Palmer, Bryan D. *Cultures of Darkness: Night Travels in the Histories of Transgression, from Medieval to Modern* (New York: Monthly Review Press, 2000).

Pasternak Slater, Ann. "Macbeth and the Terrors of the Night," *Essays in Criticism* 28 (1978): 112–28.

Paul, Markus. *Reichsstadt und Schauspiel: Theatrale Kunst im Nürnberg des 17. Jahrhunderts* (Tübingen: Niemeyer, 2002).

Pebworth, Ted-Larry. "Herbert's Poems to the Queen of Bohemia: A Rediscovered Text and a New Edition" (with text), *ELR* 9, 1 (1979): 108–20.

Perry, Adelle. *On the Edge of Empire: Gender, Race, and the Making of British Columbia, 1849–1871* (University of Toronto Press, 2001).

Persson, Fabian. *Servants of Fortune: The Swedish Court between 1598 and 1721* (Lund: Wallin & Dalholm, 1999).

Pevsner, Nikolaus. *Leipziger Barock: Die Baukunst der Barockzeit in Leipzig* (Dresden: W. Jess, 1928).

Pflugk-Harttung, Julius von. *Im Morgenrot der Reformation*, fourth edn. (Basle: A. Rohde, 1922).

Pieretti, Marie-Pascale. "Is That Seat Taken? Women and Café Life in Early Eighteenth-Century Paris," unpublished paper, 2004.

Pils, Susanne Claudine. *Schreiben über Stadt. Das Wien der Johanna Theresia Harrach 1639–1716*, Forschungen und Beiträge zur Wiener Stadtgeschichte 36 (Vienna: Deuticke, 2002).

Pincus, Steve. "'Coffee Politicians Does Create': Coffeehouses and Restoration Political Culture," *Journal of Modern History* 67 (1995): 807–34.

Pitou, Frédérique. "Jeunesse et désordre social: les coureurs de nuit à Laval au XVIIIe siècle," *Revue d'histoire moderne et contemporaine* 47, 1 (2000): 69–92.

Pitts, John Linwood. *Witchcraft and Devil Lore in the Channel Islands* (Guernsey: Guille-Allès Library, 1886).

Pollard, Nigel E. "A Short History of Public Lighting in the City of Westminster," *IPLE Lighting Journal* 49, 2 (1984): 53–58.

Porter, J.H. "Crime in the Countryside, 1600–1800," in *The Unquiet Countryside*, ed. G.E. Mingay (London and New York: Routledge, 1989), pp. 9–22.

Pünjer, Bernhard. *Geschichte der christlichen Religions-philosophie seit der Reformation* (Braunschweig: C.A. Schwetschke, 1880).

Racevskis, Roland. *Time and Ways of Knowing under Louis XIV: Molière, Sévigné, Lafayette* (Lewisburg, PA: Bucknell University Press, 2003).

Rau, Susanne, and Gerd Schwerhoff, eds. *Zwischen Gotteshaus und Taverne. Öffentliche Räume in Spätmittelalter und Früher Neuzeit*, Norm und Struktur. Studien zum sozialen Wandel in Mittelalter und früher Neuzeit 21 (Cologne: Böhlau, 2004).

Rausch, Fred G. "Karfreitagsprozessionen in Bayern," in *Hört, sehet, weint und liebt: Passionsspiele im alpenländischen Raum*, ed. Michael Henker, Eberhard Dünninger, and Evamaria Brockhoff, Veröffentlichungen zur bayerischen Geschichte und Kultur 20 (Munich: Süddeutscher Verlag, 1990), pp. 87–93.

Reichardt, Rolf. "Light against Darkness: The Visual Representations of a Central Enlightenment Concept," *Representations* 61 (1998): 95–148.

Reimbold, Ernst Thomas. *Die Nacht im Mythos, Kultus, Volksglauben und in der transpersonalen Erfahrung; eine religionsphänomenologische Untersuchung* (Cologne: Wison, 1970).

Reinbold, Anne, ed. *Georges de La Tour, ou, La nuit traversée* (Metz: Éditions Serpenoise, 1994).

Reinders, Pim, and Thera Wijsenbeek-Olthuis. *Koffie in Nederland: vier eeuwen cultuurgeschiedenis* (Zutphen: Walburg Pers, 1994).

Rendall, Steven F. "Fontenelle and His Public," *MLN* 86, 4 (1971): 496–508.

Reynolds, Elaine A. *Before the Bobbies: The Night Watch and Police Reform in Metropolitan London, 1720–1830* (Basingstoke: Macmillan, 1998).

Richter, Conrad. "Die erste öffentliche Beleuchtung der Stadt Wien," *Alt-Wien* 6 (1897): 9–11.

Richter, Horst. *Johann Oswald Harms. Ein deutscher Theaterdekorateur des Barock* (Emsdetten: Lechte, 1963).

Roche, Daniel. *Histoire des choses banales: naissance de la consommation dans les sociétés traditionnelles (XVIIe–XIXe siècle)* (Paris: Fayard, 1997).

A History of Everyday Things: The Birth of Consumption in France, 1600–1800, trans. Brian Pearce (Cambridge University Press, 2000).

Rollison, David. "Property, Ideology, and Popular Culture in a Gloucestershire Village 1660–1740," *Past & Present* 93, 1 (1981): 70–97.

Romier, Lucien. *Les origines politiques des guerres de religion*, 2 vols. (Paris: Perrin, 1913–14).

Rooijakkers, Gerard. "Spinningen in de Pre-Industriële Plattelandssamenleving," *Focaal: Tijdschrift voor Antropologie* 4 (1986): 43–61.

Roper, Lyndal. *Oedipus and the Devil: Witchcraft, Sexuality and Religion in Early Modern Europe* (London: Routledge, 2003).

"Witchcraft and the Western Imagination," *Transactions of the Royal Historical Society* 16 (2006): 117–41.

Rosseaux, Ulrich. *Freiräume: Unterhaltung, Vergnügen und Erholung in Dresden 1694–1830* (Cologne: Böhlau, 2007).

Rott, Jean and Marc Lienhard, "La communauté de 'frères suisses' de Strasbourg de 1557 à 1660," *Saisons d'Alsace* 76 (1981): 25–33.

Rudeck, Wilhelm. *Geschichte der öffentlichen Sittlichkeit in Deutschland: moralhistorische Studien* (Jena: Costenoble, 1897).

Rudrum, A.W. "Vaughan's 'The Night': Some Hermetic Notes," *Modern Language Review* 64, 1 (1969): 11–19.

Ruff, Julius R. *Crime, Justice, and Public Order in Old Regime France: The Sénéchaussées of Libourne and Bazas, 1696–1789* (London: Croom Helm, 1984).

Ruler, Han van. "Minds, Forms, and Spirits: The Nature of Cartesian Disenchantment," *Journal of the History of Ideas* 61, 3 (2000): 381–95.

Rummel, Erika. *The Confessionalization of Humanism in Reformation Germany* (Oxford University Press, 2000).

Rummel, Peter. "Katholisches Leben in der Reichsstadt Augsburg (1605–1806)," *Jahrbuch des Vereins für Augsburger Bistumsgeschichte* 18 (1984): 9–161.

Rummel, Walter. *Bauern, Herren und Hexen: Studien zur Sozialgeschichte sponheimischer und kurtrierischer Hexenprozesse 1574–1664* (Göttingen: Vandenhoeck & Ruprecht, 1991).

Rusterholz, Sibylle. "Jacob Böhmes Deutung des Bösen im Spannungsfeld von Tradition und Innovation," in *Contemplata aliis tradere. Studien zum Verhältnis von Literatur und Spiritualität,* ed. Claudia Brinker (Berne: Lang, 1995), pp. 225–40.

"Jakob Böhmes spirituelle Erfahrung als 'Grund' seiner schriftstellerischen Existenz," in *Die Morgenröte bricht an: Jakob Böhme, naturnaher Mystiker und Theosoph,* Herrenalber Forum 24 (Karlsruhe: Evangelische Akademie Baden, 1999), pp. 100–20.

Rzepinska, Maria. "Tenebrism in Baroque Painting and Its Ideological Background," *Artibus et Historiae* 13, 7 (1986): 91–112.

Sabean, David Warren. *Property, Production, and Family in Neckarhausen, 1700–1870,* Cambridge Studies in Social and Cultural Anthropology 73 (Cambridge University Press, 1990).

Salatino, Kevin. *Incendiary Art: The Representation of Fireworks in Early Modern Europe* (Santa Monica, CA: Getty Research Institute for the History of Art and the Humanities, 1997).

Sälter, Gerhard. *Polizei und soziale Ordnung in Paris: zur Entstehung und Durchsetzung von Normen im städtischen Alltag des Ancien Régime (1697–1715)* (Frankfurt: Klostermann, 2004).

Sandbank, S. "Henry Vaughan's Apology for Darkness," *Studies in English Literature 1500–1900* 7, 1 [The English Renaissance] (1967): 141–52.

Sandgruber, Roman. "Zeit der Mahlzeit. Veränderung in Tagesablauf und Mahlzeiteinteilung in Österreich im 18. und 19. Jahrhundert," in *Wandel der Volkskultur in Europa. Festschrift für Günter Wiegelmann,* ed. Nils-Arvid Bringéus and Günter Wiegelmann (Münster: Coppenrath, 1988), pp. 459–72.

Sanger, Victoria. "Military town planning under Louis XIV: Vauban's practice and methods, 1668–1707," PhD thesis, Columbia University, 2000.

Sauer, Paul, and Hansmartin Decker-Hauff. *Geschichte der Stadt Stuttgart,* vol. III, *Vom Beginn des 18. Jahrhunderts bis zum Abschluss des Verfassungsvertrags fur das Konigreich Wurttemberg 1819* (Stuttgart: Kohlhammer, 1993).

Sbriccoli, Mario, ed. *La Notte: Ordine, sicurezza e disciplinamento in eta moderna* (Florence: Ponte alle grazie, 1991).

Schalk, Fritz. "Zur Semantik von Aufklärung," in *Studien zur französischen Aufklärung* (Frankfurt: Klosterman, 1977), pp. 323–39.

Schindler, Norbert. "Guardians of Disorder: Rituals of Youthful Culture at the Dawn of the Modern Age," in *A History of Young People in the West,* 2 vols., ed. Giovanni Levi and Jean-Claude Schmitt, trans. Camille Naish (Cambridge, MA and London: Belknap Press of Harvard University Press, 1997), 1: 240–82.

"Nächtliche Ruhestörung. Zur Sozialgeschichte der Nacht in der frühen Neuzeit," in *Widerspenstige Leute: Studien zur Volkskultur in der frühen Neuzeit* (Frankfurt: Fischer Taschenbuch-Verlag, 1992), pp. 215–57.

Rebellion, Community and Custom in Early Modern Germany, trans. Pamela E. Selwyn (Cambridge University Press, 2002).

"'Und daß die Ehre Gottes mehrers befördert würde …'. Mikrohistorische Bemerkungen zur frühneuzeitlichen Karfreitagsprozession in Traunstein," *Mitteilungen der Gesellschaft für Salzburger Landeskunde* 136 (1996): 171–200.

Schivelbusch, Wolfgang. *Disenchanted Night: The Industrialization of Light in the Nineteenth Century*, trans. Angela Davies (Berkeley: University of California Press, 1988).

Schlechte, Monika. "Barocke Festkultur – Zeremoniell – Repräsentation. Ein Ausgangspunkt kunstwissenschaftlicher Untersuchungen," *Wissenschaftliche Zeitschrift der Technischen Universität Dresden (Separatreihe 1 "Gesellschaftswissenschaften")* 35, 6 (1986): 29–32.

"Barocke Festkultur in Dresden. Quellenforschung zu einem kulturgeschichtlichen Phänomen," *Wissenschaftliche Zeitschrift der Technischen Universität Dresden (Separatreihe1 "Gesellschaftswissenschaften")* 39, 6 (1990): 7–11.

Schlör, Joachim. *Nights in the Big City: Paris, Berlin, London 1840–1930*, trans. Pierre Gottfried Imhoff and Dafydd Rees Roberts (London: Reaktion Books, 1998).

Schlumbohm, Jürgen. "Gesetze, die nicht durchgesetzt werden – ein Strukturmerkmal des frühneuzeitlichen Staates?" *Geschichte und Gesellschaft* 23 (1997): 647–63.

Schmidt, Eberhard. *Der Gottesdienst am Kurfürstlichen Hofe zu Dresden* (Göttingen: Vandenhoeck & Ruprecht, 1961).

Schmidt, Roger. "Caffeine and the Coming of the Enlightenment," *Raritan* 23, 1 (2003): 129–49.

Schnapper-Arndt, Gottlieb. *Studien zur Geschichte der Lebenshaltung in Frankfurt a. M. während des 17. und 18. Jahrhunderts*, ed. Karl Bräuer, Veröffentlichungen der Historischen Kommission der Stadt Frankfurt a.M. 2: 1–2 (Frankfurt: Baer, 1915).

Schnyder, Albert. "Lichtstuben im alten Basel. Zu einer von Frauen geprägten Form frühneuzeitlicher Geselligkeit," *Schweizerisches Archiv für Volkskunde* 92, 1 (1996): 1–13.

Schön, Erich. *Der Verlust der Sinnlichkeit, oder, die Verwandlungen des Lesers: Mentalitätswandel um 1800*, Sprache und Geschichte 12 (Stuttgart: Klett-Cotta, 1987).

Schulz, Alwin. *Das häusliche Leben der europäischen Kulturvölker vom Mittelalter bis zur zweiten Hälfte des XVIII. Jahrhunderts* (Munich: R. Oldenbourg, 1903).

Schütte, Ulrich. "Das Fürstenschloß als 'Pracht-Gebäude'," in *Die Künste und das Schloss in der frühen Neuzeit*, ed. Lutz Unbehaun with the assistance of Andreas Beyer and Ulrich Schütte, Rudolstädter Forschungen zur Residenzkultur 1 (Munich: Deutscher Kunstverlag, 1998), pp. 15–29.

Schwarzwälder, Herbert. "Oberstleutnant Johann Georg von Bendeleben und sein großes Feuerwerk in Bremen zur Erinnerung an den Frieden von Habenhausen am 20. Oktober 1668," *Bremisches Jahrbuch* 58 (1980): 9–22.

Sitten und Unsitten, Bräuche und Missbräuche im alten Bremen in den Proklamen eines hochedlen, hochweisen Rathes dieser Stadt (Bremen: Schünemann, 1984).

Schwerhoff, Gerd. "Esoterik statt Ethnologie? Mit Monika Neugebauer-Wölk unterwegs im Dschungel der Hexenforschung," online at www.historicum.net/themen/hexenforschung/thementexte/forschungsdebatten/ (text dated August 1, 2007).

Köln im Kreuzverhör: Kriminalität, Herrschaft und Gesellschaft in einer frühneuzeitlichen Stadt (Bonn and Berlin: Bouvier, 1991).

Scott, Joan W. "Gender: A Useful Category of Historical Analysis," *American Historical Review* 91, 5 (1986): 1053–75.

Scott, William Robert. *The Constitution and Finance of English, Scottish and Irish Joint-Stock Companies to 1720* (Cambridge, 1912; repr. Gloucester, MA: Peter Smith, 1968).

Sébillot, Paul. *Le folk-Lore de France*, vol. 1, *Le Ciel et la Terre* (Paris: Librairie orientale & américaine, 1904).

Sennefelt, Karin. "Citizenship and the Political Landscape of Libelling in Stockholm, c. 1720–70," *Social History* 33, 2 (2008): 145–63.

Sgard, Jean. "La métaphore nocturne," in *Eclectisme et cohérence des Lumières. Mélanges offerts à Jean Ehrard*, ed. Jean-Louis Jam (Paris: Librairie Nizet, 1992), pp. 249–55.

Sharpe, Kevin. *The Personal Rule of Charles I* (New Haven: Yale University Press, 1992).

Shepardson, Nikki. "The Rhetoric of Martyrdom and the Anti-Nicodemite Discourses in France, 1550–1570," *Renaissance and Reformation/ Renaissance et Reforme* 27, 3 (2003): 37–61.

Sherman, Stuart. *Telling Time: Clocks, Diaries, and English Diurnal Form, 1660–1785* (University of Chicago Press, 1996).

Shoemaker, Robert. "Male Honour and the Decline of Public Violence in Eighteenth-Century London," *Social History* 26, 2 (2001): 190–208.

Shorter, Edward. "The 'Veillée' and the Great Transformation, in *The Wolf and the Lamb: Popular Culture in France, from the Old Régime to the Twentieth Century*, ed. Jacques Beauroy, Marc Bertrand, and Edward T.

Gargan, Stanford French and Italian Studies 3 (Saratoga, CA: Anma Libri, 1977), pp. 127–40.

Silin, Charles I. *Benserade and His Ballets de Cour* (Baltimore, MD: Johns Hopkins University Press, 1940).

Sippel, Theodor. "The Confession of the Swiss Brethren in Hesse, 1578," *Mennonite Quarterly Review* 23 (1949): 22–34.

Slack, Paul. *From Reformation to Improvement: Public Welfare in Early Modern England* (Oxford: Clarendon Press, 1999).

Smart, Sara. "Ballet in the Empire," in *Spectaculum Europaeum: Theatre and Spectacle in Europe (1580–1750) = Histoire du spectacle en Europe (1580–1750)*, ed. Pierre Béhar and Helen Watanabe-O'Kelly, Wolfenbütteler Arbeiten zur Barockforschung 31 (Wiesbaden: Harrassowitz, 1999), pp. 547–70.

Snobelen, Stephen D. "Isaac Newton, Heretic: The Strategies of a Nicodemite," *British Journal for the History of Science* 32 (1999): 381–419.

Souiller, Didier. "L'Expérience de la nuit dans la littérature européenne baroque," in *Esthétique baroque et imagination créatrice*, ed. Marlies Kronegger (Tübingen: Narr, 1998), pp. 3–21.

Speyer, Wolfgang. "Mittag und Mitternacht als heilige Zeiten in Antike und Christentum," in *Vivarium: Festschrift Theodor Klauser, Jahrbuch für Antike und Christentum, Ergänzungsband* 11 (Münster: Aschendorff, 1984), pp. 314–26.

Spielman, John P. *The City and the Crown: Vienna and the Imperial Court, 1600–1740* (West Lafayette, IN: Purdue University Press, 1993).

Spinner, Kaspar H. "Helldunkel und Zeitlichkeit: Caravaggio, Ribera, Zurbaran, G. de la Tour, Rembrandt," *Zeitschrift für Kunstgeschichte* 34, 3 (1971): 169–83.

Sponsel, Jean-Louis. *Der Zwinger, die Hoffeste und die Schloßbaupläne zu Dresden* (Dresden: Stengel, 1924).

Sreenivasan, Govind P. *The Peasants of Ottobeuren, 1487–1726: A Rural Society in Early Modern Europe* (Cambridge University Press, 2004).

Steege, Paul, Andrew Stuart Bergerson, Maureen Healy, and Pamela E. Swett. "The History of Everyday Life: A Second Chapter," *Journal of Modern History* 80, 2 (2008): 358–378.

Steger, Brigitte, and Lodewijk Brunt. *Night-Time and Sleep in Asia and the West: Exploring the Dark Side of Life* (London: Routledge, 2003).

Stewart, Alison G. "Distaffs and Spindles: Sexual Misbehavior in Sebald Beham's *Spinning Bee*," in *Saints, Sinners, and Sisters: Gender and Northern Art in Medieval and Early Modern Europe*, ed. Jane L. Carroll and Alison G. Stewart (Aldershot: Ashgate, 2003), pp. 127–54.

Stipperger, Roswitha. "Eine Karfreitagsprozession in Schladming aus dem Jahre 1671," *Österreichische Zeitschrift für Volkskunde* n.s. 33 (1979): 95–102.

Stoichita, Victor Ieronim. *A Short History of the Shadow*, trans. Anne-Marie Glasheen (London: Reaktion Books, 1997).

Stollberg-Rillinger, Barbara. "Höfische Öffentlichkeit. Zur zeremoniellen Selbstdarstellungen des brandenburgischen Hofes vor dem europäischen Publikum," *Forschungen zur Brandenburgischen und Preussischen Geschichte* n.s. 7, 2 (1997): 145–76.

Stolleis, Michael. *Arcana imperii und Ratio status: Bemerkungen zur politischen Theorie des frühen 17. Jahrhunderts* (Göttingen: Vandenhoeck & Ruprecht, 1980).

Strasser, Ulrike. *State of Virginity: Gender, Religion, and Politics in an Early Modern Catholic State* (Ann Arbor: University of Michigan Press, 2007).

Straub, Eberhard. *Repraesentatio Maiestatis oder churbayerische Freudenfeste: die höfischen Feste in der Münchner Residenz vom 16. bis zum Ende des 18. Jahrhunderts* (Munich: Stadtarchiv München et al., 1969).

Strong, Roy. *Art and Power: Renaissance Festivals 1450–1650* (Woodbridge: Boydell Press, 1984).

Sutton, Peter C. *Jan van der Heyden (1637–1712)* (Greenwich, CT: Bruce Museum, 2006).

Tanzer, Gerhard. *Spectacle müssen seyn: die Freizeit der Wiener im 18. Jahrhundert*, Kulturstudien 21 (Vienna: Böhlau, 1992).

Tavard, George H. *Poetry and Contemplation in St. John of the Cross* (Athens: Ohio University Press, 1988).

Teuteberg, Hans Jürgen. "'Alles das – was dem Dasein Farbe gegeben hat': Zur Ortsbestimmung der Alltagsgeschichte," in *Methoden und Probleme der Alltagsforschung im Zeitalter des Barock*, ed. Othmar Pickl and Helmuth Feigl (Vienna: Österreichische Akademie der Wissenschaften, 1992), pp. 11–42.

Thomas, Joseph. *L'éclairage des rues d'Amiens à travers les âges* (Cayeux-sur-Mer: P. Ollivier, 1908).

Thwing, Leroy Livingstone. *Flickering Flames: A History of Domestic Lighting through the Ages* (Rutland, VT: Published for the Rushlight Club [by] C.E. Tuttle Co., 1958).

Todd, Margo. *The Culture of Protestantism in Early Modern Scotland* (New Haven: Yale University Press, 2002).

Trénard, Louis. *Histoire de Lille: De Charles Quint à la conquête française (1500–1715)*, Histoire de Lille 2 (Toulouse: Privat, 1981).

Tschernuth, Uta. "Studentisches Leben in den Bursen," in *Das alte Universitätsviertel in Wien 1385–1985*, ed. Günther Hamann, Kurt Mühlberger, and Franz Skacel, Schriftenreihe des Universitätsarchivs 2 (Vienna: Universitätsverlag für Wissenschaft und Forschung, 1985), pp. 153–62.

Turner, Denys. *The Darkness of God: Negativity in Christian Mysticism* (Cambridge University Press, 1995).

Tutino, Stefania. "Between Nicodemism and 'Honest' Dissimulation: The Society of Jesus in England," *Historical Research* 79, 206 (2006): 534–53.

Ullmann, Sabine. "Kontakte und Konflikte zwischen Landjuden und Christen in Schwaben während des 17. und zu Anfang des 18. Jahrhunderts," in *Ehrkonzepte in der frühen Neuzeit: Identitäten und Abgrenzungen*, ed. Sibylle Backmann *et al.* (Berlin: Akademie Verlag, 1998), pp. 288–315.

Underdown, David. *Fire from Heaven: Life in an English Town in the Seventeenth Century* (New Haven: Yale University Press, 1992).

Varey, Simon. "Three Necessary Drugs," *1650–1850: Ideas, Aesthetics, and Inquiries in the Early Modern Era* 4 (1998): 3–51.

Vec, Miloš. *Zeremonialwissenschaft im Fürstenstaat. Studien zur juristischen und politischen Theorie absolutistischer Herrschaftsrepräsentation*, Studien zur Europäischen Rechtsgeschichte 106 (Frankfurt: Klostermann, 1998).

Vehse, Carl Eduard. *Geschichte des östereichischen Hofs und Adels und der östereichischen Diplomatie* (Hamburg: Hoffman und Campe, 1851).

Verdon, Jean. *Night in the Middle Ages*, trans. George Holoch (University of Notre Dame Press, 2002).

Vernus, Michel. *La Veillée: découverte d'une tradition* (Yens-sur-Morges: Cabédita, 2004).

Voth, Hans-Joachim. *Time and Work in England 1750–1830* (Oxford: Clarendon Press, 2000).

Vries, Jan de. *The Industrious Revolution: Consumer Behavior and the Household Economy, 1650 to the Present* (Cambridge University Press, 2008).

Vries, Lyckle de. *Jan van der Heyden* (Amsterdam: Meulenhoff/Landshoff, 1984).

Wagener, Hans. "Faramonds Glukseligste (sic) Insel: Eine pietistische Sozialutopie," *Symposium* 26 (1972): 78–89.

Wagner, Gerhard. *Von der Galanten zur Eleganten Welt. Das Weimarer "Journal des Luxus und der Modern" (1786–1827)* (Hamburg: Bockel, 1994).

Wagner, Helga. *Jan van der Heyden 1637–1712* (Amsterdam: Scheltema & Holkema, 1971).

Waite, Gary K. *Eradicating the Devil's Minions: Anabaptists and Witches in Reformation Europe, 1525–1600* (University of Toronto Press, 2007).

Walker, Corinne. "Du plaisir à la nécessité. L'apparition de la lumière dans les rues de Genève à la fin du XVIIIe siècle," in *Vivre et imaginer la ville XVIIIe–XIXe siècles*, ed. François Walter (Geneva: Éditions Zoé, 1988), pp. 97–124.

"Esquisse pour une histoire de la vie nocturne. Genève au XVIIIe siècle," *Revue du vieux Genève* 19 (1989): 73–85.

Walker, D.P. *The Decline of Hell: Seventeenth-Century Discussions of Eternal Torment* (University of Chicago Press, 1964).

Wappler, Paul. *Die Täuferbewegung in Thüringen von 1526–1584* (Jena: Fischer, 1913).

Watanabe-O'Kelly, Helen. *Court Culture in Dresden: From Renaissance to Baroque* (New York: Palgrave, 2002).

"From 'Société de plaisir' to 'Schönes Neben-Werck' – The Changing Purpose of Court Festivals," *German Life and Letters* 45, 3 (1992): 216–19.

Watson, Graeme J. "The Temple in 'The Night': Henry Vaughan and the Collapse of the Established Church," *Modern Philology* 84, 2 (1986): 144–61.

Weeks, Andrew. *Boehme. An Intellectual Biography of the Seventeenth-Century Philosopher and Mystic* (Albany, NY: State University of New York Press, 1991).

Wehtje, Thomas Jefferson. "Out of Darkness, Light: The Theological Implications of (Dis)Belief in Witchcraft in Early Modern English Literature and Thought," PhD thesis, Stony Brook University, 2004.

Weidenhaupt, Hugo, and Manfred Fey. *Düsseldorf: Geschichte von den Ursprüngen bis ins 20. Jahrhundert*, 4 vols. (Düsseldorf: Schwann im Patmos-Verlag, 1988–89).

Weil, Mark S. "The Devotion of the Forty Hours and Roman Baroque Illusions," *Journal of the Warburg and Courtauld Institutes* 37 (1974): 218–48.

Weiss, Ulman. "Nicodemus Martyr – ein unbekanntes Pseudonym Sebastian Francks?" *Archiv für Reformationsgeschichte* 85 (1994): 163–79.

Welten, Ruud. "The Night in John of the Cross and Michel Henry," *Studies in Spirituality* 13 (2003): 213–33.

West, Russell. "Perplexive Perspectives: The Court and Contestation in the Jacobean Masque," *Seventeenth Century* 18, 1 (2003): 25–43.

Wieder, Frederik Casparus. *De Schriftuurlijke liedekens, de liederen der Nederlandsche hervormden tot op het jaar 1566* ('s-Gravenhage: M. Nijhoff, 1900).

Wilde, Manfred. *Die Zauberei- und Hexenprozesse in Kursachsen* (Cologne, Weimar, and Vienna: Böhlau, 2003).

Wilhelmsen, Elizabeth. *Knowledge and Symbolization in Saint John of the Cross* (Frankfurt: Lang, 1993).

Williams, H. Noel. *Henri II: His Court and Times* (London: Methuen, 1910).

Wilson, Kathleen. "Empire, Gender, and Modernity in the Eighteenth Century," in *Gender and Empire*, ed. Philippa Levine (Oxford University Press, 2004), pp. 14–45.

Windt, Franziska, ed. *Preußen 1701 – eine europäische Geschichte: Katalog* (Berlin: Henschel, 2001).

Winkelhofer, Alois. "Johannes vom Kreuz und die Surius-Übersetzung der Werke Taulers," in *Theologie in Geschichte und Gegenwart; Michael Schmaus zum sechzigsten Geburtstag*, ed. Johann Auer and Hermann Volk (Munich: K. Zink, 1957), pp. 317–48.

Wohlfahrt, Cordula. "Eine Medaille auf die Einrichtung der Straßenbeleuchtung in Leipzig 1702," *Dresdner Kunstblätter* 14 (1970): 178–83.

Youngs, Deborah, and Simon Harris, "Demonizing the Night in Medieval Europe: A Temporal Monstrosity?" in *The Monstrous Middle Ages*, ed. Bettina Bildhauer and Robert Mills (University of Toronto Press, 2003), pp. 134–54.

Zika, Charles. *The Appearance of Witchcraft: Print and Visual Culture in Sixteenth-Century Europe* (London: Routledge, 2007).

Zoepfl, Friedrich. "Die Feier des Karfreitags im Mindelheim des 17. und 18. Jahrhunderts," *Jahrbuch des Historischen Vereins Dillingen an der Donau* 30 (1917): 79–94.

Zöllner, Erich. "Das barocke Wien in der Sicht französischer Zeitgenossen," in *Probleme und Aufgaben der österreichischen Geschichtsforschung: ausgewählte Aufsätze*, ed. Heide Dienst and Gernot Heiss (Munich: R. Oldenbourg, 1984), pp. 383–94.

Index